Essentials of Real Estate Law

Steven A. McCloskey, Esq.
Ann M. Cantrell, NCCP

PEARSON

Boston   Columbus   Indianapolis   New York   San Francisco   Upper Saddle River
Amsterdam   Cape Town   Dubai   London   Madrid   Milan   Munich   Paris   Montréal   Toronto
Delhi   Mexico City   São Paulo   Sydney   Hong Kong   Seoul   Singapore   Taipei   Tokyo

Editorial Director: Vernon Anthony
Executive Editor: Gary Bauer
Project Manager: Linda Cupp
Editorial Assistant: Kevin Cecil
Director of Marketing: David Gesell
Marketing Manager: Mary Salzman
Marketing Assistant: Les Roberts
Senior Art Director: Jayne Conte
Media Project Manager: April Cleland

Procurement Specialist: Deidra M. Skahill
Cover Designer: Bruce Kenselaar
Cover photo: © Steve Hamblin / Alamy
Full-Service Project Management: Integra
Composition: Integra
Text Printer/Bindery: Edwards Brothers
Cover Printer: Lehigh-Phoenix Color
Text Font: 11/13 Minion

Credits and acknowledgments borrowed from other sources and reproduced, with permission, in this textbook appear on the appropriate page within the text.

Photo Credits: Pages 1, 19, 36, 52, 76, 96, 119, 144, 188, 229, 277, 315, 339 - Shutterstock

Library of Congress Cataloging-in-Publication Data is available from the Publisher upon request.

10 9 8 7 6 5 4 3 2 1

PEARSON

ISBN 10: 0-13-511428-4
ISBN 13: 978-0-13-511428-5

Dedicated to my parents, Anita and Jack, who taught me the love of learning.

SAM

I would like to dedicate this work to my husband, Bruce, for his infinite support and patience, and his willingness to be both mom and dad to our children while I wrote.

AMC

BRIEF CONTENTS

CONTENTS

CHAPTER 10   Deeds, Mortgages, And Promissory Notes   229

PREFACE

I have taught the law of real property for several years, and have used a number of textbooks; however, I was never completely satisfied with the content and/or the presentation in those textbooks and often found myself thinking that I should author a text on real property. Pearson Education gave me that opportunity, and a challenge: to create a book that was comprehensive, interesting, and reader-friendly. Before attending law school, I worked for many years in the real estate business in sales, leasing, and property management. These experiences have informed my perspective on the application of property law and have contributed to making this a most practical and useful textbook.

CHAPTER TOPICS AND ORGANIZATION

Many of the legal concepts concerning real property are somewhat complicated, or at least relatively unknown to many students. It was not too terribly long ago that I was a student in law school, and I can recall which of the legal theories and terms were the most difficult to understand, and why. I have tried to take legal doctrines and break them into their fundamental components, and show the student how those components relate to each other. Towards this goal, an outline is included at the beginning of each chapter, which helps to illustrate how the chapter concepts are interconnected.

Chapters 1 through 3 introduce the student to several fundamental concepts relating to real property, such as estates in land, fixtures, and concurrent ownership. Chapter 4 covers the legal relationship between Landlord and Tenant. I felt it was important to address this area of law sooner, rather than later, in the text because a significant percentage of my students over the years were renters at the time they were taking my classes on real property. As such, students were eager to learn about their rights in a leasehold estate.

Chapter 5 discusses rights relating to ownership or possession of real property, such as riparian rights, littoral rights, air rights, and lateral and subjacent support.

Chapter 6 examines restrictions relating to the land such as servitudes, profits, and covenants.

Chapter 7 looks at voluntary transfers of land by way of sale, gift, or devise, as well as involuntary transfers through eminent domain and foreclosure.

Chapter 8 is devoted to an in-depth discussion of the process of selling real property, including a discussion of contract law, brokerage, and the law of agency.

Closely related to the sale of real estate are the lending process, and title searching, which are all discussed in Chapter 9.

Chapter 10 discusses the three most important documents related to the sale of real estate; that is, the deed, mortgage/deed of trust, and the promissory note.

Chapter 11 covers the process of closing the real estate transaction, and the recordation, or registering, of the deed.

Chapter 12 is devoted to common interest communities such as condominiums, cooperatives, and homeowners associations. Unlike most other texts, an entire chapter was given over to common interest communities because a very large percentage of homeowners are residents of such communities, a trend that will only increase in the future.

Chapter 13 discusses real estate development and investment, subjects not usually covered in the standard texts.

Aside from the legal theory, a secondary goal was to make students aware of the many different professionals involved in the field of real estate, including paralegals, attorneys, real estate brokers and agents, lenders, and many others. It is literally true that all of us are affected in some way by the law of real property, and it is my great hope that this book will help students to better understand their rights and obligations within this fascinating realm.

SPECIAL TEXT FEATURES

- **Definitions of key terms** have been included as margin notes that relate to the most fundamental and important ideas.
- **Many examples, hypotheticals, and actual (edited) cases** are included in each chapter, and these should help students remember how various real estate concepts and practices apply in the real world.
- **Charts and exhibits** appear throughout the text that summarize and visually illustrate a variety of concepts, forms, terms, and principles.
- **Paralegal Profiles** are included in selected chapters to provide students with a real life example of working as a real estate paralegal.
- **End of chapter features** reinforce concepts and build skills
  - **Key Terms**. A list of chapter-specific key terms appears at the end of each chapter and a Glossary appears at the end of the text.
  - **Concept Review Questions**. A series of review questions are presented at the end of each chapter to focus and reinforce content.
  - **The Building Your Professional Skills** section includes Critical Thinking Exercises, Research on the Web assignments that require students to research the law in their states, and Building Your Professional Portfolio assignments that will produce a document students can include in a portfolio.

ALTERNATE VERSIONS

Essentials of Real Estate is available in various eBook formats, including *CourseSmart* and Adobe Reader. *CourseSmart* is an exciting new choice for students looking to save money. As an alternative to purchasing the printed textbook, students can purchase an electronic version of the same content. With a *CourseSmart* eTextbook, students can search the text, make notes online, print out reading assignments that incorporate lecture notes, and bookmark important passages for later review. For more information, or to purchase access to the *CourseSmart* eTextbook, visit **www. coursesmart.com**.

INSTRUCTOR SUPPLEMENTS

- The **Online Instructor's Manual** provides suggested answers to the Concept Review Questions and the Critical Thinking Exercises, test bank questions, chapter outlines, and teaching notes.
- **MyTest:** this computerized test generation system gives you maximum flexibility in preparing tests. It can create custom tests and print scrambled versions of a test at one time, as well as build tests randomly by chapter, level of difficulty, or question type. The software also allows online testing and record-keeping and the ability to add problems to the database. This test bank can also be delivered formatted for use in popular learning

management platforms, such as BlackBoard, WebCT, Moodle, Angel, and eCollege. Visit www.PearsonMyTest.com to begin building your tests.

- **PowerPoint Lecture Presentation:** Lecture presentation screens for each chapter are available online.
- **Pearson Online Course Solutions:** *Essentials of Real Estate Law* is supported by online course solutions that include interactive learning modules, a variety of assessment tools, and supporting materials. Go to www.pearsonhighered.com or contact your local representative for the latest information.

To access supplementary materials online, instructors need to request an instructor access code. Go to www.pearsonhighered.com/irc, where you can register for an instructor access code. Within 48 hours of registering, you will receive a confirming e-mail including an instructor access code. Once you have received your code, locate your text in the online catalog and click on the Instructor Resources button on the left side of the catalog product page. Select a supplement and a log-in page will appear. Once you have logged in, you can access instructor material for all Pearson textbooks.

ACKNOWLEDGMENTS

Special thanks to the following reviewers who provided excellent technical and practical suggestions for improvement and readability for the new edition:

Heidi Getchell-Bastien, Northern Essex Community College
Patty Greer, Berkeley College
Richard Kaser, Gloucester County College
Sondi Lee, Camden County College
Elaine S. Lerner, Kaplan University
Lisa Newman, Brown Mackie College
Joy O'Donnell, Pima Community College
Annalinda Ragazzo, Bryant & Stratton College
Cheryl L. Reinhart, Pulaski Technical College
Valerie Rucker, Citgo Petroelum Company
Deborah Walsh, Middlesex Community College
Buzz Wheeler, Highline Community College
John Whitehead, Kilgore College

I would like to thank my many students over the years, who contributed to this book more than they could know. I wish to thank one of those students in particular—Melodee "Cookie" Karabin—for her dedication and invaluable assistance in locating and obtaining the many documents used throughout the text, as well as her many helpful suggestions. To my siblings and dear friends, thank you for your interest and encouragement. Finally, I would like to extend my appreciation to Gary Bauer and Linda Cupp at Pearson Education for giving me the opportunity.

STEVE MCCLOSKEY

I would like to thank Margaret Burnham, who has been a teacher, a cheerleader, and a friend to me for more than eighteen years. Her support and encouragement in this project were invaluable. I would also like to thank Jim Saintsing for recommending me to Steve, and for taking the time to read and comment on my work. I am very grateful to Steve as well, for following Jim's recommendation and opening this door for me. Thanks also for assistance from Sharon Malburg, my co-worker and friend, who happens to be the most talented title researcher in the world. Last, but far from least, I would like to thank my dad, Harry Morgan, from whom I inherited a skill in geometry, and my big brother, Eric Morgan, who inherited the same skill, and who is always willing to answer a survey question for me.

ANN CANTRELL

ABOUT THE AUTHORS

STEVEN A. MCCLOSKEY Steve McCloskey received a Bachelor of Science degree from Virginia Tech in 1974. From 1974 to 1978, he was a police officer in Greensboro, North Carolina. He then spent several years in real estate and entered the School of Law at North Carolina Central University in 1996. He earned his JD degree, cum laude, from North Carolina Central in 1999. Since 1999, McCloskey has had a law practice in Winston-Salem, where he concentrates in the areas of torts and contract law. McCloskey has taught paralegal studies since 2004, and has appeared as a guest lecturer for the North Carolina Paralegal Association.

ANN CANTRELL is a North Carolina State Bar Certified Paralegal at Nexsen Pruet, PLLC in Greensboro, North Carolina. She received a Bachelor of Science Degree in Communications from Appalachian State University in Boone, North Carolina in 1985. She began her legal career in 1989, and in 1995 she joined Adams, Kleemeier, Hagan, Hannah & Fouts, which subsequently merged with what is now Nexsen Pruet, PLLC. Ms. Cantrell concentrates in the areas of commercial real estate and foreclosure. She lives in Greensboro, North Carolina with her husband and two children.

chapter 1

OVERVIEW OF REAL PROPERTY

A. Introduction

The importance of property in our Nation's history cannot be overemphasized. The Founders believed strongly that individual ownership of real and personal property would provide a solid foundation on which to build a republic, and the protection of property interests was one of the most important functions of government. The Fifth Amendment, found in the Bill of Rights (ratified in 1791) of the United States Constitution reads in part:

> … nor [shall any person] be deprived of life, liberty, or **property**, without due process of law; nor shall **private property** be taken for public use, without just compensation.

Unlike England and the other relatively developed countries in Europe, America had a seemingly unlimited supply of available, **inexpensive land**. This appealed to a broad spectrum of colonists and immigrants, from hard-working farmers, lumbermen, and miners to the less hard-working, but "creative," real estate speculators. In some cases, the United States government actually gave land away to people who were willing to occupy and homestead the land. The government also granted huge tracts of federal lands to railroads in exchange for their laying track across the United States. For all, in one way or another, the land provided sustenance and purpose, and their legacy is found in the great farms, ranches, urban, and suburban spaces and places that we call home.

But let us not forget that the Americas were inhabited long before Columbus arrived in 1492, and even long before Eric the Red explored Newfoundland around 1000 AD. At least as early as 10,000 BC, Asian peoples were coming to North America by way of the Bering land bridge, which is now submerged under the Bering Sea. These migrants were able to cross over from present-day Russia to Alaska because sea levels were lower then, thus exposing the land bridge and making it available for travel for these first Americans.

The prevailing theory is that during the next thousand or so years, these waves of immigrants moved south through Canada, populated the western United States, and then migrated eastward across the Rockies, through the Mississippi Valley, and to the Atlantic seaboard. These were the **Native Americans** who met the Pilgrims when they landed at Plymouth Rock in Massachusetts.

As the reader undoubtedly knows, the arrival of colonists from Europe would lead to wars between the more recent European immigrants and the native peoples, which would determine who would own and control the land. The desire to own the land—to use and enjoy it, and to exercise dominion and control over it—would define not only the contours of our nation's history, but the contours of the land itself.

As you read through this book and study the legal principles associated with real property, try to discern the "why" behind those principles. What are the **public policies**—the fundamental values and priorities of the citizens—that motivate lawmakers and judges as they attempt to serve their constituents and litigants?

B. Real Property Defined

Real property
is land, anything affixed to the land,
and rights appurtenant to the land.

Real property is *land*, anything *affixed* to the land, and *rights appurtenant* to the land. Things affixed to the land include buildings, structures, trees, and shrubbery (crops for sale are a special category, and not considered real property). Rights appurtenant to the land are associated with the ownership or possession of land such as riparian (river or stream) rights, littoral (coast or shore) rights, air rights, and mineral rights.

Real estate is a term usually considered synonymous with the term *real property*. It is also the name commonly used in connection with the real estate business, including real estate brokerage—which involves the listing, sale, and purchase of real estate—as well as the development, leasing, and management of real property.

C. Characteristics of Real Property

Two of the defining characteristics of real property are its immovability and uniqueness. *Immovability* refers to the concept that real property cannot be picked up and moved to another location as with personal property. However, homeowners who live on steep hills and have experienced landslides, or those who have felt earthquakes beneath them, might take issue with the "immovability" of real property, but it is nevertheless considered a characteristic of real property.

The characteristic of **immovability** of land makes real property ideal as a source of tax revenue. Real estate cannot be hidden from the tax collector, nor can the property owner pack it up and take it somewhere else.

Each parcel of real estate is considered to be **unique**, including even adjoining building lots in subdivisions. The uniqueness of real property has consequences in the event of a breach of contract by the seller of the property. Because real property is unique, monetary damages will not adequately compensate the buyer for the breach. So, if the seller does breach by refusing to sell, a buyer may ask the court for the remedy of **specific performance**, rather than monetary damages, in which case the court will order the seller to convey the property to the buyer.

D. Personal Property

Personal property, sometimes called *chattel*, is all property that is not real property. This includes *tangible* items such as a television, an automobile, a cell phone, money, and everything that is movable. Personal property also includes *intangible* items such as ownership of shares of stock, patents, copyrights, and even the right to sue someone.

> Personal property sometimes called chattel, is all property that is not real property.

E. Ownership versus Possession

Ownership consists of a group of rights relating to a particular piece of property, and the legal recognition of one's ability to exercise those rights. Ownership of real property is always subject to limitations imposed by the **sovereign**, and therefore, no one can ever unconditionally exercise the rights of ownership to real property.

Rather, one is said to own an interest in real property known as an **estate**. These ownership rights are sometimes referred to as a **bundle of rights**, which we will examine later in this chapter.

Title has two meanings, one abstract, and the other more concrete. Title, in the abstract, is simply the ownership of real or personal property.

On a more concrete level, title refers to the documentary evidence of ownership rights, such as the physical, tangible document that is the title to your car. Ownership of most personal property is often evidenced by a bill of sale, rather than a title. In the law of real property, evidence of title is called a **deed**. Compare this to a lease, which is not evidence of title, but merely the right to use and possess real property.

Possession should not be confused with ownership or title. Possession is the right to exercise dominion and control over property, whether real property or personal property. Ownership is a matter of law, while possession is a matter of fact. For example, if the car that you own is stolen, you still have ownership, as a matter of law and as evidenced by your title, but the thief, as a matter of fact, has possession of it.

Ownership and possession most often accompany each other. You own your smart phone and are usually also in possession of it. You may own your own home and also possess, that is, occupy it.

You have probably heard the expression that "possession is nine-tenths of the law." The apparent meaning of this phrase is that mere possession of an object or parcel of real property is strong evidence of ownership. This may be true in some cases, but can just as often be false, as illustrated by the example of the thief in possession of your car. And although a tenant may be in possession of leased premises, title/ownership still resides in the landlord. This makes the point that possession, or **dominion and control** over a property, is sometimes evidenced by occupancy of the property.

The case that follows was decided by the United States Supreme Court in 1823. Note the interplay between the concepts of *possession* and *title*. As the Court

> **Sovereign**
> a governmental entity possessing independent and supreme authority. Every state in the United States is a sovereign, as is the federal government.

> **Estate**
> the nature and extent of one's legal rights and interests in a given parcel of real property.

> **Title**
> in the abstract, is the right of ownership. Title also means the evidence of ownership rights; with real estate, evidence of ownership or title is by deed.

> **Possession**
> is the exercise of dominion and control over property, whether real property or personal property.

> **Dominion and Control**
> the terms are somewhat synonymous, and therefore redundant. The exercise of dominion and control over one's property implies the ability to exclude all others from possessing or enjoying it.

makes clear, under British common law, which was adopted by the Colonists, possession of the land does not necessarily vest title in those who occupy it. Discovery of land, which sometimes included conquest of native peoples, was the vehicle by which governments claimed title to huge tracts of real estate, and sometimes entire continents. Here is the background to the case:

Plaintiff Mr. Johnson was a British subject, whose successors claimed title to a six hundred thousand acres tract of land in present-day Ohio, which he had purchased from the Piankeshaw Indians before the Revolutionary War. Defendant M'Intosh claimed title to the same land pursuant to a **land grant** from the new United States government following the Revolutionary War; these same lands had been conveyed by the British to the United States in the treaty following the War.

The legal issue is: Whose title is superior? Plaintiff Johnson's title received from the Piankeshaw, who first inhabited and occupied the land, or defendant M'Intosh's title from the United States government?

In the 1823 decision below, does the United States Supreme Court essentially say that "Might makes right"?

JOHNSON V. M'INTOSH

21 U.S. 543
February 28, 1823, Decided

Opinion

Mr. Chief Justice Marshall delivered the opinion of the Court. The plaintiffs in this cause claim the land, in their declaration mentioned, under two grants, purporting to be made, the first in 1773, and the last in 1775, by the chiefs of certain Indian tribes, constituting the Illinois and the Piankeshaw nations; and the question is, whether this title can be recognised in the Courts of the United States.

The facts show the authority of the chiefs who executed this conveyance, so far as it could be given by their own people; and likewise show, that the particular tribes for whom these chiefs acted were in rightful possession of the land they sold. The inquiry, therefore, is, in a great measure, confined to the *power of Indians to give*, and of private individuals to receive, a title which can be sustained in the Courts of this country.

While the different nations of Europe respected the right of the natives, as occupants, they asserted the ultimate *dominion* to be in themselves; and claimed and exercised, as a consequence of this ultimate dominion, a power to grant the soil, while yet in possession of the natives. These *grants* have been understood by all, to convey a title to the grantees, subject only to the Indian right of occupancy.

The United States, then, have unequivocally acceded to that great and broad rule by which its civilized inhabitants now hold this country. They hold, and assert in themselves, the title by which it was acquired. They maintain, as all others have maintained, that *discovery* gave an exclusive right to extinguish the Indian title of occupancy, either by purchase or by conquest; and gave also a right to such a degree of sovereignty, as the circumstances of the people would allow them to exercise.

The power now possessed by the government of the United States to grant lands, resided, while we were colonies, in the crown, or its grantees. The validity of the titles given by either has never been questioned in our Courts. It has been exercised uniformly over territory in possession of the Indians. The existence of this power must negative the existence of any right which may conflict with, and control it. An absolute title to lands cannot exist, at the same time, in different persons, or in different governments. An absolute, must be an exclusive title, or at least a title which excludes all others not compatible with it. All our institutions recognise the *absolute title of the crown*, subject only to the Indian right of occupancy, and recognise the absolute title of the crown to extinguish that right. This is incompatible with an absolute and complete title in the Indians.

The British government, which was then our government, and whose rights have passed to the United States, asserted a title to all the lands occupied by Indians, within the chartered limits of the British colonies. It asserted also a limited sovereignty over them, and the exclusive right of extinguishing the title which occupancy gave to them. These claims have been maintained and established as far west as the river Mississippi, by the sword.

The *title by conquest* is acquired and maintained by force. The conqueror prescribes its limits... .

But the tribes of Indians inhabiting this country were fierce savages, whose occupation was war, and whose subsistence was drawn chiefly from the forest. To leave them in possession of their country, was to leave the country a wilderness; to govern them as a distinct people, was impossible, because they were as brave and as high spirited as they were fierce, and were ready to repel by arms every attempt on their independence.

What was the inevitable consequence of this state of things? The Europeans were under the necessity either of abandoning the country, and relinquishing their pompous claims to it, or of enforcing those claims by the sword, and by the adoption of principles adapted to the condition of a people with whom it was impossible to mix, and who could not be governed as a distinct society, or of remaining in their neighbourhood, and exposing themselves and their families to the perpetual hazard of being massacred.

According to the theory of the British constitution, all vacant lands are ***vested in the crown***, as representing the nation; and the exclusive power to grant them is admitted to reside in the crown, as a branch of the royal prerogative. It has been already shown, that this principle was as fully recognised in America as in the island of Great Britain.

The Court is decidedly of opinion, that the plaintiffs do not exhibit a title which can be sustained in the Courts of the United States; and that there is no error in the judgment which was rendered against them in the District Court of Illinois.

Judgment affirmed, with costs.

F. Real Estate as a Bundle of Rights

It is sometimes said that one does not own real estate, but rather, one owns a **bundle of rights** relating to interests in the land. The types of rights that one has in the bundle of rights defines the *estate* one owns. The bundle of rights that defines a fee simple estate (the best estate one can have) includes the following rights:

> **Bundle of Rights**
> describes the nature and extent of an owner's or tenant's interests in the land.

1. The right to *possess* the property (to exercise dominion and control),
2. The right to *lease* the property,
3. The right to *mortgage* the property,
4. The right to *convey* the property (by gift, sale or will),
5. The right to *use* and *enjoy* the property,
6. The right to *exclude* all others from the property.

1. INDIVIDUALISM VERSUS POLICE POWER

Let's look at each of these rights in greater detail. But before doing so, the point must be made that none of the rights that follow are absolute. My rights end where your rights begin, and vice versa. And though the United States is a country that places a high value on *individualism*, individual rights have always been measured against, and checked by, the needs of the greater *community*.

Note that a number of the colonies referred to themselves as commonwealths, for example, the Commonwealth of Massachusetts and the Commonwealth of Pennsylvania. The "common" in Commonwealth refers to the citizenry as a whole, and to the rights enjoyed by the entire community. The importance of the communal concept is expressed through the state's **police powers**.

> **Police Power**
> is the authority that state and local governments have had for centuries to legislate in the areas of the public health, safety, morals, and the general welfare.

These police powers include the right of a state (that greater community of citizens) to legislate in areas of public health, safety, morals, and the general welfare, often in a way that diminishes or regulates one's individual rights. The states can and do delegate their police powers to local governments such as counties, cities, and towns. With the police power in mind, let us examine the bundle of rights of the greatest estate in land, the fee simple estate, sometimes called the fee simple absolute:

1. The right to possession of the property

The right of possession is the right to exercise ***dominion*** and ***control*** over property. This right is limited by the police power of the state. For example, a city housing authority, pursuant to its local building code, might condemn the property that you possess and occupy for any number of reasons, such as the structure itself being unsafe, the lot or structure being a health hazard, or the property otherwise constituting a public nuisance.

2. The right to ***lease*** the property

This right is not absolute, and can be limited by the state's police power. Most states have adopted laws that require landlords to provide "fit and habitable premises." *Habitable* means that the landlord must provide heat, running water, and a unit that is free of vermin. In addition, these statutes often impose other restrictions such as where security deposits must be held, the statutory procedure for an eviction or summary ejectment, retaliatory evictions, and so on. Further, state law may not permit a tenant to waive, or release, the landlord from these obligations.

We spoke before of "public policy"—those values, principles, and expectations of the citizens that motivate legislators when drafting statutes, and judges when interpreting common law. What, then, is the public policy behind *not* allowing the tenant to waive the landlord's duty to provide a habitable dwelling?

3. The right to ***mortgage*** the property

You may already know that to mortgage a property means that you ***pledge*** real property, say a house, as ***collateral*** to a bank in exchange for the bank lending you money for the purchase of the house. The mortgage constitutes a ***lien*** on the property, and if the owner does not make the mortgage payments, the bank will exercise its right to sell the property pursuant to a process called foreclosure. The amount owing on the loan will be paid out of the proceeds of the foreclosure sale, although in most cases, the proceeds from the foreclosure auction are not sufficient to pay off the mortgage balance.

The government—state, county, or city—really does not limit *your* right to mortgage your real property, but the federal government can and does impose regulations on banks, savings and loan associations, and other lending institutions that offer loans (secured by mortgages) for the purchase of real property. But government does have an interest in whether or not you pay your real estate taxes. Real estate taxes, like the mortgage, constitute a lien on your real property, and if the government has to foreclose, it may be paid *first* from the proceeds of the foreclosure sale.

4. The right to ***convey*** the property (by gift, sale, deed, or will)

The government, pursuant to its police powers, may prevent the owner of a property from conveying it to another, or require the owner to convey it to a specific individual. In the case of a divorce, the court may order one spouse to convey his or her ownership interest in the home to the other spouse as part of the divorce settlement.

Or perhaps the government has condemned a property under its power of eminent domain because it wants to build a highway over it. Regardless of the owner's wishes, the property will be deeded to the government in exchange for just compensation. And, of course, in almost any conveyance of property, the various government entities will tax the transfer with a gift tax, inheritance tax, estate tax, capital gains tax, sales tax, and so forth.

5. The right to **use and enjoy** the property

Your right to use and enjoy your property can be severely curtailed by the government. You may want to turn your home into an all-night discotheque, but if you live in a residential neighborhood, that probably isn't going to happen. Zoning laws limit the types of property that can be built, maintained, or operated in the various zoning districts throughout the average American town or city.

Even if you want to build a residence in a residential subdivision, governmental zoning ordinances and building codes may constrain your choice of architectural style, square footage, number of bedrooms, where the house is built on the lot, and many other preferences. Additionally, municipalities typically have noise ordinances limiting the decibel level and/or the time of day for noisy activities.

6. The right to **exclude** all others from the property

Not even this right is absolute or safe from the government's police power. If the power company wants to run a 275,000 volt electric line across your property, there is probably not much you can do about it because states legislatively grant to utility companies the right of **eminent domain**. If there is a fire next door to your property, the fire department has the right to run water hoses across your property to fight the fire, in keeping with the government's police power authority to act for the public safety and general welfare.

You know that the greatest estate one may have in real property is known as the fee simple, or sometimes, as the fee simple *absolute*. The irony being, as we have just seen, none of the rights in the bundle of rights is absolute by any stretch of the imagination.

Finally, as common sense would indicate, one cannot convey an estate greater than the estate one owns. For example, a lessee may sublease his apartment, but obviously may not sell the apartment unit because the lessee does not own it. We will examine the various types of estates—fee simple, life estate, and leaseholds—in greater depth in a later chapter.

G. Fixtures

1. DEFINITION AND SIGNIFICANCE

A *fixture* is an item of personal property or chattel, which by virtue of its attachment to real property, **becomes real property** itself. You may have heard the terms "bathroom fixtures" or "lighting fixtures." These items are typically thought of as part of the real property when the property is sold. Many a real estate sale has collapsed over disputes about what items are fixtures and should remain with the property upon a sale: window treatments, appliances, chandeliers, TV dishes and antennae, lawn ornaments, built-in appliances, children's swing sets, and even prized plants and flowers.

Let's look at three scenarios involving fixtures, but each in a different context. Assume in each case that the offer to purchase, or the rental agreement, does not adequately address the issue of fixtures:

EXAMPLES

EXAMPLE 1. RESIDENTIAL PURCHASE

Mr. and Mrs. Buyers made an offer to purchase on a house for $200,000, which was accepted by Mr. and Mrs. Sellers. This morning at the closing on the property, the Sellers casually informed Buyers that they had "a heckuva time removing the basketball backboard and rim" that had been bolted to the west wall of the house, above the garage.

The Buyers protest that their children really wanted to use the backboard, and that it is a fixture, and part of the real property, which the Sellers had no right to remove. The Buyers threaten to back out of the deal and/or sue if the backboard is not re-installed. Is the backboard a fixture that stays with the property, or are the Sellers entitled to remove it?

EXAMPLE 2. RESIDENTIAL LEASE

Tenant has a one-year residential lease at a fancy apartment complex. Six months into the lease, Tenant purchased an 84" Galactic X model, ultra-high definition plasma TV for $8,000. Following the instructions that came with the TV, Tenant bolted the heavy-duty brackets (included at no extra charge) to three separate wooden studs behind the drywall. Tenant then bolted the TV to the brackets.

Six months later, on the day Tenant's lease expires, Tenant is removing the TV from the brackets when the apartment manager stops by. The manager informs Tenant that the TV is a fixture, and that the property owner will sue—and criminally prosecute—Tenant, if the TV is removed. Who will prevail if this case goes to court, and why?

EXAMPLE 3. COMMERCIAL LEASE

Landlord owns a property, which has been rented for the last five years to Sal's Subs and Salads. The lease has expired, and Sal is moving on to greener pastures. When Landlord stops by to wish Sal farewell, Landlord observes Sal's employees removing the refrigerated deli counter, which had been bolted to the concrete floor. Landlord protests that the deli counter is a fixture, and should remain with the property; Sal, of course, disagrees.

Who will prevail if this case goes to court?

2. THE LAW OF FIXTURES

Fixture
personal property affixed or attached to real property that becomes part of the real property.

A **fixture** is personal property that has been *affixed* or attached to, real property, and thereby becomes real property. But determining whether a basketball hoop, a plasma TV, or a deli counter is a fixture is not always easy. In the event of a dispute, a court will consider the following several factors to determine if the property that was attached to a house or apartment wall is a fixture—and thus, real property—or if it is personal property that may properly be removed by a seller or departing tenant.

a. Intent of the Annexor

Annexor
one who attaches or affixes personal property to real property.

The **annexor** is the owner or tenant of a property who has attached personal property to real property. Perhaps the most important factor in determining whether that personal property has become a fixture/real property is the *intent of the annexor*. The clearest of the examples above as to the annexor's intent would be the tenant who bolted the new plasma TV to the apartment wall. Clearly, the tenant intended to remove the $8,000 TV upon departing the premises. The intent of the annexor is related to the second factor, the annexor's relationship to the land.

b. Annexor's Relationship to the Land

The second factor to be considered whether personal property has become a permanent fixture is the relationship of the annexor to the real property. In the first example above, the annexors of the basketball backboard—Mr. and Mrs. Sellers— were the **homeowners**, who are now selling the property. In the second example, the annexor of the TV was a **residential tenant**, and in the third example, the annexor of the refrigerated deli counter was a **commercial tenant**.

Generally speaking, the more permanent the relationship of the annexor to the land, the more likely that the personal property will be deemed a fixture. In the case of home ownership, the relationship would be considered more permanent than a tenancy. **Tenancies**—whether residential or commercial—are **temporary** by nature, and it is unreasonable to think that a tenant would spend thousands of dollars for a plasma TV, for example, for the use and enjoyment of the next occupant of the apartment unit.

Thus, the **rebuttable presumption** in lease cases is that the tenant may remove the affixed personal property upon leaving (although some states do take a contrary position). Of course, the tenant would be required to repair any damage caused by the removal of the personal property, and return the leased premises to its original condition. This brings up a related point: the more damage that would be done if the property were to be removed, the more likely the property will be deemed a fixture.

> **Rebuttable Presumption**
> an inference drawn from facts that establish a prima facie case, but which may be overcome by the introduction of contrary evidence.

c. Method of Attachment

A third factor to be considered in determining the fixture question is the method of attachment. The more securely that personal property is attached to the land or a structure upon it, the more likely it is that the personal property has become a fixture. A child's swing set that is secured in-ground by concrete footings is much more likely to be deemed a fixture than a swing set "attached" to the ground merely by its own weight. In the latter instance, the sellers of the property could rightfully remove the swing set upon the sale to the buyers.

By further example, consider two scenarios where a homeowner has installed walkway lights leading up to the front door of the residence. In the first scenario, the homeowner has installed walkway lights that are powered by a solar cell and battery that set atop the light; the method of attachment was simply implanting the base of each light 8 to 10 inches into the soil abutting the walkway.

The second scenario is similar, except that the lights are not solar powered, but are hard-wired by underground cables to the electrical system of the house. Although these lights have been implanted the same 8 to 10 inches into the ground, the hard-wired lights are **more securely attached**, and would almost certainly be deemed fixtures, and should remain with the property upon sale.

d. Relationship of the Affixed Property to the Land

A fourth factor that the court may consider in determining whether an item is a fixture or removable personal property is the relationship of the affixed property to the land. "Built-ins" provide a good example. If a homeowner knocks out a wall in the basement to accommodate a built-in sauna, it had better stay with the property upon sale, or the seller will get sued for removing a fixture. Built-in bookcases and appliances are generally considered fixtures. When personal property is **specially made** to be affixed to real property, it will almost certainly be deemed a fixture, and remain with the land.

e. Intent of the Parties

We have looked at the four primary factors in determining whether an item is or is not a fixture. But keep in mind that a seller and buyer, or a landlord and tenant, can always strike an agreement regarding whether an item will remain with the real property, or whether it may be removed upon sale or upon the tenant's departure.

In short, the parties to a contract may agree to anything that has a legal purpose and legal consideration. It is not an exaggeration to say that parties may agree that an ***entire house can become personal property***. You have probably witnessed the extraordinary sight of an actual house being slowly transported down the road, usually early on a Sunday morning when traffic is at a minimum. Here is the scenario:

EXAMPLE

Buyer offers to purchase a house if she can move it to a lot she owns on the other side of town. Seller agrees. The house, which is definitely real property, is subsequently lifted by hydraulic jacks, removed from its foundation, and transported across town.

In the undertaking, the house has become personal property, and will remain so until it is set down at its new location, where its sheer weight will "affix" it to the ground, and the house will once again become real property.

The lesson is that even though the *original* builder and the *original* owner of the house intended it to be real property, and even though it was "permanently" attached to the land by its foundation and sheer weight, the house may nevertheless become personal property, at least for a time. The reason is that is what the *current* owner and buyer *intend* to do with the house, that is, make it personal property, at least temporarily while it is being transported across town.

In attempting to construe any contract, a court will always look first at the ***intent of the parties*** to the contract. At first blush, that sounds simple enough. But then we realize that the parties would not be litigating the issue in court if they had the same intent as to the personal property/fixture in question. So how can it be said that there is an "intent of the parties" if the parties are in court because they disagree on the meaning of the contract?

What the court really does in deciding the *intent of the parties* is to look at how the contractual language would impress a hypothetical, objective, "reasonable person." In other words, the subjective intent or beliefs of each party to the contract does not matter when construing the terms of the contract.

Rather, what is important is how the contractual language would be construed by a neutral, objective third party, the reasonable person. In a bench trial, the judge will act as the reasonable person; in a jury trial, of course, the collective wisdom of the jurors will give voice to the reasonable person.[1]

---

[1]English barrister and humorist, A.P. Herbert, described the "Reasonable Man" in 1935:

The Reasonable Man is one who never swears, gambles, or loses his temper; who uses nothing except in moderation, and even while he flogs his child is meditating only on the golden mean. Devoid, in short, of any human weakness, with not one single saving vice, *sans* prejudice, procrastination, ill-nature, avarice, and absence of mind, as careful for his own safety as he is for that of others, this excellent but odious character stands like a monument in our Court of Justice, vainly appealing to his fellow-citizens to order their lives after his own example.... Hateful as he must necessarily be to any ordinary citizen who privately considers him, it is a curious paradox that where two or three are gathered together in one place they will with one accord pretend an admiration for him; and, when they are gathered together in the formidable surroundings of a British jury, they are easily persuaded that they themselves are, each and generally, reasonable men.

A.P. Herbert, *Uncommon Law* (International Polygonics, Ltd., 1935).

PRACTICE POINT

We have used "fixture" to mean personal property that is affixed to real property, and which becomes part of the real property. A caveat: sometimes the word "fixture" is used to convey the **opposite meaning**, that is, personal property that has been affixed to real property, but *may* be removed by the annexor.

An example of this is the term "commercial fixture." This is really an oxymoron, because a "commercial fixture" can, under the case law of most states, almost always be removed by the tenant upon departing the premises.

Unfortunately, the opposite meaning is quite commonly used by lawyers, judges, and those in the real estate profession. If you work in a law office that practices real estate law, be certain that you understand how "fixture" is being used, and if you are not sure, ask the speaker for clarification.

H. Statute of Frauds

The Statute of Frauds finds its origin in English law, but *not* in English *common* law. Common law is judge-made law, that is, law created by judges' opinions in litigated cases. Statutes, on the other hand, are enacted by legislative bodies, such as the English Parliament, or the United States Congress, or our state legislatures.

In 1677, the British Parliament enacted An Act for Prevention of Frauds and Perjuries. As its name implies, the Act was passed to prevent fraud in the conveyance of real property, and the primary method of accomplishing this goal was the requirement that such conveyances (usually, deeds) be in writing and signed by the grantor. Land was, is, and always will be, a very important source of wealth. As such, it has often been the occasion of legal disputes, sometimes involving fraud.

Every state has a statute of frauds that requires that **certain types of contracts be in writing**, and especially those involving an *interest* in real property. Obviously, a deed would involve an interest in real property, and would have to be in writing. But so, too, would a mortgage, an offer to purchase real property, an easement, and a lease. Thus, the requirement of a writing for an interest in real estate covers many more transactions than just a gift or sale of real property.

1. PURPOSE

The standard of proof in civil cases is **preponderance of the evidence**, a rather low bar to hurdle for a plaintiff. Under that standard, a plaintiff must simply prove to the trier of fact that it is "more likely than not" that the defendant engaged in the conduct alleged in the plaintiff's complaint.[2] Over the centuries, such a low standard has undoubtedly allowed many undeserving plaintiffs to prevail, and many "innocent" defendants to be found liable for some type of damages. Oftentimes in civil trials the outcome depends on which party is the better—but not necessarily more truthful—witness. Because real property is so valuable, the statutes of frauds were enacted to serve two basic purposes:

1. The statute of frauds' requirement of a writing to convey an interest in real property serves a **cautionary** function, which informs the parties that the transaction that they are entering into is very important, and that they should give all due contemplation to making the conveyance; and

---

[2]In criminal cases, the standard of proof required to convict a defendant is "proof beyond a reasonable doubt." There is another standard of proof used in special types of proceedings such as termination of parental rights and involuntary commitments. This third type of standard of proof requires that there be "clear and convincing evidence" to, for example, terminate one's parental rights or to involuntarily commit someone.

2. The statute of frauds' requirement of a writing to convey an interest in real property serves an *evidentiary* function. A court is saying in effect: "Don't bother to file a lawsuit if you cannot prove by a written document that there was a conveyance of an interest in the property." The requirement of a writing, therefore, makes it more likely that there will be a just adjudication of the lawsuit.

As with just about every legal doctrine, there can be exceptions. Such is the case with the statute of frauds. Some states take the hard line, holding that *all* contracts for the transfer of real property must be in writing.

Other states allow an exception, which is known as the doctrine of ***partial performance***. The doctrine of partial performance holds that even if a contract for the sale of real property is oral, and not written, it may still be enforceable—usually by the buyer—if the complaining party can show that she partially performed pursuant to the oral agreement. Consider the following example:

EXAMPLE

Should Partial Performance Trump the Statute of Frauds?

Owner and "Buyer" have several discussions regarding Owner's property, Greenacres. (We have put "Buyer" in quotes because it is up to you to determine his ultimate status as either a real buyer, or rather, the lessee, of Greenacres.) Owner really does not want to sell, but would prefer an arrangement involving a long-term lease, rather than an outright sale.

Buyer, on the other hand, would prefer to purchase the property. Buyer gives Owner a $2,000 deposit and takes possession of Greenacres. Over the next two years, Buyer makes monthly payments of $750 to Owner. Also during this time, Buyer has made improvements to the property by building a barn and drilling a water well.

At the end of the second year of possession, Buyer sees Owner at the local feed and seed store, approaches Owner, and says: "Isn't it about time that you gave me the deed to Greenacres?"

Owner replies: "What are you talking about? We agreed to a long-term lease. I didn't sell you Greenacres!" Owner and Buyer exchange more angry words, and almost come to blows.

If the property is located in a state that strictly adheres to the statute of frauds' requirement of a writing, Owner will prevail because there simply was no written agreement for the sale of Greenacres.

On the other hand, if the property is located in a state that has adopted the doctrine of partial performance as an exception to the statute of frauds' writing requirement, then Buyer has a pretty good chance of prevailing and taking ownership of Greenacres. Buyer will allege that the $2,000 deposit was a down payment, that the monthly payments were mortgage payments, and that the building of a barn and the drilling of a water well constitute "partial performance" that indicate that he did in fact purchase Greenacres.

Owner will argue that the $2,000 was a rental deposit (and not a down payment), that the monthly payments were rental payments, and that the building of the barn and the drilling of the well were necessary to the operation of Buyer's dairy business under a long-term lease, and is in no way evidence of a sale of Greenacres.

In light of this example, which type of statute of frauds do you prefer:

1. One that strictly adheres to the requirement of a writing, or
2. One that requires a writing, but allows an exception for partial performance?

I. The Common Law

Frequently throughout this text, we will make reference to "the common law." Common law is sometimes referred to as case law, or judge-made law. The "common" in common law means that the law is applicable to all the citizens of a region or country.

Common law is created, modified, and molded by court opinions over long periods of time, taking into consideration the beliefs, principles, and culture of the citizens. Over time, bedrock principles of law—sometimes called **black letter law**—are established. The common law allows judges to take those bedrock principles and mold them to the needs of a particular case to arrive at a just result. In other words, common law allows judges the flexibility to render fair decisions.

Thus, common law is different from statutory law, which is created by legislative bodies, such as the United States Congress or your state legislature. When interpreting statutes, judges have far less flexibility than when making decisions under common law, and are supposed to apply the statutory language as it was written and intended by the legislative body.

Our common law comes to us from England, where opinions by some courts were recorded as early as the fourteenth century. When the English colonists settled in North America in the 1600s, they brought with them their traditions of English common law. Following the Revolutionary War against the British, there was debate among the newly independent colonists as to whether, in throwing off the yoke of English rule, they would also dispose of English common law. Those in favor of retaining English common law won the debate, and that victory is memorialized in the Seventh Amendment to the United States Constitution—ratified in 1791—which reads:

> In Suits at *common law*, where the value in controversy shall exceed twenty dollars, the right of trial by jury shall be preserved, and no fact tried by a jury, shall be otherwise re-examined in any Court of the United States, than according to the rules of the *common law*.

Statutory law can always supersede common law, and this occurs when the legislature feels that a case was wrongly decided by a court of appeal. In that event, the legislative body may pass a law that will compel the court to rule differently if the same issue arises in the future. Thus, statutory law may "trump" common law because the legislature, at least in theory, represents the will of the people of a state, which takes precedence over case law made by a judge, or panel of judges. Of course, a state's statutes must be constitutional under both the state and federal constitutions.

Common Law
law that has been developed by courts, rather than legislative bodies.

Black Letter Law
bedrock principles of common law that have developed over the centuries. It is black letter law, for instance, that we each owe a duty of care to those around us to act in a manner so as not to create an unreasonable risk of harm to them.

J. Transactional or Litigation Law Office

By now, you might be thinking that you would like to work in a law office that practices in the legal area of real property. Such law offices can be divided into two basic types: the transactional law office and the litigation law office.

The **transactional law firm** engages in real property ***transactions***, meaning that these firms specialize in real estate sales, leasing, and development. They work to consummate deals, that is, transactions, by:

1. Drafting commercial lease agreements, for example, long-term lease agreements between the owner of a large parcel of land, and major corporate tenants such as Target, Home Depot or Wal-Mart;

Transactional Law Firm
the law office activities that pertain to the negotiation and the making of deals relating to real estate.

2. Assisting buyers and sellers, and lessors and lessees, usually in commercial transactions, in locating and structuring the financing by which to complete the transaction or project;

3. Assisting developers in acquiring property, as well as acquiring the licenses and permits required by various local, state, or federal agencies related to zoning ordinances, environmental regulations, and expansion of the infrastructure such as roadways and water and sewer systems. The attorneys in such law firms may make appearances at city and county council meetings regarding zoning and other legal issues related to a proposed real estate development in a community;

4. Drafting Conditions, Covenants, and Restrictions (CC&Rs) for homeowners associations and condominium projects;

5. Conducting closings on the sale of real estate.

While transactional law firms can be quite hectic at times because of looming closing deadlines, the lawyers and paralegals do not usually find themselves in a courtroom.

Litigation Law Firm
the law office activities that pertain to the process of seeking a remedy at law; a lawsuit.

Alternatively, a **litigation law firm** does just that … it litigates. These law firms specialize in trial work, and occasionally, the trials take place in other parts of the state, or even other parts of the country. Paralegals who work in litigation firms perform the type of duties that you have read about in your other paralegal texts, for example:

1. Interviewing clients and witnesses;

2. Researching the legal issues of the cases, as well as drafting legal documents including complaints, motions, and briefs;

3. Preparing for depositions, summarizing deposition testimony, and conducting other duties related to the discovery process;

4. Preparing for trial by scheduling witnesses and issuing subpoenas for their appearances in court, organizing documents and preparing the trial notebooks, arranging for presentation of exhibits, etc.; and

5. Assisting the attorney during the trial.

You might be one of those paralegals who enjoys the rough-and-tumble world of litigation, and do not mind, and may even enjoy, being in another city or state for days, weeks, or months at a time to litigate an important case. Analyze your personal characteristics and preferences with the requirements of each type of law office to determine whether you would be more comfortable in a transactional law office or a litigation law firm. Each has its own advantages and disadvantages.

Obviously, some firms have elements of both transactional and litigation practices. But when you go on your interviews, do not be shy about asking about the type of real estate activity in which the firm is primarily involved.

CHAPTER SUMMARY

The importance of land in our nation's history and development and cannot be overemphasized. The title to lands that were first occupied and claimed by Native Americans as early as 10,000 BC came to vest first in European governments, and later in the United States government.

Two of the most important characteristics of real property are its *immovability* (which makes real estate the ideal vehicle for taxation) and *uniqueness*, which is

why when a seller fails to perform pursuant to an offer to purchase, the buyer may seek the remedy of specific performance, that is, the buyer may ask the court to order seller to convey the property to the buyer.

Real property is land, and anything permanently attached to it. Real property consists of a *bundle of rights*, including the right to possess, lease, mortgage, convey, use and enjoy, and exclude all others from the property. However, these rights are not absolute, and the state may limit an owner's rights in the property by way of its *police powers*, that is, the state's authority to limit ownership rights in order to benefit the public's health, safety, morals, or general welfare.

Personal property is all property other than real property. Personal property is sometimes referred to as chattel. Personal property may be tangible or intangible. *Tangible* personal property are things that we can hold or touch, such as furniture, an automobile, or an article of clothing. Examples of *intangible* personal property include the ownership of patents, copyrights, shares of stock, and even the right to sue someone.

Title and possession are distinct, but related, concepts. *Title* is ownership, or the evidence of ownership, of real or personal property. Title to real property is evidenced by a *deed* to the property. Also, one may hold title to personal property, such as the title to a motor vehicle.

Possession is the right to exercise dominion and control of real or personal property, but not necessarily ownership. A thief may have possession of another's car, but that does not mean that the thief owns the car.

A *fixture* is an item of personal property, which by virtue of its attachment to real property, becomes real property itself. To determine whether an item is a fixture or personal property (which may be removed from the real property), courts will look at several factors, but primarily at the intent of the affixer of the personal property, and the method of its attachment to the real property.

Common law is case law, or judge-made law. The common law has descended from England and is made by judges. Common law is distinguished from *statutory law*, which is enacted by legislative bodies.

Transactional law offices engage in deal-making, including the drafting of leases and contracts relating to real property. *Litigation* law offices try cases in court. Most law offices that have a real property practice will, to a certain extent, do both transactional work and litigation.

KEY TERMS

Annexor
Black Letter Law
Bundle of Rights
Chattel
Common Law
Convey
Dominion and Control
Estate
Fixture

Immovability
Intent of the Parties
Litigation Law Office
Ownership
Personal Property
Police Powers
Possession
Real Property
Rebuttable Presumption

Sovereign
Statutory Law
Title
Title by Conquest
Transactional Law Office
Uniqueness
Use and Enjoy

CONCEPT REVIEW QUESTIONS

1. How did the availability of abundant, cheap, and sometimes even free land drive the economic development and the populating of the United States? Was this necessarily a good thing, or did it perhaps hasten the demise of the native populations?

2. What is the difference between real and personal property? Can real property become personal property? Can personal property become real property?

3. How do title and possession of real property differ? In the case of *Johnson v. M'Intosh* found earlier in this chapter, did the Piankeshaw Indians have title to, or possession of, the land in dispute, or perhaps both, or neither? In communal cultures that do not have ownership of land by individuals, do the concepts of title and possession change?

4. What rights can be contained in a land owner's "bundle of rights," and can the local, state, or federal government regulate a land owner's rights? What is the term used to describe a state or local government's powers to regulate for the purpose of public health, safety, morals, or general welfare?

5. There is a tension that exists between an individual's liberty interest—found in the Fourteenth Amendment of the U.S. Constitution—and the state's police power, which is its authority to regulate individual liberty when it conflicts with the public's health, safety, morals, and general welfare. Can you delineate any principles as to when individual liberty should trump the state's police power, or vice versa?

6. Our individual rights are very important to all of us. How does the police power check your individual liberties? Is it necessary that there be such a thing as the police power, or could our society exist without it?

ETHICS

AGREE TO **DISAGREE**

Pat Paralegal and Laura Lawyer have recently started working together on a large, commercial litigation case for one of the law firm's largest clients. Pat has extensive legal experience and has worked for the commercial litigation department for over 18 years. Laura has been practicing law for almost 6 years having joined the law firm right after law school. Pat is not fond of Laura, who can be very arrogant and bossy.

During a client meeting, Laura suggests a course of action that involves extensive motion work, which will cost the client thousands of dollars. Pat knows that the case law on the issue that Laura wants to argue is not favorable let alone persuasive, so the motion is a huge risk for the client and may even end up making the judge angry.

Based on Pat's body language and facial expressions, the client notices that Pat does not agree with Laura's advice. After the meeting ends, Pat walks the client to the elevators as Laura rushes back to her office. The client asks Pat what she thinks about Laura's advice.

Should Pat tell the client that she disagrees with the Laura and explain why?

Should Pat tell the client that she agrees with Laura and that they should move forward with the plan of action?

Should Pat say nothing to the client and discuss her disagreement with Laura privately?

BUILDING YOUR PROFESSIONAL SKILLS

CRITICAL THINKING **EXERCISES**

1. In part, we have defined real property as land, or anything affixed to it. Consider the following everyday scenario:

    You are a real estate developer and are currently engaged in the excavation of a large tract of land to be used for a shopping center. The process of excavation involves the removal of thousands of tons of rock and soil by large machines. Some of the rock and soil is loaded into large dump trucks, while some is temporarily set off to the side of the excavation site awaiting the arrival of additional dump trucks.

    How would you classify the rock and soil that has been loaded onto dump trucks—as real property or personal property? Keep in mind that such soil is often sold as "fill." How would you classify the rock and soil that has been temporarily set off to the side of the excavation site—as real property or personal property? Explain the rationale for your answers.

2. One of the rights in the so-called "bundle of rights" is the right to *exclude* unwanted persons from your property, in other words, trespassers. Imagine a situation where a farmer employs dozens of workers on a seasonal basis. Congress has recently passed an act to provide legal and medical advice to migrant farm workers. Pursuant to the act, two federal officials make entry upon the farmer's land for the purpose of providing legal and medical advice to the migrant workers.

    The farmer insists that all discussions with the workers take place in his presence. The federal officials refuse, and the farmer orders them off his land. The federal officials refuse to leave, and the farmer has them arrested for trespass.

    Does the farmer have the *right to exclude* the unwanted federal officials from his property? What are the competing interests on each side of the scale of justice?

    Does Congress have the power to force the owner of private property to allow government officials to communicate with his employees, especially if those communications could interfere with farming operations?

    See how some of these questions were answered in *State v. Shack*, 58 N.J. 297, 277 A.2d 369 (1971).

3. The concept of the state's "police powers" is very important as it relates to the ownership of private property. Recall that under its police powers, the state or governmental entity has the right to enact laws and regulations for the protection of the community. These powers fall into four broad categories: protection of the public health, public safety, public morals, and general welfare. But in protecting the public, the police power necessarily interferes with an individual's rights in his or her real property.

    The question that is frequently asked in government regulation cases is when does a regulation go so far that it actually constitutes a "taking" of the owner's property, such that compensation should be paid by the government to the owner?

Example: An owner of vacant beachfront lot wants to build a modest, 2,000-square-foot residence on the property, which is allowed under the local zoning ordinance. However, the state coastal commission, which can overrule the issuance of a permit by the local zoning commission, has been receiving many complaints that the public beaches are not readily accessible, and that new access points are necessary for the public's enjoyment of the sand and surf.

The coastal commission then demands that in exchange for the approval of the building permit, it wants the land owner to give to the state a 25-foot wide easement across the owner's property for public access to the beach. Although the state has not actually "taken" the owner's property as it would have for a school building or public hospital, it has nevertheless intruded upon the owner's "bundle of rights."

Does requiring an owner to give the easement in exchange for the issuance of the building permit constitute a taking, in violation of the Fifth and Fourteenth Amendments to the U.S. Constitution?

At what point do regulations become so burdensome upon a landowner that they would constitute a taking? Keep in mind that property owners may have paid many thousands, or even millions, of dollars for the right to use their property as they see fit. What is the proper balance between those individual property rights, and the state's police powers?

4. You are a paralegal in a transactional law office, where you have been employed for the last seven years. Much of what you do involves closings of real property sales, including a substantial amount of document preparation and review.

One of your friends, knowing that you work in a law office that handles real estate closings, has asked you to take a look at the deed to her residential property. Your friend thinks that there may be a mistake in the legal description of her lot, and wants your opinion on the matter: "It will only take you five minutes to look at the deed and tell me what you think."

Are you permitted to give your opinion? Explain the reason(s) for your answer. Is there a public policy consideration which might inform your decision to help your friend, or politely decline?

RESEARCH ON THE **WEB**

1. The definition of the word "fixture" differs from state to state. How does your state define the word "fixture," and is it defined by statute or case law, or both?

   Is there a difference between commercial fixtures and residential fixtures? Is the word used ambiguously, that is, in some contexts, does the word "fixture" mean real property that is not removable, and in other contexts does the word mean personal property that may be removed?

2. How much of the land in your state is still owned by the federal government? How much is owned by the state government?

   Can you determine how much of the government-owned land is held open to the public for recreation, is leased out to private entities for mining or timber operations, or is used for a military base or facility?

3. What *individual* owns the largest amount of land in the United States? Where is most of that owned acreage located?

4. Does your city, town, or county have building and zoning codes? When were they enacted, and by what type of governmental body (state legislature, county commissioners, or town council)?

BUILDING YOUR **PROFESSIONAL** PORTFOLIO

1. Earlier in this chapter we discovered that title to real property is transferred by a written document called a deed, while title to personal property is often transferred and evidenced by a ***bill of sale***. The requirements of the documents are very similar in some respects. What might both of the documents include? Consider the following:

   a. The parties to the transaction,

   b. A description of the property to be conveyed,

   c. The date of the conveyance,

   d. The price of the conveyed property, if any, and

   e. The signature of at least the seller (a deed), and the buyer (a bill of sale).

   Your assignment is to draft a simple bill of sale involving the transfer of several items of furniture in your house or apartment. The bill of sale should definitely include items a–e above, and *any other terms or conditions that you think necessary*.

   Do not worry about using "legalese" in drafting the document. Use simple, understandable language, but also be precise, especially in the description of the personal property to be conveyed.

After you have finished drafting the bill of sale, put it aside for a day or two and then review it with a critical eye. Is there any room for ***ambiguity*** regarding which items are to be transferred to the buyer? Is it clear who the buyer is?

Were any important terms or conditions overlooked, for example, when is the transfer of the property to be made, and are you to deliver the furniture, or will the buyer come and pick up the property at your residence?

What are the terms of the purchase, that is, cash, or payments over time, and if payments are to be made, how many payments must be made, in what amount, and where should they be sent? What rights does the seller have if the buyer defaults?

chapter 2
ESTATES IN LAND

Estates

The poorest man may in his cottage bid defiance to all the force of the Crown. It may be frail; its roof may shake; the wind may blow through it; the storms may enter, the rain may enter—but the King of England cannot enter; all his forces dare not cross the threshold of the ruined tenement!

—WILLIAM PITT, EARL OF CHATHAM (1708–1778)

An estate is the nature and extent of one's interest in the land, and can be considered a bundle of rights. The greatest bundle of rights is the present possessory[1] estate known as the *fee simple*, or *fee simple absolute*. But as we have seen, even fee simple ownership, and the rights within that bundle, are not absolute; those rights can be limited by the police power of the federal, state, or local governments.

The classification of estates can be very confusing, and the student is advised to refer often to the outline at the beginning of the chapter. In categorizing estates, the first great division is between *freehold* estates and *non-freehold* estates.

A non-freehold estate is synonymous with a leasehold estate, which is the technical term for the bundle of rights that an apartment renter has. The renter is not "seized" of the property, that is, does not have title to the property, nor any right of ownership. Unlike a fee simple estate, the duration of the leasehold estate is definite, or can be made definite. Now we will turn our attention to freehold estates.

A. Freehold Estates

Freehold estates have two primary characteristics:

1. ***Ownership*** of the property. One who has a freehold estate owns the property. Ownership is sometimes referred to as **seisin**. Think of the owner of a *free*hold estate as being free to convey the property, and
2. The freehold estate is of ***indefinite*** duration. This means that we do not know when the estate will end. The most familiar example of a freehold estate is an owner-occupied residence. In that situation, we do not know when the owner will decide to sell property, lease it, give it as a gift, or otherwise dispose of the property; that is, the duration of the estate is indefinite.

To assist you in categorizing and understanding freehold estates, review the chart on page 29.

The first category of freehold estates is the fee simple, or fee simple absolute.

The second category consists of defeasible fee simple estates, which are fee simple estates with conditions attached.

The third category of freehold estates includes the life estates.

Seisin
a term that goes back to feudal England, and is synonymous with the concept of title or ownership. If you are "seized" of the property, you have the right to convey the property.

EXAMPLE

FREEHOLD ESTATES

(two characteristics: *ownership* and *indefinite duration*)

1. Fee Simple, or Fee Simple Absolute—*the <u>best</u> estate possible*
2. *Defeasible* Fee Simple Estates—<u>*less than the best*</u> *because the estate comes with "strings"*
   a. Fee Simple Determinable
   b. Fee Simple upon Condition Subsequent
   c. Fee Simple Subject to Executory Limitation
3. Life Estates
   a. Life Estate Pur Autre Vie

NON-FREEHOLD ESTATES

Think of an apartment lease. An apartment lease is *not* a freehold estate because the tenant does not own the property, and the tenancy is of a *definite duration* (or can be made definite). Non-freehold estates will be discussed in a later chapter.

---

[1]A present estate is one which may be enjoyed immediately in the present. There is another type of estate, which can be used and enjoyed only in the future, and appropriately, is known as a future estate.

1. FEE SIMPLE ABSOLUTE

The most important type of freehold estate is the fee simple, sometimes called the fee simple absolute; these terms are synonymous. A fee simple is the estate containing the greatest bundle of rights. The language of conveyance of a fee simple estate is quite simple, for example:

> *Grantor hereby conveys Greenacres to grantee in fee simple.*

The **grantor** is transferring a fee simple estate, in its entirety, to the grantee, and the language of conveyance above is *unconditional*, meaning that there are "no strings attached" to the transfer. The **grantee**, who has become the new owner, can do whatever she pleases with the property, as long as that use is allowed by law.

Grantor
one who conveys real property to another.

Grantee
one to whom real property is conveyed.

2. *DEFEASIBLE* FEE SIMPLE ESTATES

Some conveyances of fee simple estates are conveyed with **conditions** or "strings attached," which, if the condition comes to pass, may terminate the fee simple estate. These types of estates are called *defeasible* fee simple estates because title can be *defeated* if the condition in the conveyance is breached. These defeasible, fee simple estates are still freehold estates because they retain the two important characteristics of a freehold: the owners are seized of these properties (i.e., they own them), and the estates are of indefinite duration. There are three types of conditional or defeasible fee simple estates:

a. Fee Simple Determinable

Let's look again at the conveyance of Greenacres, but notice that this time there is a condition to the conveyance of the property:

> *Grantor hereby conveys Greenacres to grantee in fee simple <u>for as long as</u> the property is not used for the sale of cigarettes.*

Here, the grantor is conveying a fee simple estate (the highest bundle of rights), *but* one which has a condition attached, that is, the non-sale of cigarettes.

What if the condition in the conveyance is breached at some point in the future? Where, or to whom, will the ownership of Greenacres go? It is a characteristic of a fee simple determinable estate that if the condition found in the conveyance is breached, that title will **automatically revert** to the grantor, or the grantor's heirs. Even if the grantee sells Greenacres to another person, the condition will run with the property, although not indefinitely (see the section on public policy later in this section).

As a result, the grantor has what is known as a **future interest** or future estate in Greenacres. Each of the three defeasible estates must have an accompanying future estate connected to it that answers the question:

> *To whom will the property go if the condition is breached?*

You may be wondering how the transfer of title occurs automatically. In fact, it does not. The grantor, or the heirs of the grantor, would have to file a **suit to quiet title**, meaning that a court would be asked to order the transfer of the title from the grantee back to the grantor, or the grantor's heirs.

Suit to Quiet Title
an action brought by a plaintiff who seeks to have a court determine that plaintiff is the owner of a piece of real property. Also called a "quiet title action."

b. Fee Simple upon Condition Subsequent

The second type of defeasible fee simple estate is known as a fee simple upon condition subsequent. It is very similar to the fee simple determinable. The difference is that with a fee simple upon condition subsequent, the property does not automatically revert to the grantor, but rather the grantor or the grantor's heirs **may elect to terminate** the grantee's ownership of Greenacres.

In a conveyance of a fee simple upon condition subsequent, the language of conveyance might read:

> *Grantor hereby conveys Greenacres to grantee in fee simple on the condition that the property is not used for the sale of cigarettes, and if it is so used, grantor <u>may</u> reenter the property and terminate the estate.*

Here again, the grantor has a future estate in Greenacres, which is known as the **right of reentry** or alternatively, as the **power of termination**. Unlike the fee simple determinable estate, the fee simple upon condition subsequent **does not automatically** revert to the grantor. Instead, the grantor must elect to exercise the right of reentry/power of termination. And if the grantor chooses to exercise the power of termination, grantor would once again have to file a suit to quiet title. However, many states have **statutes of limitation** that require that suits to enforce the power of termination be brought within a certain time following the breach of the condition.

c. Fee Simple Subject to Executory Limitation

The third and final type of defeasible fee simple estate is known as a fee simple subject to executory limitation. It differs from the first two defeasible estates (fee simple determinable and fee simple upon condition subsequent) in that if the condition is breached, and cigarettes are sold on Greenacres, the property will pass to a **third-party**, rather than the grantor.

The language in the deed conveying a fee simple subject to an executor limitation might read:

> *Grantor hereby conveys Greenacres to grantee in fee simple on the condition that the property is not used for the sale of cigarettes, but if it is so used, <u>then to the American Heart Association</u>.*

You may say that the grantee holds Greenacres in fee simple, subject to an executory limitation in favor of the American Heart Association. The American Heart Association has a future interest known as an **executory interest**.

As to all three of the defeasible or conditional fee simple estates, it can be said that as a matter of public policy, the law does not favor conditions limiting the lawful use of a property. This is especially true of a testator, or a grantor who has died, who is exercising control of property "from the grave." Thus, at some point after the grantor or testator has died, a court will remove the condition on ownership found in the conveyance of the defeasible fee simple estate, whether the transfer was by deed or by will.

Several states have enacted statutes that bar the enforcement of a condition found in conveyances of defeasible fee simple estates. For example, such a statute might make the condition in the deed or will (e.g., no gambling, no sale of cigarettes on the property) void after a period of 40 years.

Public policy also favors the ***free alienability*** (transferability) of real property by a grantee. Consistent with the high value that we place on individual property rights, the rationale underlying the public policy is that a grantee should use and enjoy the property as the grantee—who is now the owner—deems best, not the grantor.

Therefore, if there is any doubt about whether a conveyance transferred a fee simple estate, or a defeasible fee simple state (one with conditions upon use of the property), the court will favor an interpretation of the deed that favors the creation of an estate in fee simple, that is, without any conditions. Thus, it is most important that the grantor's intent be made crystal clear when the attorney drafts a deed conveying a defeasible fee simple estate.

Finally, public policy mandates that any condition of a defeasible fee estate must be stricken from the conveyance if it discriminates on the basis of race, sex, or religion, or violates some other fundamental right of the grantee.

EXAMPLE

Testator writes in her will:

"Upon my death, I do devise to my only surviving daughter, Christine, all of that property known as Greenacres, located in Our Town, USA, for as long as she remains a member of the Baptist faith. If Christine leaves the Baptist faith, Greenacres is to be conveyed in fee simple to the Town of Pleasantville to be used as a public park."

What do you believe that the public policy in your jurisdiction would have to say about the condition attached to the transfer of Greenacres?

Do you think that the condition, if breached by Karen, would be, or should be, enforced by the court?

In the following case from 1988, the plaintiffs, Mr. and Mrs. Wood, had granted land to the defendant County Board of Commissioners in 1948 to build a county hospital. Plaintiffs sought compensation for the value of the land it had conveyed to the defendant, because they alleged that approximately 40 years after the land was conveyed to the defendant, it was no longer being used for the purpose specified in the deed.

WOOD V. BOARD OF COUNTY COMM. OF FREMONT COUNTY

Supreme Court of Wyoming
759 P.2d 1250; 1988 Wyo. LEXIS 108
August 22, 1988

Opinion

Appellants Cecil and Edna Wood appeal summary judgment favoring appellee, the Board of County Commissioners for Fremont County, Wyoming. By a 1948 warranty deed appellants conveyed land in Riverton, Wyoming, to Fremont County for the construction of a county hospital. They now contend that language in the deed created either a *fee simple determinable* or a *fee simple subject to a condition subsequent* with a right of reversion in them if the land ceased to be used for the hospital. They present this issue:

Whether cessation of appellee's hospital operation by sale of public hospital facilities to a private company constituted the occurrence of an event which divested appellee of its estate in property *conditionally conveyed* by appellants.

On September 1, 1948, by warranty deed, appellants conveyed a tract of land situated in Fremont

(continued)

County, Wyoming, described as follows "... Said tract is conveyed to Fremont County for the purpose of constructing and maintaining thereon a County Hospital in memorial to the gallant men of the Armed Forces of the United States of America from Fremont County, Wyoming."

The County constructed a hospital on the land and operated it there until November 18, *1983*. At that time the County sold the land and the original hospital facility to a private company. The buyer operated a hospital on the premises until September, 1984, at which time it moved the operation to a newly constructed facility. The private company then put the premises up for sale.

Appellants filed their complaint in this case on January 16, 1986, seeking recovery of the value of the land they conveyed to the county in 1948.

Appellants' argument boils down to whether or not the language "...*for the purpose of constructing and maintaining thereon a County Hospital ...*" in the 1948 warranty deed is sufficient limiting language to create either 1) a fee simple determinable, or 2) a fee simple subject to a condition subsequent giving appellants title to the land. *W.S. 34-2-101* provides, in pertinent part:

"Every conveyance of real estate shall pass all the estate of the grantor unless the intent to pass a less estate shall expressly appear or be necessarily implied in the terms of the grant."

A fee simple estate in land that automatically expires upon the happening of a stated event, not certain to occur, is a fee simple determinable.

Words such as "so long as," "until," or "during" are commonly used in a conveyance to denote the presence of this type of special limitation. The critical requirement is that the **language of special limitation must clearly state** the particular circumstances under which the fee simple estate conveyed might expire. Language of conveyance that grants a fee simple estate in land for a special purpose, without stating the special circumstances that could trigger expiration of the estate, is not sufficient to create a fee simple determinable.

The plain language in the 1948 deed, stating that appellants conveyed the land to Fremont County for the purpose of constructing a county hospital, **does not clearly state that the estate conveyed will expire** **automatically** if the land is not used for the stated purpose. As such, it does not evidence an intent of the grantors to convey a fee simple determinable, and we hold that no fee simple determinable was created when the land was conveyed.

The language of conveyance fails to designate the time at which the hospital must be constructed as well as the time during which it must be maintained or during which the indicated memory must be preserved. The omission of such limiting language evidences an intent *not* to convey a fee simple determinable.

Similar reasoning applies to appellants' assertion that the language of conveyance created a fee simple subject to a condition subsequent. A fee simple subject to a condition subsequent is a fee simple estate in land that gives the grantor a discretionary power to terminate the grantee's estate after the happening of a stated event, not certain to occur. This type of interest is similar to the fee simple determinable in that the language of conveyance must clearly state the grantor's intent to create a discretionary power to terminate the estate he conveys. Words commonly used in a conveyance to denote the presence of a fee simple estate subject to a condition subsequent include "upon express condition that," "upon condition that," "provided that," or "if."

It is a well-settled rule that conditions tending to destroy fee simple estates, such as conditions subsequent, **are not favored** in law. They are strictly construed. Accordingly, no provision will be interpreted to create such a condition if the language will bear any other reasonable interpretation, or unless the language, used unequivocally, indicates an intention upon the part of the grantor or devisor to that effect and plainly admits of such construction.

That rule has not lost its potency. Applying it to this case, we hold that the plain language of the 1948 warranty deed, while articulating that the land conveyed was to be used for a county hospital, **does not clearly state an intent** of the grantors to retain a discretionary power to reenter the land if the land ceased to be used for the stated purpose. Appellants did not convey a fee simple subject to a condition subsequent, and we will not create one by construction some forty years after the conveyance took place.

Summary judgment is affirmed.

3. LIFE ESTATES

Consider the following language found in a deed:

> *I hereby grant to my sister Lisa a life estate in Greenacres.*

Lisa has received a **life estate**. A life estate is a *freehold* estate because: ownership of the property passes to the *life tenant* Lisa, and the estate is of indefinite duration because we do not know how long the measuring life—Lisa's life—will last.

Life Estate
an estate held only for the duration of a specified person's life, usually the possessor's life.

a. Life Tenant

Lisa is the life tenant of Greenacres, and Lisa's life is the *measuring life* of the tenancy. Although Lisa is referred to as a "tenant," her relationship with the grantor is not like the relationship between a landlord and tenant. As we will see in a section below, Lisa has many more rights in the property than would a tenant in an everyday rental situation.

b. Life Estate Pur Autre Vie

In the case of Lisa above, her life was the measuring life of the tenancy. However, the life estate may be measured by the life of someone other than the life tenant. This is called a life estate pur autre vie (French for the "life of another"). Take the following example:

> *I, Michael, grant to my brother Fredo, a life estate in my Lake Tahoe residence, for the life of our Mother.*

Here, when their Mother dies, Fredo's life estate is terminated.

c. Reversion

By definition, life estates only last as long as the measuring life, which may either be the life of the life tenant, or a third party if the tenancy is pur autre vie. The question naturally arises in the examples above, what happens to Greenacres after Lisa's death, or to the Lake Tahoe compound after the death of the Mother?

If the language of the conveyance does not direct otherwise, the life estate will automatically **revert** to the grantor of the life estate, and this is a future interest known as a **reversion**.

Reverter or Reversion
occurs when the property reverts to the grantor at the end of a life estate.

d. Remainderman

Alternatively, there may be a provision in the deed or will conveying the life estate that upon the death of the measuring life, the property will go to a third-party, who is known as the **remainderman**. Consider the example below:

Remainderman
the third person to whom the property is conveyed at the end of a life estate.

EXAMPLE

Example of a Remainderman

Anna was previously married to Arthur, and they had one child, Ashley. In the divorce settlement, Anna became the sole owner of what had been their family residence at 123 Oak St.

> Anna recently remarried. Her husband's name is Harry, and he is 15 years younger than she. At Harry's urging, Anna drafted a new will, in which she wrote:
> *"In the event that I predecease my husband Harry, I leave to him a life estate in our residence at 123 Oak St., and then to my daughter Ashley."*
> When Anna dies, Harry will receive a life estate, and will become the life tenant in the Oak Street property. But upon Harry's death, the Oak Street house will go to Anna's daughter Ashley, who is the remainderman. Ashley will take the property in fee simple.
> Anna's status as the remainderman is another example of a future interest.

Life estates are created either by **deed** or **will** and are often created when one or both spouses have been previously married, and have children from the previous marriage(s). The idea behind this arrangement is that the spouse who dies first—Anna in the example above—wants the surviving spouse, Harry, to live comfortably. At the same time, Anna wants the house that she acquired during her lifetime to go to her daughter Ashley, rather than to any of Harry's children. Harry will be allowed to live in the Oak Street house until his life estate terminates at his death, when the property will pass to the remainderman, Ashley.

The remainderman may be a male or female, or an entity such as a university, or a charitable organization like the American Red Cross.

e. Duties of the Life Tenant

In the example above, when Harry becomes the life tenant, what duties, if any, does he owe to the remainderman, Ashley? Can Harry do whatever he wants with the property, such as hold wild parties where the property is damaged, or chop down the beautiful 100-year-old trees in the yard of the residence?

The answers to the questions above are "definitely not". The life tenant cannot damage the property to the detriment of the remainderman. Life tenants have certain duties to the remainderman:

1. The life tenant must not commit **waste** on, or to, the life estate.

Waste
any use of the property by the life tenant that unreasonably reduces the value of the life estate.

Waste is any use of the property by the life tenant that **unreasonably reduces the value** of the estate. In the example of the Oak Street property, suppose that Harry, the life tenant, wants to enlarge the rear deck of the house. To do so, he must cut down two beautiful 100-year-old oak trees. Doing so would probably constitute waste upon the property, and the remainderman, Ashley, could sue to enjoin or restrain Harry's planned removal of the trees, or seek damages if the trees have already been cut down.

2. The life tenant must **maintain** the property by making any necessary repairs.

The life tenant must make any repairs that are reasonably necessary to maintain the property in approximately the same condition as when the life tenant received the estate. The life tenant is not required to improve the property.

3. The life tenant must pay all **property taxes**.
4. The life tenant must pay the **interest** on the mortgage (but not the principal, unless the deed or will granting the life estate states otherwise).

f. Rights of the Life Tenant

In addition to using and enjoying the life estate, the life tenant has two other important rights in the property.

i. Right to Profits   The life tenant is entitled to any profits from the property. If Harry, in the example above, were to rent out rooms at the Oak Street house, he would be entitled to keep any profits left over after paying the property taxes, and the routine maintenance and upkeep of the property.

The life tenant may be entitled to profits from other types of commercial operations such as mining, quarrying, or cutting timber. These activities are not considered waste if the property was previously used for such purposes.

However, if there was no such previous use, the aforementioned operations may indeed constitute waste of the life estate, for which the remainderman may seek damages.

ii. Right to Convey to Extent of Her Own Interest   A second, and rather surprising, right that life tenants have is the right to convey the property. The states differ on whether a life tenant can actually sell the property, but the important thing to remember is that the life tenant cannot convey any greater estate than what he or she possesses.

A life tenant may lease the property for an office, for example, but regardless of the length of the lease, it will terminate when the life tenant dies. The reason: Harry's life is the measuring life of the life estate. Because the life estate terminates when the life tenant dies, he cannot convey more rights in the lease than what he owns. When the life tenant dies, the property will pass to the remainderman, in fee simple. The remainderman could, of course, choose to let the tenant stay on under the terms of the lease with the life tenant, or the remainderman could negotiate a new lease.

g. Life Estate Subject to Condition

Just as fee simple estates can be made defeasible by attaching conditions to the conveyance (by deed or will), so too can life estates. Looking again at Anna's leaving in her will a life estate to Harry, she could have written the conveyance as follows, and made the life estate defeasible:

> In the event that I predecease my husband Harry, I leave to him a life estate in our residence at 123 Oak Street, _for so long as he remains unmarried_, and then to my daughter Ashley. If Harry should remarry, his life estate will immediately terminate, and 123 Oak Street shall go immediately to my daughter Ashley in fee simple.

Do you think that the condition in the clause above discriminates in an illegal way against Harry?

We stated previously that, as to a life estate, waste is that which diminishes the value of the property, and consequently, the remainderman's future interest. But suppose that the life tenant wishes to _improve_ the property so that there will be an actual increase in the value of the present life estate, as well as the remainderman's future interest. Might the life tenant's desired improvements still be deemed "waste"? The following case from New York examines that interesting question.

BROKAW V. FAIRCHILD
Supreme Court of New York, New York County
135 Misc. 70; 237 N.Y.S. 6
October 24, 1929

Opinion

This is an action in which plaintiff [the life tenant] asks that it be adjudged that he has the right to remove the present structures and improvements on No. 1 East 79th Street, and to erect new structures and improvements thereon.

In the year 1886 the late Isaac Brokaw bought for $ 199,000 a plot of ground in the borough of Manhattan, opposite Central Park, having a frontage of 102 feet on the easterly side of 5th Avenue and a depth of 150 feet on the northerly side of 79th Street. Opposite there is an entrance to the park.

Mr. Brokaw erected in the year 1887, for his own occupancy, a residence known as No. 1 East 79th Street, at a cost of over $ 300,000. That residence and corner plot is the subject-matter of this action. It is an exceedingly fine house, in construction and general condition as fine as anything in New York.

Since 1913, the year of the death of Isaac Brokaw and the commencement of the *life estate* of plaintiff [George Brokaw], there has been a change of circumstances and conditions in connection with 5th Avenue properties. Apartments were erected with great rapidity and the building of private residences has practically ceased. Plaintiff's expert testified: "It is not possible to get an adequate return on the value of that land by any type of improvement other than an apartment house. The structure proposed in the plans of plaintiff is proper and suitable for the site and show 172 rooms which would rent for $ 1,000 per room. There is an excellent demand for such apartments."

The plaintiff testified also that his expenses in operating the residence which is unproductive would be at least $ 70,542 greater than if he resided in an apartment. He claims such difference constitutes a loss and contends that the erected apartment house would change this loss into an income or profit of $ 30,000. Plaintiff claims that under the facts and changed conditions shown the demolition of the building and erection of the proposed apartment is for the best interests of himself as life tenant, and the *remaindermen*. The defendants [remaindermen] deny these contentions and assert that the proposed demolition of the residence is *waste*, which plaintiff cannot be permitted to accomplish.

It has been generally recognized that any act of the life tenant which does permanent injury to the inheritance is waste. The law intends that the life tenant shall enjoy his estate in such a reasonable manner that the land shall pass to the *reversioner* or *remainderman* as nearly as practicable unimpaired in its nature, character and improvements.

The general rule in this country is that the life tenant may do whatever is required for the general use and enjoyment of his estate as he received it. What the life tenant may do in the future in the way of improving or adding value to the estate is not the test of what constitutes waste. The act of the tenant in changing the estate, and whether or not such act is lawful or unlawful, i.e., whether the estate is so changed as to be an injury to the inheritance, is the sole question involved.

To demolish that building and erect upon the land another building, even one such as the contemplated thirteen-story apartment house, *would change the inheritance*, the use of which was given to the plaintiff as tenant for life, so that the inheritance could not be delivered to the remaindermen or reversioners at the end of the life estate. The receipt by them at the end of the life estate of a thirteen-story $ 900,000 apartment house might be more beneficial to them. Financially, the objecting remaindermen may be unwise in not consenting to the proposed change. They may be selfish and unmindful that in the normal course of time and events they probably will not receive the fee. With motives and purposes the court is not concerned.

From the foregoing I am of the opinion, that upon the present facts, circumstances and conditions as they exist and are shown in this case, the plaintiff has no right and is not authorized to remove the present structures on or affecting the real estate in question.

4. HOW ARE FEE SIMPLE AND LIFE ESTATES CONVEYED?

Suppose that Owner owns Greenacres in fee simple. If Owner wants to convey Greenacres to another, the Owner—now the grantor—must decide whether to convey the property to the grantee either:

a. In fee simple/fee simple absolute, or

b. As a defeasible fee, i.e., the three categories of fee simple with "strings attached," or

c. As a life estate, or perhaps as a life estate pur autre vie.

Owner/Grantor's conveyance of Greenacres to the grantee may be made either as a gift, or for "valuable consideration," and usually, that means money.

By what legal methods may the ownership of Greenacres be transferred? The table below indicates how the various freehold estates may be conveyed. The left column identifies the three categories of freehold estates. The right column states how the estate in the left column can be created, and conveyed, to the grantee.

Freehold Estate Being Conveyed by Grantor	How Can the Estate Be Conveyed by Grantor to the Grantee?
Fee Simple a/k/a **Fee Simple Absolute**	• Deed (gift or sale) • Will • Intestate Succession[2] *(Why can <u>only</u> a fee simple estate be transferred by intestate succession, and <u>not</u> defeasible fee estates, or a life estate?)*
Defeasible Fee Simple Estates • FS Determinable • FS on Condition Subsequent • FS Subject to Executory Interest	• Deed (gift or sale) • Will
Life Estate (including pur autre vie)	• Deed (gift or sale) • Will

a. Transfer by Deed

Transfer by deed is the most common method of conveying real property. In a deed, a grantor—the owner of the property—conveys the property to a grantee. There are several formalities that are required for a transfer by deed, including delivery and acceptance of the deed, proper description of the property, and the grantor's signature (but not the grantee's). The language of conveyance might read like the following:

> *The Grantor, for a good and valuable consideration paid by the Grantee, the receipt of which is hereby acknowledged, does hereby grant, bargain, sell and convey unto the Grantee in fee simple, all that certain lot or parcel of land situated in the City of Smallville, Any State, and more particularly described as follows (legal description).*

This language is cumbersome for classroom purposes, and so when discussing the transfer of real property in fee simple absolute, real estate

---

[2]Regarding intestate succession, the terms "grantor" and "grantee" are technically inaccurate since the transfer of the decedent's property is accomplished by operation of law, rather than a grant (an agreement that effects a transfer) made by the decedent. The proper term for a decedent who dies without a will is the "intestate," and the person who receives some or all of the decedent's property is an "heir." A "beneficiary" is one who takes property under a will.

instructors will often use a shorthand. "O" stands for Owner, and "A" stands for any grantee under a deed:

> *O to A in fee simple.*
>
> or
>
> *O to A and her heirs.*
>
> or simplest of all:
>
> *O to A (and the fee simple estate is implied).*

b. Transfer by Will

Real property may also be transferred by a will. The person who writes the will that conveys the property is called the **testator**. The grant of real property in a will is known as a *devise*, and the person who receives the property is called a **beneficiary**, or more specifically, a devisee.

The language of conveyance of real property in a will might read like the following:

> *I, Jane Doe, being of sound mind and body, do hereby give, bequeath, and devise to my sole surviving child, John Doe, all of that real property known as 123 Main St., Anytown, USA.*

In the shorthand version below, "T" stands for Testator, and "A" represents anyone receiving property pursuant to the will:

> *T to A.*

c. Transfer by Intestate Succession—Fee Simple Only

When the owner of a property dies without a will, she is said to have died intestate. The laws of the state where the real property is located will determine who will become the new owner. Statutes relating to **intestate succession** will typically give the major share of the estate property to the decedent's spouse and/or children, who will then succeed to the ownership of the property.

But if the decedent leaves no surviving spouse, children, or parents, then more distant relations may be entitled to inherit the property, for example, the decedent's siblings, nieces and nephews, and so on. However, at some point, the state intestacy statutes will draw a line, beyond which no relative of the decedent may succeed to ownership of the decedent's property. In that event, the real property **escheats** to the state.

Of the estates that we have examined in this chapter, only a fee simple may be conveyed by intestate succession, that is, when the owner of the property dies without a will. To put it differently, a life estate or defeasible fee estate cannot be transferred by intestate succession. The reason is that, without a will, there would be no way that a court could determine that the decedent, who died intestate, intended to leave anything other than a fee simple estate.

There is no language of conveyance in intestate succession because there was no will that conveyed the property. With intestate succession, the transfer of the real property occurs by operation of law, although the **heir** of the intestate may always *renounce* (refuse to take ownership of) the inherited property.

B. Future Interests/Estates

A future interest, sometimes called a future estate, is one in which the possibility of possession exists in the future, rather than the present. In both defeasible fee simple estates and life estates there is a future interest.

Testator
one who dies with a valid will.

Beneficiary
a person or entity that receives property pursuant to a will.

Intestate Succession
the state statutes that determine how a decedent's real and personal property is to be distributed when that person has died intestate, that is, without a will. The persons taking the decedent's property by intestate succession are called heirs.

Escheat
occurs when ownership of real or personal property passes to the state because the decedent has died without a will, and there are no persons qualified to receive the property under the statutes of intestate succession.

Heir
a spouse or relative of a decedent who has died intestate (without a will) and is entitled by statute to some or all of the decedent's real and personal property.

The person or entity to which the property *may* pass has a future interest in the land. One who holds a future interest will not necessarily get to own or possess the property. Remember the three defeasible fee simple estates, each of which came with a condition attached. As long as the condition contained in the conveyance—the deed or will—is not breached, then the holder of the future interest will not take possession.

The table below summarizes the relationships between the present estates and their corresponding future interests. The law of future interests answers the following question:

If and when the present estate (left column) *terminates, who <u>may</u> take title to the property in the future* (answer is in the right column)?

Present Estate	Language of Conveyance	Future Interest
Fee Simple a/k/a **Fee Simple Absolute**	"O to A." "O to A in fee simple.*"*	There is **no corresponding future estate** because no conditions are contained in the conveyance. A fee simple estate can continue *as such* indefinitely, and through successive future owners.

Each of the following three types of **defeasible fee simple estates** comes with one or more conditions or strings attached, and therefore a corresponding future interest:

Present Estate	Language of Conveyance	Future Interest
	(note the <u>conditional</u> language, which if breached, can trigger the creation of the future estate)	
1. **Fee Simple Determinable**	"O *to A <u>for as long as</u> the property is not used for gambling, and if it is so used, title shall revert to O.*"	<u>**Possibility of Reverter**</u> Title will automatically revert to **grantor** (or heirs) upon a breach.
2. **Fee Simple upon Condition Subsequent**	"O *to A <u>on the condition that</u> the property is used for educational purposes, and if it is not so used, O <u>may</u> reenter the property and terminate the estate.*"	<u>**Right of Entry**</u> or <u>**Power of Termination**</u> Title reverts to grantor upon a breach **if grantor** elects to terminate the estate.
3. **Fee Simple Subject to Executory Limitation**	"O *to A <u>on the condition that</u> the property is not used for gambling, but if it is so used, then to B.*"	<u>**Executory Interest**</u> Title will pass to a ***3rd party.***

Life estates also have a corresponding future interests (reversions or remainders):

Present Estate	Language of Conveyance	Future Interest
Life Estate[3]	(although the language below is not conditional, the estate is of definite duration; i.e., the measuring life) "*O to A for life.*"	***Reversion*** (property reverts to **grantor** when LE ends)
	"*O to A for life, then to B.*"	***Remainder*** (property goes to a ***3rd party*** when LE ends)

---

[3]Like defeasible fee simple estates, life estates may also come with conditions. For example, a testator might state in his will: "I leave my daughter a life estate in Greenacres <u>for as long as</u> she remains unmarried; but if she marries, her life estate shall immediately terminate upon her marriage, and title to Greenacres shall then vest in my son."

CHAPTER SUMMARY

Freehold estates have two primary characteristics: 1) the holder of the estate has seisin, or title, to the property, that is, the person owns the property, and 2) the estate is of indefinite duration. A grantor cannot convey to a grantee an estate larger than what the grantor possesses.

Freehold estates include the following: fee simple absolute, defeasible fee simple (three types), and life estates.

Fee simple estates are also known as fee simple absolute. Fee simple estates contain the largest "bundle of rights" relating to the use and enjoyment of a property.

The fee simple estate has no future interest associated with it because it is of potentially indefinite duration.

The three types of *defeasible* fee simple estates are fee simple determinable, fee simple upon condition subsequent, and fee simple subject to executory limitation. Each of these defeasible fee estates are conveyed with *conditions* attached, such as no gambling on the property. The law of future interests answers the questions regarding where the property will go if there is a breach of the condition:

With the fee simple determinable estate, if there is a breach of the condition, title will automatically revert to the grantor; the grantor's future estate is known as a *possibility of reverter*.

With a fee simple upon condition subsequent, if there is a breach of the condition, the grantor may reenter the premises and terminate the estate at the grantor's option; the grantor's future estate is known as a *right of reentry*, or *power of termination*.

With a fee simple subject to executory limitation, if there is a breach of the condition, the property will go to a third party (rather than to the grantor, or the grantor's heirs). The third party has a future interest known as an *executory interest*.

A *life estate* is a type of freehold estate in which the life tenant holds title to the property for an indefinite period of time measured by the life of some person. The *measuring life* may be that of the life tenant, or some other person (a life estate *pur autre vie*). Here too, the property must go somewhere when the life tenant dies.

The property may return to the grantor or the grantor's heirs, and this future estate is known as a *reversion*. Alternatively, the property may go to a third party, whose future estate is known as the *remainder*.

Life tenants have a duty not to commit *waste* upon the property, but have a right to collect *profits* generated by the life estate.

The three types of defeasible fee simple estates (FS determinable, FS upon condition subsequent, and FS subject to executory limitation) and life estates may be conveyed *by deed or by will*. Fee simple absolute estates may be conveyed by deed, by will, or through intestate succession.

CONCEPT REVIEW AND REINFORCEMENT

KEY **TERMS**

Beneficiary	Future Estate	Present Estate
Deed	Grantee	Remainderman
Defeasible Fee Simple Estate	Grantor	Reverter or Reversion
Escheat	Heir	Right of Reentry / Power of Termination
Executory Interest	Intestate Succession	Seisin
Fee Simple / Fee Simple Absolute	Life Estate	Statutes of Limitation
Fee Simple Determinable	Life Estate Pur Autre Vie	Suit to Quiet Title
Fee Simple Subject to Executory Limitation	Life Tenant	Testator
	Measuring Life	Waste
Fee Simple upon Condition Subsequent	Possibility of Reverter	Will

CONCEPT **REVIEW** QUESTIONS

1. What is the difference between a fee simple absolute estate and a defeasible fee simple estate?

2. What are the three types of defeasible fee simple estates? Why are these estates referred to as "defeasible"? What is the significance of conditions when discussing the three types of defeasible estates?

3. How would you define a life estate? What is the holder of a life estate called? How is a reversion related to a life estate, and who may hold a reversionary interest?

4. Who holds the future interest known as a remainder? How does a remainder differ from a reversion?

5. What is the difference between a life estate and a life estate pur autre vie? What is meant by the "measuring life"?

6. Does a life tenant have a right to convey his or her life estate? What is the risk for anyone purchasing a life estate from the life tenant?

7. What is a grantor, and how does a grantor differ from a testator?

ETHICS

CROSS-**TRAINING**

Alice Attorney has spent the last ten years working in criminal law. She has always had a soft spot in her heart for the underprivileged so she only charges her clients what they can afford but that has put her behind in her rent and bills for the office. In order to increase her revenue Alice has decided to start conducting real estate closings even though she does not have any experience with the closing process other than attending the closing of her own home.

Alice purchases several reference books on real estate law and a how-to book on closings to help her in her new area of practice.

Must Alice disclose to her first few prospective clients that she has no experience in real estate closings? Why or why not?

What if Alice is asked directly by a prospective client how much experience she has in real estate, and more specifically, real estate closings?

May Alice charge her clients "a little extra" for the additional time it will take her to learn this new area of the law, and to conduct the closings?

BUILDING YOUR PROFESSIONAL SKILLS

CRITICAL THINKING **EXERCISES**

1. As you know, a life tenant may convey the life estate property to another person or entity. Are there any scenarios in which you could imagine buying a life estate from the life tenant, when you know that upon the death of the life tenant the property will revert to the grantor? What if the life tenant was very young?

2. The law permits grantors to impose conditions on the transfer of real property, specifically, on the transfer of fee simple estates. Such estates are known as **defeasible** fee simple estates because the grantee's title can be defeated if the grantee violates a condition of the conveyance.

　　However, in the eyes of the law, not all conditions deserve equal deference from the courts. Which of the following conditions do you think would be declared void by a court of law, keeping in mind the concept that was introduced in the first chapter, that is, the "public policy"):

a. O to A <u>for as long as</u> the property is not used for gambling, and if it is so used, title shall revert to O.

b. In the following, assume that T is the Testator-mother, and D is her daughter:

　T to my daughter D for as long as she does not marry a person of the Muslim faith, but if she does marry a person of the Muslim faith, then title shall pass to my son, S.

c. *T to my daughter D for as long as she remains married to her husband, H, and if she does not remain married to H, then title shall pass to my son, S.*

d. *O to State University for as long as the property is used for educational purposes, but if it is not so used, then title shall revert to O or her heirs.*

e. *T to my son for as long as he remains a member of the Democrat Party, and if he does not remain a member of the Democratic Party, then title shall pass to the Democratic National Committee.*

3. The 1929 case of *Brokaw v. Fairchild* is included in this chapter. The court decided that even though the plaintiff/life tenant's proposed improvements to the life

estate could add great value to the property, allowing these improvements (which included the demolition of the then-existing mansion) would constitute **waste** upon the property and thereby violate the rights of the remaindermen.

What are the pros and cons of the court's reasoning? Should a change in the character of a neighborhood, as occurred on 5th Avenue in 1920s New York (from extravagant single-family homes to pricey high-rise apartments) be considered by the court as it attempts to define "waste"?

If the remaindermen have strong emotional ties to the life estate—in the *Brokaw* case, it was the family mansion that plaintiff wanted to demolish—should that be a factor in the court's analysis of waste?

What if it could be proven that the remaindermen have consulted with architects and engineers so that after the life tenant dies, and the remaindermen assume ownership of the property, they will demolish the existing residence and develop the property according to their own plans? Would this make you more, or less, sympathetic to the life tenant, and why?

4. Larry is the life tenant of a life estate that he received from his late mother; Roberta is the remainderman. For the last four months, Larry has been so overwrought by his mother's death that he has fallen into an alcoholic depression. Although he has not done physical damage to the life estate, for the last four months he has failed to pay the mortgage and taxes that are due on the property.

What rights, if any, does Roberta have as the remainderman? Would she prevail if she petitioned the court to have Larry removed as the life tenant, and make her the owner of the estate in fee simple? Is there some lesser alternative that the court might impose that would allow Larry to remain as the life tenant, while protecting Roberta's remainder interest?

RESEARCH ON THE **WEB**

1. Recall that with a fee simple upon condition subsequent, if the condition in the conveyance is breached, the grantor (who imposed the condition) *may* terminate the grantee's estate and retake possession of the property. Does your state have a statute of limitations, or a court opinion, regarding how long, in the case of a fee simple upon condition subsequent, the grantor has to reenter the property and terminate the estate?

2. The law does not favor unnecessary restraints on the use or alienability (transfer) of real property. The defeasible fee simple estates come with conditions, or "strings" attached.

Why does the law disfavor the imposition of conditions or restraints on real property when it is transferred? Why is this especially true when a testator has transferred property (with strings attached) by a will?

Does your state have a statute or court opinion that bars enforcement of conditions in defeasible fee estates after a certain number of years?

3. Using Westlaw, Lexis, or some other online database, determine if your jurisdiction has defined the word "waste" as it relates to life estates, either by statute, or in a court opinion. Does the concept of waste include *improvements* made by the life tenant?

4. Find the case of *Brokaw v. Fairchild* to determine if there have been any changes made in New York's case law or statutes that would alter the result in *Brokaw* if it was decided today.

5. Find 1 East 79th Street, New York City, NY, on MapQuest, Google Earth, or another such mapping site. It is just across Fifth Avenue from Central Park. How does the property look today?

6. Find your state's statutes relating to intestate succession. What chapter or chapters of your state's code cover intestate succession?

BUILDING YOUR PROFESSIONAL **PORTFOLIO**

1. Using the legal "shorthand" employed in this chapter, draft a conveyance of a fee simple subject to executory limitation wherein the fee is currently owned by O, the grantee will be A, and the entity holding the executory interest is the American Heart Association.

The condition accompanying the conveyance of the fee is that there must never be any smoking on the property.

2. You have three children, Adam (age 62), Betty (age 50), and Carla (age 45). Now in your 80s, most of what you own is the Old Homeplace, where you lived with your

(now-deceased) spouse of 50 years. This is where your children were born and raised, and you know that each has very fond memories of the house and land.

You want to show each of the three children that you love them equally, but you are most concerned about Betty, the middle child, who has a terminal illness and may die very soon. Adam, the eldest child, had an accounting business, but recently declared bankruptcy; he also has three children in college.

Although Carla is relatively young, and very healthy, she is a profligate spender, who never seems to know where her next dollar is coming from.

How would you draft a clause in your will that might give each child an interest in the property, while giving priority to the most needy?

What other facts might you require about either the children or the Old Homeplace to draft a more comprehensive clause?

chapter **3**

CONCURRENT OWNERSHIP

LEARNING OBJECTIVES

After reading this chapter, you should understand:

- The definition of concurrent ownership
- The types of concurrent ownership
- Joint tenancy with right of survivorship
- Tenancy in common
- Tenancy by the entirety
- Community property laws
- Differences between condominiums and homeowner associations
- Time shares
- Cooperatives

Concurrent Ownership

Concurrent ownership means that two or more persons own an interest in the same property *at the same time*. Fictional "persons" such as corporations and partnerships may also be concurrent owners of real property. It is important to determine the nature of a person's ownership in a property because that determines other incidents of ownership, for example, whether the owner may mortgage or convey his or her interest in the property.

The three major types of concurrent ownership are:

1. Joint tenancy with right of survivorship,
2. Tenancy in common, and
3. Tenancy by the entirety.

A. Joint Tenancy with Right of Survivorship

The first form of concurrent ownership is joint tenancy with right of survivorship. This type of concurrent ownership was the "default" under the old common law, but this is not the case today. This form of

PRACTICE POINT

Note the use of the words "tenancy" or "tenants" in each of the three categories of concurrent ownership. The word "tenant" comes from the Latin, *tenere,* meaning "to hold."

A "tenancy" or "tenant" in the context of concurrent *ownership* discussed in this chapter means just that…an ownership interest in the property.

However, you are probably more familiar with the other use of the words "tenancies" and "tenants" in the context of rental agreements.

As you know, a tenant in a rental situation does *not* own the property. You must note the contexts in which the words "tenant" or "tenancy" are used to determine whether they refer to a property owner or ownership, or to a renter.

---

concurrent ownership occurs when two or more persons own an equal and undivided interest in a property.

By an ***equal interest*** is meant that if there are two owners of the property, each owns a one-half interest in the entire property; if there are three owners, each owns a one-third interest, and so forth.

An ***undivided interest*** in the property means that each joint tenant has the right to occupy and use the whole of the property. No line can be drawn down the middle of the property separating "yours" from "mine," because no owner can exclude another owner from any portion of the property.

The most important and defining characteristic of the joint tenancy with right of survivorship is…the right of survivorship. Take the following example:

EXAMPLE

Property is owned by Adam, Beth, and Carla as joint tenants with right of survivorship. If Adam dies, what happens to his ownership interest in the property?

You can probably guess where Adam's interest goes…it is automatically (by operation of law) conveyed to his co-owners who have survived him, Beth and Carla. And thereafter, Beth and Carla own the property as joint tenants with right of survivorship. If Beth dies next, then the property will be owned entirely by Carla.

At first blush, the right of survivorship might look like a pretty good feature to have if you are a co-owner of a property (maybe because each of us expects to be the last survivor). Although joint tenancy with right of survivorship was the preferred form of concurrent ownership under the common law, it is now ***disfavored*** in modern law. This is because the term "survivors" does not refer to a decedent-owner's heirs or beneficiaries, but rather "survivors" refers to the remaining co-owners of the property, who may not be related to the decedent-owner at all.

In the example above, the surviving co-owners—Beth and Carla—will gain the decedent-Adam's share of the property under joint tenancy with right of survivorship. But in many concurrent ownership arrangements, the co-owners are business partners, rather than family members. Assume in the example above that Adam, Beth, and Carla are business partners, and not related by blood or marriage.

Because they were joint tenants with right of survivorship, when Adam died, his share went to Beth and Carla, *rather than to his estate or heirs.* Thus, Adam's wife and/or children were deprived of the benefit of Adam's interest in the property. That's fine, if that is what Adam (and his business partners) truly wanted.

However, if there is any doubt about the ownership arrangement among Adam, Beth, and Carla, the law will disfavor joint tenancy with right of survivorship.

Modern law presumes that the three partners co-owned the property as *tenants in common*. As tenants in common, and upon Adam's death, his interest in the property would go to the **beneficiaries** under his will, or to his **heirs** if he died intestate, rather than to his business partners under joint tenancy with right of survivorship.

Therefore, when a joint tenancy with right of survivorship is created—either by will or deed—the language of conveyance must be clear and unambiguous:

> *O to A, B, and C as joint tenants with rights of survivorship, and not as tenants in common.*

Why enter into a joint tenancy with right of survivorship?

The answer to this question is, in many cases, both practical and simple: a joint tenancy with right of survivorship may be the only way to make a deal happen. Suppose John and Paul want to purchase a large recording studio, but Paul is not, to say the least, fond of John's spouse, Koko.

Paul knows that if John dies before him, Paul's new co-owner in the property will be Koko, a situation that Paul would find intolerable, and therefore, a deal-breaker. So in order to make the deal happen, John and Paul might agree to become joint tenants with the right of survivorship.

The Four Unities Required for Joint Tenancy with Right of Survivorship

Aside from the right of survivorship, there are other characteristics that are associated with joint tenancy. These are known as the **four unities,** and all four must be present for there to be a joint tenancy with the right of survivorship. The four unities are possession, interest, time, and title (PITT).

1. UNITY OF POSSESSION

Unity of possession means that each of the co-owners/joint tenants has the right to *use and enjoy the whole* of the property. No joint tenant can exclude a fellow joint tenant from any portion of the property (except by mutual agreement). Unity of possession is another way of saying about the property: "What's mine is yours, and what's yours is mine."

2. UNITY OF INTEREST

Unity of interest means that each of the joint tenants must have an *equal percentage* interest in the property (one-half with two joint tenants, one-third with three joint tenants, etc.), and must have the same type of estate or bundle of rights, that is, a fee simple, fee simple determinable, or life estate.

Suppose a mother deeds a property to her son and daughter. The mother grants a fee simple estate to her son, but only a life estate to her daughter. This is *not* a joint tenancy since the same estate/bundle of rights has not been given to each grantee, that is, the son and daughter do not have a unity of interest. For there to be a joint tenancy with right of survivorship, mother would have to convey

Beneficiary
one who takes a decedent's real or personal property pursuant to the terms of the decedent's will.

Heir
one who takes a decedent's real or personal property when the decedent dies without a will; heirs are designated by a state's intestacy statutes.

Four Unities
a joint tenancy, in addition to the right of survivorship, must also carry with it the four unities of possession, interest, time, and title (PITT).

Unity of Possession
the right to use and enjoy the whole property, not just a part of it.

Unity of Interest
each joint tenant has the same percentage interest in the property, and the same type of estate, or bundle of rights.

PUBLIC POLICY

In the first chapter, we asked the reader to keep in mind the importance of *public policy* when analyzing principles of law.

What is the possible public policy reason that would compel the law to disfavor joint tenancy with right of survivorship?

the same estate/bundle of rights to both children, giving each an equal percentage interest in the property.

3. UNITY OF TIME

Unity of time means that the interests of the joint tenants in the real property vest and begin at the same time.

Suppose a father deeds a property to his son and daughter, each to receive a one-half interest. But according to the terms of the deed, the son's interest begins immediately, while the daughter's interest will begin upon the father's death. This cannot be a joint tenancy because the children's rights to use and enjoy the property—even though conveyed in the same deed—begin at different points in time, that is, there is no unity of time.

4. UNITY OF TITLE

Unity of title means that the joint tenants must acquire their interests in the property by the same conveyance, either the same deed or the same will.

To repeat, for a joint tenancy with right of survivorship to exist, the four unities (PITT) must exist, and the desire to create a joint tenancy must be explicitly stated in the deed or will.

5. PARTITION OF THE PROPERTY

What happens if there are two joint tenants, Adam and Beth, who are at odds over what use to make of the 40-acre parcel that they own? Adam may want to keep the property in its current pristine state, while Beth may want to build houses on part of the acreage. Obviously, Adam and Beth could agree to divide the property themselves. But, if for some reason they cannot agree upon how to divide the acreage, one or both of them may petition a court to partition the property. Adam or Beth may ask the court for a partition in kind or a partition by sale.

A **partition in kind** would occur if the court divided the property in two separate parcels, giving one of the two new parcels to Adam and the other to Beth. Note that a partition in kind is not necessarily an even split of the acreage, e.g., 20 acres to Adam and 20 acres to Beth. The reason is that part of the acreage may be unusable swampland, while another part of the acreage may have great views of the surrounding countryside. In that case, it would be unfair for the court to "partition in kind" by simply drawing a line down the middle of the parcel, then giving half to Adam and half to Beth. Either or both of the parties might feel that the partition was unfair and that they had been unfairly treated by the court.

As an alternative to a partition in kind, the court could order a **partition by sale**, sometimes called a **forced sale**, of the entire property. In that case, the proceeds from the sale would be split evenly between Adam and Beth.

B. Tenancy in Common—One Unity: Possession

1. THE DEFAULT TENANCY

The most important distinction between tenants in common, and joint tenants with right of survivorship, is that tenants in common have *no right of survivorship*.

As noted earlier, the law disfavors joint tenancies with the right of survivorship. Therefore, if a deed or will conveying a property is not crystal clear as to the type of tenancy being created, the law will presume that a tenancy in common has been created, in which case, there is no right of survivorship. Under *modern* common law—or in some states, pursuant to statute—tenancy in common has become the new default tenancy when there is some doubt or ambiguity about the nature of the estate being conveyed (under the *old* common law, joint tenancy with right of survivorship was the default).

Unity of Possession—The Only Required Unity

Recall that a joint tenancy with right of survivorship requires that there must be four unities: possession, interest, time, and title (PITT). Tenancy in common, on the other hand, requires only **one unity**, that is, **possession**. The unity of possession means that the tenants' ownership is "undivided," so that each tenant (owner) is entitled to use and enjoy the entire property. The three remaining unities (ITT) are not necessary in a tenancy in common.

Unity of Interest—Not Required for Tenancy in Common

Tenants in common may have **unequal interests** in the property they own. For example, Alan and Brenda are tenants in common as owners of Greenacres. Pursuant to their agreement when they purchased the property, Alan will own a 40% interest in the land, and Brenda will own a 60% interest.

What happens if there is nothing in the conveyance to indicate the percentage interests held by each owner? In the absence of an agreement or evidence indicating their respective interests, the law will presume that they own the property 50-50. However, this is a **rebuttable presumption**, meaning that Brenda might be able to produce evidence showing that she paid 60% of the purchase price of the property, and thereby rebut the presumption of 50-50 ownership.

Rebuttable Presumption
an inference drawn from certain facts that establish a prima facie case, which may be overcome by the introduction of contrary evidence.

Unity of Time—Not Required for Tenancy in Common

Tenants in common are not required to obtain their ownership interests in the property at the same time. Otis, the previous owner of Greenacres, may have sold Alan a 40% interest in the property on January 1, 2010; Otis and Adam now own the property as tenants in common.

Later, on January 1, 2011, Otis sells his remaining 60% interest to Brenda. Alan and Brenda now own Greenacres as tenants in common, in part because they became owners at different points in time. As you can see, then, the unity of time is not required for a tenancy in common.

Unity of Title—Not Required for Tenancy in Common

In the example of Otis, Alan, and Brenda above, there was no unity of title. In other words, each received his or her ownership interest under a different instrument of conveyance.

Otis may have received Greenacres by will upon his mother's death in 1986. On January 1, 2010, Otis conveyed a 40% interest to Alan by deed. A year later, on January 1, 2011, Otis conveyed the remaining 60% interest to Brenda by way of a second deed. Therefore, Alan and Brenda did not take Greenacres by the same conveyance, and so there is no unity of title.

In the following case, the Illinois Supreme Court examined whether a mortgage given by only one of the two joint tenants (two brothers) owning a property severs the joint tenancy by abolishing the unity of title:

HARMS V. SPRAGUE

Supreme Court of Illinois
105 Ill. 2d 215; 473 N.E.2d 930
November 30, 1984, Filed

Plaintiff, William H. Harms, filed a complaint to quiet title. Plaintiff had taken title to certain real estate with his [now-deceased] brother John R. Harms, as a *joint tenant*, with full right of survivorship. The plaintiff named, as a defendant, Charles D. Sprague, the executor of the estate of John Harms and the devisee of all the real and personal property of John Harms. Also named as defendants were Carl and Mary Simmons, alleged *mortgagees* of the property in question. Defendant Sprague filed a counterclaim against plaintiff, challenging plaintiff's claim of ownership of the entire tract of property and asking the court to recognize his (Sprague's) interest as a *tenant in common*, subject to a mortgage lien. At issue was the effect the granting of a mortgage by John Harms had on the joint tenancy. Also at issue was *whether the mortgage survived the death of John Harms as a lien* against the property.

The trial court held that the mortgage given by John Harms to defendants Carl and Mary Simmons severed the joint tenancy. Further, the court found that the mortgage survived the death of John Harms as a lien against the undivided one-half interest in the property which passed to Sprague by and through the will of the deceased. The appellate court reversed, finding that the mortgage given by one joint tenant of his interest in the property does not sever the joint tenancy. Accordingly, the appellate court held that plaintiff, as the surviving joint tenant, owned the property in its entirety, unencumbered by the mortgage lien. Defendant Sprague filed a petition for leave to appeal in this court. That motion was granted and the petition for leave to appeal was allowed.

Two issues are raised on appeal: (1) Is a *joint tenancy severed* when less than all of the joint tenants mortgage their interest in the property? and (2) Does such a *mortgage survive* the death of the mortgagor as a lien on the property?

Carl and Mary Simmons owned a lot and home in Roodhouse. Charles Sprague entered into an agreement with the Simmonses whereby Sprague was to purchase their property for $25,000. Sprague tendered $18,000 in cash and signed a promissory note for the balance of $7,000. Because Sprague had no security

for the $7,000, he asked his friend, John Harms, to co-sign the note and give a mortgage on his interest in the joint tenancy property. Harms agreed, and on June 12, 1981, John Harms and Charles Sprague, jointly and severally, executed a promissory note for $7,000 payable to Carl and Mary Simmons. The note states that the principal sum of $7,000 was to be paid from the proceeds of the sale of John Harms' interest in the joint tenancy property, but in any event no later than six months from the date the note was signed. The note reflects that five monthly interest payments had been made, with the last payment recorded November 6, 1981. In addition, *John Harms executed a mortgage, in favor of the Simmonses, on his undivided one-half interest in the joint tenancy property*, to secure payment of the note. William Harms was unaware of the mortgage given by his brother.

On December 10, 1981, John Harms died. By the terms of John Harms' will, Charles Sprague was the devisee of his entire estate. The mortgage given by John Harms to the Simmonses was recorded on December 29, 1981 [nineteen days after John Harms' death].

This court has considered the effect that judgment liens upon the interest of one joint tenant have on the stability of the joint tenancy. In *Peoples Trust & Savings Bank v. Haas (1927), 328 Ill. 468*, the court found that a *judgment* lien secured against one joint tenant did not serve to extinguish the joint tenancy. As such, the surviving joint tenant "succeeded to the title in fee to the whole of the land by operation of law."

If Illinois perceives a mortgage as merely a *lien* on the mortgagor's interest in property rather than a conveyance of title from mortgagor to mortgagee, the execution of a mortgage by a joint tenant, on his interest in the property, would not destroy the unity of title and sever the joint tenancy.

Early cases in Illinois, however, followed the *title theory* of mortgages. In 1900, this court recognized the common law precept that a mortgage was a conveyance of a legal estate vesting title to the property in the mortgagee. Because our cases had early recognized the unique and narrow character of the title that passed to a mortgagee under the common law title

(continued)

theory, it was not a drastic departure when this court expressly *characterized the execution of a mortgage as a mere lien* in *Kling v. Ghilarducci*. The court stated:

> "In some jurisdictions the execution of a mortgage is a severance [of title], in others, the execution of a mortgage is not a severance. In Illinois the giving of a mortgage is *not a separation of title*, for the holder of the mortgage takes only a lien thereunder."

We find that implicit in *Kling* and our more recent cases which follow the lien theory of mortgages is the conclusion that a joint tenancy is not severed when one joint tenant executes a mortgage on his interest in the property, since the **unity of title** has been preserved.

A joint tenancy has been defined as a present estate in all the joint tenants, each being seized of the whole. An inherent feature of the estate of joint tenancy is the right of survivorship, which is the right of the last survivor to take the whole of the estate. Because we find that a mortgage given by one joint tenant of his interest in the property does not sever the joint tenancy, we hold that the plaintiff's right of survivorship became operative upon the death of his brother. As such plaintiff is now the sole owner of the estate, in its entirety.

Further, we find that the mortgage executed by John Harms does not survive as a lien on plaintiff's property. A surviving joint tenant succeeds to the share of the deceased joint tenant by virtue of the conveyance which created the joint tenancy, not as the successor of the deceased. The property right of the mortgaging joint tenant is extinguished at the moment of his death. While John Harms was alive, the mortgage existed as a lien on his interest in the joint tenancy. Upon his death, his interest ceased to exist and along with it the lien of the mortgage. Under the circumstances of this case, we would note that the mortgage given by John Harms to the Simmonses was only valid as between the original parties during the lifetime of John Harms **since it was unrecorded**. In addition, recording the mortgage subsequent to the death of John Harms was a nullity. As we stated above, John Harms' property rights in the joint tenancy were extinguished when he died. Thus, he no longer had a property interest upon which the mortgage lien could attach.

For the reasons stated herein, the judgment of the appellate court is affirmed.

Q: Do you think the outcome would have/ should have been different if Mr. and Mrs. Simmons had recorded the mortgage before the death of John Harms?

C. Tenancy by the Entirety—4 Unities (PITT) + 1

Tenancy by the entirety is a form of property ownership enjoyed exclusively by **married persons**. As the common law of property developed in England, a married couple was viewed not as two separate individuals, but as a single entity. Approximately twenty states still retain the doctrine of tenancy by the entirety. About twenty other states treat the husband and wife as individuals rather than an "entirety." Nine states are governed by the law of community property.

The Four Unities

A tenancy by the entirety requires the same **four unities** as joint tenancy with right of survivorship: possession, interest, time, and title. If real property is conveyed to a husband and wife as tenants by the entirety, it must have been conveyed to them in equal shares, in the same will or deed, and ownership must become effective at the same time. If these requirements are not explicitly stated in the will or deed, there is a rebuttable presumption that the property was conveyed to the husband and wife as tenants by the entirety.

So, a tenancy by the entirety requires the familiar four unities, plus the additional requirement that the tenants (property owners) be married.

Right of Survivorship

When property is owned by tenants by the entirety, a right of survivorship exists. Suppose that Hubert and Winifred got married in 1960, and a short time later bought a house. The couple remained married and lived in their house for 45 years until Hubert died in 2010. Upon Hubert's death, title to the house automatically (by operation of law) passed to Winifred as an individual, according to the right of survivorship. The ancient English common law doctrines of **curtesy** and **dower** have been replaced in most of the states by statutes that specifically allocate the type and amount of property to be received by the surviving spouse.

Difference between Tenancy by the Entirety and Joint Tenancy with Right of Survivorship

If a tenancy by the entirety requires the same four unities, and the right of survivorship, as a joint tenancy with right of survivorship, then how are they different?

First, a tenancy by the entirety is limited to just two people—the married couple—while a joint tenancy may have more than two owners, and there is no requirement that any of the joint tenants be married.

Second, because a tenancy by the entirety is viewed as a *single entity*, rather than being comprised of two or more individuals in a joint tenancy, the rights of creditors against a tenancy by the entirety may be more limited than the **rights of creditors** against joint tenants.

Curtesy
under old common law, the rights of a widower, following the death of his wife, to property owned by her. Curtesy has been replaced in most states by statutes that specifically allocate the type and amount of property to be received by the surviving spouse.

Dower
under old common law, the rights of a widow, following the death of her husband, to property owned by him. Dower has been replaced in most states by statutes that specifically allocate the type and amount of property to be received by the surviving spouse.

EXAMPLE

Hubert and Winifred bought their house shortly after they were married in 1980, that is, as tenants by the entirety. After 25 years of making payments, they paid off their mortgage in 2005, and owned the house free and clear. The following year, Hubert and Winifred's daughter, Denise, needed money for tuition to attend college.

Hubert went to the local bank where he applied for, and obtained, a loan for the tuition. The loan was to be secured by a new mortgage on Hubert and Winifred's house, but by mistake, the lending officer only obtained Hubert's signature on the loan papers. A couple of years later, Hubert and Winifred both lost their jobs and defaulted on the loan payments.

Q: May the bank foreclose on Hubert and Winifred's house?

A: The answer to this question depends on the jurisdiction. In the majority of states, the answer would be no, the bank may not foreclose on the house. The house is owned by a tenancy by the entirety, that is, Hubert and Winifred as husband and wife. Since only Hubert signed the loan documents, the bank cannot proceed against the home owned by them as tenants by the entirety.

Having said that, however, there are differences within the majority view concerning the creditor's rights following a divorce, or the death of Hubert or Winifred.

In a minority of states, the creditor bank would be able to obtain a judgment against Hubert, and then execute on that judgment, thereby forcing a sale of the property.

D. Community Property

Nine states in the west and southwestern United States do not follow the common law of tenancy by the entirety. Instead, these states are known as **community property states**. The nine states are Arizona, California, Idaho, Louisiana, Nevada, New Mexico, Texas, Washington, and Wisconsin. These jurisdictions enacted comprehensive statutes—as opposed to English common law—that govern the ownership

Concurrent Ownership Tenancies Under Common Law

	Joint Tenancy with Right of Survivorship	Tenancy in Common	Tenancy by the Entirety
Created by:	Deed Will	Deed Will Intestate Succession	Deed Will
Requirements	4 Unities (PITT) + Right of Survivorship	Unity of Possession only	4 Unities (PITT) + Right of Survivorship + Married Couple
Possession	Undivided: each tenant has a right to possess all of the property	Undivided: each tenant has a right to possess all of the property	Undivided: each tenant has a right to possess all of the property
Interest	Equal 2 owners: 50-50 3 owners: 1/3, 1/3, 1/3	May be unequal 2 owners: 60-40 3 owners: 50-30-20	Equal
Time	Joint tenants must take ownership at the same time	Tenants in common may take ownership at different points in time	Married couple must take ownership at the same time
Title	Joint tenants must take ownership by the same conveyance	Tenants in common may take ownership by different conveyances	Married couple must take ownership by the same conveyance
Right of Survivorship	Yes	No	Yes
May tenant sell her interest	Yes, but the new owner is a tenant in common as to the remaining joint tenants	Yes	No, not during the marriage
Language of Conveyance	*"O to A and B as joint tenants with rights of survivorship, and not as tenants in common."*	*"O to A and B."* (assuming A and B are not married)	*"O to H and W."* (if H and W are married)
Miscellaneous	Disfavored in the law because upon the death of a joint tenant, his share would go to the surviving joint tenants, not his heirs or beneficiaries	The modern "default" tenancy if the type of ownership is not specified in the conveyance	TBE applies only to married couples

of real and personal property by married couples. Most of these states were originally occupied by Spanish-speaking people, who brought with them European civil law, including the law of community property.

Although the nine states above are all community property jurisdictions, their statutes are by no means identical, and there are some significant differences among them. The unities (PITT) that we discussed in the previous sections on concurrent ownership were creations of English common law. As such, the unities are not relevant in the discussion of community property.

The concept of **community property** is based on the belief that each spouse contributes equally to the marriage. Thus, community property laws are viewed as being more favorable to the wife than equitable distribution because historically, a wife's "traditional role" as homemaker and mother were undervalued by society (and mostly male judges adjudicating divorce cases) because no income was generated for the family from such activities.

Community Property
real or personal property acquired by either or both spouses during their marriage; the marital property is split equally between the divorcing parties.

Community property may be defined as real or personal property acquired by either or both spouses during their marriage. It does not include property acquired before the marriage, nor does it include property acquired during the marriage that was received by one of the spouses as a gift or an inheritance; these categories are known as *separate property*, and such property is not part of the **marital estate** and will not be divided between the spouses upon divorce.

Marital Estate
the property acquired during a marriage that will be distributed upon divorce.

1. EQUITABLE DISTRIBUTION IN *NON*-COMMUNITY PROPERTY STATES

Jurisdictions that practice the common law of tenancy by the entirety, or treat the husband and wife as separate individuals (rather than an "entirety"), have what is known as **equitable distribution**, whereby the court will attempt to distribute the marital property according to what is equitable or fair. Divorce courts in such states generally begin with a rebuttable presumption that both spouses contributed equally to the marriage and the acquisition of marital property, but will then adjust the percentage of the property allocated to either spouse based on several factors, which may include some or all of the following:

Equitable Distribution
in states other than community property states, marital property is split equitably based on several factors, rather than evenly.

a. The income, property, and liabilities of each party at the time the division of property is to become effective;
b. Any obligation for support arising out of a prior marriage;
c. The duration of the marriage and the age and physical and mental health of both parties;
d. The need of a parent with custody of a child or children of the marriage to occupy or own the marital residence and to use or own its household effects;
e. The expectation of pension, retirement, or other deferred compensation rights that are not marital property;
f. Any equitable claim to, interest in, or direct or indirect contribution made to the acquisition of such marital property by the party not having title, including joint efforts or expenditures and contributions and services, or lack thereof, as a spouse, parent, wage earner, or homemaker;
g. Any direct or indirect contribution made by one spouse to help educate or develop the career potential of the other spouse;
h. Any direct contribution to an increase in value of separate property that occurs during the course of the marriage;
i. The liquid or non-liquid character of all marital property and divisible property;
j. The difficulty of evaluating any component asset or any interest in a business, corporation, or profession, and the economic desirability of retaining such asset or interest, intact and free from any claim or interference by the other party;
k. The tax consequences to each party, including those federal and state tax consequences that would have been incurred if the marital and divisible property had been sold or liquidated on the date of valuation;
l. Acts of either party to maintain, preserve, develop, or expand; or to waste, neglect, devalue, or convert the marital property or divisible property, or both, during the period after separation of the parties and before the time of distribution;
m. The ability of the parties to produce income.

In both community property states and equitable distribution states, a *pre-nuptial agreement* may modify the distribution of assets upon divorce, notwithstanding what the statutes or common law might usually require. A "pre-nup" is simply a contract between the parties to be married in which they agree how marital property will be distributed in the event of a divorce. To be enforceable, the pre-nuptial agreement must not have been signed under duress, the spouse being asked to sign the pre-nup must have had time to consult with an attorney regarding the proposed agreement, and there must have been full disclosure of the parties' assets, liabilities, and income. In other words, a pre-nuptial agreement presented by a man to his fiancée on the day before the wedding would not be enforceable if she challenged it in a subsequent divorce action.

E. Condominiums and Homeowners Associations

We will look at condominiums and other types of planned unit developments in greater depth in a later chapter. For the time being, just note that if you own a condominium unit or residence in a planned unit development, you may have a *concurrent ownership* interest in elements of the *common area,* particularly if you live in an older common interest community. The common areas and common elements include recreational facilities and amenities, grounds and landscaping, parking spaces, elevators, walkways, and so forth.

In common interest communities that were created more recently—within the last 30 years—it is more likely that the common areas and common elements would not be owned directly by you as a tenant in common with dozens or perhaps hundreds of other tenants in common. Rather, the common area elements will be owned by the *condominium association*, in which you have an ownership interest based upon your ownership of your condominium.

The exact form of ownership may have interesting legal ramifications. Suppose you are one of 200 homeowners in a condominium association. If a stranger visits the property and breaks an ankle in a pothole in a common area such as a parking lot, who may be held liable: the association, the board of directors, you *and* the association, or perhaps just you if the plaintiff chooses to sue only you (because you have very deep pockets)? We will examine these issues in a later chapter on common interest communities.

The only unity that exists in the ownership of common area elements is the unity of *possession*. That is, generally speaking, each unit owner has a right to use all of the common areas such as the swimming pool, clubhouse, and grounds.

F. Time Shares

Time shares may be a form of ownership of real property, or may simply be a *right to use* a property for a specific amount of time each year. Regardless of whether the time share actually constitutes ownership of a property, or simply a right of use, the property in question is typically resort or vacation property, and usually relatively expensive property.

Time share ownership started in the 1960s and has been growing ever since.

One of the more appealing aspects of time shares is that oftentimes they can be *traded* for other time shares in different locations. Let's say that you have vacationed at your Hawaii time share condominium for the last three years. But now you would like a change of scenery and would like to spend a week or so in Aspen,

TIME SHARE

A developer has built a condominium project in Hawaii. The developer may decide that rather than selling each unit to one buyer, she will sell time shares in the units. Thus, for a fee of perhaps $5–$10,000, one may use the condominium for one or two weeks per year. This is essentially a lease arrangement, with a few minor twists.

Alternatively, for your $5–$10,000 you may actually be buying an ownership interest in the property, which interest is transferred by deed. In the latter case, where you actually have an ownership interest in the property, your status is as one of several tenants in common, along with the other owners of that unit.

Colorado. You may be able to trade a week in Hawaii for a week in Aspen, or any of hundreds of other time share vacation resorts located around the globe.

On the downside, time shares can be cumbersome when you consider that there may be 20 or more owners or lessees of a condominium unit. As a student of the law, you know that you must always consider potential liability. For example, as the owner of a 1/26 interest (two weeks) in a condominium time share, would you have any liability if someone were injured in a common area as a result of the negligence of one of your co-owners? This and other problems can be overcome, but buyers need to be aware of these and other legal issues that are unique to time share arrangements.

CHAPTER SUMMARY

Concurrent ownership means that two or more persons (or entities) own an interest in the same property at the same time. Remember that even though the word "tenancy" is used, what we are talking about is ownership interests. Under the common law, concurrent ownership comes in three basic varieties:

1. Joint tenancy with right of survivorship,
2. Tenancy in common, and
3. Tenancy by the entirety.

Each type of concurrent ownership requires at least one type of "unity":

1. Joint tenancy with the right of survivorship requires four unities:
   a. Unity of possession—undivided access to the whole of the property,
   b. Unity of interest—each tenant owns an equal share of the property,
   c. Unity of time—ownership of the property was acquired at the same time by all of the co-tenants, and
   d. Unity of title—ownership of the property was acquired by the same conveyance, either by deed or will.

2. Tenancy in common requires only one unity:
   a. Unity of possession—undivided access to the whole of the property.

   Tenancy in common is the "default" form of concurrent ownership. If there is any doubt about whether two or more persons own property as joint tenants with right of survivorship, or as tenants in common, the law will presume a tenancy in common. The reason for this presumption in favor of a tenancy in common is that a tenancy in common has no right of survivorship between and among co-tenants.

3. Tenancy by the entirety requires four unities (same as joint tenancy, above). Additionally, because the tenants must be a *married couple*, the right of survivorship is a characteristic of this tenancy.

   Community property laws exist in nine states, and require that marital property be evenly split between the divorcing couple. A couple contemplating marriage in either a community property state, or a tenancy-by-the-entirety state, may enter into a *pre-nuptial agreement* that can alter the distribution of assets in the event of a divorce.

Concurrent ownership of common areas may exist to a limited extent in older condominiums and homeowner associations. Homeowners either have a direct ownership interest as tenants in common in the property's common areas, or more frequently, own shares in an association, which in turn owns the common area elements.

Time shares are a method of ownership of resort and recreational properties. Time shares may actually be deeded to a buyer, in which case the buyer is a tenant in common with other such owners. Or, the time shares may nearly be a right to use the property for one or more weeks during the year.

CONCEPT REVIEW AND REINFORCEMENT

KEY **TERMS**

Beneficiary
Common Area
Community Property
Concurrent Ownership
Condominium
Conveyance by Will
Conveyance by Deed
Curtesy
Decedent
Dower

Equitable Distribution
Four Unities
Heir
Intestate
Joint Tenancy with Right of
   Survivorship
Marital Estate
Pre-Nuptial Agreement
Rebuttable Presumption
Tenancy in Common

Tenancy by the Entirety
Tenant
Testator
Time Shares
Unity of Interest
Unity of Possession
Unity of Time
Unity of Title

CONCEPT **REVIEW** QUESTIONS

1. What type of concurrent ownership exists when the co-owners of a property have an equal, undivided interest in the property, acquired the property at the same time, by way of the same conveyance, and have a right of survivorship?

2. What type of concurrent ownership exists when co-owners of a property have an equal, undivided interest in the property, acquired the property at the same time, by way of the same conveyance, but do not have a right of survivorship?

3. What are the unities that characterize the various forms of concurrent ownership, and what is the meaning of each unity?

4. Adrian, Bobby, and Charlie are business partners, and own their business property as joint tenants with right of survivorship. If Adrian dies, who will receive his interest in the business property? Is this result favored, or disfavored, in the law? Explain your answer, including the public policy issues involved.

5. Explain why a joint tenancy with right of survivorship cannot be created when the new owners acquire title through intestate succession. Can a tenancy in common be created when the new owners acquire title by way of intestate succession?

6. If the conveyance of Greenacres is ambiguous as to whether O deeded the property to X, Y, and Z as joint tenants with right of survivorship, or as tenants in common, which form of ownership would a court usually presume to have been created?

7. Who are the "survivors" when discussing a joint tenancy with right of survivorship? In the context of concurrent ownership, how does a "survivor" differ from an "heir" or "beneficiary"?

8. Why is tenancy in common preferred by the courts (the "default" tenancy) over joint tenancy with right of survivorship?

9. Do you think that a property that is owned by tenants by the entirety can be partitioned, either by sale or by an in-kind partition? What are the reasons for your conclusion?

10. How many community property states are there at present? How does equitable distribution differ from the law of distribution in community property states? Is a prenuptial agreement effective in a community property state? In an equitable distribution state?

ETHICS

YOU WERE **CC'D**

Leslie works as a paralegal for a busy attorney in a solo law office. She has over ten years of experience, is very organized, and pays close attention to detail. In addition to her other duties, she is the primary contact for the clients since the attorney is very busy and out of the office frequently. In this regard, Leslie returns client phone calls, responds to email, and drafts most of the correspondence and pleadings for the office.

Leslie has become increasingly concerned that the attorney she works for is not communicating with several important clients. She has received numerous complaints. In an effort to assist, she has sent her attorney at least five separate emails requesting that he immediately contact the clients. She has carbon copied each client on her messages to the attorney.

When Leslie finally has a chance to speak to the attorney, he claims to have never received any of her messages, which she knows is not true, and he informs her that he has withdrawn as counsel for the clients at issue. He yells at Leslie for copying the clients on her email messages to him.

Leslie knows that the attorney has not been in contact with the clients and she has not seen any filings regarding withdrawals as counsel of record from these cases.

Leslie asked to discuss these issues with her employer-attorney two weeks ago, but he has been so busy that he has not even gotten back to her with an answer. Critical deadlines are looming, and Leslie is unsure whether she should contact the clients, to at least inform them of the attorney's supposed withdrawal as counsel.

What potential ethical violations has the absentee attorney committed?

If Leslie notifies the clients of attorney's withdrawal from their cases, has she placed the attorney in jeopardy of civil liability or bar complaints for unethical behavior?

If she does not notify the clients and deadlines come and go without any action by the attorney, has she put herself in jeopardy of possible civil liability?

How would you advise Leslie to proceed?

BUILDING YOUR PROFESSIONAL SKILLS

CRITICAL THINKING **EXERCISES**

1. Alice, Billy, and Charlie decide to purchase a commercial real estate property, which they intend to own and manage as business partners. When asked by the seller how they want the deed conveyed to them, Alice, Billy, and Charlie tell the seller that they want to own the property as "joint tenants." The deed is so prepared and reads as follows:

   O to Alice, Billy, and Charlie as joint tenants.

   After the partners have successfully operated the commercial property for 15 years, Charlie dies. Alice and Billy assume that because the deed has named them as "joint tenants" they will succeed to Charlie's ownership interest in the property. However, when Charlie's will is probated, the executor of Charlie's estate determines that Charlie's spouse and sole beneficiary under the will, is entitled to Charlie's interest in the property.

   If Alice and Billy challenge the decision by the executor in court, will they prevail? What factors should the court consider in deciding who should succeed to Charlie's interest? And what weight should be given to each of those factors?

2. Owen owns and occupies one unit in a 250-unit condominium development, and as such, owns a share in the condominium association, which owns the common areas of the condo development. On Halloween night, a group of children—who do not live at the condominium—are trick-or-treating at the condominium. One of the children trips in a pothole in the parking lot and suffers a severely broken ankle. The parking lot is common area.

   You may not have taken a course on tort law, so in looking at the questions below and using your own sense of justice and fair play, state how you think a court of law would, or should, answer the following questions:

   If the child sues the condominium association for negligence, do you think he will prevail? If the child sues the condominium association, but the association does not have sufficient liability insurance to cover the child's damages, do you think that the child should be able to prevail in a suit against Owen and other owners in the condominium development, or are they shielded from liability because it is actually the association that owns the common areas, and not the individual unit owners?

Should the size of the condominium development matter, that is, would the unit owners' liability be different if the condominium development were only 15 units? Should it matter if the plaintiff who broke her ankle is a child or an adult? Does it matter that the accident happened on Halloween night?

3. Nine western states distribute property following a couple's divorce based upon a statutorily created system known as community property. In these states, assuming that there is no prenuptial agreement, the divorcing couple will evenly split the property acquired during their marriage.

The remaining states allocate property to a divorcing couple under a system generically known as equitable distribution. Under this model, the court begins by assuming that the parties are each entitled to half of the property acquired during marriage. However, this presumption can be rebutted by one or both of the parties, and the court can distribute the property acquired during the marriage based upon the parties' relative contributions to the marriage, and not necessarily according to each spouse's contribution to the acquisition of the particular property to be distributed.

Which of the methods above would you prefer, community property or equitable distribution? Enumerate the pros and cons for each method, and explained the public policy behind each method.

4. Joint tenancy with right of survivorship and tenancy by the entirety both require the four unities: possession, interest, time, and title. But there are at least two significant differences between joint tenancy with right of survivorship and tenancy by the entirety. The first has to do with the number of owners. In a joint tenancy, there can be any number of concurrent property owners; obviously, there can be only two members of a tenancy by the entirety, that is, a husband and wife.

The second significant difference has to do with the rights of creditors to proceed in a lawsuit against one of the several joint tenants, versus the much more limited rights of creditors to proceed against one of the spouses in a tenancy by the entirety.

Why are tenants by the entirety given more protection from the creditors of one of the spouses than a joint tenant with right of survivorship? In other words, what is the "public policy"? Should this protection be available to the husband and wife/tenants by the entirety if the real property is something other than their primary residence?

For example, if a creditor can get a judgment for $30,000 against the wife for unpaid credit card bills, should the creditor to be able to foreclose the couple's vacation home in the mountains, even though the husband and wife own it as tenants by the entirety? Should the protection given to tenants by the entirety extend to personal property (such as a fishing boat) as well as real property?

RESEARCH ON THE **WEB**

1. A question that frequently arises in the field of concurrent ownership concerns the rights of creditors. Research the law in your jurisdiction to determine whether when a joint tenant defaults on payments to a creditor, does the creditor have any recourse against the interests of the other joint tenants?

2. In your jurisdiction, are the unities (PITT) required for the various forms of concurrent ownership defined by common (case) law, or codified in your statutory code?

3. Does your state still abide by the common law doctrines of dower and curtesy? If not, what has replaced these doctrines?

4. The states differ considerably on how they define the various types of tenancies, particularly as to marital ownership of property. Some jurisdictions are community property states, others tenancy by the entirety, others are joint tenancies with right of survivorship. Using the Internet, examine the statutes in your state to determine how property may be owned by a married couple.

BUILDING YOUR **PROFESSIONAL** PORTFOLIO

1. Sometimes, the owners of a property will disagree on how the property is to be managed, or for what purpose it might be developed or improved. If the owners cannot find a solution to their disagreement, it may become necessary for them to partition the property. As we stated earlier in the chapter, one or more of the owners may petition the court to divide the property for them, but this may entail significant time and expense, including attorneys' fees and other related costs.

Assume that you and a partner purchased a commercial property two years ago with the general idea of developing it in some manner. However, it has become clear that you cannot agree on what is an appropriate use of the property. You have agreed to partition the property by sale, but want to avoid the costs of having the court partition the property. You have generously offered to draft an agreement to that effect.

What should you include in such an agreement? You might consider some of the following when drafting the agreement: whether or not you will use a real estate broker and how much commission should be paid to a broker, the listing price of the property, the minimum price you will accept for the purchase of the property, any financing that you and your partner would be willing to extend to a buyer, the minimum period of time that the property should be on the market for sale, the distribution of profits after paying commissions, fees and expenses, and the allocation of any tax benefits.

A final question: If you do draft such an agreement, have you engaged in the unauthorized practice of law?

2. Alternatively, consider the situation where you are one of two tenants in common, and cannot agree with your co-owner on how you want to partition the property. Draft a petition to partition the property, which will be filed with the court.

chapter 4
LANDLORD-TENANT LAW

LEARNING OBJECTIVES

After reading this chapter, you should understand:

- How a typical state's court system might be structured
- The different types of courts
- How leases are structured
- The landlord's responsibilities
- The tenant's duties
- The various types of tenancies
- The various types of residential properties
- Commercial leases
- Paralegal duties in landlord-tenant law

A. Overview—Common Law Being Replaced by Statutory Law

Landlord-tenant law is one of the oldest areas of law, and one of the most litigated. Like much of our American law, landlord-tenant law comes to us by way of English common law. However, many states have moved to replace their common law governing residential landlord-tenant relations with *statutory law*. The reason for this is that common law tended to heavily favor the landlord, at the expense of the tenant's interests.

Beginning in the 1960s, consumer protection gained national prominence, and as a result of that movement, the tenant—as a "consumer"—received greater protection under both the case law and statutory law.

Landlord-tenant relations are frequently litigated for a number of reasons:

1. Lease agreements embody one of the most fundamental of human needs—shelter;
2. Lease disputes often involve significant amounts of money, especially from the tenant's perspective. By significant, we mean an amount of money "worth fighting about"; and
3. Most states have created small claims courts—sometimes called magistrate's court—to adjudicate these disputes. These courts have been designed to be "user friendly," meaning that such courts do not require the parties to have lawyers representing them.

1. SMALL CLAIMS COURT

A typical state's court system might be structured as follows:

a. State Supreme Court
b. State Court of Appeals
c. State Trial Courts:
    i. **Superior Court**—in civil matters, superior courts adjudicate claims greater than a specific dollar amount, for example, more than $10,000. In criminal matters, superior courts usually adjudicate crimes that are felonies.
    ii. **District Court**—in civil matters, district courts adjudicate claims within a specific dollar range, for example, from $5,000 to $10,000. In criminal matters, district courts usually adjudicate crimes that are misdemeanors.
    iii. **Small Claims Court**—in civil matters, **small claims courts** only adjudicate civil actions less than a specific dollar amount, for example, less than $5,000. These actions might include residential[1] landlord-tenant disputes. In "criminal" matters, small claims courts might adjudicate infractions (which technically are not crimes) such as minor traffic violations, parking violations, and littering.[2]

Small Claims Court
a court designed to enable litigants to proceed *pro se* (without a lawyer) in order to quickly and inexpensively resolve suits involving relatively small amounts of money.

Actions in small claims court, including landlord-tenant disputes, are typically heard by a **magistrate,** rather than a judge. Small claims courts are designed for the parties to proceed ***pro se***, that is, on their own and without the assistance of an attorney. Magistrates are judicial officials who are usually appointed, rather than being elected.

Magistrate
a judicial official, usually appointed rather than elected, who presides over small claims court and who renders a judgment.

Also, the ***rules of evidence*** and the ***rules of civil procedure*** that apply in district and superior courts are relaxed in small claims court, if followed at all. Each party—such as the landlord or the tenant—will simply tell his or her side of the dispute to the magistrate and present any evidence or witnesses that they may have. The magistrate will then render a judgment. The magistrate's judgment may be appealed to a higher court where the dispute may be heard before a judge, and decided by a judge or a jury.

---

[1]Lawsuits involving *commercial* leases—as opposed to residential leases—are usually not adjudicated in small claims court. The reasons: Dollar amounts are usually much higher in commercial lease disputes, and the parties can afford to retain attorneys, and thereby proceed in district or superior court.

[2]In many jurisdictions, magistrates may also issue criminal warrants for misdemeanors and felonies based upon information provided by a victim, police officer, or witness; the standard for issuing such a criminal warrant is probable cause.

B. Residential Leases

Lease
a contract—either written or oral—that conveys an interest in real property that is known as a leasehold estate. The holder of a leasehold estate has fewer rights in the "bundle of rights" than would the owner of a fee simple.

A **lease** is a conveyance of an interest in real property. The tenant's estate, or "bundle of rights," is sometimes referred to as a *leasehold estate*. The tenant has the right to possess and use the property, but of course does not own the property, and for this reason a lease is *not* a freehold estate.

Lease agreements are *contracts*, and like all contracts, there must be mutual assent (offer and acceptance) and consideration.[3] And like all contracts, leases define the rights and duties of each of the parties to the contract. However, written residential leases are usually not as comprehensive or clear as they should be, which means that disputes will arise and may have to be litigated in small claims court. Oral lease agreements, although legal, should be avoided since there is a good possibility that a disagreement will arise over one or more of the unwritten terms and conditions. The lack of a written agreement increases the likelihood that the dispute will have to be resolved in a court of law.

Statutes of Frauds
laws in every state that hold that certain types of contracts must be in writing. The prime example is a contract for an interest in real property. Oral leases for less than a year, for example, are a common exception to the statutes of fraud.

All states have what is known as a **Statute of Frauds,** which enumerates the types of contracts that must be in writing. The states vary considerably as to what contracts must be in writing under their individual statute of frauds. The statutes of frauds in all states require that contracts for the purchase of real property must be in writing to be enforceable (as always in the law, there are exceptions to this rule). However, many states do not require that residential leases be in writing to be enforceable. This is especially true if the lease agreement is on a month-to-month basis.

1. LANDLORD'S DUTIES

The landlord's duties under a lease are, like other contracts, subject to negotiation between the parties to the contract. Having said that, however, we note that statutory codes will mandate a "floor," or minimum, as to what duties the landlord must assume, *regardless* of what the lease says. Many states have enacted statutes that require a residential landlord to provide "fit and habitable premises." This is sometimes referred to as the **warranty of habitability.**

Warranty of Habitability
a clause in a lease agreement—either express or implied by law—requiring a landlord to provide safe premises, and working electrical, plumbing, and heating systems.

What constitutes fit and habitable premises is often a matter of common law decided by the courts, sometimes by statute, and sometimes a combination of the two. At a minimum, fit and habitable premises would include adequate plumbing, electrical, and heating systems. This does not mean that the landlord has to pay for the water, electricity, or heat, but just that the systems must be adequate and operational so that the tenant may purchase and use these utility services from the local providers.

Statutory codes that mandate fit and habitable premises often make this duty of the landlord *non-waivable* by the tenant. In other words, the landlord and tenant cannot enter into a lease agreement in which the tenant waives the landlord's duty to provide fit and habitable premises in exchange for a reduction in the monthly rent, or for some other consideration, as in the following example:

---

[3]Even within the same state, case law may differ slightly on the elements of a contract. For example, some case law may list legal capacity of the parties as an element to a contract, while other case law within the same jurisdiction might state that lack of legal capacity is a *defense* to contract formation, rather than an element.

HYPOTHETICAL

Landlord owns a dilapidated house in College Town, USA. The roof leaks, the plumbing leaks, the electrical wiring is 75 years old and grossly inadequate for modern electrical demand, and the coal furnace does not work. A married student with two children approaches the landlord about renting the property. The rental market in College Town is extremely tight, that is, very few units are available for rent, and rental rates are very high, especially from the perspective of a student on a limited budget.

Landlord and the student enter into a lease agreement whereby the landlord will reduce the rental amount by $100 per month in exchange for the student-tenant waiving landlord's duty to provide fit and habitable premises.

What is the public policy that would militate *against* such a lease agreement?

Should two competent adults be allowed to freely contract for whatever lawful purpose—such as renting a house—they choose?

Other duties that may be required *by statute* relate to how the landlord must process the tenant's security deposit. Such statutes may:

a. Limit the amount of the security deposit. Such a statute might read, "Landlord shall not require a security deposit greater than the amount of two months' rent";

b. Dictate where the security deposit is to be held, for example, "in an interest-bearing trust account in a bank located in the same state where the rental property is located";

c. Limit how the landlord may use the security deposit after the tenant moves out, that is, "the deposit may be applied only against unpaid rent, and against the cost to repair damages beyond normal wear and tear"; and

d. Require that a "written accounting must be mailed to the tenant within 30 days of the termination of the lease, itemizing how the tenant's security deposit was used, and refund any unused portion of the security deposit to the tenant."

QUESTION

Why would the landlord's duties, for example, (a)–(d) above, usually *not* be found in a lease, and therefore might be required by statute?

Think of who usually drafts or provides the written lease.

It is an interesting doctrine of contract law that any ambiguity in a contract, including a lease agreement, is construed *against* the drafter. What significance does that hold in relation to a dispute between landlord and tenant?

Other duties of a landlord may be required by the lease agreement itself, rather than by statute. For example, the lease contract may require the landlord to furnish some or all of the utilities, or require the landlord to make repairs to appliances in the rental unit (not caused by tenant's negligent or intentional acts).

The extent of the landlord's duties, as determined by a lease agreement, will generally be greater when the rental property is an apartment unit in a multifamily apartment complex, rather than a free-standing rental house. This is because the market for multifamily rental units is usually more competitive between apartment owners than is the competition between owners of single family homes for rent.

EXHIBIT 4-1 Residential Lease Agreement

Residential Lease Agreement

1. This Agreement is made and entered into this _____ day of _____, 20____, between the following named persons:

    _____   _____

    _____   _____

    (herein called "Tenants") and _____ (herein called "Landlord"). Subject to the terms and conditions set forth in this Agreement, Landlord rents to Tenants, and Tenants rent from Landlord, the premises located at _____ _____, ("the premises"). The premises shall be occupied only by the above mentioned Tenants. Tenants shall use the premises for residential purposes only and for no other purpose without Landlord's prior written consent. Occupancy by guests for more than Fifteen (15) days in any six-month period is prohibited without Landlord's written consent and shall be considered a breach of this Agreement.

2. Each tenant who signs this Agreement, whether or not tenant is or remains in possession, shall be jointly and severally liable for the full performance of each and every obligation of this Agreement not limited to the payment of all rent due and the payment of costs to remedy damages to the premises, regardless of whether such damages were caused by a Tenant or invitee of a Tenant.

3. The term of this Agreement shall commence on _____, 20_____, and shall continue from that date
    a. on a month-to-month basis. This Agreement will continue for successive terms of one month each until either Landlord or Tenants terminate the tenancy by giving the other thirty (30) days written notice of an intention to terminate the premises. In the event such notice is given, Tenants agree to pay all rent up to and including the notice period.
    b. for a period of _____ months expiring on _____, 20_____. Should Tenants vacate before the expiration of the term, Tenants shall be liable for the balance of the rent for the remainder of the term, less any rent Landlord collects or could have collected from a replacement tenant by reasonably attempting to re-rent. Tenants who vacate before expiration of the term are also responsible for Landlord's costs of advertising for a replacement tenant. In the event Tenants fail to give written notice of an intention to vacate the premises at the end of the term, the tenancy shall become one of month-to-month on all terms specified in section (a) of this clause.

4. Tenant(s) shall pay Landlord rent of $ _____ per month, payable in advance on the _____ day of each month. If that day falls on a weekend or legal holiday, the rent is due on the next business day. Rent shall be paid by personal check, money order, or cashier's check only, to _____ at, _____, or at such other place as Landlord shall designate from time to time.

5. If rent is paid after the _____ day of the month, there will be a late charge of $ _____ assessed. If any check submitted the payment of rent or for any other sum due under this Agreement is returned for insufficient funds, or any other reason, Tenant(s) shall pay Landlord a returned check charge of $ _____.

6. As required by law, Tenants are hereby notified that a negative credit report reflecting on Tenants' credit history may be submitted to a credit reporting agency if Tenants fail to fulfill the terms of their financial obligations under the terms of this Agreement.

7. Before the commencement of this Agreement, Tenants shall pay Landlord $_____ as a security deposit. Landlord may use therefrom such amounts as are reasonably necessary to remedy Tenants' default in the payment of rent, repair damages to the premises exclusive of ordinary wear and tear, and to clean the premises if necessary. Landlord shall refund Tenants the balance of the security deposit after such deductions within thirty days after the expiration of this Agreement. If deductions have been made, Landlord shall provide Tenants with an itemized account of each deduction. Local law does not require Landlord to pay interest on security deposits.

8. **UTILITIES** Tenants shall pay directly for all utilities, services and charges provided to the premises, including any and all deposits required.

9. **PARKING** Tenants are assigned parking as follows:

    (Description of parking space(s).)
    This space shall be used for the parking of _____ car(s) only. Tenants may not repair vehicles of any kind anywhere on or about the property. Grease, oil, and any other drippings must be cleaned by Tenants when they occur and at Tenants' expense. Cars are not to be washed on or about the premises.

10. No animal, bird, or other pet shall be brought on or kept on the premises without Landlord's prior written consent.

11. Tenants shall be entitled to quiet enjoyment of the premises. Tenants shall not use the premises in such a way as to violate any law or ordinance, commit waste or nuisance, or annoy, disturb, inconvenience, or interfere with the quiet enjoyment of any other tenant or nearby resident.

12. No portion of the premises shall be sublet nor this Agreement assigned without the prior written consent of the Landlord. Any attempted subletting or assignment by Tenants shall, at the election of Landlord, be a breach of this Agreement and cause for immediate termination as provided by law.

13. The failure of Tenants to take possession of the premises shall not relieve them of their obligation to pay rent. If Landlord is unable to deliver possession of the premises for any reason not within Landlord's control, Landlord shall not be liable for any damage caused thereby, nor will this Agreement be void or voidable, but Tenants shall not be liable for any rent until possession is delivered. If Landlord is unable to deliver possession within fourteen calendar days after the agreed commencement date, Tenants may terminate this Agreement by giving written notice to Landlord, and shall receive a refund of all rent and security deposits paid.

14. Tenants agree to

    (i)   properly use, operate, and safeguard the premises and furnishings, appliances, and fixtures within the premises;
    (ii)   maintain the premises in clean and sanitary condition, and upon termination of the tenancy, to surrender the premises to Landlord in the same condition as when Tenants first took occupancy, except for ordinary wear and tear;
    (iii) if the surrounding grounds are part of the premises and for exclusive use of Tenants, Tenants agree to maintain the surrounding grounds in a clean and safe manner;
    (iv)   notify Landlord in writing upon discovery of any damages, defects or dangerous conditions in and about the premises; and
    (v)   reimburse Landlord for the cost of any repairs to the premises of damages caused by misuse or negligence of Tenants or their guests or invitees.

    Tenants acknowledge that they have inspected the entire interior and exterior of the premises, including plumbing, heating and electrical appliances, smoke detector(s), fixtures, carpets, and paint, and have found them to be in good, safe, and clean condition and repair, with the following exceptions: (Specify "none" if no exceptions)

    _____

    _____

    _____

    _____

15. Except as provided by law or as authorized by the prior written consent of Landlord, Tenants shall not make any repairs or alterations to the premises, including but not limited to, painting walls, installing wallpaper, murals, paneling, tile, or hanging items weighing in excess of fifteen pounds.
    If the premises are damaged or destroyed as to render them uninhabitable, then either Landlord or Tenants shall have the right to terminate this Agreement as of the date on which such damage occurs, through written notice to the other party to be given within fifteen days of occurrence of such damage. However, if such damage should occur as the result of the conduct or negligence of Tenants or Tenants' guests or invitees, Landlord shall have the right to termination and Tenants shall be responsible for all losses, including, but not limited to, damage and repair costs as well as loss of rental income.

16. Tenants shall make the premises available to Landlord or Landlord's agents for the purposes of making repairs or improvements, or to supply agreed services or show the premises to prospective buyers or tenants, or in case of emergency. Except in case of emergency, Landlord shall give Tenants reasonable notice of intent to enter. For these purposes, twenty-four (24) hour written notice shall be deemed reasonable. In order to facilitate Landlord's right of access, Tenants shall not, without Landlord's prior written consent, add or alter any locks to the premises.

17. In the event Tenants will be away from the premises for more than thirty consecutive days, Tenants agree to notify Landlord in writing of the absence. During such absence, Landlord may enter the premises at times reasonably necessary to maintain the property and inspect for damages and needed repairs.

(continued)

EXHIBIT 4-1 *Continued*

Abandonment is defined as absence of the Tenants from the premises, for at least thirty consecutive days without notice to Landlord. If the rent is outstanding and unpaid for thirty days and there is no reasonable evidence, other than the presence of the Tenants' personal property, that the Tenants are occupying the unit, Landlord may at Landlord's option terminate this agreement and regain possession in the manner prescribed by law.

18. Tenants assume full responsibility for all personal property placed, stored, or located on or about the premises. Tenants' personal property is not insured by Landlord. Landlord recommends that Tenants obtain insurance to protect against risk of loss from harm to Tenants' personal property. Landlord shall not be responsible for any harm to Tenants' property resulting from fire, theft, burglary, orders or acts of public authorities, acts of nature, or any other circumstance or event beyond Landlord's control.

19. Tenants expressly release Landlord from any and all liability for any damages or injury to Tenants, or any other person, or to any property, occurring on the premises unless the damage is the direct result of the negligence or unlawful act of Landlord or Landlord's agents.

20. The premises are equipped with a smoke detection device(s), and Tenants are responsible for reporting any problems, maintenance, or repairs to Landlord. Replacing batteries is the responsibility of Tenants.

21. **LEAD BASED PAINT DISCLOSURE** By initialing, Tenant acknowledges receipt of disclosure of information on lead-based paint and lead-based paint hazards. Landlord has no reports or knowledge of lead-based paint on the premises.

    Tenants initial here: _____ _____ _____ _____

22. Tenant shall not use or have any liquid-filled furniture, including waterbeds, on the premises without Landlord's prior written consent.

23. **ADDITIONAL PROVISIONS** (If there are no additional provisions, specify "none.")

    _____

    _____

    _____

    _____

    _____

    _____

    _____

24. This document constitutes the entire Agreement between the Tenants and Landlord. This Agreement cannot be modified except in writing and must be signed by all parties. Neither Landlord nor Tenants have made any promises or representations, other than those set forth in this Agreement and implied by law. The failure of Tenants, their guests, or invitees to comply with any term of this Agreement is grounds for termination of the tenancy, with appropriate notice to Tenants and procedures as required by law.

_____   _____
Landlord   Date

_____
Landlord/Street Address, City, State & ZIP

_____   _____
Tenant   Date

_____   _____
Tenant   Date

_____   _____
Tenant   Date

_____   _____
Tenant   Date

2. TENANT'S DUTIES

As the landlord's primary duty is to provide fit and habitable premises, the tenant's primary duty is to pay the rent. Other duties that might be imposed upon the tenant either by statute or pursuant to the lease agreement would be:

a. To keep the rental premises in a clean and safe condition,
b. To not deliberately or negligently destroy or damage any part of the premises (or permit one's guests or visitors to do so), and
c. To notify the landlord of any repairs or maintenance needed to be performed on the premises.

We have looked at a few of the respective duties of landlord and tenant. A legal issue that is frequently litigated is what duty, if any, does a landlord have to protect a tenant—or a tenant's guests or visitors—from criminal actions by third parties. The states vary considerably on this question, but the trend by the courts is toward imposing a duty of care upon a landlord when the landlord knew, or should have known, that there was a risk of harm to the tenants. This concept of "knew, or should have known" is summed up in a word which is so important in tort law: *foreseeability*.

WALLS V. OXFORD MANAGEMENT COMPANY

Supreme Court of New Hampshire
137 N.H. 653; 633 A.2d 103
1993

The United States District Court for the District of New Hampshire has certified to this court the following question: Does New Hampshire law impose a **duty on landlords** to provide security to protect tenants from the criminal attacks of third persons?

On December 13, 1988, the plaintiff, Deanna Walls, was sexually assaulted in her vehicle, which was parked on the premises of the Bay Ridge Apartment Complex in Nashua. The plaintiff lived with her mother, who leased an apartment at Bay Ridge. Gerard Buckley was arrested and subsequently convicted of sexually assaulting the plaintiff. Bay Ridge is owned by defendant Nashua-Oxford Bay Associates Limited Partnership (Nashua-Oxford), and managed by defendant Oxford Management Company, Inc. (Oxford).

It consists of 412 apartments located in fourteen buildings. During the two years prior to the assault, the Bay Ridge complex had been the site of a number of crimes directed against property, including eleven automobile thefts, three attempted automobile thefts, and thirty-one incidents involving criminal mischief/theft. No sexual assaults or similar attacks against persons had been reported.

The plaintiff brought this action in federal court, charging that the defendants:

had a duty to hire and contract with a competent management company, had a **duty to provide reasonable security** measures for the protection of residents of Bay Ridge, a duty to warn residents of its lack of security, as well as a **duty to warn** residents of the numerous criminal activities which had taken place on the premises of Bay Ridge and in the vicinity of Bay Ridge.

The plaintiff alleges that the defendants breached these duties, and that the breach was a proximate cause of the sexual assault.

(continued)

I. Landlord's Duty to Secure Tenants Against Criminal Attack

Claims for negligence rest primarily upon a violation of some duty owed by the offender to the injured party. Absent a duty, there is no negligence. Whether a duty exists in a particular case is a question of law. Only after a court has determined that a defendant owed a plaintiff a duty, and identified the standard of care imposed by that duty, may a jury consider the separate question of whether the defendant breached that duty.

The scope of the duty imposed is limited by what risks, if any, are *reasonably foreseeable*. As a general rule, a defendant will not be held liable for negligence if he could not reasonably foresee that his conduct would result in an injury or if his conduct was reasonable in light of what he could anticipate.

While we can state without reservation that *landlords owe a general duty of reasonable care* to their tenants, our efforts at resolving the question presented is complicated by the competing common law rule that private citizens ordinarily have *no duty to protect others* from criminal attacks. This rule is grounded in the fundamental unfairness of holding private citizens responsible for the unanticipated criminal acts of third parties. Although crimes do occur … they are still so unlikely that the burden of taking continual precautions against them almost always exceeds the apparent risk.

We agree that as a general principle, landlords have no duty to protect tenants from criminal attack…. We will not place on landlords the burden of insuring their tenants against harm from criminal attacks.

Our inquiry is not concluded, however, as we must further consider whether exceptions to the general rule against holding individuals liable for the criminal attacks of others apply to the landlord-tenant relationship. A review of the law suggests four such exceptions.…

A third exception is the existence of overriding *foreseeability*. Some courts have held landlords to a duty to protect tenants from criminal attacks that were clearly foreseeable, even if not causally related to physical defects on the premises.

We hold that while landlords have *no general duty* to protect tenants from criminal attack, such a duty may arise when a landlord has created, or is responsible for, a known defective condition on a premises that foreseeably enhanced the risk of criminal attack. Moreover, a landlord who undertakes, either gratuitously or by contract, to provide security will thereafter have a duty to act with reasonable care. Where, however, a landlord has made no affirmative attempt to provide security, and is not responsible for a physical defect that enhances the risk of crime, we will not find such a duty. We reject liability based solely on the landlord-tenant relationship or on a doctrine of overriding foreseeability.

A finding that an approved exception applies is not dispositive of the landlord's liability for a tenant's injury. Where a landlord's duty is premised on a defective condition that has *foreseeably enhanced the risk* of criminal attack, the question whether the defect was a proximate or legal cause of the tenant's injury remains one of fact. Moreover, where a landlord has voluntarily assumed a duty to provide some degree of security, this duty is limited by the extent of the undertaking. For example, a landlord who provides lighting for the exterior of an apartment building might be held liable for failing to insure that the lighting functioned properly, but not for failing to provide additional security measures such as patrol services or protective fencing.

Remanded.

Author's Comment: There are many cases like this one involving assaults in apartment or condominium buildings. Other cases arise in a different venue—parking garages, for example—but the legal issue is the same:

Should the owner of an apartment complex or parking garage be civilly liable for the intentionally tortious and criminal acts committed by third parties?

The Court mentioned that there had been about a dozen prior criminal acts on the property. However, those were crimes against property, and therefore qualitatively different than the physical assault against the plaintiff. The Court implied that because the previous crimes were against property, the owner could not "foresee" the violent physical assault, and therefore, was not liable.

Do you agree with the Court's analysis, or is it sufficient that knowledge of the dozen prior property crimes is sufficient to make the owner liable for negligence relating to the physical assault?

3. MUTUAL CONDITIONS—DEPENDENT OR INDEPENDENT?

Leases are contracts. In contract law, the following question frequently arises: When there is a breach of a contract term or condition by a party to the contract, when may the *non*-breaching party suspend performance? If you have taken a course in contract law, you may remember the concepts of conditions, and **material breach** and **partial breach** (substantial performance). How these concepts apply to landlord-tenant law very much depends on the following factors, listed in the order of their priority:

a. The statutory law of the jurisdiction in question,
b. The case law of the jurisdiction in question, and
c. The lease agreement between the parties.

The law of breach, and the law of conditions—whether dependent or independent—is difficult in theory and even more difficult to apply in the real world. Look at the two examples below, keeping in mind the concepts of "fit and habitable premises" (warranty of habitability), material and partial breach, dependent or independent conditions, and public policy.

Condition Precedent
in a contract, an event that must occur before a party is obligated to perform under the contract.

Material Breach
a breach by one party to a contract that is so significant that the non-breaching party is relieved from performing under the terms of the contract.

Minor/Partial Breach
a breach by one party to a contract that is relatively insignificant, and therefore does not relieve the non-breaching party of the duty to perform under the terms of the contract. When the breach is minor, the breaching party is said to have substantially performed.

EXAMPLES

EXAMPLE 1 RE DEPENDENT AND INDEPENDENT CONDITIONS

Landlord and tenant entered into a lease agreement, pursuant to which landlord had a contractual duty to furnish all of the utilities, and tenant had a contractual duty to pay rent. In the fourth month of the lease, which happened to be in January, the tenant breached the lease agreement by failing to pay the rent. In this particular case, the landlord is the *non*-breaching party. May the landlord suspend her performance by cutting off all utilities to the rental property? Or put another way:

Has there been a material breach of the rental agreement by the tenant, such that landlord would be justified in cutting off the utilities to the rental unit?

Is landlord's obligation to provide utilities dependent upon tenant's duty to pay rent? In other words, is landlord's obligation to provide heat a dependent condition of tenant's duty to pay the monthly rent?

Or is landlord's obligation to provide utilities independent of the tenant's duty to pay rent, and therefore must the landlord continue to furnish the utilities despite tenant's non-payment of the rent?

EXAMPLE 2 RE DEPENDENT AND INDEPENDENT CONDITIONS

Landlord and tenant entered into a lease agreement, pursuant to which landlord had a contractual duty to furnish all utilities, and tenant had a contractual duty to pay rent. It is July in a Southwestern state and tenant—who has no need for heat in July—*accidentally* discovers that the heat is not working in his apartment unit.

Armed with that information, and knowledge of some contract law, the tenant withholds his rent for three months until the heating unit is repaired by the landlord at the end of September. The tenant's rationale for not paying is that heat must be provided under the warranty of habitability. The tenant then resumes paying his rent for the month of October (after the heater was fixed) but still refuses to pay any of the rent for July, August, and September when the heater was not working.

Has there been a material breach of the rental agreement by the landlord, such that tenant would be justified in withholding rental payments to the landlord?

(continued)

> Conversely, has there been a material breach of the rental agreement by the tenant for failure to pay rent, such that the landlord would be justified in evicting the tenant?
>
> Do breaches exist in isolation and absolutely, that is, according to the unconditional language of the lease agreement? If so, there may be a technical breach, but is it necessarily "material"?
>
> Or should courts consider the facts and circumstances surrounding the alleged breach, such as the apartment's heater not working in July?

4. EVICTION, "SELF-HELP," AND RETALIATORY EVICTION

Eviction / Summary Ejectment / Unlawful Detainer
these are the different names used in various states for the legal process by which a tenant is removed from a rental property, whether residential or commercial. These actions, especially in residential cases, are usually litigated in small claims court.

Eviction is sometimes referred to as **summary ejectment** or an action for **unlawful detainer.** Regardless of the name, it is the legal process whereby a landlord can have the tenant removed from the leased premises, for any number of reasons, but most often for failure to pay rent. Other reasons for eviction would be if a tenant—or the tenant's guests—caused damage to the rental property beyond normal wear and tear, or if the tenant—or the tenant's guests—engaged in criminal activity on or about the rental property.

The process of eviction varies from state to state. Evictions, or complaints in summary ejectment, are usually heard in small claims court before a magistrate. Small claims court has the advantages we discussed earlier—it is informal, relatively inexpensive, the parties need not have attorneys, and the rules of evidence are less strictly applied, if they are applied at all. But perhaps most importantly— at least from the landlord's perspective—is that the time from docketing a case to its adjudication is much quicker than it would be in a state district or superior trial court, an important factor for a landlord who is not receiving rent, or whose property is being damaged by a tenant.

Self-help Eviction
the removal of a tenant by a landlord without the use of the legally required process. Self-help evictions have the potential for violence and therefore are banned in most states.

A **self-help eviction** occurs when a landlord "helps herself" by ejecting the tenant without the use of legal process. Self-help usually occurs when the landlord, or the landlord's agents, enter the leased premises for the purpose of forcing the tenant to leave immediately. The landlord may physically remove the tenant, dispose of the tenant's personal belongings, and change out the locks; the tenant may, or may not, be at home at the time.

Self-help eviction was permitted under the common law, and although some jurisdictions still permit self-help, most states have laws prohibiting the practice. It is easy to understand the public policies against a landlord's use of self-help:

First, it can be physically dangerous for all concerned, especially when one sees his or her personal property being thrown out of one's home; violence has often resulted from self-help eviction.

Second, assuming the tenant is not merely a trespasser, the tenant has a legal interest in the property, that is, a leasehold estate, and a tenant should be divested of that legal estate only by legal methods, meaning *due process* of law.

Third, when a tenant—sometimes with a family—is put out on the street, the tenant may be further victimized, and/or become a burden on the state.

Self-help evictions are much less common today than 30–40 years ago, but it still happens far too often. The reason for its demise is the passage of laws against the practice in so many states, and the trend towards increased litigation during the same time frame. *Legal Aid* offices have been in the vanguard in fighting self-help evictions.

THE RESTATEMENTS' TAKE ON SELF-HELP

The Restatements, including the Restatements of Property, are not binding on the courts, but they can be highly persuasive.

From the Restatement 2d of Prop: Landlord & Tenant, § 14.2:

§ 14.2 Effect on Self-Help Doctrine of Availability of Speedy Judicial Remedy for Recovery of Possession From Holdover Tenant.

1. *If the controlling law gives the landlord, or an incoming tenant, a speedy judicial remedy for the recovery of possession of leased property from a tenant improperly holding over after the termination of the lease, neither the landlord, nor the incoming tenant, may resort to self-help to recover possession of the leased property from such tenant, unless the controlling law preserves the right of self-help.*
2. *If the controlling law does not preserve the right of self-help, an agreement that the landlord may resort to self-help is against public policy and void.*

Retaliatory eviction occurs when a landlord attempts to remove a tenant from the leased premises solely because the tenant has exercised his or her rights to live under applicable landlord-tenant law, including, but not limited to, the right to live in a habitable dwelling.

Protected actions by a tenant might include a good faith complaint or request for repairs made to the landlord, a good faith complaint to a housing authority or governmental agency about a landlord's alleged violation of any health or safety law, or a good faith attempt to organize a tenants' association for the purpose of promoting or enforcing their legal rights under their leases and the law.

Most states have laws against retaliatory eviction.

Retaliatory Eviction
when a landlord evicts a tenant solely because the tenant has exercised rights under the law, such as the right to organize a tenant's union.

5. ASSIGNMENT OF LEASES

Because leases are contracts, they can generally be assigned. That means that if the owner of Greenacres apartment complex decides to sell the property, the leases will be **assigned** to the buyer as part of the sale, who will then have the right to collect rents from the tenants. The new owner would also assume the duties of the previous owner under the leases, for example, providing safe and habitable premises.

On the other hand, what happens if a tenant in Greenacres wants to assign her interest in the lease, that is, ***sublet*** her apartment to a third-party? Unless there is language in the lease to the contrary, the tenant will ordinarily be free to assign/sublet her apartment. However, many residential leases include language such as:

Assignment
the transfer of one's rights to another.

> *Tenant may not sublease the apartment unit <u>without the landlord's written consent</u>.*

Where such language in a lease limits the tenant's right to sublet and that issue is adjudicated, courts will often modify that contractual limitation, so that after the court reforms (re-writes) that clause in the lease, it might read:

> *Tenant may not sublease the apartment unit without the landlord's written consent, such consent <u>not to be unreasonably withheld</u>.*

A landlord has a legitimate interest in an assignment/sublet because an assignment to an unqualified sublessee could significantly ***increase the landlord's risk***. Let's say that you are the current tenant, have a solid well-paying job, and have never been late with your rent payment in the 22 months that you have lived in the rental unit.

You now want to assign the lease—that is, sublet—your apartment to your ne'er-do-well brother-in-law who hasn't had a job in 10 years, but does have a long criminal history. In this situation, the landlord's risk of nonpayment, and perhaps damage to the apartment itself, has substantially increased, and the landlord could reasonably withhold permission for the sublet.

It is worth noting that the **assignor**—the original tenant who will sublet her unit—still remains liable for the payment of the rent (and for damages) should the **assignee**—the subtenant—default on the lease. The tenant/assignor can be relieved of liability under the rental agreement if there is a novation.

A *novation* is a new contract that is created when the landlord and **assignee/subtenant** agree to a new lease, which thereby relieves the original tenant/assignor of any liability under her original lease agreement.

Assignor
one who transfers rights to another.

Assignee
one to whom rights are transferred by the assignor.

C. Types of Tenancies

In Chapter 3, you learned about the four major types of concurrent *ownership*:

1. Joint tenants with right of survivorship,
2. Tenants in common,
3. Tenants by the entirety, and
4. Community property.

The use of the words "tenants" and "**tenancy**" referred to those persons who were actually owners of the property.

In this chapter, the words "tenants" and "tenancy" refer to their more familiar, everyday meaning regarding someone who is leasing a property, as opposed to owning it. The interest that such a person has is a leasehold estate. There are four types of leasehold tenancies:

Tenancy
in the context of a leasehold estate, a tenancy defines the quality and duration of the tenant's interest in the property.

1. TENANCY FOR YEARS

The most common type of leasehold estate is a **tenancy for years.** Fair warning though—the name is a misnomer. A tenancy for years is a lease for a fixed or computable period of time, that is, the lease has a specific starting date and a specific termination date, regardless of whether the period of time is a week, a month, a year, or some other fixed period of time. Since a specific termination date is part of the rental contract, a tenancy for years may only be created by express agreement, either written or oral.

In a tenancy for years, the tenant need not give any notice of termination prior to moving out because the lease already specifies the termination date.

Tenancy for Years
the most common type of leasehold, which lasts for a fixed period of time.

EXAMPLE OF TENANCY FOR YEARS

Landlord and tenant enter into a lease which expressly states:

> *This tenancy begins on January 1, 2012, and terminates on December 31, 2012.*

This is a tenancy for years because it is for a fixed period of time, and has a specific termination date.

What if on January 1, 2013, the tenant offers, and the landlord accepts, a rental check for the month of January 2013?

Is this still a tenancy for years? (See next page.)

2. TENANCY FROM PERIOD TO PERIOD

A **tenancy from period to period,** sometimes called a periodic tenancy, is a tenancy for successive and continuous periods of time, which may be a week, a month, a year, or any other discrete unit of time. Unlike a tenancy for years, however, there is **no specific termination date**, and at the end of the rental period, the lease will "roll over" to the next rental period.

The tenancy from period to period/periodic tenancy may be created by express agreement—either oral or written—or by implication. An example of how a tenancy from period to period can be created by implication is when a tenant holds over after the expiration of a tenancy for years.

This answers the question raised above. When the tenant in the example above pays the rent for the month of January 2013, the tenancy for years becomes a tenancy from period to period, and the "period" in question will be a month, since rent was paid on a monthly basis.

The new tenancy will operate under the same terms and conditions as the previous tenancy. If the landlord wants to raise the tenant's rent or eject the tenant, landlord must give at least one month's notice before doing so. Conversely, if the tenant wants to quit the premises, tenant must give at least one month's notice.

> **Tenancy from Period to Period**
> a leasehold for successive, continuous, and discrete periods of time. There is no specific termination date, and a rental period may "roll over."

3. TENANCY AT WILL

A **tenancy at will** lasts only as long as both the landlord and tenant desire. There is no specific termination date as is required in a tenancy for years, nor is there a fixed rental period as is required in a tenancy from period to period.

Perhaps the most common example of a tenancy at will is the situation where a college student, after graduating, moves back into the home of her parents. The student may agree to pay rent with the understanding that when she is able to find a job, she will be free to terminate her tenancy.

> **Tenancy at Will**
> a leasehold that lasts for as long as the landlord and tenant agree. This is a very informal arrangement, which may be terminated at the will of either party, with reasonable notice.

EXAMPLE OF TENANCY AT WILL

Tony (barely) graduated from State University in June of 2012. He had been living in a dormitory on campus, and after the graduation ceremony announced to his parents that he would be moving back home with them.

After moving back with his parents, Tony is partying and staying out late even more than he was at State U. His parents have issued several ultimatums for Tony to cease and desist from his wild ways, "or else…"

The last straw occurs when Tony returns home at 5:00 a.m., and has to break a window to gain entry because he has lost his keys in the bushes. His parents, roused by the commotion, order Tony to leave the house by noon of that very day.

Noon comes and goes. Tony is still asleep at 2:00 p.m. If Tony's parents call the police, can they have him arrested for trespassing?

What factors figure into your answer?

4. TENANCY AT SUFFERANCE

When a tenant has held over at the expiration of his lease and has not paid any rent since then, he has become a **tenant at sufferance.** Although not considered by the law to be a trespasser, a tenant at sufferance is the next closest thing.

> **Tenancy at Sufferance**
> a tenant who has held over—remained in the property—after the expiration or termination of the lease agreement.

A tenant at sufferance is not a trespasser because the tenant originally had the landlord's permission to enter and possess the premises. The landlord may legally do one of three things:

a. Allow the tenant to remain on the property without paying rent, which is probably unlikely,

b. Negotiate a new lease with the holdover tenant, or

c. Follow the legal procedures for ejecting the tenant from the property.

A tenant at sufferance has **no rights in the property** which he occupies, and therefore has no "estate" to speak of. Rather, it is said that a tenant at sufferance merely has "naked possession," and nothing else.

Aside from an action to eject the tenant, the landlord may have a claim in tort for **restitution** for the period of unauthorized use of the property. This is true even though the landlord has not yet made a demand that the tenant depart, because the holdover is without the landlord's permission. Restitution is a claim that may be made when a defendant—in this case, the tenant at sufferance—has been unjustly enriched, by holding over on the premises without paying any rent.

In the case of the holdover, the tenant would be "unjustly enriched" if allowed to walk away without paying for the time spent in the property while holding over. The tort of restitution (sometimes called "quantum meruit") is different from a claim for breach of contract because with a restitution cause of action, there is no contract.

Restitution
a tort claim designed to prevent unjust enrichment of another in the absence of a contract between the two parties.

5. THE DIFFERENCE BETWEEN A LEASE AND A LICENSE

Suppose that Rowdy Yates and friends purchase tickets to a sporting event. Rowdy's ticket states that "The holder of this ticket may occupy Seat 8, Row 19, Section 52, for the duration of the game on Saturday, December 14, 2014." Further suppose that Rowdy lives up to his name, and as a result, he is approached by security officers who ask (order) him to leave the stadium. Security also informs Rowdy that the price of admission will be returned to him when he departs the stadium.

In response, Rowdy tells security that he has a leasehold estate for the evening of the game, in the aforementioned seat that he is currently occupying, and if stadium management wants him to leave, they will have to go to small claims court to evict him. Is Rowdy correct?

While it is true that Rowdy has paid several dollars for the use (lease?) of a particular piece of real property (Seat 8, Row 19, Section 52), you probably feel intuitively that he is mistaken. And you would be correct, because Rowdy does not have a lease or a leasehold estate that entitles him to use, possess, and enjoy that particular seat, which is, in fact, real property. Instead, he has a **license** to use the assigned seat.

License
a right to use real property for a short period of time, and which right is revocable without notice or legal process, at the will of the licensor.

The difference between a *leasehold* and a *license* is that a license is revocable, without prior notice or legal process, at the will of the person or entity granting the license (that is, the licensor), which is usually stated on the reverse side of the ticket stub. Even if there is no such language on the ticket stub identifying it as a license to use a specific, assigned seat, the extremely short duration of the permitted use of the seat would cause a reasonable person to believe that this was a license rather than a lease agreement.

D. Leased Residential Property

1. SINGLE FAMILY AND MULTIFAMILY RESIDENTIAL HOUSING

Residential rental property can be divided into two basic types of housing: single-family residential and multifamily residential.

A single-family residence (SFR) is sometimes referred to as a single-family detached residence, and generally means a stand-alone house. A **single-family residence** offers some advantages and disadvantages when compared to living in a multifamily apartment complex. Single-family rental properties often have private yards where a tenant's children may play, and dogs or other pets can be kept. Single-family properties may offer more parking and privacy than one would find in an apartment complex.

> **Single-Family Residence**
> a free-standing house having its own surrounding yards.

As far as disadvantages of single-family renting, tenants may have to perform routine maintenance inside the house, and may be required to maintain the exterior, including mowing the lawn, painting, and other such tasks. Tenants may also have to furnish their own appliances, such as refrigerators, washers, and dryers.

A **multifamily residential** property is a building containing two or more rental apartments. Perhaps the main advantage of living in a multifamily property is that the landlord will usually provide some or all of the necessary appliances, maintain the exterior, and in some cases, the interior of the apartment unit. The monthly rent may include the furnishing of some or all of the utilities, although this is not nearly as common today as it was in the 1960s and 1970s, when the cost of energy was much less expensive.

> **Multifamily Residential**
> two or more attached apartment rental units.

The presence of neighbors close by may be an advantage or disadvantage, depending on one's perspective, and perhaps most importantly, depending on the neighbors themselves.

Larger multifamily properties—for example, more than 100 units—often have on-site managers who, at least in theory, will provide better service for the tenants' needs than an absentee landlord. Good on-site managers can make a marginal, breakeven property successful and profitable.

2. SECTION 8 HOUSING

Section 8 housing is a federal program that subsidizes rent payments for low-income individuals and families. The program was authorized when Congress passed the Housing and Community Development Act of 1974, and is operated under the auspices of the Department of Housing and Urban Development (**HUD**). In addition to Section 8 and various other federal subsidized housing programs, many states, counties, and cities have their own housing agencies and subsidized rental programs. A typical subsidized program would work something like this:

An applicant for the subsidized rental program must demonstrate financial need, usually determined by having a monthly income *below* a certain amount to qualify for entry into the program. The maximum income allowed varies depending on the number of adults and children in the family that will occupy the subsidized apartment unit or house.

The *maximum* family income allowed varies widely from state to state, and even from city to city within a given state, because the cost of living, and especially the cost of housing, will vary substantially between, for example, St. Louis and a much smaller town in Missouri. Once accepted into the subsidized rental program, the tenant will be required to pay a percentage of his or her monthly income towards the rent, usually in the range of 20%–30%.

After determining that the applicant meets the income eligibility requirement, the applicant will visit one or more of the pre-inspected and *pre-approved* rental houses or apartment units on the housing agency's list of available properties. For each of the properties on the list, the housing agency will have already determined the Fair Market Rent (FMR) based upon its prior inspection of the apartment or house and the local rental housing market.

To take an example, a landlord owns a single-family residence that has already been inspected and approved for the subsidy program by the city housing authority. The housing agency has determined that the FMR is $900 per month. The applicant-tenant has a monthly income of $1,200, and under the terms of the subsidy program the tenant is required to pay 30%, or $360. The difference between the $900 FMR and the tenant's monthly payment of $360, is $540, which is the amount of the monthly subsidy paid to the landlord by the federal, state, or local government:

$1,200 Applicant's monthly income

$\times$ 30% Percent required to be paid by applicant

= $360 Rent to be paid by applicant-tenant

$900 Fair Market Rental Value

$-$ 360 Rent to be paid by applicant-tenant

$540 Amount to be subsidized by local, state or federal government

Despite its name, the Fair Market Rent (FMR) set by the local housing agency is not always the true market rent in a community, particularly if the housing market is "tight" (that is, high demand, but limited supply) in the area. The rules of Section 8 and other subsidized housing programs prohibit a landlord from charging more than the FMR.

However, particularly in tight rental markets, unscrupulous landlords have been known to demand "side agreements" whereby the tenant is forced to pay the landlord more than the agreed-upon cap of 30% of the tenant's income. This practice is illegal, and a landlord may be barred from the rental program for such practices. The tenant may also sue in tort and for breach of contract.

3. FEDERAL AND STATE FAIR HOUSING LAWS

Racially, religiously and ethnically segregated housing has been a feature of the American landscape since long before the birth of the Republic. However, it has only been in the last 40 years or so that federal and state governments have offered more than lip service to the prohibition of discrimination in the area of housing.

Section 1981 of the Civil Rights Act (CRA) of 1866 is arguably the first fair housing law passed in the United States. It was enacted shortly after the end of the Civil War and reads as follows:

Sec. 1981. Equal rights under the law

(a) Statement of equal rights

*All persons within the jurisdiction of the United States shall have the same right in every State and Territory to make and enforce **contracts**, to sue, be parties, give evidence, and to the full and equal benefit of all laws and proceedings for the security of persons and **property** as is enjoyed by white citizens, and shall be subject to like punishment, pains, penalties, taxes, licenses, and exactions of every kind, and to no other.*

However, § 1981 failed to provide for a federal enforcement mechanism. Persons who were discriminated against rarely had the financial ability to hire counsel to vindicate their rights under the statute, even if such counsel could be found. Consequently, until the last 40 years or so, § 1981 of the Civil Rights Act of 1866 had not been widely used to combat discrimination in housing.

In 1948, three years after the end of World War II, the United States Supreme Court decided the case of *Shelley v. Kraemer*, 334 U.S. 1. The Shelleys, a black family, purchased a home in a residential subdivision in 1945. However, in 1911, about 34 years earlier, the majority of homeowners in the subdivision had agreed to include a **restrictive covenant** in all of their deeds, which would prohibit the sale of any of their properties to "any person not of the Caucasian race." In a landmark decision, the Supreme Court found in favor of the Shelleys, and held that such restrictive covenants violated the Equal Protection Clause of the Fourteenth Amendment to the United States Constitution.

More than 100 years after the passage of the Civil Rights Act of 1866, Congress enacted the Civil Rights Act of 1968, including Title VIII, which is commonly known as the Fair Housing Act. Discrimination on the basis of race, color, national origin, religion, sex, disability, or familial status is prohibited under the Act.

The federal **fair housing laws** prohibit discrimination not only in the sale or rental of housing, but also ban the use of coercion, intimidation, threats, or interference with an individual's rights to fair housing under Title VIII.

> **Fair Housing Laws**
> federal and state laws enacted to prevent discrimination in the sale or rental of housing.

Title VIII was subsequently amended by the Fair Housing Amendments Act of 1988 (FHAA), which strengthened the 1968 Act, and outlawed discrimination in the *financing* of real estate. Other activities outlawed by federal and state fair housing statutes include:

1. **Steering** occurs when a real estate agent or broker "steers," manipulates, or otherwise influences a client, that is, a prospective home buyer, to purchase property in a particular neighborhood on the basis of the client's race, and the racial makeup of a given neighborhood.

   Normally, this illegal practice involves steering minority home buyers away from predominantly white neighborhoods and into minority neighborhoods. However, it is also illegal for a broker or agent to steer a white home buyer away from a predominantly minority neighborhood.

   > **Steering**
   > the illegal practice of manipulating a buyer or renter to move into, or away from, a particular community in order to maintain segregated neighborhoods.

2. **Blockbusting** occurs when a real estate agent, broker, or speculator informs the homeowners in a neighborhood that members of minority groups are, or will soon be, moving into the neighborhood. The practice is designed to frighten the existing homeowners into listing and selling their homes through the blockbusting real estate agent (generating increased sales commissions) or to a blockbusting real estate speculator who can then purchase from concerned sellers at fire sale prices.

   > **Blockbusting**
   > the illegal practice by real estate brokers or agents to frighten property owners into selling their homes by informing the owners that minorities are, or soon will be, moving into their neighborhood.

3. *False representations* regarding the unavailability of housing for rent or sale based upon a prospective renter's or buyer's race, color, religion, familial status, disability, sex, or national origin is illegal. The typical case occurs when a member of one of the aforementioned protected classes asks about the availability of an advertised rental unit or home for sale.

4. **Redlining** is another illegal real estate–related activity, usually practiced by lending institutions. The practice involves a lender excluding loan applicants from obtaining loans for the purchase of homes in certain disfavored areas. The name derives from using red lines to delineate the boundaries of the disfavored neighborhoods.

   > **Redlining**
   > the illegal practice by lending institutions when they refuse to make loans on properties in areas that are considered undesirable and poor financial risks, or to the people living in those areas

A variation of this practice involves making loans to persons in redlined neighborhoods, but charging them significantly **higher interest rates** and origination fees on home loans. Redlining is not unique to the field of real estate, and unfortunately, has been practiced in other businesses such as insurance and automobile lending.

E. Commercial Property and Leases

Thus far, we have discussed landlord-tenant law in the context of residential property. As we previously noted, in residential leases, state laws and the courts that enforce them are more inclined to be protective of the tenant's interests over the landlord's interest. Two examples of this solicitude are the implied warranty of habitability that requires the landlord to provide fit and habitable premises, and the processing and handling of tenants' security deposits.

There are at least two reasons for this legal deference towards the tenant. First, a residential lease governs a highly personal and fundamental need—housing. Our homes are our "castles" where we live and interact with our families and friends. Second, as to the landlord-tenant relationship, there is usually a considerable disparity of bargaining power and financial resources between the average residential tenant and landlord.

In situations involving unequal or disparate bargaining power, one of the two parties to a contract is perceived to be "at the mercy" of the other, stronger party. Consequently, the stronger party really does not have to bargain and can offer the contract/lease on a take-it-or-leave-it basis. Unequal bargaining power may result from a difference in wealth, education, or experience of the parties to a contract.

But the disparity may have more to do with the availability of rental units than wealth per se. As we observed earlier, in many college towns the supply of rental housing may be extremely thin in August and September, thereby giving the landlord the upper hand (i.e., superior bargaining power) over the prospective renter. However, that situation may be reversed in June and July and landlords might be offering heavily discounted rents to prospective lessees, who then would have the upper hand in lease negotiations.

Landlord-tenant law also controls leasing arrangements in the field of **commercial property**, which includes real estate where people work and transact business, such as office buildings, shopping centers, and industrial properties. In this commercial context, the law is more inclined to be neutral in its treatment of the parties to the lease.

First, a commercial lease is a business agreement, and as such does not carry with it the same personal significance and importance as a residential lease for one's home.

Second, in commercial leasing, the tenant is much more likely to be the equal of the landlord in terms of both financial resources and business sophistication, including contract (leasing) negotiation and enforcement. The parties to a commercial lease transaction are presumed to have equal bargaining power.

1. TYPES OF COMMERCIAL LEASES

Commercial leases can be highly complex and may consist of hundreds of pages. However, there are only three basic methods for determining the rental amount to be paid by the tenant to the landlord.

a. The **fixed lease** is a rental agreement where the tenant agrees to pay a flat monthly rent, just like most residential tenants would do. The main difference is that a commercial lease, because it may be for a period of five, ten, or more years, will have an escalation clause by which the monthly rental will be adjusted annually, or every few years, usually by reference to the Consumer Price Index.

> **Fixed Lease**
> a flat monthly rental paid by the commercial tenant just like the flat rate paid by an apartment renter.

Therefore, if the CPI increased by 4% during the first year of the lease, the monthly rental payments in the second year will increase by 4%. An escalation clause allows the landlord to avoid the loss of purchasing power due to inflation over the term of the lease.

b. The **fixed + percentage lease** is the second of the three most basic leasing arrangements. This lease is quite common with shopping center properties. The fixed + percentage lease has a fixed monthly rental component as we discussed in the previous paragraphs, and would likely include an escalation clause as well. In addition, the tenant—for example, a retail store—would pay to the landlord a percentage of either its net or gross receipts.

> **Fixed + Percentage Lease**
> a lease payment that has a flat monthly rate, plus a percentage of the tenant's gross or net retail receipts.

The fixed + percentage lease enables the landlord to make more money when the tenant makes more money. In this way, so the theory goes, the interests of the landlord and tenant are more closely aligned, and the landlord will be more motivated to help the tenant's profitability—perhaps with more advertising, better signage, and improved maintenance—in order to increase the landlord's profitability.

c. The **triple net lease** is the last of the three basic leasing arrangements. In triple net leases, the tenant will pay a fixed monthly rent to the landlord. The added twist in a triple net lease is that the tenant agrees to pay its pro rata portion of the taxes, insurance, and common area maintenance (a/k/a a "**CAM charge**"). Common area maintenance includes parking lot striping and repair, snow removal, landscaping, roof repairs, signage, utilities, and maintenance of the mechanical systems like the HVAC system.

> **Triple Net Lease**
> a lease in which the tenant pays its pro rata share—based on square footage—of the property taxes, property insurance, and CAM charges.

Pro rata means that a tenant in an office building who occupies 20% of the net leasable area in the building will pay 20% of the annual property taxes, property insurance, and CAM charges. Triple net leases are common in the rental of office space, as well as retail space in shopping centers. In a retail/shopping center lease agreement, the triple net lease may be combined with a percentage lease.

> **CAM Charges**
> common area maintenance charges that are billed monthly, quarterly, or annually to the tenants for things such as parking lot repair, snow removal, signage, utilities, and mechanical maintenance.

F. What Paralegals Do In the Field of Landlord-Tenant Law

Paralegals play a major role in legal firms engaged in the practice of landlord-tenant law. In transactional law offices, a paralegal's duties may include:

1. *Reviewing* lease clauses for accuracy,
2. *Drafting* lease agreements under the supervision of an attorney,
3. *Monitoring* compliance with the terms and conditions of the lease agreements, by both landlords and tenants,
4. *Collecting* rental payments,
5. *Computing* and *billing* CAM charges, and
6. Assisting in lease *negotiations* and *renewals*.

As you can see, the aforementioned activities require significant organizational skills and precision on the part of the paralegal.

Most law firms that practice transactional law also engage in litigation, and vice-versa. In law firms that have a litigation practice in the field of real estate law, paralegals will:

1. *Collect, review, and organize* the various and innumerable legal documents that may be used as exhibits at trial, including floor plans and architectural drawings, CAM billings, invoices, tax statements, witness interviews and statements, and of course, the leases themselves;
2. *Build a trial notebook* that will allow the attorneys to quickly access documents required during the trial;
3. *Inspect* the courtroom to determine what it can accommodate in terms of technology to present a coherent, understandable case to the jury;
4. Assist with *voire dire* to select a panel of jurors;
5. Assist counsel *during the trial* with any and all matters that may arise.

In addition to working in law firms, employment opportunities for paralegals can be found in governmental housing authorities and agencies, large property management firms, insurance companies, and corporate real estate offices.

CASE STUDY

In 2010, it was announced that the owners of Stuyvesant Town and Peter Cooper Village, huge multifamily apartment complexes in New York City, had turned over those two properties to the lenders, because the owners were unable to meet the mortgage payments.

To date, this was the largest (non-governmental) real estate transaction on record, totaling $5.4 billion.

It is reasonable to assume that there will be litigation related to these transactions, and that paralegals will play an important role as these matters wend their way through the court system to their conclusions.

CHAPTER SUMMARY

A residential lease is a contract that defines the rights and duties of the landlord and tenant, and creates a *leasehold* estate. The landlord's primary duty is to provide a fit and habitable dwelling to comply with the warranty of habitability.

The tenant's primary duty is to pay the rent in a timely manner. A landlord may not engage in self-help eviction, but rather must evict a tenant by following the civil process known as *eviction,* summary ejectment, or unlawful detainer, which will usually be heard in small claims or magistrate's court. Unless otherwise stated in the lease, a tenant may assign or sublease the rental unit to a third party; the tenant is the assignor, and the subtenant is the assignee. Generally, a landlord may not unreasonably withhold permission to assign the lease agreement, but the tenant does remain liable if the subtenant fails to pay the rent.

There are four types of tenancies:

1. Tenancy for Years—has a definite termination date,
2. Tenancy from Period to Period—may renew on a month-to-month or year-to-year basis,
3. Tenancy at Will—either party may give reasonable notice of termination,
4. Tenancy at Sufferance—the holdover tenant is almost a trespasser.

A *license* to use property, for example, a ticket to a sporting event, is qualitatively different from a lease. A license is of relatively short duration, and is revocable by the licensor.

Section 8 is a federal housing program that subsidizes the rent payments of low-income tenants who meet the eligibility requirements. Federal and state fair housing laws were enacted in the 1960s to protect tenants from unlawful discrimination by landlords on the basis of race, color, national origin, religion, sex, disability, or familial status. These anti-discrimination statutes also protect prospective purchasers of real property from illegal activities such as *steering* and *blockbusting* by real estate brokers, and *redlining* by real estate lending institutions.

Commercial properties consist mainly of office buildings, shopping centers, and industrial properties.

In the commercial setting, there are three basic types of lease agreements: the fixed lease, the fixed + percentage lease, and the triple net lease.

Landlord-tenant law is a subspecialty of real estate law. There are many opportunities in landlord-tenant law for the capable and well-organized paralegal. These opportunities can be found in transactional, as well as litigation, law offices. Opportunities also exist in government housing agencies, insurance companies, and real estate companies.

CONCEPT REVIEW AND REINFORCEMENT

KEY TERMS

Assignee	License	Steering
Assignment	Magistrate	Sublease
Assignor	Material Breach	Summary Ejectment
Blockbusting	Minor/Partial Breach	Tenancy
CAM Charges	Multifamily Residential	Tenancy at Sufferance
Commercial Property	Redlining	Tenancy at Will
Condition Precedent	Restitution	Tenancy for Years
Eviction	Retaliatory Eviction	Tenancy from Period to Period
Fair Housing Laws	Section 8 Housing	Title VIII
Fixed Lease	Self-help Eviction	Triple Net Lease
Fixed + Percentage Lease	Single-Family Residence	Unlawful Detainer
HUD	Small Claims Court	Warranty of Habitability
Lease	Statutes of Frauds	

CONCEPT **REVIEW** QUESTIONS

1. Why have many states created statutory law that supersedes common law in regulating landlord-tenant relations? Who has this benefited primarily, landlords or tenants, and why do you think so? What public policies or other considerations may have motivated changes to the common law schemes that had been prevalent for centuries?

2. What is the significance of the ubiquity of small claims courts, sometimes known as magistrates' courts, in landlord-tenant relations? Who has this helped primarily, landlords or tenants, and why do you think so? Who presides over a hearing in small claims court, and is that official appointed or elected?

3. What does it mean to proceed *pro se*, and how does this relate to landlord-tenant litigation?

4. Leases are contracts and subject to the many rules of contract law and contract interpretation. Regarding the lease, explain the significance of whether the landlord's duty to provide fit and habitable premises, and the tenant's duty to pay rent, are dependent, or independent, conditions. Why are the concepts of material breach or partial breach relevant to the discussion of conditions?

5. In a leasehold estate, one of the tenant's rights included in the bundle of rights is the right to use and enjoy the property. Is a tenant's leasehold estate considered to be a freehold estate? If not, why not?

6. What is meant by a "self-help" eviction? What is the public policy that prohibits self-help evictions in most states? Why did the policy come about?

7. Identify and give a brief description of each of the four types of residential tenancies. What is the most common type of tenancy?

8. What is the most significant characteristic of a tenancy for years?

9. Why is a tenant at sufferance *not* considered a trespasser? What is the significance of the legal distinction, that is, if a tenant at sufferance were a trespasser, how would that alter the remedies available to the landlord?

10. Define, or give examples of, the following terms:
    a. Redlining
    b. Blockbusting
    c. Steering

11. Define, or give examples of, the following types of commercial lease arrangement:
    a. Fixed lease
    b. Percentage lease
    c. Triple net lease

12. What is the difference between a lease and a license? Is a license an interest in real property such that it must be in writing? If not, why not?

ETHICS

EDWIN'S **EVICTIONS**

Edwin works in a large real estate office that owns and manages hundreds of residential apartment units in a major metropolitan area. The company has its own in-house attorney, for whom Edwin is the paralegal.

Edwin has not attended law school and is not a member of the state bar. In the last year, Edwin has filed eight complaints for summary ejectment (eviction) in small claims court on behalf of his employer seeking damages from past tenants.

Recently, a tenant defendant objected to Edwin's appearance in court on behalf of the employer because Edwin is not an attorney. The defendant-tenant asked the court to throw out the complaint for that reason. Edwin responded that his employer had given him express, written authority to appear on its behalf in legal matters valued at less than $5,000, the jurisdictional limit in that state's small claims court.

In your state, would Edwin have engaged in the unauthorized practice of law?

In small claims actions, must corporations in your state be represented by an attorney, or can they be represented by a corporate officer, or maybe just by an employee, such as Edwin?

Does it make a difference if Edwin is just testifying to facts known to him personally, as opposed to engaging in cross-examination and argument?

BUILDING YOUR PROFESSIONAL SKILLS

CRITICAL THINKING **EXERCISES**

1. The warranty of habitability obligates a landlord to provide "fit and habitable premises" for occupancy by a tenant. In your opinion, would the warranty of habitability obligate the landlord to ensure the physical safety of the tenant in a high-crime area? If so, to what extent? In a high-crime area, does the landlord have a duty of care to provide security officers 24/7?

   (In the case of *Walls v. Oxford Management* that you read earlier in the chapter, the court considered these very questions. Examine the case in its entirety to see how the court ruled on whether the warranty of habitability imposes a duty of care on the landlord vis-à-vis criminal conduct by third parties.)

2. Recall the example of Rowdy Yates, who was asked by security to leave the stadium during a sporting event. In the example, it was stated that stadium management would return the price of the ticket for admission to Rowdy when he left. Assume that there is no language on the back of the ticket that addresses the issue of the return of the admission price.

   Do you think that management would be legally obligated to return the admission price in exchange for making him leave the stadium, or could security remove Rowdy without having to return the price of admission? Why?

3. A residential tenant is on a month-to-month lease, but has failed to pay the rent for the past two months, despite numerous demands from the landlord. While the tenant is at home, the landlord, who is extremely irate, arrives at the rental unit and enters without notice, using a pass key. Landlord, in the presence of tenant, begins to remove the tenant's clothing and other personal belongings. Tenant, who is now also rather irate, warns landlord to "leave the premises immediately, or face the consequences."

   As landlord continues to remove tenant's personal belongings, tenant "crowns" the landlord with an iron skillet, at which point, landlord makes a tactical retreat. What, if any, civil claims will landlord have against tenant? What, if any, civil claims will tenant have against landlord?

4. A residential tenant has failed to pay the rent for the last two months, claiming that the landlord has breached the lease agreement by failing to fix a leaking commode. Tenant has also reported this alleged violation of the city's housing code to the local housing authority. Landlord has filed a suit in summary

ejectment to evict the tenant, alleging the non-payment of rent for two months.

At the hearing before the magistrate in small claims court, tenant contends that landlord is really engaging in a retaliatory eviction because tenant reported the leaking commode to the housing authority. If you were the magistrate, what additional facts would you want to know, or need to know, in order to render an equitable decision?

After obtaining those facts, how might you decide the case?

5. There are good landlords, and bad landlords, and there are good tenants and bad tenants. But generally speaking, would you agree or disagree that a landlord-owner will offer more concessions and better service when the rental property is a unit in an apartment complex, rather than a single-family rental house? If there are differences, what might account for those differences?

RESEARCH ON THE **WEB**

1. Does your state or jurisdiction prohibit retaliatory eviction, and, if so, was that tenant right created by statute or by case law? If self-help eviction is prohibited, what sanctions may be imposed by the court—civil penalties, criminal charges, or both?

2. Does your state or jurisdiction require that a landlord provide a "habitable" dwelling? If so, was that obligation created by statute or case law, and what is the language of that statute or court opinion? How is "habitable" defined in the case or statute? Is it an adequate definition, or should there be more to it…or less?

3. What types of subsidized housing does your state or jurisdiction offer, and how much money is budgeted for such programs? What are the eligibility requirements for receiving rent subsidies? Does the amount depend on the number of family members who will be occupying the rental unit or house? What other factors does the housing agency or program take into account?

4. Some states allow a tenant to pay rent to the court in the event that a landlord has materially breached the rental agreement and failed to remedy the problem. This protects the tenant from eviction due to non-payment of the rent, while at the same time motivates the landlord to fix the problem.

What provisions, if any, does your state or jurisdiction have in the event that a tenant wants to withhold the monthly rent because the landlord has breached some term or condition of the lease? Can the tenant pay the rent to the court, or clerk of court?

Do the relevant statutes allow for a partial rebate to the tenant of the withheld rent if, and when, the landlord remedies the alleged maintenance problem? If so, does this require a hearing in small claims court?

BUILDING YOUR **PROFESSIONAL** PORTFOLIO

1. You know that a lease is a contract, and can be a rather complicated contract at that. Try to draft a simple residential lease agreement. You might consider including some of the following terms and conditions:

    a. The names of the parties;

    b. A description of the leased premises;

    c. The length of the lease term, i.e., when the lease will begin and end;

    d. The rental amount and when it is to be paid, and the amount of any security deposit;

    e. When the rent will be deemed late, and whether or not there is a late fee;

    f. What happens if the tenant holds over following the expiration of the lease;

    g. Whether pets are permitted and, if so, whether there is a pet fee or deposit;

    h. Utilities or other services that are provided as part of the rental amount;

    i. Assignment of the lease by the landlord, and the tenant (subleasing).

2. You have been a tenant for six months under a one-year written lease agreement at Happy Hills Apartments. The good news is that you have been offered, and have accepted, a great job in a distant city. However, the landlord will not release you from the six months remaining on the lease term, and so you will have to assign the lease (sublet) to a friend who is interested in your apartment.

Draft an agreement between you and your friend for the sublease of your apartment unit for the six months remaining on the lease. You are the assignor, and your friend will be the assignee.

3. Obtain a Landlord-Tenant complaint form from your local magistrate or small claims court.

chapter 5

RIGHTS AND DUTIES INCIDENT TO REAL PROPERTY

Introduction

Ownership of land includes the famous "bundle of rights," including the right to mortgage, lease, donate, or sell your property. In this chapter, we will examine more of the rights and duties of landowners. These rights are said to be **incident to** land ownership. Stated somewhat differently, we do not own property in isolation, and we have certain duties to neighboring land owners, and they have reciprocal obligations to us.

The rights and duties incident to the ownership of real property that we will examine in this chapter are related more to an owner's relationships to his or her neighbors, rather than with the owner's relationship to the land itself. Remember that we are discussing rights and duties *incident to* one's ownership of a parcel of real property, and four

Incident (to)
dependent upon, subordinate to, arising out of, or otherwise connected with something else, which is usually of greater importance.

categories that we will be examining are water rights, air rights, land support, and the right to quiet enjoyment of one's property (that is, to be free from nuisances and trespasses).

Legal rights held by owner A often give rise to correlative duties from owner B, and vice-versa. This is particularly true for owners of adjoining properties, or properties that are in close physical proximity to each other.

A. Riparian Rights

Riparian rights are the rights of landowners whose properties abut rivers or streams. **Littoral rights** are the rights of landowners whose properties abut a lake, ocean, or sea. Both categories of rights—riparian and littoral—are broadly referred to as riparian rights. Note also that our discussion of riparian and *littoral rights* will be confined to the law's application to **surface waters**, such as rivers and streams, lakes, oceans, or seas.

In the eastern part of the country, riparian law was, to a large extent, shaped by the requirements of mill owners, who needed the power of flowing rivers and streams to operate their mills, especially the textile mills in the Northeastern and Southeastern United States.

In the great expanses of the Western United States, water is relatively scarce when compared to the East. In the Western states, water law was created and molded to respond to the demands of miners, farmers, and ranchers, who engaged in frequent, and often violent, disputes over rights to precious *water*.

> **Riparian Rights**
> the rights of landowners whose properties abut rivers or streams to the use of the water.
>
> **Littoral Rights**
> the rights of landowners whose properties abut a lake, ocean, or sea.
>
> **Surface Waters**
> bodies of water found on the surface of the earth, such as rivers, streams, lakes, and oceans.

1. REASONABLE USE—THE EASTERN DOCTRINE

In the East, the courts developed the doctrine of reasonable use in riparian disputes. This view holds that the owner of a property adjoining a lake or stream may use only as much water as is reasonably necessary for the beneficial use of the property, be it a mill, farm, or residence.

However, the doctrine of reasonable use is tempered by the need to consider the requirements of the downstream riparian owners, who are also entitled to the reasonable, beneficial use of the watercourse. For example, an upstream owner cannot divert so much of the water for irrigation or watering livestock so as to unreasonably impair the use of the water by downstream property owners. These competing interests, then, require, in the event of a dispute over water, that the courts balance the reasonable needs of upstream owners with the reasonable needs of the downstream owners.

Courts in some eastern states make a distinction between *natural* and *artificial* uses of the water, and generally give priority to "natural" uses, such as drinking water for humans and farm animals being raised on the property. The states sometimes differ on whether the *irrigation* of crops is a natural or artificial use, and a court's determination may hinge on the size of the commercial farming operation involved.

2. PRIOR APPROPRIATION—THE WESTERN DOCTRINE

The doctrine of prior appropriation determines the rights to water use in approximately 15 states west of the Mississippi River. To stimulate development in these Western states, particularly in the mining industry, the first claim on water was given to the first property owners to commercially develop the lands abutting the watercourses. Although this frequently worked an injustice to late-arriving downstream owners, the doctrine of prior appropriation did serve as a stimulus to economic development.

Courts and legislators believed that entrepreneurs contemplating large commercial operations that required large quantities of water—such as mining operations—would not be willing to risk the large capital investments required for such projects, unless they were *guaranteed* sufficient quantities of water. This guarantee found its voice in the doctrine of prior appropriation.

As with reasonable use doctrine in the East, there are significant variations between and among the Western states regarding the subtleties and implementation of the prior appropriation laws.

Regardless of whether a state adheres to the reasonable use doctrine, the prior appropriation doctrine, or a hybrid of the two, in the last 40 years federal and state ***environmental laws*** have had an impact on riparian rights under the common law. That is to say that federal regulations, in particular, now play a greater role in determining what is a reasonable allocation or use of a particular water source as that use relates to effects on the local, state, or regional natural environment. The Environmental Protection Agency (EPA) was created in 1970 to protect the environment and human health by monitoring and regulating use of the land, air, and water.

3. SUBTERRANEAN WATERS (a/k/a GROUNDWATERS)

Subterranean Waters
also known as groundwaters, are water sources that exist under the surface of the earth. There are two basic types: underground streams and percolating groundwaters.

Underground Streams
waters that flow through subterranean water channels.

Percolating Groundwaters
waters that are dispersed throughout an underground soil layer or layers, but do not flow through an existing water channel.

Subterranean waters, also known as groundwaters (as opposed to surface waters) exist beneath the surface of the earth. There are two basic types of groundwaters:

a. **Underground streams** are waters that flow in and through established subterranean water channels, and
b. **Percolating groundwaters** are underground waters that are dispersed throughout soil layers and, unlike underground streams, do not follow an existing underground channel. Percolating groundwaters are charged and recharged by rain water migrating through the surface and subsurface soil layers.

Aquifers are examples of subterranean waters. One of the largest aquifers in the world is the Ogallala Aquifer, sometimes known as the High Plains Aquifer. The Ogallala Aquifer occupies soil and rock layers that extend over a huge geographical area, ranging from South Dakota down to Texas.

The agricultural interests in this vast region have benefited tremendously from the irrigation water pumped out of the Ogallala Aquifer, as have we consumers of their food products. However, this heavy agricultural use has severely depleted certain parts of the aquifer, which is being drained at a much faster rate than it is being recharged by rainwater. This imbalance is of great concern to the very farmers and ranchers who irrigate their crops with waters from the aquifer. It is of utmost importance that solutions to the overuse be found in the very near future, lest the Plains states—the great bread basket of America—succumb to a lack of water.

Allocation, use, and control of subterranean waters in a given state usually follow the same legal principles that control the surface waters in the state, that is, reasonable use in the East, or prior appropriation in the West.

4. DOES THE RIPARIAN LANDOWNER OWN THE WATER?

For the answer to this seemingly simple question, let us turn to probably the greatest book ever written on real property, the 15-volume legal treatise entitled *Thompson on Real Property*, and specifically, § 50.03(b), which states:

Water rights are interesting in that, while they are real property interests, they do not embody an ownership interest in the water itself.

This one brief sentence beautifully explains the difference between real property, and rights incident to real property. A riparian landowner does not own the water, but the right to access and use the water is incident to, or connected with, the ownership of land located on a waterway.

In both a real and a practical sense, a water right must be considered as a right of access to water in order to facilitate the use of the water for only such purposes as the law deems acceptable. From this, it is apparent that the ability to properly use, rather than ownership, is the primary property attribute. . . . Indeed, the right to use is the essential feature of the water right itself. Clearly, the holder of the water right has only a right to make a permitted use of a particular quantity of water; the water right owner does not "own" that quantity of water unless and until it is lawfully reduced to possession.

Id.

5. NAVIGABLE AND NON-NAVIGABLE WATERWAYS

Navigable waterways are those that form a continuous "highway" over which commerce may be carried on within a state (e.g., Great Salt Lake, UT), or with other states or countries. The significance of classifying waterways as either navigable or **non-navigable** relates to which sovereign's (state or federal) body of law controls their use and regulation.

Navigable waterways come under ***federal maritime jurisdiction*** by virtue of the Commerce Clause in the United States Constitution. Federal regulations govern the uses of the waterways, the ship and boat traffic, and other related matters, although one or more states may still own the river or lake bed beneath the navigable waterway. A waterway is navigable for purposes of federal jurisdiction if it is susceptible of being used as an artery of commerce. The Mississippi River and the Great Lakes are two of the most prominent examples of navigable waterways.

> Navigable Waterways
> bodies of water that are capable of accommodating vessels used to transport commercial goods. Navigable waterways are regulated by federal maritime law.
>
> Non-Navigable Waterways
> bodies of water that are not capable of accommodating vessels used to transport commercial goods, and are regulated by state law.

a. Public Trust Doctrine

The **public trust doctrine** provides that lands that lie beneath tidewaters and navigable waterways within a state are owned by the state, and are to be preserved by the state for the beneficial use of the general public for such purposes as fishing, boating, diving, and other recreational activities.

The owners of land along *navigable*, public trust waterways do not own the submerged lands. Instead, those landowners own only to the shoreline, where the land and water meet. This boundary may be the high tide water mark, or the mean (average) high tide water mark.

Non-navigable waterways are regulated by the laws of the particular state wherein they are located. Submerged lands beneath non-navigable waterways are usually owned to the center of the stream or non-navigable river by the property owners abutting the body of water. Since the waterways are non-navigable, the public trust doctrine does not apply, and riparian owners own to the center of the stream or river.

> Public Trust Doctrine
> the doctrine that holds that lands beneath navigable waterways—for example, river beds, lake beds, or sea beds—are owned by the state in trust for its citizens, even though the waterway and vessels using it are governed by federal regulations

6. HOW NATURE CHANGES THE LAND . . . AND PROPERTY LINES (AREA)

AREA
this acronym may help you remember the four natural ways by which the land and boundaries may be changed: accretion, reliction, erosion, and avulsion.

Many deeds, especially older deeds, contain property descriptions that delineate boundaries by reference to waterways. For example, an old deed might read:

> On its eastern side and northern sides, the parcel is bounded by the old home place of Farmer and Mrs. Jones, and on the south and west sides by the <u>north fork of the Old Mill Stream</u>.

So what happens if the Old Mill Stream changes course because of a drought, storm, flood, or other natural force?

a. Accretion

Accretion
the slow accumulation of sand or soil through the action of water, thereby increasing the size of the affected property.

Accretion is the natural process whereby **land is added** slowly to that already in possession of the owner. Accretion is usually caused by the action of a stream, river, or other body of water. Accretion is a slow process and occurs when alluvion—sand or soil—washes onto the owner's property over time, thereby increasing the size of the land parcel.

The sand or soil probably came from upstream property owners, whose parcels were diminished in size by the loss of the alluvion. While not necessarily a zero sum game, generally speaking, when one parcel experiences an increase in size because of natural events, other parcels are usually diminished to the same extent.

b. Reliction

Reliction
the increase in land area due to the gradual subsidence or receding of a river or lake.

Reliction, like accretion, **adds land** to an owner's property. But in the case of reliction, the addition of land area is brought about by the gradual subsidence or receding of a river or lake. As an example, between 2005 and 2010, parts of the southeastern United States experienced severe droughts.

For homeowners whose properties abutted a lake, the subsidence of the waters because of the drought conditions brought about an increase in the size of their properties. When the rains came and refilled the lakes, streams, or rivers, the size of the owner's parcel was reduced accordingly.

c. Erosion

Erosion is the **gradual wearing away** of the land, primarily by the action of wind or water. The word "gradual" is relative, but in this context, it is used to mean over a period of several years, rather than just a few days. Thus, erosion may be seen as the opposite of accretion.

d. Avulsion

Avulsion
the sudden removal of land caused by a change in a river's course or by flood.

Avulsion is the **sudden loss** of land by the action of water, or a sudden change in the bed or course of a stream by, for example, an earthquake or flood. When a property boundary is defined by a stream, and an avulsion alters the course of the stream, the law generally holds that the property's boundary continues to be the boundary defined by the stream before it was avulsed. This is the opposite of the slower processes of accretion and erosion, where a property's boundary changes as the watercourse slowly changes.

With the four natural processes above in mind, let's revisit the question of what happens to property boundaries when water bodies change course. The United States Supreme Court answered this question regarding a boundary dispute between the states of Arkansas and Tennessee. The dispute followed an **avulsion**, which altered the course of the Mississippi River. In the 1918 case of *Arkansas v. Tennessee*, the U.S. Supreme Court held, in part:

ARKANSAS V. TENNESSEE

U.S. Supreme Court
246 U.S. 158, 173
1918

The next and perhaps the most important question is as to the effect of the sudden and violent change in the channel of the river that occurred in the year 1876, and which both parties properly treat as a true and typical *avulsion.*

It is settled beyond the possibility of dispute that where running streams are the boundaries between States, the same rule applies as between private proprietors, namely, that when the bed and channel are changed by the natural and gradual processes known as *erosion* and *accretion*, the boundary follows the varying course of the stream.

While if the stream from any cause, natural or artificial, suddenly leaves its old bed and forms a new one, by the process known as an *avulsion,* the resulting change of channel works *no change of boundary*, which remains in the middle of the old channel, although no water may be flowing in it, and irrespective of subsequent changes in the new channel.

Q: Now, can you tell what, if anything, happened to the boundary between Arkansas and Tennessee?

B. Air Rights

Cujus est solum, ejus est usque ad coelum et ad inferos, or translated from the Latin: "*To whoever owns the land, shall belong the earth to its center, and up to the heavens.*"

1. AIR RIGHTS AND AVIATION

Under the common law, as summarized in the Latin quotation above, the owner of a parcel of land owned not only the surface of the property, but the ground below, extending all the way to the center of the earth. Further, the ownership rights of the air and space above the parcel extended infinitely into the heavens. At least in theory, an intrusion into the airspace over one's property was a trespass, and possibly a nuisance. All that changed with the dawn of commercial aviation in the 1920s.

As with water rights and the needs of the textile industry, the law of air rights would be conformed to facilitate the growth of a nation and the nascent airline industry. You know that the *Commerce Clause* in the United States Constitution gives Congress far-reaching power to enact laws governing commerce between and among the states of the union. At the urging of the airline industry, Congress passed the *Air Commerce Act of 1926*, which opened the skies for airplane traffic.

As with most groundbreaking legislation, the Air Commerce Act was eventually challenged in court. The Fifth Amendment to the United States Constitution holds in part that "private property shall not be taken for public use *without just compensation*." Also, virtually every state has a "**takings clause**" similar to that found in the Fifth Amendment.

After the passage of the Air Commerce Act and the Civil Aeronautics Act, some private property owners challenged the federal statutes as a taking of property for which they had not been compensated by either their state or federal governments. After all, didn't the common law hold that a person's property, that is,

Takings Clause
a clause found in the Fifth Amendment to the U.S. Constitution, and practically every state constitution, that allows the taking of private property for a public use, but only on the condition that the government pay just compensation to the property owner.

Airspace
the space above a parcel of real property that may be used by commercial aircraft. Airspace must be above a minimum safe altitude, or else air traffic may constitute a nuisance.

their **airspace**, extended all the way "to the heavens"? The plaintiffs' argument, then, was that since commercial air traffic was a "public use," landowners should be justly compensated for the taking of their airspace.

In 1946, the United States Supreme Court put the issue to rest when it wrote in *United States v. Causby*:

> *The Air Commerce Act of 1926, as amended by the Civil Aeronautics Act of 1938, mandates that under those statutes the United States has complete and exclusive national sovereignty in the air space over this country. They grant any citizen of the United States a public right of freedom of transit in air <u>commerce</u> through the navigable air space of the United States. And navigable air space is defined as airspace above the minimum safe altitudes of flight prescribed by the Civil Aeronautics Authority. And it is provided that such **navigable airspace** shall be subject to a public right of freedom of interstate and foreign air navigation.*

United States v. Causby, 328 U.S. 256, 260 (1946) (emphasis added, citations and punctuation omitted).

The federal court decisions that ruled against those challenging the aforementioned statutes reasoned that typical landowners cannot make use of the airspace that is more than a couple of hundred feet above ground, and therefore had no right to be compensated by the federal government for a "taking" under the Fifth Amendment.

2. TALL BUILDINGS, LIGHT, AND UNOBSTRUCTED VIEWS

Centuries ago, English law created the doctrine of *ancient lights*, which held that the owner of a building that had received unobstructed sunlight for 20 years could prevent the construction of a structure on an adjoining lot that would diminish the amount of sunlight that the building owner had enjoyed in the past.

The *doctrine of ancient lights* never found a home in the United States because it would have completely thwarted economic growth in the early towns such as New York, Philadelphia, Boston, and Chicago. Instead, courts in our country developed a body of common law that held that property owners did *not* enjoy any right to unobstructed views or sunlight.

These early court decisions allowed developers to build high-rise buildings without fear of lawsuits brought by the surrounding property owners, who, under the old—and now discredited—doctrine of ancient lights, would have otherwise prevailed on their claims that their views or sunlight had been impaired by new high-rise buildings.

Recently, however, the pendulum has begun to swing in the opposite direction. To a significant percentage of our population, growth for its own sake is no longer as desirable as it was in the eighteenth and nineteenth centuries. Instead, towns and their citizens are now more concerned with the quality of life in their communities, rather than unrestrained growth, and the traffic, pollution, and other headaches it often brings with it.

As you will see in the case below, the Wisconsin Supreme Court significantly changed the existing common law to accommodate, and even encourage, new values that call for a "greener" economy, and energy efficiency and independence. In the future, you will see more of the same types of decisions as the courts exercise their inherent powers under common law, which allows for flexibility in addressing changing values and circumstances.

PRAH V. MARETTI

Supreme Court of Wisconsin
108 Wis. 2d 223; 321 N.W.2d 182
July 2, 1982, Decided

Plaintiff-appellant's home was the first residence built in the subdivision, and although plaintiff did not build his house in the center of the lot it was built in accordance with applicable restrictions. Plaintiff advised defendant that if the defendant's home were built at the proposed site it would cause a shadowing effect on the [plaintiff's] *solar collectors* which would reduce the efficiency of the system and possibly damage the system.

To avoid these adverse effects, plaintiff requested defendant to locate his home an additional several feet away from the plaintiff's lot line, the exact number being disputed. Plaintiff and defendant failed to reach an agreement on the location of defendant's home before defendant started construction. The Planning Commission of the City of Muskego **approved** the defendant's plans for his home, including its location on the lot.

The private **nuisance** doctrine has been employed in this state to balance the conflicting rights of landowners, and this court has recently adopted the analysis of private nuisance set forth in the Restatement (Second) of Torts. The comment in the Restatement describes the landowner's interest protected by private nuisance law as follows:

"The phrase 'interest in the **use and enjoyment of land**' is used in this Restatement in a broad sense. It comprehends not only the interests that a person may have in the actual present use of land for residential, agricultural, commercial, industrial and other purposes, but also his interests in having the present use value of the land unimpaired by changes in its physical condition. 'Interest in use and enjoyment' also comprehends the pleasure, comfort and enjoyment that a person normally derives from the occupancy of land. Freedom from discomfort and annoyance while using land is often as important to a person as freedom from physical interruption with his use or freedom from detrimental change in the physical condition of the land itself."

Although the defendant's obstruction of the plaintiff's access to sunlight appears to fall within the Restatement's broad concept of a private nuisance as a nontrespassory invasion of another's interest in the private use and enjoyment of land, the defendant asserts that he has a right to develop his property in compliance with statutes, ordinances and private covenants without regard to the effect of such development upon the plaintiff's access to sunlight.

In essence, the defendant is asking this court to hold that the private nuisance doctrine is not applicable in the instant case and that his right to develop his land is a right which is *per se* superior to his neighbor's interest in access to sunlight. The rights of the surface owner are, however, not unlimited.

This court's reluctance in the nineteenth and early part of the twentieth century to provide broader protection for a landowner's access to sunlight was premised on three policy considerations.

First, the right of landowners to use their property as they wished, as long as they did not cause physical damage to a neighbor, was jealously guarded.

Second, sunlight was valued only for aesthetic enjoyment or as illumination. Since artificial light could be used for illumination, loss of sunlight was at most a personal annoyance which was given little, if any, weight by society.

Third, society had a significant interest in not restricting or impeding land development. This court repeatedly emphasized that in the growth period of the nineteenth and early twentieth centuries change is to be expected and is essential to property and that recognition of a right to sunlight would **hinder property development**.

Considering these three policies, this court concluded that in the absence of an express agreement granting access to sunlight, a landowner's obstruction of another's access to sunlight was not actionable. These three policies are no longer fully accepted or applicable. They reflect factual circumstances and **social priorities that are now obsolete**.

First, society has increasingly regulated the use of land by the landowner for the general welfare.

Second, access to sunlight has taken on a new significance in recent years. In this case the plaintiff seeks to protect access to sunlight, not for aesthetic reasons or as a source of illumination but as a source of energy. Access to sunlight as an energy source is

(continued)

of significance both to the landowner who invests in solar collectors and to a society which has an interest in developing alternative sources of energy.

Third, the policy of favoring unhindered private development in an expanding economy is no longer in harmony with the realities of our society. The need for easy and rapid development is not as great today as it once was, while our perception of the value of sunlight as a source of energy has increased significantly.

Courts should not implement obsolete policies that have lost their vigor over the course of the years. The law of private nuisance is better suited to resolve landowners' disputes about property development in the 1980's than is a rigid rule which does not recognize a landowner's interest in access to sunlight.

This court has recognized "that the common law is susceptible of **growth and adaptation to new circumstances** and situations, and that courts have power to declare and effectuate what is the present rule in respect of a given subject without regard to the old rule…. The common law is **not immutable, but flexible**, and upon its own principles adapts itself to varying conditions."

We therefore hold that private nuisance law, that is, the reasonable use doctrine as set forth in the Restatement, is applicable to the instant case. Recognition of a nuisance claim for unreasonable obstruction of access to sunlight will not prevent land development or unduly hinder the use of adjoining land. It will promote the reasonable use and enjoyment of land in a manner **suitable to the 1980's**.

Accordingly we hold that the plaintiff in this case has stated a claim under which relief can be granted. Nonetheless we do not determine whether the plaintiff in this case is entitled to relief.

In order to be entitled to relief the plaintiff must prove the elements required to establish actionable nuisance, and the conduct of the defendant herein must be judged by the reasonable use doctrine. The judgment of the circuit court is reversed and the cause remanded for proceedings not inconsistent with this opinion.

Author's Note

One of the most important functions of the law is to provide **stability** and **predictability** in our daily lives. In this case, the defendant probably heavily relied on hundreds of years of case law relating to nuisance, and the fact that the United States had *not* adopted the doctrine of "ancient lights" from English common law, which held that a landowner did have a right to unobstructed sunlight and views.

Is it fair that the defendant, Mr. Maretti, had the legal rug pulled out from under him? That is, by a majority vote of the Wisconsin Supreme Court the stability and predictability of nuisance law was changed by 180°.

Should the Supreme Court have made its decision prospective, meaning that the holding would be applicable to all *future* cases, but would not penalize Mr. Maretti in this case?

C. Rights Incident to Land Ownership at Common Law (versus Rights Found in a Deed)

1. SUPPORT

Adjoining landowners have a reciprocal duty to **physically support** their neighbors' property in its natural state. In the absence of such support, the neighboring property would collapse or subside, thereby diminishing its utility and value. There are two types of physical support for real property.

a. Lateral Support

The right to lateral support of Owner A's property imposes a duty on Owner B, the adjoining property owner, not to excavate in such a way as to cause a subsidence or collapse of A's soil. Needless to say, A owes the same reciprocal duty to Owner B. However, Owner A's right to lateral support exists only if A's land is in its *natural state*, unaltered by the erection of buildings or other structures. Continuing with the scenario above, landowner B is entitled to excavate right up to the boundary line of A's property, but must do so in a way that A's soil will not collapse under its own weight or as a result of natural forces, such as erosion caused by flowing waters.

If A *has* constructed buildings or other structures on her land, and her property subsides or collapses due in part to the weight of A's buildings, and in part due to landowner B's excavation, Owner B will not be liable, absent some negligence on his part, such as carelessly blasting to expedite the excavation process.

b. Subjacent Support

A property owner has a right to subjacent support, which is the right to support from the soil located *beneath* one's property. The issue of subjacent support normally arises in situations where a property owner has sold the rights to the minerals beneath the surface of the parcel. In the coal mining country of Appalachia it was common for impoverished land owners to sell the mineral rights to coal seams running beneath their homes.

When the purchaser of the mineral rights—usually a coal company—failed to provide subjacent support by timbering or some other method, either during or after the mining operation, the surface owner sometimes suffered substantial and irreparable damage as a result of the collapse of the house into the underlying excavated mine. (For a slightly different scenario, see the case of *Cole v. Signal Knob Coal Co.*, below.)

COLE V. SIGNAL KNOB COAL CO.

West Virginia Supreme Court of Appeals
95 W. Va. 702
Decided: 1924

This action was instituted to recover damages for the *loss of plaintiff's horse*, which died from injuries sustained by breaking through the surface of plaintiff's land and *falling into defendant's coal mine*. Plaintiff was the owner of an undivided interest in the surface of the land and had charge and control of the other undivided interests, and had used the land where the accident occurred for pasture, for the past twenty-five years. There had been a severance of the minerals and surface many years before.

The declaration charges that it was the duty of defendant in removing the coal from its leasehold to *leave sufficient pillars or supports* to sustain the overlying surface occupied by plaintiff, so that the said surface would not crack, break or fall in, but that defendant negligently failed and refused to leave sufficient pillars and support for said surface, as a result whereof the injuries complained of occurred. The first count alleges that plaintiff's horse fell into an opening caused by a break in the surface; and the second, that the surface broke through while the horse was grazing thereon. There was a verdict and judgment for $ 200.00 in favor of plaintiff.

It is well settled in this state, as elsewhere generally, that the owner of land has an absolute **right of support** for his surface, unless such right has been waived. There is no evidence of waiver here.

The rule requiring surface support is an application of the doctrine, *sic utere tuo ut alienum non laedas,* the true legal meaning of which is defined as; "So use your own property as not to injure the rights of another."…

Has plaintiff not the right to use his land for the natural purposes to which it is adapted? Is the surface owner to be deprived of the use of his land for agricultural purposes, the use for which it is adapted by nature? If so, he could not cultivate the soil or pasture the land, or drive a wagon or other farm machinery over the excavation of the subjacent owner. Does not the rule of *sic utere tuo ut alienum non laedas* confine the owner of the subjacent strata to such use of his property as will not interfere with the use of the surface for all agricultural pursuits and purposes?

We think it does.
Affirmed.

Mining isn't the only way that subjacent support may be impaired. If your neighbor pumps large amounts of subterranean water from the aquifer beneath your property, and thereby causes your land—in its natural state—to subside or sink, your neighbor has breached the common law duty to provide subjacent support.

The states are split on this question, with some holding that your neighbor has the absolute right to make reasonable use of the subterranean water, regardless of its effects on your property. Other states maintain that your right to subjacent support is absolute, and therefore your neighbor would be liable to you for any damage to your property.

2. NUISANCE

At common law, a nuisance is a **substantial and unreasonable interference** with another's **use** and **enjoyment** of his land. The use of the word "unreasonable" in the definition is highly significant. A use that is unreasonable in a residential neighborhood may be perfectly reasonable in an industrial area, and vice versa. Excessive noise, vibrations, smoke, or noxious odors have been found to qualify as nuisances, especially in residential neighborhoods.

The outcome of a given case may—but not necessarily—hinge upon which party came to the area first, the "nuisance," or the landowner complaining about the nuisance. Nuisances may be categorized as intentional, negligent, or strict liability, and the categorization will determine the extent and type of remedy available to the injured party.

Nuisances may be further classified as either **public** or **private**, depending on the number of landowners who are affected by the condition constituting the alleged nuisance. There is no hard and fast rule about how many persons must be affected by some condition in order to constitute a public nuisance. However, in the case of a public nuisance, the plaintiff is often a governmental agency—a city, county, or state—suing on behalf of its many citizens damaged by the nuisance.

a. Nuisance Per Se and Nuisance Per Accidens

Nuisance Per Se
a nuisance in and of itself, at all times, under all circumstances, and regardless of the surrounding land uses. A nuisance per se always involves a violation of a statute or ordinance.

A **nuisance per se** is an act, occupation, condition, or structure that is a nuisance at **all times** and **under any circumstances** regardless of the location or surroundings. A nuisance per se is inimical to the injured party's health, safety, morals, or welfare. In all situations involving a nuisance per se, the activity or condition will be prohibited by statute or a city ordinance, and that is why it is called a nuisance *per se*, meaning a nuisance in and of itself. Examples of nuisances per se include illegal drug laboratories ("meth labs"), marijuana growing operations, brothels, liquor or gambling houses, and other activities constituting a breach of the peace against the *community*, even if the next door neighbor is not bothered by, or even aware of, the illegal activity.

A **nuisance per accidens**, or **nuisance in fact,** is an act, condition, or structure which may become a nuisance by virtue of its construction, location, or operation. Such activities are lawful but become nuisances when the use is unreasonable under certain conditions. Consider this situation:

EXAMPLE OF NUISANCE PER ACCIDENS

A church and a drag strip have coexisted as neighbors for many years because the church held services on Sunday morning and early afternoon, and the drag strip was open only on Saturdays. The owners of the drag strip decided that they could make more money by holding races on Sundays, and changed the race schedules accordingly.

Consequently, the drag strip has become a nuisance per accidens because its operation on Sundays is a substantial and unreasonable interference with the church's use and enjoyment of its land, that is, the church's holding of Sunday church services. If the church sues, it may obtain monetary damages, *injunctive relief* prohibiting the drag strip from operating on Sunday, or both.

---

b. Coming to the Nuisance

When discussing nuisance cases, one of the first questions asked by the courts is: "Which of the parties to the lawsuit was there first?" Traditionally, courts have been less sympathetic to plaintiffs who have come *to* an existing "nuisance," such as a factory, farm, ranch, or other commercial operation that existed before the plaintiff asserting the claim for nuisance ever arrived in the neighborhood.

The opinion in the Spur Industries v. Del E. Webb Industries case is one of the most famous of the category of cases known as "coming to the nuisance." As you read the opinion, try to determine what factors the court weighed to arrive at its holding. Do you agree with the court's reasoning, or is it somewhat strained? While the decision seems very unfair to the defendant, Spur Industries, was it nevertheless necessary for "the greater good," and perhaps even inevitable?

SPUR INDUSTRIES [DEFENDANT] V. DEL E. WEBB DEVELOPMENT CO.[1]

Supreme Court of Arizona
108 Ariz. 178; 494 P.2d 700
March 17, 1972

Maricopa County, Arizona is 15 miles west of the urban area of Phoenix. Farming started in this area about 1911. By 1950, the only urban areas in the vicinity were the agriculturally related communities of Peoria, El Mirage, and Surprise. The area is well suited for *cattle feeding* and in 1959, there were 25 cattle feeding pens or dairy operations within a 7 mile radius of the location developed by defendant Spur's predecessors. In April and May of 1959, the Northside Hay Mill was feeding between 6,000 and 7,000 head of cattle and Welborn approximately 1,500 head on a combined area of 35 acres.

In May of 1959, plaintiff Del Webb began to plan the development of an urban area to be known as Sun City. For this purpose, the Marinette and the Santa Fe Ranches, some 20,000 acres of farmland, were purchased for $15,000,000 or $750.00 per acre.

By September 1959, Del Webb had started construction of a golf course south of Grand Avenue and Spur's predecessors had started to level ground for more feedlot area. In 1960, Spur purchased the property in question and began a rebuilding and expansion program extending both to the north and south of the original facilities. By 1962, Spur's expansion program

---

[1]Del Webb was a fascinating man who dropped out of high school to become a carpenter. Through hard work and dedication, his fortunes changed and he became one of the premier developers in the United States. He is perhaps best remembered for his numerous Sun City retirement communities. Additionally, Webb was part-owner of the New York Yankees in the early 1960s, and owned and developed a number of casinos in Las Vegas. Among the casinos he developed was the iconic Flamingo Hotel, which he built for the legendary mobster Benjamin "Bugsy" Siegel. Shortly after the Flamingo opened, Siegel was murdered by his mob brethren, who believed that Siegel and/or his girlfriend were skimming money from the construction accounts.

(*continued*)

was completed and had expanded from approximately **35 acres to 114 acres.**

Accompanied by an extensive advertising campaign, homes were first offered by Del Webb in January 1960. By 2 May 1960, there were 450 to 500 houses completed or under construction. At this time, Del Webb did not consider odors from the Spur feed pens a problem and Del Webb continued to develop in a southerly direction, until **sales resistance** became so great that the parcels were difficult if not impossible to sell. Del Webb filed its original complaint alleging that in excess of 1,300 lots in the southwest portion were unfit for development for sale as residential lots because of the operation of the Spur feedlot.

Del Webb's suit complained that the Spur feeding operation was a public nuisance because of the flies and the odor which were drifting or being blown over the southern portion of Sun City. At the time of the suit, Spur was feeding between **20,000 and 30,000 head of cattle**, and the facts amply support the finding of the trial court that the feed pens had become a nuisance to the people who resided in the southern part of Del Webb's development.

The cattle in a commercial feedlot will produce 35 to 40 pounds of wet manure per day, per head, or over a million pounds of wet manure per day for 30,000 head of cattle, and that despite the admittedly good feedlot management by Spur, the resulting odor and flies produced an annoying if not unhealthy situation as far as the senior citizens of southern Sun City were concerned. There is no doubt that some of the citizens of Sun City were unable to enjoy the outdoor living which Del Webb had advertised and that Del Webb was faced with sales resistance from prospective purchasers as well as strong and persistent complaints from the people who had purchased homes in that area.

The difference between a **private nuisance** and a **public nuisance** is generally one of degree. A private nuisance is one affecting a single individual or a definite small number of persons in the enjoyment of private rights not common to the public, while a public nuisance is one affecting the rights enjoyed by citizens as a part of the public. To constitute a public nuisance, the nuisance must affect a considerable number of people or an entire community or neighborhood.

We have no difficulty, however, in agreeing with the conclusion of the trial court that Spur's operation was an **enjoinable public nuisance** as far as the people in the southern portion of Del Webb's Sun City were concerned. In the so-called "**coming to the nuisance**" cases, the courts have held that the residential landowner may not have relief if he knowingly came into a neighborhood reserved for industrial or agricultural endeavors and has been damaged thereby. Were Webb the only party injured, we would feel justified in holding that the doctrine of "coming to the nuisance" would have been a bar to the relief asked by Webb.

There was no indication in the instant case at the time Spur and its predecessors located in western Maricopa County that a new city would spring up, full-blown, alongside the feeding operation and that the developer of that city would ask the court to order Spur to move because of the new city. **Spur is required to move** not because of any wrongdoing on the part of Spur, but because of a proper and legitimate regard of the courts for the rights and interests of the public.

Del Webb, on the other hand, is entitled to the relief prayed for (a permanent injunction), **not because Webb is blameless, but because of the damage to the people** who have been encouraged to purchase homes in Sun City. It does not equitably or legally follow, however, that Webb, being entitled to the injunction, is then free of any liability to Spur if Webb has in fact been the cause of the damage Spur has sustained. It does not seem harsh to require a developer, who has taken advantage of the lesser land values in a rural area as well as the availability of large tracts of land on which to build and develop a new town or city in the area, to indemnify those who are forced to leave as a result.

Having brought people to the nuisance to the **foreseeable detriment of Spur**, Webb must **indemnify Spur for a reasonable amount of the cost of moving or shutting down**. It is therefore the decision of this court that the matter be remanded to the trial court for a hearing upon the damages sustained by the defendant Spur as a reasonable and direct result of the granting of the permanent injunction.

In the wake of the *Del Webb* opinion by the Arizona Supreme Court, a number of states passed legislation to preclude the possibility of similar decisions in their jurisdictions. One such example is North Carolina, which enacted the following statute in 1979, about six years after the *Del Webb* decision:

N.C. Gen. Stat. § 106-701. When agricultural and forestry operation, etc., not constituted nuisance by changed conditions in locality

a. *No agricultural or forestry operation or any of its appurtenances shall be or become a nuisance, private or public, by any changed conditions in or about the locality thereof after the same has been in operation for more than one year, when such operation* **was not a nuisance at the time the operation began**; *provided, that the provisions of this subsection shall not apply whenever a nuisance results from the negligent or improper operation of any such agricultural or forestry operation or its appurtenances.*

b. *For the purposes of this Article, "agricultural operation" includes, without limitation, any facility for the production for commercial purposes of crops, livestock, poultry, livestock products, or poultry products....*

c. Spite Fences and Structures

In his poem entitled "Mending Wall," published in 1914, Robert Frost wrote: "Good fences make good neighbors."

Well, maybe, but then again … maybe not. There is a body of law that has grown up around the infamous **spite fence**, defined as "a fence erected for no benefit or pleasure to the person erecting it, but solely with the *malicious* motive of injuring the adjoining owner by shutting out his light, air, and view.[2]

The legal question is whether building a fence or other structure for the *sole* purpose of annoying a neighbor is included in a landowner-fence builder's bundle of rights. The almost universal answer is no, the rights of property ownership do not include such a malicious use of one's land. However, if the fence or structure has a legitimate purpose, its construction and use are permitted despite its interference with a neighbor's light, air, or view.

The construction of spite fences is less common today than it was 60 or more years ago. This is due primarily to two factors:

a. The **building codes** adopted by many counties, cities, and towns are more comprehensive today than in the past, and often limit the height of improvements to a property, including fences, and even the residence itself, and

b. A significant portion of our population now resides in **homeowners associations**. Such associations are required to have recorded conditions, covenants, and restrictions (CC&Rs), which almost always provide architectural guidelines, including limits on the size and types of fences allowed in the association. As a further check on the erection of spite fences in an association, the board of directors often empowers an architectural committee to review, and hold hearings, for all proposed construction.

Spite Fence
a fence erected solely to injure an adjoining landowner by shutting out or diminishing the landowner's light, air, or view.

3. TRESPASS TO LAND

Trespass to land is a tort, meaning a civil wrong for which the law will provide a remedy. The interest protected by the tort of trespass is the possessor's right to be free from interference of the possessor's dominion and control of his or her real property. The following are three methods by which one may trespass on the land of another:

a. One's **intentional, unauthorized entry** upon the land of another.

Example 1: You are out for a walk in the country and intentionally climb over Farmer Jones' fence and enter his pasture to pet the bull. You have committed a trespass, although that may be the least of your immediate worries.

Trespass to Land
the intentional tort by which one enters, or causes an object to enter, the land of another. Trespass also includes refusing to leave another's real property after being ordered to do so.

[2]*Racich v. Mastrovich*, 65 S.D. 321, 323 (1937).

Example 2: You are out for a walk in the country on public land, and *accidentally* wander on to Farmer Smith's property. You have committed a trespass.[3]

b. One's ***refusal to leave*** another's real property after being ordered to depart.

Example: You are having a party at your home. One of your guests becomes disorderly. When you tell her to leave, she refuses, and she has thereby committed a trespass.

c. One's intentionally ***causing an object to enter*** the land of another.

Example: You are practicing your golf game by hitting golf balls onto— and over—your next door neighbor's yard. You have committed a trespass regardless of whether the balls land in your neighbor's yard, or merely pass through the neighbor's "airspace."

Assume that in the golf ball scenario above, your next door neighbor is renting the residential property from the owner. In an action against you for trespass, who has standing to bring the lawsuit … the tenant, the owner, or both?

Answer: The tenant is the only person who has ***standing*** to bring the lawsuit for trespassing, and not the owner of the residence. The reason is that in renting the property, the tenant has acquired a leasehold estate. One of the rights in the tenant's "bundle of rights" is the right to exercise ***dominion and control*** over the leasehold, a right that the owner transferred to the tenant when the lease became effective.

4. ENCROACHMENT

An encroachment is the intrusion of a building or other structure, such as a fence or stone wall, onto the property of an adjoining landowner, either ***above or below the surface***. Some states hold that ***trees*** and ***shrubs*** may constitute an encroachment as well as the previously mentioned man-made structures. An encroachment may constitute a trespass if it is a physical invasion of a neighboring property. However, an encroachment necessarily involves *adjoining* landowners; trespass does not. Also, an encroachment is not a tort *per se*, but it may become one if it meets the elements of either trespass to real property, or nuisance.

The interplay of trespass, encroachment, and nuisance can be complicated for students, and even experienced legal practitioners. The categories are not necessarily mutually exclusive, and sometimes the same condition on the land, such as a building, may simultaneously be an encroachment, a trespass, and a nuisance.

---

[3]This scenario requires an explanation: Even though your entry on to Farmer Smith's property was *accidental* and *unintentional*, you nevertheless committed the *intentional* tort of trespass to real property. The reason is that liability for trespass depends on ***intentionally doing the act that constitutes the physical invasion*** of the property. Since you intended to walk on to Farmer Smith's property it is a trespass, even though you mistakenly believed you were still on public lands. In the real world, assuming that you did no damage to Smith's property, you might be liable for, at most, nominal damages.

Examine the table below to see some of the similarities and differences between and among the three categories of interference with the land of another:

Type of Interference	Trespass	Encroachment	Nuisance
Definition or Elements	An intentional, unauthorized entry upon the land of another by a person or an object (or refusing to leave when ordered to do so).	A building or other structure intruding onto the property of an adjoining landowner, either above or below the surface; some states include plants or trees planted or nourished by the offending landowner.	A substantial and unreasonable interference with another's use and enjoyment of her property.
Is the interference tortious conduct?	Yes, trespass is tortious conduct.	Usually, no. But if the encroachment is not abated after notice, it may become both a trespass and a nuisance.	Yes, a nuisance is tortious conduct, and may be the result of either negligent or intentional conduct.
Must the interference be by the <u>adjoining</u> landowner?	No, a trespasser may be a stranger to the land.	Yes, by definition, encroachments involve neighboring property owners.	No, a nuisance such as noxious gases or odors may come from miles away.
May the interference be by a building or other structure?	Yes	Yes, and in some states, *only* man-made buildings or structures can constitute an encroachment (and not flora).	Yes
Plants or Trees	*Natural growth* plants or trees are usually not a trespass because of the required element of intent. But if an owner or previous owner planted the offending tree or plant—or in some states, *nourishes the natural growth* plants or trees—she may be liable for trespass.	The states vary considerably in deciding if trees or plants are an encroachment. The states also differ on whether there is an absolute right by the aggrieved owner to cut the offending roots, for example, or whether the root-cutting must be reasonable; if not, the cutter may have liability if the tree dies or falls, causing damage.	Generally, a tree or plant that drops pine needles, flowers, or fruit on a neighbor's property is *not* considered a nuisance, unless there is actual damage, for example, to a swimming pool filter. This is because the aggrieved owner has the right to trim back the overhanging branches to the property line (which may not always be an effective or convenient remedy for wind-blown pine needles, etc.).

CHAPTER SUMMARY

This chapter dealt with rights and duties incident to the possession or ownership of land, that is, rights and duties of neighboring landowners to each other.

There are two broad categories of water rights. First, **riparian rights** are the rights of owners whose properties abut rivers or streams. Second, **littoral rights** are the rights of owners whose properties abut an ocean, sea, or lake.

In the Eastern United States, the doctrine of **reasonable use** controls in riparian disputes; that is, an owner of property adjoining a lake or stream may use only as much water as is reasonably necessary for the beneficial use of the property, tempered by considering the needs of the downstream riparian owners. In the Western United States, the doctrine of **prior**

appropriation determines the rights to water use. This doctrine stimulated economic development, particularly in the mining industry, where the first claim on water was given to the first property owners to commercially develop the lands abutting the watercourses.

Navigable waterways are those that form a continuous "highway" over which commerce may be carried on with other states or countries. The significance of classifying waterways as either navigable, or non-navigable, relates to which body of law controls their use. Navigable waterways are regulated by federal law. **Non-navigable waterways** are regulated by state law.

The **public trust** doctrine is one whereby a state holds public land, including river, lake, and sea beds, for the benefit of the general public.

Nature can work drastic changes on the land, and change property lines and even the boundaries between states. *Accretion* is the natural process whereby land is slowly added to an owner's property, often caused by the action of a stream, river, or other body of water.

Reliction, like accretion, adds land to an owner's property, but through the gradual subsidence or receding of the stream, river, or lake.

Erosion is the gradual removal or wearing away of the land, primarily by the action of wind or water.

Avulsion is the sudden loss of land by the action of water, or a sudden change in the bed or course of a stream.

Air rights are the rights of a landowner to reasonably use and enjoy the air and space above the owned parcel of land. Under the common law, one owned not only the surface of the land, but to the center of the earth and to the heavens above. The common law was altered by federal law in the 1920s to accommodate the arrival of commercial aviation.

Adjoining landowners have a reciprocal duty to physically support their neighbors' property in its natural state so that the land will not collapse or sink. The physical support owed is either *lateral*, that is, side support, or *subjacent*, that is, support from below.

A *nuisance* is a substantial and unreasonable interference with another's use and enjoyment of his land. A *nuisance per se* is an act, occupation, condition, or structure that is a nuisance at all times and under any circumstances, regardless of the location or surroundings. A *nuisance per accidens*, or *nuisance in fact* is a structure or use of property that may become a nuisance by virtue of its construction, location, or operation. Cases of *coming to the nuisance* can be difficult for a court to balance fairness to the owner of the nuisance property (who was there first) with the needs of newly arrived owners.

A *trespass* to land involves an intentional, unauthorized entry by a person upon the land of another; trespass to land includes a tortfeasor's intentionally causing entry upon the land of another by an object, for example, hitting golf balls onto—or over—your neighbor's property constitutes a trespass.

An *encroachment* is the intrusion of a building or other structure, such as a fence or stone wall, onto the property of an adjoining landowner, either above or below the surface. An encroachment is not a tort, but may eventually become a trespass and/or a nuisance if the offending structure is not removed.

CONCEPT REVIEW AND REINFORCEMENT

KEY TERMS

Accretion
Air Commerce Act
   of 1926
Air Rights
Airspace

AREA
Ancient Lights
Avulsion
Coming to the Nuisance
Encroachment
Erosion

Lateral Support
Littoral Rights
Navigable Waterways
Non-Navigable Waters
Nuisance Per Se
Nuisance Per Accidens
Percolating Groundwaters
Prior Appropriation
Private Nuisance
Public Nuisance
Public Trust Doctrine

Reasonable Use
Reliction
Surface Waters
Riparian Rights
Spite Fence
Subjacent Support
Subterranean Waters
Takings Clause
Trespass
Trespass to land
Underground Streams

CONCEPT REVIEW QUESTIONS

1. How are rights *incident* to property ownership different from property rights *per se*? Does one's ownership of property *necessarily* mean that one has incidental property rights and obligations, as well?

2. What are riparian rights?

3. What are littoral rights?

4. What is the water use doctrine applied in the eastern United States? What is the water use doctrine applied in the western United States? What were the factors that motivated the use of the two different theories in the East and West?

5. What is the public trust doctrine, and to what types of real property does it apply? What are the public policies that underlie the public trust doctrine?

6. What are the four ways that boundaries may be altered by natural forces (AREA)?

7. Under common law, owners of land owned "to the heavens." What technological invention forced a change in the common law? Could our society have developed to the extent it has without the changes to the common law concept of "owning to the heavens"?

8. Under common law, what are the two types of support to which a landowner is entitled from his or her neighboring land owners?

9. Nuisance, like trespass, is a tort. How is nuisance defined, or stated differently, what are the elements of nuisance? What are the elements of trespass? May the two property-related torts sometimes overlap, that is, may one act constitute both a nuisance and a trespass? Give some examples.

10. What is a nuisance *per se*? What is a nuisance *per accidens*? What is "coming to the nuisance"?

11. What is an encroachment, and how does it differ from trespass and nuisance. May an encroachment become a trespass or nuisance?

12. You know that under the reasonable use doctrine, a riparian owner has a right to make reasonable use of a reasonable quantity of water. But does the property right in water include a reasonable quality, as well as a reasonable quantity, of water? Why?

ETHICS

KEEP ON ROCKIN' . . . **MAYBE**

Annie Attorney is a real estate lawyer. A quiet fellow named Ben Boring comes to her and asks Annie to sue "whatever idiot" owns the piece of property next to Ben's property, where he lives. It seems that Ben is not fond of all the partying, loud music, and dancing that goes on next door.

Annie tells Boring: "I certainly do sympathize with you. But I will have to find out who the owner of the noisy property is, and then check for any conflicts before we proceed. I will call you tomorrow."

Annie checks the county real estate ownership database. It turns out that the owner of the offending property is indeed one of her best clients.

Annie notifies Ben that she is unable to represent him due to a conflict of interest. Ben hires another attorney who files a lawsuit for nuisance against the neighboring property owner, who is Annie's client.

When does the attorney-client relationship begin?

Did Annie and Ben establish an attorney-client relationship by virtue of their meeting?

Can Annie represent her existing (noisy) client in the lawsuit which has now been filed by Ben?

BUILDING YOUR PROFESSIONAL SKILLS

CRITICAL THINKING **EXERCISES**

1. Neighbor D (defendant) has a unique type of pine tree, which is close to the boundary of Neighbor P's property, and in fact, its limbs overhang P's (plaintiff's) property. Last fall, the pine trees lost a large amount of pine needles and pine cones, many of which ended up clogging P's pool filter and causing a significant amount of damage.

   Assuming that P had not previously mentioned the problem to D, what remedy, if any, does P have in this situation?

2. Neighbor P lives in a condominium where neighbor D in the adjoining unit is fond of smoking stogies— a cheap cigar—several times a day. Neighbor P knows this because the smoke from the cigars gets into the HVAC duct work, which is shared by the unit owners.

   Under the law of your state, would P have a claim for trespass or nuisance (or maybe even battery?), and if so, could those claims be asserted against D, the homeowners association, or both?

3. Both land owners P and D own property abutting the River Styx. Landowner D owns a parcel of land upstream from landowner P. In the last few years, D has used ever-increasing amounts of water to irrigate a small, but growing, organic farming operation. Landowner P has never used any of the water in the river for commercial purposes, but does enjoy the river's aesthetic beauty, and canoeing on the river.

   Because of D's use of the river water for irrigation, P has noticed that the depth of the river has been diminished by half, and the river's subsidence has exposed the muddy banks. Does P have a viable claim against D for P's diminished enjoyment of the river views? Does P have a claim against D for an unreasonable use of the water?

4. Landowner P has a beautiful ocean view, but learns that D, the owner of the currently vacant lot between P's house and the ocean, intends to build a three-story residence that will obstruct practically all of P's view of the ocean. The plans for the new house conform in every way to the town's existing zoning laws and building codes.

    Should P be allowed to enjoin the anticipated construction in order to limit the height of D's new residence, and/or reduce the square footage, and/or force the house to be built on another part of the lot?

5. The case of *Spur Industries v. Del Webb* was an example of "coming to the nuisance." Many students are struck by the seeming unfairness of Spur Industries being forced to move from a location where it had conducted business operations for years, even though the move was paid for by Del Webb.

    Should the law always strive to do what is "fair," or should other considerations—for example, economic growth, or increasing the tax base—outweigh the importance of a fair result? How would the suburban Phoenix/Sun City area be different today if Spur Industries had been allowed to stay in business as a cattle feed lot at the same location?

6. On April 20, 2010, there was a catastrophic explosion on British Petroleum's (BP) Deepwater Horizon drilling platform in the Gulf of Mexico. The accident took the lives of 11 workers on the rig, injured 17 others, and polluted thousands of square miles of ocean and Gulf Coast beaches with oil sludge.

    After the explosion, the well was very difficult to cap because it was approximately 5,000 feet under water. There were devastating effects on the wildlife in and around the Gulf, and also to the regional economy. Some scientists claim that this was the worst environmental and ecologic disaster ever in the United States.

    How far should BP's liability extend? Clearly, it should compensate the residents of the Gulf who engage in fishing, oyster farming, and shrimping operations. But for how long … for the next 5, 10, or 20 (or more) years?

    Suppose you own a string of eateries—Ollie's Oyster Bars—located throughout the central United States. You have several Ollie's in Louisiana and Mississippi, and several others up to a hundred miles from the Gulf of Mexico. Almost all of your oysters came from the Gulf. You have experienced a 50% decline in business because customers are concerned about the safety of eating oysters. Would you have a claim against BP, or are your damages "too remote," that is, indirect?

    How about the trucking companies that carried the oysters to your several franchises—should they have claims against BP? At what point, and on what bases, should the courts draw the line in imposing liability?

    Aside from BP, should the federal government be held liable for the damage? In April of 2009, a year before the accident, the Department of Interior waived the requirement of an environmental impact report, which was required under the National Environmental Policy Act (NEPA). If BP is unable to pay for all of the billions of dollars in damages, should the federal government be responsible? Should criminal charges be filed against BP, or its employees? Could criminal charges be filed against the United States government?

RESEARCH ON THE WEB

1. You are involved in a boating accident on a large, navigable lake located entirely within your state or jurisdiction. Research the question of venue. That is, if you sue the captain and owner of the other boat that ran into you for negligence in causing the accident, does venue properly lie in state court, federal court, or either? This question involves the issue of subject matter jurisdiction, that is, what courts—state or federal—can hear certain types of cases, such as maritime accidents.

2. Same facts as in the preceding question except that the lake lies not only in your state but extends into a neighboring state as well. In that case, where would proper venue lie?

3. The case of *Spur Industries v. Del Webb* was decided in 1972. In response, a number of states enacted statutes addressing the issue of "coming to the nuisance." Research whether your state enacted such a statute, or set of statutes, and if so, whose interests are mainly protected, the owner of the existing "nuisance"—for example, hog farmers or timber mill owners—or those who "came to the nuisance," like the owners in a new residential development such as Sun City in the *Del Webb* case?

4. Research the question of whether your state has case law or statutes regarding an avulsion (a sudden loss of land, usually due to the action of water) working a permanent change in the boundary between land owners.

   If so, does your state law comport with the holding of the United States Supreme Court in the 1918 case of *Arkansas v. Tennessee*?

5. In your state or jurisdiction, what rights does a property owner have to cut the roots of a tree on an adjacent property, which have encroached on the land of another?

   Assuming the aggrieved property owner has a right to cut encroaching roots, does that owner have an absolute right to do so, regardless of the consequences, or must the aggrieved owner use reasonable care so as not to damage the tree or other property?

6. Identify some navigable waterways in your jurisdiction.

BUILDING YOUR **PROFESSIONAL** PORTFOLIO

1. Your next door neighbor owns what she thinks is a beautiful peach tree, which is located close to the property line separating your land from hers. You have pruned back the branches which extended over the property line, but peaches continue to fall on your lot.

   Not only do the decaying peaches smell bad, but they attract wasps and vermin. You have asked your neighbor several times to completely remove the tree, but she has refused.

   Draw up two claims as if you were drafting a complaint, one for nuisance and the other for trespass. Make sure to include the necessary elements for each claim.

2. You are the Zoning Commissioner in Any Town, USA. You have noticed in the last few years that more and more of the residents of Any Town have applied for residential building permits for homes incorporating expensive solar cell technology.

   Several of the applicants for building permits have expressed concerns that new construction on parcels adjoining their building sites could block some or even all of the sun's rays from their solar cells, thereby thwarting their efforts to reduce their "carbon footprint," and costing them more in utility bills.

   Draft a proposed ordinance for consideration by the town council that would protect owners of homes with solar cells from being blocked from access to the sun by new construction on neighboring lots.

   Do you think that such an ordinance would survive a legal challenge by a landowner who is forced to build on another, less appealing part of her lot, just because her neighbors want to install a few solar panels on their roofs?

chapter 6

RESTRICTIONS ON THE USE OF REAL PROPERTY

LEARNING OBJECTIVES

After reading this chapter, you should understand:

- The types of restrictions that can be placed on real property

- Private property restrictions

- Easements

- Public property restrictions and the takings clause

- Servitudes

- How zoning laws work

Restrictions On the Use of Real Property

This chapter deals with restrictions on the use of real property. The first part of the chapter concerns restrictions called **servitudes**, which are placed on the land by private parties, rather than by government. The second part of the chapter covers restrictions put on the land by governmental entities.

Suppose that a 40-acre tract of vacant land has been in your family for many generations. But you now feel that it is time to subdivide property into several residential lots. Is it possible for you to impose restrictions on future purchasers of the lots as to the minimum size of the individual lots? May you set a minimum and maximum square footage on the size of the houses to be built on the lots?

What about restrictions on the architectural style that may be used for the new homes, such as Dutch Colonial, Spanish, or Victorian? The answer is yes, you can impose these and other restrictions on the individual lots that you have subdivided from the main 40-acre parcel. This is accomplished through servitudes.

A. Servitudes—*Private* Restrictions on Land

A **servitude** is a general term describing a legal device that creates a right or an obligation in land, and that **runs with the land.**[1]

There are three major categories of servitudes:

1. Easements,
2. Profits, and
3. Covenants.

Regardless of which type of the servitudes above that we are discussing, they all have at least three characteristics in common:

1. Servitudes **run with the land.** This means that after the easement, profit, or covenant has been created, it will automatically *bind subsequent owners* and occupiers of a property, without the necessity of creating the servitude again.

In the example above where you subdivided your 40 acres, assume that you imposed a restriction (that is, a restrictive covenant) on each of the buyers that the minimum lot size is to be 3 acres. Buyer purchases a 3-acre parcel. But after purchasing the parcel, Buyer (now Owner) wants to then subdivide his newly acquired lot into three 1-acre parcels so that he can build three houses, one on each 1-acre lot. The question is: Can he do it?

The answer is no, he cannot subdivide the 3-acre parcel. The reason, of course, is the restrictive covenant that you imposed on the original subdivided lots, and that "runs with the land." Because the covenant runs with the land, it binds all of the current and future owners and occupiers of the land.[2]

To determine if a right or obligation is in fact a servitude that runs with the land, we look to the ***intent of the parties*** to the conveyance, whether the transfer of the property is made by deed or by will. The parties' intent may either be ***express*** (usually in a writing, but sometimes orally), or ***implied*** from the parties' conduct, and the facts and circumstances surrounding the parcel of land.

2. The second characteristic common to servitudes is that in creating the servitude, the creation of a **dominant estate** and a **servient estate** usually follows.

Servitude
a right or obligation in land that runs with the land.

Runs with the Land
when a right or obligation relating to land is binding on successive owners.

Dominant Estate
the estate or parcel of land that benefits from an easement.

Servient Estate
the estate or parcel of land that is burdened by an easement.

---

[1]Restatement 3d of Property – Servitudes, § 1.1.
[2]In an earlier chapter we discussed *licenses*. Recall that a license is permission granted by the licensor to the licensee to use the licensor's property for some limited purpose, such as fishing in the licensor's pond. A license is *not* a servitude because it does not run with the land; that is, the license may be used only by the specific licensee.

The dominant estate is the property that *benefits* from a servitude, whereas a servient estate is the property that is *burdened* by the servitude, whether it is an easement, profit, or covenant.

3. The third characteristic common to servitudes is that they are *non-possessory* interests in the land. Looking again at the example of subdividing your 40-acre parcel, the fact that you can impose a 3-acre minimum on future purchasers does not mean that you also have some *possessory* interest in their properties.

To take another example, even though one has an easement to cross the property of another, that is merely a right to use—and not a right to possess—the property that the easement crosses.

1. EASEMENTS

Easement
a type of servitude in which one acquires the right to use another's land for a specific purpose.

An **easement** is a non-possessory right to enter and *use the land* of another for a specific purpose. Perhaps the most familiar type of the easement is created when property is subdivided. In Exhibit 6-1 Owner has split her property in two, selling off the eastern half to Buyer, while keeping ownership of the western half.

On the western side, adjacent to Owner's parcel, is a public road. In fact, it is the only public road within two miles of the property. Thus, there is no public road that abuts Buyer's parcel, and so Buyer is **landlocked**.

Landlocked
when there is no access to a parcel of land by way of a public road.

Under the facts given here, the law will not permit the Buyer to be landlocked. Usually, at the time of sale, the parties will create an easement and include it in the deed of conveyance. The easement will give Buyer the right to use—specifically, the right to travel over—Owner's property in order that Buyer may access his property.

Easement by Necessity
an easement created by operation of law because the easement is indispensable to the reasonable use of nearby property, such as an easement connecting a parcel of land to a road.

However, if the parties forget to provide for an easement in a deed, the law will allow Buyer to have an **easement by necessity**. If Owner refuses to voluntarily allow Buyer an easement over Owner's property, then Buyer will have to file an action to obtain the easement.

EXHIBIT 6-1   EASEMENT APPURTENANT

P U B L I C R O A D	Owner-seller— keeps ownership of the western parcel, but sells the eastern half of the property to Buyer. Owner-seller must provide the easement appurtenant (below) so that Buyer will not be "landlocked." ------------------ Easement Appurtenant	Buyer— is the new owner of the eastern half of the property. Without the easement, Buyer would have been landlocked since there is no direct access to a public road.

a. Dominant and Servient Estates

Servitudes are generally characterized by the presence of a dominant estate and a servient estate. In the example above, is Owner or Buyer the *dominant estate*? The answer is counterintuitive, and students sometimes assume that because Owner gave the easement to Buyer, that Owner must have the "dominant estate." But this is not the case.

When determining which estate (parcel of land) is dominant, look to see which property and which owner **benefits** from the easement.

Conversely, to determine which estate is servient, look to see which property and which owner is **burdened** by the easement.

With that distinction in mind, it is easy to determine that in Exhibit 6-1, Buyer holds the dominant estate because he is the one who benefits from the easement by gaining access to his property. Owner, on the other hand, holds the **servient estate**, because it is her property that is being used by another—the Buyer—and is therefore burdened by the easement.

The easement created will "run with the land." This means that if Buyer sells his property a few years from now, the new buyer will have a right to use the easement just like the previous owner because the servitude/easement runs with the land. Alternatively, if the Owner sells or gives her property to another, that new owner must continue to allow Buyer to use the easement. As you can see, both the benefit *and* the burden run with the land.

It is sometimes difficult to determine whether the right to use another's property runs with the land, or not. Consider the following example:

SERVITUDE OR LICENSE?

You own and reside on a lovely piece of property that includes a small lake, which is chock-full of fish. You have told your next-door neighbor Pat that she and her family can fish in the lake anytime they like.

Pat and her family members gratefully take advantage of your generosity by fishing the lake for several years. But recently, Pat decided to sell her residence. Will the person who buys Pat's residence be able to fish your lake just like Pat did? Put differently, does the right to fish the lake run with (Pat's) land?

What we must explore here are two possibilities:

The first possibility is that the right to fish the lake is a **servitude**, either an easement or a covenant. If the right is an easement or covenant, that right to fish would run with Pat's land, and would benefit not only Pat, but also the future owners of her property. And if the right to fish is an easement or covenant, then Pat's land would be the dominant estate because it is her property that benefits from the servitude.

The second possibility is that the right to fish is merely a **license**, and not a servitude. If that is the case, then the license was given by you (the licensor) to Pat and her family members (the licensees), and it does *not* run with the land. And if the right to fish is merely a license, it is revocable by you, the licensor.

On what bases do you make your determination whether the right to fish the pond is a servitude, or a license?

b. Easements Appurtenant, and Easements in Gross

Easements may be broadly categorized as either easements appurtenant (meaning "next to" or "connected with"), or easements in gross. An example of an easement appurtenant was given above in the case of Owner and the landlocked Buyer, and the creation and use of the easement to access Buyer's property.

An **easement appurtenant** is one created or given for the benefit of another parcel of land. In this case, the easement was created by the parties for the benefit of the parcel purchased by Buyer. As you would imagine, the parcel benefited—the dominant estate—is almost always a parcel adjoining the servient estate, which is why it is described as "appurtenant."

Easement Appurtenant
an easement conveyed by one landowner—the servient estate—to benefit another (usually adjoining) parcel of land, the dominant estate.

EXHIBIT 6-2   Appurtenant Easement

Grant of Easement

THIS AGREEMENT, made _____ (date) between _____ _____ Grantor, and _____ Grantee.

Whereas, the Grantor is owner of an estate in fee simple of a parcel of land described as the _____ _____ [legal description] County and State, and marked Exhibit "A" attached hereto across which there runs a private road shown on Exhibit "A"

Whereas, Grantee is owner in fee simple of another parcel of land described as the _____ _____ County of Any and State of _____, upon which is erected a private dwelling house; and

Whereas, for the consideration hereinafter mentioned, the Grantor has agreed to grant to the Grantee such easement and right of way over said private road as hereinafter expressed;

WITNESSETH, that in pursuance of said agreement and in consideration of the sum one thousand dollars ($1000) paid by the Grantee to the Grantor, the receipt whereof is hereby acknowledged, the Grantor hereby grants to the Grantee, her heirs and assigns:

Full and free right and liberty for Grantee; Grantee and his tenants, servants, visitors, and licensees, in common with all other persons having the like right, at all times hereafter, on foot or on horseback or in vehicles to pass and repass along the said private road from said _____ Road to _____ _____ Road for all lawful purposes connected with the use and enjoyment of said premises of the Grantee as a single private dwelling house, but for no other purposes.

To have and to hold said right of way hereby granted to the Grantee, his heirs and assigns, as appurtenant to said premises.

In Witness Whereof, the Grantor has hereunto set his hand and seal the day and year first above written.

_____

Grantor

[Acknowledgment/Notarization]

Easement in Gross
an easement to benefit a specific person or entity, such as the electric company, rather than another parcel of land.

An **easement in gross** is created or given *not* for the benefit of another parcel of land, but rather for the benefit of a specific person or entity, such as the power company or city water district. Note that the person or entity that benefits from an easement in gross is *not* the owner of an adjoining piece of property. See the following example:

EXHIBIT 6-3 Express Easement In Gross

Grant of Easement to Lay Sewer Line

Mutual agreement, made this _____ day of _____, 20___, between (name) of the City of _____, State of _____, Grantor, and (construction company name) of the City of _____, State of _____, Grantee.

WITNESSETH, that for and in consideration of the sum of $_____ and other consideration hereinafter set out, the parties agree:

The Grantor gives and grants to the Grantee the right to construct and maintain a sewer line under and through his/her property located in _____ Subdivision, an addition to the City of _____, County of _____, State of _____, being Lot Nos. _____ through _____ inclusive of said Subdivision.

In consideration of said right, the Grantee agrees to lay said sewer line at sufficient depth not to interfere with the Grantor's use and enjoyment of said property; and to place an intake connection in said sewer line for use of the Grantor at a point to be designated by him/her, and further agrees to pay to the Grantor any damage which may result to his property by reason of the laying, maintenance, repairing, and operation of the sewer line.

In witness whereof, the parties have executed this agreement on the day and year first above written.

_____
Grantor

Construction Company, Inc., Grantee

by _____

Title _____

[Acknowledgment/Notarizations]

EASEMENTS IN GROSS

FOR SEWER, POWER + PHONE LINES

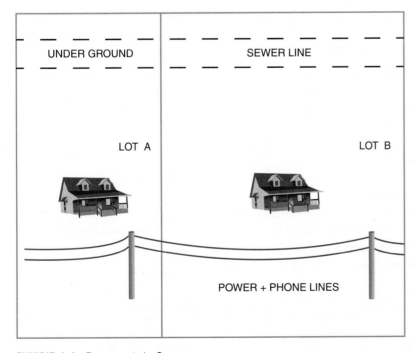

EXHIBIT 6-4 Easements in Gross

c. How Easements Are Created and Types of Easements

Express Easement
an easement that is created by the written agreement of the parties.

i. Express Easement   Easements are usually created through the express, *written* agreement of the parties to a deed.[3] In the example of Owner and Buyer above, when they contracted for the sale of the property, they should have included in the offer to purchase a requirement that the deed contain an easement allowing access for Buyer across Owner's property.

After the closing, the deed should be **recorded** or registered at the office of the Register of Deeds. The purpose of **recording** a deed or other legal instrument is to put the world (especially potential buyers) **on notice** of one's interest in a particular property. In this case, the deed containing the easement declares that Buyer not only owns the eastern parcel, but that he also has a right of access across Owner's property. Recording that deed puts all interested parties on notice of the existence of the easement.

Implied Easement
an easement implied from the facts and circumstances relating to a parcel of real property. The conduct of the parties may also shed light on whether an easement has been created by implication.

ii. Implied Easement   Using the same example of Owner and Buyer above, what if they included the conveyance of an easement in the purchase agreement, but forgot to include Buyer's access easement in the deed? If Buyer were denied access to his property by Owner, and Buyer sued Owner for access, the court would almost certainly declare that there was an **implied easement**. This means that a trier of fact (a judge or jury) would make the assumption that Owner and Buyer *would* have intended to include an access easement in the deed had they not forgotten about it. The existence of an easement may be implied from the facts and circumstances surrounding a given transaction, and perhaps from the conduct of the parties themselves.

Note that an implied easement is an exception to the Statute of Frauds, which requires that all *interests* in (and not just ownership of) real property be put in writing. Because an easement is undoubtedly an interest in real property, albeit the property of another, it would normally be required under the Statute of Frauds that the easement be in writing. However, in order not to leave Buyer landlocked, the law has carved out an exception for implied easements and other types of easements that follow.

If it became necessary for Buyer to file suit, and if the court ruled that an implied easement existed, it would behoove Buyer to record that judicial order at the Register of Deeds office.

iii. Easement by Necessity   If a landowner would be deprived of the use of his or her property due to the absence of an express easement over the adjoining property, then the law may provide that owner with an easement by necessity. Assume that the owner of lot A has built a one-story residence in which she has invested thousands of dollars for solar panels on the roof of the residence to provide electricity for her home.

The owner of the adjoining property, lot B, which is currently a vacant parcel, has announced plans to build a three-story home on the lot, in a location that will completely block the sun's rays from owner A's solar panels. If the owner of lot B refuses to build in another location on his lot, the owner of lot A may be able to sue and obtain an **easement by necessity**, which would allow owner A to receive the benefit of the sun's rays.

---

[3] An express agreement means that it is either oral or written. Technically then, an **oral** agreement for an easement would be an "express" agreement, just like a written agreement. However, if there was a dispute between the parties about the terms of their oral agreement, they could run into a problem, because the Statute of Frauds requires that any *interest* in real property be in writing. Although there are some exceptions to the Statute of Frauds for implied (i.e., not expressed) easements, it is not certain that a court would enforce an express *oral* easement agreement.

This, of course, would force the owner of lot B to build in another location on his parcel of land. The easement would be necessary (thus, an easement by necessity) to enable the owner of lot A to enjoy the use of her property, and more specifically, enjoy the benefit of her solar heating system. If she were not allowed to obtain the easement, she would suffer considerable **economic injury**. Not only has she paid a considerable sum to purchase and install the solar panels, but she will have to pay higher utility bills since she cannot generate electricity from the panels.

Note that to obtain an easement by necessity, one would have to file a lawsuit. If an easement were granted by the court, its order should be filed at the office of the Register of Deeds.

iv. Easement by Prescription   An **easement by prescription** is created through the **long and continuous use** of another's property. Suppose the owner of parcel A has walked over parcel B, owned by A's neighbor, to access a common water well serving all the property owners in the area. If A's use of B's property is long enough that it meets the statutory time period required for an easement by prescription, then A's continuous use will ripen into such an easement. This type of easement is similar to obtaining title to property by what is known as **adverse possession**. Here again, the easement is unwritten, and is an exception to the Statute of Frauds.

To summarize the creation of easements, most are created by express, written agreements. However, those that are not put in writing—implied easements, easements by necessity, and easements by prescription—are exceptions to the Statute of Frauds' general rule that all interests in real property be put in writing to be enforceable.

Easement by Prescription
an easement created as a result of one's long and continuous use of another's property.

SCOPE OF THE EASEMENT

Let us revisit our old friends Owner and Buyer. Assume that when Owner sold the eastern half of the property to Buyer, they included an express, written easement in the deed, which read:

> Buyer is permitted to use a 20-foot-wide strip of land running along the southern boundary of Owner's property for the purpose of access between Buyer's property and the public road. Buyer is permitted to pave the easement, or lay down crushed stone upon the easement, at Buyer's sole expense.

At the time that Owner sold the property to Buyer, it was assumed, at least by Owner, that Buyer would only use the newly acquired property for residential purposes. However, since purchasing the property, Buyer has learned that there are valuable mineral deposits on the far eastern side of his property. As a result, Buyer is now conducting a small-scale mining operation on his property, which includes large dump trucks using the easement 30 to 40 times per day, five days per week.

There was nothing in the quoted clause above that prohibits the use of the easement by dump trucks. Nor is there anything in the clause that limits the number of trips that can be made in a day. It would appear that the only hard and fast rule in the easement-creating language is that the roadway was not to exceed 20' in width.

So, has Buyer exceeded the **scope of the easement**? Is there even such a thing as the "scope of the easement"? If not, should there be? Are there any limits to the use of the easement, assuming that Buyer keeps the truck traffic within the boundaries of the 20' wide easement?

If Owner sues for an injunction to prohibit the use of the easement by the dump trucks, will she succeed? What factors should the court consider when making its decision whether or not to award the injunction?

Would it matter whether Buyer had the mining operation in mind when he bought his parcel from A, or whether he came up with the idea after he purchased and moved on to the land?

d. How Easements Are Terminated

Easements may be terminated in several ways, and some of the more common methods are described below.

i. Agreement   Just as two adjoining land owners can agree to create an easement, so they can agree to a **termination of easement**. Whether or not the original easement was in writing, the agreement terminating the easement should be in writing, and filed with the Register of Deeds. This will put all future owners of the properties on notice that the easement has been extinguished. As an example of when the parties might terminate an easement, consider the landlocked buyer. If a new road has been built that now abuts the formerly landlocked property, then the need for an easement over the servient property disappears.

ii. Expiration   When easements are created by agreement, they will often have a *termination date* on which the easement will expire. If a definite termination date is agreed to, it may be for a period of several years or may only be for a few months, or could terminate upon the occurrence of a specific event.

An example of a situation involving a short-term easement is when governmental entities are constructing roadways or installing water and sewer pipes. In these events, a city or a state's department of transportation may purchase easements from landowners along the construction site for a specific, but relatively brief, period of time, for the sole purpose of parking its heavy construction equipment, rather than hauling the machines back and forth to the site each day.

An example of a longer-term easement is a mining or timber operation for which you grant an easement to allow the heavy trucks associated with those operations to travel across a road over your land "until the expiration date of December 31, 2020, or until a public road is built on the eastern boundary of the grantor's property, whichever comes first."

iii. Merger   Again using the example of Owner and Buyer, several years have gone by since Owner sold the eastern half of her property to Buyer, and over those years, Buyer has been using the easement for access between the public road and his property. Buyer was recently offered a new job in a distant city, and now offers to sell back his (eastern) parcel to Owner.

Owner accepts the offer, the deal is closed, and Owner once again owns both parcels. The *merger* of the two parcels back into one parcel terminates the easement, as there is no need for Owner to give an easement to herself.

The result would be the same if Buyer had purchased Owner's parcel, or if a third party had purchased both Owner's and Buyer's individual parcels. The rule is that once the two parcels are *merged* under a single ownership, the easement terminates.

iv. Abandonment   Assume that after Buyer has lived on the property for several years, the state finally builds a new public road along the eastern side of Buyer's parcel. Buyer is delighted that he now has easy and convenient access to the new public road.

Buyer no longer has need of the easement that he had obtained from Owner years before, and never uses it after the completion of the new road. That easement will be extinguished because of Buyer's *abandonment* of it.

2. PROFITS ARE EASEMENTS +

Profits, the second category of servitudes, are simply *easements plus*. That means that if you have a profit, you have:

   a. The right to enter the land of another (just like a regular easement), *plus*
   b. The right to take something of value from that land (the profit), such as oil, gas, timber, minerals, or wild animals.

When the servitude involves a **profit**, there is usually just one parcel of land involved, that is, the burdened parcel. The profit may take the form of a royalty payment made to the property owner based upon the quantity of oil, stone, and so forth, extracted from the property.

In the past, a profit was sometimes called a profit à prendre,[4] from the French, meaning a "profit to take." Profit à prendre has been shortened in legal parlance to simply "profit."

Profit
an easement to enter the land of another, coupled with the right to take something of value from the land.

3. COVENANTS

Remember that servitudes are agreements concerning rights and obligations in land, and between private parties, as opposed to governmentally imposed obligations. The first two servitudes that we studied were easements and profits ("easements +"). The third and final type of servitude is a **covenant**. A covenant is simply a promise relating to real property.

a. Covenants Are of Two General Types

i. *Affirmative covenants* are those that require the **covenantor** (the promissor) to perform some specific act, to a **covenantee** (the promisee). For example, condominium owners covenant or promise to the covenantee-homeowners association to make monthly, quarterly, or annual payments for the upkeep and maintenance of the common areas, and to comply with other obligations under the Conditions, Covenants & Restrictions (CC&Rs).

In return, the condominium or homeowners association (HOA) may make an affirmative covenant to keep the common areas in a clean, safe, and well-maintained condition.

ii. *Negative covenants*, also known as ***restrictive covenants*,** restrict or limit in some way an owner's use of his or her property. Using the example of a homeowners association, many such associations prohibit/restrict property owners from using certain colors when painting the exteriors of their homes.

Like easements and profits, covenants run with the land if either the burden or benefit of the covenant is binding on future owners of the property.

Covenant
a formal promise in a contract or deed, and often relating to real property.

Affirmative Covenant
a formal promise by the covenantor to take some specific action, or do some specific thing.

Covenantor
the person or entity making a formal promise in a contract or deed.

Covenantee
the person or entity to whom a covenant or formal promise is made in a contract or deed.

Negative Covenant
prohibits or restricts an owner's use of his property; it is also called a restrictive covenant.

b. Covenants Are Common in Common Interest Communities

Covenants have become commonplace as more and more ***common interest communities*** (CIC) have been built throughout the country. Depending on certain legal characteristics, these communities may be called homeowners associations, condominiums, cooperatives, and even some time-share arrangements.

Regardless of the particular type of common interest community, one of the principal motivations for purchasing a home in such a community is the buyer-owner's desire to increase, or at least maintain, the value of the residential property. One important method of accomplishing this goal is by having property owners agree to certain conditions—more accurately, ***covenants***—by which they are bound when they purchase homes in the common interest community. These covenants, and other conditions and obligations of ownership, are embodied in a document

---

[4]Students sometimes ask: If our law has descended from English common law, why are there so many French legal terms in use, such as *profit à prendre* and life estate *pur autre vie.*

It is a good question, and the answer is … the Norman Conquest, which occurred in the year 1066. Normandy is in northwestern France, just across the English Channel from England. When William the Conqueror, Duke of Normandy, defeated the English troops at the Battle of Hastings in 1066, English culture and language were forever transformed. Among other things, this transformation included the importation of many French words and terms into the English language and English common law, from which much of our jurisprudence descends.

known as a Declaration of Covenants, Conditions & Restrictions, often shortened to the *Declaration*, or *CC&Rs*.

Because common interest communities are *quasi-governmental* in nature, the Covenants, Conditions & Restrictions (CC&Rs) may impose restrictions on virtually every aspect of community living. However, since covenants restrict the use of one's "castle," many courts have held that covenants, to be enforceable, must be *reasonable*. Some of the more common covenants found in common interest communities concern the following:

    i.   The amount and frequency of dues payments,

   ii.   Fines and other penalties for infractions of the rules,

  iii.   Residential color schemes,

   iv.   Architectural styles,

    v.   Landscaping and types of plantings permitted,

   vi.   Whether and what type of fences are allowed,

  vii.   The types of pets permitted (and even the size and weight of the pets),

 viii.   Whether and how frequently a residence can be rented out to non-residents,

   ix.   Restrictions on the number and types of vehicles and parking arrangements,

    x.   What you may or may not have on your patio or balcony (BBQs, laundry, or carpeting, for example),

   xi.   The size and type of signs, flags, or other symbols that may be posted in or on one's property, and

  xii.   Just about anything else you can imagine.

While this regimen may seem oppressive to some, for others it provides a sense of security and a feeling of control over one's community and property value.

When a piece of property is developed for residential purposes, the developer will seek to maximize profit. In doing so, the developer may determine that the property is best suited as a condominium property, a homeowners association, or some other type of common interest community. Regardless of which type of development is selected, the developer will have an attorney draft appropriate CC&Rs for the future governance of the property by the homeowners. It can be stated with absolute certainty that without the CC&Rs, common interest communities could not exist. It is vitally important that the CC&Rs then be *recorded* or *registered* at the office of the Register of Deeds for the county where the residential community is located.

Recordation is essential because it provides notice to future buyers of the lots or homes in the development exactly what is required of them. If the Declaration requires homeowners to pay monthly dues, and the Declaration has been recorded, future purchasers of residences in the condominium or association cannot claim that they were unaware of their obligation to pay monthly dues. On the other hand—and there are actually far too many cases like this—if the Declaration has not been properly recorded, then home buyers will not be bound by the conditions, covenants, and restrictions found in the Declaration; such a scenario would doom the common interest community.

You are probably already aware that notice is a very important concept in the law. This is especially true in the law of real property. There are two basic types of notice:

    i.   *Actual notice* is notice given directly to, or received personally by, a person, including entities such as corporations, LLCs, and partnerships;

   ii.   *Constructive notice* arises by presumption of law from the existence of certain facts and circumstances that a party had a duty to take notice of, such as a registered deed.[5]

---

[5]Black's Law Dictionary, 9th Ed.

When a prospective purchaser is thinking of buying a property in a condominium or homeowners association, the selling broker, or perhaps the property management company, may provide the prospective purchaser with a copy of the Declaration of Covenants, Conditions & Restrictions. This is an example of **actual notice** being given to the buyer.

However, if a prospective purchaser is not given a copy of the CC&Rs, the purchaser will be deemed by a court of law to have received **constructive notice** of the CC&Rs, assuming that they have been recorded at the office of the Register of Deeds in the county where the residential community is situated. In other words, the law will impose a duty on a prospective buyer to investigate the possible existence of CC&Rs or any other recorded restrictions on the property to be purchased. This investigation is conducted in the files of the county's Register of Deeds.

B. *Public* Restrictions on Land

We have just looked at some of the burdens and benefits that can run with the land through three types of servitudes: easements, profits, and covenants. These servitudes are created and attached to real property by *private* persons or entities.

Now we will turn our attention to burdens and obligations that are placed on property by governmental agencies or entities. From the mid-1930s through the 1970s, our nation witnessed the ascendance of individual, personal and civil rights, while the importance of property rights experienced a period of relative decline, at least as far as constitutional law was concerned. However, from the mid-1980s forward, landowners and the courts have more jealously guarded, asserted, and sought to protect rights in real property. This effort received support from certain decisions from the United States Supreme Court under Chief Justice William Rehnquist.

In an earlier chapter, we noted that government taxes both real and personal property. In the case of real property, government—be it federal, state, or local—places certain limits on a property owner's incorporeal "bundle of rights," such as the right to possess, use, mortgage, and lease real property. The point is that property rights, and even individual rights such as freedom of speech, are not absolute. In the case of property, government may not only tax and regulate its use, but may even take possession of it, regardless of the owner's wishes.

1. THE TAKINGS CLAUSE OF THE FIFTH AMENDMENT

Before we examine the topic of zoning regulations in the next section, we must first lay the groundwork with a brief look at the **Takings Clause** that is found in the Fifth Amendment to the federal Constitution.

The United States Constitution was ratified in 1789. The Bill of Rights, consisting of the first ten amendments, was ratified and became part of the Constitution on December 15, 1791. The amendment of most interest and importance to our present discussion is the Fifth Amendment. It is interesting that all of the Fifth Amendment's clauses except the last—the Takings Clause—deal with criminal matters. The **Fifth Amendment** reads in its entirety:

> No person shall be held to answer for a capital, or otherwise infamous crime, unless on a presentment or indictment of a Grand Jury, except in cases arising in the land or naval forces, or in the Militia, when in actual service in time of War or public danger; nor shall any person be subject

Takings Clause
a protection found in the Fifth Amendment, and almost all state constitutions, that commands government to pay just compensation when it takes an individual's property for a public use.

for the same offense to be twice put in jeopardy of life or limb; nor shall be compelled in any criminal case to be a witness against himself, nor be deprived of life, liberty, or property, without due process of law; *nor shall private property be taken for public use, without just compensation.*

As you can see, the **Takings Clause** requires that if government takes one's private property for a ***public use***, then the owner of that property must be paid "just compensation." The Takings Clause seems reasonably clear, yet there has been a great deal of litigation concerning the *applied* meaning of those 12 words. Everyone reading this text arrived in class by way of a public road. In all likelihood, the land for that roadway was previously owned by a private individual, who was compelled to sell that property to the government for a "public use," that is, a public road.[6]

The power of a governmental entity to take private land for a public use under the Fifth Amendment is known as ***eminent domain***. The legal process by which the land is taken is called ***condemnation***.[7]

As we have previously observed, there is a fundamental tension between an individual's ***liberty*** and ***property rights***, and the right of the government to exercise its ***police powers*** for the public's health, safety, morals, and general welfare. As to real property, the primary method by which government asserts its police power to protect the public's health and safety is through the process of zoning.

2. ZONING

Zoning law is usually made at the county or town level of government. The authority for a county, city, or town to enact zoning regulations and ordinances comes from the state. The state then ***delegates its police powers*** to protect the public's health and safety in these purely local land-use matters to the local governments, which are best able to determine the needs of their localities, and most appropriate regulatory schemes for their residents.

Zoning is:

> *The division of a city or town by legislative regulation into* districts *and the prescription and application in each district of regulations having to do with the structural and architectural design of buildings and of regulations prescribing the* use *to which buildings within designated districts may be put. Division of land into zones, and within those zones, the regulation of both the nature of land usage and the physical dimensions of uses including height, setbacks, and minimum area.*[8]

In the mid to late 1800s, due mostly to the Industrial Revolution, there was a tremendous migration in the United States from the farms to urban areas, where

---

[6]The Bill of Rights, including the Fifth Amendment, originally applied as a check only against the power of the *federal* government. However, in 1868 in the wake of the Civil War, the Fourteenth Amendment was ratified and served to check the power of *state* governments. Through what is known as the **Incorporation Doctrine**, the Supreme Court has held that most of the protections found in the federal Constitution's Bill of Rights, including those in the Fifth Amendment, are now applicable against the states. For our purposes, the significance of the Incorporation Doctrine is that the Fifth Amendment's Takings Clause now protects individuals from takings by a state government, as well as the federal government.

[7]We will discuss eminent domain and condemnation in detail in a later chapter.

[8]BLACK'S LAW DICTIONARY, 6th Ed., p. 1618, citing *Cheyenne Airport Board v. Rogers, Wyo.*, 707 P. 2d 717, 726 (emphasis added).

vast industrial facilities were being built, and employers were looking for labor to work in their plants and factories. At the same time, there was also a tremendous inflow of millions of people from Europe, who migrated mainly to the major cities of the northeastern United States.

As population **density** increased in these urban areas, residents found themselves living almost on top of one another in incredibly cramped tenements, and next to noisy plants and smoke-belching factories. Local governments soon realized that chaotic, haphazard, and explosive population growth was destroying the quality of life for new and existing residents of the cities. Not surprisingly, New York City, in 1916, became the first municipality in the United States to enact a systematic zoning plan. Many other cities and towns quickly followed suit.

Examples of different types of **zoning districts** include single-family residential, multifamily residential, institutional, commercial, and industrial. Within each category are subcategories, for example, a single-family residential zoning district might include **subdistricts** based upon the square footage of the residence. One subdistrict might require that any home built within its boundaries must be a minimum of 3,000 square feet; another subdistrict may require that any home built within its boundaries must be a minimum of 2,000 square feet, etc.

The zoning subdistricts tend to sort residential communities by property values because they restrict houses being built in the subdistrict by square footage and lot size. The square footage of a house, and the size of the lot on which it sets, are highly correlated to its fair market value. So, a subdistrict where houses must be built on lots of at least three acres and have a livable area of at least 3,000 square feet will, generally speaking, have higher fair market values than a subdistrict in the same city where the minimum lot size is ½ acre and the houses must contain at least 1,500 square feet.

From the example in the previous paragraph, you can see that zoning districts maintain and enhance **property values**, especially in higher-priced neighborhoods. But it is equally true that zoning excludes classes of people who cannot afford to purchase property in these more expensive areas. In that regard, it has sometimes been alleged that residential zoning laws have been implemented for the sole purpose of segregating residents on the basis of race or ethnicity, and the subject of fair housing is one that we examine elsewhere in the text.

In addition to minimum square footage and lot size requirements, residential zoning ordinances may impose **height** limitations and **setback requirements**. The latter requires that a residence be "setback" a certain number of feet from the street or your neighbors' property lines. Zoning ordinances may even dictate the architectural style that is allowed in a particular neighborhood. This is especially in the many cities and towns across the United States that are home to **historic districts**, also known as **heritage districts**.

3. CONSTITUTIONAL ISSUES RELATED TO ZONING

By way of introduction, let us begin this discussion with a very important point. As you have seen, when a property is taken by government for a public use, the landowner must receive just compensation from the government for the taking; this is required by the Fifth Amendment. Put succinctly, a government agency must pay "just compensation" when it **takes** property.

Setback Requirement
a zoning restriction that requires that a structure be built at some minimum distance from a street or a neighbor's property line.

Historic/Heritage District
sections or neighborhoods in a city or town where, for historic or architectural reasons, zoning regulations require the preservation of the exteriors of the local buildings, and may prohibit their demolition.

On the other hand, when government *merely regulates* the use of property pursuant to its police powers (for the public health safety, morals and general welfare), then it is *not obligated to pay* a landowner for any diminution in the property's value resulting from the regulation. However, as we will see later, a police power regulation of property may be so burdensom that it effectively constitutes a taking for which compensation must be paid to the landowner.

As zoning became more prevalent, its constitutionality was bound to be challenged. Where zoning regulations and the Takings Clause meet, the constitutional issue is whether the zoning regulation has become so restrictive and burdensome on the landowner that a taking has occurred, and if so, the government "taking" the property must pay just compensation to the landowner. Consider the following scenario based on an actual case:

JUST A ZONING REGULATION, OR AN UNCONSTITUTIONAL TAKING?

You own a piece of prime land consisting of 68 acres that lies directly in the path of a rapidly growing urban area. You intend to develop the property for industrial use, and as such, the land would have a value of approximately $10,000 per acre, or $680,000.

However, your local government has recently enacted a comprehensive zoning plan. As a result, your property has been zoned for residential use, rather than industrial use. Under the residential zoning plan, the appraised value of your now-residential acreage is $2,500 per acre. This constitutes a "paper loss" of $7,500 per acre ($10,000 − $2,500 = $7,500). When multiplied by 68 acres, your paper loss is $510,000.

This case actually made its way to the United States Supreme Court in 1926, and so the $510,000 decrease in the value of your property then would be the equivalent of about $13–$15 million today.

Issue: Does a city's zoning ordinance that *significantly* reduces the value of one's real property (75% in this case) constitute a "taking" for a public use in violation of the Fifth Amendment?

The "public use" in question here would be the general betterment of the public's health, safety, and welfare that presumably flows from zoning laws, which are enacted pursuant to the government's police powers.

As is often the case, the clash here is between the government's right to enact laws for the public's benefit, by authority of its *police powers*, versus an individual's *right to use* property as he or she pleases.

To see how the Supreme Court ruled on these facts, visit the decision of *Village of Euclid v. Ambler Realty Co.*, 272 U.S. 365 (1926).

In the case of *Village of Euclid v. Ambler Realty Co.*, summarized above, the Supreme Court decided that even though Ambler Realty had lost hundreds of thousands of dollars in land value, the Village of Euclid's zoning regulations did not violate the Takings Clause of the Fifth Amendment, and therefore, the Village did *not* have to pay any compensation to the property owner.

In light of the Supreme Court's holding in *Village of Euclid*, we might ask whether zoning regulations can ever be so restrictive as to constitute a *taking* in violation of the Fifth Amendment. The answer is yes, but only rarely has the Supreme Court found a land-use regulation so oppressive and restrictive of an owner's use of property that it is a *de facto* taking. One such case is *Lucas v. South Carolina Coastal Council*, 505 U.S. 1003 (1992), summarized on the next page:

SUMMARY OF LUCAS V. SOUTH CAROLINA COASTAL COUNCIL

David Lucas was a developer who purchased two residential building lots for a total of almost $1 million on the Isle of Palms, off the coast of Charleston, South Carolina. After buying the lots, but before building on them, South Carolina enacted the Beachfront Management Act (technically, not a zoning ordinance, but a law regulating land use).

That law prohibited building in certain coastal areas, including the two lots that had been purchased by Lucas. The State of South Carolina refused to compensate Lucas, claiming that it had not **taken** the developer's property.

Lucas sued the State, and eventually the case was heard by the United States Supreme Court. The Court decided that the Beachfront Management Act had effectively deprived Lucas of **all economically beneficial use** of his land, and was, therefore, a taking in violation of the Fifth Amendment, and for which Mr. Lucas must be paid "just compensation" by the State of South Carolina.

The *Lucas* case illustrates how difficult it is for a landowner to prevail on a takings case based on a zoning restriction. That is because it is rare indeed that a zoning regulation would deprive an owner of "*all* economically beneficial use" of his property, but that was the requirement laid down by the Supreme Court in Lucas, and one that Mr. Lucas was able to meet. Of course, when the state of South Carolina paid Mr. Lucas just compensation for the two lots,, it took title to the lots.

4. EXCEPTIONS TO ZONING LAWS

By now, you are well aware that there are almost always exceptions to most every body of law, and even exceptions to the exceptions. That truism is no different when it comes to zoning regulations. There are three major exceptions to zoning restrictions.

a. Non-Conforming Use

A non-conforming use is one that does not comply with present zoning classification but that existed lawfully prior to the enactment of the current zoning provision. Such a use is sometimes said to be **grandfathered**.

Non-conforming uses arise when areas are in a state of transition. As towns grow, streets in once-quiet residential neighborhoods may experience large increases in traffic volume. To encourage commercial activity (and increase sales and property tax revenue), the local planning department or zoning board may re-zone the properties fronting the now-busy thoroughfares, changing the zoning classification from residential to an office or commercial use.

Obviously it would be unfair (and unconstitutional) to make the people living in those houses move out to make way for commercial development, or to make them turn their homes into businesses. And so the property owners are free to keep living in their homes on property that is now zoned commercial, that is, they are grandfathered.

Sooner or later, most if not all of the homeowners will sell to a developer who is willing to pay a premium price for property that is now zoned commercial. When that happens, the homes will be torn down and a commercial property built in what was once a quiet residential neighborhood. And so it goes.

b. Variances

The second exception that a property owner may be allowed under an existing zoning plan is a variance. This exception allows a builder or property owner to deviate from the normal building or site requirements, when constructing a new structure, or adding onto an existing structure. The purpose of a variance is to **prevent undue hardship** for the builder/owner.

For example, the planning board may allow a variance from the normal requirements regarding a structure's size, height, construction material, setback, or location on the property. However, the new structure's use must conform to the current zoning classification in that district. In other words, if the property on which the new structure is to be built is zoned residential, the new structure must be used as a residence.

c. Conditional Use Permit

The third category of exceptions to the existing zoning plan is a conditional use. A conditional use of real property is one that does not strictly comply with an area's zoning classification, but which is not necessarily incompatible with that classification either.

Take the example of an area that is zoned residential. The owner of a 10-acre tract of land in that particular area wants to donate the acreage to his church for the purpose of constructing a new church building on his property. It should be noted that churches and schools are sometimes categorized for zoning purposes as **institutional uses**, which is obviously different from a residential use. While the proposed church would not be in strict compliance with the current zoning requirements, it is very likely that the planning board would nevertheless allow that use for the benefit of the community. However, such an exception would undoubtedly come with "strings attached."

In allowing for the construction of a church on the 10 acres, the planning board would impose conditions (thus, the "*conditional* use permit") to minimize any negative impact that the new church would have upon the neighborhood. Such conditions might include:

i. Requiring the church to have a minimum and/or maximum number of parking spaces,
ii. A buffer zone of trees or large shrubs between the church's property and the neighboring properties,
iii. Limiting the use to worship services only, and not allowing ancillary uses on the site, such as a day care center, or
iv. Requiring the presence of police officers for traffic control before, during and after church services.

Zoning has made for a better quality of life, particularly in urban areas, but at the expense of restricting certain uses of one's property. To the extent that some zoning restrictions can sometimes be harsh and burdensome, that burden may be eased by the three major exceptions to zoning classifications: non-conforming uses (grandfathering), variances, and conditional use permits.

EXHIBIT 6-5 Restrictive Covenant—Conditional Use Permit

Page_____of_____

After recording return to:

_____

_____

_____

Restrictive Covenant
Conditional Use Permit

The undersigned, being the record owners of all of the real property described as follows: _____
_____ and further identified by "Exhibit A" attached hereto, do hereby make the following restrictive covenant(s) for the above-described real property, specifying that the covenant(s) shall run with the land and shall be binding on all persons claiming under such land, and that these restrictions shall be for the benefit of and limitation on all future owners of said real property.

In consideration of approval by Klamath County, Oregon of a land use permit to construct a single family dwelling on property designated by the Klamath County Assessor's Office as Tax Lot _____ in Township _____ South, Range _____ East, Section _____, the following restrictive covenant(s) hereafter bind the subject property:

> "Declarant and Declarant's heirs, legal representatives, assigns, and lessees hereby recognize(s) the rights of adjacent and nearby landowners to conduct farm and forest operations consistent with accepted farming practices and Forest Practices Act, ORS 30,090 and Rules for uses authorized by this Code."

This covenant shall not be modified or terminated except by the express written consent of the owners of the land at the time, and the Klamath County Community Development Department, as hereafter provided.

KLAMATH COUNTY, a political subdivision of the State of Oregon, shall be considered a party to this covenant and shall have the right, if it so desires, to enforce any or all of the covenant(s) contained herein by judicial or administrative proceeding. This covenant is made pursuant to the provisions of the Klamath County Land Development Code.

Dated this _____ day of _____, 20____.

_____   _____
Record Owner   Record Owner

STATE OF OREGON   )
) ss.
County of Klamath   )

Personally appeared the above names _____ and acknowledged the foregoing instrument to be his/her voluntary act and deed before me this_____day of_____, 20____.

By _____.

_____
Notary Public for State of Oregon
My Commission Expires:

Note: A copy of the recorded instrument must be returned to Community Development before permits can be issued.
\\mady\cdd\shared\PLANNING\Planning Forms\Covenant-CUP.doc

CHAPTER SUMMARY

This chapter covers the law of *servitudes*, which are restrictions on land imposed by private parties, rather than by government. One of the defining characteristics of a servitude is that it runs with the land, meaning that it is binding on successive owners of the land. There are three basic types of servitudes: *easements* ("appurtenant" and "in gross"), *profits*, and *covenants* (affirmative and negative/restrictive).

An easement appurtenant almost always involves two adjoining parcels of land. The parcel of land that benefits as a result of the easement is the *dominant estate*. The parcel of land that is burdened by the easement is the *servient estate*. Easements in gross involve only one parcel of land, the burdened parcel, and the benefit flows to a person or entity, such as a utility company.

Easements may be created expressly (orally or written), impliedly, by necessity, or by prescription. Easements may be terminated by agreement, expiration, merger, or abandonment.

Profits are a type of servitude that could be described as "easements plus." That is, in addition to an easement to enter the land of another, the holder of a profit also has the right to take from the property minerals, timber, wild animals, or some other natural resource connected with the land.

Covenants are promises relating to real property. They are commonly found in recorded Declarations of Conditions, Covenants & Restrictions (CC&Rs), which are widely used to govern property owners in common interest communities such as condominiums, cooperatives, homeowners associations, and other types of planned communities.

Covenants may be *affirmative*, such as a requirement that homeowners pay association maintenance dues; or covenants may be *negative* or *restrictive* such as a prohibition on certain types of architecture, landscaping, color schemes, and so on. CC&Rs must be *recorded* at the office of the Register of Deeds in order to provide prospective homebuyers *notice* of the covenants. Notice may be either *actual* or *constructive*.

The most common type of public restrictions on land use is *zoning* regulation, which first became common in the early twentieth century. The *Takings Clause* of the Fifth Amendment to the United States Constitution prohibits the taking of private land for public use without just compensation.

The power of a governmental entity to take private land for a public use is known as *eminent domain*; the legal process by which the land is taken is called *condemnation*.

Zoning laws are enacted pursuant to a state's *police power* to provide for the public's safety, health, morals, and general welfare. A state delegates its police power regarding zoning matters to a county, city, or town, to be tailored to a municipality's specific needs. The ordinances are designed to promote efficient use of the land, while avoiding incompatible uses in a given locale.

There are three major exceptions to zoning regulations. The first is the *nonconforming use* which allows existing uses to be "*grandfathered*" under the current zoning classification.

The second major exception to zoning regulations is a *variance*, which is granted by a zoning board to prevent an undue hardship for the property owner. The variance allows for some modification of a proposed building's height, square footage, setback, or some other requirement relevant to that zoning district. However, the proposed structure's use must conform to the current zoning classification in that district.

The third major exception to zoning regulations is the *conditional use permit*, which allows a use that may not comply with an area's zoning classification, but which is not necessarily incompatible with that classification either, for example, allowing the construction of a church in an area zoned for residential use.

CONCEPT REVIEW AND REINFORCEMENT

KEY **TERMS**

Actual Notice	Covenant	Easement by Necessity
Affirmative Covenant	Covenantee	Easement by Prescription
CC&Rs	Covenantor	Easement in Gross
Condemnation	Dominant Estate	Eminent Domain
Conditional Use	Easement	Express Easement
Constructive Notice	Easement Appurtenant	Fifth Amendment

Heritage District	Police Powers	Servitude
Historic District	Profit	Setback Requirement
Implied Easement	Recording	Takings Clause
Landlocked	Register of Deeds	Termination of Easement
Negative Covenant	Runs with the Land	Variance
Non-conforming Use	Servient Estate	Zoning

CONCEPT **REVIEW** QUESTIONS

1. What is a servitude? What does it mean that a servitude "runs with the land"? How does a court know if the servitude runs with the land?

2. What are the three types of servitudes? What is the difference between an easement and a profit?

3. What is the difference between an easement appurtenant and an easement in gross?

4. In the context of easements, what is the difference between a dominant estate and a servient estate? Which estate benefits from the easement, and which estate is burdened by the easement.

5. Why are profits sometimes call "easements plus"? Being a type of servitude, would a profit run with the land?

6. What is the type of servitude that is of the most significance in common interest communities? Why? Why is it important that this specific type of servitude be recorded with the Register of Deeds?

7. What types of activities do covenants—both affirmative and negative/restrictive—control in common interest communities?

8. What is the most common type of public control restricting the use of real property? By what authority or power does government presume to issue such restrictions relating to real property?

9. What is the power that a government has to take private property for public use? How is that power related to the Fifth Amendment to the United States Constitution? What is the legal process by which private property is taken for public use?

10. How many major types of exceptions are there to zoning regulations, and what are they?

11. What is the nickname or slang term sometimes associated with a non-conforming use? Explain how the slang term relates to the concept of a non-conforming use.

12. What is a variance, and what characteristics of a parcel or proposed structure might a zoning committee consider when deciding whether to grant a variance?

13. What is a conditional use? In granting a conditional use permit, what conditions might a zoning committee impose on the proposed use of the property?

14. You know that the Statute of Frauds requires certain kinds of contracts to be in writing. However, we noted in this chapter that easements may be created by implication (rather than being written).

    What public policy reasons might there be for making an exception to the Statute of Frauds when easements have not been memorialized in a writing? Do you think that an exception for unwritten easements should be allowed?

ETHICS

STAR **STRUCK**!

Samantha is a paralegal in a mid-size law firm in a fairly small, sleepy town. One of the town's favorite sons is an actor who went off to Hollywood and became famous almost overnight starring as the teenage vampire-son in a family of vampires.

The actor has returned to his hometown for a visit and to purchase a home for his mother. The actor has contacted the law firm where Samantha works for assistance with the transaction. The actor stops by the law firm and meets with two of the lawyers; Samantha, who is thrilled that she is meeting the star of her favorite television show, attends the meeting with the actor and lawyers to take notes. The actor informs everyone present that he has his eye on a particular property for his mother, but wants to keep that confidential

for fear that the purchase price might increase dramatically if it is learned that he will be the buyer.

Later that evening, Samantha and a friend are having dinner at a restaurant. Samantha swears her friend to secrecy, and then tells her friend about the meeting with the actor in her law office earlier that day. Two days later, the local newspaper carries a story that the actor has returned to town to purchase a property for his mother; the apparent source of the story is Samantha's friend.

After reading the story, the actor is livid and it turns out that he did have to pay considerably more than the fair market value for the property that he purchased for his mother. The seller of the house later bragged: "When I read the story that the vampire guy had come back to town to buy a house for his mother, I knew I could squeeze a little extra blood out of him, ha ha."

Has Samantha violated an ethical duty of confidentiality by sharing client information with her friend, and as a result, the rest of the town?

Has Samantha's law firm violated an ethical duty of confidentiality to the actor-client because of Samantha's actions?

Does the actor have any sort of a claim against Samantha and/or her law firm, and if so, for what claim or claims? What are the actor's damages?

BUILDING YOUR PROFESSIONAL SKILLS

CRITICAL THINKING **EXERCISES**

1. You have lost the deed to your home, and go to the office of the Register of Deeds in the county where the property is located in order to obtain a copy. Upon obtaining a copy of the deed, you notice that the property description references a plat map. You ask to see a copy of a plat map, locate your residential lot on the plat, and notice that there are some easements running across your land, including water and sewer easements and utility easements.

   The water and sewer easements are held by the city, obviously a governmental entity. But the utility easement is held by Lotsa Volts Power Company, which is clearly not a governmental entity. You have never received any payment from Lotsa Volts for the easement over your property. Shouldn't they have to pay you or move their power lines? What type of easement is this, if it is, in fact, an easement? And by what authority does Lotsa Volts presume to run high power lines across your property?

2. Last year Pat purchased a residence in a homeowners association, which had duly recorded its CC&Rs several years ago when the property was first developed. One of the conditions in the CC&Rs states that "any flag, sign, insignia, or symbol displayed on an owner's property shall not exceed four square feet."

   In the week before July 4, Pat displays a large American flag on her front yard, which measures $4' \times 5'$, or 20 square feet, five times the size permitted under the CC&Rs. The president of the HOA informs Pat that she will have to remove the flag, or be fined $100 per day by the homeowners association. Pat replies: "I never even read the CC&Rs and if you interfere with my right of right of free speech I'll sue the association for $1 million."

   What are the competing interests in this scenario? Does it matter that Pat has not read the CC&Rs, and if not, why not? Does it make any difference that Pat is displaying the American flag rather than, for example, a For Sale sign of the same size? What are the ramifications if the association does not try to enforce this particular condition of the CC&Rs? Is there a federal law that controls in this particular case involving the display of the Stars and Stripes?

3. Tidal lands and waters are usually owned by the state under the public trust doctrine, to be used for the public's recreation and enjoyment. But consider the situation where long stretches of privately owned lots and homes abut and run parallel to the public beach.

   Can one or more of the beachfront owners be compelled to provide public access, that is, a public easement, to the beach over their private properties? The homeowners might argue that there is public access to the beach available, say, 15 blocks to the north. Beachgoers would argue that a 30-block round-trip with folding chairs, beach balls, and children in tow makes the stretch of beach in question effectively inaccessible to the public.

   Discuss the pros and cons of forcing (through eminent domain) one or more of the private land owners to convey an easement over their private property so that the public can more easily access that stretch of beach. For insight, review the following cases:

   Matthews v. Bay Head Improvement Association, 95 N.J. 306, 471 A.2d 355 (1984), and

   City of Malibu v. California Coastal Com., 128 Cal. App. 4th 897 (this case involves, in part, billionaire entertainment executive David Geffen and his home on Malibu Beach).

4. The Tahoe Regional Planning Agency was created for the purpose of monitoring growth and minimizing the environmental impact of development on both the California and Nevada sides of Lake Tahoe. In order to study growth patterns and devise recommendations concerning future growth, a moratorium on construction was enacted which prevented property owners from building on their lots for a period of 32 months.

   Due to the building moratorium, several landowners sued, claiming that the moratorium was an uncompensated taking in violation of the Takings Clause found in the Fifth Amendment of the United States Constitution.

   Discuss the merits of the moratorium from the Planning Agency's standpoint, and then discuss the merits of the land owners' argument that they should be compensated because they were deprived of the use of their properties for almost three years.

You might want to review the actual case that this question is based on, that is, *Tahoe-Sierra Pres. Council v. Tahoe Reg'l Planning Agency*, 535 U.S. 302 (2002).

5. A suburban subdivision is governed by several covenants, one of which reads:

> *No lot shall ever be used for any purpose other than <u>single-family residence purposes</u>. No dwelling house located thereon shall ever be used for other than <u>single-family residence purposes</u>, nor shall any outbuildings or structure located thereon be used in a manner other than incidental to such <u>family residence purposes</u>.*

Residents in the subdivision noticed that one house seems to be drawing significantly more traffic than in the past, and soon discover that the house has been leased to four unrelated individuals with AIDS, each of whom required some in-home care. The neighbors filed an injunction against the group home, claiming that the term "single-family residence" in the restrictive covenant does not include group homes such as the house in which the four unrelated people live.

Without revealing whether the language below comes from the majority opinion or a dissent, discuss its utility in analyzing the concept of a "single-family residence," and thereby framing the argument for, or against, enforcement of the restrictive covenant (previously quoted above):

> *It is undisputed that the group home is designed to provide the four individuals who live in the house with a <u>traditional family structure</u>, setting, and atmosphere, and that the individuals who reside there use the home much as would any family with a disabled family member. The four residents <u>share communal meals</u>. They <u>provide support</u> for each other socially, emotionally, and financially. They also receive spiritual guidance together from religious leaders who visit them on Tuesday evenings.*

What is the significance of the underlined language? Should the court adopt a broad definition of the term "single family" to encompass group living arrangements described above? To what extent, if any, should it matter to the court that the four unrelated occupants suffer from AIDS? If the court finds in favor of the four roommates, could the decision be extended to other unrelated individuals living in "group homes," such as sororities or fraternities?

After you have discussed these questions, you might want to read the case of *Hill v. Community of Damien of Molokai*, 121 N.M. 353, 911 P.2d 861(1996).

Just as an aside, consider the situation where an ordinance allows unrelated individuals with disabilities such as AIDS to live together in a group home environment. But the same ordinance forbids more than six fraternity brothers or sorority sisters from living in group homes.

Do you think that such an ordinance would survive constitutional scrutiny? Specifically, would the ordinance survive a fraternity's equal protection challenge pursuant to the Fourteenth Amendment to the United States Constitution?

Here is a hint: For there to be an equal protection violation, the individual or group discriminated against (in this case, the frats' and sororities' members) must be "similarly situated" to the individual or group favored by the legislation (in this case, the HIV house mates). Are those two groups "similarly situated"? How are they alike, and how are they different?

6. A Tale of Two Cities:

Houston, Texas, and Portland, Oregon, are two of the most beautiful and vibrant cities in the United States. However, they are at opposite ends of the spectrum when it comes to land-use controls. Houston is the largest city in America without a comprehensive zoning plan, although private land transactions usually contain restrictive covenants, which serve, to a certain extent, as substitutes for zoning regulations.

Portland, on the other hand, pursuant to Oregon state law, has adopted a comprehensive and extensive set of land-use controls, including a concept called Urban Growth Boundaries (the urban growth boundaries promote development within the boundary; that is, within the metro area, while keeping the areas outside the boundaries relatively undeveloped).

Discuss the public policies that underlie each of the above land-use models. What are the consequences, good and bad, on individual property owners and the community at large, of relatively unrestricted development that one might see in Houston?

What are the consequences, good and bad, on individual property owners and the community at large, of relatively restricted development that one might see in Portland? Let's assume that you own several acres of land outside of the Urban Growth Boundary that is zoned strictly for agricultural use, and would like to develop a large apartment project on the property. If prohibited from doing so by the comprehensive land use statutes, would you be able to prevail on a claim that the State has taken your property without just compensation? Explain the reasons for your answer, and cite any case law from this chapter that you think might be relevant to your answer.

RESEARCH ON THE **WEB**

1. In Critical Thinking Exercise # 1, you probably discovered that Lotsa Volts Power Company has an easement across your property for the construction and maintenance of its power lines. Since utility providers are not typically governmental agencies, in your state are they entitled to exercise the power of eminent domain for the purpose of obtaining easements, or an outright taking of private property? You might begin by checking your state's statutory code, as opposed to case law. Why?

2. In Critical Thinking Exercise # 2, Pat flew a rather large American flag on her property, despite a condition in the CC&Rs prohibiting such. You may, or may not, be surprised to learn that the issue of flying the American flag in violation of CC&Rs has been raised fairly often over the years since the inception of common interest communities. On the Web, try and determine if Congress has taken any action to resolve these disputes.

3. In the case of *Hill v. Community of Damien of Molokai* cited and discussed in the previous section, the four unrelated roommates suffered from AIDS, which is defined as a disability under the Americans with Disabilities Act (ADA).

   Find the ADA on the Web to learn what other physical and/or mental disorders are covered by the word "disability," and the significance of the term "reasonable accommodation" as relates to one with a disability. Also, find the relevant federal and state housing laws to learn how they address the disability issue as it relates to the rental or purchase of residential real property.

4. Hundreds, if not thousands, of municipalities and counties now post their zoning ordinances and regulations online. Check to see if your city, town or county has posted its zoning code.

   If so, ascertain the specifics for the various categories and subcategories relating to residential development, such as limits on square footage, the size of a structure's "footprint," maximum and minimum number of bedrooms and/or bathrooms, and setback requirements.

BUILDING YOUR PROFESSIONAL **PORTFOLIO**

1. In Critical Thinking Exercise # 5, we looked at the case of *Hill v. Community of Damien of Molokai*. The Supreme Court of New Mexico held that the covenant that defined a single-family residence encompassed the four unrelated individuals in a group home, who were suffering from AIDS.

   Draft a zoning ordinance for a residential neighborhood that would allow for the presence of group homes for unrelated persons suffering from disabilities, but that would also prohibit the presence of unrelated persons, such as in sororities or fraternities.

2. Common interest communities often have covenants that govern the types of pets that homeowners may have living in their units, and sometimes, may limit the size and/or weight. Often these limitations are actually part of the CC&Rs. More commonly, however, the CC&Rs authorize the association's board of directors to craft the specifics of limitations and restrictions on pets. Your assignment is to draft a reasonable rule that would limit the size of pets to 25 pounds.

   Should the same weight requirement be imposed on both cats and dogs, or should cats have a lower weight limitation, such as 15 pounds? How is the rule to be enforced; that is, is every pet in the community to be weighed on a regular basis, or only when someone complains about a neighbor's pet possibly violating the limit? Should an owner/pet which violates the weight limit be immediately fined, or should they be given a certain grace period by which to comply with the rule?

chapter 7

TRANSFERS OF REAL PROPERTY

LEARNING OBJECTIVES

After reading this chapter, you should understand:

- The four methods by which real property may be voluntarily transferred

- The difference between eminent domain and condemnation, and how they relate to the Takings Clause of the Fifth Amendment

- The elements of a valid contract for the purchase of real property

- The elements of adverse possession

- The difference between judicial foreclosure and nonjudicial foreclosure/power of sale foreclosure

Transfers of Real Property

There are two ways that real property can be transferred by an owner—either voluntarily or involuntarily. A conveyance that is "voluntary" means that the owner is making the conveyance of his or her own volition.

An involuntary transfer is just the opposite. A property owner is either forced to convey the property to another person or entity, or the property is taken by operation of law. That is, the landowner is compelled to convey the property by some entity, such as the government—through eminent domain/condemnation—or by court order, for example, a foreclosure.

A. Voluntary Transfer

1. VOLUNTARY TRANSFER BY SALE

The most common type of voluntary transfer of real property is by sale.[1] In the last several years, sales of *existing* homes—including condominiums and cooperative units—have averaged about 5 million per year. However, sales of *new* homes declined dramatically from about 1.2 million units in 2005 to approximately 340,000 units in 2010.

The construction and sale of new homes are particularly important to the economy because they drive demand for a whole host of building-related goods and services, including concrete, brick, lumber, carpeting, appliances, and all the construction specialists needed to build a home such as carpenters, plumbers, brick and stone masons, and electricians. Of course, there is also a market for new and existing commercial properties such as office buildings, shopping centers, and apartment projects.

a. Contracts for the Sale of Real Property

> **Contract**
> an enforceable agreement between two or more persons to do, or not to do, some act.

Let us review a few of the basic requirements for making a valid contract. On the most basic level, there are really only two elements of a valid, enforceable contract … mutual assent and consideration.

i. First Element of a Valid Contract—Mutual Assent   Mutual assent is sometimes described as the parties coming to a "***meeting of the minds***" regarding the terms and conditions of the specific transaction. To have mutual assent or a meeting of the minds, there must be an ***offer*** by the **offeror,** and an ***acceptance*** by the **offeree.**

> **Offeror**
> the person who makes an offer to another.

> **Offeree**
> the person to whom an offer is made.

Mutual assent implies that the offer is made in ***terms sufficiently definite*** and certain so that there is a meeting of the minds. In other words, the parties must agree to the same thing; if they do not, then no contract has been formed. There are two facets to the element of mutual assent: an offer and an acceptance.[2]

a. Offer

According to the Restatement 2d of Contracts:

> *An offer is the <u>manifestation of willingness</u> to enter into a bargain, so made as to justify another person in understanding that his assent to that bargain is invited and will conclude it.*

---

[1]According to the United States Census Bureau there are approximately 2.5 million deaths in the United States each year. Even if every person who died in a given year owned one piece of real property, which passed to another by will or intestacy, that would still only amount to about one-half of the transfers by sale. Of course, a relatively small percentage of the population owns multiple real properties that could pass at death, and there are also inter-vivos ("between the living") gifts of real property. However, it still seems a reasonable assumption that the majority of voluntary transfers are by sale.

[2]We have stated that there are two elements to an enforceable contract: mutual assent (i.e., offer and acceptance) and consideration. Some contracts instructors prefer to present the elements as offer, acceptance, and consideration. There are still other formulations of the elements, but for simplicity's sake, we prefer mutual assent and consideration.

b. Acceptance

Again, let us rely on the Restatement 2d of Contracts for the definition:

> *Acceptance of an offer is a <u>manifestation of assent</u> to the terms thereof made by the offeree in a manner invited or required by the offer.*

Here is an example of a simple offer and acceptance:

Offer made by the offeror: "*I promise to sell my house to you for $200,000.*"

Acceptance by the offeree: "*I promise to pay you $200,000 to buy your house.*"

Because of the requirements of the **Statute of Frauds**, in an agreement involving real property, the "manifestation of willingness to enter into a bargain" (the offer), and the "manifestation of assent to the terms" (the acceptance), only become enforceable when committed to writing. The writing is usually embodied in an **Offer to Purchase and Contract of Sale**.

ii. Second Element of a Valid Contract—Consideration   One of the more difficult legal concepts to understand in any area of law is consideration. Essentially, consideration involves an exchange. In a **bilateral contract,** there is an exchange of two promises. The first promise is the offer, and it is made by the offeror. The second promise is the acceptance, and this return promise is made by the offeree. The return promise by the offeree must accept the exact terms of the offer for there to be an acceptance of the offer; this is known as the **mirror-image rule.** If the offeree changes any of the terms of the offer, then the offeree has rejected the offer, and made a counteroffer. Here is an example:

Offeror: "*I promise to sell my house to you for $200,000.*"

Offeree: "*I promise to pay you $199,999 to buy your house.*"

The offeree has rejected the offer because the offeree's reply does not exactly mirror the terms of the offer. In addition to rejecting and terminating the original offer, the offeree has made a **counteroffer,** which is a completely new offer. In the process of making a counteroffer, the offeree has switched hats and has now become the offeror.

The examples above are bilateral in nature, meaning that a promise is given by the offeror who seeks a return promise from the offeree. In shorthand, a bilateral contract is "a promise for a promise."

There is another type of contract called a **unilateral contract**. With a unilateral contract, a promise is made by the offeror, that is, the offer. The offeror is not seeking a promise from the offeree, but rather a **performance**, and if the offeree so chooses, he can accept the offer by performing the act sought by the offeror:

Offeror: "I'll pay you $50 if you mow my lawn this afternoon."

Offeree: Says nothing, but accepts the offer by mowing the offeror's lawn this afternoon.

The shorthand way of describing a unilateral contract is that it is "a promise for a performance."

Although the word "promise" is used in the definitions of both an offer and an acceptance, and in describing a unilateral and bilateral contract, it is not necessary

Bilateral Contract
a promise made in exchange for a return promise.

Mirror-Image Rule
for there to be an acceptance of an offer, the offeree may not change, add, or qualify any of the offeror's terms.

Counteroffer
an offeree's new offer that varies one or more terms of the original offer. A counteroffer both rejects and terminates the original offer.

Unilateral Contract
a promise made in exchange for a return performance.

that the word "promise" be actually used in the offer or acceptance. Consider the following offers:

    i. "I *promise* to sell my house to you for $200,000."
   ii. "I *will* sell my house to you for $200,000."

The first statement includes the word "promise," while the second statement does not. In contract law, however, there is no legal difference between the two statements, because both "*manifest a willingness to enter into a bargain*," which, you will recall, is the Restatement's definition of an offer.

Contracts for the sale of real property are almost always bilateral contracts, that is, a promise for a promise: a promise to sell in exchange for a promise to buy.

Why is it important to classify a contract as bilateral or unilateral? The main reason concerns the **remedy** that is available. The lawn mowing example involved a unilateral contract; that is, a promise for a performance. Assume that the offeree had mowed half of the offeror's yard when the offeror says: "I'm withdrawing my offer. Get off my property."

If the offeree sues the offeror, the court would likely award one-half of the originally offered amount of $50, that is, $25. That is because a *unilateral* contract can only be accepted by the offeree's *full and complete performance*. It seems unfair, but the offeror is entitled to terminate her offer of a unilateral contract *at any time before full performance* has been rendered. When she does withdraw her offer halfway through the mowing, she has not breached the "contract" because the offeree had not accepted by fully performing. However, to avoid injustice, the court will make an award in "quantum meruit," that is, "as much as he deserves," or a pro-rata $25.

Alternatively, assume that the contract had been *bilateral*, a promise for a promise, and the exchange went like this:

Offeror: "I'll pay you $50 if you mow my lawn this afternoon."

Offeree: "I accept."

Let's assume that once again, halfway through the offeree's mowing of the lawn, the offeror states: "I'm withdrawing my offer. Get off my property."

In this case of a bilateral contract, the offeror has breached the contract, and if the offeree sues for breach, he will be awarded the full $100, what is known as expectation damages, or the "benefit of the bargain."

How to Determine If Consideration Is Present

Consideration
that which motivates or induces another to enter into a bargain or agreement. Consideration may consist of either a promise, or a performance.

You may find the following four-step analysis helpful in determining whether consideration is present to support either a bilateral (promise for a promise) or unilateral (promise for a performance) contract. For there to be consideration—and thus, a contract—you must receive a "yes" answer to each of the four questions below. Let's make the transaction a simple one based on our example above.

Offeror/Seller: "*I will sell my house to you for $200,000, closing to occur on or before December 31 of this year.*"

Offeree/Buyer: "*I will pay you $200,000 to buy your house, and agree to close on the property on or before December 31 of this year.*"

It is apparent that we have the first element-mutual assent-between the parties, that is, an offer and an acceptance. But do we have the second necessary element, consideration? Here is the four-step analysis. If you do not get an affirmative response to each of the four questions, then there is no consideration, and therefore, no contract.

   1. *Was there a <u>promise by offeror/seller</u>?*
      Answer: Yes, she promised to sell her house on specific terms.

2. *Was there a <u>return promise or performance</u> by the offeree/buyer?*
Answer: Yes, he promised to buy the offeror's house on her specific terms.

3. *Was the offeree's return promise or performance <u>sought by the offeror/seller</u>?*
Answer: Yes, she wanted him to accept her offer.

4. *Was the offeree/buyer's promise or performance <u>given in exchange for</u> the offeror/seller's promise?*
Answer: Yes.

Because we received affirmative answers to each of the four questions, we have consideration from each party that will support the contract. Since there is mutual assent (for example, they both have in mind the same house as the one for sale), the parties will have a valid, enforceable contract, keeping in mind that the transaction must be memorialized in writing to comply with the Statute of Frauds.

PRACTICE POINTER

Using the example above, it would be quite common for judges, lawyers, and paralegals to refer to the house being sold, and the $200,000 paid for the house, as the "consideration" that supports the contract.

Technically speaking, however, that is incorrect. As you may glean from the four-step analysis, it is the parties' *mutual promises* that constitute the actual consideration, and not the house, or the $200,000.

What Is the Relationship Between the Contract of Sale and a Deed?

The contract of sale—sometimes referred to as an ***offer to purchase***—and the deed to the property are two separate legal instruments. The promises contained in the ***contract of sale*** bind the parties to perform the terms and conditions of their agreement, that is, at the closing, the seller must convey the title, and the buyer must pay for the house.

The **deed** is the written instrument that actually conveys title—the evidence of ownership—to the property. To sell a property, there must first be a valid contract of sale, followed by a closing on the property, at which time the deed is transferred from the seller to the buyer, the seller is paid by the buyer, and then the deed should be immediately **recorded** at the office of the Register of Deeds.

> **Deed**
> a written legal document that proves title to, and ownership of, real property.
>
> **Recordation**
> a deed is recorded or registered at the office of the Register of Deeds to put the world on notice of one's ownership of real property, and to make a record of when such notice was filed, in the event of a competing claim of ownership.

c. Land Sale Contract and Lease-Purchase Option: Buyer Beware

Another type of contract for the sale of real property is a ***lease-purchase option***, also known as a ***land sale contract***, or ***contract for the sale of land***. In the vast majority of residential real estate sales, the deed is transferred from seller to buyer at the closing, and recorded at the office of the Register of Deeds either at the time of the closing, or very shortly thereafter. The conveyance of the deed at closing has the effect of immediately vesting title to the property in the buyer.

With a land sale contract or lease-purchase contract, the contract specifies that title to the property will not transfer to the buyer until after all payments have been made to the seller. These payments may extend over many years, during which time the seller retains title to the property. This arrangement presents considerable risks to the buyer, as demonstrated by the example on the next page.

Unfortunately, the example scenario is all too common. While the owner *may* have been within his rights to evict the family under the lease-purchase option agreement, the outcome seems very unfair. Also common with land sale contracts and lease-purchase options is the unscrupulous owner who mortgages the property

LEASE-PURCHASE OPTION NIGHTMARE

Buyers are a just-married young couple. Husband and wife each have some blemishes on their credit histories, and relatively low incomes from their jobs. Thus, they are unable to secure financing from a bank for the purchase of a home. The couple sees an ad for a home in the local newspaper:

"Lease with option to buy. Low credit or no credit not a problem—owner will finance. House needs some work but is in a fine neighborhood. For more information, call …

The newlyweds visit the house, which does require extensive repairs and renovation. Nevertheless, the couple enters into a lease-option agreement with the owner. They agree that the purchase price of the house will be the current fair market value of $85,000, and the newlyweds will make monthly payments in the amount of $710 for the next 10 years. At the end of 10 years, if all payments have been timely made, the owner will convey title to the property to the buyers.

During their first five years in the house, the couple makes extensive repairs to the house, including painting all of the rooms, installing new electrical wiring and carpet, and remodeling the master bathroom. These improvements have increased the fair market value of the property to approximately $130,000.

In year six, the couple has a baby and, for the first time, they are late with four consecutive monthly payments. The owner has threatened to rescind the lease-purchase agreement and evict them from the property if they are late with one more payment, which he has the right to do under the terms of the lease option agreement. The couple continues to experience financial distress and is late with two more payments in the next six months. At that point, the owner files eviction papers. The suit is heard in small claims court where the owner prevails, and the couple and their child are evicted.

The most obvious economic result is that the couple has lost, and the owner has gained, approximately $45,000 in equity in the property, that is, the difference between the current fair market value of $130,000 and the fair market value at the time of purchase, $85,000. To the extent that the monthly payments of $710 may have been in excess of the fair market *rental* value of the property during the years of occupancy, the couple will have lost additional money. Finally, the couple is out-of-pocket the cost of the improvements (new electrical wiring, carpet and bathroom remodel) that they made to the property, plus the value of their labor.

A court of law would probably award the couple some monetary damages to compensate them for the improvements made to the property, and to prevent unjust enrichment of the owner. The couple's claim would be for restitution or quantum meruit. But lawsuits are expensive, time-consuming and rarely make plaintiffs whole. And the couple has lost what it really wanted, the house.

(and gets cash out) during the option period. If the buyers do manage to make all the payments over the term of the agreement, they may find themselves having to pay off a mortgage that they knew nothing about. Some owners have even engaged in outright fraud and sold the property to a third party, that is, right out from under the lease-option buyers.

Because the deed is not transferred from the seller to the buyer "up front" at a closing, land sale contracts and lease-option agreements are very risky for the buyers, who are often young, inexperienced in business and legal transactions, and have bad or no credit. However identified—land-sale contract, lease-option contract, or contract for the sale of land—these transactions are best avoided. If such a contract is contemplated, the prospective buyers should always consult an attorney before signing any documents.

2. VOLUNTARY TRANSFER BY WILL

Real property may be voluntarily transferred to another by means of a will. A **will** is the legal document and method by which people dispose of their real and personal property upon death. Usually, a will is a written document; most commonly, a will is typewritten, but it may also be handwritten and this is called a **holographic will**.

A will may even be made orally, and this is known as a **nuncupative will**. Nuncupative wills are rare and made by persons who are in imminent peril of death and for whom there is insufficient time to write a will. In some states, a nuncupative will can only devise the decedent's personal property, not real property.

A **devise** is a gift of property—real or personal—made in a will. The **testator** is the person who makes a will with the intent of leaving his or her real or personal property to one or more **beneficiaries** after the testator's death.

In order for a testator's real or personal property to pass successfully by will to a beneficiary, certain legal formalities must be observed. These requirements vary considerably from state to state, but generally speaking:

a. A will must be *in writing*, and *signed* by the testator. Alternatively, the will may be signed by someone other than the testator *if* this occurs at the testator's direction and in the presence of the testator. This might occur if the testator is physically too feeble to sign the will;

b. A will must be *witnessed*. Many states require at least two competent witnesses, that is, the witnesses must be mentally competent and over the age of 18. Some jurisdictions have prohibitions against the witnesses, or even their spouses, being beneficiaries under a will that they intend to witness. Witnesses are required to sign the will in the presence of the testator, although the witnesses do not necessarily have to witness or sign the will at the same time;

c. The clause by which property is transferred by will is commonly referred to as the devising clause. It must clearly identify the *devisee*, also known as a *beneficiary*, of the gift, as well as the property which is to be conveyed. In the case of real estate, it is not necessary that the will include a *legal* description; usually, a street address, town, and state is sufficient to identify the property.

Wills, trusts, and estates make up an interesting area of law that almost inevitably is intertwined with the law of real property, as well as tax law. The reason is that in any conveyance of real property, whether by gift, sale, trust or will, one of the primary objectives of the grantor or testator, and the grantee or beneficiary, is to reduce the taxes that must be paid to the local, state, and federal governments.

a. Transfer by Intestacy

What happens when a person dies owning real or personal property, but does not have a will?

In that case, the decedent is said to have died **intestate.** Every state has **intestacy statutes** that mandate how a decedent's property will be distributed in the absence of a will. The persons who receive property from the decedent pursuant to the intestacy statutes are known as **heirs.** The terms "**heirs**" and "*beneficiaries*" are often, but mistakenly, used interchangeably. As stated above, beneficiaries are persons (or entities, such as a charitable organization) who take pursuant to a gift in a will, whereas heirs are those who are legally entitled to receive the property when someone dies intestate.

Whether one is an heir under a state's intestacy statutes depends on the family relationship that existed between the intestate and the putative heir. The states

---

Will
the legal document that describes how one's real and personal property is to be distributed upon death.

Holographic Will
a will that was handwritten by the testator.

Nuncupative Will
an oral will.

Devise
a gift of real or personal property made in a will, although it is most commonly understood to mean a gift of real property.

Testator
the person who makes a will with the intent of leaving real or personal property to one or more beneficiaries.

Beneficiary
one who receives real or personal property under a will.

Intestate
one who dies without a will.

Intestacy Statutes
a state's body of laws that determines who qualifies as an heir of an intestate, and is thus entitled to receive the intestate's real and personal property.

Heir
one who is entitled by statute to the real or personal property of a decedent who dies intestate.

vary considerably about how closely related a person must be to the decedent in order to receive property as an heir. Many states' intestacy statutes give priority to a surviving spouse in the distribution of the intestate's property. Next in priority are usually the decedent's children, if any, and then the decedent's parents, if one or both are still living. In some jurisdictions, that is the end of the line of heirs; if none of the aforementioned survive the intestate, then the property will *escheat* to the state.

Other jurisdictions may define heirs more broadly to include the intestate's siblings, cousins, or aunts and uncles, or even more distant family relatives before the decedent's property escheats to the state.

b. Escheat

When a person dies without a will, and without heirs, the decedent's property will escheat to the state. In fact, it is sometimes said that "the State is the last heir." It is difficult to say whether escheat should be characterized as a voluntary, or involuntary, transfer of property. Since there is no coercive taking of the property during the intestate's lifetime by the government, a bank, or mortgagee, we have placed it in the category of a "voluntary" transfer.

By one estimate, the states currently hold about $35 billion in escheated real and personal property. Typically, the property is held by the state for a certain number of years before being sold. The proceeds from a sale may then be placed in the state's general fund, a special escheat fund, or allocated to a specific use, such as the state's public schools.

If a previously unknown heir comes forward to claim some or all of the intestate's property after the sale of the decedent's property, the state would pay the heir the money it received from the sale of the property. Some states pay interest on the money paid to the heir; others do not.

3. VOLUNTARY TRANSFER BY INTER VIVOS GIFT

The third method by which real property may be transferred is by gift. A gift is the voluntary transfer of property without compensation. As we have seen in a previous section, gifts of real property may be made by will from a decedent to a living beneficiary. But this section covers the gift transfer of real property from one living person to another living person. Such a conveyance is called an **inter vivos gift**, from the Latin meaning "between the living."

Inter Vivos ("between the living") Gift
a transfer of property by gift from a living person to another living person.

As with any transfer of real property, there must be a written deed in order to comply with the Statute of Frauds. Gifts of real property can be made to natural persons, of course, but may also be made to charitable and nonprofit organizations, colleges, and universities. The grantor-donor of an inter vivos gift of real property to one of the aforementioned organizations may be entitled to a tax deduction based on the fair market value of the gifted property.

4. VOLUNTARY TRANSFER BY DEDICATION

The fourth method by which real property may be voluntarily transferred is by dedication. A **dedication** is essentially a gift of the property to the government. Why would anyone make a gift of their land to the government?

Dedication
a gift of real property to a local, state, or federal government.

a. Conservation

Many landowners have made gifts of property to local, state, and the federal governments. These gifts often involve large tracts of raw land from several hundred acres, to several thousands of acres. The gifts are usually given on the condition that the properties stay in their pristine state, never to be developed or used for commercial purposes.

Other landowners have made gifts of smaller parcels of real property. These might be dedicated to the local government to be used for local parks, or building sites for schools, hospitals, or other public uses. Aside from charitable motivations, real property that is dedicated to the government—whether a large or small parcel—may be used as a tax deduction that will reduce the grantor-donor's taxable income.

b. Subdivision

Frequently, real estate developers dedicate the roads within the development or subdivision to the local government. This saves the developer and the homeowners within the new subdivision the cost of maintaining the roads, which costs would be considerable over a period of many years.

The local government is usually amenable to accepting the dedication from the developer, if the roadways have been constructed to local and state standards. If the roads have not been built to acceptable standards, the government will either refuse to take ownership, or will require the roadways be brought up to standards before accepting the dedication.

B. Involuntary Transfer

1. EMINENT DOMAIN (THE POWER) AND CONDEMNATION (THE PROCESS)

Eminent domain is the power of government to take private property for a public use if the government pays **just compensation** to the owner of the property. Although the phrase "eminent domain" is not found in the Constitution, the government's power of eminent domain is implicit in the Takings Clause of the Fifth Amendment:

> ... *nor shall private property be taken for **public use**, without just compensation.*

The quintessential public uses for which property may be taken are public roads, public parks, public hospitals, public airports, and public schools. The repeated use of the word "public" is not accidental, but rather underscores the important point that the Takings Clause commands that any confiscation of property by government must be for a public use, as opposed to a private use. And in that situation, of course, the landowner must be paid just compensation by the government.

Eminent domain is the power to take property, and **condemnation** is the name of the legal process by which property is actually taken. As with zoning issues, eminent domain cases involve the fundamental tension between the common good, and individual liberty and property rights.

Eminent Domain
the power of federal, state, or local government to take private property for a public use, and for which it must pay just compensation.

Just Compensation
usually, the fair market value of a property paid to a land owner by the government for taking part or all of the owner's real property under its power of eminent domain.

Condemnation
the legal process by which government exercises its rights of eminent domain.

PRACTICE POINTER

Condemnation is the process by which the federal, state, or local government takes a property for a public use, and for which it pays just compensation to the owner.

Do not confuse this condemnation with the scenario when a city or town **condemns** a structure (or perhaps a vacant lot) because it is a menace to the community's health or safety, or is dilapidated or otherwise unfit for human occupancy. In that type of condemnation, the government acts pursuant to its police power, and if the owner does not remedy the violations of the building or health codes, the structure will be torn down (or a vacant lot will be cleared) and the cost of the demolition and removal of the structure will be billed to the non-complying landowner.

de facto
Latin "in fact"—having effect even though not formally recognized in the law.

de jure
Latin "as a matter of law"—existing as a matter of law, or as a result or consequence of a legal act.

a. A Fifth Amendment Taking: Kelo v. City of New London

Zoning regulations, although not an actual seizure of property by the government, may be so burdensome that they constitute a **de facto** taking. In those rare, zoning-related takings, the government must compensate the landowner, as in the case of *Lucas v. South Carolina Coastal Council*. The test that a landowner such as developer Mr. Lucas has to meet is difficult indeed: the owner must prove that he is deprived of *all* economically beneficial use of the property.

In contrast to the rare zoning-related takings, in this section we will examine the fairly common **de jure** takings where the government takes actual possession of the landowner's property for a public use.

The most famous case in recent years involving an actual physical taking by a government pursuant to its power of **eminent domain** under the Fifth Amendment[3] is *Kelo v. City of New London*, decided by the Supreme Court in 2005.

Background of the *Kelo* Case

Susette Kelo and eight of her neighbors lived in the Fort Trumbull area of the City of New London, Connecticut, which is at the confluence of the Thames River and Long Island Sound. Although Ms. Kelo's home and other residential properties in the neighborhood were old, they were not dilapidated, and the neighborhood was not blighted.

During the 1990s, the City of New London had experienced an economic decline, and in an attempt to improve its future economic prospects, the City adopted a development plan that would purportedly generate approximately 3,000 new jobs, and raise an additional $1.2 million in local tax revenues for the City coffers.

The plan called for the City to exercise its power of **eminent domain** and to **condemn** the Kelo residence and other nearby properties, and then convey the land to a private developer, the New London Development Corporation (NLDC). The NLDC planned to construct office buildings, shops, a hotel, and new multifamily residential units. Pursuant to the plan, the City had already purchased dozens of properties in the Fort Trumbull area, but Ms. Kelo and her eight neighbors refused to sell.

The legal question presented was whether the City of New London could lawfully take Ms. Kelo's home, pursuant to the City's power of eminent domain under the Fifth Amendment, for the purpose of commercially developing the Fort Trumbull area. The answer to that question hinged on the Supreme Court majority's interpretation of the phrase "public *use*" in the Fifth Amendment, which it determined actually meant "public *purpose*."

The Supreme Court's 5-4 decision was written by now-retired Justice John Paul Stevens, and has been heavily criticized by property rights groups. The following case is edited, but still rather lengthy due to its great importance to the law of real property. The edited dissents of both Justice O'Connor and Justice Thomas are included because their respective analyses are quite incisive and illuminate many of the concepts that we have been discussing. Note, in particular, how the majority and minority differ in their interpretations of the term found in the Fifth Amendment, that is, "public *use*."

---

[3]The ten amendments found in the Bill of Rights originally acted as a check only against the power of the *federal* government. However, the Supreme Court has held in various cases that the Due Process Clause in the Fourteenth Amendment makes most of the rights found in the Bill of Rights applicable against the *states*, including the Takings Clause found in the Fifth Amendment. This is known as the Incorporation Doctrine.

KELO, ET AL. V. CITY OF NEW LONDON

Supreme Court of the United States
545 U.S. 469
June 23, 2005, Decided

It has long been accepted that the sovereign may not take the property of A *for the sole purpose of transferring it to another* <u>private</u> *party B*, even though A is paid just compensation. On the other hand, it is equally clear that a State may transfer property from one private party to another if future "use by the public" is the purpose of the taking; the condemnation of land for a railroad with common-carrier duties is a familiar example.

The City would no doubt be forbidden from taking petitioners' land for the purpose of *conferring a private benefit on a particular private party*. Nor would the City be allowed to take property under the mere pretext of a public purpose, when its actual purpose was to bestow a private benefit. The takings before us, however, would be executed pursuant to a "carefully considered" development plan.

On the other hand, this is not a case in which the City is planning to open the condemned land—at least not in its entirety—to use by the general public. This Court long ago rejected any literal requirement that condemned property be put into use for the general public. Indeed, while many state courts in the mid-19th century endorsed "use by the public" as the proper definition of public use, that narrow view steadily eroded over time. Accordingly, when this Court began applying the Fifth Amendment to the States at the close of the 19th century, it embraced the broader and more natural interpretation of *public use* as *"public purpose."* The disposition of this case therefore turns on the question whether the City's development plan serves a "public purpose."

Viewed as a whole, our jurisprudence has recognized that the **needs of society** have varied between different parts of the Nation, just as they **have evolved over time** in response to changed circumstances. Our earliest cases in particular embodied a strong theme of federalism, emphasizing the "great respect" that we owe to state legislatures and state courts in discerning local public needs. For more than a century, our public use jurisprudence has wisely eschewed rigid formulas and intrusive scrutiny in favor of affording legislatures broad latitude in determining what public needs justify the use of the takings power.

Those who govern the City **were not confronted with the need to remove blight** in the Fort Trumbull area, but their determination that the area was sufficiently distressed to justify a **program of economic rejuvenation** is entitled to our deference. The City has carefully formulated an economic development plan that it believes will provide appreciable benefits to the community, including—but by no means limited to—new jobs and increased tax revenue. Given the comprehensive character of the plan, the thorough deliberation that preceded its adoption, and the limited scope of our review, it is appropriate for us to resolve the challenges of the individual owners, not on a piecemeal basis, but rather in light of the entire plan. Because that plan unquestionably serves a **public purpose**, the takings challenged here satisfy the **public use** requirement of the Fifth Amendment.

Dissent (by Justice O'Connor)

Today under the banner of economic development, all private property is now vulnerable to being taken and transferred to another private owner, so long as it might be upgraded—i.e., given to an owner who will use it in a way that the legislature deems more beneficial to the public—in the process. To reason, as the Court does, that the incidental public benefits resulting from the subsequent ordinary use of private property render economic development takings "for public use" is to wash out any distinction between private and public use of property—and thereby effectively to **delete the words "for public use"** from the Takings Clause of the Fifth Amendment.

The Fifth Amendment to the Constitution, made applicable to the States by the Fourteenth Amendment, provides that "private property [shall not] be taken for public use, without just compensation." When interpreting the Constitution, we begin with the unremarkable presumption that *every word in the document has independent meaning, that no word was unnecessarily used, or needlessly added*. In keeping with that presumption, we have read the Fifth

(*continued*)

Amendment's language to impose two distinct conditions on the exercise of eminent domain: the Taking must be for a *"public use"* and "just compensation" must be paid to the owner.

While the Takings Clause presupposes that government can take private property without the owner's consent, the just compensation requirement spreads the cost of condemnations and thus prevents the public from loading upon one individual more than his just share of the burdens of government. The *public use* requirement, in turn, imposes a more basic limitation, circumscribing the very scope of the eminent domain power: Government may compel an individual to forfeit her property for the public's use, but not for the benefit of another private person. This requirement promotes fairness as well as security.

Dissent (by Justice Thomas)

If such "economic development" takings are for a *"public use,"* then *any taking is*, and the Court has erased the Public Use Clause from our Constitution, as Justice O'Connor powerfully argues in dissent. I do not believe that this Court can eliminate liberties expressly enumerated in the Constitution and therefore join her dissenting opinion. Regrettably, however, the Court's error runs deeper than this. Today's decision is simply the latest in a string of our cases construing the Public Use Clause to be a virtual nullity, without the slightest nod to *its original meaning*. In my view, the Public Use Clause, originally understood, is a meaningful limit on the government's eminent domain power. Our cases have strayed from the Clause's original meaning, and I would reconsider them.

Tellingly, the phrase "public use" contrasts with the very different phrase "general Welfare" used elsewhere in the Constitution (preamble—Constitution established "to promote the general Welfare"). The Framers would have used some such broader term if they had meant the Public Use Clause to have a similarly sweeping scope.

There is no justification, however, for affording almost insurmountable deference to legislative conclusions that a use serves a "public use." To begin with, a court owes no deference to a legislature's judgment concerning the quintessentially legal question of whether the government owns, or the public has a legal right to use, the taken property. We would not defer to a legislature's determination of the various circumstances that establish, for example, when a search of a home would be reasonable, or when a convicted double-murderer may be shackled during a sentencing proceeding without on-the-record findings, or when state law creates a property interest protected by the Due Process Clause.

Our current Public Use Clause jurisprudence, as the Court notes, has rejected this natural reading of the Clause. The Court adopted its modern reading blindly, with little discussion of the Clause's history and *original meaning*, in two distinct lines of cases: first, in cases adopting the "public purpose" interpretation of the Clause, and second, in cases deferring to legislatures' judgments regarding what constitutes a valid public purpose. Those questionable cases converged in the boundlessly broad and deferential conception of "public use" adopted by this Court in *Berman* v. *Parker*, and *Hawaii Housing Authority* v. *Midkiff*.

The *"public purpose" test* applied by *Berman* and *Midkiff* also cannot be applied in a principled manner. When we depart from the natural import of the term *"public use,"* and substitute for the simple idea of a public possession and occupation, that of public utility, public interest, common benefit, general advantage or convenience … we are afloat without any certain principle to guide us. Once one permits takings for public purposes in addition to public uses, no coherent principle limits what could constitute a valid public use.

For all these reasons, I would revisit our Public Use Clause cases and consider returning to the original meaning of the Public Use Clause: that the government may take property only if it actually uses or gives the public a legal right to use the property.

When faced with a clash of constitutional principle and a line of unreasoned cases wholly divorced from the text, history, and structure of our founding document, we should not hesitate to resolve the tension in favor of the Constitution's original meaning.

Kelo—The Aftermath

As a result of the Supreme Court's *Kelo* holding in 2005, anger spread across the country among advocates of individual property rights. Both Justice Souter and Justice Breyer were in the majority in the *Kelo* decision, and both own homes in New Hampshire. Shortly after the controversial opinion there were attempts by property rights groups to have the Breyer and Souter homes condemned and used for "public purposes," such as so-called "freedom parks" or a "liberty hotel.[4] Those efforts failed, and were probably less than serious. But to some, the attempts made the point that what is good for one (taking Ms. Kelo's home) should be good for everyone (taking Breyer's and Souter's homes).

One practical result of the decision was that many states passed legislation to effectively ban, at least to some extent, the kind of action taken by the City of New London, or to pass laws that otherwise strengthened the rights of property owners.

Finally, Susette Kelo's house was physically moved from the Fort Trumbull site to another location in New London. The homes of her eight neighbors who were co-plaintiffs in the lawsuit against the City were demolished. What of the promised 3,000 jobs and $1.2 million in additional tax revenue from the redevelopment plan?

The jobs and tax revenues never materialized, because after the homes were leveled, the private developer to whom the tract was sold was not able to obtain financing to implement the redevelopment plan. And so several years after the Supreme Court's decision upholding the City of New London's powers of eminent domain, the properties that were condemned by the City lie vacant and unused.

b. Inverse Condemnation

As we have just seen, governmental entities have the power of eminent domain by which they can, and often do, condemn private property for, ostensibly, a public use (or a "public *purpose*" as in the *Kelo* case). Thus, the usual scenario involves the government initiating the condemnation process.

However, there are situations where private landowners may actually ask the government to condemn their property. This process is called ***inverse condemnation,*** or sometimes, reverse condemnation. Consider the following example:

SMALLVILLE GROWS UP

Fifty years ago, Smallville, USA, was a sleepy town with a population of only 10,000 people. At that time, it did have a small airport about 8 miles west of the town center, with a few small subdivisions 3 to 4 miles from the airport's sole, relatively short, runway.

In the ensuing decades, a new interstate highway was constructed, which passes close to Smallville and its airport. This brought increased economic activity to the area, and today the population has increased by tenfold, to well over 100,000 people. The town, and the regional planning commission, now want to construct a second runway, which will have the capability of accommodating commercial jet aircraft. Residents who were once a comfortable three miles away from the old runway have learned that they will be directly under the glide path for the jet aircraft using the new runway.

The prospect of deafening jet engines, increased pollution, and rattling windows compels some of the residents to petition the local and state governments to ***inversely condemn*** their properties, that is, they want the government to buy them out—for "just compensation"—so that they can purchase homes elsewhere.

Whether the local and state government choose to do so will depend on several factors, including the anticipated impact of the new runway on the homeowners, the availability of funds, and the fair market values of the several affected properties.

---

[4]As to the attempt to condemn Justice Breyer's residence, see, for example: "Eminent domain this! Justice's [Breyer's] farm is target" at http://www.msnbc.msn.com/id/8406056/ns/us_news-weird_news/t/eminent-domain-justices-farm-target/.

Regarding the effort to condemn Justice Souter's home, see, for example, "Lost Liberty Hotel, at http://en.wikipedia.org/wiki/Lost_Liberty_Hotel.

The scenario above is fairly common today because, in the last approximately 30 years, only a very few major airports have been constructed in the United States. As a result, many older airports—in large urban areas, as well as in relatively small cities—had to expand their airport operations, often encroaching on small, quiet neighborhoods like those in Smallville.

2. ADVERSE POSSESSION—"LEGALIZED THEFT"?

Adverse Possession

the process by which one who is essentially a trespasser may obtain lawful title to real property by openly, exclusively, and actually possessing and using it for a specified number of years.

Another method by which real property may be involuntarily transferred is through **adverse possession,** sometimes referred to as "legalized theft," whereby someone who is essentially a trespasser may legally claim title to a property after possessing it for a statutorily prescribed holding period. The states have various formulations, but the basic elements of adverse possession are listed below. As you will see, there is some overlap between and among the elements:

  a. Hostile intent,
  b. Actual possession,
  c. Open and notorious possession,
  d. Exclusive possession, and
  e. Continuous and uninterrupted possession.

a. Hostile Intent

Hostile intent does not imply any sort of malice on the part of the adverse possessor or the true owner of the property. Rather, it simply means that the adverse possessor possesses the property *without the consent* of the true owner. Thus, if the owner grants the adverse possessor permission to use the property, this will defeat a claim for adverse possession.

b. Actual Possession

Actual possession is *physical control and dominion* over a property, and implies that the property is being put to some use by the adverse possessor. It is not necessary that the property be occupied or used 24/7/365, but it does mean that the property should be possessed as is appropriate for a particular use.

Consider the situation involving a hunting cabin in the woods that is only used a few times a year by the adverse possessor (but not at all by the actual owner). Even though the cabin is used for only 8–10 days per year, this would be sufficient to meet the requirement of actual possession because although the use is minimal, it is nonetheless appropriate for that type of property.

If a large tract of land is being claimed by adverse possession, and if the court found in favor of the adverse possessor, it would likely award only that portion of the land actually used by the adverse possessor, rather than the entire tract.

c. Open and Notorious Use

The requirement that the adverse possession be open and notorious simply means that the *possession must be visible*, considering the nature of the property. That is, if one is adversely possessing property in an urban area, the court would expect the use of that property to be more visible than the hunting cabin in the woods, described in the previous section on actual possession. Here again, the nature of the property being adversely possessed will be considered by the court in its analysis of the elements of adverse possession.

d. Exclusive Possession

The adverse possessor must possess the property exclusively. One of the characteristics of land ownership is dominion and control of a property, specifically, the *right to exclude others*. If the adverse possessor shares possession with the actual owner or some other person, then the claim for adverse possession is defeated because the claimant's possession is not exclusive.

> **QUESTION**
>
> If the adverse possessor leases the property to a tenant, would this mean that the adverse possessor cannot meet the element of exclusive possession?

e. Continuous and Uninterrupted Use

The adverse possessor must possess the property *continuously and without interruption*. This requirement expands on what is required under the element of actual possession. Like the requirement of actual possession, the requirement of "continuous and uninterrupted use" does not mean that the property must be used, or even occupied, by the adverse possessor 24/7/365. Continuous use means that use which is appropriate for that particular type of property. Uninterrupted use means that the adverse possessor has not abandoned the property during the statutorily required holding period.

> **QUESTION**
>
> Regarding the example of the hunting cabin in the woods, is the adverse possessor's use "continuous and uninterrupted" if he uses the cabin an average of four times per year for 20 years?

f. Statutory Holding Period: With and Without "Color of Title"

The states have various requirements concerning the period of time that a property must be adversely possessed in order for the adverse possessor to prevail on a claim of adverse possession. A typical holding period is 20 years when the adverse possessor claims *without* the benefit of color of title. However, the holding period may be reduced to as little as five or seven years under claim of color of title.

Color of title means that there is a writing or some other evidence that purports to show that the adverse possessor is the real owner of the property, but falls short of actually proving ownership. The law in most states shortens the required holding period for one who claims under color of title, perhaps to acknowledge at least the possibility that the adverse possessor's claim is bona fide.

The question often arises about how, in an adverse possession case, title is actually transferred from the true owner to the adverse possessor. The answer is by way of a suit for an ***action to quiet title***. Usually, it is the adverse possessor who files the suit after possessing the property for the required holding period. But sometimes it is the original owner who will sue for trespass, and then the adverse possessor will make a counterclaim to quiet title. In either case, the court may order that a deed be drafted and conveyed to the prevailing party, and recorded at the office of the register of deeds so as to remove the **cloud on title.**

Color of Title
a writing or other evidence purporting to show that a claimant to property, such as an adverse possessor, is the actual owner of the property.

Cloud on Title
a defect or potential defect in one's title arising from another's claim to the same property.

Tacking
the joining of consecutive periods of
ownership or possession by different
persons and treating them as one
continuous period.

g. Tacking

Tacking allows one adverse possessor's time of possession to be added on to, or tacked on to, a second (or third, fourth, etc.) adverse possessor's time of possession in order to meet the legally required holding period to adversely possess real property. Assume that the first adverse possessor exclusively uses and possesses the property for seven years. She then sells the property to a buyer who adversely possesses the property for 13 years. If their periods of ownership are tacked together, they have met the required 20-year holding period for a claim of adverse possession.

Reverse tacking, sometimes called inverse tacking, relates to adding together consecutive periods of ownership by the *true* owners of the property that is being adversely possessed:

REVERSE TACKING ON THE PONDEROSA

Ben Cartwright is the owner of the Ponderosa ranch, which covers several thousand acres in Nevada. Squatters are openly using about 20 of the Ponderosa's acres to graze their sheep, which they claim that they have a right to do *under color of title*. Ben does not like it, but is too busy to evict "those trespassers." The squatters' have adversely possessed the acreage for 3 years, after which Ben dies. In his will, Ben leaves the ranch to his son, Hoss. However, for the next 2½ years, Hoss is very busy with the Ponderosa's timber and mining operations, and neglects to take any action against the squatters.

In Nevada, when one adversely possesses property under color of title, the required time of possession is only 5 years. The question relating to *inverse tacking* is whether the squatters' adverse possession "clock" had to be reset and start all over again after Ben died, and Hoss became the new owner.

In states that allow inverse tacking, the answer is no, the adverse possession clock is not reset, and continues to count time. The squatters adversely possessed the 20 acres for the last 3 years of Ben's life, which is tacked on to the 2½ years that they adversely possessed since Hoss became the owner of the ranch. Therefore, the squatters have met the required 5-year requirement to adversely possess under color of title. When the squatters file suit to quiet title, they will become the new owners of 20 acres of what used to be Ponderosa land.

---

h. Public Policy

What public policy could possibly justify the so-called "legalized theft" of real property, otherwise known as adverse possession? Why is it that one who is a trespasser can, if he trespasses long enough, obtain title to a property that was never his, and that he perhaps *knew* was never his? In that regard, some states do allow adverse possession by one who *knows* that the property does not belong to her; other states do not.

The public policy behind the law of adverse possession is that *land should be used*. If a person, even a trespasser, is willing to put the land to some use, then the law will reward that person's industry and initiative, because at least in theory, the use of land contributes to economic productivity and the creation of wealth.

Governments are constantly searching for ways to generate **tax revenue**, and land that is being used productively can be taxed at a higher rate than a property that is not being used. And of course the activity that constitutes the adverse use—be it farming, ranching, mining, and so on—can be taxed, in addition to the tax on the land.

Today, we may be uncomfortable with the policy promoting adverse possession because we live in a nation that is already highly developed, economically and in terms of land utilization. Thus, the policy justifying adverse possession may seem anachronistic. In fact, we honor persons and groups who donate large tracts of land for preservation and conservation purposes, rather than developing those parcels for commercial gain.

In our time, adverse possession is much less common than it was during the first two centuries of our nation's history. One reason is that *surveying* has become a science so that property boundaries are much more reliable and less susceptible to misinterpretation; thus, there are many fewer claims under color of title than in the past. Also, the practice of *recording deeds*, now universally required by lenders and title companies, has drastically reduced the opportunity to adversely possess a property through the fraudulent manipulation of deeds, and property descriptions found in deeds. Finally, lawyers are better trained today than a century ago, which has undoubtedly resulted in better drafting of real estate contracts, deeds, and related documents.

Before we leave the subject of adverse possession, take a few minutes to read the story of Marengo Cave, one of the most famous and interesting cases of adverse possession in American jurisprudence:

MARENGO CAVE CO. V. ROSS

Supreme Court of Indiana
212 Ind. 624; 10 N.E.2d 917
November 5, 1937, Filed

In 1883 one Stewart owned the real estate now owned by appellant [Marengo Cave Co.], and in September of that year some young people who were upon that land discovered what afterwards proved to be the entrance to the cavern since known as Marengo Cave, this entrance being approximately *700 feet from the boundary line* between the lands now owned by appellant [and adverse possessor Marengo Cave Co.] and appellee Ross, and the only entrance to said cave. The then owner of the real estate upon which the entrance was located took complete possession of the entire cave as now occupied by appellant and used for exhibition purposes, and began to charge an admission fee to those who desired to enter and view the cave, and to exclude therefrom those who were unwilling to pay for admission.

For a period of approximately twenty-five years prior to the time appellee Ross purchased his land, and for a period of twenty-one years afterwards, *exclusive possession* of the cave has been held by appellant Marengo Cave Co., and its immediate and remote grantors. The cave, as such, has never been listed for

taxation separately from the real estate wherein it is located, and the owners of the respective tracts of land have paid the taxes assessed against said tracts.

A part of said cave at the time of its discovery and exploration extended beneath real estate now owned by appellee Ross, but this fact was not ascertained until the year 1932, when the boundary line between the respective tracts through the cave was established by means of a survey made by a civil engineer pursuant to an order of court entered in this cause. Previous to this survey neither of the parties to this appeal, nor any of their predecessors in title, knew that any part of the cave was in fact beneath the surface of a portion of the land now owned by appellee Ross.

It is appellant's contention that it has a fee simple title to all of the cave. That it owns that part underlying Ross's land by adverse possession. All the authorities agree that before the owner of the legal title can be deprived of his land by another's possession, through the operation of the statute of limitation, the possession must have been *actual, visible, notorious, exclusive, under claim of ownership* and *hostile* to

(continued)

the owner of the legal title and to the world at large (except only the government) and continuous for the full period prescribed by the statute.

1. The possession must be *actual*. It must be conceded that appellant, in the operation of the "Marengo Cave," used not only the cavern under its own land but also that part of the cavern that underlaid appellee's land, and assumed dominion over all of it. Yet it must also be conceded that during all of the time appellee was in constructive possession, as the only constructive possession known to the law is that which inheres in the legal title and with which the owner of that title is always endowed. Whether the possession was actual under the peculiar facts in this case we need not decide.

2. The possession must be *visible*. The owner of land who, having *notice* of the fact that it is occupied by another who is claiming dominion over it, nevertheless stands by during the entire statutory period and makes no effort to eject the claimant or otherwise protect his title, ought not to be permitted, for reasons of public policy, thereafter to maintain an action for the recovery of his land. But, the authorities assert, in order that the possession of the occupying claimant may constitute notice in law, it must be visible and open to the common observer so that the owner or his agent on visiting the premises might readily see that the owner's rights are being invaded.

3. The possession must be *open* and *notorious*. The mere possession of the land is not enough. It is knowledge, either actual or imputed, of the possession of his lands by another, claiming to own them bona fide and openly, that affects the legal owner thereof. Where there has been no actual notice, it is necessary to show that the possession of the disseisor was so *open, notorious and visible* as to warrant the inference that the owner must, or should have, known of it.

4. The possession must be *exclusive*. It is evident that two or more persons cannot hold one tract of land adversely to each other at the same time. It is essential that the possession of one who claims adversely must be of such an exclusive character that it will operate as an ouster of the owner of the legal title.

The facts as set out above show that appellee Ross and his predecessors in title have been in actual and continuous possession of his real estate since the cave was discovered in 1883. At no time were they aware that anyone was trespassing upon their land. No one was claiming to be in possession of appellee's land. It is true that appellant was asserting possession of the "Marengo Cave." There would seem to be quite a difference in making claim to the "Marengo Cave," and making claim to a portion of appellee's land, even though a portion of the cave extended under appellee's land, when this latter fact was unknown to anyone. The evidence on both sides of this case is to the effect that the "Marengo Cave" was thought to be altogether under the land owned by appellant, and this erroneous supposition was not revealed until a survey was made at the request of appellee and ordered by the court in this case.

Even though it could be said that appellant's possession has been actual, exclusive and continuous all these years, we would still be of the opinion that appellee Ross has not lost his land. It has been the uniform rule in equity that the *statute of limitation does not begin to run until the injured party discovers, or with reasonable diligence might have discovered*, the facts constituting the injury and cause of action. Until then the owner cannot know that his possession has been invaded. Until he has knowledge, or ought to have such knowledge, he is not called upon to act, for he does not know that action in the premises is necessary and the law does not require absurd or impossible things of anyone.

So in the case at bar, appellant pretended to use the "Marengo Cave" as his property and *all the time he was committing a trespass* upon appellee's land. After twenty years of secret use, he now urges the statute of limitation as a bar to appellee's action. Appellee did not know of the trespass of appellant, and had no reasonable means of discovering the fact. It is true that appellant took no active measures to prevent the discovery, except to deny appellee the right to enter the cave for the purpose of making a survey, and disclaiming any use of appellee's lands, but nature furnished the concealment, or where the wrong conceals itself.

We cannot assent to the doctrine that would enable one to trespass upon another's property through a subterranean passage and under such circumstances that the owner does not know, or by the exercise of reasonable care could not know, of such secret occupancy, for twenty years or more and by so doing obtained a fee simple title as against the holder of the legal title. The fact that appellee Ross had knowledge that appellant was claiming to be the owner of the "Marengo Cave," and advertised it to the general public, was no knowledge to him that it was in possession of appellee's land or any part of it. We are of the opinion that appellant's possession for twenty years or more of that part of "Marengo Cave," underlying appellee's land, *was not open, notorious, or exclusive*, as required by the law applicable to obtaining title to land by adverse possession.

Judgment affirmed.

3. FORECLOSURE

The third method by which real property may be involuntarily transferred is through a foreclosure action. When a buyer purchases a piece of property, it is usually necessary for that buyer to obtain a loan. In return for a bank or other lender making the loan, the buyer pledges the property as security for the loan.

Foreclosure is the legal process whereby the **lender can force the sale** of the property because the buyer/borrower/owner has defaulted on the loan by failing to make the monthly mortgage payments. There are two basic types of foreclosure: judicial foreclosure, and non—judicial/power of sale foreclosure.

a. Judicial Foreclosure

Judicial foreclosure is so named because the process is very similar to the regular litigation process. That is, a formal complaint is filed by the lender (the mortgagee) against the defaulting borrower (the mortgagor), who must be served with the complaint. Proper notice of the foreclosure hearing must be given, and then a judicial hearing is conducted. Further, as in the regular litigation process, the borrower may be permitted to appeal from the decision rendered at the hearing.

A judicial foreclosure *sale*, which is not to be confused with the *hearing*, is sometimes conducted by the sheriff, or clerk of court, of the county wherein the property is located.

You know that litigation can be, and often is, lengthy and expensive, which is why **lenders do not prefer judicial foreclosure**. On the other hand, a borrower who has allegedly defaulted can take advantage of the due process protections that are inherent in a judicial foreclosure. However, as a practical matter, most borrowers going through judicial foreclosure probably cannot afford legal counsel.

Judicial Foreclosure
a method of foreclosure that is very similar to a regular lawsuit, and requires the filing of a complaint, service on the borrower, a formal hearing, and the opportunity to appeal.

b. Foreclosure Pursuant to Power of Sale Clause (Non-Judicial Foreclosure)

When compared to judicial foreclosure, foreclosure pursuant to a **power of sale** clause—sometimes called a *non-judicial foreclosure*—is much quicker and less expensive. Therefore, in those states where it is available, non-judicial foreclosure is preferred by lenders over judicial foreclosure. However, because a power of sale foreclosure "short-circuits" many of a borrower's due process rights, the power of sale clause must be clearly expressed in the mortgage or deed of trust, and the foreclosing lender must strictly follow the requirements of the power of sale clause, and the relevant statutes. Non-judicial/power of sale foreclosures are disfavored and many states have outlawed non-judicial foreclosure.

Whether discussing a judicial foreclosure, or a power of sale/non-judicial foreclosure, the most important requirement is *notice* to the defaulting borrower that the lender intends to foreclose on the property. Such notice may consist of sending certified letters to the borrower, posting notice of the foreclosure at the courthouse, or publishing a notice of foreclosure in a newspaper of general circulation for a certain period of time, or perhaps all three.

Power of Sale
a clause found in a mortgage or deed of trust that allows the lender to foreclose without giving the borrower the right to a formal judicial hearing.

Equitable Right of Redemption
the right of a borrower in foreclosure to pay off the entire loan balance at any time up until the foreclosure sale.

Upset Bid
a bid that overturns the winning bid at a foreclosure sale. State law will dictate the amount or percentage by which the upset bid must exceed the winning bid, and the length of time after the foreclosure sale in which the upset bid must be submitted to the clerk of court.

Deficiency Judgment
a judgment for the difference between what the borrower owed to the lender and the proceeds from the foreclosure sale.

Up until the moment of foreclosure, a borrower in default has an **equitable right of redemption.** This means that if the borrower can pay the principal, interest, and other costs related to the foreclosure, the borrower may cure the default and stop the foreclosure process. Some states even allow a defaulting homeowner to exercise the right of redemption for several months *after* the foreclosure sale. As a practical matter, very few borrowers who are in default can take advantage of the equitable right of redemption. If the borrowers had, or could have obtained, funds with which to pay off their loan balance, they would have been able to stay current on their monthly mortgage payments.

When a property is sold at a foreclosure sale, a notice of sale is filed with the clerk of court. But that is not necessarily the end of the foreclosure sale process. Many states allow for submission of an **upset bid,** which overturns the winning bid at the foreclosure sale. State law will usually require that an upset bid be at least 5% more than the original winning bid, or a minimum of $500 to $1,000 more than the winning bid, whichever is greater. State law will also determine the amount of time after the foreclosure sale that one may submit an upset bid; a typical timeframe might be 7 to 10 days. Several upset bids may be submitted, and in theory, the upset process can go on indefinitely.

What happens if, at the foreclosure sale, the property sells for less than the amount owed to the lender by the defaulting borrower? Many states allow the lender to obtain a **deficiency judgment** against the borrower for the deficiency or shortfall between what the borrower owed to the lender and the foreclosure sale price. Even those states allowing for deficiency judgments will require that the lender's right to obtain a deficiency judgment be expressly stated in the loan documents.

Assume that the outstanding loan balance on a house headed to foreclosure is $150,000, and there are foreclosure costs of $5,000, for a total of $155,000 owed to the bank. However, at the foreclosure sale the property is sold for only $115,000. Thus, there is a deficiency or shortfall of $40,000, for which the defaulting borrower may be liable in some states.

Other states view *deficiency judgments* as allowing the lender to "pile on" the borrower, and have enacted anti-deficiency judgment statutes, which severely restrict a lender's right to obtain a deficiency judgment.

A Final Note About Foreclosures

Beginning in 2008, the United States real estate market experienced the greatest number of residential foreclosures since the Great Depression of the 1930s. The foreclosures occurred when millions of homeowners defaulted on their monthly mortgage payments to their lenders. There was plenty of blame to go around for causing the foreclosure crisis, including:

   i. *Appraisers* who made overly optimistic or even fraudulent estimates of value, which were then used to justify loans in excess of the properties' fair market values, and/or borrowers' ability to afford the monthly mortgage payments.
   ii. *Lenders* were willing to make questionable loans because more loans generated more loan origination fees for the banks, and for several years, residential real estate had been steadily and predictably appreciating in value (or so the banks and borrowers thought). In many cases, lenders were making loans that exceeded the property value by 20% to 30%, for the purpose of generating greater fees. The lenders thought that even if a borrower did default today it was not a problem because there was strong buyer-demand, and the property would just be worth more tomorrow. This so-called real estate "bubble" finally burst, and property values collapsed. At the same time,

unemployment increased dramatically, and many homeowners were not able to make their mortgage payments.

iii. *Congress* enacted the original Community Reinvestment Act (CRA) in 1977, which was designed to encourage banks and other lending institutions to reinvest more of their funds in the communities in which they were located. The Act was amended a number of times, and usually the result was a loosening of lending standards so as to allow more low- and moderate-income earners to become homeowners. Although this was a worthy goal, these would later become known as "subprime loans," which many borrowers could not repay.

iv. *Borrowers* who were otherwise unqualified to obtain home loans managed to get loans under the reduced lending standards of the CRA. Some of these loans were "adjustable rate mortgages" (ARMs) which carried an artificially low-interest "teaser" rate in the first three to five years of the loan, but thereafter, a borrower's monthly payments increased by two or three times, from perhaps $1,000 per month to $3,000 per month. Many borrowers found themselves unable to make the increased payments, especially as unemployment rapidly increased.

v. The *secondary mortgage market*, including Fannie Mae and Freddie Mac, as well as giant insurance companies, banks, and pension funds, bought the high-risk subprime loans as investments without conducting the proper due diligence as to the safety and security of those loans. These entities mistakenly assumed that the underlying value of the homes (the "bubble") that secured the loans would increase steadily and indefinitely. When millions of borrowers were unable to make their mortgage payments, those institutions lost hundreds of billions of dollars, which necessitated a "bailout" by the U.S. Treasury.

CHAPTER SUMMARY

Real estate may be transferred either voluntarily or involuntarily. *Voluntary* transfers of real estate may be made by sale, devise (by a will), inter vivos gift, or dedication. When real property is sold, the contract of sale must be in writing to comply with the Statute of Frauds. A **contract for sale** of property or a **lease-option** agreement can be very risky for the buyer of the property because the seller retains title until the full amount of the purchase price is received from the buyer after several years. During this time, an unscrupulous seller could take out a second or third mortgage on the property, for which the buyer could become liable, or might even sell the property out from under the buyer.

Under the category of a voluntary transfer, we also included *escheat*, which occurs when a decedent dies **intestate** (without a will) but has no surviving heirs who can take the property, in which case title or custody of the property will go to the state. A **dedication** involves the donation of real property to the local, state, or federal government.

Involuntary transfers of real property may occur by three methods. The first occurs when a governmental entity or public utility exercises its power of eminent domain and condemns property for a public use, such as roadways, power lines, water and sewer lines, and public schools or parks. *Eminent domain* is the power of government to take private land for public use, while **condemnation** is the name of the legal process employed to do so. As with zoning issues, eminent domain cases involve the fundamental tension between the common good and individual liberty.

The *Takings Clause* of the Fifth Amendment to the United States Constitution prohibits the taking of private property for **public use** without payment of just compensation to the owner. In the case of *Kelo v. City of New London*, the legal issue was whether the City's proposed redevelopment plan of the Kelo property it had condemned was a genuine public use.

The second method by which real property may be involuntarily transferred is through *adverse possession*, which is sometimes called "legalized theft." The elements of adverse possession are hostile intent, actual possession, open and notorious use, exclusivity of use, and continuous and uninterrupted use. The person who claims title by adverse possession must meet all of the aforementioned requirements for a period of time required by statute, for example, 7 years under *color of title*, or 20 years without color of title.

The third method by which real property may be involuntarily transferred is by *foreclosure.* When a property owner has borrowed money from a lender for the purchase of the property, the owner will pledge the property as collateral for the loan. If the owner defaults, the lender may foreclose pursuant to either a *judicial foreclosure* sale, or a *power of sale*/non-judicial foreclosure sale. A judicial foreclosure takes more time and is more expensive, but gives the defaulting borrower greater due process rights. Conversely, a foreclosure pursuant to a power of sale clause in a mortgage or deed of trust is quicker and less expensive, and is therefore preferred by lenders.

CONCEPT REVIEW AND REINFORCEMENT

KEY **TERMS**

Acceptance
Actual Possession
Adverse Possession
Beneficiary
Bilateral Contract
Cloud on Title
Color of Title
Condemnation
Consideration
Contract
Counteroffer
Dedication
Deed
de facto
Deficiency Judgment
de jure
Devise
Eminent Domain

Equitable Right of
    Redemption
Escheat
Foreclosure
Heir
Holographic Will
Inter Vivos Gift
Intestacy Statutes
Intestate
Inverse Condemnation
Involuntary Transfer
Judicial Foreclosure
Just Compensation
Kelo v. City of New London
Land Sale Contract /
    Lease-Purchase Option
Legalized Theft
Mirror-Image Rule

Mutual Assent
Nuncupative Will
Offer
Offer to Purchase
Offeree
Offeror
Power of Sale/
    Non-Judicial Foreclosure
Recordation
Statute of Frauds
Tacking
Takings Clause of the Fifth
    Amendment
Testator
Unilateral Contract
Upset Bid
Voluntary Transfer
Will

CONCEPT **REVIEW** QUESTIONS

1. What are the four methods by which real property may be voluntarily transferred?

2. What is an inter vivos gift, and how is it different from a gift that is conveyed by way of a will?

3. What is a dedication of real property, and to whom is the real property dedicated? Why would a property owner dedicate real property?

4. What is the difference between eminent domain and condemnation, and how do those concepts relate to the Takings Clause found in the Fifth Amendment to the United States Constitution?

5. What is inverse condemnation, who would pursue an action for inverse condemnation, and what is an example of when such an action might be brought?

6. What are the elements of a valid contract for the purchase of real property?

7. Why is a lease-option for the purchase of real property potentially very dangerous for the buyer? What precautions might the buyer take to reduce the risks associated with a lease-option agreement?

8. What are the elements of adverse possession, and what overlap, if any, exists between or among those elements?

9. What is color of title? If someone purports to adversely possess property under color of title, does that increase or decrease the statutorily required holding period when compared with someone who adversely possesses without color of title? Why?

10. How would you define "public policy," and what was the public policy behind the doctrine of adverse possession? Is that public policy still as relevant today as it was, for example, 150 years ago?

11. What is the difference between judicial foreclosure and non-judicial/power of sale foreclosure? Which gives greater rights of due process to the defaulting borrower? Which method of foreclosure is preferred by lenders, and why?

12. What is the equitable right of redemption, and when may the right of redemption be exercised, and by whom?

13. What is an upset bid, when is it used, and by whom is it used?

ETHICS

ATTORNEY ADVERTISES FREE FORECLOSURE CLINIC TO DISTRESSED HOMEOWNERS

Alex Attorney is a licensed attorney specializing in real estate law. Due to the housing collapse, much of his practice now consists of representing underwater homeowners with foreclosure litigation and proceedings.

In an effort to increase his client base, Alex hosts a free clinic in the ballroom of a local hotel every Saturday morning where he provides general information to the attendees regarding their rights and responsibilities in the foreclosure process. Alex's paralegal also attends, handing out brochures containing information about the foreclosure process, some statistical data about the number of foreclosures nationally and locally, and Alex's photograph and contact information.

As a result of these general information sessions, on average, four or five attendees ask for a more in-depth consultation at Alex's office. Of those, two or three of the five consultations will result in the representation of the clients in the foreclosure proceedings.

In holding such information sessions, has Alex violated any ethical rules regarding solicitation and/or advertising? Why, or why not?

Does it matter that people who may be facing foreclosure of their homes could be seen as a group particularly "vulnerable" to an attorney's marketing of legal services?

If your answer to the question above is yes, does that place a higher ethical burden on Alex as to the marketing of legal services to such a vulnerable group?

Assume that Alex normally bills for services after the services are rendered to clients. However, knowing that these foreclosure clients are in precarious financial straits, Alex asks for, and gets, a $4,000 retainer "up front." Is this discrimination? If so, is it illegal discrimination that would be actionable by Alex's clients?

BUILDING YOUR PROFESSIONAL SKILLS

CRITICAL THINKING **EXERCISES**

1. A residential property has been listed for sale by Bobbie Broker. About a month after the listing, Broker receives an Offer to Purchase from Mr. and Mrs. Byers, including an earnest money deposit of $20,000. The Offer contains a clause that reads:

   Closing on the property to take place on or before December 31 of this year. This offer is contingent upon Buyers obtaining financing in the amount of $200,000, at a rate of interest not to exceed 5%, for a term of 25 years.

   Shortly after making the offer, Mr. and Mrs. Byers come down with a case of cold feet, and are reluctant to follow through on the purchase. They make one attempt to obtain financing, and that lender tells them that although it will loan them $200,000 for a term of 25 years, the interest rate will be 5.5 %, rather than the 5% called for in the Offer to Purchase. Shortly

   thereafter, Mr. and Mrs. Byers inform Bobbie Broker that they were unable to obtain financing for the purchase of the property, and demand the return of their $20,000 earnest money deposit.

   Under the circumstances described above, do you think that Mr. and Mrs. Byers are entitled to the return of their earnest money? They did make one attempt to obtain financing, but do you think that that satisfies their obligation as written in the contract clause above? If this issue is litigated, should the court read into the contract an implied duty on the part of Mr. and Mrs. Byers to use their best efforts to obtain financing, or perhaps reasonable efforts to obtain financing, or perhaps some other standard, or no implied duty at all? Explain the reasoning behind your answers.

2. The Statute of Frauds is alive and well in all 50 states, and requires that certain contracts be in writing,

including contracts for the transfer of any interest in real property. The Statute was originally enacted in England in 1677, more than 330 years ago. What is the reason for the Statute of Frauds? People in our time are far more literate, better educated, and informed than they were in 1677, and so is the Statute as necessary today as it was then? Explain.

3. In the case of *Kelo v. City of New London*, the City decided that it wanted to condemn the waterfront properties of Ms. Kelo and her neighbors in order to build a large commercial development that would include office buildings, a shopping mall, and high-end townhouses and condominiums. The City informed the citizens that the development would generate millions of dollars in tax revenue, and create 3,000 jobs.

   Ms. Kelo, through her attorneys, argued in the Supreme Court that the Fifth Amendment allowed the taking of her private property only for public *use*, and that turning the properties over to a developer to build offices and condominiums did not meet that constitutional criterion. The City argued that "public use" actually embraced within its meaning a public *purpose*.

   In your opinion, which side had the better argument, and why? Should the Supreme Court interpret the words of the Constitution literally, or should the justices permit themselves to interpret language in the Constitution more expansively to adapt to the ever-changing conditions of our modern world?

4. Article I, Section 10 of the Constitution states that "No State shall … pass any law impairing the obligation of contracts." This is the so-called Contracts Clause, and the original motivation for its inclusion in the Constitution was to prevent the 13 states from reneging on their debts or obligations to their citizens who were Loyalists and supported the British Crown during the Revolutionary War.

   In the last few years, millions of homes in America have gone to foreclosure. In light of the Contracts Clause above, would it be constitutional for a state to adopt legislation that would declare a moratorium on residential foreclosures? Would such a law "impair the obligations" in contracts (mortgages or deeds of trust) between borrowers or lenders?

   There are few, if any, absolutes in the Constitution … even the right to free speech can be limited. Are there any circumstances in which a state-ordered moratorium on foreclosures might be appropriate? You might want to review the case of *Home Building & Loan Association v. Blaisdell*, 290 U.S. 398 (1934), which was decided at the height of lender foreclosures during the Great Depression.

RESEARCH ON THE **WEB**

1. Critical Thinking Exercise # 2 above concerned the Statute of Frauds. Go online and locate the Statute of Frauds for your state. What types of contracts must be in writing? What other requirements, if any, are there that are specific to contracts for an interest in real property? Does the writing requirement apply only to contracts for the sale of real property, or are other real estate interests covered by the Statute of Frauds, such as easements, leases, and covenants found in declarations for homeowners associations?

2. In Critical Thinking Exercise # 3 above, we discussed the case of *Kelo v. City of New London*. After the Supreme Court's decision, the homes that were condemned by the City were razed to clear the tract for development. At the time of this writing, about six years after the homes were demolished, the developer still had not obtained financing and begun construction of the new development. Check the Web and see if you can get an update on the property. Is it still vacant? Has the developer obtained financing? Does the City still intend to follow through with its original plans, or has it gone to some "Plan B"?

3. Locate a few of your state's statutes (or common law cases) that pertain to adverse possession. What are the elements of adverse possession in your state? Are they similar to those described in the text? What is the required holding period for someone adversely possessing under color of title? What is the required holding period for someone adversely possessing without the benefit of color of title? Does your state allow for adverse possession when the adverse possessor *knows* that the land being adversely possessed does not belong to him or her? Can someone adversely possess real property that is owned by the state?

BUILDING YOUR **PROFESSIONAL** PORTFOLIO

1. In the case of *Home Building & Loan Association v. Blaisdell*, 290 U.S. 398 (1934), the State of Minnesota enacted legislation that placed a moratorium on foreclosures by lenders in that state. One of the reasons that the U.S. Supreme Court did not overturn the law was because the moratorium was temporary, and to last only as long as the Depression-related foreclosure emergency existed. Draft a short statute that would protect homeowners in default on their loans from foreclosure, as well as those who are already in the foreclosure process.

2. Recall that when someone dies without a will, a state's intestacy statutes will determine who are the

decedent's heirs, and consequently, who will inherit the decedent's real and personal property. But also recall that if the decedent dies intestate, and is not survived by any statutorily determined heirs, then the decedent's property will escheat to the state. Draft a short statute that deals with when property will escheat. Decide how inclusive (or exclusive) you want the list of heirs to be. Should you include immediate family only, in which case, more property will escheat to the state, than if you define heirs to include collateral relatives such as aunts, uncles, and cousins? What about heirs who were adopted into the family; should they be entitled to inherit property, and if so, should they inherit as much property as blood relations?

3. Locate your state's intestacy statutes and prepare a summary of the statutory headings.

4. Draft a restrictive covenant limiting the range of square footages for new residential construction in the subdivision to between 2,000 and 3,000 square feet.

chapter **8**
REAL ESTATE SALES

LEARNING OBJECTIVES

After reading this chapter, you should understand:

- What real estate brokers do

- Certain aspects of the legal theory of agency, and ethical considerations

- How real property is valued in the appraisal process

- The process of selling residential property

Real Estate Sales

A real estate sale is the ***transfer of title*** to real property and title thereto, for an amount of money, or other valuable consideration.

In previous chapters we have discussed the sale of real property in terms of just a buyer and a seller. In reality, transactions for the sale of real property are often accomplished with the assistance of a real estate broker. In this chapter, we will examine the real estate brokerage profession and how brokers facilitate the sale of real property.

A. Real Estate Brokers

A real estate **broker** is a person who assists prospective buyers and sellers in negotiating the terms and conditions of real estate offers to purchase, and helps bring to fruition the sale and closing of real property. Simply put, a real estate broker is a *facilitator*, and is paid a fee to assist the buyer and seller in coming to an agreement. The broker's fee usually takes the form of a **commission**, which is a percentage of the sales price of the property.

1. BROKERS AND REALTORS

Real estate brokers are **licensed** by the state in which they operate. In order to obtain a real estate broker's license, states typically require that an individual takes several real estate–related courses, and passes a state licensing examination. Broker examinations cover topics very similar to the ones covered in this book, such as mortgages, deeds, easements, zoning, and so forth. Many states also require that an applicant for a broker's license must have previous sales experience under the supervision of someone who is already a licensed broker.

When one becomes a licensed real estate broker, she may open her own brokerage business and have licensed salespersons or **agents** working for her. Salespersons are licensed as such, but may not have the necessary course requirements or experience to be a broker. One of a broker's main responsibilities is to oversee and supervise the activity of her sales agents so that they provide appropriate service to their clients and comply with state law and ethical codes of conduct.

Some brokers are also **Realtors.** A Realtor® is a licensed real estate broker who is a member of the National Association of Realtors® (NAR). The NAR is a trade organization, which was founded in 1908, and its members are people engaged in the real estate **profession**. In addition to brokers, sales agents who are not brokers may also be members of the NAR, as can appraisers and property managers.

2. STATE SUPERVISION OF REAL ESTATE BROKERS AND AGENTS

Real estate brokerage is a business, and it is also a profession. Brokers handle large sums of money and are involved in transactions that may be worth millions of dollars. Additionally, brokers have a **fiduciary relationship**—a relationship of trust—with their clients, the buyers and sellers of real property.

Consequently, most states have real estate departments or divisions that supervise and monitor the licensing and conduct of its real estate agents and brokers. If a state rule, regulation, or ethical code is allegedly violated by an agent or broker, the state may conduct an investigation of the violation, and then, if appropriate, sanction the individual. **Sanctions** are punishments that may include monetary penalties, and/or the suspension or revocation of an agent's or broker's license.

A state's real estate department or division may order the broker or agent to pay compensation to anyone financially injured as a result of their illegal or unethical conduct. Some states even have special compensation funds in reserve to make payments to the victims in the event that the offending broker or agent is unable to do so. The compensation accounts are usually funded by a portion of the dues paid by all of the brokers and agents in the state.

Broker
one who facilitates the purchase of real property by assisting buyers and sellers in coming to an agreement on the terms and conditions of the transaction. Brokers are licensed by the state wherein they conduct business.

Profession
an occupation requiring advanced training and education, and often adhering to a professional code of ethics.

Sanctions
penalties imposed on a broker or agent by the state's department or division of real estate. Sanctions include monetary penalties, and/or the suspension or revocation of an agent's or broker's license.

B. The Law of Agency

In typical real estate transactions, the seller of the property will employ a real estate broker to assist in marketing the property to prospective buyers. It is the contractual relationship between the seller and the broker that constitutes the *agency relationship* (and *not* the contractual relationship between the seller and buyer).

An **agency** is a fiduciary relationship created by *express or implied* contract, or by law, in which one party—the agent—may act on behalf of another party—the principal—and bind the **principal** by the agent's words or actions.

A *fiduciary relationship* is one in which an agent is under a duty to act for the benefit of a principal on matters within the scope of the agency relationship. Fiduciary relationships, such as trustee-beneficiary, guardian-ward, principal-agent, and attorney-client, require an unusually high degree of care.[1] This is so because if the agent exceeds the scope of the agency, then the *principal may become liable* for breach of contract (e.g., if the agent, without authority to do so, signs a contract on principal's behalf) or for some tort, such as misrepresentation.

Ideally, the **scope of the agency** relationship should be explicitly defined by the parties to the agency contract, that is, the principal-seller and the agent-broker. Establishing the agency relationship, and the scope of the relationship—the extent of the agent's authority—is accomplished in the real estate business by the use of a standardized form known as the listing agreement.

1. AGENT'S DUTIES TO PRINCIPAL

As part and parcel of the agency relationship, an agent owes several different duties to the principal. Those duties include the following.

a. Duty of Loyalty

The *duty of loyalty* means that an agent should *not* use her position to further her own personal interest rather than those of the principal, or engage in self-dealing. **Self-dealing** occurs when the agent participates in a business deal that benefits the agent, to the detriment, or possible detriment, of her principal. An example of self-dealing would be when an agent, at a foreclosure sale, bids on the same property as her principal.

b. Duty of Performance

The **agent has a duty to perform** for the principal's benefit in accordance with the express and implied terms of their agency agreement. Bear in mind, though, that generally speaking, an agency contract need not be written, but may be implied from the conduct of the parties, just as with most other types of contracts.

An agent's duty to perform includes a *duty to obey* the principal's directives that are lawful, and within the scope of the agency agreement. By way of example, suppose a seller of real estate (the principal) lists his house for sale with a real estate broker (the agent) with an asking price of $300,000. At that price, there are very few interested buyers.

After the house has been on the market for a month, the seller directs the broker to lower the price to $250,000. The broker is obligated to obey the seller, even though the broker may believe that $50,000 is too much of a price reduction, and even though the broker will likely collect a much lower commission if and

---

Agency
a fiduciary relationship wherein the agent acts on behalf of a principal and, in the process, may bind the principal to a contract. In real estate transactions, the agent will be the real estate broker.

Principal
the person for whom an agent acts. In most real estate transactions, the principal will be the seller of the property.

Scope of the Agency
the extent of an agent's authority to act on behalf of a principal.

Self-dealing
occurs when an agent participates in a business deal that benefits the agent to the principal's detriment, or possible detriment.

Agent's Duty to Perform
the obligation of the agent to act in accordance with the terms of the agency agreement. The duty to perform includes the agent's subsidiary duty to obey, and the duty of diligence.

---

[1] BLACK'S LAW DICTIONARY, 9th Ed.

when the property is sold. This does not mean that the broker cannot advise the principal, but ultimately, the broker must act according to the principal's directives.

An agent's duty to perform also includes a *duty of diligence* for the principal's benefit. In the example in the previous paragraph, the broker reluctantly agreed to lower the price of the seller's home to $250,000. But a $50,000 reduction in price means that she will make about $3,000 less on her sales commission (6% of the $50,000 reduction). The broker has a fiduciary obligation to market the property as diligently as she did when it was priced at $300,000.

c. Duty to Render an Accounting

When requested by the principal, or as the terms of the agency contract require, **an agent must render an accounting** of how the principal's funds have been used by the agent. For example, a property management firm that manages a shopping center for the owner is an agent for the owner. The property manager may have received money from the principal, or may have used money from the property's cash flow, to advertise the shopping center, to maintain the common areas, to pay the property taxes, and to make the monthly mortgage and interest payments on the property's loan. In this situation, the agent-property manager is obligated to provide an accounting of how the owner's monies have been allocated.

Agent's Duty to Render an Accounting
the agent's obligation to report to the principal on the monies received, and disbursed, by the agent on the principal's behalf.

2. PRINCIPAL'S DUTIES TO AGENT

Just as an agent has duties to a principal, so the principal has duties to the agent. However, a principal's duties to an agent are fewer in number because it is the principal who entrusts the agent with the principal's money or property, and as previously noted, it is the agent who can create liability for the principal in tort and/or for breach of contract if the agent acts inappropriately.

a. Duty to Deal Fairly and in Good Faith

The *duty to deal fairly* and in *good faith* is not much of a surprise because it is implicit in all contracts, and you will recall that an agency relationship is a matter of contract, whether express or implied. Fair dealing and good faith are very broad terms, and somewhat synonymous. Fair dealing means *full disclosure* of all relevant information, and adherence to one's contractual duties and obligations. Good faith simply means *honesty* in executing one's obligations under the contract.

b. Duty to Cooperate

A principal has a *duty to cooperate* with the agent in carrying out the purposes of the agency relationship. Occasionally, a real estate broker (the agent) may become frustrated with the home seller (the principal) when the seller fails to cooperate with the showing of the listed property. The broker may go to great lengths to set up appointments for prospective buyers to visit the seller's property, or to hold an open house on the weekend. Assuming the broker has given the seller notice of these activities, the seller has a duty to reasonably cooperate in their execution.

Real estate brokers are sometimes frustrated when told something like the following by their sellers: "I don't want anybody to see the house because it's not clean." Or, conversely: "I just cleaned the house, and I don't want any strangers tromping through it."

There are a multitude of other reasons—some legitimate, and some not—why sellers might not want prospective buyers visiting their homes on a given occasion. Maybe the basement was flooded by last night's big rain, a legitimate reason to postpone a showing. Quite often sellers will get cold feet, meaning that they are having second thoughts about selling the property at all. If the seller is having such thoughts, it is only fair that the seller inform the broker of this fact. Otherwise, the broker would spend considerable time, energy, and money attempting to market a property that the "seller" has no intention of selling. This is why the law imposes a duty to cooperate upon the seller.

c. Duty to Compensate

The principal/seller of a property has a **duty to compensate** the agent/real estate broker when the broker has produced a prospective buyer who is **ready, able, and willing** to purchase the property. Note that the sale of the property need not actually be consummated in order for the seller to be liable to the broker for the payment of a commission.

If the broker performs pursuant to the listing agreement and produces a buyer who is ready, able, and willing to purchase the property, and the seller then refuses to sell, the seller is still obligated to pay the broker the real estate sales commission, which is typically 5%–6% of the sales price. Suppose that a house is listed for sale at $200,000, and the broker presents a legitimate offer to the seller for that amount, and with no conditions. The seller may very well be liable to the broker for the 6% commission—$12,000—even if the seller refuses to close on the property.

3. AGENT'S DUTIES TO THIRD PARTIES

An agent will be subject to **liability to a third-party**—someone other than the principal, for example a prospective buyer, or a lender—who is harmed by the agent's improper conduct. *Rest. 2d § 7.01.*

That is a rather broad statement and does not offer much guidance to an agent regarding what is proper, or improper, conduct by the agent acting on behalf of the principal. But remember that real estate professionals must adhere to a code of ethics promulgated and enforced by the state's department of real estate. Returning to the Restatement, it does make clear that an agent can be held liable by a third party for statements that constitute the negligent misrepresentation of **material information** about the property, or facts and circumstances otherwise relevant to the transaction. And of course, agents can be held liable for material statements that are fraudulent, including the concealment of material information.

In the case below, the New York Court of Appeals examined the question of whether a seller's failure to disclose the presence of poltergeists in the house being sold was of such a material nature as to allow the buyer to rescind the contract of purchase.

Material Information
that which would be important to a reasonable person in making a financial decision, for example, of whether to buy or sell real property.

STAMBOVSKY V. ACKLEY

Supreme Court of New York, Appellate Division, First Department
169 A.D.2d 254; 572 N.Y.S.2d 672; 1991 N.Y. App. Div. LEXIS 9873
July 18, 1991
[*Stambovsky is the buyer-plaintiff-appellant; Ackley is the seller-defendant-appellee*]

Plaintiff, to his horror, discovered that the house he had recently contracted to purchase was widely reputed to be possessed by poltergeists, reportedly seen by defendant seller and members of her family on numerous occasions over the last nine years. Plaintiff promptly commenced this action seeking rescission of the contract of sale. Supreme Court reluctantly dismissed the complaint, holding that plaintiff has no remedy at law in this jurisdiction.

Not being a "local," plaintiff could not readily learn that the home he had contracted to purchase is haunted. Whether the source of the spectral apparitions seen by defendant seller are parapsychic or psychogenic, having reported their presence in both a national publication (Reader's Digest) and the local press (in 1977 and 1982, respectively), **defendant is estopped to deny their existence** and, as a matter of law, the house is haunted. More to the point, however, no divination is required to conclude that it is defendant's promotional efforts in publicizing her close encounters with these spirits which fostered the home's reputation in the community. In 1989, the house was included in a five-home walking tour of Nyack and described in a November 27th newspaper article as "a riverfront Victorian (with ghost)." The impact of the reputation thus created goes to the very essence of the bargain between the parties, greatly *impairing both the value of the property and its potential for resale*. The extent of this impairment may be presumed for the purpose of reviewing the disposition of this motion to dismiss the cause of action for rescission and represents merely an issue of fact for resolution at trial.

While I agree with Supreme Court that the real estate broker, as agent for the seller, is under **no duty to disclose** to a potential buyer the phantasmal reputation of the premises and that, in his pursuit of a legal remedy for fraudulent misrepresentation against the seller, plaintiff hasn't a ghost of a chance, I am nevertheless moved by the spirit of equity to allow the buyer to seek rescission and recovery of his down payment. New York law fails to recognize any remedy for damages incurred as a result of the seller's mere silence, applying instead the strict rule of **caveat emptor.**

From the perspective of a person in the position of plaintiff herein, a very practical problem arises with respect to the discovery of a paranormal phenomenon: "Who you gonna' call?" as a title song to the movie "Ghostbusters" asks.... It has been suggested by a leading authority that the ancient rule which holds that mere nondisclosure does not constitute actionable misrepresentation "finds proper application in cases where the fact undisclosed is patent, or the plaintiff has equal opportunities for obtaining information which he may be expected to utilize, or the defendant has no reason to think that he is acting under any misapprehension" However, with respect to transactions in real estate, *New York adheres to the doctrine of caveat emptor* and imposes no duty upon the vendor to disclose any information concerning the premises unless there is a confidential or fiduciary relationship between the parties or some conduct on the part of the seller which constitutes "active concealment." Normally, some affirmative misrepresentation is required to impose upon the seller a duty to communicate undisclosed conditions affecting the premises.

The doctrine of caveat emptor requires that a buyer act prudently to assess the fitness and value of his purchase and operates to bar the purchaser who fails to exercise due care from seeking the equitable remedy of rescission.... It should be apparent, however, that the most meticulous inspection and the search would not reveal the presence of poltergeists at the premises or unearth the property's ghoulish reputation in the community. Therefore, there is no sound policy reason to deny plaintiff relief for failing to discover a state of affairs which the most prudent purchaser would not be expected to even contemplate.

The most salient distinction is that existing cases invariably deal with the *physical condition* of the premises. No case has been brought to this court's attention in which the property value was impaired as the result of the *reputation* created by information disseminated to the public by the seller (or, for that matter, as a result of possession by poltergeists).

Where a *condition which has been created by the seller materially impairs the value* of the contract and is peculiarly within the knowledge of the seller or unlikely to be discovered by a prudent purchaser exercising due care with respect to the subject transaction, **nondisclosure** constitutes a basis for rescission as a matter of equity. Any other outcome places upon the buyer not merely the obligation to exercise care in his purchase but rather to be omniscient with respect to any fact which may affect the bargain.

Defendant's contention that the contract of sale, particularly the merger or "as is" clause, bars recovery of the buyer's deposit is unavailing. Even an express disclaimer will not be given effect where the facts are peculiarly within the knowledge of the party invoking it. If the language of the contract is to be construed as broadly as defendant urges to encompass the presence of poltergeists in the house, it cannot be said that she has delivered the premises "vacant" in accordance with her obligation under the provisions of the contract rider.

In the case at bar, defendant seller deliberately fostered the public belief that her home was possessed.

(continued)

Having undertaken to inform the public-at-large, to whom she has no legal relationship, about the supernatural occurrences on her property, she may be said to owe no less a duty to her contract vendee. Where, as here, the seller not only takes unfair advantage of the buyer's ignorance but has created and perpetuated a condition about which he is unlikely to even inquire, enforcement of the contract (in whole or in part) is offensive to the court's sense of equity. Application of the remedy of rescission, within the bounds of the narrow exception to the doctrine of caveat emptor set forth herein, is entirely appropriate to relieve the unwitting purchaser from the consequences of a most unnatural bargain.

Dissent

I would affirm the dismissal of the [plaintiff-buyer's] complaint by the motion court. Plaintiff seeks to rescind his contract to purchase defendant Ackley's residential property and recover his down payment. Plaintiff alleges that Ackley and her real estate broker, defendant Ellis Realty, made material misrepresentations of the property in that they failed to disclose that Ackley believed that the house was haunted by poltergeists. Moreover, Ackley shared this belief with her community and the general public through articles published in Reader's Digest (1977) and the local newspaper (1982). In November 1989, approximately two months after the parties entered into the contract of sale but subsequent to the scheduled October 2, 1989 closing, the house was included in a five-house walking tour and again described in the local newspaper as being haunted.

Prior to closing, plaintiff learned of this reputation and unsuccessfully sought to rescind the $650,000 contract of sale and obtain return of his $32,500 down payment without resort to litigation. The plaintiff then commenced this action for that relief and alleged that he would not have entered into the contract had he been so advised and that as a result of the alleged poltergeist activity, the market value and resaleability of the property was greatly diminished. Defendant Ackley has counterclaimed for specific performance.

It is settled law in New York State that the seller of real property is under no duty to speak when the parties deal at arm's length. The mere silence of the seller, without some act or conduct which deceived the purchaser, does not amount to a concealment that is actionable as a fraud. The buyer has the duty to satisfy himself as to the quality of his bargain pursuant to the doctrine of caveat emptor, which in New York State still applies to real estate transactions.

The parties herein were represented by counsel and dealt at arm's length. This is evidenced by the contract of sale which, *inter alia*, contained various riders and a specific provision that all prior understandings and agreements between the parties were merged into the contract, that the contract completely expressed their full agreement and that neither had relied upon any statement by anyone else not set forth in the contract. There is no allegation that defendants, by some specific act, other than the failure to speak, deceived the plaintiff. Nevertheless, a cause of action may be sufficiently stated where there is a confidential or fiduciary relationship creating a duty to disclose and there was a failure to disclose a material fact, calculated to induce a false belief. However, plaintiff herein has not alleged and there is no basis for concluding that a confidential or fiduciary relationship existed between these parties to an arm's length transaction such as to give rise to a duty to disclose. In addition, there is no allegation that defendants thwarted plaintiff's efforts to fulfill his responsibilities fixed by the doctrine of caveat emptor.

Finally, if the doctrine of caveat emptor is to be discarded, it should be for a reason **more substantive than a poltergeist**. The existence of a poltergeist is no more binding upon the defendants than it is upon this court. Based upon the foregoing, the motion court properly dismissed the complaint.

Author's Comment

If sellers do have an obligation to disclose information, then one of the requirements is that the information be *material*. The majority opinion above is replete with puns and wisecracks about ghosts and poltergeists (even more so in the full-length, unedited opinion). If the majority thinks that the "presence" of ghosts is a matter of levity, how material can that "fact" be?

Should the materiality of the presence of ghosts be judged by a reasonable person standard (does the reasonable person believe in ghosts?), or by the buyer's subjective frame of mind?

Since the seller had to return the buyer's $32,500 earnest money deposit, and the contract was rescinded, why was the broker—the seller-principal's agent—relieved of any liability for failing to disclose the presence of ghosts?

It was apparently relevant to the Court's holding that the sellers had previously told *Reader's Digest*, the press, and others that the property was haunted. The Court implied that since that "fact" was disclosed to the general public, that information should also have been disclosed to the buyers. Is the Court correct, or is this a case of apples and oranges?

Was the Court correct to assume that the property's reputation as haunted necessarily impairs its value? Wouldn't some buyers pay a premium for a haunted house, for example, a buyer who purchases the property as a tourist attraction, or as an unusual bread and breakfast establishment?

4. ETHICAL ISSUES OF AGENCY

Ethical issues in agency law are more complicated than in situations involving only two parties. The reason is that ethical questions that arise in the context of agency relationships are characterized by the presence of at least three parties, that is, the principal, the agent, and the "third party." In real estate transactions, the third party is often the prospective buyer, or could be a lender or someone else involved in the transaction. Consider the following example.

EXAMPLE

Battle of the Duties

A homeowner wants to sell her home, and she and a real estate broker sign a listing agreement, which defines the scope and duties of the agency relationship. The homeowner is the principal, and the real estate broker is the agent. The "third party" is the prospective buyer that the broker has procured through an advertisement in the local newspaper.

The broker takes the prospect on a tour of the home, and the prospect expresses a desire to make a full-price offer on the property within the next 24 hours. Broker conveys this good news to the seller, who gleefully exclaims, "I guess you didn't tell him about the crack in the foundation!"

The surprised broker replies, "I didn't know there *was* a crack in the foundation."

The seller responds, "Sure, why do you think I have all those boxes stacked against the wall in the basement?"

The broker tells the seller that the he—the broker—believes that he has an *affirmative duty to inform* the prospective buyer of the crack in the foundation.

The homeowner thunders: "Nonsense! I've read books on the law of agency, and know that you have a duty of loyalty to *me*. You have a duty to obey *me*. And I am ordering you not to disclose that information. If you do, I will sue you for breach of our agency [listing] contract."

The seller/principal is no doubt correct, to a certain extent. The broker/agent *does* have a duty of loyalty to the principal, and a duty to obey the principal. But how comprehensive is that duty, and does the broker have a duty to the third party/prospective buyer, even though the broker and buyer do not have an agency relationship?

If the broker does also have a duty to the prospective buyer, which duty should take precedence, the broker's duty to the seller, or the broker's duty to the prospective buyer? What are the reasons for your answer, or if you prefer, what are the *public policy* reasons for your answer?

If you feel that the broker does have a duty to the third party, what should the broker do about it given the scenario presented?

In the poltergeist case of *Stambovsky v. Ackley*, above, the Court repeatedly referred to the Latin maxim of **caveat emptor**, or "let the buyer beware." As its Roman origins imply, the doctrine has been in existence for a long time, and was incorporated into English common law centuries ago. Under the doctrine of caveat emptor, the buyer had to beware because the seller was under no affirmative duty to disclose even hidden defects in the property or goods being sold.

Caveat Emptor
Latin for "Let the buyer beware." It meant that the seller of property had no affirmative duty to disclose defects in the property, even hidden defects.

But in modern times, the pendulum has swung in the opposite direction (despite the holding in *Stambovsky*, which was decided more than 20 years ago), although not completely, and sellers frequently do have a duty to disclose information that is material to the transaction. Material information is that which is:

i. important to the transaction, and

ii. might influence the buyer's decision to purchase or not.

In order for a buyer to obtain an FHA or VA loan, or other lender financing, sellers may be required to fill out **disclosure statements** regarding the condition of a home's plumbing, heating, and electrical systems, as well as the roof and other major components of the house. Some states require sellers to make disclosure statements. Prospective buyers may also request sellers to voluntarily fill out such a form.

EXHIBIT 8-1 Residential Property Condition Disclosure Report

State of Connecticut
Department of Consumer Protection
165 Capitol Avenue ✦ Hartford, CT 06106

RESIDENTIAL PROPERTY CONDITION DISCLOSURE REPORT

Seller's Name:		
Property Street Address:		
Property City:	State:	Zip Code:

The Uniform Property Condition Disclosure Act <u>Connecticut General Statutes Section 20-327b</u> requires the seller of residential property to provide this disclosure to the prospective purchaser prior to the prospective purchaser's execution of any binder, contract to purchase, option or lease containing a purchase option. These provisions apply to the transfer of residential real property of four dwelling units or less made with or without the assistance of a licensed broker or salesperson. The seller will be required to credit the purchaser with the sum of $300.00 at closing if the seller fails to furnish this report as required by this act.

Please note that Connecticut law requires the owner of any dwelling in which children under the age of 6 reside to abate or manage materials containing toxic levels of lead

Pursuant to the Uniform Property Condition Disclosure Act, the seller is obligated to disclose here any knowledge of any problem regarding the following:

YES	NO	UNKN	I. GENERAL INFORMATION
			1. How long have you occupied the property? _____ Age of structure _____
☐	☐	☐	2. Does anybody other than yourself have any right to use any part of your property or does anybody else claim to own any part of your property? If yes, explain _____
☐	☐	☐	3. Is the property in a flood plain area or an area containing wetlands? _____
☐	☐	☐	4. Do you have any reason to believe that the municipality may impose any assessment for purposes such as sewer installation, sewer improvements, water main installation, water main improvements, sidewalks or other improvements? _____
☐	☐	☐	5. Is the property located in an historic village or special tax district? Explain _____

YES	NO	UNKN		II. SYSTEM/UTILITIES	

☐   ☐   ☐   6. HEATING SYSTEM problems? Explain _____
   a. Heating System and Fuel Type _____
   b. Is there an underground fuel tank? If yes, location and age _____
   _____

☐   ☐   ☐   7. HOT WATER HEATER problems? Explain
   Type of hot water heater _____ Age _____

☐   ☐   ☐   8. PLUMBING SYSTEM problems? Explain _____
   _____

☐   ☐   ☐   9. SEWAGE SYSTEM problems? Explain _____
   a. Type of sewage disposal system
      (central sewer, septic, cesspool, etc.) _____
   b. If private: (a) Name of service company _____
      (b) Date last pumped _____ Frequency _____
   c. If public:
      (1) Is there a separate charge made for sewer use? yes _____ no _____
      (2) If separate charge, is it a flat amount or metered? _____
      (3) If flat amount, please state amount and payment dates
      _____
      (4) Are there any unpaid sewer charges, and if so state
         the amount _____

☐   ☐   ☐   10. AIR CONDITIONING problems? Explain _____
   Air Conditioning type: Central _____ Window _____ Other _____

☐   ☐   ☐   11. ELECTRICAL SYSTEM problems? Explain _____

☐   ☐   ☐   12. DRINKING WATER problems? Quality or Quantity? Explain _____
   _____
   If public drinking water:
   a. Is there a separate charge made for water use? Yes _____ No _____
   b. If separate charge, is it a flat amount or metered? _____
   c. If flat amount, please state amount and payment dates
   _____
   d. Are there any unpaid water charges, and if so state the amount _____

☐   ☐   ☐   13. ELECTRONIC SECURITY SYSTEM problems? Explain _____

☐   ☐   ☐   14. CARBON MONOXIDE OR SMOKE DETECTOR problems? Explain _____

☐   ☐   ☐   15. FIRE SPRINKLER SYSTEM problems? Explain _____

(continued)

EXHIBIT 8-1 *Continued*

YES	NO	UNKN	III. BUILDING/STRUCTURE/IMPROVEMENTS
☐	☐	☐	16. FOUNDATION/SLAB problems/settling? Explain _____
☐	☐	☐	17. BASEMENT Water/Seepage/Dampness? Explain amount, frequency and location. _____
☐	☐	☐	18. SUMP PUMP problems? If yes, explain _____
☐	☐	☐	19. ROOF leaks, problems? Explain _____ Roof type _____ Age _____
☐	☐	☐	20. INTERIOR WALLS/CEILING problems? Explain _____
☐	☐	☐	21. EXTERIOR SIDING problems? Explain _____
☐	☐	☐	22. FLOOR problems? Explain _____
☐	☐	☐	23. CHIMNEY/FIREPLACE/WOOD OR COAL STOVE problems? Explain: _____
☐	☐	☐	24. Any knowledge of FIRE/SMOKE damage? Explain _____
☐	☐	☐	25. PATIO/DECK problems? _____ If made of wood, is wood treated or untreated? _____
☐	☐	☐	26. DRIVEWAY problems? Explain _____
☐	☐	☐	27. TERMITE/INSECT/RODENT/PEST INFESTATION problems? Explain _____
☐	☐	☐	28. IS HOUSE INSULATED? Type _____ Location _____
☐	☐	☐	29. ROT AND WATER DAMAGE problems? Explain _____
☐	☐	☐	30. WATER DRAINAGE problems? Explain _____
☐	☐	☐	31. Are ASBESTOS CONTAINING INSULATION OR BUILDING MATERIALS present? _____ If yes, location _____
☐	☐	☐	32. Is LEAD PAINT present? If yes, location _____
☐	☐	☐	33. Is LEAD PLUMBING present? If yes, location _____
☐	☐	☐	34. Has test for RADON been done? If yes, attach copy. State whether a radon control system is in place _____

The Seller should use this area to further explain any item above. Attach additional pages if necessary and indicate here _____ the number of additional pages attached.

I. Seller's Certification

To the extent of the Seller(s) knowledge as a property owner, the Seller acknowledges that the information contained above is true and accurate for those areas of the property listed. In the event a real estate broker or salesperson is utilized, the Seller authorizes the broker or salesperson to provide the above information to prospective buyers, selling agents or buyer's agents.

DATE _____SELLER _____SELLER _____
                              (Signature)   (Type or Print)

DATE _____SELLER _____SELLER _____
                              (Signature)   (Type or Print)

II. Responsibilities of Real Estate Brokers

This report in no way relieves a real estate broker of his or her obligation under the provisions of Section 20-328-5a of the Regulations of Connecticut State Agencies to disclose any material facts. Failure to do so could result in punitive action taken against the broker, such as fines, suspension or revocation of license.

III. Statements Not to Constitute a Warranty

Any representations made by the seller on this report shall not constitute a warranty to the buyer.

IV. Nature of Disclosure Report

This residential disclosure report is not a substitute for inspections, tests, and other methods of determining the physical condition of the property.

V. Information on the Residence of Convicted Felons

Information concerning the residence address of a person convicted of a crime may be available from law enforcement agencies or the department of public safety.

VI. Buyer's Certification

The buyer is urged to carefully inspect the property and, if desired, to have the property inspected by an expert. The buyer understands that there are areas of the property for which the seller has no knowledge and this disclosure statement does not encompass those areas. The buyer also acknowledges that the buyer has read and received a signed copy of this statement from the seller or seller's agent.

DATE _____BUYER _____BUYER _____
                              (Signature)   (Type or Print)

DATE _____BUYER _____BUYER _____
                              (Signature)   (Type or Print)

Questions or Comments? Consumer Problems?

Contact the Department of Consumer Protection at (860) 713-6150 or occprotrades@po.state.ct.us

---

As you know, the typical agency relationship involves a principal/home seller and the agent/listing broker. The listing broker, as the name implies, will list the home for sale and attempt to market the property by advertising it and usually by placing it on the local Multiple Listing Service. Quite often it is another brokerage firm (that is, one other than the listing broker's firm) that may produce one or more prospective buyers; we will identify this firm as the "selling broker."

You also know that the listing broker has an agency relationship with the home seller, and therefore, that broker's fiduciary duty is owed to the seller. But to whom does the selling broker's duty run, the home seller or the prospective buyer? Consider the following scenario:

HYPOTHETICAL

Seller tells his listing broker: "Even though the house is listed for sale at $300,000, I would probably take $250,000 for it."

The listing broker conveys this information to the selling broker, who in turn conveys that tidbit to the prospective buyer.

Lo and behold, the prospective buyer tells her selling broker that she wants to make an offer on the property for … $250,000.

Has either the listing broker or the selling broker breached a duty to the seller? The listing broker undoubtedly has a duty of loyalty to the seller. Has the listing broker breached that duty by telling listing broker what the seller said about accepting an offer of $250,000?

Does the selling broker, who has been working with the buyer, owe a duty of loyalty to the seller, or to the prospective buyer?

Does the answer depend on whether selling broker has an agency agreement with the buyer? Does it matter if the selling broker will receive her commission from the seller's proceeds when the closing takes place?

The answers to these questions have changed over the years. Twenty or so years ago, the selling broker would have been deemed a *subagent* of the seller, and therefore, the selling broker's duty would have run to the seller, and not to the buyer.

However, the scenario described in the hypothetical happened all too often, and as you can see, set up a number of potential conflicts of interest and ethical questions, That is why it is now quite common for buyers to hire brokers to represent the buyers exclusively, rather than the those brokers being subagents of the sellers. This arrangement precludes many of the ethical problems that were inherent when a buyer's broker was deemed to be a subagent of the seller. But it is interesting to note that even under the new arrangement—seller hires a broker, buyer hires a broker—the buyer's broker is still quite often paid her commission out of the seller's proceeds at closing.

5. DUAL AGENCY

Dual Agency
when a broker represents both buyer and seller in the same transaction. Dual agency is fraught with the danger of ethical conflicts, and is therefore illegal in some states.

When the same broker represents both the seller and the buyer, this is known as a **dual agency,** and raises special ethical concerns. As you might imagine, a dual agency relationship is fraught with danger for seller, buyer, and broker because the broker cannot properly serve two masters. A buyer and seller have inherently *conflicting interests*: the seller wants to sell the property for the highest possible price, while the buyer wants to purchase the property for the lowest possible price.

It would seem almost impossible for a dual agency broker to walk this tightrope of his clients' competing interests. Revealing even a seemingly insignificant piece of information may benefit one principal over the other, and thereby breach the duty of loyalty to that principal. It is for that and other reasons that many states prohibit real estate brokers to engage in dual agency.

In states that do permit dual agency, brokers must expressly—in writing—and explicitly inform both the buyer and the seller of the dual agency relationship, and the possible conflicts that it presents. In states that permit dual agency, as long as the parties are informed, they may consent to the dual agency representation by the broker.

C. Valuation and Appraisal of Real Property

1. DETERMINING A LISTING PRICE: MARKET COMPARISON METHOD

After a seller and broker discuss the possibility of marketing the seller's house, they may sign an exclusive right to sell listing agreement. One of the most important terms in that contract is the **list price,** or the seller's offering price. The list price should not simply be pulled out of the air, but rather the listing broker will research the sale of similar properties that have taken place in the neighborhood in the preceding year or two. This method of valuation is called the **market comparison**, *or* **market comparable** ("market comp") approach.

When assigning a list price to the **subject property**—the house the broker has just listed—the listing broker will note the similarities and differences between the subject property and homes that have previously sold in the neighborhood. Important categories for comparison of the subject property and the other home sales would include:

i. The square footage of the comparables and the subject property, and the average prices per square foot,

ii. The number of bedrooms and bathrooms,

iii. The lot sizes, and

iv. Amenities such as swimming pools and spas.

The differences between the properties are probably more significant than the similarities. You may have heard the old expression that "The three most important things about real estate are location, location, location." This phrase underscores the importance of not only a property's scenic views—whether of the ocean, the mountains, or a landfill operation—but also the proximity of the property to good schools, convenient shopping, recreational areas, healthcare facilities, and other amenities.

Market Comparable
a property that has recently sold and is compared with the subject property to derive an appropriate list price for the subject property. It is important that the sale of the "comp" property be in the same neighborhood as the subject property, and have been sold recently.

Subject Property
the property that is being listed for sale by the broker.

EXHIBIT 8-2 Uniform Residential Appraisal Report

UNIFORM RESIDENTIAL APPRAISAL REPORT   FILE

The purpose of this summary appraisal report is to provide the lender/client with an accurate, and adequately supported, opinion of the market value of the subject property.	

Property Address	City	State Zip Code
Borrower Owner of Public Record		County
Legal Description		
Assessor's Parcel #	Tax Year	R.E. Taxes $
Neighborhood Name	Map Reference	Census Tract
Occupant ☐ Owner ☐ Tenant ☐ Vacant Special Assessments $	☐ PUD HQA$	☐ per year ☐ per month
Property Rights Appraised ☐ Fee Simple ☐ Leasehold ☐ Other (describe)		
Assignment Type ☐ Purchase Transaction ☐ Refinance Transaction ☐ Other (describe)		
Lender/Client Address		
Is the subject property currently offered for sale or has it been offered for sale in the twelve months prior to the effective date of this appraisal? ☐ Yes ☐ No		
Report data source(s) used, offering price(s), and date(s).		

(continued)

EXHIBIT 8-2 *Continued*

UNIFORM RESIDENTIAL APPRAISAL REPORT   FILE

C O N T R A C T

I ☐ did ☐ did not analyze the contract for sale for the subject purchase transaction. Explain the results of the analysis of the contract for sate or why the analysis was not performed.

Contract Price $ Dale of Contract   is the property seller the owner of public record?   ☐ Yes   ☐ No   Data Source(s)

Is there any financial assistance (loan charges, sale concessions, gift or downpayment assistance, etc.) to be paid by any party on behalf of the borrower? ☐ Yes ☐ No
If Yes, report the total dollar amount and describe the items to be paid.

N E I G H B O R H O O D

Note: Race and the racial composition of the neighborhood are not appraisal factors.

Neighborhood Characteristics			One-Unit Housing Trends				One-Unit Housing		Present Land Use %	
Location ☐ Urban	☐ Suburban	☐ Rural	Property Values ☐ Increasing		☐ Stable ☐ Declining		PRICE	AGE	One-Unit	%
Built-Up ☐ Over 75% ☐ 25-75%		☐ Under 25%	Demand/Supply ☐ Shortage		☐ In Balance	☐ Over Supply	$(000)	(yrs)	2-4 Unit	%
Growth ☐ Rapid	☐ Stable	☐ Slow	Marketing Time ☐ Under 3 mths		☐ 3-6 mths	☐ Over 6 mths	Low		Multi-Family	%
Neighborhood Boundaries							High		Commercial	%
							Pred.		Other	%

Neighborhood Description

Market Conditions (Including support for the above conclusions)

S I T E

Dimensions   Area   Shape   View

Specific Zoning Classification   Zoning Description

Zoning Compliance ☐ Legal   ☐ legal Nonconforming (Grandfathered Use)   ☐ No Zoning   ☐ illegal (describe)

Is the highest and best use of the subject property as Improved (or as proposed per plans and specifications) the present use? ☐ Yes ☐ No If No, describe

Utilities	Public	Other (describe)		Public	Other (describe)	Off-site Improvements—Type	Public	Private
Electricity	☐	☐	Water	☐	☐	Street	☐	☐
Gas	☐	☐	Sanitary Sewer	☐	☐	Alley	☐	☐

FEMA Special Flood Hazard Area ☐ Yes ☐ No   FEMA Feed Zone   FEMA Map #   FEMA Map Date

Are the utilities and off-site Improvements typical for the market area? ☐ Yes ☐ No If No, describe

Are there any adverse site conditions or external factors (easements, encroachments, environmental conditions, land uses, etc.)? ☐ Yes ☐ No   if Yes, describe

I M P R O V E M E N T S

General Description		Foundation		Exterior Description materials/condition	Interior materials/condition
Units ☐ One ☐ One with Accessory Unit		☐ Concrete Slab ☐ Crawl Space		Foundation Walls	Floors
# of Stories		☐ Full Basement ☐ Partial Basement		Exterior Walls	Walls
Type ☐ Det. ☐ Att. ☐ S-Del/End Unit		Basement Area sq. ft.		Roof Surface	Trim/Finish
☐ Existing ☐ Proposed ☐ Under Const.		Basement Finish %		Gutters & Downspouts	Bath Floor
Design (Style)		☐ Outside Entry/Exit ☐ Sump Pump		Window Type	Bath Wainscot
Year Built		Evidence of ☐ Infestation		Storm Sash/Insulated	Car Storage ☐ None
Effective Age (Yrs)		☐ Dampness ☐ Settlement		Screens	☐ Driveway # of Cars
Attic	☐ None	Healing ☐ FWA ☐ HWBB ☐ Radiant		Amenities ☐ Woodslove(s) #	Driveway Surface
☐ Drop Stair	☐ Stairs	☐ Other	Fuel	☐ Fireplace(s) # ☐ Fence	☐ Garage #of Cars
☐ Floor	☐ Scuttle	Cooling ☐ Central Air Conditioning		☐ Patio/Deck ☐ Porch	☐ Carport #of Cars
☐ Finished	☐ Heated	☐ Individual	☐ Other	☐ Pool ☐ Other	☐ Att. ☐ Det. ☐ Built-in

Appliances ☐ Refrigerator ☐ Range/Oven ☐ Dishwasher ☐ Disposal ☐ Microwave ☐ Washer/Dryer ☐ Other (describe)

Finished area above grade contains: Rooms   Bedrooms   Bath(s)   Square Feet of Gross Living Area Above Grade

Additional features (special energy efficient items, etc.)

Describe the condition of the property (including needed repairs, deterioration, renovations, remodeling, etc.).

Are there any physical deficiencies or adverse conditions that affect the livability, soundness, or structural integrity of the property? ☐ Yes ☐ No   If Yes, describe

Does the property generally conform to the neighborhood (functional utility, style, condition, use, construction, etc.)?   ☐ Yes   ☐ No   If No, describe

UNIFORM RESIDENTIAL APPRAISAL REPORT

FILE #

SALES COMPARISON APPROACH

There are comparable properties currently offered for sale in the subject neighborhood ranging In price from $ to $

There are comparable sales in the subject neighborhood within the past twelve months ranging in sale price from $ to$

FEATURE	SUBJECT	COMPARABLE SALE #1		COMPARABLE SALE #1		COMPARABLE SALE #3	
Address							
Proximity to Subject							
Sale Price	$		$		$		$
Sale Price/Gross Liv. Area	$ sq.ft.	$ sq.ft.		$ sq.ft.		$ sq.ft.	
Data Source(s)							
Verification Source(s)							
VALUE ADJUSTMENTS	DESCRIPTION	DESCRIPTION	+(−)$Adjustment	DESCRIPTION	+(−)$Adjustment	DESCRIPTION	+(−)$Adjustment
Sale or Financing Concessions							
Date of Sale/Time							
Location							
Leasehold/Fee Simple							
Site							
View							
Design (Style)							
Quality of Construction							
Actual Age							
Condition							
Above Grade Room Count	Total / Bdrms. / Baths	Total / Bdrms. / Baths		Total / Bdrms. / Baths		Total / Bdrms. / Baths	
Gross Living Area	sq.ft.	sq.ft.		sq.ft.		sq.ft.	
Basement & Finished Rooms Below Grade							
Functional Utility							
Heating/Cooling							
Energy Efficient items							
Garage/Carport							
Porch/Patio/Deck							
Net Adjustment (Total)		☐ + ☐ −	$	☐ + ☐ −	$	☐ + ☐ −	$
Adjusted Sale Price of Comparables		Net Adj. % Gross Adj. %	$	Net Adj. % Gross Adj. %	$	Net Adj. % Gross Adj. %	$

I ☐ did ☐ did not research the sale or transfer history of the subject property and comparable sales. If not explain.

My research ☐ did ☐ did not reveal any prior sales or transfers of the subject property for the three years prior to the effective date of this appraisal.

Data source(s)

My research ☐ did ☐ did not reveal any prior sales or transfers of the comparable sales for the year prior to the date of sale of the comparable sale.

Data source(s)

Report the results of the research and analysis of the prior sale or transfer history of the subject property and comparable sales (report additional prior sales on page 3).

ITEM	SUBJECT	COMPARABLE SALE #1	COMPARABLE SALE #2	COMPARABLE SALE #3
Dale of Prior Sale/Transfer				
Price of Prior Sale/Transfer				
Date Source(s)				
Effective Date of Data Source(s)				

Analysis of prior sale or transfer history of the subject property and comparable sales

Summary of Sales Comparison Approach

Indicated Value by Sales Comparison Approach $

RECONCILIATION

Indicated Value by: Sales Comparison Approach $ Cost Approach (if developed) $ Income Approach (if developed) $

This appraisal is made ☐ "as is", ☐ subject to completion per plans and specifications on the basis of a hypothetical condition that the improvements have been completed, ☐ subject to the following repairs or alterations on the basis of a hypothetical condition that the repairs or alterations have been completed, or ☐ subject to the following required inspection based on the extraordinary assumption that the condition or deficiency does not require alteration or repair:

Based on a complete visual Inspection of the interior and exterior areas of the subject property, defined scope of work. statement of assumptions and limiting conditions, and appraiser's certification, my (our) opinion of the market value, as defined, of the real property that is the subject of this report is $,as of ,which is the date of Inspection, and the effective date of this appraisal.

(continued)

EXHIBIT 8-2 *Continued*

UNIFORM RESIDENTIAL APPRAISAL REPORT

FILE #

ADDITIONAL COMMENTS

COST APPROACH TO VALUE (not required by Fannie Mae)

Provide adequate information for the lender/client to replicate the below cost figures and calculations.

Support for the opinion of site value (summary of comparable land sales or other methods for estimating site value)

COST APPROACH

ESTIMATED ☐ REPRODUCTION OR ☐ REPLACEMENT COST NEW	OPINION OF SITE VALUE.. = $		
Source of cost data	Dwelling	Sq.Ft.@$	.... = $
Quality rating from cost service Effective date of cost data		Sq.Ft.@$	.... = $
Comments on Cost Approach (gross living area calculations, depreciation, etc.)			
	Garage/Carport	Sq.Ft.@$	.... = $
	Total Estimate of Cost-New		.... = $
	Less Physical	Functional	External
	Depreciation		= $( )
	Depreciated Cost of Improvements		.... = $
	"As-is" Value of Site Improvements		.... = $
Estimated Remaining Economic Life (HUD and VA only) Years	Indicated Value By Cost Approach.. = $		

INCOME APPROACH TO VALUE (not required by Fannie Mas)

Estimated Monthly Market Rent $ X Gross Rent Multiplier   = $ Indicated Value by Income Approach

Summary of Income Approach (including support for market rent and GRM)

PROJECT INFORMATION FOR PUDs (If applicable)

Is the developer/builder in control of the Homeowners' Association (HOA)?   ☐ Yes   ☐ No   Unit type(s) ☐ Detached   ☐ Attached

Provide the following Information for PUDs ONLY if the developer/builder is in control of the HOA and the subject property is an attached dwelling unit.

Legal name of project

Total number of phases   Total number of units   Total number of units sold

Total number of units rented   Total number of units for sale   Data source(s)

Was the project created by the conversion of an existing building(s) into a PUD?   ☐ Yes   ☐ No   If Yes, date of conversion

Does the project contain any multi-dwelling units?   ☐ Yes   ☐ No   Data source(s)

Are the units, common elements, and recreation facilities complete?   ☐ Yes   ☐ No   If No, describe the status of completion.

Are the common elements leased to or by the Homeowners' Association?   ☐ Yes   ☐ No   if Yes, describe the rental terms and options.

Describe common elements and recreational facilities

Uniform Residential Appraisal Report

File #

This report form is designed to report an appraisal of a one-unit property or a one-unit property with an accessory unit, including a unit in a planned unit development (PUD). This report form is not designed to report an appraisal of a manufactured home or a unit in a condominium or cooperative project.

This appraisal report is subject to the following scope of work, intended use, intended user, definition of market value, statement of assumptions and limiting conditions, and certifications. Modifications, additions, or deletions to the intended use, intended user, definition of market value, or assumptions and limiting conditions are not permitted. The appraiser may expand the scope of work to include any additional research or analysis necessary based on the complexity of this appraisal assignment. Modifications or deletions to the certifications are also not permitted. However, additional certifications that do not constitute material alterations to this appraisal report, such as those required by law or those related to the appraiser's continuing education or membership in an appraisal organization, are permitted.

SCOPE OF WORK: The scope of work for this appraisal is defined by the complexity of this appraisal assignment and the reporting requirements of this appraisal report form, including the following definition of market value, statement of assumptions and limiting conditions, and certifications. The appraiser must, at a minimum: (1) perform a complete visual inspection of the interior and exterior areas of the subject property, (2) inspect the neighborhood, (3) inspect each of the comparable sales from at least the street, (4) research, verify, and analyze data from reliable public and/or private sources, and (5) report his or her analysis, opinions, and conclusions in this appraisal report.

INTENDED USE: The intended use of this appraisal report is for the lender/client to evaluate the property that is the subject of this appraisal for a mortgage finance transaction.

INTENDED USER: The intended user of this appraisal report is the lender/client.

DEFINITION OF MARKET VALUE: The most probable price which a property should bring in a competitive and open market under all conditions requisite to a fair sale, the buyer and seller, each acting prudently, knowledgeably and assuming the price is not affected by undue stimulus. Implicit in this definition is the consummation of a sale as of a specified date and the passing of title from seller to buyer under conditions whereby: (1) buyer and seller are typically motivated; (2) both parties are well informed or well advised, and each acting in what he or she considers his or her own best interest; (3) a reasonable time is allowed for exposure in the open market; (4) payment is made in terms of cash in U.S. dollars or in terms of financial arrangements comparable thereto; and (5) the price represents the normal consideration for the property sold unaffected by special or creative financing or sales concessions* granted by anyone associated with the sale.

*Adjustments to the comparables must be made for special or creative financing or sales concessions. No adjustments are necessary for those costs which are normally paid by sellers as a result of tradition or law in a market area; these costs are readily identifiable since the seller pays these costs in virtually all sales transactions. Special or creative financing adjustments can be made to the comparable property by comparisons to financing terms offered by a third-party institutional lender that is not already involved in the property or transaction. Any adjustment should not be calculated on a mechanical dollar for dollar cost of the financing or concession but the dollar amount of any adjustment should approximate the market's reaction to the financing or concessions based on the appraiser's judgment.

STATEMENT OF ASSUMPTIONS AND LIMITING CONDITIONS: The appraiser's certification in this report is subject to the following assumptions and limiting conditions:

1. The appraiser will not be responsible for matters of a legal nature that affect either the property being appraised or the title to it, except for information that he or she became aware of during the research involved in performing this appraisal. The appraiser assumes that the title is good and marketable and will not render any opinions about the title.

2. The appraiser has provided a sketch in this appraisal report to show the approximate dimensions of the improvements. The sketch is included only to assist the reader in visualizing the property and understanding the appraiser's determination of its size.

3. The appraiser has examined the available flood maps that are provided by the Federal Emergency Management Agency (or other data sources) and has noted in this appraisal report whether any portion of the subject site is located in an identified Special Flood Hazard Area. Because the appraiser is not a surveyor, he or she makes no guarantees, express or implied, regarding this determination.

4. The appraiser will not give testimony or appear in court because he or she made an appraisal of the property in question, unless specific arrangements to do so have been made beforehand, or as otherwise required by law.

5. The appraiser has noted in this appraisal report any adverse conditions (such as needed repairs, deterioration, the presence of hazardous wastes, toxic substances, etc.) observed during the inspection of the subject property or that he or she became aware of during the research involved in performing this appraisal. Unless otherwise stated in this appraisal report, the appraiser has no knowledge of any hidden or unapparent physical deficiencies or adverse conditions of the property (such as, but not limited to, needed repairs, deterioration, the presence of hazardous wastes, toxic substances, adverse environmental conditions, etc.) that would make the property less valuable, and has assumed that there are no such conditions and makes no guarantees or warranties, express or implied. The appraiser will not be responsible for any such conditions that do exist or for any engineering or testing that might be required to discover whether such conditions exist. Because the appraiser is not an expert in the field of environmental hazards, this appraisal report must not be considered as an environmental assessment of the property.

6. The appraiser has based his or her appraisal report and valuation conclusion for an appraisal that is subject to satisfactory completion, repairs, or alterations on the assumption that the completion, repairs, or alterations of the subject property will be performed in a professional manner.

(continued)

EXHIBIT 8-2 *Continued*

UNIFORM RESIDENTIAL APPRAISAL REPORT   FILE

APPRAISER'S CERTIFICATION: The Appraiser certifies and agrees that:

1. I have, at a minimum, developed and reported this appraisal in accordance with the scope of work requirements stated in this appraisal report.

2. I performed a complete visual inspection of the interior and exterior areas of the subject property. I reported the condition of the improvements in factual, specific terms. I identified and reported the physical deficiencies that could affect the livability, soundness, or structural integrity of the property.

3. I performed this appraisal in accordance with the requirements of the Uniform Standards of Professional Appraisal Practice that were adopted and promulgated by the Appraisal Standards Board of The Appraisal Foundation and that were in place at the time this appraisal report was prepared.

4. I developed my opinion of the market value of the real property that is the subject of this report based on the sales comparison approach to value. I have adequate comparable market data to develop a reliable sales comparison approach for this appraisal assignment. I further certify that I considered the cost and income approaches to value but did not develop them, unless otherwise indicated in this report.

5. I researched, verified, analyzed, and reported on any current agreement for sale for the subject property, any offering for sale of the subject property in the twelve months prior to the effective date of this appraisal, and the prior sales of the subject property for a minimum of three years prior to the effective date of this appraisal, unless otherwise indicated in this report.

6. I researched, verified, analyzed, and reported on the prior sales of the comparable sales for a minimum of one year prior to the date of sale of the comparable sale, unless otherwise indicated in this report.

7. I selected and used comparable sales that are locationally, physically, and functionally the most similar to the subject property.

8. I have not used comparable sales that were the result of combining a land sale with the contract purchase price of a home that has been built or will be built on the land.

9. I have reported adjustments to the comparable sales that reflect the market's reaction to the differences between the subject property and the comparable sales.

10. I verified, from a disinterested source, all information in this report that was provided by parties who have a financial interest in the sale or financing of the subject property.

11. I have knowledge and experience in appraising this type of property in this market area.

12. I am aware of, and have access to, the necessary and appropriate public and private data sources, such as multiple listing services, tax assessment records, public land records, and other such data sources for the area in which the property is located.

13. I obtained the information, estimates, and opinions furnished by other parties and expressed in this appraisal report from reliable sources that I believe to be true and correct.

14. I have taken into consideration the factors that have an impact on value with respect to the subject neighborhood, subject property, and the proximity of the subject property to adverse influences in the development of my opinion of market value. I have noted in this appraisal report any adverse conditions (such as, but not limited to, needed repairs, deterioration, the presence of hazardous wastes, toxic substances, adverse environmental conditions, etc.) observed during the inspection of the subject property or that I became aware of during the research Involved in performing this appraisal. I have considered these adverse conditions in my analysis of the property value, and have reported on the effect of the conditions on the value and marketability of the subject property.

15. I have not knowingly withheld any significant information from this appraisal report and, to the best of my knowledge, all statements and information in this appraisal report are true and correct.

16. I stated in this appraisal report my own personal, unbiased, and professional analysis, opinions, and conclusions, which are subject only to the assumptions and limiting conditions in this appraisal report.

17. I have no present or prospective interest in the property that is the subject of this report, and I have no present or prospective personal interest or bias with respect to the participants in the transaction. I did not base, either partially or completely, my analysis and/or opinion of market value in this appraisal report on the race, color, religion, sex, age, marital status, handicap, familial status, or national origin of either the prospective owners or occupants of the subject property or of the present owners or occupants of the properties in the vicinity of the subject property or on any other basis prohibited by law.

18. My employment and/or compensation for performing this appraisal or any future or anticipated appraisals was not conditioned on any agreement or understanding, written or otherwise, that I would report (or present analysis supporting) a predetermined specific value, a predetermined minimum value, a range or direction In value, a value that favors the cause of any party, or the attainment of a specific result or occurrence of a specific subsequent event (such as approval of a pending mortgage loan application).

19. I personally prepared all conclusions and opinions about the real estate that were set forth in this appraisal report. If I relied on significant real property appraisal assistance from any individual or individuals in the performance of this appraisal or the preparation of this appraisal report, I have named such individual(s) and disclosed the specific tasks performed in this appraisal report. I certify that any individual so named is qualified to perform the tasks. I have not authorized anyone to make a change to any item in this appraisal report; therefore, any change made to this appraisal is unauthorized and I will take no responsibility for it.

20. I identified the lender/client In this appraisal report who is the Individual, organization, or agent for the organization that ordered and will receive this appraisal report.

UNIFORM RESIDENTIAL APPRAISAL REPORT   FILE

21. The lender/client may disclose or distribute this appraisal report to: the borrower; another lender at the request of the borrower; the mortgagee or its successors and assigns; mortgage insurers; government sponsored enterprises; other secondary market participants; data collection or reporting services; professional appraisal organizations; any department, agency, or instrumentality of the United States; and any state, the District of Columbia, or other Jurisdictions; without having to obtain the appraiser's or supervisory appraiser's (if applicable) consent. Such consent must be obtained before this appraisal report may be disclosed or distributed to any other party (including, but not limited to, the public through advertising, public relations, news, sales, or other media).

22. I am aware that any disclosure or distribution of this appraisal report by me or the lender/client may be subject to certain laws and regulations. Further, I am also subject to the provisions of the Uniform Standards of Professional Appraisal Practice that pertain to disclosure or distribution by me.

23. The borrower, another lender at the request of the borrower, the mortgagee or its successors and assigns, mortgage insurers, government sponsored enterprises, and other secondary market participants may rely on this appraisal report as part of any mortgage finance transaction that involves any one or more of these parties.

24. If this appraisal report was transmitted as an "electronic record" containing my "electronic signature," as those terms are defined In applicable federal and/or state laws (excluding audio and video recordings), or a facsimile transmission of this appraisal report containing a copy or representation of my signature, the appraisal report shall be as effective, enforceable and valid as If a paper version of this appraisal report were delivered containing my original hand written signature.

25. Any intentional or negligent misrepresentation(s) contained In this appraisal report may result in civil liability and/or criminal penalties including, but not limited to, fine or imprisonment or both under the provisions of Title 18, United States Code, Section 1001, et seq., or similar state laws.

SUPERVISORY APPRAISER'S CERTIFICATION: The Supervisory Appraiser certifies and agrees that:

1. I directly supervised the appraiser for this appraisal assignment, have read the appraisal report, and agree with the appraiser's analysis, opinions, statements, conclusions, and the appraiser's certification.

2. I accept full responsibility for the contents of this appraisal report including, but not limited to, the appraiser's analysis, opinions, statements, conclusions, and the appraiser's certification.

3. The appraiser identified in this appraisal report is either a sub-contractor or an employee of the supervisory appraiser (or the appraisal firm), is qualified to perform this appraisal, and is acceptable to perform this appraisal under the applicable state law.

4. This appraisal report complies with the Uniform Standards of Professional Appraisal Practice that were adopted and promulgated by the Appraisal Standards Board of The Appraisal Foundation and that were in place at the time this appraisal report was prepared.

5. If this appraisal report was transmitted as an "electronic record" containing my "electronic signature," as those terms are defined in applicable federal and/or state laws (excluding audio and video recordings), or a facsimile transmission of this appraisal report containing a copy or representation of my signature, the appraisal report shall be as effective, enforceable and valid as if a paper version of this appraisal report were delivered containing my original hand written signature.

APPRAISER

Signature _____
Name _____
Company Name _____
Company Address _____

Telephone Number _____
Email Address _____
Date of Signature and Report _____
Effective Date of Appraisal _____
Slate Certification # _____
or State License # _____
or Other (describe) _____ State # _____
State _____
Expiration Date of Certification or License _____

ADDRESS OF PROPERTY APPRAISED

_____
_____

APPRAISED VALUE OF SUBJECT PROPERTY $ _____

LENDER/CLIEN

Name _____
Company Name _____
Company Address _____

Email Address _____

SUPERVISORY APPRAISER (ONLY IF REQUIRED)

Signature _____
Name _____
Company Name _____
Company Address _____

Telephone Number _____
Email Address _____
Date of Signature _____
State Certification # _____
or State License # _____
State _____
Expiration Date of Certification or License _____

SUBJECT PROPERTY

☐ Did not inspect subject property
☐ Did inspect exterior of subject property from street
   Date of inspection _____
☐ Did inspect interior and exterior of subject property
   Date of inspection _____

COMPARABLE SALES

☐ Did not inspect exterior of comparable sales from street
☐ Did inspect exterior of comparable sales from street
   Date of Inspection _____

2. LIST PRICE VERSUS APPRAISED VALUE

In the previous section we discussed how a listing broker will arrive at a list price for the property to be sold using the "market comp" method. What is the difference between the list price and the appraised value?

First, an **appraisal** is the process of determining an *opinion of value*. The opinion of the value in question is that of a licensed appraiser. In generating an appraised value of a residential property, the appraiser will almost always use the same method as the listing broker, that is, the market comparables approach. As you can see from the Uniform Residential Appraisal Report (Exhibit 8-2), an appraisal is very comprehensive, and certainly more so than the market comparable valuation for listing purposes.

The dollar difference between the list price and the appraised value may be practically nil, or it may be significant. The real difference has to do with the purpose: the list price is the price at which the property is offered for sale by the seller.

The *appraised value,* on the other hand, is the value *used by the lender*—usually a bank—to determine how much money it will loan to the buyer of the house. That is why appraisers must take extensive coursework in the appraisal process, pass rigorous examinations, and be licensed by the state in which they practice.

> **Appraisal**
> the process of determining an opinion of value by a licensed appraiser, which is used by a lender to determine the amount to be loaned for the purchase price.

EXAMPLE

The listing broker has conducted a market comparison, and suggests to the seller that the property be listed at $300,000, to which the seller agrees. A prospective buyer makes a written offer to purchase of $290,000, which the seller accepts.

The buyer will then apply to a lender about making a loan on the property. Assume that the buyer qualifies for an 80% loan. The lender then hires an appraiser to issue an appraisal opinion of the property's fair market value.

In this example, the appraisal comes in at $280,000, that is, $10,000 less than the purchase price of $290,000. The lender will make a loan for 80% of the *appraised* value of $280,000, which is $224,000, and *not* 80% of the purchase price of $290,000, which is $232,000.

This means that the buyer will have to come up with an extra $8,000 ($232,000 − $224,000) in order to have a 20% down payment, and close on the property. In the wake of the collapse of the real estate market, lenders became far more conservative in their lending practices, in large part because of the requirements of the Dodd–Frank Wall Street Reform and Consumer Protection Act (Pub. L. 111-203).

D. The Process of Selling a Home

Although our discussion below focuses on the sale of residential real estate, the principles apply to the sale of commercial properties, or even vacant land. In the United States, most sales of residential real estate are accomplished with the assistance of a real estate broker.

1. THE LISTING AGREEMENT

The listing agreement is the contract between the seller of a property and the broker employed by the seller, for the purpose of selling real property. The listing agreement establishes the agency relationship that we discussed earlier, and identifies the duties and obligations that the seller and broker owe to each other. There are three basic types of listing agreements.

a. Exclusive Right to Sell Listing Agreement

The exclusive right to sell is the listing agreement **most preferred by real estate brokers** because it gives the broker the most control, and the most security in terms of being paid. An exclusive right to sell is a written contract between the seller and a real estate broker in which the seller gives to the broker a right to sell the property, to the exclusion of all other brokers. However, the word "exclusive" is a little confusing here: Although the listing broker is considered the exclusive broker, other brokers are allowed to bring offers to purchase from their prospective buyers for the listing broker to present to the seller.

If such an offer is accepted by the seller, the listing broker will split the commission with the selling broker. What the word "exclusive" really means in the context of an "exclusive right to sell" listing contract is that the listing broker has the exclusive right to receive the commission for the sale of the property, which the listing broker is then obligated to split with the selling broker.

The listing agreement should specify each of the following terms and conditions of the seller and broker's contract:

i. The **parties** to the listing agreement, that is, the seller and the listing broker;
ii. The identity of the **property** to be sold;
iii. The **list price** of the property. This is the price at which the property is offered for sale, although it is not necessarily the final selling price;
iv. The **term** of the listing agreement, specifically, the beginning and ending dates. A typical term for a listing agreement might be 180 days. Commercial properties and raw land take longer to sell, and the term of such listings would likely be for at least a year;
v. The amount of **compensation** to be paid to the listing broker, which is usually a percentage of the selling price, and is usually in the range of 5%–6% for residential properties. For commercial properties, 10% is a typical commission because commercial properties are more complicated transactions, more expensive to market, and take considerably longer to sell;
vi. The listing agreement will usually require that the broker use **reasonable efforts** to market the property, including advertising the property and placing the property on the local Multiple Listing Service, and often placing a For Sale sign on the property;
vii. The **exclusivity provision** (this is an *exclusive* right to sell listing contract), which states that a commission will still be owed to the listing broker in the event that the property is sold by the seller herself, or if it is sold by another broker who presents an offer directly to the seller, rather than going through the listing broker.

The exclusivity provision in number (vii) above is the reason that brokers prefer the **exclusive right to sell listing agreement.** Even if the seller finds a buyer without the assistance of the listing broker, the listing broker is still entitled to a commission. If it were otherwise, the listing broker would be very reluctant to risk the time, money, and energy to market the property. If a prospective buyer makes an offer to purchase directly to the seller, the seller should inform the prospect to contact the listing broker and make the offer through the listing broker.

Exclusive Right to Sell Listing Agreement
the listing contract preferred by brokers because it offers the most protection to the broker. The broker will be paid a commission regardless of who sells the property.

EXHIBIT 8-3 Listing Agreement

LISTING AGREEMENT

THIS AGREEMENT made by and between _____
& _____, hereinafter collectively referred to as
"Owner" and "Broker."

Recitals:

1. Owner is the owner of that certain real property situated in _____ County, State
of _____, commonly known as _____
and hereinafter referred to as the "Property," and more particularly described as (legal description):

2. Owner desires to sell the Property and, accordingly, Owner desires to grant to Broker the [exclusive and irrevocable] right to sell the
Property in accordance with the provisions of this Agreement. Broker is a duly licensed real estate salesman [or broker] in the State of
_____, and desires to have the [exclusive] authority to sell the Property in accordance with the provisions of and
for the compensation provided for in this Agreement.

THEREFORE, Owner and Agent agree as follows:

1. Grant of Right. Owner hereby grants to Broker the [exclusive and irrevocable] right, commencing on_____, and
expiring at _____.m. on _____, to sell the Property.

2. Personal Property Included. In addition to the real property described above, the Property to be sold [or exchanged or sold] includes the
personal property itemized in the inventory attached hereto as Exhibit _____, which exhibit is incorpo-
rated in and made a part of this Agreement.

3. Incorporation of Information Checklist. As a further description of the Property, the parties have jointly prepared statements and information, which appear in the Property Information Checklist, which checklist is attached to and incorporated in this Agreement as Exhibit A.

4. Terms of Sale. The selling price of the Property shall be $_____, which shall be paid on the following
terms: _____ or at such price and terms as shall be acceptable to Owner, and to accept a
deposit thereon.

[ ] 5. Open Listing. This Agreement is commonly known in the trade as an open listing and if, during the period of this Agreement, the sale
of the Property is consummated and the deed or other evidence of the transfer of title is recorded other than through the efforts of Broker,
but rather through the efforts of other agents, or of anyone else, including Owner, the aforesaid compensation for the sale shall not be paid
to Broker as set forth in this Agreement.
[or]
[ ] 5. Exclusive Agent Listing. This Agreement is commonly known in the trade as an exclusive agency listing and if, during the period of this
Agreement, the sale of the Property is consummated and the deed or other evidence of the transfer of title is recorded other than through
the efforts of Broker, but rather through the efforts of other agents, or of anyone else, excluding Owner, compensation shall be paid to
Broker as set forth in this Agreement.

[or]
[ ] 5. Exclusive Right to Sell Listing. This Agreement is commonly known in the trade as an exclusive right to sell listing and if, during the
period of this Agreement, the sale of the Property is consummated and the deed or other evidence of the transfer of title is recorded other
than through the efforts of Broker, but rather through the efforts of other agents, or of anyone else, including Owner, compensation shall be
paid to Broker as set forth in this Agreement.

It is understood that Broker is a member of _____ and that such listing service and its mem-
bers shall act in cooperation with Broker in procuring or attempting to procure a purchaser in accordance with this Agreement.

6. Compensation of Broker. The amount or rate of real estate commissions is not fixed by law. They are set by each Broker individually and may be negotiable between the Seller and Broker. Owner agrees to pay Broker as compensation for services rendered a fee of _____ percent of the purchase price.

7. Cooperation of Owner. Owner agrees to make available to Broker and prospective purchasers all data, records, and documents pertaining to the Property, to allow Broker, or any other broker with whom Broker chooses to cooperate, to show the Property at reasonable times and upon reasonable notice, and to place a "For Sale" sign upon the Property. Owner agrees to commit no act which might tend to obstruct the Broker's performance hereunder. Broker may furnish the information provided herein to third parties, and after close of escrow, may disclose the terms of sale to interested parties.

8. Sales Facilitation.
By initializing here: [_____] Owner instructs Broker to list the herein Property with the local Multiple Listing Service.

By initializing here: [_____] Owner authorizes Broker to install a Lock Box upon the Property.

9. Delivery of Papers by Owner. In the event of a sale, Owner will promptly, upon Broker's request, deposit in escrow all instruments necessary to complete the sale.

10. Distribution of Sales Information. In the event Owner has signed a PROPERTY DISCLOSURE STATEMENT, Broker is authorized to furnish copies to potential purchasers.

11. Owner's Representations. Owner warrants the accuracy of the information furnished herein with respect to the above described Property and agrees to hold the Broker harmless from any liabilities or damages arising out of incorrect or undisclosed information. Owner agrees to notify Broker within _____ (_____) days of any changes in rentals and/or expenses of the Property. The undersigned Owner warrants further that he is the owner of record of the Property or has the authority to execute this Agreement.

12. Broker Indemnified. If suit is brought to collect the compensation of Broker, or if Broker successfully defends any action brought against Broker by Owner relating to this authorization or under any sales agreement relating to said Property, Owner agrees to pay all costs incurred by Broker in connection with such action, including a reasonable attorney's fee.

13. Escrow Instructions and Closing Date. Escrow instructions to Escrow Agent shall be signed by the purchasers and Owner and shall be delivered to said escrow within _____ days from acceptance of the terms and conditions of the sale of the Property. Said instructions shall provide for closing and the recording of the deed or other evidence of the transfer of title within _____ days from the date the instructions are delivered to said escrow.

14. Title Defects. Title shall be free of liens, encumbrances, easements, restrictions, rights, and conditions of record or known to Owner other than the following:

15. Owner Default. If Owner fails to deliver title as herein provided, any deposit, together with any other money paid on account of the purchase price, shall there upon be returned to the purchasers.

In consideration of the execution hereof, the undersigned Broker agrees to use diligence in effecting a sale of the Property.

Dated : _____
Broker _____

Broker's
Address/Phone _____

Seller_____   Seller_____

b. Exclusive Agency Listing Agreement

Exclusive Agency Listing Agreement
this offers less protection to a broker because if the property owner finds a buyer, she will not have to pay a commission to the broker. If the listing broker or another broker procures a buyer, seller must pay a brokerage commission to the listing broker.

An **exclusive agency listing agreement** offers much *less protection* to the listing broker, and therefore, is much less popular with brokers. The **exclusive agency** is the same as the exclusive right to sell in that the seller will pay a commission to the listing broker if the listing broker, or any other broker acting through the listing broker (a subagent), procures a buyer.

The major difference between an exclusive agency agreement (versus the exclusive right to sell agreement) is that the *owner may sell the property herself*, and thereby save the commission. The benefit to the seller is obvious, and so are the *dis*advantages to the listing broker, who may expend significant effort, time, and money marketing the property, only to be cut out of a commission if the seller herself finds a buyer for the property. To discourage sellers from using this type of listing agreement, a property listed pursuant to an exclusive agency agreement cannot be placed on the local Multiple Listing Service.

c. Open Listings and FSBOs

Open Listing Agreement
an ad hoc contract whereby seller agrees to pay a commission to *any* broker who procures a buyer. Seller also reserves the right to sell the property herself without having to pay a commission at all.

An **open listing agreement** is one whereby the seller agrees to pay a commission to *any* broker who produces a prospective buyer who purchases the property, but reserves the right to sell the property herself. This situation is most frequently encountered with a **FSBO** (pronounced "*fiz-bo*"), meaning For Sale By Owner.

No broker would spend any money advertising or otherwise trying to market the property. It is just too much of a risk that the seller, or some other broker, will find a buyer. On the other hand, if a broker has a client who is looking for a house like the FSBO in question, the broker can still get a commission from the seller—usually 3%—without incurring the expenses involved in marketing the property. In FSBO situations, when the prospective buyers and their broker draw up the offer to purchase, they should include the requirement that the broker is to be paid a commission, and what percentage of the selling price it will be.

Sellers tend to be FSBOs and use an exclusive agency agreement in "hot" markets, that is, when buyer demand is very high relative to the supply of desirable real estate, and there are plenty of prospective buyers (which implies that the overall economy is good, loan money is available, and interest rates are relatively low).

2. MARKETING

Let us retrace our steps back to where the seller and the broker have signed the Exclusive Right to Sell listing agreement, and have determined and agreed that the listing price will be $300,000. The next step is to market the property, and this is where the broker's knowledge and experience comes to the fore.

a. Advertising

There are numerous methods by which the broker can market the property, including advertisements in newspapers, on radio, and perhaps even on TV on one of the local cable channels. Traditionally, Sunday is the day on which most brokers advertise their properties for sale in the local newspaper, which might have a pullout section of several pages of homes for sale. The advertisements generate significant income for the newspapers, and prospective buyers have more time on Sunday to peruse the ads, and perhaps later drive by the properties that interest them. Many brokerage firms hold **open houses** on weekends where buyers may visit the property, have a walk through, and ask questions of the real estate agent; the homeowner-seller is usually not present during an open house.

The Internet has greatly expanded the capability of the broker to market listed properties. Most firms have their own websites where prospective buyers can go to look at properties online that the firm has listed. A buyer may be able to take a virtual tour of the broker's listings without ever leaving home. This makes the marketing process much more efficient, although some might argue that it undermines the personal relationship between a buyer and a broker.

Additionally, the listing broker may have collected the names of prospective buyers who have called or contacted the broker in the past about other listed properties. The brokers will contact them and determine if they have any interest in the purchase of the broker's just-listed property. If the listing broker can also sell the property, she will not have to split the commission with any other broker. Thus, a property that sold for $300,000 would generate a commission of $18,000, assuming a typical commission rate of 6%.

b. Multiple Listing Service

The **Multiple Listing Service (MLS)** is a generic term for any system that employs a database made up of local real property that is listed for sale by local brokers. Various localities may have different names for their local databases, but the concept and practices described below are basically the same for all such systems and locales.

Most of the residential brokers in a geographic area—usually a city or county—are members of the local Multiple Listing Service. The MLS usually requires that any broker who lists a property under an exclusive right to sell listing agreement must place the listing on the MLS within a certain number of hours of signing the listing agreement. This gives the listing broker a limited window in which to interest one of her own buyer-clients in purchasing the house, as described above.

Assuming that the listing broker cannot get one of her client-buyers to make an offer within the prescribed time window, the listing broker will place the listed property on the MLS. The MLS is basically a **computerized database** of properties currently for sale within a given geographical area. In placing the listed property on the MLS, the listing broker is agreeing to split the commission with any other broker who procures a buyer for the property.

Because the listed house is now part of a database of properties, any broker who is a member of the MLS can access and query the database using a variety of filters, such as price range, location or school district, number of bedrooms and baths, age of the property, and other variables. The database will then display the properties meeting the selected criteria, with photographs, and more and more commonly, will allow the viewer to take a virtual tour of the listed property.

The MLS system, in its various local incarnations, has been a tremendous asset in facilitating the sale of real estate. After posting the new listing on the MLS, the seller now effectively has several brokers trying to sell the property to their buyer-clients, rather than just the listing broker, which will result in a much quicker sale.

The listing broker, although probably having to split the commission with a selling broker, will get half of the commission much quicker, and still has the opportunity to sell the listed property. The broker who represents the client who ultimately buys the house will receive half the commission, and provides an efficient service for the client-buyer.

c. "Puffing"

For most people, the purchase of a home is the largest and most important financial transaction that they will make in their lives. As such, sellers and buyers will attach great importance to representations made by their brokers. Therefore, in

Fraud
intentionally deceiving another as to a material fact. Fraud also includes concealment of a material fact by one who has an affirmative duty to disclose such material information.

Misrepresentation
negligently conveying erroneous, material information to one to whom a duty of care is owed regarding the information being conveyed.

Puffing
the expression of an exaggerated opinion about real or personal property that is being sold to another. Puffing is "just sales talk," and is generally not considered to be tortious conduct.

trying to sell a property, a real estate broker must avoid making a statement that might constitute misrepresentation, or even fraud.

Fraud is an intentional and knowing misrepresentation of a material fact, or the concealment of a material fact, for the purpose of inducing someone to act to his or her detriment. Fraud is an intentional tort because there is an intent by the one making the misrepresentation to deceive another.

Misrepresentation, on the other hand, is a tort in the nature of negligence, and is not intentional. Misrepresentation is the false assertion of a material fact to one to whom a duty of care is owed as to the statement.[2]

You may have heard of the word "puffing" as it relates to selling, and in the context of the torts of misrepresentation or fraud. **Puffing** is the expression by a seller or broker of an opinion—often exaggerated—rather than an assertion of fact, and is sometimes described as "just sales talk." Ordinarily, a buyer cannot prevail on a claim of fraud or misrepresentation when based on puffing. Consider the following statements made by a real estate broker to a prospective buyer:

JUST PUFFING, OR TORTIOUS CONDUCT?

Statement # 1 by the broker: *"This is the best little house in this neighborhood, and is low maintenance, too."*

Statement # 2 by the broker: *"This is the best little house in this neighborhood, and hasn't had a maintenance problem since it was built in 2001."*

Is either or both of the statements above merely "puffing"?

Are the statements different in some qualitative way, or are they basically the same?

If the statements are different, how are they different? Does the difference make one of the statements tortious, and therefore actionable as either misrepresentation or fraud?

Steering
the illegal practice by a broker of manipulating, directing, or "steering" a buyer or renter of one race into a neighborhood comprised mainly of residents of the buyer's (or renter's) own race.

d. Prohibited Practices—Steering and Blockbusting

The federal ***Fair Housing Act of 1968*** (and its amendments) prohibits discrimination in the sale or leasing of real property based on race, religion, national origin, or gender. The Fair Housing Act is actually Title VII of the Civil Rights Act of 1968.

Steering is an illegal practice that has been engaged in by some real estate brokers and agents. The practice involves manipulating, directing, funneling, or steering a buyer (or renter) of one race into neighborhoods comprised primarily of the buyer's own race. The practice tends to keep neighborhoods segregated, and discourages integration. Steering has ripple effects that are felt in the racial composition of local school districts, which often draw school district boundary lines based on neighborhood housing patterns. The ripple effect of steering may sometimes be observed in employment patterns as well as housing, thereby perpetuating segregation in the workplace.

To combat steering, local, state, and federal enforcement agencies may engage in testing. ***Testing*** involves blacks and whites posing as prospective renters or homebuyers to determine whether a real estate broker shows the black prospects the same properties as the white prospects, and vice versa. The white and black

---

[2]In some states, the torts are called "intentional misrepresentation" (fraud) and "negligent misrepresentation" (misrepresentation). Regardless of the nomenclature, intentionally deceiving another will carry with it the prospect of punitive damages, whereas the remedy for a careless or negligent misrepresentation is compensatory damages.

testers will purport to have similar incomes, job stability, and other socioeconomic factors, to eliminate the possibility that any discrimination in the showing of properties could be explained by a factor other than race.

Blockbusting is the illegal practice whereby a real estate broker will attempt to generate listings and sales by telling homeowners in a relatively segregated neighborhood that a racial, ethnic, or religious minority is beginning to move into their neighborhood. The broker tells the homeowners that they had better list their homes for sale now before housing prices decline further, as more minorities move into the community.

Blockbusting
the illegal practice by a broker who is attempting to generate sales of real estate by telling homeowners in a segregated neighborhood that a racial, ethnic, or religious minority is beginning to move into their neighborhood.

Blockbusting, to a certain degree, encouraged and caused "white flight" from major urban areas during the 1960s and 70s. More recently, demographers have observed the phenomenon of "black flight" as more African-Americans have entered the middle class and moved from the cities to the suburbs. An example can be found in affluent Prince George's County, Maryland, which over the years has changed from a predominantly white to a predominantly black suburb of Washington, DC.

3. THE OFFER TO PURCHASE

Let's assume that the listing broker has signed an Exclusive Right to Sell listing contract with the home owner. The broker has placed the property in the MLS database, and has begun to receive calls from other brokers asking to show the house to their client-buyers. One of those prospective buyers visits the house with her broker, likes the house, and wants to make an offer. Buyer's broker will then begin to fill out a standardized form called the Offer to Purchase contract.

a. Mutual Assent + Consideration = Contract

We have already looked at the basic elements of a contract, which are **mutual assent** (including an offer and an acceptance) and **consideration**. As to the latter, we said that technically, consideration consists of mutual promises (rather than the house or the purchase money):

> Buyer: "I offer $200,000 to purchase your house."

> Seller: "I accept your offer and will sell you my house for $200,000."

Recall that the word "promise" need not be used in the statements, and the statements above constitute a contract for the sale of real property once they are put into writing, and signed by the parties. The need for a written agreement is mandated by the **Statute of Frauds**, which requires that certain types of contracts be in writing, including contracts for the conveyance of interests in real property.

As you can see from the Offer to Purchase, the broker will have to assist the buyer in filling out several pieces of information. (See Exhibit 8-4, Contract for the Sale and Purchase of Real Property, at the end of this chapter.) Much of this information can be gleaned from the listing information submitted to MLS by the listing broker. The offer to purchase should include the following basic provisions:

i. The **identity of the buyers and sellers**, and their **marital statuses**. This is important to determine whether the buyers want to take ownership as partners (tenants in common), or possibly as husband and wife (tenants by the entirety), or some other arrangement (joint tenants with right of survivorship).

ii. The **identity of the property**. At this stage, a street address is sufficient, although when the property ultimately closes, a new deed will have been drafted that includes the legal description of the property.

iii. The **offered purchase price**, which is usually going to be less than the listing price. However, in a "seller's market," where there is great demand for housing, buyers have been known to offer more than the seller's asking (list) price of the property.

iv. The *earnest money* deposit, which evinces the buyers' good faith and intent to carry through with the transaction; it is usually in the range of 1%–5% of the offering price. If the buyer fails to perform under one or more of the terms of the finalized contract, the earnest money may be forfeited to the seller.

v. The *terms of the financing*, which specify the loan amount that the buyer will seek to obtain from a lender, the interest rate of the loan, and the term (number of years) of the loan, and any other financial provisions, such as a balloon payment.

vi. Any of the seller's *personal property* that the buyer wants to be included along with the conveyance of the real property. Many a closing has fallen apart because of a dispute over what is classified as a fixture, or personal property. For example, are window treatments (drapes, curtain rods) fixtures that should remain with the real property upon sale, or are these items personal property that the sellers may take with them when they move out?

vii. The *closing date* by which time the closing of the property—the transfer of the deed/title in exchange for the money to buy the house—must occur. Frequently the contract will include language in this section that "time is of the essence," which we will discuss below.

viii. The *signatures* of the parties. Sometimes the word "Seal" is next to the signature line, which is significant because it may extend the statute of limitations for either the seller or buyer to file a lawsuit related to the sale of the property.

After the buyers and their broker have filled out the Offer to Purchase, the broker will deliver the Offer and the buyer's earnest money check to the listing broker. If the offer is accepted by the seller, the check may be deposited in the listing broker's *trust account*. This account is reserved exclusively for funds related to real estate transactions, and the broker may not commingle her personal funds with trust funds. This is a serious ethical violation and will subject the commingling broker to disciplinary action by the state. In those states where closings are conducted by escrow companies, the earnest money will be deposited to that company's *escrow account*.

b. Counteroffers

The listing broker will convey the written offer to the seller, and they will discuss its pros and cons. The seller may not like one or more of the terms in the Offer to Purchase, in which case the seller may cross out the item, and write in a different amount of money, closing date, or change or add some other term.

For example, the listed price of the house was $300,000, but the buyer offered only $250,000. The seller may cross out the "$250,000" written in the Offer, and replace it with a figure of "$275,000."

Any change made to an offer by the offeree is a rejection of the offer, and becomes a *counteroffer.* In the example above, the seller, who was the offeree, has now become the offeror, by virtue of the counteroffer; conversely, the buyer has become the offeree. The Offer to Purchase may go back and forth between buyer and seller several times before the offer is finalized and either becomes a contract, or the negotiations end and the deal falls apart.

Time Is of the Essence
a clause in a contract that requires that a particular act, such as a closing on real property, must occur by a specific date.

c. Is Time Really "of the Essence"?

A fairly common reason for lawsuits relating to real property is the phrase: "**Time is of the essence.**" This contract term is used quite often in association with the scheduled *closing date*. Let's say that in the standardized Offer to Purchase used by the buyer above, the section reads:

> *Closing on the property to occur on or before _____ (insert date). Time is of the essence.*

In the space for the date, the buyer makes the handwritten entry: "July 31, 2015."

Assume that the offer of $275,000 has been accepted by the seller, including the condition that the closing is "to occur on or before July 31, 2015. Time is of the essence." The buyer has been approved for a loan in accordance with the terms in the Offer to Purchase. Everything is going according to plan and the **closing date** is finalized and scheduled for July 31.

On July 20, the buyer informs her broker that she has just learned that she needs to have a biopsy performed as soon as possible, and the only date in the next 30 days that the surgeon can perform the operation is on July 31. The buyer will have to postpone the closing for a day or two.

The buyer's broker says he will pass that along to the listing broker and is confident that there won't be a problem. Listing broker then conveys the information to the seller, who is adamant that the closing take place on or before July 31, because, according to the seller:

> *Look. It says right there in the contract that "time is of the essence"! I need the proceeds from this sale to close on my new house on August 3rd. Tell the buyer that if she doesn't close on or before July 31, the deal is off and I'll keep her $15,000 earnest money deposit.*

Is time really "of the essence" in this case? Should it be? The seller is correct that the contract does say that closing must occur on or before July 31, and that "time is of the essence." But will the courts enforce this provision? The answer may depend on whether the "time is of the essence" clause is deemed by the court to be **boilerplate.** If time really is of the essence, is there a way that the parties can ensure that the provision is enforced by the courts if a dispute arises over that language?

Does it make a difference whether the need for a postponement of the closing is because the buyer needs a medical procedure, or if the buyer just wants to stay on vacation at the beach for an extra day or two?

Closing Date
the deadline by which the closing of the transaction must occur. At closing, the seller transfers title to the property to the buyer in exchange for the buyer's payment of the sale price to the seller.

Boilerplate
language in a contract that has become standardized, and therefore, is rarely negotiated.

NORMILE V. MILLER

N.C. Supreme Court
313 N.C. 98; 326 S.E.2d 11
February 27, 1985

Defendant-seller Hazel Miller owned real estate located in Charlotte, North Carolina. On *4 August 1980*, the property was listed for sale with a local realtor, Gladys Hawkins. On that same day, Richard Byer, *a real estate broker* with the realty firm Gallery of Homes, showed the property to the prospective purchasers, Plaintiffs Normile and Kurniawan. Afterwards, Byer helped plaintiffs prepare a written *offer to purchase* the property. A Gallery of Homes form, entitled "Deposit Receipt and Contract for Purchase and Sale of Real Estate," containing blanks for the insertion of terms pertinent to the purchasers' offer, was completed in quadruplicate and signed by Normile and Kurniawan. One specific standard provision in Paragraph 9 included a blank that was filled in with the time and date to read as follows: "Offer & Closing Date: Time is of the essence, therefore *this offer must be accepted on or before 5:00 p.m. Aug. 5th* 1980. A signed copy shall be promptly returned to the purchaser."

Byer [buyers' agent] took the offer to purchase form to [listing broker] Gladys Hawkins, who

(continued)

presented it to defendant-seller Miller. Later that evening of *August 4*, [listing broker] Hawkins returned the executed form to Byer. It had been signed by defendant, with *several changes in the terms* having been made thereon and initialed by defendant.

That same evening of *August 4*, Byer presented defendant-seller's counteroffer to plaintiff-buyers. Plaintiff Normile thought he had first option on the property and that "nobody else could put an offer in on it and buy it while he had this counteroffer, so he was going to wait awhile before he decided what to do with it." Normile, however, neither accepted nor rejected the counteroffer at this point, according to Byer. When this meeting closed, Byer left the pink copy of the offer to purchase form containing defendant-seller's counteroffer with Normile. Byer stated that he thought that Normile had rejected the counteroffer at this point.

At approximately *12:30 a.m. on 5 August*, Byer went to the home of [another of his clients,] Segal, who *signed an offer to purchase* with terms very similar to those contained in defendant Miller's counteroffer to Plaintiff Normile. This *offer was accepted*, without change, by defendant-seller. Later that same day, *August 5*, at approximately *2:00 p.m.*, Byer informed Plaintiff Normile that defendant had revoked her counteroffer by commenting to Normile, "You snooze, you lose; the property has been sold." Prior to 5:00 p.m. on that same day, August 5, Normile and Kurniawan initialed the offer to purchase form containing defendant-seller's counteroffer and delivered the form to the Gallery of Homes' office, along with the earnest money deposit of $500.

The first issue on this appeal is *whether a time limit* within which an offer must be accepted that is contained in a prospective purchaser's written offer to purchase real property *becomes a term of the seller's subsequent counteroffer*, transforming the counteroffer into an option contract or irrevocable offer for the time stated. We conclude that it does not.

Plaintiff-appellants argue that the counteroffer made by Defendant-seller Miller to plaintiffs became a binding and irrevocable option to purchase within the time for acceptance contained in their original offer to purchase.

We begin with a brief description of how a typical sale of real estate is consummated. The broker, whose primary duty is to secure a ready, willing, and able buyer for the seller's property, generally initiates a potential sale by procuring the prospective purchaser's signature on an offer to purchase instrument.

Usually, this *offer to purchase* is a printed form with blanks that are filled in and completed by the broker. Among the various clauses contained in such an instrument, it is not uncommon for the form to contain "a clause stipulating that the seller must accept the offer and approve the sale within a certain specified period of time, … The inclusion of a date within which the seller must accept simply indicates that the offer will automatically expire at the termination of the named period if the seller does not accept before then." Such a clause is contained in Paragraph 9 of the offer to purchase form in the case *sub judice*.

In the instant case, the offerors-buyers (plaintiff-appellants) submitted their offer to purchase defendant's property. This offer contained a Paragraph 9, requiring that "this offer must be accepted *on or before 5:00 p.m. Aug. 5th* 1980." Thus the offeree's, defendant-seller's, power of acceptance was controlled by the duration of time for acceptance of the offer.

This offer to purchase remains only an offer until the seller accepts it on the terms contained in the original offer by the prospective purchaser. If the seller does accept the terms in the purchaser's offer, he denotes this by signing the offer to purchase at the bottom, thus forming a valid, binding, and irrevocable purchase contract between the seller and purchaser. However, if the seller purports to accept but changes or modifies the terms of the offer, he makes a *counteroffer* and a rejection of the buyer's offer.

This assent, or *meeting of the minds*, requires an *offer and acceptance* in the exact terms and that the acceptance must be communicated to the offeror. The offeree (defendant-seller) changed the original offer in several material respects, most notably in the terms regarding payment of the purchase price. In substance, defendant's conditional acceptance modifying the original offer did not manifest any intent to accept the terms of the original offer, including the time-for-acceptance provision, unless and until the original offeror accepted the terms included in defendant's counteroffer. Thus, the time-for-acceptance provision contained in plaintiff-appellants' original offer did not become part of the terms of the counteroffer.

It is more significant that *defendant's counteroffer did not contain any promise or agreement that her counteroffer would remain open* for a specified period of time. There is no language indicating that defendant-seller in any way agreed to sell or convey her real property to plaintiff-appellants at their request within a specified period of time. There is, however, language contained within the prospective purchasers' offer to purchase that does state, "Description: I/we Michael M. Normile and Wawie Kurniawan hereby agree to purchase from the sellers, ..." and "*this* offer must be accepted on or before 5:00 p.m. Aug. 5th 1980." Nowhere is there companion language to the effect that Defendant Miller "hereby agrees to sell or convey to the purchasers" if they accept by a certain date.

Accordingly, we hold that defendant's counteroffer was not transformed into an irrevocable offer for the time limit contained in the original offer because the defendant's conditional acceptance did not include the time-for-acceptance provision as part of its terms and because defendant did not make any promise to hold her counteroffer open for any stated time.

The foregoing preliminary analysis of both the Court of Appeals' opinion and plaintiff-appellants' argument in their brief prefaces what we consider to be decisive of the ultimate issue to be resolved. Basic contract principles effectively and logically answer the primary issue in this appeal. That is, if a seller rejects a prospective purchaser's offer to purchase but makes a counter-offer that is not accepted by the prospective purchaser, *does the prospective purchaser have the power to accept after he receives notice that the counteroffer had been revoked?* The answer is no. The net effect of defendant-seller's counteroffer and rejection is twofold. First, plaintiff-appellants' original offer was rejected and ceased to exist. Secondly, the counteroffer by the offeree requires the original offeror, plaintiff-appellants, to either accept or reject.

Accordingly, the *next question is did plaintiff-appellants, the original offerors, accept or reject defendant-seller's counteroffer?* Plaintiff-appellants in their brief seem to answer this question when they state, "At the time Byer presented the counteroffer to Normile, Normile neither accepted nor rejected it. ..." Therefore, plaintiff-appellants did not manifest any intent to agree to or accept the terms contained in defendant's counteroffer. Normile instead advised Byer that he, though mistakenly, had an option on the property and that it was off the market for the duration of the time limitation contained in his original offer. Although Normile's mistaken belief that he had an option is unfortunate, he still failed to express to Byer his agreement to or rejection of the counteroffer made by defendant-seller.

Plaintiff-appellants in the instant case did not accept, either expressly or by conduct, defendant's counteroffer. In addition to disagreeing with the change in payment terms, Normile stated to Byer that "he was going to wait awhile before he decided what to do with the counteroffer." Neither did plaintiffs explicitly reject defendant's counteroffer. Instead, plaintiff-appellants in this case chose to operate under the impression, though mistaken, that they had an option to purchase and that the property was "off the market." Absent either an acceptance or rejection, there was no meeting of the minds or mutual assent between the parties, a *fortiori*, there was no contract.

It is evident from the record that after plaintiff-appellants failed to accept defendant's counteroffer, there was a second purchaser, Segal, who submitted an offer [through Byer] to defendant-seller that was accepted. This offer and acceptance between the latter parties, together with consideration in the form of an earnest money deposit from plaintiff-appellee, ripened into a valid and binding purchase contract.

By entering into the contract with Plaintiff-appellee Segal, defendant-seller **manifested her intention to revoke** her previous counteroffer to plaintiff-appellants. It is a fundamental tenet of the common law that an offer is generally freely revocable and can be countermanded by the offeror **at any time before it has been accepted** by the offeree. The revocation of an offer terminates it, and the offeree has no power to revive the offer by any subsequent attempts to accept.

Generally, notice of the offeror's revocation must be communicated to the offeree to effectively terminate the offeree's power to accept the offer. It is enough that the offeree receives reliable information, even indirectly that the offeror had taken definite action inconsistent with an intention to make the contract.

In this case, plaintiff-appellants received notice of the offeror's revocation of the counteroffer in the afternoon of August 5, when Byer saw Normile and told him, "You snooze, you lose; the property has been sold." Later that afternoon, plaintiff-appellants initialed the counteroffer and delivered it to the Gallery of Homes, along with their earnest money deposit of $ 500.

These subsequent attempts by plaintiff-appellants to accept defendant's revoked counteroffer were fruitless, however, since their *power of acceptance had been effectively terminated by the offeror's revocation.* Since defendant's counteroffer could not be revived, the practical effect of plaintiff-appellants' initialing defendant's counteroffer and leaving it at the broker's office before 5:00 p.m. on August 5 was to resubmit a new offer. This offer was not accepted by defendant since she had already contracted to sell her property by entering into a valid, binding, and irrevocable purchase contract with Plaintiff-appellee Segal.

For the reasons stated herein, the decision of the Court of Appeals is

Modified and affirmed.

EXHIBIT 8-4 Contract For The Sale and Purchase of Real Estate

CONTRACT FOR THE SALE AND PURCHASE OF REAL ESTATE
(NO BROKER)

WARNING: THIS CONTRACT HAS SUBSTANTIAL LEGAL CONSEQUENCES AND THE PARTIES ARE ADVISED TO CONSULT LEGAL AND TAX COUNSEL.

FOR VALUABLE CONSIDERATION OF TEN DOLLARS and other good and valuable consideration, the receipt and sufficiency of which is hereby acknowledged, _____ (Seller), whether one or more, and _____ (Buyer), whether one or more, do hereby covenant, contract and agree as follows:

1. AGREEMENT TO SALE AND PURCHASE: Seller agrees to sell, and Buyer agrees to buy from Seller the property described as follows: (*complete adequately to identify property*)

    _____ County, Connecticut.

    Address: _____

    Legal Description (or see attached exhibit): _____
    _____
    _____

    Together with the following items, if any: (*Strike items to be retained by Seller*) curtains and rods, draperies and rods, valances, blinds, window shades, screens, shutters, awnings, wall-to-wall carpeting, mirrors fixed in place, ceiling fans, attic fans, mail boxes, television antennas and satellite dish system with controls and equipment, permanently installed heating and air-conditioning units, window air-conditioning units, built-in security and fire detection equipment, plumbing and lighting fixtures including chandeliers, water softener, stove, built-in kitchen equipment, garage door openers with controls, built-in cleaning equipment, all swimming pool equipment and maintenance accessories, shrubbery, landscaping, permanently installed outdoor cooking equipment, built-in fireplace screens, artificial fireplace logs and all other property owned by Seller and attached to the above described real property except the following property which is not included (*list items not included*):

    _____
    _____

    All property sold by this contract is called the "Property."

2. SALES PRICE: The parties agree to the following sales price:

	Amount	Amount
Purchase Price	$	
Earnest Money		$
New Loan		$
Assumption of Loan		$
Seller Financing		$
Cash at Closing		$
Total (both columns should be equal)	$	$

Both columns should be an equal amount.

If the unpaid principal balance(s) of any assumed loan(s), if any, as of the Closing Date varies from the loan balance(s) stated above, the cash payable at closing will be adjusted by the amount of any variance.

Buyer Initials _____ _____   Seller Initials _____ _____

3. FINANCING: The following provisions apply with respect to financing:

☐ CASH SALE: This contract is not contingent on financing.

☐ OWNER FINANCING: Seller agrees to finance _____ dollars of the purchase price pursuant to a promissory note from Buyer to Seller of $_____, bearing _____% interest per annum, payable over a term of _____ years with even monthly payments, secured by a deed of trust or mortgage lien with the first payment to begin on the _____ day of _____, 20 _____.

☐ NEW LOAN OR ASSUMPTION: This contract is contingent on Buyer obtaining financing. Within _____ days after the effective date of this contract Buyer shall apply for all financing or noteholder's approval of any assumption and make every reasonable effort to obtain financing or assumption approval. Financing or assumption approval will be deemed to have been obtained when the lender determines that Buyer has satisfied all of lender's financial requirements (those items relating to Buyer's net worth, income, and creditworthiness). If financing or assumption approval is not obtained within _____ days after the effective date hereof, this contract will terminate and the earnest money will be refunded to Buyer. If Buyer intends to obtain a new loan, the loan will be of the following type:

☐ Conventional ☐ VA ☐ FHA ☐ Other: _____

The following provisions apply if a new loan is to be obtained:

FHA. It is expressly agreed that notwithstanding any other provisions of this contract, the Purchaser (Buyer) shall not be obligated to complete the purchase of the Property described herein or to incur any penalty by forfeiture of earnest money deposits or otherwise unless the Purchaser (Buyer) has been given in accordance with HUD/FHA or VA requirements a written statement by the Federal Housing Commissioner, Veterans Administration, or a Direct Endorsement lender setting forth the appraised value of the Property of not less than $ _____. The Purchaser (Buyer) shall have the privilege and option of proceeding with consummation of the contract without regard to the amount of the appraised valuation. The appraised valuation is arrived at to determine the maximum mortgage the Department of Housing and Urban Development will insure. HUD does not warrant the value nor the condition of the Property. The Purchaser (Buyer) should satisfy himself/herself that the price and condition of the Property are acceptable.

VA. If Buyer is to pay the purchase price by obtaining a new VA-guaranteed loan: It is agreed that, notwithstanding any other provisions of this contract, Buyer shall not incur any penalty by forfeiture of earnest money or otherwise be obligated to complete the purchase of the Property described herein, if the contract purchase price or cost exceeds the reasonable value of the Property established by the Veterans Administration. Buyer shall, however, have the privilege and option of proceeding with the consummation of this contract without regard to the amount of the reasonable value established by the Veterans Administration.

Existing Loan Review. If an existing loan is not to be released at closing, Seller shall provide copies of the loan documents (including note, deed of trust or mortgage, modifications) to Buyer within _____ calendar days from acceptance of this contract. This contract is conditional upon Buyer's review and approval of the provisions of such loan documents. Buyer consents to the provisions of such loan documents if no written objection is received by Seller from Buyer within _____ calendar days from Buyer's receipt of such documents. If the lender's approval of a transfer of the Property is required, this contract is conditional upon Buyer's obtaining such approval without change in the terms of such loan, except as may be agreed by Buyer. If lender's approval is not obtained on or before _____ this contract shall be terminated on such date. The Seller ☐ shall ☐ shall not, be released from liability under such existing loan. If Seller is to be released and release approval is not obtained, Seller may nevertheless elect to proceed to closing, or terminate this agreement in the sole discretion of Seller.

Buyer Initials _____ _____

Seller Initials _____ _____

(continued)

EXHIBIT 8-4 *Continued*

Credit Information. If Buyer is to pay all or part of the purchase price by executing a promissory note in favor of Seller or if an existing loan is not to be released at closing, this contract is conditional upon Seller's approval of Buyer's financial ability and creditworthiness, which approval shall be at Seller's sole and absolute discretion. In such case: (1) Buyer shall supply to Seller on or before _____, _____, at, Buyer's expense, information and documents concerning Buyer's financial, employment and credit condition; (2) Buyer consents that Seller may verify Buyer's financial ability and creditworthiness; (3) any such information and documents received by Seller shall be held by Seller in confidence, and not released to others except to protect Seller's interest in this transaction; (4) if Seller does not provide written notice of Seller's disapproval to Buyer on or before _____, _____, then Seller waives this condition.

4. EARNEST MONEY: Buyer shall deposit $ _____ as earnest money with _____ upon execution of this contract by both parties.

5. PROPERTY CONDITION:

PROPERTY TO BE MAINTAINED; PROPERTY CONDITION DISCLOSURE; Except as may be set forth elsewhere in this Contract, the Property is being sold "as-is". Seller agrees to maintain property with all buildings, landscaping and other improvements thereon, and any personal property included in the sale in the same condition, reasonable wear and tear excepted, as they were on the date of this Contract. Buyer shall have the right to make a final inspection of the real property during a 48-hour period prior to closing. **In the event the Seller failed to provide Buyer with a copy of the Uniform Property Condition Disclosure Report required by Public Act 95-311 and is not exempt from the Act, Seller shall credit Buyer with the sum of $300,00 at closing as required by law**.

Buyer is notified that the Department of Environmental Protection is required pursuant to Section 22a-134f of the Connecticut General Statutes to furnish lists of hazardous waste facilities located within the town to the Town Clerk office. Buyer should refer to these lists and the Department of Environmental Protection for information on environmental questions concerning the Property and the lands surrounding the Property.

SELLER'S DISCLOSURE OF LEAD-BASED PAINT AND LEAD-BASED PAINT HAZARDS is required by Federal law for a residential dwelling constructed prior to 1978. An addendum providing such disclosure ☐ is attached ☐ is not applicable.

Buyer hereby represents that he has personally inspected and examined the above-mentioned premises and all improvements thereon. Buyer hereby acknowledges that unless otherwise set form in writing elsewhere in this contract neither Seller nor Seller's representatives, if any, have made any representations concerning the present or past structural condition of the improvements, Buyer and Seller agree to the following concerning the condition of the property:

☐ Buyer accepts the property in its "as-is" and present condition.
☐ Buyer may have the property inspected by persons of Buyer's choosing and at Buyer's expense. If the inspection report reveals defects in the property, Buyer shall notify Seller within 5 days of receipt of the report and may cancel this contract and receive a refund of earnest money, or close this agreement notwithstanding the defects, or Buyer and Seller may renegotiate this contract, in the discretion of Seller. All inspections and notices to Seller shall be complete within _____ days after execution of this agreement.

☐ Buyer accepts the Property in its present condition; provided Seller, at Seller's expense, shall complete the following repairs and treatment: _____
_____
_____

Buyer agrees that he will not hold Seller or its representatives responsible or liable for any present or future structural problems or damage to the foundation or slab of said property. **If the subject residential dwelling was constructed prior to 1978, Buyer may conduct a risk assessment or inspection for the presence of lead-based paint and/or lead-based paint hazards, to be completed within _____ days after execution of this agreement. In the alternative, Buyer may waive the opportunity to conduct an assessment/inspection by indicating said waiver on the attached Lead-Based Paint Disclosure form.**

Buyer Initials _____ _____   Seller Initials _____ _____

MECHANICAL EQUIPMENT AND BUILT IN APPLIANCES: All such equipment is sold ☐ "as-is" without warranty, or ☐ shall be in good working order on the date of closing. Any repairs needed to mechanical equipment or appliances, if any, shall be the responsibility of ☐ Seller ☐ Buyer.

UTILITIES: Water is provided to the property by _____, Sewer is provided by _____. Gas is provided by _____. Electricity is provided by _____.

Other: _____
_____
_____
_____

The present condition of all utilities is accepted by Buyer.

6. CLOSING: The closing of the sale will be on or before _____, 20_____, unless extended pursuant to the terms hereof.

   Closing may be extended to within 7 days after objections to matters disclosed in the title abstract, certificate or Commitment or by the survey have been cured.

   If financing or assumption approval has been obtained, the Closing Date will be extended up to 15 days if necessary to comply with lender's closing requirements (for example, appraisal, survey, insurance policies, lender-required repairs, closing documents). If either party fails to close this sale by the Closing Date, the non-defaulting party will be entitled to exercise the remedies contained herein. The closing date may also be extended by written agreement of the parties.

7. TITLE AND CONVEYANCE: Seller is to convey title to Buyer by Warranty Deed or _____ (as appropriate) and provide Buyer with a Certificate of Title prepared by an attorney, title or abstract company upon whose Certificate or report title insurance may be obtained from a title insurance company qualified to do and doing business in the state of Connecticut. Seller will also execute a Bill of Sale, if necessary, for the transfer of any personal property. Seller shall, prior to or at closing, satisfy all outstanding mortgages, deeds of trust, and special liens affecting the subject property which are not specifically assumed by Buyer herein. Title shall be good and marketable, subject only to (a) covenants, conditions, and restrictions of record, (b) public, private utility easements and roads and rights-of-way, (c) applicable zoning ordinances, protective covenants, and prior mineral reservations, (d) special and other assessments on the property, if any, (e) general taxes for the year _____ and subsequent years and (e) other: _____. A title report shall be provided to Buyer at least 5 days prior to closing. If there are title defects, Seller shall notify Buyer within 5 days of closing and Buyer, at Buyer's option, may either (a) if defects cannot be cured by designated closing date, cancel this contract, in which case all earnest money deposited shall be returned, (b) accept title as is, or (c) if the defects are of such character that they can be remedied by legal action within a reasonable time, permit Seller such reasonable time to perform curative work at Seller's expense. In the event that the curative work is performed by Seller, the time specified herein for closing of this sale shall be extended for a reasonable period necessary for such action. Seller represents that the property may be legally used as zoned and that no government agency has served any notice to Seller requiring repairs, alterations, or corrections of any existing condition except as stated herein.

8. APPRAISAL, SURVEY, AND TERMITE INSPECTION: Any appraisal of the property shall be the responsibility of ☐ Buyer ☐ Seller. A survey is: ☐ not required ☐ required, the cost of which shall be paid by ☐ Seller ☐ Buyer. A termite inspection is ☐ not required ☐ required, the cost of which shall be paid by ☐ Seller ☐ Buyer. If a survey is required it shall be obtained within 5 days of closing.

9. POSSESSION AND TITLE: Seller shall deliver possession of the Property to Buyer at closing. Title shall be conveyed to Buyer, if more than one as ☐ Joint tenants with rights of survivorship, ☐ tenants in common, ☐ Other _____ Prior to closing the property shall remain in the possession of Seller and Seller shall deliver the property to Buyer in substantially the same condition at closing, as on the date of this contract, reasonable wear and tear excepted.

Buyer Initials _____ _____

Seller Initials _____ _____

(continued)

EXHIBIT 8-4 *Continued*

10.   CLOSING COSTS AND EXPENSES: The following closing costs shall be paid as provided. *(Leave blank if the closing cost does not apply.)*

Closine Costs	Buyer	Seller	Both*
Attorney Fees	☐	☐	☐
Title Insurance	☐	☐	☐
Title Abstract or Certificate	☐	☐	☐
Property Insurance	☐	☐	☐
Recording Fees	☐	☐	☐
Appraisal	☐	☐	☐
Survey	☐	☐	☐
Termite Inspection	☐	☐	☐
Origination fees	☐	☐	☐
Discount Points	☐	☐	☐
If contingent on rezoning, cost and expenses of rezoning	☐	☐	☐
Other:			
	☐	☐	☐
	☐	☐	☐
	☐	☐	☐
	☐	☐	☐
	☐	☐	☐
All other closing costs	☐	☐	☐

* 50/50 between buyer and seller.

11.   PRORATIONS: Taxes for the current year, interest, maintenance fees, assessments, dues and rents, if any, will be prorated through the Closing Date. If taxes for the current year vary from the amount prorated at closing, the parties shall adjust the prorations when tax statements for the current year are available. If a loan is assumed and the lender maintains an escrow account, the escrow account must be transferred to Buyer without any deficiency. Buyer shall reimburse Seller for the amount in the transferred account. Buyer shall pay the premium for a new insurance policy. If taxes are not paid at or prior to closing, Buyer will be obligated to pay taxes for the current year.

12.   CASUALTY LOSS: If any part of the Property is damaged or destroyed by fire or other casualty loss after the effective date of the contract, Seller shall restore the Property to its previous condition as soon as reasonably possible. If Seller fails to do so due to factors beyond Seller's control, Buyer may either (a) terminate this contract and the earnest money will be refunded to Buyer, (b) extend the time for performance and the Closing Date will be extended as necessary, or (c) accept the Property in its damaged condition and accept an assignment of insurance proceeds.

13.   DEFAULT: If Buyer fails to comply with this contract, Buyer will be in default, and Seller may terminate this contract and receive the earnest money as liquidated damages, thereby releasing both parties from this contract. If, due to factors beyond Seller's control, Seller fails within the time allowed to make any non-casualty repairs or deliver evidence of clean title, Buyer may either (a) extend the time for performance up to 15 days and the Closing Date will be extended as necessary or (b) terminate this contract as the sole remedy and receive a refund of the earnest money. If Seller fails to comply with this contract for any other reason, Seller will be in default and Buyer may either (a) enforce specific performance, seek such other relief as may be provided by law, or both, or (b) terminate this contract and receive the earnest money, thereby releasing both parties from this contract.

14.   ATTORNEY'S FEES: The prevailing party in any legal proceeding brought under or with respect to the transaction described in this contract is entitled to recover from the non-prevailing party all costs of such proceeding and reasonable attorney's fees.

15.   REPRESENTATIONS: Seller represents that as of the Closing Date (a) there will be no liens, assessments, or security interests against the Property which will not be satisfied out of the sales proceeds unless securing payment of any loans assumed by Buyer and (b) assumed loans will not be in default. If any representation in this contract is untrue on the Closing Date, this contract may be terminated by Buyer and the earnest money will be refunded to Buyer. All representations contained in this contract will survive closing.

Buyer Initials _____ _____   Seller Initials _____ _____

16. FEDERAL TAX REQUIREMENT: If Seller is a "foreign person", as defined by applicable law, or if Seller fails to deliver an affidavit that Seller is not a "foreign person", then Buyer shall withhold from the sales proceeds an amount sufficient to comply with applicable tax law and deliver the same to the Internal Revenue Service together with appropriate tax forms. IRS regulations require filing written reports if cash in excess of specified amounts is received in the transaction.

17. AGREEMENT OF PARTIES: This contract contains the entire agreement of the parties and cannot be changed except by their written agreement.

18. NOTICES: All notices from one parry to the other must be in writing and are effective when mailed to, hand-delivered at, or transmitted by facsimile machine as follows:

To Buyer at:

_____

_____

_____

Telephone (_____)_____

Facsimile (_____)_____

To Seller at:

_____

_____

_____

Telephone (_____)_____

Facsimile (_____)_____

19. ASSIGNMENT: This agreement may not be assigned by Buyer without the consent of Seller. This agreement may be assigned by Seller and shall be binding on the heirs and assigns of the parties hereto.

20. PRIOR AGREEMENTS: This contract incorporates all prior agreements between the parties, contains the entire and final agreement of the parties, and cannot be changed except by their written consent. Neither party has relied upon any statement or representation made by the other party or any sales representative bringing the parties together. Neither party shall be bound by any terms, conditions, oral statements, warranties, or representations not herein contained. Each party acknowledges that he has read and understands this contract. The provisions of this contract shall apply to and bind the heirs, executors, administrators, successors, and assigns of the respective parties hereto. When herein used, the singular includes the plural and the masculine includes the feminine as the context may require.

21. NO BROKER OR AGENTS: The parties represent that neither party has employed the services of a real estate broker or agent in connection with the property, or that if such agents have been employed, that the party employing said agent shall pay any and all expenses outside the closing of this agreement.

22. EMINENT DOMAIN: If the property is condemned by eminent domain after the effective date hereof, the Seller and Buyer shall agree to continue the closing, or a portion thereof, or cancel this Contract. If the parties cannot agree, this contract shall ☐ remain valid with Buyer being entitled to any condemnation proceeds at or after closing, or ☐ be cancelled and the earnest money returned to Buyer.

23. OTHER PROVISIONS

_____

_____

_____

_____

_____

_____

_____

_____

_____

_____

_____

24. TIME IS OF THE ESSENCE IN THE PERFORMANCE OF THIS AGREEMENT.

25. GOVERNING LAW: This contract shall be governed by the laws of the State of Connecticut.

Buyer Initials _____ _____

Seller Initials _____ _____

(continued)

EXHIBIT 8-4 *Continued*

26 DEADLINE LIST *(Optional) (complete all that apply)*. Based on other provisions of Contract.

Deadline	Date
Loan Application Deadline, if contingent on loan	
Loan Commitment Deadline	
Buyer(s) Credit Information to Seller	
Disapproval of Buyers Credit Deadline	
Survey Deadline	
Title Objection Deadline	
Survey Deadline	
Appraisal Deadline	
Property Inspection Deadline	

Whether or not listed above, deadlines contained in this Contract may be extended informally by a writing signed by the person granting the extension except for the closing date which must be extended by a writing signed by both Seller and Buyer.

EXECUTED the _____ day of _____, 20_____ (THE EFFECTIVE DATE).

_____ _____

Buyer Seller

_____ _____

Buyer Seller

EXHIBIT FOR DESCRIPTION OR ATTACH SEPARATE DESCRIPTION

RECEIPT

Receipt of Earnest Money is acknowledged.

Signature: _____

By: _____

_____

Address

_____

City   State   Zip Code

Date: _____, 20

Telephone (_____) _____

Facsimile (_____) _____

Buyer Initials _____ _____

Seller Initials _____ _____

CHAPTER SUMMARY

Real estate brokers are persons who have been **licensed by the state** to assist others in the sale and purchase of real property. **Realtors** are brokers who are also members of the National Association of Realtors®.

Agency is the relationship by which a principal empowers an agent (e.g., a real estate broker) to act on the principal's behalf and in the principal's best interests. Brokers and their clients, be they sellers or buyers, have a **fiduciary relationship**, which embodies the duties each owes to the other. An agent's duties to a principal include the duty of loyalty, the duty to obey, and the duty of performance. A principal's duties to an agent include the duty to cooperate and the duty to compensate.

Listing agreements are contracts between a seller and a broker that describe the obligations of the two parties. The broker agrees to use reasonable efforts to market the property and to procure a buyer who is ready, able, and willing to purchase the property. In return, the seller agrees to cooperate with the marketing of the property and to pay a commission to the broker. There are three types of listing agreements:

exclusive right to sell (the most common, and preferred by brokers), **exclusive agency**, and an **open listing** agreement.

The seller and broker agree to a list price for the property, usually after the broker has performed a **market comparables** analysis to determine what similar properties have sold for in the previous year or two. In contrast, an **appraisal** is performed by a licensed appraiser (who also uses the market comparison/comparables approach) to determine the fair market value of the property for lending purposes.

If the listing agreement is an exclusive right to sell, the property will then be entered into the Multiple Listing Service (MLS), which is a computerized database of properties for sale in a given locality. The MLS system has been very successful in bringing sellers and buyers together, and with the assistance of their brokers, closing on countless pieces of real estate.

If interested in a property, a buyer—with the assistance of a broker—will fill out, sign, and present to the seller an **Offer to Purchase**. The seller may accept the offer, in which case a contract is formed, which includes a closing date on which title to the property will transfer to the buyer; the closing clause typically contains language to the effect that *"time is of the essence"* as to the closing date. Alternatively, the seller may reject the offer outright, or more likely, will make a *counteroffer*, which both rejects the buyer's offer and makes the seller the new offeror.

Steering and blockbusting are two illegal, discriminatory practices prohibited by the Fair Housing Act of 1968. *Steering* involves a broker trying to influence a prospective buyer to purchase a home in a neighborhood comprised predominantly of homeowners of the buyer's race, ethnicity or religion; the purpose is to keep residential neighborhoods segregated. *Blockbusting* occurs when a broker informs homeowners in a neighborhood that minorities are beginning to move into the community and that the homeowner should sell before housing prices decline.

CONCEPT REVIEW AND REINFORCEMENT

KEY **TERMS**

Agency
Agent
Agent's Duty to Perform
Agent's Duty to Render an Accounting
Appraisal
Appraised Value
Blockbusting
Boilerplate
Broker
Caveat Emptor
Closing
Closing Date
Conflict of Interest
Counteroffer
Disclosure Statement
Dual Agency

Duty of Loyalty
Duty to Compensate
Duty to Cooperate
Exclusive Agency
Exclusive Agency Listing Agreement
Exclusive Right to Sell
Exclusive Right to Sell Listing
    Agreement
Fair Housing Act of 1968
Fiduciary Relationship
Fraud
List Price
Listing Agreement
Market Comparable
Material Information
Misrepresentation

Multiple Listing Service (MLS)
Offer to Purchase
Open Listing
Open Listing Agreement
Principal
Profession
Puffing
Realtor
Sanctions
Scope of the Agency
Self-dealing
Self-dealing
Statute of Frauds
Steering
Subject Property
Testing
Time Is of the Essence

CONCEPT **REVIEW** QUESTIONS

1. What is the difference between a real estate broker and a Realtor?

2. What is the difference between the exclusive right to sell listing agreement, and an exclusive agency listing agreement? Why do real estate brokers prefer the former type of listing agreement?

3. What is a dual agency? Describe the ethical problems that may inhere in such a relationship.

4. How is the list price different from the appraised value? Usually, who comes up with the list price, and who generates the appraised value?

5. What is a fiduciary relationship? Does a fiduciary relationship exist between the seller of a home and the seller's listing broker? Does a fiduciary relationship exist between the seller of a home and the buyer of that home?

6. What is the doctrine of caveat emptor, and is it still viable in the realm of home sales? How does a seller's

disclosure statement relate to the doctrine of caveat emptor?

7. What is the statute of frauds, and what, in your opinion, are the public policy reasons for such a statute?

8. Should real estate agents and brokers have to be licensed by the state? Explain the reasons behind your conclusion.

9. What is steering, and how does it contribute to racial segregation in housing patterns and school districts?

10. What is blockbusting, and what is its relationship to "white flight"?

11. What is the Multiple Listing Service? What are its advantages for home sellers, home buyers, and brokers? Can you think of any disadvantages for any of those parties?

12. What is a FSBO?

ETHICS

INCIDENTAL **TO** …

Angela is a real estate broker with 15 years of experience, and owns her own residential realty office in town. Recently, her buyer-clients sat down with her to make an offer on a home that Angela had showed them earlier that day.

As Angela and the buyers are going through the Offer to Purchase and filling in the various blanks on the contract, the buyers begin to ask Angela questions such as:

"What happens if the seller backs out of the deal; will we be able to get our $10,000 earnest money deposit back?"

"What happens if we can't close on the specified closing date, but need a few more days to close? Will the seller be able to back out of the deal and keep our earnest money deposit?"

"This clause here that states that 'time is of the essence' as to the date by which we must obtain a lender's loan commitment letter … is that really enforceable if we need a little extra time to obtain the loan commitment letter?"

Angela answers each one of the buyers' questions based on her many years of experience as a real estate broker and the owner of a real estate brokerage office.

Has Angela engaged in the unauthorized practice of law? Why or why not?

If Angela is wrong about one of the answers to the buyers' inquiries, and the buyers lose their $10,000 earnest money deposit, would they be able to prevail in a lawsuit against Angela? What type of claims might the buyers assert?

Do you think that these types of questions are typically asked by real estate buyers and sellers, and answered by real estate brokers?

How would you handle this recurring situation if you were Angela?

BUILDING YOUR PROFESSIONAL SKILLS

CRITICAL THINKING **EXERCISES**

1. Rock Starr is a famous musician who has hired Agnes Agent (on a handshake) to book musical gigs and venues for Rock and his band. Agnes has performed this service very well for three years. While visiting some friends in Del Boca Vista Estates, a very expensive neighborhood, Agnes spots a home that sports a sign: For Sale by Owner. Agnes knocks on the front door, and when Mr. Costanza, the owner/seller answers, Agnes presents him with a business card that reads "Agnes Agent—Exclusive Agent for Rock Starr".

   Seller Costanza tells Agnes that he wants $15 million for the property. Agnes offers $14.5 million *on behalf of Rock*, and Mr. Costanza eagerly accepts. Seller and Agnes sit down and commit the offer and acceptance to writing, which Agnes signs as Rock's agent.

   Later that day, Agnes Agent calls Rock to give him the "good news" that he will soon be the proud new owner of the Costanza property. Rock exclaims, "Are you kidding? I've heard that only kooks live at Del Boca Vista. You better get me out of that deal and get back to your business of booking me gigs!"

   Do you see any problems on the horizon? Has Agnes operated "within the scope" of her agency (oral) agreement with Rock? If she has not, can Rock escape from the deal, or must he go through with it, and then sue Agnes?

2. Broker has listed the property at 123 Elm St. for sale. It has been vacant for the last three years, according to some, because of the horrible and sensational murders and suicide that occurred in the house. The property is sold to a young couple from out of town who have three children, ages 9, 6, and 3. Although the broker is well aware of the crimes that occurred inside the house three years ago, broker does not inform the buyers of this information.

   Two weeks after moving in, the neighborhood welcoming committee visits the new homeowners and recounts the grisly story of the murders and suicide. The new homeowners are appalled and afraid to live in their new house. The buyers sue the broker and seller for fraudulent concealment and misrepresentation, for failing to disclose material information about the events that occurred in the house. Buyers also want to rescind or revoke the contract of sale, and make the seller take back the property and return their money.

   Did the broker and seller have an affirmative duty to inform the home buyers that there had been terrible crimes committed in the house? Is that material information? Would it matter if the home buyers were a middle-aged couple with no children, rather than a young couple with three children? Should the couple's religious beliefs be of any interest to the court?

3. Every state has adopted laws prohibiting the unauthorized practice of law by persons not licensed by the state bar. Typically, those statutes state something to the effect that unlicensed persons may not "prepare legal documents or offer legal advice, with or without compensation."

Bobbie Broker is helping the Buyers to fill out an Offer to Purchase for a 4,000 square foot home on 4 acres. Buyers will submit a $10,000 earnest money deposit with the Offer, but are anxious about not getting the deposit back if the deal falls through. Mr. Buyer asks Broker if they will get their deposit back if they are unable to obtain the financing they have specified in the Offer, that is, a loan in the amount of $250,000, at 6% interest, for a term of 25 years. Mrs. Buyer asks if they can void the contract and get their deposit back if the lot survey reveals that the property is actually 1/10th of an acre less than the 4 acres indicated on the listing sheet.

Bobbie Broker answers both of their questions, and also explains in general the circumstances under which a seller can, and cannot, retain a buyer's earnest money deposit. Has Bobbie Broker just engaged in the unauthorized practice of law? What are the reasons for your conclusion? What is the public policy that underlies statutes that prohibit non-lawyers from practicing law?

4. Broker has been trying to sell the Sellers' house for more than six months. The property is listed for $199,999, and the market has been very slow. Broker has advertised the property in the local newspapers, taken several prospective buyers to view the house, and has held open houses on six separate weekends. Finally, Broker finds a buyer who makes an offer on the property for $195,000, with no conditions attached to the offer. The Sellers reject the offer, claiming that it is not for the full asking price; in reality, they have decided not to sell the property because Mr. Seller has been diagnosed with a serious illness and he wants to remain in the home where he has lived with his wife for the last 30 years.

The Exclusive Right to Sell listing agreement that the Sellers and Broker signed states: "Broker shall be entitled to a commission of 6% of the offering price if broker procures a buyer who is ready, able, and willing to purchase the property."

Sellers inform Broker of their decision to reject the offer and that they wish to take their house off the market. Broker says that's fine, but wants to be paid the 6% commission on the $195,000 offering price. If the Sellers refuse, and Broker sues for the commission, who will prevail, and why?

5. Broker has an exclusive right to sell listing agreement with Seller for a period of 180 days; the list price for the house is $300,000, and the stated commission is 6%. On day 179, Broker shows the property to Buyer, who is secretly very interested in the property.

However, Buyer knows that the listing agreement is about to expire, and so Buyer tells Broker that he is not ready to make a commitment. On day 183, three days after the listing agreement has expired, Buyer approaches Seller directly, with an offer of $285,000. Buyer explains that this is really more than the Seller's asking price because now that the listing agreement has expired, Seller will not have to pay an $18,000 commission to Broker.

If Buyer and Seller consummate the sale without paying Broker a commission, have they acted unethically? Have they acted illegally?

What if this situation is not covered in the listing agreement, can Broker still enforce the 6% commission, and why?

RESEARCH ON THE **WEB**

1. Are real estate agents and brokers required to be licensed in your state? What is the name of the state department, division, or agency that licenses brokers and agents, investigates alleged ethical and legal violations, and disciplines agents and brokers by suspension or revocation of their licenses?

2. What are the requirements to be licensed as a real estate broker in your jurisdiction? What are the requirements to be licensed as a real estate sales agent in your jurisdiction? Can one become a broker immediately, or must the applicant first work under the supervision of a licensed broker?

3. In your state, what is the significance of "time is of the essence" clauses in offers to purchase real property? Is the clause strictly enforced, and if so, under what circumstances? Under what circumstances have the courts in your state found the time is *not* of the essence? In the cases that you examine, do the opinions make reference to the word "boilerplate"?

4. Research instances of racial, ethnic, or religious steering in your city, town, or state. How many such instances have there been? Were testers used to determine if there were violations? Was anyone found civilly liable or criminally convicted?

5. Does your jurisdiction impose any restrictions upon what real estate agents and brokers may disclose about deaths in a property that is for sale? Check federal law regarding a broker's disclosure that someone died of AIDS in the house listed for sale.

BUILDING YOUR **PROFESSIONAL** PORTFOLIO

1. An offer to purchase real estate can be a daunting legal document. How many terms and conditions can you think of that are important to a proper offer to purchase? Obviously you would start with the names of the parties, the identification of the property, and the offering price.

   From the seller's perspective, what might you be very interested in, and therefore want to be incorporated in the contract? Think money and how you will want to be paid. Is the earnest money deposit adequate—it is usually construed as a measure of the buyer's interest in the property, good faith, and willingness to consummate the transaction?

   What if, after making the offer, buyers get cold feet and really don't try very hard to find a loan?

   Now try the exercise from the buyer's point of view. Think about what you *don't* know about the property, and how you can protect yourself. Was there any property that you really liked, but which could be construed as the seller's personal property, and therefore can be taken by the sellers when they move out?

   What happens if, after the offer is accepted by the seller, but before the closing date, the home is heavily damaged by a fire, storm, hurricane, tornado, earthquake, or some other act of nature? Contract law is, to a great extent, about allocating risk. To which party will you allocate the risk of such occurrences?

chapter **9**

LENDING AND THE TITLE SEARCH

LEARNING OBJECTIVES

After reading this chapter, you should understand:

- Amortization
- Loan principal and interest
- The definition and purpose of collateral
- The purpose of a title search
- Encumbrances

A. Real Estate Lending

1. OVERVIEW

a. Principal & Interest

Why do banks, credit unions, and even individuals make **mortgage** loans for the purchase of residential and commercial property? The obvious answer: To make money. The **lender** makes money by charging the borrower/buyer interest on the loan principal.

The **principal** is the amount of money borrowed from the lender for the purchase of the real property. It is sometimes referred to as the "face amount" of the loan. If the property being sold is owned by the seller free and clear (has no liens against it), then at the closing the lion's share of the principal being lent to the buyer will be paid to the seller. On the other hand, if the seller has an outstanding loan for which the property being sold is collateral, then the principal amount of the *new* (buyer's) loan will first go to paying off the *existing* (seller's) loan. Whatever funds remain after payoff of the seller's existing loan and any other liens will then be disbursed to the seller at the closing. This amount constitutes the seller's equity in the property being sold.

Interest is the money charged to the borrower by the lender for the use of the borrowed loan funds (principal), or as is sometimes stated, interest is "the cost of money." Interest is calculated by using the prevailing interest rate. Interest rates fluctuate according to a multitude of conditions that affect the lending market. These conditions are affected by local, state, national, and even international events. Examples of such events and conditions run the gamut from wars and natural disasters to the availability of money from the federal government, to national, state and local unemployment rates.

The **interest rate** set by the lender for any given borrower is also influenced by the borrower's credit history, employment record, and any income from sources other than the borrower's salary. The less risk the lender perceives in making a loan to an individual, the lower that individual's interest rate for the loan will be.

Lenders make money by lending funds to home buyers, but they receive additional income by charging **loan origination fees,** which are usually 1%–3% of the amount lent. For example, if the lender makes a loan of $200,000 for the purchase of a property, and the loan origination fee is 2%, then the borrower will pay $4,000 as a loan origination fee. Over the life of a loan, which may have a term ranging from 5 to 30 years, the lender also makes money from the interest charged to the borrower on the outstanding loan balance. And finally, lenders usually charge administrative **service fees** to the borrower for "servicing the loan."

b. Amortization

The first time people learn about residential mortgage lending, they are usually quite surprised to learn that, over the life of the loan, particularly those with lengthy terms of 20 to 30 years, they will pay back to the lender much more than the amount they borrowed. With the addition of interest, a home loan of $100,000, **amortized** (paid off) over 30 years will result in a total payback to the lender of approximately $170,000 at 4% and approximately $240,000 at 7%.

Lenders will provide a borrower with an **amortization schedule,** which is a list of the monthly payments over the 15–30 year life of the loan. In the early years of the loan payments, most of each monthly payment is allocated to interest, whereas in the later years, most of each monthly payment is applied against the principal. Below is the first-year amortization table for a $100,000 loan, at

Principal
the amount of money borrowed from the lender.

Interest
the amount of money paid by a borrower for the use of the borrowed funds.

Interest Rate
the percentage of the loan amount that a borrower must pay to a lender in return for the use of the borrowed money.

Loan Origination Fee
the fee charged by a lender to cover the administrative costs of making a loan. It is usually 1%–3% of the amount lent.

Amortize
to pay off a debt over a period of time, usually in equal payments, for example, monthly payments, with a portion of each payment paying off interest and a portion paying off principal.

Amortization Schedule
a listing of the periodic payments indicating how much of any given payment is applied against principal, and how much is applied to the interest component of the loan.

4.00% interest payable over 20 years. Note that the monthly payments stay the same ($605.98), while the amount of each payment allocated to principal increases ever so slightly over time, and the amount allocated to interest ever so slightly decreases:

Payment	Interest	Principal	Balance
# 1	$333.33	$272.65	$99,727.35
# 2	$332.42	$273.56	$99,453.80
# 3	$331.51	$274.47	$99,179.33
# 4	$330.60	$275.38	$98,903.95
# 5	$329.68	$276.30	$98,627.65
# 6	$328.76	$277.22	$98,350.42
# 7	$327.83	$278.15	$98,072.28
# 8	$326.91	$279.07	$97,793.21
# 9	$325.98	$280.00	$97,513.20
# 10	$325.04	$280.94	$97,232.27
# 11	$324.11	$281.87	$96,950.39
# 12	$323.17	$282.81	$96,667.58
...			
# 240	$2.01	$603.97	$0.00

The reason is that in the early years of the loan, the major portion of each monthly payment is applied against interest on the *outstanding* loan amount, and only a small fraction of the payment goes to reducing the **principal** amount of the loan. In the later years of the loan term as the principal is reduced, the trend is reversed, with most of the monthly payments being applied against principal, and less to the interest component of the loan.

2. LENDERS WANT SECURITY

It is no accident that a bank vault is often referred to as a "safe." Lenders want their funds to be safe and secure, but the business of lending money is inherently risky, so lenders seek to reduce their risk in many ways, including the following:

a. Ascertaining, through the loan application process, that the buyer is credit worthy;
b. Ascertaining, through an appraisal, that the value of the real property being purchased is sufficient collateral for the loan being given;
c. Ascertaining, through a **title** search, that the buyer-borrower will obtain marketable title from the seller.

Needless to say, it is important that the lender also "qualify" the borrower to ascertain that the borrower will have sufficient income to meet the monthly loan payments. We will look at that process in a later chapter.

As we examine the concepts relating to the title search, it will be easier to understand the process if you put yourself in the shoes of the lender. In the example that follows, you—the lender—have been asked by the prospective buyers of a residential property to lend them the amount of $400,000 for the purchase of their dream home, on which they have made an offer to purchase of $500,000, and which offer was accepted by the seller.

3. COLLATERAL

As the lender, you want to be assured that your loan is secured first and foremost by the value of the property that is the **collateral** for the loan. The collateral is property that is pledged as security for a loan, that is, something the lender may take from the borrower to recoup or lessen its loss if the borrower does not pay back the loan as agreed. That means the property should be worth somewhat more than the $400,000 you will be lending to the buyers, because foreclosed properties almost never bring their fair market value ($500,000 in this case) at foreclosure sales.

Collateral
property that is pledged as security for a loan. The real property being purchased is pledged as collateral in the mortgage or deed of trust as security for the loan.

4. LOAN-TO-VALUE RATIO

The **loan-to-value ratio** is the ratio or percentage of the loan amount to the fair market value (FMV) of the property to be purchased. The formula is simple:

Loan-to-Value Ratio
the ratio (percentage) of the loan amount to the fair market value of the property to be purchased.

$$\frac{\text{Loan Amount (Ex: \$400,000)}}{\text{FMV of Property (Ex: \$500,000)}} = \text{LTV Ratio} = 80\%$$

In the formula above, if a bank lends 80% of the FMV, which we will assume is the same as the purchase price of $500,000, the buyer will have to provide a down payment of the other 20%, or $100,000.

The higher the LTV ratio (say, 90%–95%), *the greater the risk* the lender is taking in making the loan. Again, the reason is that if a lender has to foreclose on a property because the owner is in default on the monthly payments, the property will almost always sell for much less at the foreclosure auction than its fair market value. Therefore, the greater the "cushion" (i.e., homeowner's equity) there is between the fair market value and the loan amount, the less money the lender might lose in the event of a foreclosure sale.

Lenders have become more conservative following the decline of real estate values in the last several years, the so-called bursting of the bubble. The bubble in question was the seemingly inexorable increase, pretty much nationwide, in housing values from the 1990s through about 2007.

Lenders had a false sense of security, believing that even if a borrower did default, the ever-expanding bubble of home values would protect the lender from losing its loan principal in the event of a foreclosure sale. Therefore, they were making loans with a much thinner cushion of protection, often making loans with loan-to-value ratios of 95%–120% (meaning that lenders were often making loans in excess of the appraised value of the property). When the bubble was still expanding, very few homes went to foreclosure because distressed homeowners could always put their properties up for sale, and buyers/speculators would pay a premium, believing, like the lenders, that home values (the bubble) would continue rising.

Let us get back to the example above. A less conservative lender would permit a higher loan-to-value ratio of, for example, 90%, in which case the loan amount would be $450,000:

$$\$500,000 \text{ Fair Market Value} \times 90\% \text{ Loan-to-Value Ratio}$$
$$= \$450,000 \text{ Amount of the loan}$$

In return for the greater risk (i.e., only a 10% cushion in case of a default and foreclosure), the lender would require a greater reward, charging the buyers a higher interest rate for this greater loan-to-value ratio and requiring that the borrower obtain *mortgage insurance,* which would pay off the loan in the event the borrower defaulted and the property were foreclosed.

B. The Title Search/Examination

1. OVERVIEW AND PURPOSE

a. Cloud on Title

The purpose of the title search is to determine if the seller is, in fact, the owner, and has the right to transfer the property being sold, and to find any ***encumbrances of record*** on the property, such as mortgages, tax liens, ***easements***, covenants, and judgments, which could put the lender in a junior, or subordinate, position in a foreclosure sale, or perhaps ***cloud the buyer's title***.

A **cloud on title** makes the title less marketable, that is, less desirable from the buyer's and lender's standpoint. Imagine that you are a buyer and the title search of the property you want to purchase reveals that there is an old, unpaid city tax lien against the property in the amount of $7,500. Because tax liens attach to the property, the city may foreclose its lien even after title has been conveyed to you.

If the lien is not satisfied prior to or at closing, would you want to assume that debt, and the risk of foreclosure? Obviously not, and neither would your lender. Understandably, lenders will not lend money for the purchase of a property when there is a cloud on the title, because the buyer's ownership free of liens may be challenged in a court of law. Such a cloud/claim impairs the lender's collateral—the property—which is the lender's security for the loan.

b. The Title Examination in Practice

A **title search**, put simply, is a search of the public records in the name of each owner of the property over a period of time. Each owner's name is researched for the time period he or she owned the property.

The first step is to clearly identify the entire property being conveyed. Find the document(s) that created the current owner's interest, which will usually be a deed. A reference to the deed recording information may usually be found in the tax records. It may also be found by checking the *grantee* index in that owner's name, going backward in time from the present. Once the vesting deed has been established, check the *grantor* index, civil records, and any other real estate records in the jurisdiction, in that owner's name (in all owners' names if more than one, even in the case of a married couple), from the date of the deed going forward in time, to determine what liens and encumbrances have been recorded in his or her name that will affect the property. This completes the search of the current owner. Then do the same for each prior owner. Find each prior chain deed by checking the *grantee* index in the prior owner's name, going backward in time, and search the same records in that name from that deed going forward in time to the current owner's deed.

In some databases, the grantor and grantee indices are combined, and the paralegal must be able to distinguish between the two. Both indices should be reviewed in each owner's name, as most instruments will only appear in one or the other.

All variations of each name should be searched, including initials only. Registrars enter documents in their indices exactly as the names are shown (usually even typographical errors), and a person may sign his or her name in multiple ways over time. If the party's name is Timothy Andrew Baker, the index should also be searched under Timothy A. Baker, Timothy Baker, Tim A. Baker, Tim Baker, Timmy A. Baker, Timmy Baker, Timmy Andrew Baker,

---

Cloud on Title

a defect or potential defect in the owner's title to a piece of land arising from some claim or encumbrance such as a lien, easement, or court order.

Title Search

a thorough search of all types of public records to discover any liens or other encumbrances that may affect the quality of the title of the property to be conveyed.

T. Baker, T. A. Baker, T. Andrew Baker, Andrew Baker, T. Andy Baker, Andy Baker, Timmy Andy Baker, and A. Baker, and perhaps even under Drew or Andrew Timothy.

It is not necessary to type each variation individually, as many will appear in the same partial-name search. The results of a query using the last name "Baker" and the first initial "T" will reflect most of the names shown above. If Mr. Baker has been known as "Buddy" for most of his life, this name should be searched too. If his middle name or initial is not known, the search parameters are broadened significantly until the name can be determined from the records. But it is not necessary to search outside the known initials for a male individual; that is, there is no need to search under Timothy B. Baker, as Mr. Baker's initials are not likely to have changed. On the other hand, a woman's name should be searched using all variations of her first, middle, and maiden names, as the possible variations are more numerous. Some women use their middle names after marriage (Jacqueline Sue Oliver) and some use their maiden names (Jacqueline Miller Oliver). Some women do not take their husband's names, and some hyphenate the two. A woman may have received title to property prior to marriage, meaning index entries may be in both her maiden and her married name. If she has married multiple times during her ownership of the property, each of her husband's last names must be searched.

Also consider the variations between spellings of names, e.g., "Lee" vs. "Leigh" or "Catherine" vs. "Katherine." A lender may have printed an incorrectly spelled name on a mortgage, and if the discrepancy was not realized at the closing, the document will be indexed under the incorrect spelling.

Obviously, a title examination is much easier to perform using an unusual name than a common name, and most title researchers will choose a search on Jedediah Quentin McCorquodale's property over John Smith's any day, but misspellings in indices are much more common with unusual names. Consider the difference between the common name "Durham" and the similar but much less common "Dunham." It can be assumed that a registry clerk has at some point looked at "Dunham" and assumed "Durham."

In some areas title records are indexed under parcel identification numbers in addition to owner names, and both should be searched for complete results.

A title examination is *certified* as accurate by the closing agent/attorney or title agency, and the records must be researched thoroughly to reduce the risk of a title claim. Most registries provide a brief description of the property affected by each instrument in the index entry. Some even provide cross-references to other related instruments. These entries are helpful, but should never be relied upon as accurate. Sometimes there is not enough room for the entire description in the document entry, particularly if it includes multiple tracts. Every document should be opened or pulled from the file and read from beginning to end for any hidden terms or defects that may affect the property. Internet records are also convenient and are utilized more and more frequently, but only the records available onsite at the providers' physical locations should be relied upon for a certified title examination, unless the agent or attorney has authorized otherwise. If this is the case, a disclosure of the search methods should be included in the certification or opinion.

After the title research is complete, a summary of findings should be prepared for the closing agent/attorney's review, and where applicable, a preliminary opinion of title drafted to be signed and submitted to the title insurance company or agency, which will issue a title commitment prior to closing showing all the requirements for the issuance of the final policy and the exceptions that will be set out therein.

Once the closing has occurred, an abbreviated title examination is performed, only in the current owner's name, from the date of the prior search to the present, and assuming no new liens or encumbrances have been filed since the preliminary examination, record the deed and/or mortgage immediately thereafter. Any new matters of record should be reported to the closing agent/attorney prior to recording.

After recording, where applicable, a final opinion is prepared, containing all new matters affecting the title, through and including the documents recorded in conjunction with closing, which will be included in the title policies when issued in final. Any cancellations or terminations of prior liens, including UCC financing statements, must be completed in a reasonable, usually statutory, time.

c. Chain of Title

Chain of Title
the ownership history of a piece of real property, showing the grantors and grantees who owned the property over a period of time.

Many title insurance companies require that the title searcher review the **chain of title** for a specified period of time, usually 30 to 40 years.[1] The chain of title is a summary of the ownership history of a property for a given period of time. A chain of title is established using the records of the county Register of Deeds and/or Clerk of Court/Circuit Clerk of Court, depending on where these records are housed in your state. The "Grantor" index reflects grants, or "out conveyances" of property, and the "Grantee" index reflects receipts, or "in conveyances." So a deed may be found in both indices, in the grantor index under the seller's name, and the grantee index under the buyer's name.

A title researcher may want to establish the chain of title in reverse since the current owner's name is known. A good place to start is by locating the property in the current year's tax records, which are updated annually. Tax records are usually searchable by owner's name, property address, or parcel number. The tax record for the tract will typically reference the deed to the current owner, or the "vesting" deed, and sometimes prior chain deeds as well, which is convenient for the title researcher. Another way to find the vesting deed is to review the grantee index under the name of the current owner, starting with recent records and going back in time until the deed is located.

Never assume the property was received by the current owner via a single deed, even if the tax records and/or the purchase contract only reflect one. When looking at the tax map, consider adjacent tracts in the same owner's name—does one look as though it should be part of the property? Perhaps there was a boundary-line agreement with a neighbor that added a small parcel to the property, but it was not combined with the larger parcel for tax purposes. This would result in two separate parcels that make up the property, but only one may come up under the street address, and one will certainly be missed under a search only by parcel number. Does the tax map show a structure lying across the line between two parcels? If so, perhaps both parcels are being conveyed but this was not set out clearly in the contract. This is why it is important to identify the property by checking the records under the name, the parcel number, and the street address.

Once the vesting deed has been found, the title researcher then finds the prior deed in the chain, sometimes called the "derivation" deed, by starting with the date of the vesting deed and going back in time, checking the grantee index

---

[1] For a summary of the process of title searching, see "Overview of a Title Search" at the end of this chapter.

in the name of the grantor who conveyed the property to the current owner. Often a deed will contain the prior deed reference, which is another convenience for the title researcher. The title researcher continues in this way until the chain has been established for the desired time period, typically 30-40 years for a full title search, but the period varies by state. In the case where the existing owner has owned the property for more than 40 years, the researcher still may need to go back even further to find that deed, because many title companies require the ownership history be established to at least one valid "link" in the chain, even if it means a longer search period than 40 years. The grantor on each chain deed should match the grantee on the prior deed exactly, and if it does not, further research will be necessary to establish whether it is due to an error that must be corrected before title can be conveyed to the new buyer, or there is a valid reason for the discrepancy. Perhaps a husband and wife divorced and the surviving spouse remarried. Perhaps an owner died and the subsequent deed is from his or her heirs. Perhaps a corporation went through a merger or name change.

Searching a chain of title can be complicated by events like the subdivision of a larger parcel into lots, the death of an owner, the conveyance of only a portion of a tract, the conveyance of a partial ownership interest, a boundary-line agreement, a defect in a deed, and so forth. It is essential to prepare an abstract for each chain deed. Also, a title researcher should not rely entirely on deed references shown in tax records or chain deeds. These references may be abbreviated due to lack of space, or incomplete due to lack of diligence on the preparer's part. The property description should be plotted for closure errors and checked carefully for consistency from each deed to the next.

Older deeds may contain legal descriptions that use terms like "chains," "rods," "links," "perches," and/or "poles." These units of measurement are no longer used, and they may be converted to feet and inches using online converters. Conversion tables for both linear and square measure are also available from title insurance companies/agents.

Older documents may also contain typed names followed by a slash mark and the letter "s" ("/s") rather than actual signatures. In these cases, the actual signatures were present on the original documents, but copiers had not yet been invented, so the entire documents, including the signatures, were typed and "conformed" for the record books.

Deeds contain different levels of "warranties" of title, as discussed in detail in Chapter 10. "General warranty" deeds provide the grantee with the highest level of assurance from the grantor. "Special warranty" deeds contain more limited warranties, and are typically used for special purpose conveyances, such as a trustee's deed in foreclosure. "Non-warranty" and "quitclaim" deeds contain no warranties and are generally used for "cleanup" purposes, without purporting to convey any interest unless it is actually owned. If the contract calls for anything other than a general warranty deed, the title company should be notified, as it may not be willing to provide insurance coverage.

Sometimes title is passed without a deed, as in the case of an inheritance from a deceased owner. In this case, there may be an estate file in the county where the owner died, which will indicate the heir(s) of the deceased. If the deceased had a will, or died **testate**, the will is **probated** by the Clerk of Superior Court, or determined to be legally valid, and the instructions in the will are followed unless contested. If the deceased had no will, or died **intestate**, the property passes to his or her legal heirs according to the intestacy laws of the state in which he or she died.

Testate
having left a will at death.

Probate
the judicial process by which a testamentary document is established to be a valid will; to administer a decedent's estate.

Intestate
of or relating to a person who has died without a will.

A title researcher should provide an "abstract," or a summary of the estate file, to the attorney certifying title so he or she may disclose any potential issues to the title insurance company. If no estate file for a deceased owner in the chain of title can be found in the public records, the suspected heirs may be determined if there is a deed on record granted by individuals other than the deceased owner, hopefully describing them as the heirs, but a title company will be wary of insuring title in this case as the potential for a future claim against the policy increases. It is possible that a previously unknown heir will come forward to claim an interest in the property after it has been conveyed by the other heirs, possibly even years later after it may have changed hands multiple times.

One way to mitigate this risk is to have all known heirs sign an affidavit and indemnity that there are no other heirs. If it happens that an unknown heir comes forward, and the owner has purchased title insurance, he or she may make a claim against the policy. The title insurance company, after hiring an attorney to research the claim, will find evidence that either the heir has no valid interest in the property, or that he or she does, and will pay damages to the heir so the current owners will not lose title to the property. In the latter circumstance, the title company's attorney will require that the heir sign a deed conveying any interest he or she had in the property to the current owners. Note: The loss under a title policy is limited pursuant to the terms of the policy, for example, the maximum loss will be either the amount of title insurance purchased or the value of the property, whichever is less.

There are multiple ways title may be held jointly by more than one individual, and each has its specific outcome when the parties convey the property or sever their relationship. Married couples may own property by the "entireties," meaning they are treated as one ownership entity, and 100% interest in the property passes automatically to the surviving spouse if one dies. Only married couples may hold property by the entireties. "Joint tenants with right of survivorship" are treated similarly, but are not necessarily married. "Tenants in common" own the property jointly and each owns a partial interest (equal unless otherwise designated in the deed). Tenants in common do not have a right of survivorship, and upon the death of one co-tenant, her interest will pass to her heirs if she dies intestate, or to her beneficiaries under a will.

If a married couple separates, a separation agreement may determine how the parties may convey or encumber the property with or without the consent of the other while they are still married. After divorce, absent an agreement stating otherwise, the spouses become tenants in common until one conveys his or her interest to the other. If the property was initially conveyed to an individual and the individual was married at the time or married later, an interest by entireties is not created; the property must be conveyed to both parties to create an interest by entireties. Some states require that the couple's marital status be shown on the face of the deed to create tenancy by the entireties.

In some counties, tax records are only updated once per year on January 1, so they may not reflect the most recent conveyance, and therefore not the current owner. Accordingly, the title researcher's first step should be to check the out conveyances of the owner reflected in the tax records, beginning with January 1 and going forward to the present date, to make sure the property has not changed hands since the tax records were last updated. It is possible it has been conveyed more than once, so each subsequent owner must be searched from the date of his or her deed forward until the most recent deed has been found. The search may even need to be retroactive beginning with January 1 of the *prior* year, as some counties' records are only current through January 1 of the "current tax year," meaning the most recent year for which tax bills have been generated.

Some counties index their real estate records by tax parcel number in addition to grantor/grantee indices, and these indices should be reviewed as well, even though the results of both searches should be the same.

Title searching is a job for experienced professionals. The process is complex, and errors can be costly for the title insurance company. A high percentage of ***malpractice claims*** against attorneys arise out of the title searching process, and therefore, lawyers—or their paralegals—who perform title searches should specialize in the area of real estate law.

A **title insurance** company will not insure against title defects if a title search has not been conducted. In applicable states, an attorney must issue a favorable **opinion of title** to the title company. Also, the buyer or grantee wants assurance that he or she will not have to defend against lawsuits claiming title to the property. Therefore, any liens must be cleared before the lender will make the loan and the buyer will accept the property.

When properties are sold, a closing is conducted to complete the transaction and transfer title to the property to the buyer. But before the closing occurs, and before the lender will make the final loan commitment, the lender will require that a title search be conducted, and that a title insurance policy be issued for the buyer's and lender's benefit. The cost of the title search is usually the buyer's responsibility.

A title search is necessary because, as we indicated previously, lenders like to feel their funds are secure. The same is true for the buyer of the property, and for the title insurance company that will issue the title insurance policy insuring the buyer against defects in the title. Therefore, a title insurance company will not issue a policy of title insurance, and a lender will not make a loan for the purchase of a property unless they know that:

i.   There are no ***liens*** or other encumbrances on the property, nor any actual or potential ***clouds on the title***, and

ii. In the case of the lender, it is confident that it has, or will have a first-priority position for its lien, also referred to as ***priority of lien***.

2. LIENS AND OTHER ENCUMBRANCES

A property is usually encumbered by liens of one sort or another, which must be satisfied by the seller before the buyer will take title of the property. Perhaps the most important function of a title search (described later) is to identify the **liens** that **encumber** the property to be sold. The buyer and new lender want to make sure that any outstanding liens are *satisfied* prior to or at the closing so that none of the lien holders may go against the property after the buyer has closed and taken possession.

The most common and expected type of lien is the one held by the existing mortgage lender—also known as the mortgagee—which must be paid off at the closing when the property is transferred to a new owner, unless arrangements have been made with the lender for the buyer to assume the seller's loan. Other types of liens are not so common—or expected—which is why a title searcher must be diligent in investigating for possible liens.

As you will see, if the liens below are not paid off when the property changes hands, the lienholder can and will foreclose on the property, a situation the new

Title Insurance
a policy issued by a title insurance company that protects the buyer of a property against losses related to a defect in the title of the real property.

Opinion of Title
a certification offered by an attorney, after reviewing the title search and abstract of title, stating whether a parcel of real property is marketable

Lien
a legal claim, right, or interest that a creditor has in another's property, lasting until the debt or duty that it secures is satisfied.

Encumbrance
an encumbrance is a broader term than "lien," and encompasses liens, as well as claims against, or interests in, a property that may reduce its value, such as an easement or possible legal claim against the property, which would cloud the title.

buyers and their lender obviously want to avoid. A lien on a property might consist of one or more of the following:

a. Mortgage Lien

This is the most common type of lien on a property. It is the lender's security for the funds it lends for purchase or refinance of the property, and must be paid in full before its borrower conveys the property to another party. For example, when the current owners purchased the property, they obtained a mortgage from ABC Mortgage Co. in order to buy the residence. That loan must now be satisfied—paid off—at closing when the sellers convey the property to the buyers, so that ABC will not have a claim on the property, the purchase of which is to be financed by the buyers' new lender, YOU Financing. If ABC is not paid off at the closing, and payments are no longer made to ABC, it will foreclose on the property, after which the new owners will be evicted.

Mortgages and Deeds of Trust are usually recorded in the Register of Deeds or the Clerk of Court/Circuit Court, depending on the state. Since the borrower, or mortgagor, grants the mortgage or deed of trust to the beneficiary or the trustee, it will be indexed in the grantor index as an out conveyance, under the name of the owner of the property during the time the mortgage was executed and recorded. It will also be in the grantee index under the lender or trustee's name. The registry may have all real estate records in a combined index, or may have separate indices for mortgages and deeds of trust, and all separate indices must be searched since they may not be linked or cross-referenced. The paralegal should report the document in his or her title summary, and will want to note specific elements in the document, including the amount of the loan, date of maturity, proper execution and notarization, and presence and correctness of the legal description. It is also important to report whether the document secures future advances or an equity line.

If a mortgage or deed of trust has already been satisfied and canceled of record, the satisfaction or cancellation should appear in both the grantor and grantee index under the borrower/owner's name. But a *release* of deed of trust may only appear in the grantee index in some counties, as it is granted by the lender to the borrower/owner. When reviewing the grantor/grantee indices, it is a good idea to note all cancellations first, so the corresponding mortgages may be eliminated immediately. This will simplify the process of determining which mortgages remain active, and which is in a senior lien position. But *all* mortgages securing the subject property should be reported to the closing agent/attorney, even those marked as canceled or released, as the cancellation or release instrument may be defective.

b. Tax Lien

If the owner/seller of the property has not paid taxes to any one of several governmental entities, that governmental entity may have placed a **tax lien** on the property. The federal, state, and local governments—cities, towns, villages—may all encumber a property with a tax lien. In some jurisdictions, the taxing authority does not have to "file" a lien—unpaid taxes are automatically a lien. If the tax lien is not paid, the government has the authority to force the sale of the house via foreclosure. A buyer will want to make sure any tax lien is satisfied prior to taking ownership to avoid a tax foreclosure after he or she has taken possession.

The title paralegal should check the status of payment of taxes for at least a ten-year period, or as instructed by the title insurance company and the supervising attorney. Tax bills should be searched using the owner's name, the street address, and the tax parcel number(s) to ensure capture of all taxes due.

Taxes are assessed on personal property separately from real property, and if personal property is being included in the sale, these taxes must be reported along with the real property taxes so they may also be prorated between the parties at closing.

If the property lies within the boundaries of a city or town, taxes will likely be assessed by that municipality in addition to those assessed by the county in which it lies. There may also be separate taxes assessed for fire and ambulance services. In some areas, arrangements are made between municipalities and the counties in which they are located, so that the city and county tax bills are combined and collected by one of the governmental entities, usually the county. But a title researcher should not assume this is the case in all areas. All potential taxing entities' records must be checked. The paralegal should report in his or her summary the year through which the taxes are paid, along with any delinquent taxes.

In some states, counties are authorized to require the payment of any delinquent taxes on real property before a deed may be recorded. In these areas, the paralegal may be required to obtain a certification on the deed at the tax office to show evidence of the payment of taxes before presenting the deed for recording.

Real property tax records are broken down by land and buildings. It is possible to determine whether improvements (structures) are located on the property, and their specific value, by checking tax assessment records. If these records only provide a land value, it can be assumed the property was vacant at the time taxes were last assessed. But construction may be in progress, in which case the building value will appear in the records at the next annual assessment.

A parcel being used for certain purposes, e.g., agricultural, may have the benefit of **deferred taxes**, sometimes called **rollback taxes**, meaning payment of a portion of the taxes may be deferred to a later date. Any deferred taxes must be reported to the closing agent/attorney; they must normally be paid at closing, as the exemption would typically expire upon sale or transfer.

c. Mechanic's or Materialmen's Lien

If a person or company was not paid for work performed on, or materials supplied for, a property's construction, repair, or renovation, the contractor or supplier may file a claim of lien, followed by a lawsuit in which he or she obtains and forecloses a judgment to satisfy the lien. For example, if a plumber installs new plumbing facilities at a residential property and is not paid, the plumber can file a mechanic's lien and actually force the foreclosure of the property to satisfy the unpaid bill. The same applies to others who may perform work on or relating to real property, such as architects, building contractors, landscapers, electricians, roofers, and so on. Foreclosure of **judgment liens** is fairly uncommon because construction work is usually done in conjunction with a loan, in which the lender would have protected itself by requiring subordination by the contractor of his lien to the mortgage or deed of trust, putting the mortgage in a senior position to the potential claim of lien.

Claims of lien must be reported and followed up on prior to closing, because a claim of lien is simply a notice that the contractor intends to file suit, which could result in a judgment lien and subsequent foreclosure. If a suit is not filed within a statutory period following the last date of work, the claim of lien expires, but the lien must be paid by the seller prior to closing or from closing funds, since the change of ownership will not extinguish the lien should the contractor file suit within the statutory time period. If the contractor forecloses its judgment, the real property is sold at auction by the county sheriff, and conveyed to the purchasing party by a Sheriff's Deed, which is recorded in the register of deeds, creating a public record of the new "link" in the chain of title.

d. Notice of Lis Pendens

Lis pendens
a pending lawsuit; a notice, recorded in the chain of title to real property, required or permitted in some jurisdictions to warn all persons that certain property is the subject matter of litigation, and that any interest acquired during the pendency of the suit are subject to its outcome.

A Notice of Lis Pendens is filed in the civil records that states a civil action has been filed, which could ultimately impact title to the property. A Notice of Lis Pendens should be reported to the closing attorney/agent, even if dismissed. The suit may have been voluntarily dismissed either with or without prejudice. As with mechanic's/materialmen's liens, if the dismissal is without prejudice, the plaintiff reserves the right to re-file the suit, typically within one year.

e. Judgment Liens

If the sellers of the property lost a lawsuit, there may be a monetary judgment against them. The judgment must be satisfied or the judgment creditor (the party who won the lawsuit) may force the sale of the house to satisfy the judgment. In some states, unpaid homeowners association dues may become a lien on the property of the delinquent homeowner.

Judgments attach to and run with land, so if a judgment is entered against a person during his or her ownership of a parcel, the judgment constitutes a lien on that parcel (and all other parcels owned by the party against whom the judgment was obtained), and remains so even if that owner conveys the parcel. Therefore the names of all prior owners of the parcel must be searched during their ownership and for the statutory time period prior to their ownership.

For example, say a closing is scheduled on 02/01/2014 and the property has changed hands three times during the state's 10-year period for expiration of judgments: John Brown conveyed the property to Jane White on 03/11/2005; Jane conveyed it to David Smith on 08/15/2008; and David conveyed it to Mary Jones on 09/19/2012. Each of these owners' names must be searched during his or her corresponding time period of ownership *and* the prior statutory period during which a lien would have attached to the property when he or she obtained it. But the search need not extend more than 10 years prior to the date of closing as any judgments prior to that will have expired, so the search periods would be as follows: John Brown from 02/01/2004 through 03/11/2005, Jane White from 02/01/2004 through 08/15/2008, David Smith from 02/01/2004 through 09/19/2012, and Mary Jones from 02/01/2004 through the present. This search method will reveal any judgment entered during any party's ownership and during the statutory time period prior to his or her ownership, which judgment would have attached to the parcel and remained a lien on the land until it was paid and satisfied.

Judgment records are usually kept in the civil division of the Clerk of Superior Court. There may be an online index providing access to statewide records, searchable by county. Judgments are indexed by plaintiff and defendant rather than grantor and grantee. Judgments in favor of the Internal Revenue Service for federal taxes, sometimes referred to as federal tax liens or IRS tax liens, are also indexed with civil judgments, as are liens filed by the state Employment Security Commission. Tax liens filed by the federal government can be in large amounts, and are not as easily extinguished by foreclosure as are other liens junior to a mortgage or deed of trust. Claims of lien, or notices filed by contractors who have not been paid for construction work performed or materials provided for construction work on the property, are also filed with civil judgments.

The status of satisfaction, cancellation, or dismissal of a judgment lien or claim of lien may be determined by the public records. But the language should be reviewed carefully to confirm the lien was properly *satisfied* or *paid in full* and *canceled of record*, as opposed to being reduced by a partial payment. All civil judgments and liens for the search period should be reported to the attorney or title agency, whether satisfied or not, so that the attorney or title agency may determine whether the civil judgments or liens should be included in the title opinion.

f. Restrictive Covenants

Restrictive covenants are recorded by the developer in the establishment of the planned subdivision, condominium complex, or townhome development, and govern common elements so that the owners may enjoy certain aspects of community living. They may be amended from time to time to change the terms and/or incorporate newly improved phases of the subdivision. Some of the matters governed by restrictive covenants include:

Building setback requirements (how far away from the street or property lines buildings must be placed),

Exterior paint colors of homes,

Regular maintenance of yards and or building exteriors,

The use of any clubhouses or other amenities,

Types of structures permitted,

The size and/or height of buildings,

Temporary buildings,

The size of flags or signs,

The visibility of garages and automobiles,

Noise,

Parking, and

Types of animals allowed as pets.

Restrictive covenants ensure all owners may enjoy a well-maintained and quiet community. Before ground was broken for the construction of the property, the developer should have recorded the covenants at the office of the county's Register of Deeds. Covenants "run with the land" and any prospective buyer of a property subject to such covenants should be provided a copy of the covenants prior to closing. In this way, the buyer will have actual notice of the restrictive covenants.

   i. Dues. In most cases owners are required to pay monthly or quarterly homeowners' dues to the management association, which are used by the association for the upkeep and maintenance of the clubhouses and common areas, and building exteriors and yards for condominiums and townhomes. The status of payment of these dues should be checked by the title paralegal. He or she may need written authorization from the seller to obtain this information from the association.

   ii. Right of Reversion. Some older restrictive covenants contained a right of reversion or forfeiture, meaning that title reverted to the developer if a lot owner failed to pay association dues or violated the covenants. For this reason, restrictive covenants should be reviewed to make sure they do not contain a right of reversion, and if they do, it should be disclosed to the title agent and included in the preliminary title opinion.

   iii. *Unenforceable Restrictions.* Some older covenants contained restrictions that were discriminatory in nature, and are fortunately unenforceable today due to laws preventing illegal discrimination. These specific restrictions no longer carry weight and are ignored by lenders, closing agents, and title insurance companies, but the documents that contain them should still be reported, as their other enforceable terms remain an encumbrance on the property.

   iv. *Restrictions in Deeds.* Not all restrictions are contained in standalone documents governing an entire community, but they are no less binding. Many restrictive covenants may be set out in deeds <u>and</u> pertain only to the one parcel they convey. The title paralegal should read each deed in the chain of title and report any restrictions contained therein.

   v. *Zoning Restrictions.* In addition to restrictive covenants, there will be similar restrictions in accordance with the county, city, village, or town's zoning ordinance, which apply generally to all properties lying within their boundaries. These ordinances are provided by the planning department in the jurisdiction. There may be a discrepancy between the restrictions shown in the covenants and the zoning ordinance (e.g., setback distance), and the title searcher should make the title insurance company aware of any such discrepancies.

g. Easements and Rights of Way

An easement or a right of way is not a lien because it is not security for money owed, but a grant of access to the property to a third party for a specific reason. Nevertheless, it is an encumbrance that affects the title to the property, so a prospective lender wants to know about any existing easements before making the loan. Usually a neighbor or public utility company is the beneficiary of an easement as opposed to a creditor. The terms "easement" and "right of way" are essentially interchangeable as they serve the same purpose. There are many types of easements:

   i. *Vehicular Access to a Public Right of Way.* One example of an easement is for vehicular access (sometimes referred to as the right of "ingress, egress, and regress") to a public right of way in the case of an otherwise landlocked parcel. If the property does not directly adjoin a public street, as in the case of a subdivision lot on a privately maintained road, or a parcel that was carved out of a larger parcel and no longer abuts a public street, there must be another means of access to the public street, perhaps via the private road in the first example, or over an adjoining property owner's tract in the second. The style of vehicular access will be recorded in the registry so there is public evidence of the property owner's right to cross the land described in the easement, which will run with the land and therefore benefit future owners as well. In the case of a subdivision, the easement over the private road will be reflected on the subdivision plat or map. In the case of a landlocked parcel, an easement between the owner and the adjacent parcel will be recorded to evidence the right of access across the adjoining parcel.

   A title researcher should understand the difference between an *appurtenant* easement and a *burdensome* easement. An easement between parties for access across one parcel for the benefit of another is *appurtenant* to the party granted access across the tract, and *burdensome* to the party who owns the tract across which access was granted. In both cases, the easement should be described as part of the legal description in a deed, the style of which depends on whether the benefited tract or the burdened tract is being conveyed. If the benefited tract is being conveyed, the easement is appurtenant to that tract, and should be described at the end of the legal description as a benefit, for example:

> "Being all of Tract 1 of Shady Oaks Subdivision, Phase One, as recorded in Plat Book 123, Page 56 of the Any County Registry, TOGETHER WITH an easement for public access across Tract 2 of said plat, as described in the easement agreement recorded in Book 12345, Page 6789 of the Any County Registry." The words "together with" provide evidence that there is a benefit added to the property. If the burdened tract is being conveyed, the same applies, except the description should be worded something like, "Being all of Tract 2 of Shady Oaks Subdivision, Phase One, as recorded in Plat Book 123, Page 56 of the Any County Registry, SUBJECT TO an easement for public access across said tract for the benefit of Tract 1 of said plat, as described by the easement agreement recorded in Book 12345, Page 6789 of the Any County Registry."

This reflects that the conveyance includes a restriction, or an encumbrance, on the title to the burdened parcel. The "together with" and "subject to" phrases should be included in the legal description in each deed in the chain of title subsequent to the easement agreement for both tracts. The grantee in the deed to the burdened parcel is bound to provide access to the owner of the benefited tract according to the terms of the easement until such time as the easement agreement is modified or terminated by both parties. Any such modification or termination must be recorded in the registry just as is the easement, so there is a public record of the change.

A title researcher should also make sure that an easement for vehicular access over an adjacent parcel provides full and complete access. An easement extending from one tract across another to a public road must have enough frontage for a vehicle to cross into the public road without entering any portion of the burdened tract that is not encumbered by the easement. In Figure 9-1, the initial easement from the tract to the road, which crosses two tracts, reaches the street, but it is insufficient as there is not enough space for a vehicle to pass into the street without leaving the easement. The additional highlighted easement across the third tract is necessary to complete the tract's access to the street.

An easement for vehicular access should also contain the right to access public utilities. If vehicular access is across an adjacent tract, as is the case in Figure 9-1, the residence will also need the right to have utility lines extended from the street to the tract.

Not every encumbrance that affects the title to a parcel of land is evidenced in the public record, which is the reason for the need for title insurance and a *survey* of the property. Some access easements are not on record. An example of this is a *prescriptive* easement, discussed in detail in Chapter 6. Prescriptive easements are acquired via *adverse possession*, meaning that a property owner has used a means of access across another tract for at least a statutory time period without the consent of the property owner, and therefore the claim to the easement may be upheld in a court of law. This is uncommon, but will occur mainly in the case of a tract that has been owned by the same party for many years as opposed to those that have been conveyed, and particularly surveyed, in recent years. The title researcher

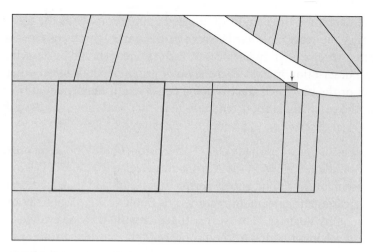

FIGURE 9-1 Vehicular Access

should review aerial photographs of the parcel, which are available through county tax records and many online mapping resources, and report any evidence of dirt roads or pathways to the closing attorney. This implied easement is sometimes referred to as a "cart-way" easement, dating back to the days of a horse and cart crossing a beaten path.

Vehicular access is included in title insurance, so the style of access must be reported to the title insurance company in the title opinion so the policy may be worded accordingly. In some cases access may be questionable, as in the case of adverse possession, or there may be shared access, as in the case of a shopping center, and the lender will request an endorsement to the title policy specifically insuring there is legal access to the tract.

ii. *Utility Easements*. Companies that provide utility services to the general public, like electricity, natural gas, water/sewer, phone, and cable services, must have the ability to install and maintain the equipment used to provide those services, such as underground pipes, overhead wires, telephone poles, and so forth. Utility easements already encumber the vast majority of land in urban areas via easements that were granted in the early-to-mid 1900s when these utility companies began providing mass services. A title researcher going back that far in a search will likely find some "blanket" easements or permits, meaning the utility company is granted unlimited access to the entire parcel rather than to a specified area, although different laws may come into play binding the utility company to the area where the utilities were located on the ground. These easements will have been granted by the owners of the parcels at the time they were granted, and earlier ones may be handwritten. They may be called "General Permits" or "Agreements."

A title researcher will want to establish the location of structures on the property to make sure none lies within an easement, particularly one held by a utility company, which may have the right to force the property owner to remove the encroaching structure, even if it does not interfere with the utility company's ability to maintain its lines. Structure locations may be determined by reviewing the survey, tax maps, and aerial photographs.

iii. *Railroad Right of Way*. Railroad charters were established beginning in the 1800s and are still a frequent source of difficulty for title agents and title insurance companies. Before general incorporation statutes came about, railroads were granted charters by the states and the federal government, which granted the railroads eminent domain, giving them almost unlimited power to take property and construct their tracks on the most favorable routes for public use. They were not written with specifics regarding the proposed locations or method of installment of tracks, making it difficult to argue with the railroad company over the powers granted. In some states, there has been debate over the actual width of the rights of way granted in these charters because of the nebulous terms.

If a charter described a 100-foot right of way, did that mean the width of the entire right of way was 100 feet, or that the right of way extended 100 feet in each direction from the centerline of the track? Arguments for the former have not been very successful, so it is better to err on the side of caution and assume the latter. The original charters were granted for the initial "main" east/west lines, but it is generally assumed that their terms extend to subsequent tracks and even spur tracks on private property for access to loading docks. There may be special statutory exceptions to recordation of railroad deeds and rights of way.

A railroad right of way is legally considered abandoned after a period of non-use, but given the scope of powers granted in the charters, abandonment of a portion of track should never be assumed without written evidence from the appropriate railroad company. Any evidence of a present or past railroad track or right of way should be disclosed to the title company via the opinion of title, even if a track was never constructed or the track no longer appears to be in use.

iv. *Highway Right of Way*. Streets, roads, and highways are necessities, as is the ability to get our vehicles to them in order to drive on them. Over time, the needs for streets and highways change as areas thrive or diminish, and the government must have the authority to widen, relocate, or close them as necessary to provide for the safe flow of traffic. As with railroads, the federal and state governments have the power of eminent domain and may condemn or "take" property for these purposes, but this is usually handled via a civil action, which will be discovered in the title research.

v. *Controlled Access*. Many public rights of way are not accessible directly by vehicle due to the danger of driveway access. This may not be obvious on a tax map or aerial map.

h. Leases

Leases may or may not be recorded, and typically a full lease is not. But it is in the tenant's interest to record a memorandum of the lease to protect its interest in the property. The memorandum should contain the basic terms of the lease, including the term, the expiration date, and whether the tenant has the option to renew the lease at the end of the initial term.

i. Foreclosures/Partitions

Obviously foreclosure or a partition action affects the status of the property, so a title researcher must make sure one is not ongoing and a sale imminent. These records are usually kept in the civil division of the Clerk of Court's office.

j. Brokers' Liens

In some areas, brokers are permitted to file liens against real property for their commissions, based on written contracts signed by the property owner. These are typically filed in the civil clerk's records.

k. Bankruptcy

It is extremely important to know whether the current owner of the property has filed a bankruptcy petition, considering the automatic stay imposed on the petitioner's assets and debts. Bankruptcy petitions are filed with the proper district of the federal courts.

l. Matters Specific to Location

Properties located in certain areas will have matters and exceptions specific to the region, like the use of beach areas, navigable waters, and boat slips in coastal areas, or access to adjacent ski areas in mountain regions.

m. Other Matters Specific to States and Counties

This text does not purport to address all matters revealed by title examinations in every state. Title examinations are performed in all states for a common purpose, but the methods and elements that must be researched lack uniformity across states. It is the paralegal's responsibility to determine what records are specific to his or her state, county, and municipality, and to include all relevant records in his or her research.

3. PRIORITY OF LIEN

Priority of lien determines the order in which lienholders will be paid, in the event that a homeowner does not make the monthly mortgage payments (defaults on the loan), and it becomes necessary to foreclose on the property. The lower a lienholder is in priority, the less likely that it will be paid. The priority of each lien is determined by the date on which the lien was filed against the property; liens filed earlier have priority over liens filed more recently. The mortgage lender is usually first in priority. As a practical matter, however, the proceeds of the foreclosure sale are not usually sufficient to fully satisfy even the first lienholder, which leaves nothing for the junior lienholders.

In some cases, a lender whose mortgage or deed of trust is on record will agree to the borrower obtaining a new loan that will be in a higher priority lien position. How can this be accomplished where the first recorded document takes priority? The existing lender will sign a *subordination agreement* stating that it agrees the new mortgage or deed of trust will take a senior position to its existing mortgage or deed of trust already on record. This agreement is recorded in the real estate records to publicly acknowledge the existing lender's agreement to take a junior priority position to the new lender, and once the new lender's mortgage or deed of trust is recorded, it has first priority.

4. HOW FAR BACK SHOULD THE TITLE SEARCH GO?

In order for the lender, title insurance company, and buyer to feel comfortable with the title of the property to be purchased, how far back in time should the title search extend? A typical answer is *40 years*, but this may vary by state, lender, and title insurance company. Many states have passed statutes generally known as **marketable title** acts. These statutes hold that if a property owner can establish good title going back a certain period of time, for example, 40 years, then anyone making a claim against the title arising from events more than 40 years ago cannot prevail on that claim. But *marketable title acts* are riddled with exceptions, so a title paralegal should perform every search in thorough detail without assuming any level of protection.

Marketable Title
a title that is free of any defects that could diminish the value of the property, and impair the owner's ability to guarantee quiet enjoyment of the property to a grantee.

a. Tacking

Suppose the current owner of a property bought the property two years ago and now wants to sell it. A full title search was conducted in connection with the transaction for the benefit of the existing owner, and a title insurance policy was issued in that owner's name. The new buyer would prefer not to pay for a title search going back 40 years since the current owner (seller) had a full title search performed only two years ago and title to the property was insured at that time.

Thus, a question that frequently arises in obtaining title insurance is whether the attorney for the new buyer can *tack* to the existing title insurance policy,[2] and search only the two-year period during which the current owner has owned the property, thereby saving the buyer the expense of a full 40-year title search. In states that permit tacking, the attorney conducting the title search is usually required to make *full disclosure* to the buyer, and in some cases that disclosure must be in writing.

Tacking should only be performed in connection with an owner's title insurance policy, not a lender's policy, because owner's policies are more restrictive and therefore contain more exceptions than loan policies. Tacking to a loan policy may mean missing an encumbrance affecting title to the property. The existing owner's title policy may be obtained from the seller, and he or she may be legally bound by the purchase contract to provide it. If the seller cannot provide a copy, the existing lender's policy, which the existing lender may be able to provide, may contain a reference to the owner's policy. If not, the paralegal may call title companies in the area to try to locate a policy to which to tack. But they may be reluctant to provide copies of their policies without the closing agent's agreement to reinsure the property through their company or agency.

A paralegal performing a title search in a tacking situation may begin the search with the date of the existing policy and come forward to the present time. This does not mean he or she will not need to review any records prior to that date, because many new index entries relate to or modify prior ones, so it may be necessary to read the terms of the prior instruments. It is also possible the prior title researcher did not search for judgments in the *grantee's* name when he or she recorded in connection with that closing, and any judgment already in the grantee's name at that time would have immediately attached to the property once it was conveyed to him or her. Also, it is very common to find mortgages remaining on record from prior closings, which were paid in full but never canceled of record.

The title paralegal should include all matters he or she finds on record relating to the property in the title summary, even those canceled or terminated, and let the closing agent or attorney decide which do not apply. Responsibility falls to the closing attorney or agent for any inaccuracies or missing exceptions in the opinion, and these mistakes can be extremely costly, so it is crucial that the paralegal disclose all matters found in the title examination to the attorney. In the same vein, full disclosure to the title insurance company is important, so that it may decide which matters it is comfortable insuring and to which it will take exception. The title opinions should be drafted with this in mind. See the *White vs. Western Title* case at the end of this subsection.

Tacking saves time and money, but it is not without risk. Remember that the prior policy is based on a title examination performed by someone else, and the title attorney or closing agent may not feel comfortable tacking to an existing policy, particularly if the prior title research on which it is based was performed by an unknown title searcher or one with a questionable reputation.

---

[2]You may remember the term "tacking" from another context, that is, adverse possession, whereby successive adverse possessors were allowed to tack their times of possession so as to meet the statutorily mandated period of time to adversely possess a property.

Upon receipt of the prior policy, the title paralegal should confirm that the owner and property description shown therein are consistent with the vesting deed. He or she should then determine whether the mortgage or deed of trust insured by the policy (if applicable) has been canceled of record, then check the status of the other exceptions shown. All exceptions and insured documents shown in the policy will remain as exceptions unless canceled or terminated, so the paralegal must include exceptions from the policy in the title summary and draft title opinion along with new matters of record. This may be accomplished by setting them out individually as he or she would do with new exceptions, or adding a statement that all exceptions contained in the prior policy are incorporated in the opinion.

WHITE V. WESTERN TITLE INSURANCE

Supreme Court of California
40 Cal. 3d 870; 710 P.2d 309; 221 Cal. Rptr. 509
December 31, 1985

Summary

The purchasers of two parcels of property filed suit against a title insurance company for breach of contract and were awarded damages of $8,400 for breach of contract. The preliminary title insurance reports issued by defendant **did not mention recorded water easements** on the property. The insurance policies purported to insure a "fee" interest, free from any defect in title or any lien or encumbrance on title, subject to certain specific exceptions including unrecorded easements, and water rights, claims, or title to water. After plaintiff-landowners learned of the existence of the easements, their appraiser estimated the loss in value of their lots resulting from the potential loss of ground water at $62,947. Plaintiffs made a demand on defendant—Western Title Insurance— for that sum. Defendant declined to pay their claim. Plaintiffs filed suit for **breach** of the insurance contract and negligence in the preparation of the preliminary title reports.

Opinion

In 1975, William and Virginia Longhurst owned 84 acres of land on the Russian River in Mendocino County. The land was divided into two lots, one unimproved, the other improved with a ranch house, a barn and adjacent buildings. It contained **substantial subsurface water.**

On December 29, 1975, the Longhursts executed and delivered an "Easement Deed for Waterline and Well Sites," conveying to River Estates Mutual Water Corporation an "easement for a right-of-way for the construction and maintenance of a water pipeline and for the drilling of a well or wells within a defined area and an easement to take water, up to 150 gallons per minute, from any wells within said defined area." The deed was **recorded** the following day.

In 1978 plaintiffs agreed to purchase the property from the Longhursts. Plaintiffs, who **were unaware of the water easement**, requested preliminary title reports from defendant. Each report purported to list all easements, liens and encumbrances of record, but **neither mentioned the recorded water easement**.

Plaintiffs and the Longhursts opened two escrows, one for each lot. Upon close of escrow defendant issued to plaintiffs two standard CLTA title insurance policies, for which plaintiffs paid $1,467.55. **Neither policy mentioned the water easement.**

The title insurance policies provided:

"*Subject to Schedule B and the Conditions and Stipulations Hereof, Western Title Insurance Company* **insures the insured against** *loss or damage, and costs, attorneys' fees and expenses incurred by said insured by reason of:*

2. Any defect in or lien or encumbrance on such title;...

Schedule B provided in part that "*this policy* **does not insure against** *loss or damage which arises by reason of the following:*

3. Easements, liens or encumbrances, or claims thereof, which are **not shown by the public records.**"

About six months after the close of escrow, River Estates Mutual Water Corporation notified plaintiffs of its intention to enter their property to implement the easement. Plaintiffs protested, and River Estates filed an action to quiet title to the easement. Plaintiffs notified defendant, who agreed to defend the proceeding. Plaintiffs, however, declined defendant's offer, preferring representation by an attorney who was then representing them in an unrelated action. River Estates eventually decided not to enforce its easement and dismissed the suit.

Plaintiffs' appraiser estimated the loss in value of their lots resulting from the potential loss of groundwater at $62,947. Plaintiffs then made a demand on defendant for that sum. Defendant acknowledged its responsibility for **loss of value due to the easement** (the loss attributable to the occupation of plaintiffs' land by wells and pipes, and to the water company's right to enter the property for construction and maintenance). It maintained, however, that **any loss in value attributable to loss of groundwater** was excluded by the policy, and since plaintiffs' claim of loss was based entirely on diminution of groundwater, declined to pay their claim.

Plaintiffs filed suit alleging causes of action for breach of the insurance contract and negligence in the preparation of the preliminary title reports. Defendant moved for summary judgment; after briefing and argument the motion was denied.

The jury returned a special verdict finding defendant in breach of the covenant, awarding compensatory damages of $20,000, and denying punitive damages. Defendant appeals from the judgment.

Defendant relies on this last exclusion to avoid coverage in the present case.

Schedule B, part one, reads in part:

This policy does not insure against loss or damage, nor against costs, attorneys' fees or expenses, any or all of which arise by reason of the following:

3. Easements, liens or encumbrances, or claims thereof, which are not shown by the public records....

Construction of the policy, however, is controlled by the well-established rules on interpretation of insurance agreements. **Any ambiguity or uncertainty in an insurance policy** is to be resolved against the insurer and if semantically permissible, the contract will be given such construction as will fairly achieve its object of providing indemnity for the loss to which the insurance relates. The purpose of this canon of construction is to **protect the insured's**

reasonable expectation of coverage in a situation in which the insurer-draftsman controls the language of the policy. Coverage clauses are interpreted broadly so as to afford the greatest possible protection to the insured...exclusionary clauses are interpreted narrowly against the insurer.

In the present context, these rules require coverage of water rights shown in public records within the scope of an ordinary title search. The structure of the policy itself creates the impression that coverage is provided for claims of record, while excluded for unrecorded claims. This impression is reinforced by the specific language of the policy.

Coverage of claims of record also accords with the purpose of the title policies and the reasonable expectations of the insured. This standard CLTA policy is a policy based upon an inspection of records and, unlike more expensive policies, does not involve inspection of the property. The purchaser of such a policy could not reasonably expect coverage against unrecorded claims, but he could **reasonably expect that the title company had competently searched the records**, disclosed all interests of record it discovered and agreed to protect him against any undisclosed interests. Nothing in the policy makes it clear that there may be interests of record undisclosed by the policy yet excluded from coverage.

We conclude that the title insurance policies here in question, construed to carry out their purpose of protecting against undisclosed recorded interests, **provide coverage for water rights which appear of record** within the scope of the ordinary title search. The trial court reached the same conclusion, but by a different route. It reasoned that the water rights here at issue are inseparable from the recorded easement permitting River Estates Mutual Water Corporation to construct and maintain wells and pipelines. No provision of the policies excluded such easement, and defendant from the beginning has acknowledged liability for any loss in value attributable to the easement. The loss of water rights, the trial court concluded, is a loss attributable to the easement.

We raise no objection to this line of reasoning, but prefer to rest our holding upon the broader ground that a purchaser of a title policy could reasonably expect protection against recorded water rights even if they were not connected to an easement for wells or pipes.

Affirmed.

5. TITLE EXAMINATION V. TITLE INSURANCE

If the prospective buyer of a property has paid an attorney to perform a title search, why does the buyer have to pay for a title insurance policy? Is the title search not designed to bring to light potential clouds on the title?

The answer is that the title search is designed to disclose all liens and other encumbrances **of record**, that is, those that are apparent from the public records to be found in the register of deeds office, tax office, estates office, clerk's office, office of vital statistics, and other public records. (See the Overview of a Title Search at the end of this chapter.)

A title insurance policy is designed to protect the buyer against defects in title, or clouds on title, that *cannot* be found in the public record, that is, defects which are not "of record." Title insurance may also insure over known title defects such as an old mortgage or deed of trust that the lender failed to cancel after payoff. A bit of good news for the buyer is that, unlike automobile and medical insurance policies, a one-time title insurance premium protects the buyers as long as they own the property.

As its name implies, title insurance insures title to, and protects the owner against, persons claiming an ownership interest in—or title to—the property. However, title insurance does not protect the owner against an imprudent deal that the owner made when he or she bought the property. That is, title insurance will not protect the buyer against a bad investment when the purchased property is significantly less valuable than what the owner paid for it. Nor does title insurance protect the owner if the property cannot be used for the purpose that the owner intended.

There are two types of title insurance policies: one for the lender and one for the property owner. The lender's policy insures the mortgage or deed of trust. The owner's policy insures title to the property.

A title insurance policy has two main sections, Schedule A and Schedule B. Schedule A contains information about the insurance coverage: the insured's name, the insured property description, the type of interest insured (usually fee simple), the vested owner's name, and a description of the insured document (the mortgage or deed of trust in a loan policy). Schedule B contains the exceptions to the coverage, including easements, restrictive covenants, railroad and highway rights of way, and unpaid taxes. Schedule B will also contain other exceptions that may not be of record but that the title company will not agree to insure, like rights of any parties in possession of the property other than the fee owner (e.g., a tenant), rights of others to the uninterrupted flow of creeks or other waterways crossing the property (riparian rights), environmental issues, and matters that would be disclosed by a current survey of the property, if one was not obtained in connection with the closing.

6. TITLE INSURANCE COMPANY, TITLE AGENCY, OR TITLE ATTORNEY?

A title insurance company issues title insurance policies. A title agency is an independently owned office that underwrites policies for at least one title insurance company, and sometimes more. A title attorney, or closing attorney, issues an opinion, or a certification of the status of title to a title insurance company or title agency, who then issues a policy based on that opinion. State

EXAMPLE

CLOUD ON TITLE THAT IS NOT DISCOVERABLE FROM THE PUBLIC RECORD

Suppose a man had been in a common-law marriage in a state recognizing such marriages. A common-law marriage would not be a matter of public record. Assume that he leaves his common-law wife, and moves by himself to another state where he purchases a house. The man lives in the house for 10 years and then dies. His estate sells the property to Mr. and Mrs. Buyer.

After living in the house for two years, there is a knock at the Buyers' door; it is the decedent's common-law wife who claims that she is the actual owner of the property. Regardless of whether the common-law wife prevails, if she sues, the Buyers will have to defend against that suit. The Buyers' title insurance policy *will* defend them against the claim of the common-law wife because that cloud on the title was *not* part of the public record.

law governs who is authorized to issue a title opinion and a title policy, and whether a title company, escrow company, or attorney is authorized to conduct closings.

For examples of an Owner's Policy of Title Insurance, see Exhibit 9-1 at the end of the chapter.

7. ABSTRACT OF TITLE AND ATTORNEY'S OPINION OF TITLE

Based on the information that the title searcher has acquired during the title search, he or she will draft an **abstract of title,** which summarizes the history of the property to be sold, including all conveyances, liens, and other encumbrances that may affect title to the property.

Abstract of Title
a summary of the history of a piece of real property, showing not only the grantors and grantees, but also liens and other encumbrances that may affect the quality of title of the property.

In applicable states, the attorney who was retained by the buyer will review the abstract of title, and then issue a preliminary **opinion of title** based on the abstract. If the opinion of title is negative, the title company will not issue title insurance, nor will the lender make the mortgage loan, at least not until all title defects or clouds on the title are removed. If the opinion of title is favorable, and all conditions of the purchase agreement have been satisfied or will be satisfied at closing, then the parties will proceed to closing for the purpose of transferring title to the property.

In some states, attorneys are permitted to own title insurance companies, and therefore may serve both as closing agent and title agent. In these cases, the title examination is handled within the same office as issuance of the commitment and policy.

Opinion of Title
a certification offered by an attorney, after reviewing the title search and abstract of title, stating whether a parcel of real property is marketable.

An opinion of title is usually submitted in two parts: the preliminary opinion prior to closing and the final opinion after closing. The preliminary opinion discloses all matters affecting title from the beginning of the search period to the date of the title examination the paralegal has just performed, so that any unfavorable matters may be dealt with prior to or at closing. Note that in tacking situations, there is a difference between the search period and the coverage period. The opinion must include all matters of record during the search period *and* the period covered by the prior policy, so the title company receives a report of the entire 40-year period, even if a portion of it is via the prior policy. Depending on the title attorney's preference, the preliminary opinion may be prepared with each exception from the prior policy set out individually, or it may simply include an exception stating that all matters shown in the prior policy, referenced by the policy number, are incorporated therein. But even in the former case, the opinion should include a disclosure that it is being tacked to a prior policy.

The preliminary opinion should include instructions for whether to issue an *insured closing letter*, also known as a *closing protection letter*. This letter is provided along with the commitment and indemnifies the lender against any loss as a result of specific forms of misconduct by the closing agent, such as failure to follow the lender's closing instructions. The closing agent will be on the title company's approved agent list after a vetting process. The insured closing letter is for the lender's benefit, and will not be applicable in purchase transactions involving no loan.

The final opinion discloses all new matters of title since the date of the preliminary opinion, mainly the ones recorded in conjunction with the closing. It also provides evidence of the satisfaction or other handling of the unfavorable matters shown in the preliminary opinion, so the title company will have written certification to rely on when deleting those items as exceptions in the title policy. The final opinion covers a much shorter period of time, only from the date of the preliminary opinion to the date of recording.

Once the preliminary title opinion has been submitted, the title company issues a commitment or binder, which is its commitment to issue a title insurance policy once certain requirements are met in connection with the closing. Depending on the state, the title research is performed either by the title company or by an attorney who certifies the status of title to the title company in the form of an opinion. In attorney-based states, the commitment is based on the preliminary opinion submitted by the closing attorney, which is based on the title research performed by the closing attorney or his or her paralegal. The preliminary opinion discloses all matters to which the title company might take exception when issuing a policy.

The requirements that must be met are listed in the commitment, and many will be satisfied by default because the closing occurred, like the conveyance document and payment of the consideration. Some requirements may be dealt with prior to closing, like a survey or zoning certification. Others will be satisfied post-closing in conjunction with disbursement of closing funds, like the payoff of an existing mortgage or deed of trust, payment of the title insurance premium, payment of taxes or other liens, or cancellation of the existing mortgage.

There will also be exceptions set out in the commitment that will remain when the policy is issued, which are matters the title company does not agree to insure over, mostly matters of record, but that are acceptable to the lender because they are inextinguishable or they benefit the property. Examples of these exceptions are utility easements and rights of way, leases and other agreements of record, riparian rights (rights of others to the uninterrupted flow of creeks or waterways crossing the property), taxes that are payable but not yet due, and matters that would be revealed by a current survey of the property (if a new one was not obtained). The closing attorney will want to eliminate as many exceptions as possible to provide the best coverage for his or her client. There will sometimes be more exceptions in the owner's policy than in the lender's policy.

Endorsements to the title policy may be requested by the owner or the lender. These add additional coverage for specific matters like access to a public right of way, environmental matters, compliance with local zoning ordinances, and so on. They are provided by the California Land Title Association (CLTA) and the American Land Title Association (ALTA). Most endorsements have specific requirements that must be met, which are listed in the commitment. For example, for a zoning endorsement, which insures that the property is in compliance with the zoning ordinance, a certification or letter should be obtained from the zoning authority and provided to the title insurance company.

The closing agent or attorney may provide certification for some endorsements, like a tax parcel endorsement, which states that the property described in the legal description is the same as the tax parcel shown in the tax records. But it is preferable to obtain the certification from the proper authority, in this case the tax department, to limit the closing agent's potential liability.

Another type of endorsement is what is sometimes called a "date-down" endorsement. A date-down endorsement is typically issued in conjunction with a modification of the loan, which the lender will want insured. This endorsement brings the date of the policy current through the modification, and incorporates any new exceptions based on a current title update (and, where applicable, a new certification or opinion from the closing agent/attorney). A date-down endorsement should not be confused with an endorsement that simply reports any new matters reflected by a title update, but does not bring the policy date forward. This latter endorsement does not affect the level of insurance provided in the policy.

A list of CLTA and ALTA endorsements is available from any title company or agency.

Once the closing occurs and all requirements are met, the final opinion is provided to the title company based on the title update performed immediately prior to recording, and the final policy is issued. The final opinion provides recording information for the closing documents and discloses all matters of record for the time period between the preliminary opinion and the recording date, so that there is no gap in the title examination. It also discloses the method of satisfaction of the requirements contained in the commitment.

In some states, gap coverage is available in conjunction with the title insurance policy, covering the period between the title commitment and recording.

The lender may require a "marked commitment" immediately after closing has occurred and closing documents have been recorded. This simply means that the title insurance company revises or marks up the commitment by hand to include the recording information and delete the satisfied requirements, effectively converting it to a policy in handwritten form. If a marked commitment is required, the closing attorney must provide the title company with the final opinion and any accompanying documents like the lien affidavit, immediately upon recording. An efficient paralegal will have the opinion prepared except for the information that is unknown, such as recording information, so that it may be inserted and the document finalized immediately after recording.

A paralegal may draft the title opinions for the agent's/attorney's review, and standard forms may be obtained from the title company insuring the mortgage. Some title companies provide an online database for submitting preliminary information electronically, and will issue title commitments based on data submitted. This method is convenient, but without the accompaniment of a signed opinion or the electronic equivalent of a signature, it is not an official certification of the status of title since it is not signed by the closing agent/attorney. Moreover, a *final* opinion may never be submitted in this way, and a title company will not issue a final policy based on this database. The final opinion should always be signed by the certifying agent/attorney and the original delivered to the title company, as it represents certification of the entire search period, even though it technically covers a shorter time period.

a. Title Update Prior to Recording

The title paralegal will perform a title update, or limited title examination, immediately after closing and before recording. This update should cover the period from the date of the initial title examination, on which the preliminary title opinion is based, through the second the deed and/or mortgage are recorded. The purpose of this update is to ensure that no new encumbrances have been recorded before the current deed goes on record. It also completes the title exam, so that the entire time period has been searched and no gap remains. The paralegal should check all the same records he or she checked in the initial exam, including any documents that have been submitted for filing but not yet keyed into the index. This should be done manually after all electronic records have been checked, by looking at each filing that has not been keyed in each office that keeps records affecting title.

Is this kind of diligence really necessary? Yes, because it ensures that a document causing an encumbrance on the property is not "slipped in," or filed just before the paralegal records. If this occurs, the property is conveyed subject to an unexpected and unknown encumbrance that takes a senior lien position to the mortgage, which is a violation of the lender's closing instructions, which the closing attorney has signed to evidence his or her compliance, as well as a breach of the seller's covenants and warranties in the deed conveying the property free and clear of encumbrances other than those agreed upon prior to closing. If the paralegal finds any new matters of record in his or her title update, he or she should contact the attorney before recording in case they have a negative effect on the closing.

It is a good idea to check the records again after the documents have been recorded, to ensure they are reflected correctly in the index.

b. Recording

Upon authorization and immediately following the title update, the deed, mortgage, and any other documents should be presented in the proper order to the registry for recording. (See Chapter 11 for a comprehensive discussion of recording.) A book and page number will be assigned to each document. Sometimes it is necessary to fill in the book and page number from one document into another, as in the case of an assignment of the mortgage, and the blanks in the assignment should be flagged as a reminder to the paralegal to do so while at the recording desk.

The recording clerk may ask the paralegal whether the documents should be recorded at the same time or if the seconds should be allowed to run between them. This may seem a strange question to ask, but there is a good reason. Say the paralegal has updated title and is at the recording desk with the documents. At the same time, a subcontractor is in the civil clerk's office filing a lien against the property. If the time is allowed to run between the deed and mortgage, the lien may actually be filed between the two, meaning it has priority over the mortgage. If the mortgage had been recorded at the same time as the deed, the lien would be after both, and therefore in a junior position to the mortgage.

Although there may be statutory recording standards for matters like margins, size of type, color of ink, and so on, each county has its own requirements for the recording process that should be followed to avoid delays. Examples of these include the tax parcel number being shown on the front of the deed, or specific forms being completed and attached to the instruments. Once the documents have been recorded, the paralegal should report immediately to the closing agent/attorney so the disbursements may be made in a timely manner.

c. Order of Recording

In pure-race states, the deed should be recorded before the mortgage so that title to the property transfers to the new owner before the new owner grants an interest in that property to the lender. An assignment of the mortgage should follow the mortgage for obvious reasons, as should any other document recorded in connection with the mortgage. But what about a release or cancellation of the prior mortgage?

The natural inclination is record the new deed first and mortgage second since they are the most important documents, but if the release or cancellation is not recorded until after the mortgage, then technically, the property has been conveyed and a mortgage has secured it while it still has a **mortgage lien** against it, which is a breach of the loan commitment letter, the loan instruction letter the attorney signed, and the warranties within the deed. But realistically, a release or cancellation is not likely to be available prior to payoff of the loan, so it may not be recorded until later. This does not present a practical problem as there is written evidence of the payoff having been made by the closing agent, and the payoff statement, evidencing the lender's intent to cancel. But if the release is available prior to recording, the proper method is to record it first. Order of recording is very important and should be confirmed with the closing attorney, not assumed by the paralegal.

8. OVERVIEW OF A TITLE SEARCH

Title searching is a task that requires patience, diligence and organization. Because searching a title may be so complex, the following is offered for illustrative purposes only. Any person searching a title should do so only with proper training.

To begin the **title search**, one should obtain as much information as possible from the Offer To Purchase and loan application documents, if available, such as the names of the seller(s), and the description of the property, which may include the street address and tax parcel identification number. Armed with this information, the title searcher goes to the Register of Deeds or the Clerk of Court's office in the county where the property is located. Many Register of Deeds offices now have deeds and other records on computerized databases. The process of title searching will usually begin with the **Grantor/ Grantee Index** database.

The first step is to learn how the current owner/seller obtained title to the property being conveyed. The seller's name should appear in the Grantee Index (the seller should be the most recent grantee of the property). The index will display the deed by which the seller acquired the property, or at least the book and page number of the deed book in which the actual deed is recorded. As ownership of the property is traced back in time, the status of previous owners will change from grantee (when taking title to the property) to grantor (when transferring the property to another). The title searcher should make a copy of the *vesting deed*, which will include a legal description of the property.

If the property was purchased—rather than gifted—the deed may also reflect the **excise tax/revenue tax** and/or **transfer tax** indicating the amount of the purchase price, for example, $1 of tax stamps for each $1,000 of the purchase price. Thus, one can determine the price paid for a property by looking at the stamps, although the prices paid would not necessarily be important to the title searcher.

Excise/revenue tax, transfer tax, and recording fees help to support the operations in the register of deeds office. Inflation causes the costs of such operations to increase over time, and thus stamps may have increased from, for example, $1 to $2 per $1,000 of the purchase price. So, if one is interested in the amount paid for the subject property in a specific conveyance, he or she must determine what ratio of stamps-to-value was required at the time the deed or other legal document was recorded. If the property was gifted, the space for stamps will not reflect an excise or transfer tax as there was no consideration paid for the conveyance, but this should be evidenced on the deed by the words: "Gift deed" or "no taxable consideration" in lieu of an amount.

Suppose the deed for the property now under contract was transferred in 1995 to "Mr. and Mrs. Seller, as husband and wife." But if the purchase agreement is signed only by Mrs. Seller, that would require further investigation to determine if Mr. Seller died, or there was a divorce, or there is some other reason why only Mrs. Seller signed the purchase agreement as the seller. If Mr. and Mrs. Seller were divorced, the index may reference a **quitclaim deed** giving ownership to Mrs. Seller as part of the divorce settlement. If Mr. Seller died, that fact should be recorded in the Vital Records section located at the Register of Deeds office, and/or in the Estates division of the office of the Clerk of Court (assuming he died in that jurisdiction). The important thing to note is that a title search is not confined to just the information available in the registrar's office.

The Register of Deeds' index may have separate book types/databases for different types of documents, which are not necessarily cross-referenced. If this is the case, each book type or database must be checked. These books/databases may include: Deed of Trust, Mortgage, Plat, Condo Plat, Terminations, and Uniform Commercial Code (UCC) financing statements. UCC filings, also referred to as "fixture filings" or "financing statements," function like a mortgage or deed of trust, but rather than securing the real property itself, they secure personal property that has been attached to the real property, or "*fixtures*," for example, an HVAC unit. Such UCC filings constitute liens against the real property.

The purpose of a UCC filing statement is to put prospective lenders or purchasers of real property **on notice** that there is an existing lien on, for example, the HVAC unit. If you were going to buy a shopping center, you would certainly want to know that there is an outstanding, and possibly very large loan, on the HVAC system that heats and cools the entire mall. Just as a mortgage lender can foreclose and repossess real property if the mortgage payments are not made, so can a secured party (e.g., the company that sold the HVAC system to the shopping center developer) either repossess the secured fixture, or force the sale of the real property to satisfy the outstanding debt on the HVAC system. Thus, a prospective buyer of the shopping mall is very interested in any and all UCC filing statements relating to the real property.

UCC **financing statements** may also secure non-fixture personal property like construction equipment, vehicles, or boats, even intangibles and accounts receivable, but they are typically *filed with the Secretary of State* rather than the county. To be thorough, UCC filings should be checked at both the county and state level. UCC financing statements expire after a statutory time period, so the UCC search must be performed on all owners of the property during that time period.

In counties where the indices are not combined, all the aforementioned databases should be checked by seller's name, and by the property address/parcel identifier, where applicable. For example, if the current seller bought the property in 2002 with a loan, there is probably a mortgage or deed of trust listed in the Mortgage or Deed of Trust book/database (note that the seller was listed as the grantee in the Deed Book/database, but will be the grantor in the Mortgage or Deed of Trust database because he or she granted the mortgage to the Beneficiary or the deed of trust to the trustee).

The status of any existing mortgage or deed of trust must be determined, that is, whether it has been canceled of record, and if not, whether it was paid and satisfied but cancellation was overlooked. Any documents affecting the status of the mortgage or deed of trust should be recorded. Examples of these include an assignment or modification, an assumption of the loan by another party, substitution of the trustee (for a deed of trust), or satisfaction/cancellation of the instrument.

The title searcher should visit the *Vital Records* section to check for births, deaths, marriages, or divorces that could affect the chain of title to the property. The process of checking for liens, encumbrances or other events such as a divorce that could affect title should be repeated for the corresponding time period of each previous owner going back as much as the title company requires, often 40 years.

The city and/or county *tax office* must also be checked for any outstanding or delinquent tax bills in the seller's name or in a prior owner's name, because *unpaid local taxes automatically constitute a lien* on a property.

The title researcher will also need to check with the office of the Clerk of Court for *civil judgment liens* against the seller or buyer, as well as *mechanics' or materialmen's liens* and other claims of lien on the property that could affect title to the property. State and federal tax liens should appear in the judgment book/database in the Clerk's office, listed by owner's name. The title searcher should pay particular attention to liens filed by governmental agencies like the Employment Security Commission or the Internal Revenue Service. Review the *lis pendens* index for *pending* lawsuits which could become a lien or judgment in the future. Also, where applicable, check the Clerk's book/database of *Special Proceedings*, which includes information regarding foreclosures, legal name changes, adoptions, and incompetency.

Financing Statement
a document filed in the public records to notify third parties, usually buyers and lenders, of a secured party's security interest in goods or real property.

9. GENERAL CHECKLIST FOR TITLE EXAMINATIONS

The following is a checklist that will help those engaged in title examinations:

1. Status of payment of current and prior years' taxes;
2. Chain of title (to the extent required outside the search period);

3. Grantor/Grantee index for mortgages or deeds of trust and any modifications to same, including releases;
4. Grantor/Grantee index for other liens and encumbrances;
5. Civil records for judgments and pending actions;
6. Special Proceedings records for foreclosures, partitions, or non-competency actions (in applicable states);
7. Estates records (if applicable);
8. Utility liens (where they are a lien on real property);
9. Bankruptcy records;
10. Compliance with setback requirements and subdivision ordinances;
11. Any additional records applicable in the state;
12. Prepare summary for title agent/attorney's review;
13. Prepare title opinion for agent's/attorney's review and signature;
14. Update title immediately prior to recording;
15. Prepare final title opinion for agent's/attorney's review and signature;
16. Obtain final policies from title company and forward to respective owner and lender;
17. Obtain original recorded documents and forward to respective parties.
18. Follow up on cancellations, terminations, and releases of prior liens.

10. THE PROPERTY SURVEY

At or about the same time a title search is requested by the buyer, a survey of the real property being purchased may also be requested, and may, in fact, be required in the jurisdiction. Since the title search and property survey are deemed to protect primarily the buyer's interest, the buyer will usually pay for the title search and survey.

A property survey involves a physical inspection and analysis of the property with sophisticated measuring devices, as well as the inspection of legal and other documents, including plat maps of the subdivision, historical records, topographic maps, and previous surveys. A survey of the property to be purchased is necessary in order to determine:

a. The boundary lines of the lot or acreage;
b. Whether there are any encroachments onto or off of the subject property from neighboring properties, such as encroaching buildings, fence lines, or trees;
c. The locations of utility and other easements and possible encroachments into them;
d. The locations of public rights of way belonging to the federal, state, or local governments.

The art and science of surveying have lacked uniformity across the United States and across the decades. In an effort to promote uniformity, the American Land Title Association (ALTA) and the American Congress on Surveying and Mapping (ACSM) have cooperated to craft uniform, minimum standards for professional surveyors. An ALTA/ACSM survey will include at least the four items mentioned above, thereby promoting reliance by title companies.

EXHIBIT 9-1 Vehicular Access

OWNER'S POLICY OF TITLE INSURANCE

Issued by

BLANK TITLE INSURANCE COMPANY

Any notice of claim and any other notice or statement in writing required to be given to the Company under this Policy must be given to the Company at the address shown in Section 18 of the Conditions.

COVERED RISKS

SUBJECT TO THE EXCLUSIONS FROM COVERAGE, THE EXCEPTIONS FROM COVERAGE CONTAINED IN SCHEDULE B, AND THE CONDITIONS, BLANK TITLE INSURANCE COMPANY, a Blank corporation (the "Company") insures, as of Date of Policy and, to the extent stated in Covered Risks 9 and 10, after Date of Policy, against loss or damage, not exceeding the Amount of Insurance, sustained or incurred by the Insured by reason of:

1. Title being vested other than as stated in Schedule A.

2. Any defect in or lien or encumbrance on the Title. This Covered Risk includes but is not limited to insurance against loss from

    (a) A defect in the Title caused by

        (i) forgery, fraud, undue influence, duress, incompetency, incapacity, or impersonation;

        (ii) failure of any person or Entity to have authorized a transfer or conveyance;

        (iii) a document affecting Title not properly created, executed, witnessed, sealed, acknowledged, notarized, or delivered;

        (iv) failure to perform those acts necessary to create a document by electronic means authorized by law;

        (v) a document executed under a falsified, expired, or otherwise invalid power of attorney;

        (vi) a document not properly filed, recorded, or indexed in the Public Records including failure to perform those acts by electronic means authorized by law; or

        (vii) a defective judicial or administrative proceeding.

    (b) The lien of real estate taxes or assessments imposed on the Title by a governmental authority due or payable, but unpaid.

    (c) Any encroachment, encumbrance, violation, variation, or adverse circumstance affecting the Title that would be disclosed by an accurate and complete land survey of the Land. The term "encroachment" includes encroachments of existing improvements located on the Land onto adjoining land, and encroachments onto the Land of existing improvements located on adjoining land.

3. Unmarketable Title.

4. No right of access to and from the Land.

5. The violation or enforcement of any law, ordinance, permit, or governmental regulation (including those relating to building and zoning) restricting, regulating, prohibiting, or relating to

    (a) the occupancy, use, or enjoyment of the Land;

    (b) the character, dimensions, or location of any improvement erected on the Land;

    (c) the subdivision of land; or

    (d) environmental protection.

    If a notice, describing any part of the Land, is recorded in the Public Records setting forth the violation or intention to enforce, but only to the extent of the violation or enforcement referred to in that notice.

6. An enforcement action based on the exercise of a governmental police power not covered by Covered Risk 5 if a notice of the enforcement action, describing any part of the Land, is recorded in the Public Records, but only to the extent of the enforcement referred to in that notice.

7. The exercise of the rights of eminent domain if a notice of the exercise, describing any part of the Land, is recorded in the Public Records.

8. Any taking by a governmental body that has occurred and is binding on the rights of a purchaser for value without Knowledge.

9. Title being vested other than as stated in Schedule A or being defective

    (a) as a result of the avoidance in whole or in part, or from a court order providing an alternative remedy, of a transfer of all or any part of the title to or any interest in the Land occurring prior to the transaction vesting Title as shown in Schedule A because that prior transfer constituted a fraudulent or preferential transfer under federal bankruptcy, state insolvency, or similar creditors' rights laws; or

(continued)

EXHIBIT 9-1 *Continued*

  (b) because the instrument of transfer vesting Title as shown in Schedule A constitutes a preferential transfer under federal bankruptcy, state insolvency, or similar creditors' rights laws by reason of the failure of its recording in the Public Records

      (i) to be timely, or

      (ii) to impart notice of its existence to a purchaser for value or to a judgment or lien creditor.

10. Any defect in or lien or encumbrance on the Title or other matter included in Covered Risks 1 through 9 that has been created or attached or has been filed or recorded in the Public Records subsequent to Date of Policy and prior to the recording of the deed or other instrument of transfer in the Public Records that vests Title as shown in Schedule A.

The Company will also pay the costs, attorneys' fees, and expenses incurred in defense of any matter insured against by this Policy, but only to the extent provided in the Conditions.

[Witness clause optional]

BLANK TITLE INSURANCE COMPANY

BY: **PRESIDENT**

BY: **SECRETARY**

EXCLUSIONS FROM COVERAGE

The following matters are expressly excluded from the coverage of this policy, and the Company will not pay loss or damage, costs, attorneys' fees, or expenses that arise by reason of:

1. (a) Any law, ordinance, permit, or governmental regulation (including those relating to building and zoning) restricting, regulating, prohibiting, or relating to

      (i) the occupancy, use, or enjoyment of the Land;

      (ii) the character, dimensions, or location of any improvement erected on the Land;

      (iii) the subdivision of land; or

      (iv) environmental protection;

     or the effect of any violation of these laws, ordinances, or governmental regulations. This Exclusion 1(a) does not modify or limit the coverage provided under Covered Risk 5.

  (b) Any governmental police power. This Exclusion 1(b) does not modify or limit the coverage provided under Covered Risk 6.

2. Rights of eminent domain. This Exclusion does not modify or limit the coverage provided under Covered Risk 7 or 8.

3. Defects, liens, encumbrances, adverse claims, or other matters

  (a) created, suffered, assumed, or agreed to by the Insured Claimant;

  (b) not Known to the Company, not recorded in the Public Records at Date of Policy, but Known to the Insured Claimant and not disclosed in writing to the Company by the Insured Claimant prior to the date the Insured Claimant became an Insured under this policy;

  (c) resulting in no loss or damage to the Insured Claimant;

  (d) attaching or created subsequent to Date of Policy (however, this does not modify or limit the coverage provided under Covered Risk 9 and 10); or

  (e) resulting in loss or damage that would not have been sustained if the Insured Claimant had paid value for the Title.

4. Any claim, by reason of the operation of federal bankruptcy, state insolvency, or similar creditors' rights laws, that the transaction vesting the Title as shown in Schedule A, is

  (a) a fraudulent conveyance or fraudulent transfer; or

  (b) a preferential transfer for any reason not stated in Covered Risk 9 of this policy.

5. Any lien on the Title for real estate taxes or assessments Imposed by governmental authority and created or attaching between Date of Policy and the date of recording of the deed or other instrument of transfer in the Public Records that vests Title as shown in Schedule A.

SCHEDULE A

Name and Address of Title Insurance Company:

[File No.:   ]   Policy No.:
Address Reference:
Amount of Insurance: $ [Premium: $]
Date of Policy: [at a.m/p.m.]

1. Name of Insured:

2. The estate or interest in the Land that is insured by this policy is:

3. Title is vested in:

4. The Land referred to in this policy is described as follows:

SCHEDULE B

[File No.   ] Policy No.

EXCEPTIONS FROM COVERAGE

This policy does not insure against loss or damage, and the Company will not pay costs, attorneys' fees, or expenses that arise by reason of:

1. [Policy may include regional exceptions if so desired by the issuing Company.]

2. [Variable exceptions such as taxes, easements, CC&R's, etc., shown here]

(continued)

EXHIBIT 9-1 *Continued*

CONDITIONS

1. DEFINITION OF TERMS

The following terms when used in this policy mean:

(a) "Amount of Insurance": The amount stated in Schedule A, as may be increased or decreased by endorsement to this policy, increased by Section 8(b), or decreased by Sections 10 and 11 of these Conditions.

(b) "Date of Policy": The date designated as "Date of Policy" in Schedule A.

(c) "Entity": A corporation, partnership, trust, limited liability company, or other similar legal entity.

(d) "Insured": The Insured named in Schedule A.

    (i) the term "Insured" also includes

        (A) successors to the Title of the Insured by operation of law as distinguished from purchase, including heirs, devisees, survivors, personal representatives, or next of kin;

        (B) successors to an Insured by dissolution, merger, consolidation, distribution, or reorganization;

        (C) successors to an Insured by its conversion to another kind of Entity;

        (D) a grantee of an Insured under a deed delivered without payment of actual valuable consideration conveying the Title

            (1) if the stock, shares, memberships, or other equity interests of the grantee are wholly-owned by the named Insured;

            (2) if the grantee wholly owns the named Insured;

            (3) if the grantee is wholly-owned by an affiliated Entity of the named Insured, provided the affiliated Entity and the named Insured are both wholly-owned by the same person or Entity; or

            (4) if the grantee is a trustee or beneficiary of a trust created by a written instrument established by the Insured named in Schedule A for estate planning purposes.

    (ii) with regard to (A), (B), (C), and (D) reserving, however, all rights and defenses as to any successor that the Company would have had against any predecessor Insured.

(e) "Insured Claimant": An Insured claiming loss or damage.

(f) "Knowledge" or "Known": Actual knowledge, not constructive knowledge or notice that may be imputed to an Insured by reason of the Public Records or any other records that impart constructive notice of matters affecting the Title.

(g) "Land": The land described in Schedule A, and affixed improvements that by law constitute real property. The term "Land" does not include any property beyond the lines of the area described in Schedule A, nor any right, title, interest, estate, or easement in abutting streets, roads, avenues, alleys, lanes, ways, or waterways, but this does not modify or limit the extent that a right of access to and from the Land is insured by this policy.

(h) "Mortgage": Mortgage, deed of trust, trust deed, or other security instrument, including one evidenced by electronic means authorized by law.

(i) "Public Records": Records established under state statutes at Date of Policy for the purpose of imparting constructive notice of matters relating to real property to purchasers for value and without Knowledge. With respect to Covered Risk 5(d), "Public Records" shall also include environmental protection liens filed in the records of the clerk of the United States District Court for the district where the Land is located.

(j) "Title": The estate or interest described in Schedule A.

(k) "Unmarketable Title": Title affected by an alleged or apparent matter that would permit a prospective purchaser or lessee of the Title or lender on the Title to be released from the obligation to purchase, lease, or lend if there is a contractual condition requiring the delivery of marketable title.

2. CONTINUATION OF INSURANCE

The coverage of this policy shall continue in force as of Date of Policy in favor of an Insured, but only so long as the Insured retains an estate or interest in the Land, or holds an obligation secured by a purchase money Mortgage given by a purchaser from the Insured, or only so long as the insured shall have liability by reason of warranties in any transfer or conveyance of the Title. This policy shall not continue in force in favor of any purchaser from the Insured of either (i) an estate or interest in the Land, or (ii) an obligation secured by a purchase money Mortgage given to the Insured.

3. NOTICE OF CLAIM TO BE GIVEN BY INSURED CLAIMANT

The Insured shall notify the Company promptly in writing (i) in case of any litigation as set forth in Section 5(a) of these Conditions, (ii) in case Knowledge shall come to an Insured hereunder of any claim of title or interest that is adverse to the Title, as insured, and that might cause loss or damage for which the Company may be liable by virtue of this policy, or (iii) if the Title, as insured, is rejected as Unmarketable Title. If the Company is prejudiced by the failure of the Insured Claimant to provide prompt notice, the Company's liability to the Insured Claimant under the policy shall be reduced to the extent of the prejudice.

4. PROOF OF LOSS

In the event the Company is unable to determine the amount of loss or damage, the Company may, at its option, require as a condition of payment that the Insured Claimant furnish a signed proof of loss. The proof of loss must describe the defect, lien, encumbrance, or other matter insured against by this policy that constitutes the basis of loss or damage and shall state, to the extent possible, the basis of calculating the amount of the loss or damage.

5. DEFENSE AND PROSECUTION OF ACTIONS

(a) Upon written request by the Insured, and subject to the options contained in Section 7 of these Conditions, the Company, at its own cost and without unreasonable delay, shall provide for the defense of an Insured in litigation in which any third party asserts a claim covered by this policy adverse to the insured. This obligation is limited to only those stated causes of action alleging matters insured against by this policy. The Company shall have the right to select counsel of its choice (subject to the right of the Insured to object for reasonable cause) to represent the Insured as to those stated causes of action. It shall not be liable for and will not pay the fees of any other counsel. The Company will not pay any fees, costs, or expenses incurred by the Insured in the defense of those causes of action that allege matters not insured against by this policy.

(b) The Company shall have the right, in addition to the options contained in Section 7 of these Conditions, at its own cost, to institute and prosecute any action or proceeding or to do any other act that in its opinion may be necessary or desirable to establish the Title, as insured, or to prevent or reduce loss or damage to the Insured. The Company may take any appropriate action under the terms of this policy, whether or not it shall be liable to the Insured. The exercise of these rights shall not be an admission of liability or waiver of any provision of this policy. If the Company exercises its rights under this subsection, it must do so diligently.

(c) Whenever the Company brings an action or asserts a defense as required or permitted by this policy, the Company may pursue the litigation to a final determination by a court of competent jurisdiction, and it expressly reserves the right, in its sole discretion, to appeal any adverse judgment or order.

6. DUTY OF INSURED CLAIMANT TO COOPERATE

(a) In all cases where this policy permits or requires the Company to prosecute or provide for the defense of any action or proceeding and any appeals, the Insured shall secure to the Company the right to so prosecute or provide defense in the action or proceeding, including the right to use, at its option, the name of the Insured for this purpose. Whenever requested by the Company, the Insured, at the Company's expense, shall give the Company all reasonable aid (i) in securing evidence, obtaining witnesses, prosecuting or defending the action or proceeding, or effecting settlement; and (ii) in any other lawful act that in the opinion of the Company may be necessary or desirable to establish the Title or any other matter as insured. If the Company is prejudiced by the failure of the Insured to furnish the required cooperation, the Company's obligations to the Insured under the policy shall terminate, including any liability or obligation to defend, prosecute, or continue any litigation, with regard to the matter or matters requiring such cooperation.

(b) The Company may reasonably require the Insured Claimant to submit to examination under oath by any authorized representative of the Company and to produce for examination, inspection, and copying, at such reasonable times and places as may be designated by the authorized representative of the Company, all records, in whatever medium maintained, including books, ledgers, checks, memoranda, correspondence, reports, e-mails, disks, tapes, and videos whether bearing a date before or after Date of Policy, that reasonably pertain to the loss or damage. Further, if requested by any authorized representative of the Company, the Insured Claimant shall grant its permission, in writing, for any authorized representative of the Company to examine, inspect, and copy all of these records in the custody or control of a third party that reasonably pertain to the loss or damage. All information designated as confidential by the Insured Claimant provided to the Company pursuant to this Section shall not be disclosed to others unless, in the reasonable judgment of the Company, it is necessary in the administration of the claim. Failure of the Insured Claimant to submit for examination under oath, produce any reasonably requested information, or grant permission to secure reasonably necessary information from third parties as required in this subsection, unless prohibited by law or governmental regulation, shall terminate any liability of the Company under this policy as to that claim.

7. OPTIONS TO PAY OR OTHERWISE SETTLE CLAIMS; TERMINATION OF LIABILITY

In case of a claim under this policy, the Company shall have the following additional options:

(a) To Pay or Tender Payment of the Amount of Insurance.

To pay or tender payment of the Amount of Insurance under this policy together with any costs, attorneys' fees, and expenses

(continued)

EXHIBIT 9-1 *Continued*

incurred by the Insured Claimant that were authorized by the Company up to the time of payment or tender of payment and that the Company is obligated to pay.

Upon the exercise by the Company of this option, all liability and obligations of the Company to the Insured under this policy, other than to make the payment required in this subsection shall terminate, including any liability or obligation to defend, prosecute, or continue any litigation.

(b) To Pay or Otherwise Settle With Parties Other Than the insured or With the Insured Claimant.

(i) To pay or otherwise settle with other parties for or in the name of an Insured Claimant any claim insured against under this policy. In addition, the Company will pay any costs, attorneys' fees, and expenses incurred by the Insured Claimant that were authorized by the Company up to the time of payment and that the Company is obligated to pay; or

(ii) To pay or otherwise settle with the Insured Claimant the loss or damage provided for under this policy, together with any costs, attorneys' fees, and expenses incurred by the Insured Claimant that were authorized by the Company up to the time of payment and that the Company is obligated to pay.

Upon the exercise by the Company of either of the options provided for in subsections (b)(i) or (ii), the Company's obligations to the Insured under this policy for the claimed loss or damage, other than the payments required to be made, shall terminate, including any liability or obligation to defend, prosecute, or continue any litigation.

8. DETERMINATION AND EXTENT OF LIABILITY

This policy is a contract of indemnity against actual monetary loss or damage sustained or incurred by the Insured Claimant who has suffered loss or damage by reason of matters insured against by this policy.

(a) The extent of liability of the Company for loss or damage under this policy shall not exceed the lesser of

(i) the Amount of Insurance, or

(ii) the difference between the value of the Title as insured and the value of the Title subject to the risk insured against by this policy.

(b) If the Company pursues its rights under Section 5 of these Conditions and is unsuccessful in establishing the Title, as insured,

(i) the Amount of Insurance shall be increased by 10%, and

(ii) the Insured Claimant shall have the right to have the loss or damage determined either as of the date the claim was made by the Insured Claimant or as of the date it is settled and paid.

(c) In addition to the extent of liability under (a) and (b), the Company will also pay those costs, attorneys' fees, and expenses incurred in accordance with Sections 5 and 7 of these Conditions.

9. LIMITATION OF LIABILITY

(a) If the Company establishes the Title, or removes the alleged defect, lien, or encumbrance, or cures the lack of a right of access to or from the Land, or cures the claim of Unmarketable Title, all as insured, in a reasonably diligent manner by any method, including litigation and the completion of any appeals, it shall have fully performed its obligations with respect to that matter and shall not be liable for any loss or damage caused to the Insured.

(b) In the event of any litigation, including litigation by the Company or with the Company's consent, the Company shall have no liability for loss or damage until there has been a final determination by a court of competent jurisdiction, and disposition of all appeals, adverse to the Title, as insured.

(c) The Company shall not be liable for loss or damage to the Insured for liability voluntarily assumed by the insured in settling any claim or suit without the prior written consent of the Company.

10. REDUCTION OF INSURANCE; REDUCTION OR TERMINATION OF LIABILITY

All payments under this policy, except payments made for costs, attorneys' fees, and expenses, shall reduce the Amount of Insurance by the amount of the payment.

11. LIABILITY NONCUMULATIVE

The Amount of Insurance shall be reduced by any amount the Company pays under any policy insuring a Mortgage to which exception is taken in Schedule B or to which the Insured has agreed, assumed, or taken subject, or which is executed by an Insured after Date of Policy and which is a charge or lien on the Title, and the amount so paid shall be deemed a payment to the Insured under this policy.

12. PAYMENT OF LOSS

When liability and the extent of loss or damage have been definitely fixed in accordance with these Conditions, the payment shall be made within 30 days.

13. RIGHTS OF RECOVERY UPON PAYMENT OR SETTLEMENT

(a) Whenever the Company shall have settled and paid a claim under this policy, it shall be subrogated and entitled to the rights of the Insured Claimant in the Title and all other rights and remedies in respect to the claim that the Insured Claimant has against any person or property, to the extent of the amount of any loss, costs, attorneys' fees, and expenses paid by the Company. If requested by the Company, the Insured Claimant shall execute documents to evidence the transfer to the Company of these rights and remedies. The Insured Claimant shall permit the Company to sue, compromise, or settle in the name of the Insured Claimant and to use the name of the Insured Claimant in any transaction or litigation involving these rights and remedies.

If a payment on account of a claim does not fully cover the loss of the Insured Claimant, the Company shall defer the exercise of its right to recover until after the Insured Claimant shall have recovered its loss.

(b) The Company's right of subrogation includes the rights of the Insured to indemnities, guaranties, other policies of insurance, or bonds, notwithstanding any terms or conditions contained in those instruments that address subrogation rights.

14. ARBITRATION

Either the Company or the Insured may demand that the claim or controversy shall be submitted to arbitration pursuant to the Title Insurance Arbitration Rules of the American Land Title Association ("Rules"). Except as provided in the Rules, there shall be no joinder or consolidation with claims or controversies of other persons. Arbitrable matters may include, but are not limited to, any controversy or claim between the Company and the Insured arising out of or relating to this policy, any service in connection with its issuance or the breach of a policy provision, or to any other controversy or claim arising out of the transaction giving rise to this policy. All arbitrable matters when the Amount of Insurance is $2,000,000 or less shall be arbitrated at the option of either the Company or the Insured. All arbitrable matters when the Amount of insurance is in excess of $2,000,000 shall be arbitrated only when agreed to by both the Company and the Insured. Arbitration pursuant to this policy and under the Rules shall be binding upon the parties. Judgment upon the award rendered by the Arbitrator(s) may be entered in any court of competent jurisdiction.

15. LIABILITY LIMITED TO THIS POLICY; POLICY ENTIRE CONTRACT

(a) This policy together with all endorsements, if any, attached to it by the Company is the entire policy and contract between the Insured and the Company. In interpreting any provision of this policy, this policy shall be construed as a whole.

(b) Any claim of loss or damage that arises out of the status of the Title or by any action asserting such claim shall be restricted to this policy.

(c) Any amendment of or endorsement to this policy must be in writing and authenticated by an authorized person, or expressly incorporated by Schedule A of this policy.

(d) Each endorsement to this policy issued at any time is made a part of this policy and is subject to all of its terms and provisions. Except as the endorsement expressly states, it does not (i) modify any of the terms and provisions of the policy, (ii) modify any prior endorsement, (iii) extend the Date of Policy, or (iv) increase the Amount of Insurance.

16. SEVERABILITY

In the event any provision of this policy, in whole or in part, is held invalid or unenforceable under applicable law, the policy shall be deemed not to include that provision or such part held to be invalid, but all other provisions shall remain in full force and effect.

17. CHOICE OF LAW; FORUM

(a) Choice of Law: The Insured acknowledges the Company has underwritten the risks covered by this policy and determined the premium charged therefor in reliance upon the law affecting interests in real property and applicable to the interpretation, rights, remedies, or enforcement of policies of title insurance of the jurisdiction where the Land is located.

Therefore, the court or an arbitrator shall apply the law of the jurisdiction where the Land is located to determine the validity of claims against the Title that are adverse to the Insured and to interpret and enforce the terms of this policy. In neither case shall the court or arbitrator apply its conflicts of law principles to determine the applicable law.

(b) Choice of Forum: Any litigation or other proceeding brought by the Insured against the Company must be filed only in a state or federal court within the United States of America or its territories having appropriate jurisdiction.

18. NOTICES, WHERE SENT

Any notice of claim and any other notice or statement in writing required to be given to the Company under this policy must be given to the Company at [fill in].

NOTE: Bracketed [] material optional

CHAPTER SUMMARY

Lenders make loans to make money. Money is made by the lenders not only via the *interest* paid by the borrower on the loan, but through *loan origination fees* and *loan servicing fees*. Lenders want to feel secure about the quality of their loans, and this need for security influences the *loan-to-value ratio* offered by the lender. The LTV is the percentage of the purchase price that the lender will finance, usually from a minimum of 80% to as high as 95% of the purchase price. The higher the LTV, the greater risk for the lender.

A *title search* of the property to be sold will be required by both the lender and a title insurance company, which will insure the quality of the title to the property by protecting the buyer against encumbrances not of record. A title search typically involves going back as much as 40 or more years to determine the *chain of title*, that is, identify the previous owners of the property, and the *encumbrances* established via the deeds and other documents in the chain of title on the property, such as liens, easements, and rights of way. Existing liens, such as the existing mortgage loan on the property, must be satisfied at or before the closing on the sale of the property. In addition to a mortgage lien on a property, there may also be tax liens, mechanics' liens, homeowners' association (HOA) dues, assessment liens for infrastructure, and judgment liens. The priority of each lien determines which lien will be paid first in the event of a foreclosure of a property.

After the *title search* is conducted and the *chain of title* established, an *abstract of title* is prepared by the title searcher. The abstract of title provides a summary of the ownership and lien history of the property, as well as a snapshot of the current status of title, including existing liens, easements, rights of way, and any other possible encumbrance on the property, which could reduce the value of the property or impair the seller's ability to convey title by way of a general warranty deed.

Based on the title search and the abstract of title, the closing agent/attorney will issue an *opinion of title* describing the quality of the title, and whether it may be conveyed via a general warranty deed, the best assurance of title that a buyer may obtain. There are at least two ethical pitfalls that may confront the closing attorney. The first is the issue of *tacking*, that is, whether the title researcher may "tack to" a prior title policy issued on the property, as opposed to performing a "full" search covering at least 30 years. The second ethical problem is the attorney's representation of both the seller and buyer at the closing, known as *dual representation*. Dual representation is permitted if the buyer and seller have given their informed consent and thereby waived the conflict.

In conjunction with the title search, a *property survey* may be conducted to determine the legal boundaries of the property, and the existence of any *encroachments* onto the property from a neighboring parcel, such as an encroaching fence or driveway. If such an encroachment is found, the lender and/or title company may insist that it be removed prior to closing, or else the sale may not be consummated. The survey will also reflect the locations of utility and other easements, and rights of way held by federal, state, or local governments, as well as any encroachments of the existing improvements into those easements.

CONCEPT REVIEW AND REINFORCEMENT

KEY TERMS

Abstract of Title	Interest Rate	Opinion of Title
Amortization Schedule	Judgment Lien	Principal
Amortize	Lender	Priority of Lien
Chain of Title	Lien	Survey
Cloud on Title	Loan Origination Fee	Tax Lien
Collateral	Loan-to-Value Ratio	Title
Easement	Marketable Title	Title Search
Encumbrance	Mechanics/Materialmen's Lien	Title Insurance
Financing Statement	Mortgage	
Interest	Mortgage Lien	

CONCEPT **REVIEW** QUESTIONS

1. How does an amortization schedule show the shift in application of payments to principal and interest over time?

2. What is loan interest, and how is it related to loan principal?

3. What is collateral, and why does it make a lender feel more secure?

4. What is a loan origination fee, and how is it usually computed? What are loan servicing fees, and who pays those? To whom are they paid?

5. What is the loan-to-value ratio (LTV)? Is a lender more secure, or less secure, with a higher LTV? Why?

6. What is an abstract of title, and how does it differ from the chain of title?

7. What is the purpose of a title search? Who benefits from the title search?

8. What is the difference between encumbrances of record, and encumbrances not on the record? Which of these does the typical title insurance policy insure against?

9. What is a marketable title? What are marketable title statutes?

10. What is a typical period of time that a title searcher will examine to determine ownership of a property, and whether there are any liens or other encumbrances on a property?

11. What is an opinion of title, and who issues it? To whom is the opinion of title issued?

ETHICS

THE PARALEGAL AND THE TITLE COMPANY

Paula Paralegal is employed by Secure Title Company. The company handles all of the title work for three large residential homebuilders in her state. Due to the large volume of work, many of the employees have been working long overtime hours, including Paula. Paula is worried that the heavy workload is taking a toll on the quality of their work. In particular she has noticed significant title search mistakes and incomplete paperwork generated by two different employees. In addition, late one night she walked in on one of the employees shredding several boxes of files that she had recently reviewed and returned to the employee because they were incomplete.

She brought her concerns to the attention of her supervisor who assured her that her suspicions were unfounded.

Paula later learned that the two employees she complained about were being transferred in order to open and supervise a satellite office for the company.

Do any of the ethical rules of professional conduct apply to Paula since the title company is not a law firm and has no attorneys employed?

Does Paula have an ethical duty to report the potential fraud to another company authority?

If under state law an attorney is required to supervise all real estate title reports and Secure Title uses Paula Paralegal for this purpose, does your response change?

BUILDING YOUR PROFESSIONAL SKILLS

CRITICAL THINKING **EXERCISES**

1. During the late 1970s through the mid-1980s, Owner had three children (A, B & C) by his wife, Wilma. For the last 40 years, Owner and Wilma lived on their large estate, Greenacres. Wilma passed away in 2005, and in 2006 Owner, after learning that he had a terminal illness, updated his will, which read: "I devise Greenacres to my children who survive me at my death." Owner died in late 2006, and the property descended to the children.

In 2009, the children decided to sell Greenacres for a large sum of money to a real estate developer, who built a shopping center on the property.

In 2011, the attorney for A, B & C received a phone call from D. D informed the attorney that she had conducted some genealogy research that indicated that she was the out-of-wedlock daughter of Owner. D has a DNA test performed which proves that she is Owner's daughter (of course, D's mother is someone other than Wilma).

Does the fact that D is Owner's daughter raise a cloud on the title of Greenacres? Is D's possible claim on Greenacres a problem primarily for A, B & C, or the developer?

This case involves what is known as "the undisclosed heir," and is not at all uncommon in the annals of real estate law.

Would D's claim to being Owner's out-of-wedlock daughter be the type of information that would be discoverable from a title search; that is, would it be "of record"? Would it matter if D was born not in the county where the property was located, but rather in another part of the state?

2. Timber Company purchased a property. A title search was conducted prior to the closing. After Timber Company acquired title, it learned that it could not remove trees from a substantial portion of the property because that part of the property was in a watershed (a large area of land drained by a stream or river). To prevent excess runoff and erosion in the watershed, a protective buffer zone had been created by county ordinance prior to Timber Company's purchase of the property. Timber Company sued the title insurance company when it refused to compensate Timber Company for losses related to the watershed and its inability to cut timber therein.

While the existence of the watershed and protective buffer zone may have diminished the value of the property to Timber Company, it did not prevent Timber Company from cutting and removing trees on other parts of the property. In other words, the property still had economic value. Should this be a consideration in the court's determination of whether the title insurance policy provides coverage in this situation?

Is Timber Company correct in that this type of claim should be covered by a title insurance policy?

Is the existence of the watershed and the protective buffer zone a title defect, or a claim by an outsider to an interest in the property?

See *Haw River Land & Timber v. Lawyers Title Insurance*, 152 F.3d 275 (4th Cir. 1990).

3. Using the name of one of this book's co-authors, Steven A. McCloskey, how many variations of the name would need to be researched in a thorough title examination? (Examples: "Steven" could be spelled as "Stephen," or even "Stefan," and "McCloskey" could be spelled "McLoskey," "McCluskey," "McClosky," etc.) How could a middle initial be obtained to narrow the search? Why might this process be more difficult with a woman's name?

RESEARCH ON THE **WEB**

1. Critical Thinking Exercise # 1 involves the situation of the "undisclosed heir." Run a query using that term in your state's cases database. How many hits do you get? Refine the search by adding terms such as "real property" or "real estate." How many hits do you get now?

2. Conduct a search on the web to determine how many of the following are listed in your town or city: title insurance companies, property or land surveyors, title search attorneys, real estate closing attorneys.

3. Many counties now have much information relating to real property available online, such as tax information, plat maps, aerial surveys and even grantor-grantee deed-related information. If your county has such a system, check the aforementioned databases to obtain as much information as you can about a particular piece of property.

BUILDING YOUR **PROFESSIONAL** PORTFOLIO

1. Create a simple loan application. What factors, besides the applicant's income, age, and employment history, would a lender want to consider in deciding whether to lend funds to a potential borrower?

2. Locate two or three lending applications from different lenders. What differences, if any, are there in questions/requirements of the applications?

chapter **10**

DEEDS, MORTGAGES, AND PROMISSORY NOTES

LEARNING OBJECTIVES

After reading this chapter, you should understand:

- The purpose of a deed

- The purpose of a mortgage and deed of trust

- The difference between the granting clause and habendum clause in a deed

- The three types of legal descriptions found in a deed

- The difference between a patent ambiguity and a latent ambiguity

- The purpose of a quitclaim deed

- The difference between the primary and secondary mortgage market

A. Deeds

1. OVERVIEW AND DEFINITION

In real estate law, there are many important documents related to the sale of real property and the closing. No doubt this is related to the fact that real estate transactions involve large amounts of money. Perhaps the three most important documents in a real-estate sale are:

  i. The deed,
 ii. The mortgage (or deed of trust), and
iii. The promissory note.

This chapter examines these three documents, including the formalities required for each, and their significance to the real estate transaction.

A deed is a written document that **conveys an interest** in real property, and is **evidence of title** to a property.

Although *Black's Law Dictionary* (9th Ed.) lists approximately 50 definitions under the word "deed," we will look at only a few types of deeds. Let us review the necessary elements of a deed.

2. NECESSARY ELEMENTS OF A DEED

a. Language of Conveyance

In a legal instrument that purports to convey title, there must be **language of conveyance**. The language must be in writing so as to comply with the Statute of Frauds, which requires certain types of agreements to be written, including any agreement to convey an interest in real property.

The language of conveyance is embodied in two types of clauses found in a deed:

Granting Clause
language in a deed that transfers some or all of a grantor's interest in real property to a grantee.

  i. The **granting clause** simply consists of language in the deed that transfers some or all of the grantor's interest in the real property to the grantee. An example of such language might be:

The Grantor does hereby grant, bargain, sell, and convey unto the Grantee all of that certain lot or parcel of real property in Any County, Any State, USA, described as follows: (followed by the legal description of the property).

Habendum Clause
language in a deed that describes the extent of the estate being conveyed by the grantor to the grantee.

 ii. The **habendum clause** describes the *extent* of the estate being granted or conveyed. In earlier chapters we referred to an estate as a "bundle of rights." The habendum clause states the type of estate that the grantor is conveying, for example, a fee-simple estate, a fee-simple determinable estate, a life estate, and so on. The habendum clause is also known as the "to Have and to Hold Clause" because of language such as the following:

To have and to hold the aforesaid lot or parcel of land and all privileges and appurtenances thereto belonging to the Grantee <u>in fee simple</u>. And the Grantor covenants with the Grantee, that Grantor is seized of the premises in fee simple, has the right to convey the same in fee simple, that title is marketable, free and clear of all encumbrances, and that Grantor will warrant and defend the title against the lawful claims of all persons whomsoever.

Typically, the granting clause and/or the habendum clause will describe how the grantees (if more than one grantee) are taking title: as tenants in common, joint tenants with right of survivorship, or tenants by the entirety.

PRACTICE POINTER

A large volume of legal documents pass through every law office, but especially a real estate law office. Many of these documents require notarization. It is a decided advantage in searching for a paralegal position for the student to have obtained a notary license.

Each state has its own requirements for becoming a notary public. Quite often, the Secretary of State's office has the responsibility for the licensing and oversight of notaries.

b. Grantor's Signature and Competent Grantor

The grantor must sign (or "execute") the deed. Some states require the grantor's signature be **notarized**—also known as an **acknowledgment**—for the deed to be valid. Other states require the grantor's signature to be notarized or acknowledged only if the deed is going to be recorded at the office of the register of deeds. In those states, the deed itself is valid without the acknowledgement, but since it cannot be recorded, the grantee runs a significant risk that an unscrupulous grantor could sell the property again, to a second buyer, who would record that deed, and thereby be deemed the valid owner of the property. Some states require witnesses to the grantor's signature in addition to notary acknowledgment.

The grantor must also be **competent,** meaning at least 18 years of age, and mentally competent. If the grantor had been adjudicated mentally incompetent in a court of law prior to his or her execution of the deed, the deed would be **void.** On the other hand, if the grantor had not been adjudicated mentally incompetent in a court of law, but there was evidence of mental disability when the deed was signed, the deed would be **voidable.**

Unlike the grantor, the grantee's signature on the deed is *not* necessary. In most states, the grantee must be identified in the deed before its delivery. However, there is case law from a few states indicating that where the grantee is "in blank," (no name indicated on the deed), the property can still be conveyed if the grantee's name is written on the deed *after* its delivery.

Standard deed forms contain language that the terms "Grantor" and "Grantee" include the parties' **heirs, successors, and assigns**, so that if the owner dies, title to the property passes to that party's legal heirs.

On most deeds, the grantor(s) and grantee(s) may be further identified by their **marital status**. This information is important not only to help identify the parties to the current conveyance, but will also assist future title searchers to better understand the chain of title. The marital status might be conveyed as follows on the deed:

"Grantors John and Mary Smith, a <u>married couple</u>, do hereby grant and convey to Grantee Margaret Jones, an <u>unmarried person</u> (or, a "<u>single person</u>"), all of that parcel described as follows…"

In many states, execution by both spouses is necessary, even if the property was only conveyed to one of the parties, or if the spouses are separated, to convey any marital interest the non-vested spouse may own, such as a spouse's right to claim an interest in the land upon the death of the spouse holding title.

c. Delivery

Delivery of the deed by the grantor to the grantee is required for a valid conveyance of the property. However, states differ on whether there must be an **actual delivery** of the deed, or whether **constructive delivery** suffices to convey the property. An example of an actual delivery would be when the grantor hands the signed deed to the grantee or the grantee's agent.

An example of constructive delivery might occur if the grantee is very ill and bedridden, and the grantor inserts the deed into the grantee's Bible, which is lying

Competent
of a suitable age, usually 18, and mental capacity to engage in a legal transaction, for example, the conveyance of real property.

Void
without legal force or effect, a nullity; the word is generally used in regard to a contract.

Voidable
a contract or conveyance that is valid until it is voided at the option of the grantor.

on the grantee's night table. To determine whether there has been a delivery of a deed, courts will first try to discern the **grantor's intent**: Did the grantor *intend* to deliver the deed?

d. Acceptance

For the real property to transfer, there must not only be a delivery of the deed by the grantor, but an acceptance of the deed by the grantee. The requirement of an acceptance by the grantee means that an unwanted property (such as a toxic waste site) cannot be foisted upon the grantee without the grantee's knowledge. Whether

WIGGILL v. CHENEY

Supreme Court of Utah
597 P.2d 1351
July 16, 1979, Filed

Opinion

This case involves the disposition of certain real property located in Weber County, State of Utah. The judgment before us invalidated a Warranty Deed, because of **no valid delivery**. We affirm. No costs awarded.

The material facts are undisputed. Specifically, on the 25th day of June, 1958, <u>Lillian</u> W. Cheney [the decedent] signed a deed to certain real property located in the city of Ogden, Utah, wherein the defendant, <u>Flora</u> Cheney, was *named grantee*. Thereafter Lillian Cheney placed this deed in a sealed envelope and deposited it in a safety deposit box in the names of herself and the plaintiff, Francis E. Wiggill.

Following the deposition of the deed, Lillian Cheney advised plaintiff [Francis Wiggill] that his name was on the safety deposit box and instructed plaintiff that upon her death, he was to go to the bank where he would be granted access to the safety deposit box and its contents. Lillian Cheney further instructed, "in that box is an envelope addressed to all those concerned. All you have to do is give them that envelope and that's all." At all times prior to her death, Lillian Cheney was in possession of a key to the safety deposit box and had *sole and complete control over it*. Plaintiff was *never given the key* to the safety deposit box.

Following the death of Lillian Cheney, plaintiff, after gaining access to the safety deposit box, delivered the deed contained therein to Flora Cheney, the named grantee.

The *sole issue* presented here on appeal is whether or not the acts of plaintiff constitute a delivery of the deed such as will render it enforceable as a valid conveyance.

The rule is well settled that a deed, to be operative as a transfer of the ownership of land, or an interest or estate therein, **must be delivered**. It was equally settled in this and the vast majority of jurisdictions that a valid delivery of a deed requires it *pass beyond the control or domain of the grantor*. The requisite relinquishment of control or dominion over the deed may be established, notwithstanding the fact the deed is in possession of the grantor at her death, by proof of facts which tend to show delivery had been made with the *intention to pass title* and to explain the grantor's subsequent possession. However, in order for a delivery effectively to transfer title, the grantor must part with possession of the deed or the right to retain it.

The evidence presented in the present case establishes Lillian Cheney remained in *sole possession and control* of the deed in question until her death. Because *no actual delivery* of the deed occurred prior to the death of the grantor, the subsequent manual delivery of the deed by plaintiff to defendant conveyed no title to the property described therein, or any part thereof, or any of its contents.

Concerning the contention that the grantor intended title to pass, the applicable rule was explained in *Singleton v. Kelly, supra.*, at 66, where this court stated, "that is true the courts will carry out the grantor's intention whenever this is possible, but without any evidence of delivery, it can be of no importance whatever what the intentions of the grantor in this case were. One may have an intention to convey his property to another, but unless the deed is delivered to the grantee, or someone for him, title cannot pass, and the undelivered deed is a nullity."

the intended grantee has accepted is not always clear-cut. In the example above where the grantor laid the deed on the intended bedridden grantee's night table, assume that the intended grantee died a short time later. Assume further that no words were exchanged between the grantor and the intended grantee. Was there an acceptance by the grantee?

In 1970, Stevie Wonder released a hit song entitled "Signed, Sealed, Delivered (I'm Yours)." If you add the words "and Accepted," the song might help you remember a few of the elements for a valid conveyance by deed, that is "Signed, Sealed, Delivered, and Accepted (I'm Yours)."

e. The Seal

Placing the word "seal" on a deed (or any contract) is a practice that dates back many centuries to the very beginning of English common law. The earliest seals were created by pressing one's unique ring or coat of arms into warm wax that had been dripped onto a legal document. The seal served to **authenticate the validity** of the document, as well as the **identity** of the party signing and sealing it.

Today, many states have abolished the requirement of a seal (or the word "seal") next to the grantor's signature on a deed as described above. In states that still allow instruments to be sealed, the seal may have the legal effect of **extending the statute of limitations**. For example, if the statute of limitations for a breach of contract in a state is usually 3 years, the limitations period may be extended to 10 years if the contract is signed "under seal." This type of seal should not be confused with the impressed or printed seals still used by **notaries public** and corporate secretaries for purposes of authentication of signatures,

Under English common law, later adopted in the American Colonies, a seal also served as a substitute for consideration. Suppose a father made a gift of real property to his daughter. There is no consideration by either party, that is, there was no promise to convey the property made by the grantor-father, and there was no promise or performance by the grantee-daughter. Until the arrival of the seal, many of these gifts were held to be invalid.

This underscores a significant point: Unlike a contract, there is *no requirement for consideration* in the conveyance of property by deed (although deeds often recite that some minimal consideration has been given by the grantee, for example, $10—this is to avoid a possible challenge to the conveyance for a lack of consideration).

f. Legal Description of the Property

The property to be transferred by the deed must be correctly and adequately described if there is to be a valid transfer. It is not ideal to simply identify the property in the deed or mortgage by the street address or tax map number, as this vagueness opens the description to a potential challenge, but it may be found legally sufficient in some states if the intent to convey the specific property can be shown. There are three main types of legal descriptions of real property:

i. Metes-and-Bounds Legal Description The metes-and-bounds legal description is probably the most widely used in America today. The metes-and-bounds method consists of distances (the "metes"—think of meters) and directions (the bounds):

> *Beginning at an existing iron stake located in the northern right-of-way line of Little Brook Lane marking its intersection with the east right-of-way margin of Elm Tree Drive, and running thence North 02° 22' East a total distance of 156.43 feet to a point; running thence North 00° 55' 40" East 38.21 feet to a point; running thence South 87° 41' 35" East 189.07 feet*

to a point; running thence with the western right-of-way line of Lochraven Place South 2° 12' West a total distance of 177.51 feet to an existing iron pipe; running thence along said west margin along a curve to the right having a radius of 25.00 feet, an arc length of 26 feet and a chord bearing and distance of South 47° 45' West a distance of 31.80 feet to an existing concrete monument; running thence along the northern right-of-way line of Little Brook Lane, North 85° 54' 05" West 166.07 feet to the point and place of the beginning, containing 0.8518 acre, or less.

From the example above, you can see that a metes-and-bounds legal descriptions can be very accurate, describing distances to one one-hundredth of a foot, and directions and angles to the second. However, this same detail also invites **transcription errors**, which have been the cause of countless title defects, costing property owners and title insurance companies untold amounts to remedy.

Older metes-and-bounds descriptions often used natural features such as large trees, boulders, and streams as **monuments** from which to take measurements. But over time, trees die, boulders move, and streams change course, which can be a source of confusion for later surveyors relying on the previous metes-and-bounds description. Modern metes-and-bounds descriptions use man-made monuments that are usually iron stakes driven into the ground or into a street, and are much less likely to be moved or move by natural shifting.

A paralegal drafting a legal description from a survey must be diligent in transcribing calls correctly from the survey to the document. Once the description has been drafted, it should be plotted to confirm the calls were typed accurately; today, this can be done with readily-available computer software.

ii. Plat/Map Legal Description

The plat map legal description was developed in urban areas in the 1800s. But it was the dramatic increase in the development of residential subdivisions following World War II that provided the impetus for the ascendance of the plat map legal description.

A plat/map description is much simpler than using metes and bounds because it simply correlates the identity of the property with a plat/subdivision map, which is recorded in a county office such as the register of deeds. For example, the property described above using metes and bounds could just as easily be described using the following plat/map description:

The property being conveyed is all of Lot Number 38 as shown on the plat map of Greenacres Estates, Block Number 2, as recorded in Plat Book 20, page 3, of the Any County Registry.

The plat/map itself still relies on metes-and-bounds descriptions. That is, the plat/map was likely based upon a metes-and-bounds description of a much larger tract of land that was subsequently subdivided into smaller parcels or lots. And on the plat/map, the individual lots are delineated using metes-and-bounds (distances and directions) descriptors. But all that is necessary for the legal description *in the deed* are the simple Lot, Block, and (plat) Map numbers. The plat/maps may be stored in the county's register of deeds office, or perhaps the office of the county engineer, or zoning department.

iii. Public Land Survey System

When English colonists settled the original 13 colonies, they used the English system of metes and bounds described above to measure property boundaries. However, it soon became apparent that there were immense lands—almost an entire continent—beyond the Appalachians, and the metes and bounds system was simply inadequate to survey such huge tracts of land.

The system that was adopted to survey the large expanses west of the 13 colonies was the Public Land Survey System (PLLS). In addition to being better suited for setting boundaries for large tracts of land, the PLLS enabled much faster surveys of the land. That was important because thousands of soldiers who fought in the Revolutionary War were promised large tracts of land in lieu of wages. After the War, these soldiers wanted to homestead their lands as quickly as possible. Consequently, Congress enacted the Land Ordinance of 1785, which established the Public Land Survey System, by which the federal government measured, described, and divided immense tracts of Western land into territories, states, and their constituent townships. Many of these tracts were sold to investors and speculators in order to partly pay off the large federal debt incurred during the Revolutionary War. Despite these grants to soldiers, and sales to speculators, the federal government still owns millions of acres of land across the United States.

The PLLS system employs **base lines**, which run east and west and are correlated with lines of latitude, and the **principal meridian**, which runs north and south, thereby creating the starting point for a grid. This large area is subdivided into **townships**, which are 6 miles long × 6 miles wide, that is, 36 square miles.

Townships are subdivided into 36 **sections** of one square mile each; each section consists of 640 acres. Sections are further subdivided into **quarter sections**, comprised of 160 acres. The quarter section was the smallest unit of land surveyed by the government under the PLSS. If the owner of a quarter section wanted to further subdivide the property—for example, to distribute to one's children—the owner would have to hire a surveyor to do so.

3. AMBIGUITIES IN A DEED'S PROPERTY DESCRIPTION

As you observed in the section on metes-and-bounds legal descriptions, it can be very easy to make a mistake in transcribing the description from an earlier deed to the deed now being used to convey a particular piece of property. Mistakes in legal descriptions are referred to as **ambiguities**, and they are of two general types:

a. Patent Ambiguities

The first type of ambiguity that may appear in the legal description of a deed is a **patent ambiguity.** *Patent* in this context is pronounced with a "long a" sound, as in "pay," and it means that something is obvious. An example would be an ***obvious or self-evident mistake*** in a deed's legal description such as the omission or contradiction of necessary words. A patent ambiguity in a deed renders the deed ***void***, that is, without any legal effect.

In these instances, the ambiguity is patent because it appears "on the face of the deed," and is obvious. Patent ambiguities may *not* be resolved by relying on extrinsic or parol evidence.

Ambiguity
that which is reasonably susceptible to two different interpretations.

Patent Ambiguity
an obvious mistake in the legal description of real property, and is found on the face of the deed. A patent ambiguity renders the deed void.

EXAMPLE OF A PATENT AMBIGUITY

Suppose that the grantor is a developer who is conveying a lot to a grantee on which to build a house. One portion of the legal description indicates that the lot being conveyed is "Lot 15." But another part of the same legal description indicates that the lot being conveyed is "Lot 16."

This is a patent ambiguity because of the contradictory description of the lot in question, which is readily discernible from the face of the deed (i.e., it is a "patent" mistake), and therefore the deed is void.

b. Latent Ambiguities

Latent Ambiguity
a defect in the legal description of a property in a deed that is hidden, or not obvious. A latent ambiguity does not necessarily void the deed, and may be cured by extrinsic evidence.

The second type of ambiguity that may occur in the legal description of a deed is a **latent ambiguity**. Latent in this context means hidden, or not obvious from the face of the deed. The ambiguity does not manifest itself until the document's terms are applied or carried out, and some fact or circumstance external to the deed makes the description ambiguous.

A latent ambiguity in a legal description will not necessarily void the deed because the ambiguity can be resolved by looking to extrinsic evidence (such as the deed description of an adjoining property), or *parol evidence* from the parties to the transaction or witnesses to explain the ambiguity.

EXAMPLE OF A LATENT AMBIGUITY

A grandmother has 18 grandchildren. Grandmother draws up a standard deed form in which she writes:

> *"I hereby grant and convey in fee simple my property known as the Homestead, more fully described below, to the grantee, my grandson John Jones...."*

Grandmother actually has two grandchildren legally named John Jones, one of whom goes by that name. The other grandson, whose legal name is also John, has been called "Jay" (his middle name) by his extended family, including grandmother, for 35 years.

Extrinsic evidence, meaning evidence from outside the deed itself, may be used to cure this latent ambiguity. Grandmother may simply identify the actual John to whom she wished to deed the property. Or, if the grandmother is now deceased, other relatives could testify that the second John had been known as Jay for his entire life, and therefore, that grandmother meant to convey title to the first John.

4. TYPES OF DEEDS

a. General Warranty Deed

General Warranty Deed
the best kind of deed because it contains the most warranties or guarantees from the grantor, and thereby, the greatest protection for the grantee.

Warranty
a promise or guarantee made by the grantor and found in a deed.

A **general warranty deed** is the best type of deed that a grantee can receive from the grantor.

A **warranty** is simply a *guarantee*. When you last purchased a car, TV, or large appliance, you may have received a warranty with the product, which was a guarantee that it would be repaired or replaced if it did not operate according to specifications. With a general warranty deed, the grantor makes several guarantees to the grantee. As we review some of the warranties below, put yourself in the grantee's position to better appreciate the importance of each guarantee/warranty.

i. Warranties in a General Warranty Deed

(a) *Seisin*. Seisin is a concept that dates back to medieval England. As originally used, the concept was rather complicated. Today, however, the warranty of seisin means that the grantor guarantees that he or she has the **right to convey** the property to the grantee. The word is sometimes spelled "seizin."

(b) *Quiet Enjoyment*. The warranty of quiet enjoyment has nothing to do with noise violations. It does mean that the grantee will not be disturbed by *third parties making claims* of superior title to the ownership of the property.

If such claims are made, the grantor guarantees or warrants that he will defend the title that he has conveyed to the grantee from such third-party claims. As a practical matter, a title insurance company would be obligated to defend the grantee.

(c) *Against Encumbrances*. The warranty against encumbrances means that the property being conveyed is not encumbered by mortgages, liens, or easements, and therefore, the grantor can convey **marketable title.** There may be acceptable exceptions, like ad-valorem taxes, governmental regulations, or restrictive covenants for a subdivision, which run with the property and are not extinguished upon conveyance, and these are usually set out as exceptions in the deed.

(d) *Further Assurance*. The warranty of further assurance guarantees the grantee that, following the transfer of the property (usually at a closing), the grantor will provide and sign any legal instrument that may be required to perfect the title that was supposed to have been conveyed to the grantee.

Exhibit 10-1 is an example of a general warranty deed.

> **Marketable Title**
> a title that a reasonable buyer would accept because the title has no defects.

b. Limited Warranty Deed a/k/a Special Warranty Deed

A **limited warranty deed** is also known as a special warranty deed. In either case, the grantor does not guarantee to defend the title against the whole world as in the general warranty deed. Instead, the grantor merely guarantees to defend the title to the property against the ***grantor's own claims***, or those claiming through the grantor. Special warranty deeds are often used by trustees and executors of decedents' estates. In conveying the title to a ***beneficiary***, the trustee or executor is only warranting the deed against the trustee's or executor's own errors or omissions, and not to any clouds or encumbrances prior to the trustee or executor taking title. Exhibit 10-2 is an example of a special warranty deed.

> **Limited Warranty Deed**
> also known as a Special Warranty Deed. Because this type of deed offers fewer warranties or guarantees to the grantee than a general warranty deed, it is not preferred by grantees.

c. Non-Warranty or Quitclaim Deed

With a non-warranty or **quitclaim deed**, the grantor makes ***no warranties*** or guarantees to the grantee, but simply conveys any interest that the grantor *may* have in the property. The question immediately arises as to why a grantee would want a deed that guarantees nothing. The answer is that the purpose of the quitclaim deed is usually to *quiet title*, or lay to rest any potential clouds on the title or claims to the property.

Quitclaim deeds are useful when an unknown "heir" (fourth cousin, twice removed) shows up at the front door to claim an interest in a property devised to the grandchildren-grantees by their grandfather-testator. Maybe Cuz does have a colorable claim but would be willing to sign a quitclaim deed and go away for a few dollars. These situations are sometimes described as **will contests.** A will is usually challenged or *contested* by two classes of individuals:

> **Quitclaim Deed**
> a deed wherein the grantor makes no warranties or guarantees to the grantee, but simply conveys any interest that the grantor *may* have in the property. Quitclaim deeds are commonly used to quiet title in will contests and divorce actions.

i. Someone who is not named in the will, but believes that she should have been named in the will; or

ii. Someone who is named as a beneficiary in the will, but believes that he should have received more property than he did under the terms of the will.

> **Will Contest**
> the litigation of a will's validity, usually based on allegations that the testator lacked capacity or was under undue influence.

Aside from will contests, quitclaim deeds are frequently employed in ***divorce*** actions, where one of the divorcing spouses will quitclaim his or her interest in the family residence, for example, to the other divorcing spouse. Exhibit 10-3 on page 242 is an example of a quitclaim deed.

A few other, less common types of deeds include the following:

d. Deed in Lieu of Foreclosure

When foreclosure on a property by the lender is imminent, the property owner-borrower can offer the lender a deed in lieu of (instead of) foreclosure. If the lender agrees, title to the property is conveyed to the lender in return for which the lender will extinguish the outstanding mortgage debt.

EXHIBIT 10-1 General Warranty Deed

General Warranty Deed

This Deed is made on this date, _____, 20_____, between the

Grantor _____ (name) _____

of _____ (address) _____ and the

Grantee_____ (name) _____of_____

(address)_____.

For consideration of the sum of $ _____, the Grantor hereby bargains, deeds and conveys the following described real property to the Grantee forever, free and clear with WARRANTY COVENANTS:

Property Address:

_____

Legal Description:

_____

_____

Grantor, for itself and its heirs, hereby covenants with Grantee, its heirs and assigns, that Grantor is lawfully seized in fee simple of the above described property; that it has a good right to convey the described property; and that the property is free from all encumbrances. The Grantor and its heirs or assigns, and all persons acquiring any interest in the property granted, through or for Grantor, will, on demand of Grantee or its heirs or assigns, and at the expense of Grantee or its heirs or assigns, execute any instrument necessary for the further assurance of the title to the property that may be reasonably required. Grantor and its heirs will forever warrant and defend all of the property so granted to Grantee and its heirs or assigns against every person lawfully claiming the same or any part thereof.

EXECUTED this day of _____, 20_____.

Grantor Name: _____

Grantor Signature: _____

Witness Name: _____
Witness Signature : _____

Witness Name: _____
Witness Signature: _____

STATE OF _____
COUNTY OF_____

On this day, _____personally appeared before me, known to be the person(s) described in and who executed this instrument, and acknowledged that he/she voluntarily signed this deed, for the uses and purposes mentioned therein.

Witness my hand and official seal hereto affixed on this day of _____, 20_____.

Notary's Public Signature: _____

My commission expires _____.

EXHIBIT 10-2 Special Warranty Deed

SPECIAL WARRANTY DEED

This Special Warranty Deed is made by hereinafter referred to as "Grantor," of _____ (address) _____, of _____ (address) _____, hereinafter referred to as "Grantee."

Grantor, in consideration of the sum of Dollars and for other good and valuable consideration, the receipt of which is hereby acknowledged, hereby conveys to Grantee the following described real property in:

(insert legal description of property)

The Property Appraiser's Parcel Identification Number for the above described property is _____.

Subject to valid easements and restrictions of record, governmental regulations and real property taxes for the current year.

The Grantor hereby covenants with Grantee that the property is free of all encumbrances made by Grantor and that Grantor does hereby warrant and defend the title to the property against the lawful claims of all persons claiming by, through or under Grantor, but not otherwise.

Executed on the _____ day of _____, 200 _____.

WITNESSES:

_____   By: _____

Print Name: _____   GRANTOR

_____

Print Name: _____

_____

STATE OF _____

COUNTY OF _____

The foregoing instrument was acknowledged before me this _____ day of _____ 20_____ by

_____

Notary Public

_____

My Commission Expires: _____

A deed in lieu of foreclosure saves the lender the time and expense of what could be a long foreclosure process. It also saves the owner of the property from having a foreclosure appear on the owner's credit history, and the owner may be able to remain in the property as a tenant. But a lender will only agree to accept a deed in lieu from the owner/borrower if the title to the property is clear of liens and encumbrances, because a foreclosure action will render almost all liens junior to the lender's mortgage unenforceable, where a deed in lieu will not. Since a foreclosure will give the lender clear title to the property, a title search must be performed before the lender may determine whether it will accept a deed in lieu as opposed to foreclosing.

EXHIBIT 10-3 Quitclaim Deed

Quitclaim Deed

This DEED, executed on this the _____ day of _____,

20_____, by _____, Grantor of _____

(address)_____ to Grantee, _____, of

_____(address)_____.

For the sum of $_____ and other good and valuable consideration, the receipt of which is hereby acknowledged,

GRANTOR does hereby convey unto GRANTEE forever all the rights, title, interest, and any claim which Grantor has in and to the following described property:

(insert legal description of property)

IN WITNESS whereof, _____(name of Grantor) _____ has signed and sealed these presents the day and year written above.

_____ Grantor

STATE OF_____
COUNTY OF _____

Subscribed and sworn before me this _____ day of _____,

20_____.

_____
Notary Public
My commission expires: _____

---

e. Sheriff's Deed

A sheriff's deed is the method by which title to real property is conveyed following a sheriff's sale. The reason the sheriff is conducting a sheriff's sale is to satisfy a *civil judgment*, and in some states, the foreclosure of a mortgage is deemed to be a sheriff's sale. When a plaintiff prevails at a civil trial, a monetary judgment—for example, $20,000—is entered in that county's judgment book, and becomes a lien on the property.

The defendant becomes the *judgment-debtor* after the verdict and is obligated to pay the $20,000, which is probably accruing interest following the entry of the court's judgment in the civil judgment book. The plaintiff is the *judgment-creditor*. If the defendant cannot or will not pay the $20,000, the plaintiff can request that the clerk of court issue a *writ of execution*, which authorizes the sheriff to *seize* or *levy* the defendant's property in order to satisfy the judgment.

The sheriff will usually seize the defendant's personal property first. However, if that is not sufficient to satisfy the judgment debt, the sheriff will then "seize" any real property owned by the defendant, which will be auctioned at the sheriff's sale.

EXHIBIT 10-4 Sheriff's Deed

SHERIFF'S DEED

WITNESSETH, that _____ (Sheriff's name), as Sheriff of County, State of conveys to _____, in

consideration of the sum of $_____ Dollars, the receipt of which is hereby acknowledged, on sale made by

virtue of a decree judgment, issued from _____ Court of County, in the State of pursuant to the laws of said State on

the _____ day of _____, _____, in Case no.

_____ wherein _____ was Plaintiff, and _____ was Defendant,

in consideration of said sum aforesaid, the following described real estate in County, to-wit:

To have and to hold the premises aforesaid with the privileges and appurtenances to said purchaser, their grantees and assigns, forever, with all rights, title and interest held or claimed by the aforesaid Defendants.

IN WITNESS WHEREOF, I, THE UNDERSIGNED, Sheriff aforesaid have set my hand and seal, this _____

day of _____, 20_____.

SHERIFF OF _____ County, State of _____

_____

Frank J. Anderson

On the _____ day of _____, 20_____ Sheriff's name personally appeared to me, in the
capacity of Sheriff of said County, and acknowledged the execution of the foregoing deed.

IN WITNESS WHEREOF, I have hereunto set my hand and official seal.

_____	_____
COUNTY OF _____	NOTARY PUBLIC
STATE OF _____	
_____	_____
COMMISSION EXPIRES	PRINTED NAME

Following the sale of the real property at auction, a *sheriff's deed* is issued to the successful bidder. Sheriffs' deeds rarely come with any warranties, so purchasing property at a sheriff's sale is like buying a car "as is." Exhibit 10-4 is an example of a sheriff's deed.

f. Tax Deed

The process by which a buyer at a tax sale auction receives a tax deed is about the same as at a sheriff's sale. When the owner of a property fails to pay property taxes, a *tax lien* will be entered against the real property by the federal, state, county, or municipal government to which the taxes are owed. If the property owner does not satisfy the tax lien, the governmental entity will sell the owner's real property to pay the taxes owed.

If a title search reveals delinquent taxes, the paralegal should check with the tax office to find out if a tax foreclosure has been initiated. Generally, if the tax office knows that either the property is being sold or foreclosed, it will hold off on initiating the tax foreclosure to save the expense, because it is likely the taxes will be paid by the closing attorney or the foreclosing lender.

As with a sheriff's deed, a tax deed does not generally come with warranties.

5. DRAFTING A DEED

The paralegal drafting the deed must use the type of warranty-deed form specified in the purchase contract. To preserve the integrity of the chain of title, the information must be entered carefully and proofed. The sellers' (grantor) names must be exactly as shown in the vesting deed to the seller, unless there is a valid reason for a difference, like the addition of a spouse's name where the property was vested in only one of the parties' names, conveyance by heirs in the case of the death of the vested owner, or an organizational name change in a commercial transaction. The names in the signature lines and notary acknowledgments should match the seller's names as shown in the grantor clause.

The buyer (grantee) name(s) on the deed should match that shown on the purchase contract, unless there is a written record evidencing the reason for the difference, such as an assignment of the purchase contract from the buyer to another party. In commercial transactions, this may occur if the buyer wants to create a limited liability company to hold title to the property, but the entity had not yet been formed at the time the contract was executed by the parties.

Marital status may be required on the deed to properly convey title, even where title is vested in only one spouse, because some states have statutes protecting a spouse's interest in real property.

In the case of multiple grantees other than a married couple, due care should be taken to reflect the proper status of the buyers so it is clear what type of interest each is receiving, for instance, "Joseph J. Jones and Jim B. White as tenants in common," or "as joint tenants with right of survivorship."

If an individual owner marries, he or she may want to create a tenancy by entireties by conveying the property to himself or herself and the spouse. It seems unnecessary to convey property to oneself, but both names are needed as grantee in order to create the tenancy by entireties interest. A statement of intent to create the tenancy by entireties should be added to the deed for clarification, and may include a statutory reference. In the same vein, tenancy by the entireties may be dissolved by conveying from both spouses to one. Again, a statement of intent should be added to the deed.

Correct spelling of party names is important for proper indexing in the public records. If the seller's last name is "Bartlett" but it was spelled incorrectly as "Bartlet" in the vesting deed, it will be indexed as "Bartlet." This particular instrument may not necessarily be corrected, but for cross-referencing purposes, the most thorough way to phrase the grantor clause in the new deed is "David R. Bartlett, also known as David R. Bartlet," which will cause the document to be indexed under both spellings. This will help a future title researcher "connect the dots" and locate the incorrect deed by using the information provided in the new deed.

To preserve the integrity of the chain of title, it is crucial that the legal description be consistent with the prior deed, to the extent that the description has not been legally changed since the prior deed was recorded. An example of this legal change might be the purchase of one subdivision lot, where the vesting deed conveyed the entire parcel by metes and bounds prior to the subdivision of lots and plat recording. Note that it is very easy to forget to attach the legal description if it is on a separate page as an exhibit, as opposed to being typed into the text of the document.

If a new survey has been obtained, the paralegal may be asked to prepare a new metes-and-bounds legal description. See the guide for drafting the legal description, in the "Property Survey" section under Closing Documents. The legal description should include references to any applicable appurtenant or burdensome easements (using "together with" or "subject to").

The warranties contained within the deed must match the type of deed designated in the purchase contract. The title of the document may not be changed without changing the language pertaining to warranties, as the actual language prevails over the title. In other words, if the contract calls for a special warranty deed and the paralegal has erroneously drafted a general warranty deed, he or she may not simply change the title to "Special Warranty Deed." The corresponding warranties given are set out in the text of the document, and this text must be revised in accordance with correction of the title.

Any exceptions to the warranties should be specified in the deed. Examples of typical exceptions are payment of the current year's taxes (which cannot be paid if the bill has not yet been issued), governmental regulations, and easements and restrictions of record. If a mortgage or deed of trust is not being canceled in conjunction with the conveyance, as in the case where an individual conveys title to himself and his wife to create tenancy by the entireties, or an assumption of seller's loan by the buyer, it should be included in the exceptions.

The amount of excise tax and/or transfer tax should be shown on the face of the deed, as should the parcel identification number where required.

The buyer does not need to sign the deed unless it contains a clause pertaining to an agreement between the parties, like the assumption by the buyer of the seller's existing loan.

Any additional forms or information required by the county for the facilitation of recording should be included with the deed and any other applicable documents prior to recording.

Laws are evolving with respect to the property rights for owners in nontraditional marriages, and the laws of each state must be checked for the requirements of conveyance of title in these circumstances, and what bundle of rights are conveyed to such buyers.

B. Mortgages and Deeds of Trust

1. OVERVIEW

A **mortgage** and deed of trust are both written legal documents that *pledge* real property as collateral for the loan made by the lender for the purchase of the property. Because mortgages and deeds of trust have the same purpose, we will use the generic term "mortgage" in our discussion below, except when pointing out a few differences between the two legal documents. Because mortgages convey an interest in real property, they must be written to satisfy the Statute of Frauds.

Mortgage
a pledge of real property as collateral/security for a loan.

a. Mortgage

We will use the terms "mortgagor" and "mortgagee" repeatedly in our discussion and so, as a preliminary matter, let us discuss the terminology, which is somewhat counterintuitive. The **mortgagor** is the borrower of the loan proceeds, *not* the lender.

Mortgagor
the party giving the pledge to the lender as collateral for a loan. Thus, the mortgagor is the borrower.

This will be easier to remember if you know that mortgage derives from two French words: "mort," meaning dead, and "gage," meaning pledge. In other words, the mortgage is a pledge of the real property by the buyer/borrower to the lender, as collateral for the loan. The pledge is extinguished or "dies" (mort) when the loan has been repaid by the borrower.

The **mortgagee** is the lender because it is the party that receives the pledge (mortgage) of the real property/collateral from the borrower.

An excerpt from a typical mortgage might read as follows:

This Mortgage is made by and between Mortgagor, Bobbie Borrower, a single person residing at 123 N. Elm St., Anytown, Any State, USA, and Mortgagee, Large Lender, Inc., of 212 Commerce Pl., Metropolis, USA.

Mortgagor declares that she is indebted to Mortgagee in the principal amount of $250,000, as evidenced by the Promissory Note from the Mortgagor to the Lender of the same date, in the amount of $250,000, and which loan of $250,000, as evidenced by the said Promissory Note, was made by Mortgagee to Mortgagor to be secured by the real property described as follows: all of Lot 13 of Block 8, of Plat Map 108, located in the Office of the Register of Deeds in Any County, USA.

To secure payment of the aforementioned Promissory Note, Mortgagor does hereby pledge and mortgage the above-described real property to Mortgagee.

The pledge of the real property as collateral is followed by several pages of covenants or promises relating to the mortgage, which we will discuss later.

Most jurisdictions in the United States are "mortgage states," where the principal method for financing the purchase of real property is by the use of a mortgage. As you have gleaned from the language in the mortgage clause above, mortgages involve two parties: the mortgagor/borrower, and the mortgagee/lender. See Exhibit 10-5 for a sample mortgage.

b. Deed of Trust

As compared to mortgage states, there are significantly fewer states that use the deed of trust to finance real property. Although the purpose of the deed of trust is the same as the mortgage—to pledge the real property as collateral for the loan—a deed of trust involves ***three parties***:

i. ***Borrower/Trustor***—the borrower is sometimes called the trustor because it is the borrower who essentially creates the trust for the benefit of the lender;

ii. ***Trustee***—the trustee is a neutral third-party—often an attorney—who holds the deed of trust. If the borrower defaults, under the terms of the deed of trust, the trustee will proceed to foreclose on the property;

iii. ***Lender/Beneficiary***—because the deed of trust is to protect the lender, the lender is the beneficiary of the trust.

For the lender, there are two major advantages of using a deed of trust over a mortgage. The first advantage is that the foreclosure process can be carried out much *more quickly* under a deed of trust than under a mortgage.

The second advantage is that because the trustee is a supposedly neutral third-party, the *lender can bid* on the property at the foreclosure auction. Because the parties to a mortgage are just the borrower and lender, there is not a neutral trustee to insure the fairness of the foreclosure process, and therefore, a mortgagee/lender cannot bid on the property in foreclosure. See Exhibit 10-6 for a sample deed of trust on page 263.

c. Lien Theory States v. Title Theory States

We have seen that both a mortgage and a deed of trust pledge the real property to the lender as collateral for the loan to purchase the property. Technically, both the mortgage and the deed of trust not only pledge real property, but also actually *convey title* from the homeowner-borrower to the lender, or from the homeowner-borrower to the trustee when a deed of trust is used; that is why it is called a *deed* of trust, because of the actual conveyance of title to the real property.

In light of the previous paragraph, one might ask: Who actually holds title, that is, who owns, the real property?

Lien theory states are almost always states wherein the mortgage is the predominant method of financing the purchase of the real property. Generally speaking:

Lien Theory States = Mortgage States

As the name implies, in a lien theory state what the borrower conveys to the lender is a lien on (an interest in) the real property, and *not* the legal title to it.

Alternatively, deed of trust states are those that follow the title theory, and generally speaking:

Title Theory States = Deed of Trust States

In jurisdictions where the deed of trust is the primary method of financing real estate transactions, the borrower conveys **legal title** to the neutral trustee until the loan is satisfied by the borrower. When that occurs, the trustee will cancel the deed of trust and thereby return legal title to the borrower, who is then reinstated as the legal owner.

In title theory/deed of trust states, even though "legal title" resides in the trustee, the borrower still holds what is known as "equitable title," and therefore can enjoy the full bundle of rights usually associated with a fee-simple estate, such as using and enjoying the property, leasing it, raising crops, and selling the property.

d. Purchase-Money Mortgage

A purchase-money mortgage (also called seller financing) is considered a mortgage because it does pledge real property as collateral for the money with which to purchase the property. But in a purchase-money mortgage there is a slight twist: it is the owner-seller of the property who finances the purchase of the property for the buyer.

Suppose that traditional lenders such as banks and credit unions are not lending as much as usual, or are requiring stronger credit histories from prospective borrowers. A young, newly-married couple is unable to obtain traditional financing but locates the owner of a home who will sell it to them *and* finance the purchase of the property. Assume that the owner-seller owns the property free and clear of any debt, and makes this offer to the couple:

> *"I will sell you my property, Greenacres, for $90,000 and convey the deed to you at closing if you give me a $10,000 down payment at closing, and sign a promissory note and mortgage or deed of trust securing said promissory note, for which Greenacres is the collateral, promising to pay me the remaining $80,000 in equal monthly installments over the next 10 years."*

This is a purchase-money mortgage because it is the owner-seller—and not a traditional lender—who is financing the sales transaction. It is sometimes said that the owner-seller will **"carry paper"** for the buyers, the "paper" in question being the promissory note that the buyers will sign and that is the evidence of their debt to the seller.

Note that the deed will convey title to the property *at the time of the closing*, and the buyers will become the owners of an estate in fee simple. As you will see in the next section, this provides much more safety for the buyers than if this were a land-sale contract.

In some states, statutory provisions govern and protect consumers. One such protection is **anti-deficiency**, meaning that upon default on the purchase-money loan, the seller may foreclose but not sue on the promissory note.

e. Contract for Deed/Land Sale Contract

A contract for deed resembles a purchase-money mortgage in that the owner-seller finances the purchase of the property. Technically, however, a *contract for deed is not a mortgage* because the buyer cannot pledge the real property as collateral for the purchase of the property, because the buyer will not take title to the property for many years. Let's look at the same example as above, except for a few changes in the language of the offer. Put yourself in the buyers' shoes as you analyze this scenario:

> *"I will sell you this property for $90,000 if you give me a $10,000 down payment, and sign a promissory note promising to pay me the remaining $80,000 in equal monthly installments over the next 10 years. At the end of the 10 years, if you have made all monthly payments as promised, I will sign the deed over to you."*

(In reading the last sentence, you can understand why this type of financing is called a "contract for deed.")

From the buyers' perspective, does a contract for deed provide them with more or less protection than a purchase money mortgage where title conveys at the closing?

The answer is obvious, and it is negative. No, a contract for deed/land sale contract can be very **dangerous for the buyers** if the seller is unscrupulous. The seller, for example, might collect the monthly payments from the young couple for 10 years, and then refuse to turn over the deed as promised. Or, in year nine of the transaction, seller may mortgage the property to the hilt, taking the money and leaving the property encumbered with a huge debt when the deed is turned over to the buyers at the end of year 10.

Needless to say, a contract for deed is not favored by buyers, and someone considering the purchase of real property using a contract for deed should exercise extreme caution. Although the buyer prevailed in the below case, one does not want to endure the expense, worry, and time involved in a trial.

BEAN v. WALKER

Supreme Court of New York, Appellate Division, Fourth Department
95 A.D.2d 70; 464 N.Y.S.2d 895
July 11, 1983

Opinion

Presented for our resolution is the question of the relative rights between a vendor [seller] and a defaulting vendee [buyer] under a **land purchase contract**. Special Term, in granting summary judgment in favor of plaintiffs, effectively held that the defaulting vendee has no rights. We cannot agree.

In January, 1973 plaintiffs [Sellers] agreed to sell and defendants [Buyers] agreed to buy a single-family home in Syracuse for the sum of $15,000. (The house now has an alleged market value of $44,000.) The contract provided that this sum would be paid over a 15-year period at 5% interest, in monthly installments of $118.62. The ***sellers retained legal title*** to the property which they agreed to convey upon payment in full according to the terms of the contract. The purchasers were entitled to possession of the property, and all taxes, assessments and water rates, and insurance became the obligation of the purchasers. The contract also provided that in the event purchasers defaulted in making payment and ***failed to cure*** the default within 30 days, the sellers could elect to call the remaining balance immediately due or elect to declare the contract terminated and repossess the premises. If the latter alternative was chosen, then a forfeiture clause came into play whereby the seller could retain all the money paid under the contract as "liquidated" damages and "the same shall be in no event considered a penalty but rather the payment of rent."

Defendants went into possession of the premises in January, 1973 and in the ensuing years claim to have made substantial improvements on the property. They made the required payments under the contract until August, 1981 when they ***defaulted following an injury*** sustained by defendant Carl Walker. During the years while they occupied the premises as contract purchasers defendant paid to plaintiff $12,099.24, of which $7,114.75 was applied to principal. Thus, at the time of their default, ***defendants had paid almost one half*** of the purchase price called for under the agreement. After the required 30-day period to cure the default, plaintiffs [Sellers] commenced this action sounding in ***ejectment*** seeking a judgment that they be adjudged the owner in fee of the property and granting them possession thereof. The trial court granted summary judgment to plaintiffs [Sellers].

Defendants' offer to bring the payments up to date and pay a higher interest rate on the balance due were unavailing.

If the only substantive law to be applied to this case was that of contracts, the result reached would be correct. However, under the facts presented herein the law with regard to the transfer of real property must also be considered. The reconciliation of what might appear to be conflicting concepts is not insurmountable.

It is well settled that the owner of the real estate from the time of the execution of a valid contract for its sale is to be treated as the owner of the purchase money and the purchaser of the land is to be treated as the equitable owner thereof. The purchase money becomes personal property. Thus, notwithstanding

the words of the contract and implications which may arise therefrom, the law of property declares that, upon the execution of a contract for sale of land, the vendee acquires ***equitable title***. The vendor holds the ***legal title*** in trust for the vendee and has an equitable lien for the payment of the purchase price. The vendee in possession, for all practical purposes, is the owner of the property with all the rights of an owner subject only to the terms of the contract. The vendor may enforce his lien by foreclosure or an action at law for the purchase price of the property.

The conclusion to be reached, of course, is that upon the execution of a contract an interest in real property comes into existence by operation of law, superseding the terms of the contract. An analogous result occurs in New York if an owner purports to convey title to real property as security for a loan; the conveyance is deemed to create a lien rather than an outright conveyance, even though the deed was recorded.

Cases from other jurisdictions are more instructive. In *Skendzel v Marshall (261 Ind 226* [addressing itself to a land sale contract]), the court observed that while legal title does not vest in the vendee until the contract terms are satisfied, he does acquire a vested equitable title at the time the contract is consummated. When the parties enter into the contract all incidents of ownership accrue to the vendee who assumes the risk of loss and is the recipient of all appreciation of value. The status of the parties becomes like that of mortgagor-mortgagee. Viewed otherwise would be to elevate form over substance. The doctrine that equity [fairness] deems as done that which ought to be done is an appropriate concept which we should apply to the present case.

We perceive no reason why the instant vendees should be treated any differently than the mortgagor at common law. Thus the contract vendors may not summarily dispossess the vendees of their equitable ownership without first bringing an action to foreclose the vendees' equity of redemption. This view reflects the modern trend in other jurisdictions.

The key to the resolution of the rights of the parties lies in whether the vendee under a land sale contract has acquired an interest in the property of such a nature that it must be extinguished before the vendor may resume possession. We hold that such an interest exists since the ***vendee acquires equitable title*** and the vendor merely holds the ***legal title in trust*** for the

(continued)

vendee, subject to the vendor's equitable lien for the payment of the purchase price in accordance with the terms of the contract. The vendor may not enforce his rights by the simple expedient of an action in *ejectment* but must instead proceed to *foreclose* the vendee's equitable title [which allows buyers the equitable right of redemption, which they tried to exercise] or bring an action at law for the purchase price, neither of which remedies plaintiffs have sought.

The effect of the judgment granted in the trial court is that plaintiffs [Sellers] will have their property with improvements made over the years by defendants, along with over $7,000 in principal payments on a purchase price of $15,000, and over $4,000 in interest. The *basic inequity* of such a result requires no further comment. If a forfeiture would result in the inequitable disposition of property and an exorbitant monetary loss, equity can and should intervene.

By our holding today we do not suggest that forfeiture would be an inappropriate result in all instances involving a breach of a land contract. If the vendee abandons the property and absconds, logic compels that the forfeiture provisions of the contract may be enforced. Similarly, where the vendee has paid a minimal sum on the contract and upon default seeks to retain possession of the property while the vendor is paying taxes, insurance and other upkeep to preserve the property, equity will not intervene to help the vendee. Such is not the case before us. Accordingly, the judgment should be reversed, the motion should be denied and the matter remitted to Supreme Court [in New York, the trial courts are called the Supreme Court] for further proceedings in accordance with this opinion.

Judgment unanimously reversed, with costs, motion denied and matter remitted to Supreme Court, Onondaga County, for further proceedings, in accordance with this opinion.

f. Standard Mortgage/DoT Clauses/Covenants

Regardless of which of the three legal documents above is used to pledge the property as security for the loan—mortgage, deed of trust, or purchase-money mortgage—the document should contain most, if not all, of the standard clauses or **covenants** below. As you can see, some of these requirements benefit the borrower, while others benefit the lender:

Covenant
a promise in a contract or deed.

i. All taxes, charges, dues, liens, and assessments to be paid by the Borrower;
ii. Property insurance to be maintained on the property by the Borrower;
iii. Promissory note payments are to be kept current by the Borrower;
iv. Waste on the property prohibited;
v. *Acceleration Clause.* The lender will exercise the acceleration clause when the borrower defaults on one or more monthly payments. Pursuant to the acceleration clause, if the borrower defaults the lender can "accelerate the loan payments," that is, demand not just the delinquent payments, but the entire outstanding loan balance.

If there were no acceleration clause, the lender would have to sue the borrower for a few missed payments, which the borrower would probably pay just before trial. After a few months of steady payments, the borrower might default again, and the lender would have to sue again. To avoid the time and expense of the recurring lawsuits, the lender calls the entire loan due so there is only one lawsuit, which is the foreclosure action.

If the lender accepts late payments on a regular basis, it may have waived its rights to insist on prompt payments until the lender has notified the borrower that it now expects prompt payments or a default will be declared.

vi. *Due-On-Sale Clause*. A due on sale clause states that if the borrower-owner conveys the property, the entire mortgage balance must be paid to the lender.

This allows the lender to control its risk regarding the payment of the principal and interest. For example, if the current owner-borrower sells or gives the property to his ne'er-do-well brother-in-law, the risk of a default has substantially increased. If the lender wants to make a new loan to the ne'er-do-well brother-in-law for the purchase of the property, it can certainly do so. Another advantage for the lender with a due-on-sale clause is that if the existing mortgage carries a relatively low interest rate, the lender can increase the interest rate if it chooses to lend to the new buyer of the property.

vii. *No Prepayment Penalty Clause*. In older mortgages, lenders often included a prepayment penalty if the borrower paid off the loan before the final payment was due. The purpose was to keep the borrower as a "customer" and paying interest to the lender. Prepayment penalties are still legal in many states, although some jurisdictions have banned prepayment penalties in mortgages and other types of loan agreements.

viii. *Right of Accounting*. This clause allows the borrower to request an accounting of the borrower's payments over the years.

C. Promissory Notes

We have examined two of the three major documents involved in a real estate transaction, the deed and the mortgage/deed of trust. The third of the three important documents, and probably the simplest, is the **promissory note**.

Promissory Note
a written promise to pay a debt of a specific sum of money, for a specific term, and at a stated interest rate.

1. PURPOSE

A promissory note is a *written promise to pay* a debt of a specific sum of money, for a specific term, and at a stated interest rate. Payment of the promissory note by the buyer-borrower is secured by the mortgage, which pledges the property as collateral if the buyer-borrower defaults on payments required by the promissory note.

Even though the purchased property is pledged as security if the borrower defaults, the lender may protect itself further by requiring that the borrower be *personally liable* on the note.

2. REQUIREMENTS

A typical promissory note might include language such as the following:

> *For value received, the undersigned promises to pay Large Lender, Inc. the principal sum of $250,000, with interest thereon at the rate of 7% per annum on the unpaid balance until paid in full. The monthly payment is $1,938.25, which is due and payable at the office of Large Lender, Inc. beginning on January 1, 2014, with the final monthly payment due on December 1, 2033.*

The promissory note is usually only signed by the buyer-borrower. It should also include, at a minimum, the principal amount of the loan, the interest rate, the monthly payment, and the term (number of years) of the loan.

If there are two or more buyer-borrowers, the lender-promisee will require that they be jointly (together) and severally (individually) liable for the full amount of the debt. In the event of a default on the promissory note, the lender may choose to pursue and obtain payment from one, some, or all of the borrowers, for the entire amount owed.

D. The Mortgage Market

The "mortgage market" is the name given to the vast complex of financial institutions that keeps mortgage money circulating through the mortgage banking system, enabling ever-increasing numbers of Americans to purchase homes. As recent events have demonstrated, however, the mortgage market is far from perfect and not necessarily efficient. It is also susceptible to the risks inherent in any investment, and the risk of corrupt practices by appraisers, buyers and sellers, lenders, insurance companies, and real estate speculators.

1. THE PRIMARY MORTGAGE MARKET

Primary Mortgage Market
banks, employee credit unions, and savings and loan associations that make residential mortgage loans directly to borrowers.

The **primary mortgage market** is made up of the front-line money lenders such as *banks*, *savings and loan associations* (S&Ls), and employee *credit unions*. The job of these financial institutions is to make residential and commercial real estate loans. Lenders want security in the form of collateral from the borrower. The purpose of the mortgage or deed of trust is to pledge the property being purchased as security, or collateral, for the lender.

Aside from looking to the property for security, lenders have to evaluate prospective borrowers. When someone walks into a bank asking for a loan of $300,000, the loan officer has two overarching questions: what is the risk, and what is the reward? The answer to both of those questions lies with the borrower. Lenders are "rewarded" for making loans by the interest payments that they receive on the outstanding loan balance. The reward side of the equation can be calculated to the penny because the lender can compute exactly how much it will earn in interest over the life of the loan. But lenders must also assess the risk of default by any given loan applicant, and to do so the lender will consider several factors:

i. Debt-to-Income Ratio

This calculation looks at how much debt the applicant carries as compared to the applicant's monthly income. The loan applicant will complete the lender's loan application form listing his or her major monthly financial obligations, including payments for housing, car payments, utilities, and food.

ii. Employment

Perhaps the most important aspect regarding this factor is not the applicant's business or occupation, or even the applicant's annual income, but whether the applicant has been steadily employed in that occupation. The applicant's job stability reflects on the ability of the applicant to meet the monthly mortgage payments.

iii. Credit Report

After the loan application is submitted, or even while it is being filled out by the applicant, the loan officer will obtain the applicant's **credit report,** sometimes known as a credit history. The credit history will include entries pertaining to how many times the applicant has been late on payments for: credit cards, mortgage or rent, automobile, utilities, and so forth.

The credit report will also note if the applicant has filed for bankruptcy, or has ever had a civil judgment entered against him or her. Based upon this information, the credit reporting agency that compiles and provides the applicant's credit report will have assigned a numerical credit rating based on the applicant's credit history. The credit rating is very important to the lender in determining whether to make a home loan to the borrower. Any discrepancies between outstanding debts listed on the credit report and the debts listed by the borrower on the loan application will have to be explained by the borrower.

Assume that the loan applicant has been approved by the lender, a local savings and loan association. The S&L will issue a check on the borrower-buyer's behalf in the amount of $300,000. That check will be made payable to closing attorney's trust account, or to the escrow company's escrow account. At closing, these borrowed loan funds will be disbursed and used to pay off the current lender, the owner-seller, the closing attorney/escrow company, and so forth.

2. THE SECONDARY MORTGAGE MARKET

Lenders—even the biggest national banks—can make only so many loans before they exhaust the cash that they have on deposit. There needs to be a way by which loan funds can be replenished so that more prospective buyers can obtain loans. The method by which this is accomplished is the **secondary mortgage market.**

The purpose of the secondary mortgage market is to provide liquidity to the mortgage market. *Liquidity* means that one's assets—for example, a mortgage held by lender—can quickly be converted into cash. *Real property is not liquid* because it may take many months or even a year or more before a property sells and closes. Liquidity is valued by investors because it allows them to quickly and efficiently move into and out of investments when they see better opportunities for making money in other investments. Although real estate is not liquid in and of itself, the secondary mortgage market has managed to bring liquidity to the system as explained below.

Once a bank or other primary lender has made and holds several loans, it will bundle the loans according to the rate of return; that is, the interest rate, and other factors such as risk, property type, and region. The bundled loans—called **mortgage-backed obligations** (MBOs)—are then sold on the secondary mortgage market, which is comprised of huge insurance companies, pension funds, Fannie Mae and Freddie Mac, as well as other large investors. The institutions involved in the secondary mortgage market pay the primary mortgage market lenders, which will then use those funds to make new loans. And so the cycle continues.

As investment vehicles, home loans have traditionally been thought of as being very safe and offering a consistent, predictable return, although that reputation has been somewhat tarnished in the last few years. Notwithstanding recent history, a **pension fund** that is obligated to pay retirement benefits to its current and future retirees may want to buy one or more bundles of those relatively safe, reliable mortgages, which will provide the income stream for the pension fund to pay its retirees.

In 2007, there was a danger that this system would collapse. The reason was that primary mortgage lenders were making loans that were very risky, the so-called **subprime loans**. Lenders were not properly vetting loan applicants, meaning that the lenders would ignore the poor credit histories of their applicants, questionable employment histories, inadequate income to carry the loan, and other factors that would have dissuaded prudent lenders from making such loans.

Mortgage lenders felt safe making these questionable loans because the real estate bubble had been expanding for years, meaning residential real estate values were increasing steadily and significantly, and there seemed to be no end in sight.

However, around 2007, many homeowners began to default on their subprime loans (as well as regular loans) because the economy had slipped into a *recession*, producing higher unemployment. Higher unemployment caused more loan defaults, which exacerbated the recession, causing more unemployment, causing a vicious downward economic spiral.

Secondary Mortgage Market large financial institutions, including Fannie Mae and Freddie Mac, which buy bundles of mortgages from primary mortgage lenders, and thereby enable the primary lenders to continue making loans for the purchase of real property.

Also, many of the subprime loans made by the lenders were *adjustable rate mortgages* (ARMs). Adjustable rate mortgages have a below-market (teaser) interest rate for the first few years of the loan but thereafter, the monthly mortgage payments may double, triple, or in some cases, even quadruple. Thus, in the early years of an ARM, the buyer-borrower might make monthly mortgage payments of $1,000. After the teaser rate expires, the interest rate increases to the then-market rate, or higher, increasing the monthly payment to $3,000 or more.

The growing number of homeowners defaulting on their loans rippled through to the huge financial institutions involved in the secondary mortgage market—the pension funds, insurance companies, and so forth. If homeowners are not paying their monthly mortgages, then the pension funds are not receiving that income, and cannot pay their retirees. The same principle applies to the insurance companies, which might cause them to default on their obligations.

The collapse of one or more of these giant institutions could have destroyed confidence in the economic system, and did cause significant disruptions in the national and international economies. It was said that these large institutions were "*too big to fail,*" because if one or more did fail, it could send the national and international markets into chaos and possibly a severe depression. Thus, the federal government was forced to step in and "bail out" the financial institutions by making loans of approximately $800 billion.

a. Fannie Mae & Freddie Mac

Fannie Mae and Freddie Mac are the two biggest buyers of mortgages in the *secondary mortgage market*. Fannie Mae is the nickname given to the Federal National Mortgage Association (FNMA). For many years, beginning in 1938, Fannie Mae was the *only* player in the secondary mortgage market.

Congress created Fannie Mae to staunch the deluge of foreclosures during the *Great Depression* of the 1930s by the same method described above, that is, by buying bundles of mortgages from local banks, which would then make new home loans with the funds paid to them by Fannie Mae. Originally, the only mortgages that could be purchased by Fannie Mae were those which were insured against default by the Federal Housing Administration (FHA). The Federal Housing Administration was created by Congress pursuant to the National Housing Act of 1934; Fannie Mae was born in 1938 when the Act was amended.

Fannie Mae was originally chartered as an agency of the federal government. Later, however, Congress allowed Fannie Mae to issue stock to the public for investment purposes (as previously noted, home mortgages were, and still are, considered relatively safe investments, and therefore popular with the investing public). In 1968, Fannie Mae, which had been a child of the federal government for 30 years, became a publicly held corporation.

In 1970, Congress passed legislation creating the Federal Home Loan Mortgage Corporation, better known as *Freddie Mac.* Although created by Congress, Freddie Mac was, and still is, a private corporation. The purpose of Freddie Mac is essentially the same as that of Fannie Mae, that is, making the mortgage markets more liquid.

Congress believed that Freddie Mac would provide competition for Fannie Mae in the secondary mortgage market, and make the secondary mortgage market more efficient, which would redound to the benefit of the public. At first, the idea seemed to work. But in the last decade, both Fannie Mae and Freddie Mac have been vehemently criticized by some as bloated, inefficient, and engaged in highly questionable management practices.

Between them, Fannie Mae and Freddie Mac own or guarantee residential loans of approximately $7 trillion ($7,000,000,000,000).

EXHIBIT 10-5 Mortgage

After Recording Return To:

_____

_____

_____

_____

_____ **[Space Above This Line For Recording Data]** _____

MORTGAGE

DEFINITIONS

Words used in multiple sections of this document are defined below and other words are defined in Sections 3, 11, 13, 18, 20, and 21. Certain rules regarding the usage of words used in this document are also provided in Section 16.

(A) **"Security Instrument"** means this document, which is dated _____, _____, together with all Riders to this document.

(B) **"Borrower"** is _____. Borrower is the mortgagor under this Security Instrument.

(C) **"Lender"** is _____. Lender is a _____ organized and existing under the laws of _____. Lender's address is _____. Lender is the mortgagee under this Security Instrument.

(D) **"Note"** means the promissory note signed by Borrower and dated _____, _____. The Note states that Borrower owes Lender _____ Dollars (U.S. \$_____) plus interest. Borrower has promised to pay this debt in regular Periodic Payments and to pay the debt in full not later than _____.

(E) **"Property"** means the property that is described below under the heading "Transfer of Rights in the Property."

(F) **"Loan"** means the debt evidenced by the Note, plus interest, any prepayment charges and late charges due under the Note, and all sums due under this Security Instrument, plus interest.

(G) **"Riders"** means all Riders to this Security Instrument that are executed by Borrower. The following Riders are to be executed by Borrower [check box as applicable]:

☐ Adjustable Rate Rider	☐ Condominium Rider	☐ Second Home Rider
☐ Balloon Rider	☐ Planned Unit Development Rider	☐ Other(s)[specify]_____
☐ 1–4 Family Rider	☐ Biweekly Payment Rider	

(H) **"Applicable Law"** means all controlling applicable federal, state, and local statutes, regulations, ordinances, and administrative rules and orders (that have the effect of law) as well as all applicable final, non-appealable judicial opinions.

(I) **"Community Association Dues, Fees, and Assessments"** means all dues, fees, assessments and other charges that are imposed on Borrower or the Property by a condominium association, homeowners association, or similar organization.

(J) **"Electronic Funds Transfer"** means any transfer of funds, other than a transaction originated by check, draft, or similar paper instrument, which is initiated through an electronic terminal, telephonic instrument, computer, or magnetic tape so as to order, instruct, or authorize a

(continued)

EXHIBIT 10-5 *Continued*

financial institution to debit or credit an account. Such term includes, but is not limited to, point-of-sale transfers, automated teller machine transactions, transfers initiated by telephone, wire transfers, and automated clearinghouse transfers.

(K) "Escrow Items" means those items that are described in Section 3.

(L) "Miscellaneous Proceeds" means any compensation, settlement, award of damages, or proceeds paid by any third party (other than insurance proceeds paid under the coverages described in Section 5) for: (i) damage to, or destruction of, the Property; (ii) condemnation or other taking of all or any part of the Property; (iii) conveyance in lieu of condemnation; or (iv) misrepresentations of, or omissions as to, the value and/or condition of the Property.

(M) "Mortgage Insurance" means insurance protecting Lender against the nonpayment of, or default on, the Loan.

(N) "Periodic Payment" means the regularly scheduled amount due for (i) principal and interest under the Note, plus (ii) any amounts under Section 3 of this Security Instrument.

(O) "RESPA" means the Real Estate Settlement Procedures Act (12 U.S.C. §2601 et seq.) and its implementing regulation, Regulation X (24 C.F.R. Part 3500), as they might be amended from time to time, or any additional or successor legislation or regulation that governs the same subject matter. As used in this Security Instrument, "RESPA" refers to all requirements and restrictions that are imposed in regard to a "federally related mortgage loan" even if the Loan does not qualify as a "federally related mortgage loan" under RESPA.

(P) "Successor in Interest of Borrower" means any party that has taken title to the Property, whether or not that party has assumed Borrower's obligations under the Note and/or this Security Instrument.

TRANSFER OF RIGHTS IN THE PROPERTY

This Security Instrument secures to Lender: (i) the repayment of the Loan, and all renewals, extensions, and modifications of the Note; and (ii) the performance of Borrower's covenants and agreements under this Security Instrument and the Note. For this purpose, Borrower does hereby mortgage, grant, and convey to Lender, with power of sale, the following described property located

in the_____ of _____:
     [Type of Recording Jurisdiction]   [Name of Recording Jurisdiction]

which currently has the address of _____
                                                    [Street]

_____, Hawaii _____ ("Property Address"):
          [City]   [Zip Code]

TOGETHER WITH all the improvements now or hereafter erected on the property, and all easements, appurtenances, and fixtures now or hereafter a part of the property. All replacements and additions shall also be covered by this Security Instrument. All of the foregoing is referred to in this Security Instrument as the "Property."

BORROWER COVENANTS that Borrower is lawfully seised of the estate hereby conveyed and has the right to mortgage, grant, and convey the Property and that the Property is unencumbered, except for encumbrances of record. Borrower warrants and will defend generally the title to the Property against all claims and demands, subject to any encumbrances of record.

THIS SECURITY INSTRUMENT combines uniform covenants for national use and nonuniform covenants with limited variations by jurisdiction to constitute a uniform security instrument covering real property.

UNIFORM COVENANTS. Borrower and Lender covenant and agree as follows:

1. **Payment of Principal, Interest, Escrow Items, Prepayment Charges, and Late Charges.** Borrower shall pay when due the principal of, and interest on, the debt evidenced by the Note and any prepayment charges and late charges due under the Note. Borrower shall also pay funds for Escrow Items pursuant to Section 3. Payments due under the Note and this Security Instrument shall be made in U.S. currency. However, if any check or other instrument received by Lender as payment under the Note or this Security Instrument is returned to Lender unpaid, Lender may require that any or all subsequent payments due under the Note and this Security Instrument be made in one or more of the following forms, as selected by Lender: (a) cash; (b) money order; (c) certified check, bank check, treasurer's check, or cashier's check, provided any such check is drawn upon an institution whose deposits are insured by a federal agency, instrumentality, or entity; or (d) Electronic Funds Transfer.

Payments are deemed received by Lender when received at the location designated in the Note or at such other location as may be designated by Lender in accordance with the notice provisions in Section 15. Lender may return any payment or partial payment if the payment or partial payments are insufficient to bring the Loan current. Lender may accept any payment or partial payment insufficient to bring the Loan current, without waiver of any rights hereunder or prejudice to its rights to refuse such payment or partial payments in the future, but Lender is not obligated to apply such payments at the time such payments are accepted. If each Periodic Payment is applied as of its scheduled due date, then Lender need not pay interest on unapplied funds. Lender may hold such unapplied funds until Borrower makes payment to bring the Loan current. If Borrower does not do so within a reasonable period of time, Lender shall either apply such funds or return them to Borrower. If not applied earlier, such funds will be applied to the outstanding principal balance under the Note immediately prior to foreclosure. No offset or claim which Borrower might have now or in the future against Lender shall relieve Borrower from making payments due under the Note and this Security Instrument or performing the covenants and agreements secured by this Security Instrument.

2. **Application of Payments or Proceeds.** Except as otherwise described in this Section 2, all payments accepted and applied by Lender shall be applied in the following order of priority: (a) interest due under the Note; (b) principal due under the Note; (c) amounts due under Section 3. Such payments shall be applied to each Periodic Payment in the order in which it became due. Any remaining amounts shall be applied first to late charges, second to any other amounts due under this Security Instrument, and then to reduce the principal balance of the Note.

If Lender receives a payment from Borrower for a delinquent Periodic Payment which includes a sufficient amount to pay any late charge due, the payment may be applied to the delinquent payment and the late charge. If more than one Periodic Payment is outstanding, Lender may apply any payment received from Borrower to the repayment of the Periodic Payments if, and to the extent that, each payment can be paid in full. To the extent that any excess exists after the payment is applied to the full payment of one or more Periodic Payments, such excess may be applied to any late charges due. Voluntary prepayments shall be applied first to any prepayment charges and then as described in the Note.

Any application of payments, insurance proceeds, or Miscellaneous Proceeds to principal due under the Note shall not extend or postpone the due date, or change the amount, of the Periodic Payments.

3. **Funds for Escrow Items.** Borrower shall pay to Lender on the day Periodic Payments are due under the Note, until the Note is paid in full, a sum (the "Funds") to provide for payment of amounts due for: (a) taxes and assessments and other items which can attain priority over this Security Instrument as a lien or encumbrance on the Property; (b) leasehold payments or ground rents on the Property, if any; (c) premiums for any and all insurance required by Lender under Section 5; and (d) Mortgage Insurance premiums, if any, or any sums payable by Borrower to Lender in lieu of the payment of Mortgage Insurance premiums in accordance with the provisions of Section 10. These items are called "Escrow Items." At origination or at any time during the term of the Loan, Lender may require that Community Association Dues, Fees, and Assessments, if any, be escrowed by Borrower, and such dues, fees, and assessments shall be an Escrow Item. Borrower shall promptly furnish to Lender all notices of amounts to be paid under this Section. Borrower shall pay Lender the Funds for Escrow Items unless Lender waives Borrower's obligation to pay the Funds for any or all Escrow Items. Lender may waive Borrower's obligation to pay to Lender Funds for any or all Escrow Items at any time. Any such waiver may only be in writing. In the event of such waiver, Borrower shall pay directly, when and where payable, the amounts due for any Escrow Items for which payment of Funds has been waived by Lender and, if Lender requires, shall furnish to Lender receipts evidencing such payment within such time period as Lender may require. Borrower's obligation to make such payments and to provide receipts shall for all purposes be deemed to be a covenant and agreement

(continued)

EXHIBIT 10-5 *Continued*

contained in this Security Instrument, as the phrase "covenant and agreement" is used in Section 9. If Borrower is obligated to pay Escrow Items directly, pursuant to a waiver, and Borrower fails to pay the amount due for an Escrow Item, Lender may exercise its rights under Section 9 and pay such amount and Borrower shall then be obligated under Section 9 to repay to Lender any such amount. Lender may revoke the waiver as to any or all Escrow Items at any time by a notice given in accordance with Section 15 and, upon such revocation, Borrower shall pay to Lender all Funds, and in such amounts, that are then required under this Section 3.

Lender may, at any time, collect and hold Funds in an amount (a) sufficient to permit Lender to apply the Funds at the time specified under RESPA, and (b) not to exceed the maximum amount a lender can require under RESPA. Lender shall estimate the amount of Funds due on the basis of current data and reasonable estimates of expenditures of future Escrow Items or otherwise in accordance with Applicable Law.

The Funds shall be held in an institution whose deposits are insured by a federal agency, instrumentality, or entity (including Lender, if Lender is an institution whose deposits are so insured) or in any Federal Home Loan Bank. Lender shall apply the Funds to pay the Escrow Items no later than the time specified under RESPA. Lender shall not charge Borrower for holding and applying the Funds, annually analyzing the escrow account, or verifying the Escrow Items, unless Lender pays Borrower interest on the Funds and Applicable Law permits Lender to make such a charge. Unless an agreement is made in writing or Applicable Law requires interest to be paid on the Funds, Lender shall not be required to pay Borrower any interest or earnings on the Funds. Borrower and Lender can agree in writing, however, that interest shall be paid on the Funds. Lender shall give to Borrower, without charge, an annual accounting of the Funds as required by RESPA.

If there is a surplus of Funds held in escrow, as defined under RESPA, Lender shall account to Borrower for the excess funds in accordance with RESPA. If there is a shortage of Funds held in escrow, as defined under RESPA, Lender shall notify Borrower as required by RESPA, and Borrower shall pay to Lender the amount necessary to make up the shortage in accordance with RESPA, but in no more than 12 monthly payments. If there is a deficiency of Funds held in escrow, as defined under RESPA, Lender shall notify Borrower as required by RESPA, and Borrower shall pay to Lender the amount necessary to make up the deficiency in accordance with RESPA, but in no more than 12 monthly payments.

Upon payment in full of all sums secured by this Security Instrument, Lender shall promptly refund to Borrower any Funds held by Lender.

4. Charges; Liens. Borrower shall pay all taxes, assessments, charges, fines, and impositions attributable to the Property which can attain priority over this Security Instrument, leasehold payments, or ground rents on the Property, if any, and Community Association Dues, Fees, and Assessments, if any. To the extent that these items are Escrow Items, Borrower shall pay them in the manner provided in Section 3.

Borrower shall promptly discharge any lien which has priority over this Security Instrument unless Borrower: (a) agrees in writing to the payment of the obligation secured by the lien in a manner acceptable to Lender, but only so long as Borrower is performing such agreement; (b) contests the lien in good faith by, or defends against enforcement of the lien in, legal proceedings which in Lender's opinion operate to prevent the enforcement of the lien while those proceedings are pending, but only until such proceedings are concluded; or (c) secures from the holder of the lien an agreement satisfactory to Lender subordinating the lien to this Security Instrument. If Lender determines that any part of the Property is subject to a lien which can attain priority over this Security Instrument, Lender may give Borrower a notice identifying the lien. Within 10 days of the date on which that notice is given, Borrower shall satisfy the lien or take one or more of the actions set forth above in this Section 4.

Lender may require Borrower to pay a one-time charge for a real estate tax verification and/or reporting service used by Lender in connection with this Loan.

5. Property Insurance. Borrower shall keep the improvements now existing or hereafter erected on the Property insured against loss by fire, hazards included within the term "extended coverage," and any other hazards including, but not limited to, earthquakes and floods, for which Lender requires insurance. This insurance shall be maintained in the amounts (including deductible levels) and for the periods that Lender requires. What Lender requires pursuant to the preceding sentences can change during the term of the Loan. The insurance carrier providing the insurance shall be chosen by Borrower subject to Lender's right to disapprove Borrower's choice, which right shall not be exercised unreasonably. Lender may require Borrower to pay, in connection with this Loan, either: (a) a one-time charge for flood zone determination, certification and tracking services; or (b) a one-time charge for flood zone determination and certification services and subsequent charges each time remappings or similar changes occur which reasonably might affect such determination or certification. Borrower shall also be responsible for the payment of any fees imposed by the Federal Emergency Management Agency in connection with the review of any flood zone determination resulting from an objection by Borrower.

If Borrower fails to maintain any of the coverages described above, Lender may obtain insurance coverage, at Lender's option and Borrower's expense. Lender is under no obligation to purchase any particular type or amount of coverage. Therefore, such coverage shall cover Lender, but might or might not protect Borrower, Borrower's equity in the Property, or the contents of the Property, against any risk, hazard, or liability and might provide greater or lesser coverage than was previously in effect. Borrower acknowledges that the cost of the insurance coverage so obtained might significantly exceed the cost of insurance that Borrower could have obtained. Any amounts disbursed by Lender under this Section 5 shall become additional debt of Borrower secured by this Security Instrument. These amounts shall bear interest at the Note rate from the date of disbursement and shall be payable, with such interest, upon notice from Lender to Borrower requesting payment.

All insurance policies required by Lender and renewals of such policies shall be subject to Lender's right to disapprove such policies, shall include a standard mortgage clause, and shall name Lender as mortgagee and/or as an additional loss payee. Lender shall have the right to hold the policies and renewal certificates. If Lender requires, Borrower shall promptly give to Lender all receipts of paid premiums and renewal notices. If Borrower obtains any form of insurance coverage, not otherwise required by Lender, for damage to, or destruction of, the Property, such policy shall include a standard mortgage clause and shall name Lender as mortgagee and/or as an additional loss payee.

In the event of loss, Borrower shall give prompt notice to the insurance carrier and Lender. Lender may make proof of loss if not made promptly by Borrower. Unless Lender and Borrower otherwise agree in writing, any insurance proceeds, whether or not the underlying insurance was required by Lender, shall be applied to restoration or repair of the Property, if the restoration or repair is economically feasible and Lender's security is not lessened. During such repair and restoration period, Lender shall have the right to hold such insurance proceeds until Lender has had an opportunity to inspect such Property to ensure the work has been completed to Lender's satisfaction, provided that such inspection shall be undertaken promptly. Lender may disburse proceeds for the repairs and restoration in a single payment or in a series of progress payments as the work is completed. Unless an agreement is made in writing or Applicable Law requires interest to be paid on such insurance proceeds, Lender shall not be required to pay Borrower any interest or earnings on such proceeds. Fees for public adjusters, or other third parties, retained by Borrower shall not be paid out of the insurance proceeds and shall be the sole obligation of Borrower. If the restoration or repair is not economically feasible or Lender's security would be lessened, the insurance proceeds shall be applied to the sums secured by this Security Instrument, whether or not then due, with the excess, if any, paid to Borrower. Such insurance proceeds shall be applied in the order provided for in Section 2.

If Borrower abandons the Property, Lender may file, negotiate, and settle any available insurance claim and related matters. If Borrower does not respond within 30 days to a notice from Lender that the insurance carrier has offered to settle a claim, then Lender may negotiate and settle the claim. The 30-day period will begin when the notice is given. In either event, or if Lender acquires the Property under Section 22 or otherwise, Borrower hereby assigns to Lender (a) Borrower's rights to any insurance proceeds in an amount not to exceed the amounts unpaid under the Note or this Security Instrument, and (b) any other of Borrower's rights (other than the right to any refund of unearned premiums paid by Borrower) under all insurance policies covering the Property, insofar as such rights are applicable to the coverage of the Property. Lender may use the insurance proceeds either to repair or restore the Property or to pay amounts unpaid under the Note or this Security Instrument, whether or not then due.

6. Occupancy. Borrower shall occupy, establish, and use the Property as Borrower's principal residence within 60 days after the execution of this Security Instrument and shall continue to occupy the Property as Borrower's principal residence for at least one year after the date of occupancy, unless Lender otherwise agrees in writing, which consent shall not be unreasonably withheld, or unless extenuating circumstances exist which are beyond Borrower's control.

7. Preservation, Maintenance, and Protection of the Property; Inspections. Borrower shall not destroy, damage, or impair the Property; allow the Property to deteriorate; or commit waste on the Property. Whether or not Borrower is residing in the Property, Borrower shall maintain the Property in order to prevent the Property from deteriorating or decreasing in value due to its condition. Unless it is determined pursuant to Section 5 that repair or restoration is not economically feasible, Borrower shall promptly repair the Property if damaged to avoid further deterioration or damage. If insurance or condemnation proceeds are paid in connection with damage to, or the taking of, the Property, Borrower shall be responsible for repairing or restoring the Property only if Lender has released proceeds for such purposes. Lender may disburse proceeds for the repairs and restoration in a single payment or in a series of progress payments as the work is completed. If the insurance or condemnation proceeds are not sufficient to repair or restore the Property, Borrower is not relieved of Borrower's obligation for the completion of such repair or restoration.

Lender or its agent may make reasonable entries upon and inspections of the Property. If it has reasonable cause, Lender may inspect the interior of the improvements on the Property. Lender shall give Borrower notice at the time of or prior to such an interior inspection specifying such reasonable cause.

8. Borrower's Loan Application. Borrower shall be in default if, during the Loan application process, Borrower or any persons or entities acting at the direction of Borrower or with Borrower's knowledge or consent gave materially false, misleading, or inaccurate information or statements to Lender (or failed to provide Lender with material information) in connection with the Loan. Material representations include, but are not limited to, representations concerning Borrower's occupancy of the Property as Borrower's principal residence.

(continued)

EXHIBIT 10-5 *Continued*

9. Protection of Lender's Interest in the Property and Rights Under this Security Instrument. If (a) Borrower fails to perform the covenants and agreements contained in this Security Instrument, (b) there is a legal proceeding that might significantly affect Lender's interest in the Property and/or rights under this Security Instrument (such as a proceeding in bankruptcy, probate, for condemnation or forfeiture, for enforcement of a lien which may attain priority over this Security Instrument or to enforce laws or regulations), or (c) Borrower has abandoned the Property, then Lender may do and pay for whatever is reasonable or appropriate to protect Lender's interest in the Property and rights under this Security Instrument, including protecting and/or assessing the value of the Property, and securing and/or repairing the Property. Lender's actions can include, but are not limited to: (a) paying any sums secured by a lien which has priority over this Security Instrument; (b) appearing in court; and (c) paying reasonable attorneys' fees to protect its interest in the Property and/or rights under this Security Instrument, including its secured position in a bankruptcy proceeding. Securing the Property includes, but is not limited to, entering the Property to make repairs, change locks, replace or board up doors and windows, drain water from pipes, eliminate building or other code violations or dangerous conditions, and have utilities turned on or off. Although Lender may take action under this Section 9, Lender does not have to do so and is not under any duty or obligation to do so. It is agreed that Lender incurs no liability for not taking any or all actions authorized under this Section 9.

Any amounts disbursed by Lender under this Section 9 shall become additional debt of Borrower secured by this Security Instrument. These amounts shall bear interest at the Note rate from the date of disbursement and shall be payable, with such interest, upon notice from Lender to Borrower requesting payment.

If this Security Instrument is on a leasehold, Borrower shall comply with all the provisions of the lease. If Borrower acquires fee title to the Property, the leasehold and the fee title shall not merge unless Lender agrees to the merger in writing.

10. Mortgage Insurance. If Lender required Mortgage Insurance as a condition of making the Loan, Borrower shall pay the premiums required to maintain the Mortgage Insurance in effect. If, for any reason, the Mortgage Insurance coverage required by Lender ceases to be available from the mortgage insurer that previously provided such insurance and Borrower was required to make separately designated payments toward the premiums for Mortgage Insurance, Borrower shall pay the premiums required to obtain coverage substantially equivalent to the Mortgage Insurance previously in effect, at a cost substantially equivalent to the cost to Borrower of the Mortgage Insurance previously in effect, from an alternate mortgage insurer selected by Lender. If substantially equivalent Mortgage Insurance coverage is not available, Borrower shall continue to pay to Lender the amount of the separately designated payments that were due when the insurance coverage ceased to be in effect. Lender will accept, use, and retain these payments as a non-refundable loss reserve in lieu of Mortgage Insurance. Such loss reserve shall be non-refundable, notwithstanding the fact that the Loan is ultimately paid in full, and Lender shall not be required to pay Borrower any interest or earnings on such loss reserve. Lender can no longer require loss reserve payments if Mortgage Insurance coverage (in the amount and for the period that Lender requires) provided by an insurer selected by Lender again becomes available, is obtained, and Lender requires separately designated payments toward the premiums for Mortgage Insurance. If Lender required Mortgage Insurance as a condition of making the Loan and Borrower was required to make separately designated payments toward the premiums for Mortgage Insurance, Borrower shall pay the premiums required to maintain Mortgage Insurance in effect, or to provide a non-refundable loss reserve, until Lender's requirement for Mortgage Insurance ends in accordance with any written agreement between Borrower and Lender providing for such termination or until termination is required by Applicable Law. Nothing in this Section 10 affects Borrower's obligation to pay interest at the rate provided in the Note.

Mortgage Insurance reimburses Lender (or any entity that purchases the Note) for certain losses it may incur if Borrower does not repay the Loan as agreed. Borrower is not a party to the Mortgage Insurance.

Mortgage insurers evaluate their total risk on all such insurance in force from time to time, and may enter into agreements with other parties that share or modify their risk, or reduce losses. These agreements are on terms and conditions that are satisfactory to the mortgage insurer and the other party (or parties) to these agreements. These agreements may require the mortgage insurer to make payments using any source of funds that the mortgage insurer may have available (which may include funds obtained from Mortgage Insurance premiums).

As a result of these agreements, Lender, any purchaser of the Note, another insurer, any reinsurer, any other entity, or any affiliate or any of the foregoing, may receive (directly or indirectly) amounts that derive from (or might be characterized as) a portion of Borrower's payments for Mortgage Insurance, in exchange for sharing or modifying the mortgage insurer's risk, or reducing losses. If such agreement provides that an affiliate of Lender takes a share of the insurer's risk in exchange for a share of the premiums paid to the insurer, the arrangement is often termed "captive reinsurance." Further:

(a) Any such agreements will not affect the amounts that Borrower has agreed to pay for Mortgage Insurance, or any other terms of the Loan. Such agreements will not increase the amount Borrower will owe for Mortgage Insurance, and they will not entitle Borrower to any refund.

(b) Any such agreements will not affect the rights Borrower has – if any – with respect to the Mortgage Insurance under the Homeowners Protection Act of 1998 or any other law. These rights may include the right to receive certain disclosures, to request and obtain cancellation of the Mortgage Insurance, to have the Mortgage Insurance terminated automatically, and/or to receive a refund of any Mortgage Insurance premiums that were unearned at the time of such cancellation or termination.

11. **Assignment of Miscellaneous Proceeds; Forfeiture.** All Miscellaneous Proceeds are hereby assigned to and shall be paid to Lender.

If the Property is damaged, such Miscellaneous Proceeds shall be applied to restoration or repair of the Property, if the restoration or repair is economically feasible and Lender's security is not lessened. During such repair and restoration period, Lender shall have the right to hold such Miscellaneous Proceeds until Lender has had an opportunity to inspect such Property to ensure the work has been completed to Lender's satisfaction, provided that such inspection shall be undertaken promptly. Lender may pay for the repairs and restoration in a single disbursement or in a series of progress payments as the work is completed. Unless an agreement is made in writing or Applicable Law requires interest to be paid on such Miscellaneous Proceeds, Lender shall not be required to pay Borrower any interest or earnings on such Miscellaneous Proceeds. If the restoration or repair is not economically feasible or Lender's security would be lessened, the Miscellaneous Proceeds shall be applied to the sums secured by this Security Instrument, whether or not then due, with the excess, if any, paid to Borrower. Such Miscellaneous Proceeds shall be applied in the order provided for in Section 2.

In the event of a total taking, destruction, or loss in value of the Property, the Miscellaneous Proceeds shall be applied to the sums secured by this Security Instrument, whether or not then due, with the excess, if any, paid to Borrower.

In the event of a partial taking, destruction, or loss in value of the Property in which the fair market value of the Property immediately before the partial taking, destruction, or loss in value is equal to or greater than the amount of the sums secured by this Security Instrument immediately before the partial taking, destruction, or loss in value, unless Borrower and Lender otherwise agree in writing, the sums secured by this Security Instrument shall be reduced by the amount of the Miscellaneous Proceeds multiplied by the following fraction: (a) the total amount of the sums secured immediately before the partial taking, destruction, or loss in value divided by (b) the fair market value of the Property immediately before the partial taking, destruction, or loss in value. Any balance shall be paid to Borrower.

In the event of a partial taking, destruction, or loss in value of the Property in which the fair market value of the Property immediately before the partial taking, destruction, or loss in value is less than the amount of the sums secured immediately before the partial taking, destruction, or loss in value, unless Borrower and Lender otherwise agree in writing, the Miscellaneous Proceeds shall be applied to the sums secured by this Security Instrument whether or not the sums are then due.

If the Property is abandoned by Borrower, or if, after notice by Lender to Borrower that the Opposing Party (as defined in the next sentence) offers to make an award to settle a claim for damages, Borrower fails to respond to Lender within 30 days after the date the notice is given, Lender is authorized to collect and apply the Miscellaneous Proceeds either to restoration or repair of the Property or to the sums secured by this Security Instrument, whether or not then due. "Opposing Party" means the third party that owes Borrower Miscellaneous Proceeds or the party against whom Borrower has a right of action in regard to Miscellaneous Proceeds.

Borrower shall be in default if any action or proceeding, whether civil or criminal, is begun that, in Lender's judgment, could result in forfeiture of the Property or other material impairment of Lender's interest in the Property or rights under this Security Instrument. Borrower can cure such a default and, if acceleration has occurred, reinstate as provided in Section 19, by causing the action or proceeding to be dismissed with a ruling that, in Lender's judgment, precludes forfeiture of the Property or other material impairment of Lender's interest in the Property or rights under this Security Instrument. The proceeds of any award or claim for damages that are attributable to the impairment of Lender's interest in the Property are hereby assigned and shall be paid to Lender.

All Miscellaneous Proceeds that are not applied to restoration or repair of the Property shall be applied in the order provided for in Section 2.

12. **Borrower Not Released; Forbearance By Lender Not a Waiver.** Extension of the time for payment or modification of amortization of the sums secured by this Security Instrument granted by Lender to Borrower or any Successor in Interest of Borrower shall not operate to release the liability of Borrower or any Successors in Interest of Borrower. Lender shall not be required to commence proceedings against any Successor in Interest of Borrower or to refuse to extend time for payment or otherwise modify amortization of the sums secured by this Security Instrument by reason of any demand made by the original Borrower or any Successors in Interest of Borrower. Any forbearance by Lender in exercising any right or remedy including, without limitation, Lender's acceptance of payments from third persons, entities, or Successors in Interest of Borrower or in amounts less than the amount then due, shall not be a waiver of or preclude the exercise of any right or remedy.

13. **Joint and Several Liability; Co-signers; Successors and Assigns Bound.** Borrower covenants and agrees that Borrower's obligations and liability shall be joint and several. However, any Borrower who co-signs this Security Instrument but does not execute the Note (a "co-signer"): (a) is co-signing this Security Instrument only to mortgage, grant, and convey the co-signer's interest in the Property under the terms of this Security Instrument; (b) is not personally obligated to pay the sums secured by this Security Instrument; and (c) agrees that Lender and any other Borrower can agree to extend, modify, forbear, or make any accommodations with regard to the terms of this Security Instrument or the Note without the co-signer's consent.

Subject to the provisions of Section 18, any Successor in Interest of Borrower who assumes Borrower's obligations under this Security Instrument in writing, and is approved by Lender, shall obtain all of Borrower's rights and benefits under this Security Instrument. Borrower shall not be released from Borrower's obligations and liability under this Security Instrument unless Lender agrees to such release in writing. The covenants and agreements of this Security Instrument shall bind (except as provided in Section 20) and benefit the successors and assigns of Lender.

(continued)

EXHIBIT 10-5 *Continued*

14. Loan Charges. Lender may charge Borrower fees for services performed in connection with Borrower's default, for the purpose of protecting Lender's interest in the Property and rights under this Security Instrument, including, but not limited to, attorneys' fees, property inspection, and valuation fees. In regard to any other fees, the absence of express authority in this Security Instrument to charge a specific fee to Borrower shall not be construed as a prohibition on the charging of such fee. Lender may not charge fees that are expressly prohibited by this Security Instrument or by Applicable Law.

If the Loan is subject to a law which sets maximum loan charges, and that law is finally interpreted so that the interest or other loan charges collected or to be collected in connection with the Loan exceed the permitted limits, then: (a) any such loan charge shall be reduced by the amount necessary to reduce the charge to the permitted limit; and (b) any sums already collected from Borrower which exceeded permitted limits will be refunded to Borrower. Lender may choose to make this refund by reducing the principal owed under the Note or by making a direct payment to Borrower. If a refund reduces principal, the reduction will be treated as a partial prepayment without any prepayment charge (whether or not a prepayment charge is provided for under the Note). Borrower's acceptance of any such refund made by direct payment to Borrower will constitute a waiver of any right of action Borrower might have arising out of such overcharge.

15. Notices. All notices given by Borrower or Lender in connection with this Security Instrument must be in writing. Any notice to Borrower in connection with this Security Instrument shall be deemed to have been given to Borrower when mailed by first class mail or when actually delivered to Borrower's notice address if sent by other means. Notice to any one Borrower shall constitute notice to all Borrowers unless Applicable Law expressly requires otherwise. The notice address shall be the Property Address unless Borrower has designated a substitute notice address by notice to Lender. Borrower shall promptly notify Lender of Borrower's change of address. If Lender specifies a procedure for reporting Borrower's change of address, then Borrower shall only report a change of address through that specified procedure. There may be only one designated notice address under this Security Instrument at any one time. Any notice to Lender shall be given by delivering it or by mailing it by first class mail to Lender's address stated herein unless Lender has designated another address by notice to Borrower. Any notice in connection with this Security Instrument shall not be deemed to have been given to Lender until actually received by Lender. If any notice required by this Security Instrument is also required under Applicable Law, the Applicable Law requirement will satisfy the corresponding requirement under this Security Instrument.

16. Governing Law; Severability; Rules of Construction. This Security Instrument shall be governed by federal law and the law of the jurisdiction in which the Property is located. All rights and obligations contained in this Security Instrument are subject to any requirements and limitations of Applicable Law. Applicable Law might explicitly or implicitly allow the parties to agree by contract or it might be silent, but such silence shall not be construed as a prohibition against agreement by contract. In the event that any provision or clause of this Security Instrument or the Note conflicts with Applicable Law, such conflict shall not affect other provisions of this Security Instrument or the Note which can be given effect without the conflicting provision.

As used in this Security Instrument: (a) words of the masculine gender shall mean and include corresponding neuter words or words of the feminine gender; (b) words in the singular shall mean and include the plural and vice versa; and (c) the word "may" gives sole discretion without any obligation to take any action.

17. Borrower's Copy. Borrower shall be given one copy of the Note and of this Security Instrument.

18. Transfer of the Property or a Beneficial Interest in Borrower. As used in this Section 18, "Interest in the Property" means any legal or beneficial interest in the Property, including, but not limited to, those beneficial interests transferred in a bond for deed, contract for deed, installment sales contract, or escrow agreement, the intent of which is the transfer of title by Borrower at a future date to a purchaser.

If all or any part of the Property or any Interest in the Property is sold or transferred (or if Borrower is not a natural person and a beneficial interest in Borrower is sold or transferred) without Lender's prior written consent, Lender may require immediate payment in full of all sums secured by this Security Instrument. However, this option shall not be exercised by Lender if such exercise is prohibited by Applicable Law.

If Lender exercises this option, Lender shall give Borrower notice of acceleration. The notice shall provide a period of not less than 30 days from the date the notice is given in accordance with Section 15 within which Borrower must pay all sums secured by this Security Instrument. If Borrower fails to pay these sums prior to the expiration of this period, Lender may invoke any remedies permitted by this Security Instrument without further notice or demand on Borrower.

19. Borrower's Right to Reinstate After Acceleration. If Borrower meets certain conditions, Borrower shall have the right to have enforcement of this Security Instrument discontinued at any time prior to the earliest of: (a) five days before sale of the Property pursuant to any power of sale contained in this Security Instrument; (b) such other period as Applicable Law might specify for the termination of Borrower's right to reinstate; or (c) entry of a judgment enforcing this Security Instrument. Those conditions are that Borrower: (a) pays Lender all sums which then would be due under this Security Instrument and the Note as if no acceleration had occurred; (b) cures any default of any other covenants or agreements; (c) pays all expenses incurred in enforcing this Security Instrument, including, but not limited to, reasonable attorneys' fees, property inspection and valuation fees, and other fees incurred for the purpose of protecting Lender's interest in the Property and rights under this Security Instrument; and (d) takes such action as Lender may reasonably require to assure that Lender's interest in the Property and rights under this Security Instrument, and Borrower's obligation to pay the sums secured by this Security Instrument, shall continue unchanged. Lender may require that Borrower pay such reinstatement sums and expenses in one or more of the following forms, as selected by Lender: (a) cash; (b) money order; (c) certified check, bank check, treasurer's check, or cashier's check, provided any such check is drawn upon an institution whose deposits are insured by a federal agency, instrumentality or entity; or (d) Electronic Funds Transfer. Upon reinstatement by Borrower, this Security Instrument and obligations secured hereby shall remain fully effective as if no acceleration had occurred. However, this right to reinstate shall not apply in the case of acceleration under Section 18.

20. Sale of Note; Change of Loan Servicer; Notice of Grievance. The Note or a partial interest in the Note (together with this Security Instrument) can be sold one or more times without prior notice to Borrower. A sale might result in a change in the entity (known as the "Loan Servicer") that collects Periodic Payments due under the Note and this Security Instrument and performs other mortgage loan servicing obligations under the Note, this Security Instrument, and Applicable Law. There also might be one or more changes of the Loan Servicer unrelated to a sale of the Note. If there is a change of the Loan Servicer, Borrower will be given written notice of the change which will state the name and address of the new Loan Servicer, the address to which payments should be made and any other information RESPA requires in connection with a notice of transfer of servicing. If the Note is sold and thereafter the Loan is serviced by a Loan Servicer other than the purchaser of the Note, the mortgage loan servicing obligations to Borrower will remain with the Loan Servicer or be transferred to a successor Loan Servicer and are not assumed by the Note purchaser unless otherwise provided by the Note purchaser.

Neither Borrower nor Lender may commence, join, or be joined to any judicial action (as either an individual litigant or the member of a class) that arises from the other party's actions pursuant to this Security Instrument or that alleges that the other party has breached any provision of, or any duty owed by reason of, this Security Instrument, until such Borrower or Lender has notified the other party (with such notice given in compliance with the requirements of Section 15) of such alleged breach and afforded the other party hereto a reasonable period after the giving of such notice to take corrective action. If Applicable Law provides a time period which must elapse before certain action can be taken, that time period will be deemed to be reasonable for purposes of this paragraph. The notice of acceleration and opportunity to cure given to Borrower pursuant to Section 22 and the notice of acceleration given to Borrower pursuant to Section 18 shall be deemed to satisfy the notice and opportunity to take corrective action provisions of this Section 20.

21. Hazardous Substances. As used in this Section 21: (a) "Hazardous Substances" are those substances defined as toxic or hazardous substances, pollutants, or wastes by Environmental Law and the following substances: gasoline, kerosene, other flammable or toxic petroleum products, toxic pesticides and herbicides, volatile solvents, materials containing asbestos or formaldehyde, and radioactive materials; (b) "Environmental Law" means federal laws and laws of the jurisdiction where the Property is located that relate to health, safety, or environmental protection; (c) "Environmental Cleanup" includes any response action, remedial action, or removal action, as defined in Environmental Law; and (d) an "Environmental Condition" means a condition that can cause, contribute to, or otherwise trigger an Environmental Cleanup.

Borrower shall not cause or permit the presence, use, disposal, storage, or release of any Hazardous Substances, or threaten to release any Hazardous Substances, on or in the Property. Borrower shall not do, nor allow anyone else to do, anything affecting the Property (a) that is in violation of any Environmental Law, (b) which creates an Environmental Condition, or (c) which, due to the presence, use, or release of a Hazardous Substance, creates a condition that adversely affects the value of the Property. The preceding two sentences shall not apply to the presence, use, or storage on the Property of small quantities of Hazardous Substances that are generally recognized to be appropriate to normal residential uses and to maintenance of the Property (including, but not limited to, hazardous substances in consumer products).

Borrower shall promptly give Lender written notice of (a) any investigation, claim, demand, lawsuit, or other action by any governmental or regulatory agency or private party involving the Property and any Hazardous Substance or Environmental Law of which Borrower has actual knowledge, (b) any Environmental Condition, including but not limited to, any spilling, leaking, discharge, release or threat of release of any Hazardous Substance, and (c) any condition caused by the presence, use or release of a Hazardous Substance which adversely affects the value of the Property. If Borrower learns, or is notified by any governmental or regulatory authority, or any private party, that any removal or other remediation of any Hazardous Substance affecting the Property is necessary, Borrower shall promptly take all necessary remedial actions in accordance with Environmental Law. Nothing herein shall create any obligation on Lender for an Environmental Cleanup.

(continued)

EXHIBIT 10-5 *Continued*

NON-UNIFORM COVENANTS. Borrower and Lender further covenant and agree as follows:

22. Acceleration; Remedies. Lender shall give notice to Borrower prior to acceleration following Borrower's breach of any covenant or agreement in this Security Instrument (but not prior to acceleration under Section 18 unless Applicable Law provides otherwise). The notice shall specify: (a) the default; (b) the action required to cure the default; (c) a date, not less than 30 days from the date the notice is given to Borrower, by which the default must be cured; and (d) that failure to cure the default on or before the date specified in the notice may result in acceleration of the sums secured by this Security Instrument and sale of the Property. The notice shall further inform Borrower of the right to reinstate after acceleration and the right to bring a court action to assert the non-existence of a default or any other defense of Borrower to acceleration and sale. If the default is not cured on or before the date specified in the notice, Lender at its option may require immediate payment in full of all sums secured by this Security Instrument without further demand and may invoke the power of sale and any other remedies permitted by Applicable Law. Lender shall be entitled to collect all expenses incurred in pursuing the remedies provided in this Section 22, including, but not limited to, reasonable attorneys' fees and costs of title evidence.

If Lender invokes the power of sale, Lender shall give Borrower notice of sale in the manner provided in Section 15. Lender shall publish a notice of sale and shall sell the Property at the time and place and under the terms specified in the notice of sale. Lender or its designee may purchase the Property at any sale. The proceeds of the sale shall be applied in the following order: (a) to all expenses of the sale, including, but not limited to, reasonable attorneys' fees; (b) to all sums secured by this Security Instrument; and (c) any excess to the person or persons legally entitled to it.

23. Release. Upon payment of all sums secured by this Security Instrument, Lender shall release this Security Instrument. Borrower shall pay any recordation costs. Lender may charge Borrower a fee for releasing this Security Instrument, but only if the fee is paid to a third party for services rendered and the charging of the fee is permitted under Applicable Law.

24. Waivers. Borrower relinquishes all right of dower and curtesy in the Property.

BY SIGNING BELOW, Borrower accepts and agrees to the terms and covenants contained in this Security Instrument and in any Rider executed by Borrower and recorded with it.

_____   _____ (Seal)
                Witness   Borrower

_____   _____ (Seal)
                Witness   Borrower

_____ [Space Below This Line For Acknowledgment] _____

EXHIBIT 10-6 Deed of Trust

After Recording Return To:

_____

_____

_____

_____

_____ [Space Above This Line For Recording Data] _____

DEED OF TRUST

DEFINITIONS

Words used in multiple sections of this document are defined below and other words are defined in Sections 3, 11, 13, 18, 20 and 21. Certain rules regarding the usage of words used in this document are also provided in Section 16.

(A) "Security Instrument" means this document, which is dated _____,
_____, together with all Riders to this document.

(B) "Borrower" is _____. Borrower is the trustor under this Security Instrument. Borrower's mailing address is _____.

(C) "Lender" is _____. Lender is a _____
_____ organized and existing under the laws of _____
_____. Lender's mailing address is _____.
Lender is the beneficiary under this Security Instrument.

(D) "Trustee" is _____. Trustee's mailing address is _____
_____.

(E) "Note" means the promissory note signed by Borrower and dated _____,
_____. The Note states that Borrower owes Lender _____
_____ Dollars (U.S. $_____
_____) plus interest. Borrower has promised to pay this debt in regular Periodic Payments and to pay the debt in full not later than _____.

(F) "Property" means the property that is described below under the heading "Transfer of Rights in the Property."

(G) "Loan" means the debt evidenced by the Note, plus interest, any prepayment charges and late charges due under the Note, and all sums due under this Security Instrument, plus interest.

(H) "Riders" means all Riders to this Security Instrument that are executed by Borrower. The following Riders are to be executed by Borrower [check box as applicable]:

☐ Adjustable Rate Rider	☐ Condominium Rider	☐ Second Home Rider
☐ Balloon Rider	☐ Planned Unit Development Rider	☐ Other(s) [specify] _____
☐ 1–4 Family Rider	☐ Biweekly Payment Rider	

(continued)

EXHIBIT 10-6 *Continued*

(I) "**Applicable Law**" means all controlling applicable federal, state, and local statutes, regulations, ordinances, and administrative rules and orders (that have the effect of law) as well as all applicable final, non-appealable judicial opinions.

(J) "**Community Association Dues, Fees, and Assessments**" means all dues, fees, assessments and other charges that are imposed on Borrower or the Property by a condominium association, homeowners association, or similar organization.

(K) "**Electronic Funds Transfer**" means any transfer of funds, other than a transaction originated by check, draft, or similar paper instrument, which is initiated through an electronic terminal, telephonic instrument, computer, or magnetic tape so as to order, instruct, or authorize a financial institution to debit or credit an account. Such term includes, but is not limited to, point-of-sale transfers, automated teller machine transactions, transfers initiated by telephone, wire transfers, and automated clearinghouse transfers.

(L) "**Escrow Items**" means those items that are described in Section 3.

(M) "**Miscellaneous Proceeds**" means any compensation, settlement, award of damages, or proceeds paid by any third party (other than insurance proceeds paid under the coverages described in Section 5) for: (i) damage to, or destruction of, the Property; (ii) condemnation or other taking of all or any part of the Property; (iii) conveyance in lieu of condemnation; or (iv) misrepresentations of, or omissions as to, the value and/or condition of the Property.

(N) "**Mortgage Insurance**" means insurance protecting Lender against the nonpayment of, or default on, the Loan.

(O) "**Periodic Payment**" means the regularly scheduled amount due for (i) principal and interest under the Note, plus (ii) any amounts under Section 3 of this Security Instrument.

(P) "**RESPA**" means the Real Estate Settlement Procedures Act (12 U.S.C. §2601 et seq.) and its implementing regulation, Regulation X (24 C.F.R. Part 3500), as they might be amended from time to time, or any additional or successor legislation or regulation that governs the same subject matter. As used in this Security Instrument, "RESPA" refers to all requirements and restrictions that are imposed in regard to a "federally related mortgage loan" even if the Loan does not qualify as a "federally related mortgage loan" under RESPA.

(Q) "**Successor in Interest of Borrower**" means any party that has taken title to the Property, whether or not that party has assumed Borrower's obligations under the Note and/or this Security Instrument.

TRANSFER OF RIGHTS IN THE PROPERTY

This Security Instrument secures to Lender: (i) the repayment of the Loan, and all renewals, extensions, and modifications of the Note; and (ii) the performance of Borrower's covenants and agreements under this Security Instrument and the Note. For this purpose, Borrower irrevocably grants and conveys to Trustee, in trust, with power of sale, the following described property located in the

_____ of _____:
   [Type of Recording Jurisdiction]   [Name of Recording Jurisdiction]

which currently has the address of _____
                                                                    [Street]

_____, Arizona _____ ("Property Address"):
                            [City]   [Zip Code]

TOGETHER WITH all the improvements now or hereafter erected on the property, and all easements, appurtenances, and fixtures now or hereafter a part of the property. All replacements and additions shall also be covered by this Security Instrument. All of the foregoing is referred to in this Security Instrument as the "Property."

BORROWER COVENANTS that Borrower is lawfully seised of the estate hereby conveyed and has the right to grant and convey the Property and that the Property is unencumbered, except for encumbrances of record. Borrower warrants and will defend generally the title to the Property against all claims and demands, subject to any encumbrances of record.

THIS SECURITY INSTRUMENT combines uniform covenants for national use and non-uniform covenants with limited variations by jurisdiction to constitute a uniform security instrument covering real property.

UNIFORM COVENANTS. Borrower and Lender covenant and agree as follows:

1. **Payment of Principal, Interest, Escrow Items, Prepayment Charges, and Late Charges.** Borrower shall pay when due the principal of, and interest on, the debt evidenced by the Note and any prepayment charges and late charges due under the Note. Borrower shall also pay funds for Escrow Items pursuant to Section 3. Payments due under the Note and this Security Instrument shall be made in U.S. currency. However, if any check or other instrument received by Lender as payment under the Note or this Security Instrument is returned to Lender unpaid, Lender may require that any or all subsequent payments due under the Note and this Security Instrument be made in one or more of the following forms, as selected by Lender: (a) cash; (b) money order; (c) certified check, bank check, treasurer's check, or cashier's check, provided any such check is drawn upon an institution whose deposits are insured by a federal agency, instrumentality, or entity; or (d) Electronic Funds Transfer.

Payments are deemed received by Lender when received at the location designated in the Note or at such other location as may be designated by Lender in accordance with the notice provisions in Section 15. Lender may return any payment or partial payment if the payment or partial payments are insufficient to bring the Loan current. Lender may accept any payment or partial payment insufficient to bring the Loan current, without waiver of any rights hereunder or prejudice to its rights to refuse such payment or partial payments in the future, but Lender is not obligated to apply such payments at the time such payments are accepted. If each Periodic Payment is applied as of its scheduled due date, then Lender need not pay interest on unapplied funds. Lender may hold such unapplied funds until Borrower makes payment to bring the Loan current. If Borrower does not do so within a reasonable period of time, Lender shall either apply such funds or return them to Borrower. If not applied earlier, such funds will be applied to the outstanding principal balance under the Note immediately prior to foreclosure. No offset or claim which Borrower might have now or in the future against Lender shall relieve Borrower from making payments due under the Note and this Security Instrument or performing the covenants and agreements secured by this Security Instrument.

2. **Application of Payments or Proceeds.** Except as otherwise described in this Section 2, all payments accepted and applied by Lender shall be applied in the following order of priority: (a) interest due under the Note; (b) principal due under the Note; (c) amounts due under Section 3. Such payments shall be applied to each Periodic Payment in the order in which it became due. Any remaining amounts shall be applied first to late charges, second to any other amounts due under this Security Instrument, and then to reduce the principal balance of the Note.

If Lender receives a payment from Borrower for a delinquent Periodic Payment which includes a sufficient amount to pay any late charge due, the payment may be applied to the delinquent payment and the late charge. If more than one Periodic Payment is outstanding, Lender may apply any payment received from Borrower to the repayment of the Periodic Payments if, and to the extent that, each payment can be paid in full. To the extent that any excess exists after the payment is applied to the full payment of one or more Periodic Payments, such excess may be applied to any late charges due. Voluntary prepayments shall be applied first to any prepayment charges and then as described in the Note.

Any application of payments, insurance proceeds, or Miscellaneous Proceeds to principal due under the Note shall not extend or postpone the due date, or change the amount, of the Periodic Payments.

3. **Funds for Escrow Items.** Borrower shall pay to Lender on the day Periodic Payments are due under the Note, until the Note is paid in full, a sum (the "Funds") to provide for payment of amounts due for: (a) taxes and assessments and other items which can attain priority over this Security Instrument as a lien or encumbrance on the Property; (b) leasehold payments or ground rents on the Property, if any; (c) premiums for any and all insurance required by Lender under Section 5; and (d) Mortgage Insurance premiums, if any, or any sums payable by Borrower to Lender in lieu of the payment of Mortgage Insurance premiums in accordance with the provisions of Section 10. These items are called "Escrow Items." At origination or at any time during the term of the Loan, Lender may require that Community Association Dues, Fees, and Assessments, if any, be escrowed by Borrower, and such dues, fees, and assessments shall be an Escrow Item. Borrower shall promptly furnish to Lender all notices of amounts to be paid under this Section. Borrower shall pay Lender the Funds for Escrow Items unless Lender waives Borrower's obligation to pay the Funds for any or all Escrow Items. Lender may waive Borrower's obligation to pay to Lender Funds for any or all Escrow Items at any time. Any such waiver may only be in writing. In the event of such waiver, Borrower

(continued)

EXHIBIT 10-6 *Continued*

shall pay directly, when and where payable, the amounts due for any Escrow Items for which payment of Funds has been waived by Lender and, if Lender requires, shall furnish to Lender receipts evidencing such payment within such time period as Lender may require. Borrower's obligation to make such payments and to provide receipts shall for all purposes be deemed to be a covenant and agreement contained in this Security Instrument, as the phrase "covenant and agreement" is used in Section 9. If Borrower is obligated to pay Escrow Items directly, pursuant to a waiver, and Borrower fails to pay the amount due for an Escrow Item, Lender may exercise its rights under Section 9 and pay such amount and Borrower shall then be obligated under Section 9 to repay to Lender any such amount. Lender may revoke the waiver as to any or all Escrow Items at any time by a notice given in accordance with Section 15 and, upon such revocation, Borrower shall pay to Lender all Funds, and in such amounts, that are then required under this Section 3.

Lender may, at any time, collect and hold Funds in an amount (a) sufficient to permit Lender to apply the Funds at the time specified under RESPA, and (b) not to exceed the maximum amount a lender can require under RESPA. Lender shall estimate the amount of Funds due on the basis of current data and reasonable estimates of expenditures of future Escrow Items or otherwise in accordance with Applicable Law.

The Funds shall be held in an institution whose deposits are insured by a federal agency, instrumentality, or entity (including Lender, if Lender is an institution whose deposits are so insured) or in any Federal Home Loan Bank. Lender shall apply the Funds to pay the Escrow Items no later than the time specified under RESPA. Lender shall not charge Borrower for holding and applying the Funds, annually analyzing the escrow account, or verifying the Escrow Items, unless Lender pays Borrower interest on the Funds and Applicable Law permits Lender to make such a charge. Unless an agreement is made in writing or Applicable Law requires interest to be paid on the Funds, Lender shall not be required to pay Borrower any interest or earnings on the Funds. Borrower and Lender can agree in writing, however, that interest shall be paid on the Funds. Lender shall give to Borrower, without charge, an annual accounting of the Funds as required by RESPA.

If there is a surplus of Funds held in escrow, as defined under RESPA, Lender shall account to Borrower for the excess funds in accordance with RESPA. If there is a shortage of Funds held in escrow, as defined under RESPA, Lender shall notify Borrower as required by RESPA, and Borrower shall pay to Lender the amount necessary to make up the shortage in accordance with RESPA, but in no more than 12 monthly payments. If there is a deficiency of Funds held in escrow, as defined under RESPA, Lender shall notify Borrower as required by RESPA, and Borrower shall pay to Lender the amount necessary to make up the deficiency in accordance with RESPA, but in no more than 12 monthly payments.

Upon payment in full of all sums secured by this Security Instrument, Lender shall promptly refund to Borrower any Funds held by Lender.

4. Charges; Liens. Borrower shall pay all taxes, assessments, charges, fines, and impositions attributable to the Property which can attain priority over this Security Instrument, leasehold payments, or ground rents on the Property, if any, and Community Association Dues, Fees, and Assessments, if any. To the extent that these items are Escrow Items, Borrower shall pay them in the manner provided in Section 3.

Borrower shall promptly discharge any lien which has priority over this Security Instrument unless Borrower: (a) agrees in writing to the payment of the obligation secured by the lien in a manner acceptable to Lender, but only so long as Borrower is performing such agreement; (b) contests the lien in good faith by, or defends against enforcement of the lien in, legal proceedings which in Lender's opinion operate to prevent the enforcement of the lien while those proceedings are pending, but only until such proceedings are concluded; or (c) secures from the holder of the lien an agreement satisfactory to Lender subordinating the lien to this Security Instrument. If Lender determines that any part of the Property is subject to a lien which can attain priority over this Security Instrument, Lender may give Borrower a notice identifying the lien. Within 10 days of the date on which that notice is given, Borrower shall satisfy the lien or take one or more of the actions set forth above in this Section 4.

Lender may require Borrower to pay a one-time charge for a real estate tax verification and/or reporting service used by Lender in connection with this Loan.

5. Property Insurance. Borrower shall keep the improvements now existing or hereafter erected on the Property insured against loss by fire, hazards included within the term "extended coverage," and any other hazards including, but not limited to, earthquakes and floods, for which Lender requires insurance. This insurance shall be maintained in the amounts (including deductible levels) and for the periods that Lender requires. What Lender requires pursuant to the preceding sentences can change during the term of the Loan. The insurance carrier providing the insurance shall be chosen by Borrower subject to Lender's right to disapprove Borrower's choice, which right shall not be exercised unreasonably. Lender may require Borrower to pay, in connection with this Loan, either: (a) a one-time charge for flood zone determination, certification and tracking services; or (b) a one-time charge for flood zone determination and certification services and subsequent charges each time remappings or similar changes occur which reasonably might affect such determination or certification. Borrower shall also be responsible for the payment of any fees imposed by the Federal Emergency Management Agency in connection with the review of any flood zone determination resulting from an objection by Borrower.

If Borrower fails to maintain any of the coverages described above, Lender may obtain insurance coverage, at Lender's option and Borrower's expense. Lender is under no obligation to purchase any particular type or amount of coverage. Therefore, such coverage shall cover Lender, but might or might not protect Borrower, Borrower's equity in the Property, or the contents of the Property, against any risk, hazard, or liability and might provide greater or lesser coverage than was previously in effect. Borrower acknowledges that the cost of the insurance coverage so obtained might significantly exceed the cost of insurance that Borrower could have obtained. Any amounts disbursed by Lender under this Section 5 shall become additional debt of Borrower secured by this Security Instrument. These amounts shall bear interest at the Note rate from the date of disbursement and shall be payable, with such interest, upon notice from Lender to Borrower requesting payment.

All insurance policies required by Lender and renewals of such policies shall be subject to Lender's right to disapprove such policies, shall include a standard mortgage clause, and shall name Lender as mortgagee and/or as an additional loss payee. Lender shall have the right to hold the policies and renewal certificates. If Lender requires, Borrower shall promptly give to Lender all receipts of paid premiums and renewal notices. If Borrower obtains any form of insurance coverage, not otherwise required by Lender, for damage to, or destruction of, the Property, such policy shall include a standard mortgage clause and shall name Lender as mortgagee and/or as an additional loss payee.

In the event of loss, Borrower shall give prompt notice to the insurance carrier and Lender. Lender may make proof of loss if not made promptly by Borrower. Unless Lender and Borrower otherwise agree in writing, any insurance proceeds, whether or not the underlying insurance was required by Lender, shall be applied to restoration or repair of the Property, if the restoration or repair is economically feasible and Lender's security is not lessened. During such repair and restoration period, Lender shall have the right to hold such insurance proceeds until Lender has had an opportunity to inspect such Property to ensure the work has been completed to Lender's satisfaction, provided that such inspection shall be undertaken promptly. Lender may disburse proceeds for the repairs and restoration in a single payment or in a series of progress payments as the work is completed. Unless an agreement is made in writing or Applicable Law requires interest to be paid on such insurance proceeds, Lender shall not be required to pay Borrower any interest or earnings on such proceeds. Fees for public adjusters, or other third parties, retained by Borrower shall not be paid out of the insurance proceeds and shall be the sole obligation of Borrower. If the restoration or repair is not economically feasible or Lender's security would be lessened, the insurance proceeds shall be applied to the sums secured by this Security Instrument, whether or not then due, with the excess, if any, paid to Borrower. Such insurance proceeds shall be applied in the order provided for in Section 2.

If Borrower abandons the Property, Lender may file, negotiate, and settle any available insurance claim and related matters. If Borrower does not respond within 30 days to a notice from Lender that the insurance carrier has offered to settle a claim, then Lender may negotiate and settle the claim. The 30-day period will begin when the notice is given. In either event, or if Lender acquires the Property under Section 22 or otherwise, Borrower hereby assigns to Lender (a) Borrower's rights to any insurance proceeds in an amount not to exceed the amounts unpaid under the Note or this Security Instrument, and (b) any other of Borrower's rights (other than the right to any refund of unearned premiums paid by Borrower) under all insurance policies covering the Property, insofar as such rights are applicable to the coverage of the Property. Lender may use the insurance proceeds either to repair or restore the Property or to pay amounts unpaid under the Note or this Security Instrument, whether or not then due.

6. Occupancy. Borrower shall occupy, establish, and use the Property as Borrower's principal residence within 60 days after the execution of this Security Instrument and shall continue to occupy the Property as Borrower's principal residence for at least one year after the date of occupancy, unless Lender otherwise agrees in writing, which consent shall not be unreasonably withheld, or unless extenuating circumstances exist which are beyond Borrower's control.

7. Preservation, Maintenance, and Protection of the Property; Inspections. Borrower shall not destroy, damage, or impair the Property; allow the Property to deteriorate; or commit waste on the Property. Whether or not Borrower is residing in the Property, Borrower shall maintain the Property in order to prevent the Property from deteriorating or decreasing in value due to its condition. Unless it is determined pursuant to Section 5 that repair or restoration is not economically feasible, Borrower shall promptly repair the Property if damaged to avoid further deterioration or damage. If insurance or condemnation proceeds are paid in connection with damage to, or the taking of, the Property, Borrower shall be responsible for repairing or restoring the Property only if Lender has released proceeds for such purposes. Lender may disburse proceeds for the repairs and restoration in a single payment or in a series of progress payments as the work is completed. If the insurance or condemnation proceeds are not sufficient to repair or restore the Property, Borrower is not relieved of Borrower's obligation for the completion of such repair or restoration.

Lender or its agent may make reasonable entries upon and inspections of the Property. If it has reasonable cause, Lender may inspect the interior of the improvements on the Property. Lender shall give Borrower notice at the time of or prior to such an interior inspection specifying such reasonable cause.

8. Borrower's Loan Application. Borrower shall be in default if, during the Loan application process, Borrower or any persons or entities acting at the direction of Borrower or with Borrower's knowledge or consent gave materially false, misleading, or inaccurate information or statements to Lender (or failed to provide Lender with material information) in connection with the Loan. Material representations include, but are not limited to, representations concerning Borrower's occupancy of the Property as Borrower's principal residence.

9. Protection of Lender's Interest in the Property and Rights Under this Security Instrument. If (a) Borrower fails to perform the covenants and agreements contained in this Security Instrument, (b) there is a legal proceeding that might significantly affect Lender's

(continued)

EXHIBIT 10-6 *Continued*

interest in the Property and/or rights under this Security Instrument (such as a proceeding in bankruptcy, probate, for condemnation or forfeiture, for enforcement of a lien which may attain priority over this Security Instrument or to enforce laws or regulations), or (c) Borrower has abandoned the Property, then Lender may do and pay for whatever is reasonable or appropriate to protect Lender's interest in the Property and rights under this Security Instrument, including protecting and/or assessing the value of the Property, and securing and/or repairing the Property. Lender's actions can include, but are not limited to: (a) paying any sums secured by a lien which has priority over this Security Instrument; (b) appearing in court; and (c) paying reasonable attorneys' fees to protect its interest in the Property and/or rights under this Security Instrument, including its secured position in a bankruptcy proceeding. Securing the Property includes, but is not limited to, entering the Property to make repairs, change locks, replace or board up doors and windows, drain water from pipes, eliminate building or other code violations or dangerous conditions, and have utilities turned on or off. Although Lender may take action under this Section 9, Lender does not have to do so and is not under any duty or obligation to do so. It is agreed that Lender incurs no liability for not taking any or all actions authorized under this Section 9.

Any amounts disbursed by Lender under this Section 9 shall become additional debt of Borrower secured by this Security Instrument. These amounts shall bear interest at the Note rate from the date of disbursement and shall be payable, with such interest, upon notice from Lender to Borrower requesting payment.

If this Security Instrument is on a leasehold, Borrower shall comply with all the provisions of the lease. If Borrower acquires fee title to the Property, the leasehold and the fee title shall not merge unless Lender agrees to the merger in writing.

10. **Mortgage Insurance.** If Lender required Mortgage Insurance as a condition of making the Loan, Borrower shall pay the premiums required to maintain the Mortgage Insurance in effect. If, for any reason, the Mortgage Insurance coverage required by Lender ceases to be available from the mortgage insurer that previously provided such insurance and Borrower was required to make separately designated payments toward the premiums for Mortgage Insurance, Borrower shall pay the premiums required to obtain coverage substantially equivalent to the Mortgage Insurance previously in effect, at a cost substantially equivalent to the cost to Borrower of the Mortgage Insurance previously in effect, from an alternate mortgage insurer selected by Lender. If substantially equivalent Mortgage Insurance coverage is not available, Borrower shall continue to pay to Lender the amount of the separately designated payments that were due when the insurance coverage ceased to be in effect. Lender will accept, use, and retain these payments as a non-refundable loss reserve in lieu of Mortgage Insurance. Such loss reserve shall be non-refundable, notwithstanding the fact that the Loan is ultimately paid in full, and Lender shall not be required to pay Borrower any interest or earnings on such loss reserve. Lender can no longer require loss reserve payments if Mortgage Insurance coverage (in the amount and for the period that Lender requires) provided by an insurer selected by Lender again becomes available, is obtained, and Lender requires separately designated payments toward the premiums for Mortgage Insurance. If Lender required Mortgage Insurance as a condition of making the Loan and Borrower was required to make separately designated payments toward the premiums for Mortgage Insurance, Borrower shall pay the premiums required to maintain Mortgage Insurance in effect, or to provide a non-refundable loss reserve, until Lender's requirement for Mortgage Insurance ends in accordance with any written agreement between Borrower and Lender providing for such termination or until termination is required by Applicable Law. Nothing in this Section 10 affects Borrower's obligation to pay interest at the rate provided in the Note.

Mortgage Insurance reimburses Lender (or any entity that purchases the Note) for certain losses it may incur if Borrower does not repay the Loan as agreed. Borrower is not a party to the Mortgage Insurance.

Mortgage insurers evaluate their total risk on all such insurance in force from time to time, and may enter into agreements with other parties that share or modify their risk, or reduce losses. These agreements are on terms and conditions that are satisfactory to the mortgage insurer and the other party (or parties) to these agreements. These agreements may require the mortgage insurer to make payments using any source of funds that the mortgage insurer may have available (which may include funds obtained from Mortgage Insurance premiums).

As a result of these agreements, Lender, any purchaser of the Note, another insurer, any reinsurer, any other entity, or any affiliate of any of the foregoing, may receive (directly or indirectly) amounts that derive from (or might be characterized as) a portion of Borrower's payments for Mortgage Insurance, in exchange for sharing or modifying the mortgage insurer's risk, or reducing losses. If such agreement provides that an affiliate of Lender takes a share of the insurer's risk in exchange for a share of the premiums paid to the insurer, the arrangement is often termed "captive reinsurance." Further:

(a) Any such agreements will not affect the amounts that Borrower has agreed to pay for Mortgage Insurance, or any other terms of the Loan. Such agreements will not increase the amount Borrower will owe for Mortgage Insurance, and they will not entitle Borrower to any refund.

(b) Any such agreements will not affect the rights Borrower has – if any – with respect to the Mortgage Insurance under the Homeowners Protection Act of 1998 or any other law. These rights may include the right to receive certain disclosures, to request and obtain cancellation of the Mortgage Insurance, to have the Mortgage Insurance terminated automatically, and/or to receive a refund of any Mortgage Insurance premiums that were unearned at the time of such cancellation or termination.

11. Assignment of Miscellaneous Proceeds; Forfeiture. All Miscellaneous Proceeds are hereby assigned to and shall be paid to Lender.

If the Property is damaged, such Miscellaneous Proceeds shall be applied to restoration or repair of the Property, if the restoration or repair is economically feasible and Lender's security is not lessened. During such repair and restoration period, Lender shall have the right to hold such Miscellaneous Proceeds until Lender has had an opportunity to inspect such Property to ensure the work has been completed to Lender's satisfaction, provided that such inspection shall be undertaken promptly. Lender may pay for the repairs and restoration in a single disbursement or in a series of progress payments as the work is completed. Unless an agreement is made in writing or Applicable Law requires interest to be paid on such Miscellaneous Proceeds, Lender shall not be required to pay Borrower any interest or earnings on such Miscellaneous Proceeds. If the restoration or repair is not economically feasible or Lender's security would be lessened, the Miscellaneous Proceeds shall be applied to the sums secured by this Security Instrument, whether or not then due, with the excess, if any, paid to Borrower. Such Miscellaneous Proceeds shall be applied in the order provided for in Section 2.

In the event of a total taking, destruction, or loss in value of the Property, the Miscellaneous Proceeds shall be applied to the sums secured by this Security Instrument, whether or not then due, with the excess, if any, paid to Borrower.

In the event of a partial taking, destruction, or loss in value of the Property in which the fair market value of the Property immediately before the partial taking, destruction, or loss in value is equal to or greater than the amount of the sums secured by this Security Instrument immediately before the partial taking, destruction, or loss in value, unless Borrower and Lender otherwise agree in writing, the sums secured by this Security Instrument shall be reduced by the amount of the Miscellaneous Proceeds multiplied by the following fraction: (a) the total amount of the sums secured immediately before the partial taking, destruction, or loss in value divided by (b) the fair market value of the Property immediately before the partial taking, destruction, or loss in value. Any balance shall be paid to Borrower.

In the event of a partial taking, destruction, or loss in value of the Property in which the fair market value of the Property immediately before the partial taking, destruction, or loss in value is less than the amount of the sums secured immediately before the partial taking, destruction, or loss in value, unless Borrower and Lender otherwise agree in writing, the Miscellaneous Proceeds shall be applied to the sums secured by this Security Instrument whether or not the sums are then due.

If the Property is abandoned by Borrower, or if, after notice by Lender to Borrower that the Opposing Party (as defined in the next sentence) offers to make an award to settle a claim for damages, Borrower fails to respond to Lender within 30 days after the date the notice is given, Lender is authorized to collect and apply the Miscellaneous Proceeds either to restoration or repair of the Property or to the sums secured by this Security Instrument, whether or not then due. "Opposing Party" means the third party that owes Borrower Miscellaneous Proceeds or the party against whom Borrower has a right of action in regard to Miscellaneous Proceeds.

Borrower shall be in default if any action or proceeding, whether civil or criminal, is begun that, in Lender's judgment, could result in forfeiture of the Property or other material impairment of Lender's interest in the Property or rights under this Security Instrument. Borrower can cure such a default and, if acceleration has occurred, reinstate as provided in Section 19, by causing the action or proceeding to be dismissed with a ruling that, in Lender's judgment, precludes forfeiture of the Property or other material impairment of Lender's interest in the Property or rights under this Security Instrument. The proceeds of any award or claim for damages that are attributable to the impairment of Lender's interest in the Property are hereby assigned and shall be paid to Lender.

All Miscellaneous Proceeds that are not applied to restoration or repair of the Property shall be applied in the order provided for in Section 2.

12. Borrower Not Released; Forbearance By Lender Not a Waiver. Extension of the time for payment or modification of amortization of the sums secured by this Security Instrument granted by Lender to Borrower or any Successor in Interest of Borrower shall not operate to release the liability of Borrower or any Successors in Interest of Borrower. Lender shall not be required to commence proceedings against any Successor in Interest of Borrower or to refuse to extend time for payment or otherwise modify amortization of the sums secured by this Security Instrument by reason of any demand made by the original Borrower or any Successors in Interest of Borrower. Any forbearance by Lender in exercising any right or remedy including, without limitation, Lender's acceptance of payments from third persons, entities, or Successors in Interest of Borrower or in amounts less than the amount then due, shall not be a waiver of or preclude the exercise of any right or remedy.

13. Joint and Several Liability; Co-signers; Successors and Assigns Bound. Borrower covenants and agrees that Borrower's obligations and liability shall be joint and several. However, any Borrower who co-signs this Security Instrument but does not execute the Note (a "co-signer"): (a) is co-signing this Security Instrument only to mortgage, grant, and convey the co-signer's interest in the Property under the terms of this Security Instrument; (b) is not personally obligated to pay the sums secured by this Security Instrument; and (c) agrees that Lender and any other Borrower can agree to extend, modify, forbear, or make any accommodations with regard to the terms of this Security Instrument or the Note without the co-signer's consent.

Subject to the provisions of Section 18, any Successor in Interest of Borrower who assumes Borrower's obligations under this Security Instrument in writing, and is approved by Lender, shall obtain all of Borrower's rights and benefits under this Security Instrument. Borrower shall not be released from Borrower's obligations and liability under this Security Instrument unless Lender agrees to such release in writing. The covenants and agreements of this Security Instrument shall bind (except as provided in Section 20) and benefit the successors and assigns of Lender.

(continued)

EXHIBIT 10-6 *Continued*

14. Loan Charges. Lender may charge Borrower fees for services performed in connection with Borrower's default, for the purpose of protecting Lender's interest in the Property and rights under this Security Instrument, including, but not limited to, attorneys' fees, property inspection, and valuation fees. In regard to any other fees, the absence of express authority in this Security Instrument to charge a specific fee to Borrower shall not be construed as a prohibition on the charging of such fee. Lender may not charge fees that are expressly prohibited by this Security Instrument or by Applicable Law.

If the Loan is subject to a law which sets maximum loan charges, and that law is finally interpreted so that the interest or other loan charges collected or to be collected in connection with the Loan exceed the permitted limits, then: (a) any such loan charge shall be reduced by the amount necessary to reduce the charge to the permitted limit; and (b) any sums already collected from Borrower which exceeded permitted limits will be refunded to Borrower. Lender may choose to make this refund by reducing the principal owed under the Note or by making a direct payment to Borrower. If a refund reduces principal, the reduction will be treated as a partial prepayment without any prepayment charge (whether or not a prepayment charge is provided for under the Note). Borrower's acceptance of any such refund made by direct payment to Borrower will constitute a waiver of any right of action Borrower might have arising out of such overcharge.

15. Notices. All notices given by Borrower or Lender in connection with this Security Instrument must be in writing. Any notice to Borrower in connection with this Security Instrument shall be deemed to have been given to Borrower when mailed by first class mail or when actually delivered to Borrower's notice address if sent by other means. Notice to any one Borrower shall constitute notice to all Borrowers unless Applicable Law expressly requires otherwise. The notice address shall be the Property Address unless Borrower has designated a substitute notice address by notice to Lender. Borrower shall promptly notify Lender of Borrower's change of address. If Lender specifies a procedure for reporting Borrower's change of address, then Borrower shall only report a change of address through that specified procedure. There may be only one designated notice address under this Security Instrument at any one time. Any notice to Lender shall be given by delivering it or by mailing it by first class mail to Lender's address stated herein unless Lender has designated another address by notice to Borrower. Any notice in connection with this Security Instrument shall not be deemed to have been given to Lender until actually received by Lender. If any notice required by this Security Instrument is also required under Applicable Law, the Applicable Law requirement will satisfy the corresponding requirement under this Security Instrument.

16. Governing Law; Severability; Rules of Construction. This Security Instrument shall be governed by federal law and the law of the jurisdiction in which the Property is located. All rights and obligations contained in this Security Instrument are subject to any requirements and limitations of Applicable Law. Applicable Law might explicitly or implicitly allow the parties to agree by contract or it might be silent, but such silence shall not be construed as a prohibition against agreement by contract. In the event that any provision or clause of this Security Instrument or the Note conflicts with Applicable Law, such conflict shall not affect other provisions of this Security Instrument or the Note which can be given effect without the conflicting provision.

As used in this Security Instrument: (a) words of the masculine gender shall mean and include corresponding neuter words or words of the feminine gender; (b) words in the singular shall mean and include the plural and vice versa; and (c) the word "may" gives sole discretion without any obligation to take any action.

17. Borrower's Copy. Borrower shall be given one copy of the Note and of this Security Instrument.

18. Transfer of the Property or a Beneficial Interest in Borrower. As used in this Section 18, "Interest in the Property" means any legal or beneficial interest in the Property, including, but not limited to, those beneficial interests transferred in a bond for deed, contract for deed, installment sales contract, or escrow agreement, the intent of which is the transfer of title by Borrower at a future date to a purchaser.

If all or any part of the Property or any Interest in the Property is sold or transferred (or if Borrower is not a natural person and a beneficial interest in Borrower is sold or transferred) without Lender's prior written consent, Lender may require immediate payment in full of all sums secured by this Security Instrument. However, this option shall not be exercised by Lender if such exercise is prohibited by Applicable Law.

If Lender exercises this option, Lender shall give Borrower notice of acceleration. The notice shall provide a period of not less than 30 days from the date the notice is given in accordance with Section 15 within which Borrower must pay all sums secured by this Security Instrument. If Borrower fails to pay these sums prior to the expiration of this period, Lender may invoke any remedies permitted by this Security Instrument without further notice or demand on Borrower.

19. Borrower's Right to Reinstate After Acceleration. If Borrower meets certain conditions, Borrower shall have the right to have enforcement of this Security Instrument discontinued at any time prior to the earliest of: (a) five days before sale of the Property pursuant to any power of sale contained in this Security Instrument; (b) such other period as Applicable Law might specify for the termination of Borrower's right to reinstate; or (c) entry of a judgment enforcing this Security Instrument. Those conditions are that Borrower: (a) pays Lender all sums which then would be due under this Security Instrument and the Note as if no acceleration had occurred; (b) cures any default of any other covenants or agreements; (c) pays all expenses incurred in enforcing this Security Instrument, including, but not limited to, reasonable attorneys' fees, property inspection and valuation fees, and other fees incurred for the purpose of protecting Lender's interest in the Property and rights under this Security Instrument; and (d) takes such action as Lender may reasonably require to assure that Lender's interest in the Property and rights under this Security Instrument, and Borrower's obligation to pay the sums secured by this Security Instrument, shall continue unchanged. Lender may require that Borrower pay such reinstatement sums and expenses in one or more of the following forms, as selected by Lender: (a) cash; (b) money order; (c) certified check, bank check, treasurer's check, or cashier's check, provided any such check is drawn upon an institution whose deposits are insured by a federal agency, instrumentality or entity; or (d) Electronic Funds Transfer. Upon reinstatement by Borrower, this Security Instrument and obligations secured hereby shall remain fully effective as if no acceleration had occurred. However, this right to reinstate shall not apply in the case of acceleration under Section 18.

20. Sale of Note; Change of Loan Servicer; Notice of Grievance. The Note or a partial interest in the Note (together with this Security Instrument) can be sold one or more times without prior notice to Borrower. A sale might result in a change in the entity (known as the "Loan Servicer") that collects Periodic Payments due under the Note and this Security Instrument and performs other mortgage loan servicing obligations under the Note, this Security Instrument, and Applicable Law. There also might be one or more changes of the Loan Servicer unrelated to a sale of the Note. If there is a change of the Loan Servicer, Borrower will be given written notice of the change which will state the name and address of the new Loan Servicer, the address to which payments should be made and any other information RESPA requires in connection with a notice of transfer of servicing. If the Note is sold and thereafter the Loan is serviced by a Loan Servicer other than the purchaser of the Note, the mortgage loan servicing obligations to Borrower will remain with the Loan Servicer or be transferred to a successor Loan Servicer and are not assumed by the Note purchaser unless otherwise provided by the Note purchaser.

Neither Borrower nor Lender may commence, join, or be joined to any judicial action (as either an individual litigant or the member of a class) that arises from the other party's actions pursuant to this Security Instrument or that alleges that the other party has breached any provision of, or any duty owed by reason of, this Security Instrument, until such Borrower or Lender has notified the other party (with such notice given in compliance with the requirements of Section 15) of such alleged breach and afforded the other party hereto a reasonable period after the giving of such notice to take corrective action. If Applicable Law provides a time period which must elapse before certain action can be taken, that time period will be deemed to be reasonable for purposes of this paragraph. The notice of acceleration and opportunity to cure given to Borrower pursuant to Section 22 and the notice of acceleration given to Borrower pursuant to Section 18 shall be deemed to satisfy the notice and opportunity to take corrective action provisions of this Section 20.

21. Hazardous Substances. As used in this Section 21: (a) "Hazardous Substances" are those substances defined as toxic or hazardous substances, pollutants, or wastes by Environmental Law and the following substances: gasoline, kerosene, other flammable or toxic petroleum products, toxic pesticides and herbicides, volatile solvents, materials containing asbestos or formaldehyde, and radioactive materials; (b) "Environmental Law" means federal laws and laws of the jurisdiction where the Property is located that relate to health, safety, or environmental protection; (c) "Environmental Cleanup" includes any response action, remedial action, or removal action, as defined in Environmental Law; and (d) an "Environmental Condition" means a condition that can cause, contribute to, or otherwise trigger an Environmental Cleanup.

Borrower shall not cause or permit the presence, use, disposal, storage, or release of any Hazardous Substances, or threaten to release any Hazardous Substances, on or in the Property. Borrower shall not do, nor allow anyone else to do, anything affecting the Property (a) that is in violation of any Environmental Law, (b) which creates an Environmental Condition, or (c) which, due to the presence, use, or release of a Hazardous Substance, creates a condition that adversely affects the value of the Property. The preceding two sentences shall not apply to the presence, use, or storage on the Property of small quantities of Hazardous Substances that are generally recognized to be appropriate to normal residential uses and to maintenance of the Property (including, but not limited to, hazardous substances in consumer products).

Borrower shall promptly give Lender written notice of (a) any investigation, claim, demand, lawsuit, or other action by any governmental or regulatory agency or private party involving the Property and any Hazardous Substance or Environmental Law of which Borrower has actual knowledge, (b) any Environmental Condition, including but not limited to, any spilling, leaking, discharge, release or threat of release of any Hazardous Substance, and (c) any condition caused by the presence, use or release of a Hazardous Substance which adversely affects the value of the Property. If Borrower learns, or is notified by any governmental or regulatory authority, or any private party, that any removal or other remediation of any Hazardous Substance affecting the Property is necessary, Borrower shall promptly take all necessary remedial actions in accordance with Environmental Law. Nothing herein shall create any obligation on Lender for an Environmental Cleanup.

NON-UNIFORM COVENANTS. Borrower and Lender further covenant and agree as follows:

22. Acceleration; Remedies. Lender shall give notice to Borrower prior to acceleration following Borrower's breach of any covenant or agreement in this Security Instrument (but not prior to acceleration under Section 18 unless Applicable Law provides otherwise). The notice shall specify: (a) the default; (b) the action required to cure the default; (c) a date, not less than 30 days from the date the notice is given to Borrower, by which the default must be cured; and (d) that failure to cure the default on or before the date specified in the notice may result in acceleration of the sums secured by this Security Instrument and sale of the Property. The notice shall further inform Borrower of the right to reinstate after acceleration and the right to bring a court action to assert the non-existence of a default or any other defense of

(continued)

EXHIBIT 10-6 *Continued*

Borrower to acceleration and sale. If the default is not cured on or before the date specified in the notice, Lender at its option may require immediate payment in full of all sums secured by this Security Instrument without further demand and may invoke the power of sale and any other remedies permitted by Applicable Law. Lender shall be entitled to collect all expenses incurred in pursuing the remedies provided in this Section 22, including, but not limited to, reasonable attorneys' fees and costs of title evidence.

If Lender invokes the power of sale, Lender shall give written notice to Trustee of the occurrence of an event of default and of Lender's election to cause the Property to be sold. Trustee shall record a notice of sale in each county in which any part of the Property is located and shall mail copies of the notice as prescribed by Applicable Law to Borrower and to the other persons prescribed by Applicable Law. After the time required by Applicable Law and after publication and posting of the notice of sale, Trustee, without demand on Borrower, shall sell the Property at public auction to the highest bidder for cash at the time and place designated in the notice of sale. Trustee may postpone sale of the Property by public announcement at the time and place of any previously scheduled sale. Lender or its designee may purchase the Property at any sale.

Trustee shall deliver to the purchaser Trustee's deed conveying the Property without any covenant or warranty, expressed or implied. The recitals in the Trustee's deed shall be prima facie evidence of the truth of the statements made therein. Trustee shall apply the proceeds of the sale in the following order: (a) to all expenses of the sale, including, but not limited to, reasonable Trustee's and attorneys' fees; (b) to all sums secured by this Security Instrument; and (c) any excess to the person or persons legally entitled to it or to the county treasurer of the county in which the sale took place.

23. Release. Upon payment of all sums secured by this Security Instrument, Lender shall release this Security Instrument. Borrower shall pay any recordation costs. Lender may charge Borrower a fee for releasing this Security Instrument, but only if the fee is paid to a third party for services rendered and the charging of the fee is permitted under Applicable Law.

24. Substitute Trustee. Lender may, for any reason or cause, from time to time remove Trustee and appoint a successor trustee to any Trustee appointed hereunder. Without conveyance of the Property, the successor trustee shall succeed to all the title, power, and duties conferred upon Trustee herein and by Applicable Law.

25. Time of Essence. Time is of the essence in each covenant of this Security Instrument.

BY SIGNING BELOW, Borrower accepts and agrees to the terms and covenants contained in this Security Instrument and in any Rider executed by Borrower and recorded with it.

_____   _____ (Seal)
Witness   Borrower

_____   _____ (Seal)
Witness   Borrower

_____ [Space Below This Line for Acknowledgment] _____

CHAPTER SUMMARY

The three major documents involved in the sale of real property are the deed, the mortgage or deed of trust, and the promissory note.

A *deed* is a written document that conveys an interest in real property, and is evidence of title to a property. There are several requirements for a valid deed, including language of conveyance in the granting clause and habendum clause, grantor's signature and mental competency, delivery and acceptance of the deed, and an adequate legal description of the property being conveyed.

There are three primary types of *legal descriptions* of the property to be conveyed: metes and bounds, plat map, and the public land survey system (PLSS). *Ambiguities* in the deed's legal description are either patent (obvious), or latent (hidden).

There are several types of deeds, but the best that can be conveyed is the *general warranty deed*. The warranties contained in a deed are guarantees made by the grantor to the grantee, and include the warranties of seisin and quiet enjoyment, as well as the warranty against encumbrances, and the warranty of further assurances. A *limited warranty deed*, also known as a special warranty deed, has fewer warranties or guarantees than a general warranty deed. A *quitclaim deed* is often used to quiet title in a divorce action, and is also useful to dispel clouds on title in will contests. Other types of deeds are deed in lieu of foreclosure, sheriffs' deeds, and tax deeds.

Mortgages and *deeds of trust* are written legal instruments that both had the purpose of pledging property to the lender as security for the lender making the loan to purchase the property. A mortgage involves two parties: the *mortgagor*, who is the buyer-borrower, and the *mortgagee*, which is the lender.

A deed of trust requires three parties: the borrower-trustor, the trustee, and the lender-beneficiary.

Mortgage states are usually *lien theory states,* and deed of trust states are usually *title theory states.*

A *purchase money mortgage* occurs when the seller of a property finances the property for the buyer by "carrying paper." In a purchase money mortgage, the deed/title is conveyed at closing. A *contract for deed/land sale contract* is similar to a purchase money mortgage in that the seller finances the property for the buyer, but title does not transfer to the buyer until all payments have been made after several years; thus, contracts for deeds/land sale contracts are risky for the property buyers.

Mortgages, deeds of trust, and purchase money mortgages contain standard clauses, some of which benefit the mortgage lender and others of which benefit the buyer. The main clauses that benefit the lender are the acceleration clause and the due on sale clause. The main clauses that benefit the borrower are the no prepayment penalty clause and the right of accounting clause.

A *promissory note* is a written promise to pay a debt, and specifies the terms of the repayment including the principal amount of the loan, interest rate, and the term of the loan.

The *mortgage markets* consist of the primary mortgage market and the secondary mortgage market. The primary mortgage market is made up of front-line lenders, such as banks, savings and loans, and credit unions, as well as Fannie Mae and Freddie Mac, which were created by the federal government. In order to replenish the money it has lent, that is, maintain *liquidity*, lenders will bundle their mortgage loans into packages (MBOs—mortgage-backed obligations), which are then sold on the secondary mortgage market to the aforementioned large financial institutions.

CONCEPT REVIEW AND REINFORCEMENT

KEY **TERMS**

Acceleration Clause	Credit Rating	Freddie Mac
Acknowledgment	Credit Report/History	General Warranty Deed
Ambiguity	Debt-to-Income Ratio	Grantee
Beneficiary	Deed	Granting Clause
Collateral/Security	Deed in Lieu of Foreclosure	Grantor
Competent	Deed of Trust	Habendum Clause
Contract for Deed/Land Sale Contract	Delivery and Acceptance	Latent Ambiguity
Covenant	Due on Sale Clause	Legal Description
Conveyance	Fannie Mae	Lien Theory State

Limited Warranty Deed/Special
  Warranty Deed
Liquidity
Marketable Title
Metes and Bounds
Mortgage
Mortgage Market
Mortgagee
Mortgagor
No Prepayment Penalty Clause
Notarize
Patent Ambiguity
Plat Map

Primary Mortgage Market
Promissory Note
Public Land Survey System (PLSS)
Purchase-Money Mortgage
Quiet Enjoyment
Quitclaim Deed
Seal
Secondary Mortgage Market
Seisin
Sheriff's Deed
Tax Deed
Title
Title Theory State

Too Big to Fail
Trustee
Trustor
Void
Voidable
Warranty
Warranty Against Encumbrances
Warranty of Further Assurance
Will Contest

CONCEPT **REVIEW** QUESTIONS

1. What are the three most important legal documents in the sale of real property?

2. What is a deed, and what is its purpose? What are the requirements for a valid deed? Must they deed be in writing? Why?

3. What is the purpose of the mortgage and deed of trust? What is the main difference between them? How many parties are there to a mortgage, and who are they? How many parties are there to a deed of trust, and who are they? Must the mortgage and deed of trust be in writing?

4. What is the difference between the granting clause and habendum clause in a deed?

5. What are the three types of legal descriptions that are found in a deed? Which type is predominant in the eastern United States? Which type is predominant in the western United States?

6. Why are ambiguities in the legal descriptions in deeds problematic? What is the difference between a patent ambiguity and a latent ambiguity? Which type of ambiguity may be "cured" by extrinsic evidence such as parol testimony?

7. What is the best type of deed that a grantor can convey to a grantee, and why is it the best?

8. What is the purpose of a quitclaim deed? Does a quitclaim deed offer any warranties (guarantees)?

9. What is a special warranty deed, also known as a limited warranty deed?

10. What is the warranty of seisin? What is the warranty against encumbrances? What is the warranty

of quiet enjoyment? What is the warranty of further assurance?

11. What is an acceleration clause, and in what legal document is it found? What is a due on sale clause, and in what legal document is it found? Do these clauses protect the borrower or the lender?

12. What is the name of the clause in a mortgage or deed of trust that prevents a lender from imposing a penalty on the borrower, if the borrower pays off the loan early?

13. What is a purchase money mortgage, and who are the parties to the PMM?

14. What is a contract for deed/land sale contract? Why is this a dangerous type of contract for the purchaser of real property?

15. What is a promissory note? Who is the promisor on a promissory note, and must the promisor sign the note? Who is the promisee on a promissory note, and must the promisee sign the note?

16. What is the primary mortgage market, and what types of financial institutions make loans in the primary mortgage market?

17. What is the purpose of the secondary mortgage market, and what types of financial institutions are involved in it?

18. Who, or what, are Fannie Mae and Freddie Mac?

19. What is liquidity, and why is it important to an investor?

20. What is the significance of the term "too big to fail" in the context of federal government bailouts of certain financial institutions?

ETHICS

TO NOTARIZE OR NOT TO NOTARIZE—THAT IS THE QUESTION

Margaret is a paralegal and works for James, a very busy real estate attorney. James is very conscientious and has an excellent reputation for the work he does for his clients. One day James brings Margaret a handful of closing-related documents, including a deed, and asks her to notarize each document.

Margaret is a registered notary. James explains to her that he finalized a deal late last night at the airport as his clients were leaving town. James did not want to disturb Margaret after hours so he decided to have the clients sign, after he checked their drivers' licenses; James also took down the appropriate driver's license numbers for Margaret's notary book.

What should Margaret do? Should she notarize the documents based upon James' having examined the clients' licenses?

Would James' conduct be considered deceitful or dishonest considering he checked his clients' licenses for Margaret?

BUILDING YOUR PROFESSIONAL SKILLS

CRITICAL THINKING **EXERCISES**

1. There were two brothers named Jesse and Frank, and for several years they had had a disagreement over which of them owned a small parcel of land. Jesse and Frank each had two children. One day, Frank became seriously ill, and fell into a coma. Jesse felt guilt and remorse about the arguments he'd had with his brother over the piece of land. In a gesture of brotherly love, Jesse drew up a deed, went into Frank's bedroom, and slipped the deed into the Bible lying on Frank's nightstand, just beside his bed. While doing so, Jesse said: "Forgive me dear brother. I want you to have the land that we have been arguing about."

   This moving scene was witnessed by several members of the family. Unfortunately, the next day Frank died, never having come out of his coma. A short time later, Jesse was killed as the result of a gun accident.

   Jesse's children have filed suit against their cousins, the children of Frank, claiming that there was not a legal transfer of the property by Jesse to Frank. Assume that Jesse was seised of the property, meaning that he did have the authority to convey it to his brother Frank. What is the legal issue to be resolved by the court relating to the deed? In your opinion, which brother's children will ultimately own the property, and why?

2. Grantor has a son from whom he has been estranged for many years. His son has a daughter (grantor's granddaughter), age 20, whom grantor dearly loves. Grantor-grandfather wants to convey title to his ranch to his granddaughter by way of a gift deed. Grandfather has an attorney prepare the gift deed, and tells the attorney that he will sign it later.

   A few days later, grandfather remembers that he has to sign the deed and give it to his granddaughter. Grandfather sits down, writes in his *first name and middle initial* on the deed when he is interrupted by a knock at the door. Distracted, grandfather puts the pen down, and answers the door. The visitor is his granddaughter, and grandfather says, "I'm so glad to see you, I wanted to give you the deed." Grandfather walks to the writing table, folds the deed, and gives it to his granddaughter, who gratefully accepts it, but without looking at it or noticing that grandfather has yet to write his last name on the deed. Just a few hours after his granddaughter has departed, grandfather suffers a fatal heart attack, dying without a will.

   Grandfather's son—the father of granddaughter—challenges the validity of the conveyance because grandfather did not sign his full name. Since his father died intestate, the son is the sole heir under state law. Who will prevail in this lawsuit, granddaughter or her father? On what legal grounds do you base your decision?

3. Mother has three children, Adam, Betty, and Charlie. Of the three children, Charlie is mother's favorite. Mother signs and delivers a general warranty deed conveying a large, fairly valuable tract of land known as Greenacres to Charlie, who eagerly accepts the deed. Charlie does not look at the deed, and assumes that Mother has given identical interests in the property to his siblings, Adam and Betty.

A few months later, Charlie is speaking with Adam and Betty, and says: "Wasn't that generous of Mother to deed the property to us?" Adam and Betty are stunned, and Adam says: "What are you talking about? Mother didn't give Betty or me anything!" Charlie feels guilty and the next day visits Mother. Charlie hands the deed back to Mother, stating:

"If Adam and Betty were not to receive part of the property, then I can't accept it either." A few days later, Mother has a stroke and dies. Mother died intestate.

Who owns Greenacres? Can Charlie "revoke" the conveyance of Greenacres? When did title to Greenacres transfer from Mother to Charlie?

RESEARCH ON THE **WEB**

1. Conduct a search on the web to determine if your jurisdiction is a mortgage state or a deed of trust state. After making that determination, see if your state is a title-theory state, or a lien theory state.

2. Search the web to see if you can find any examples of latent ambiguities and patent ambiguities and deeds. How do these two types of ambiguities differ? Are there more examples of the former, or the latter, type of ambiguity?

3. Run a query on the Internet for "too big to fail." How many hits did you receive? Narrow the search by adding the term "AIG". Further narrow your search by adding "Fannie Mae." Who, or what, is AIG? How are Fannie Mae (and Freddie Mac) related to the concept of "too big to fail"?

4. If you have access to Lexis, Westlaw, or some other type of case database, run a query using the terms:

   "contract for deed" or "land sale contract" and "fraud" or "defrauded"

   Depending upon the size of the case database(s) that you are using, you may have gotten hundreds or even thousands of hits. If so, try to reduce that number by using "proximity connectors" between the terms above. For example, some databases will allow you to search for terms such as "contract for deed" in the same sentence as "fraud." The proximity connector "in the same sentence as" helps to narrow the number of hits considerably.

5. Searching online, try to discover the value of the loan portfolios for Fannie Mae and Freddie Mac. Have those amounts increased or decreased significantly in the last 10 years? As to Fannie Mae, what if any involvement does the federal government have with that institution? Has that relationship changed over the years?

6. Research the Public Land Survey System (PLSS) on the Internet to learn about its history. When was it first employed in the United States, and pursuant to what authority? Is it still in use, and if so, where? How does its accuracy compare with a metes-and-bounds description, and are these two types of legal descriptions ever used in conjunction with each other?

BUILDING YOUR **PROFESSIONAL** PORTFOLIO

1. Draft a simple general warranty deed conveying Greenacres to your best friend. Keep in mind the requirements of a valid deed: Grantor's (your) signature, an adequate legal description of the property, and language of conveyance (the granting and habendum clauses). Remember also that there must be a delivery of the deed by you, and an acceptance by the grantee.

2. Draft a simple mortgage document. Remember that a mortgage is a pledge of real property used to secure the loan made to purchase the property. Who are the parties to a mortgage? A mortgage must include an adequate legal description of the property being pledged as collateral for the loan.

3. Draft a simple contract for deed/land sale contract. Remember that in this type of transaction, title (the deed) does not transfer until the buyer has paid for the property in full, which is why a contract for deed can be very risky from the buyer's perspective.

chapter 11

THE CLOSING AND RECORDING

A. The Closing—Conveyance of Title

Closing
the final step in a real estate transaction during which the grantor (usually a seller) conveys title to the grantee (usually a buyer), most often in exchange for financial consideration.

The real-estate **closing** is the final step in a real estate transaction. The closing is the meeting at which the buyer and seller sit down together to sign the documents that finalize the conveyance of title from the seller to the buyer, and if applicable, put the buyer's loan into effect.

The overarching purpose of the closing is for the seller to **convey title** of the real property to the buyer, in exchange for payment of the agreed-upon purchase price by the buyer. The closing funds, including the purchase price, the loan funds, and the earnest-money deposit, are collected by the closing agent and deposited into his or her trust account immediately prior to closing, and are then disbursed by the closing agent to the appropriate parties after the closing has been completed and the documents have been recorded. Let us review what happens prior to closing:

1. The property is put on the market for sale by the owner, who may have employed a real estate broker to list the property, perform a market comparable analysis to determine a listing price, place the property on the Multiple Listing Service (MLS), advertise the property, conduct open houses and otherwise show the property to prospective buyers, and receive any offers to purchase, to be presented to the seller;

2. The owner/seller and the real estate broker review the offer to purchase and may make a counteroffer to the prospective buyer;

3. The executed offer to purchase contains a closing date, which may include language that "time is of the essence" to avoid unnecessary delays on either party's part;

4. The buyer qualifies for a real estate loan from a bank or other lender to purchase the property, and the lender requires certain reports to determine the property's fair market value and the potential risks involved with the loan, including an appraisal; inspections of the home's plumbing, electrical, and HVAC components; the septic tank and/or well-water systems; and inspections to reveal issues like termites, lead paint, and radon gas, which is a naturally occurring radioactive gas that is common in all parts of the United States. Acceptable levels are determined by the Environmental Protection Agency.

   The offer to purchase form contains a clause allowing the buyer a period of time to have the property inspected so he or she may formally address any necessary repairs to the property with the seller. This called the **due diligence** or **inspection** period. The closing paralegal should calendar the deadline for this inspection period and ensure that all pending inspections, the survey, and other due-diligence research is completed within the designated time period.

5. A title agency, or closing agent/attorney, is engaged to perform a title examination, and issue an opinion of title, if applicable to the state.

Although the tasks in (4) and (5) above can be performed more or less simultaneously, they still require a considerable amount of time, which is why a closing date is typically scheduled for a date at least 30 days after the purchase contract has been executed by the parties. For the real estate paralegal, orchestrating the intricacies of the closing process is of paramount importance, and explains why organizational skills are essential for a paralegal.

Once the closing agent or attorney has been engaged, the paralegal's participation in the closing process begins. If the paralegal is responsible for title research, he or she should begin the examination as soon as the purchase contract (offer to purchase) is received. He or she should then calendar all deadlines in connection with the closing and the closing date. If the seller has engaged his or her own attorney, the closing paralegal or attorney should contact that attorney to ask whether he or she plans to provide the seller's documents or if the closing attorney will be responsible for preparing them. A paralegal should only contact the adverse party or his or her counsel with the supervising attorney's authorization to do so. It is very easy for an inexperienced paralegal to cross ethical lines without realizing he or she has done so.

The lender may make first contact with the closing agent/attorney's office, but if not, the paralegal should contact the lender to determine when the loan package will be forwarded. Many times it will not be until the day before, or even the day of, closing, so it is a good idea to ask whether the lender is willing to send at least its closing instruction letter in advance so the paralegal may know what is expected well in advance of closing.

B. What Happens at Closing?

Many persons and entities have an interest in the closing of real property, and are entitled to be paid from the distribution of funds at closing. Not all of these interested persons attend the closing; they rely on the closing attorney or **escrow** agent to appropriately disburse the funds owed to them.

In almost all states, the closing is conducted by an *escrow agent* or a *title agency,* but in some states the closing is conducted by an attorney. Attorneys, especially, are frequently assisted at the closings by their paralegals, who have compiled the large number of documents to be executed by the buyer and seller. Many of these documents must be notarized, and so it is important that the paralegal assisting with the closing be a **notary public.**

Many states in the eastern United States require an attorney to conduct a closing, whereas in many western states, closings are conducted by an escrow agent for an escrow company. In either case, the events that take place at a closing are generally the same.

Attorneys must be especially careful and aware of the dangers of *dual representation,* meaning the closing attorney represents both the seller and buyer at the closing. Such representation is permitted, and the conflict can be waived by the parties if the parties have given their informed consent. While both the seller's and buyer's interests are aligned in that they want to consummate the transaction, there is always a risk that their interests may become adverse. If the attorney is representing both parties, the attorney may not ethically advocate on behalf of one party to the detriment of the other party.

The *buyer* and *seller* are usually present at the closing, although in the seller's case this is not an absolute necessity if the seller has signed the appropriate documents beforehand, most importantly, the deed conveying title to the property. Many closing agents or attorneys will require that all closing documents be notarized in the case of a "mail-away" closing like this, even those that would typically not be notarized, to minimize the chance of fraud on the seller's part, and the paralegal may be asked to take additional steps to verify the signatures are authentic. The attendance of the buyer at closing is usually required by the lender because of the number of loan documents that must be signed and the risk involved in having them signed outside the closing agent's presence.

The buyer's and seller's respective real estate *brokers* are not required to attend the closing, but frequently do so to offer "moral support" for their clients, who may be experiencing stress related to the closing. Many a real estate transaction has fallen apart at the closing because of some disagreement between the buyer and seller, oftentimes relating to a fixture or item of personal property that the seller expected to take upon departing the property, and that the buyer expected to remain with the property. Because of their professional experience and their relationships with their clients, the agents and brokers can often smooth over any such disagreements so that the property may close as planned. The brokers may

Escrow
a legal document such as a deed, or property such as money, held by a person not a party to the real estate transaction, that is, the escrow agent. Upon the satisfaction of the conditions in the contract for sale of the property, at the closing the escrow agent will deliver the deed to the buyer, and will disburse proceeds to the seller.

Notary Public
a person authorized by a state to administer oaths, certify documents, and attest to the authenticity of signatures.

also choose to wait after closing to receive their commission checks, and they will usually want a copy of the fully executed *settlement statement* as well.

The paralegal's role at closing varies by state and by closing attorney or agent. In some states paralegals are allowed to conduct closings without an attorney present, as long as their role is restricted to having documents executed and not providing legal advice. For an inexperienced paralegal this can be a difficult line to define, so he or she should always err on the side of caution and avoid any explanation of the closing documents.

In other states paralegals are not authorized to conduct closings. But universally, an experienced paralegal is a valuable asset at a closing. Before the closing begins, the paralegal should make sure all closing documents, including the transaction documents (deed, settlement statement), the loan documents (mortgage or deed of trust and related documents), the title insurance documents (lien affidavit, any indemnities), and any other agreements or affidavits are prepared in their final form and organized in a manner that makes it simple for the closing agent to have them signed efficiently at closing such as marking all signature blanks with flags. The paralegal should make sure the legal description and any other exhibits or attachments are present in the corresponding documents.

As documents are signed, the paralegal should ascertain all signatures match the names on the fronts of the documents and those typed under the signature lines. These discrepancies in signatures are simple to remedy while the closing is in process and all the parties are still present. The closing paralegal should be in contact with the title paralegal about coordinating the title update and having the documents that are to be recorded delivered into his or her hands for recording.

1. NOTARIZATION OF DOCUMENTS

Notaries public are commissioned by the states, and applications are typically made through the office of the Secretary of State. Many law firms are willing to pay the fees for their paralegals to become and remain certified as notaries public.

At the closing, the paralegal should carefully notarize each signature using the proper acknowledgment form and make sure to place his or her seal on each **acknowledgment** if required, and even if not for those documents being recorded. The paralegal-notary's signature must match the notary seal exactly. Identification should be checked carefully for any person who is not personally known to the paralegal. In states where a journal entry or fingerprint is required for each notary acknowledgment, the paralegal must be diligent about entering/obtaining them.

Notary laws should be followed to the letter and not be taken lightly. Many come with harsh sanctions for violations, including misdemeanor and felony, and for good reason. Consider the husband who wants to sell a rental house he owns with his estranged wife, with whom he does not have a good relationship. He knows she will not agree to sign the deed, so he asks or hires another woman to attend the closing and pretend to be his wife. A diligent paralegal will check the identification of the woman and suspect she is not who she claims to be. But the paralegal should never accuse a person of fraud in a closing; rather, she should convey her concerns to the attorney privately and let him or her decide how to proceed.

Consider another case where a couple is selling property but only the husband comes to closing. He says his wife is busy and cannot attend, so he has had her sign the deed at home and brought it to closing for the paralegal to notarize. In no case may a paralegal notarize this deed, acknowledging that he or she witnessed the signature of the wife, even if the wife is personally known to the paralegal. It can be very difficult to refuse to notarize a document when a client is being pushy

Acknowledgment
a formal declaration made in the presence of an authorized officer, such as a notary public, by someone who signs a document and confirms that the signature is authentic.

and feels the refusal is trivial, but the paralegal is statutorily required to stand his or her ground, so this is as much for his or her own protection as for that of the closing agent by whom he or she is employed.

a. Basic Acknowledgment Form

The notary public should complete the form of acknowledgment that corresponds with the style of signature on the document. In residential closings, a basic form of signature by an individual will almost always be appropriate. In commercial closings, a document may be signed by an entity, and sometimes another entity may sign as a member or partner of the signing entity. In some states the chain of signature must be set out in the acknowledgment form. Where a paralegal is provided with a document containing an incorrect form of acknowledgment, he or she *may not* tell the signatory the form is incorrect or suggest the proper form, even though he or she has been through the certification process and knows what form should be used. This may be interpreted as the providing of legal advice and should be left to the attorney. In the case of an incorrect form of acknowledgment, the paralegal should refuse to notarize the document, but should discuss the issue with the supervising attorney, not with the signatory.

It is also important that the notary always remember to place his or her seal on the acknowledgment in states where it is required, and even in those where it is not when it comes to documents being recorded. The seal should be stamped or impressed firmly enough to be clearly legible, and darkened in the case of an impressed seal so it is photographically reproducible. Seal darkeners are convenient and are available at most office-supply vendors.

Some states, like South Carolina, have statutory requirements for the witnessing of signatures on documents in addition to notarization. The paralegal should be familiar with all requirements for the acknowledgment of execution of documents in his or her state.

b. Subscribing Witness

There is an option for notarization of a document that has already been signed outside the presence of the notary public, called a ***subscribing witness***, where the acknowledgment form states that the notary is acknowledging the signature of *another person* who saw the signatory sign the instrument. Say John Goodfriend has an aging neighbor who is home-bound, and she needs to have her signature on a document notarized. She signs the document in front of Mr. Goodfriend, and he offers to bring it to the attorney's office for notarization. As long as Mr. Goodfriend actually witnessed the neighbor's signature on the instrument, he may, in the presence of the notary public, add his signature to the document near his neighbor's as evidence of this, and the notary may acknowledge *Mr. Goodfriend's* signature rather than the neighbor's.

A subscribing witness acknowledgment is not acceptable in the case in which a husband brings documents previously signed by his wife to closing, because the husband stands to gain something from that transaction. Mr. Goodfriend is not involved in his neighbor's transaction, and may sign as a subscribing witness because he is a disinterested party.

c. Attorney in Fact

Sometimes one party signs a document on behalf of the other as his or her attorney-in-fact. In this case, the person signing has been given the power to act on behalf of the other party by a ***power of attorney***. A power of attorney may grant a wide range of authority, or may be specific to one transaction, and sometimes even one document. A specific form of notary acknowledgment is usually required in connection with signature by an attorney-in-fact. The paralegal must be careful to notarize the signature of the person serving as attorney-in-fact, not the person on whose behalf the attorney-in-fact is signing.

d. Jurat

Jurat
(from the Latin, "to swear") a certification added to an affidavit or deposition stating when and before what authority the affidavit or deposition was made.

Affidavits are sworn statements, and a **jurat** form of acknowledgment should be used for an affidavit, in which the signatory signs the document under oath. In the case of a sworn statement, the notary must administer an oath in accordance with the appropriate statute. The jurat must contain the required elements of a notary acknowledgment, such as the date, the seal, and the notary's printed name and signature, and reads generally as follows: "Sworn to and subscribed before me this the ___ day of _____, 2015."

As long as a notary public has actually witnessed a signature and has confirmed the identity of the signatory, then the signature may be illegible, or as simple as an "X" and still be valid and binding.

The notary's role is strictly to verify in writing and under official seal that he or she has witnessed a person's signature on a document, and has confirmed the identity of the person who has signed. A notary acknowledgment is not proof of the legality, authenticity, or enforceability of a document, and in fact, the notary public has no need to know the contents of the document. The text of a confidential document may be covered, and the notary may still notarize signatures at the end.

After a document has been signed, the notary public should make sure the signatures match the names in the documents and under the signature lines exactly; for instance, if the grantor name is typed "Jeffrey L. Parker" he should not sign as "Jeff Parker." The paralegal should also make sure the notary acknowledgment is complete, including all elements required by the state, such as correctly spelled names, date of acknowledgment, the printed name of the notary, and notary seal.

C. The Closing Documents

RESPA
the Real Estate Settlement Procedures Act is a federal law that requires lenders to provide homebuyers with information about known or estimated settlement costs.

Truth in Lending Act
also known as the Consumer Credit Protection Act, the TILA is a federal statute that requires full disclosure of the terms of consumer loans, including mortgage loans, including the interest rate, the annual percentage rate, and the term of the loan.

The number of documents at a typical closing has increased dramatically in the last 30 years, driven by two forces. First, since the mid-1970s, the federal government has required a substantial amount of documentation for loans insured by the government, for example, FHA and VA loans; the documentation requirements benefit not only the government, but borrowers as well. These documents and disclosures are required by the **Real Estate Settlement Procedures Act (RESPA)**[1] and the federal **Truth in Lending Act (TILA)**.[2]

The second force driving the increase in closing documentation has been an increase in the number of lawsuits, mostly by buyers/borrowers. These lawsuits usually make claims for fraud, misrepresentation, or unfair and deceptive trade practices, alleging that some relevant, material fact was not disclosed to the borrower, to the buyer's financial detriment.

[1]RESPA was enacted in 1974, and is codified at Title 12, Chapter 27 of the United States Code, 12 U.S.C. §§ 2601–2617.
[2]The Truth in Lending Act was originally enacted in 1968. The TILA covers a broad range of consumer-related loans, including loans for the purchase of residential real property. The law is codified at 12 CFR § 226.

The buyer will typically select the closing/escrow agent or title attorney to conduct the closing. The lender will then forward a ***loan package*** or ***settlement package*** to the escrow agent or closing attorney. The package will contain all the documents the buyer is expected to sign in connection with the loan, and sometimes copies of additional documents that are relevant to the closing, like the offer to purchase executed by the buyer and seller. Following is a general list of documents common to most closings:

1. TRANSACTION DOCUMENTS

The transaction documents are, for the most part, executed only by the seller. If the seller has engaged the services of an attorney to represent him or her in connection with the closing, this attorney will usually prepare the seller's documents on the seller's behalf and forward them to the closing agent/attorney prior to or at closing. In the case of dual representation, the seller's documents may be prepared by the closing attorney. In this case, he or she may charge a document preparation fee to the seller, which should be reflected in the settlement statement. In a closing of a loan refinance, where the transaction only involves a loan and the property is not being conveyed by one party to another, there will be no need for pure "transaction" documents, but certain affidavits relating to the status of the property may still apply, and they will be signed by the borrower as the current owner, rather than the seller.

a. Deed

As we discussed in the previous chapter, the deed is the legal document that actually ***conveys title*** to the property from the seller to the buyer. The buyer will want a general warranty deed as this type of deed offers the highest degree of protection to the buyer because of its extensive warranties (promises), for example, the warranty of quiet enjoyment. We will discuss deeds and warranties in greater detail in a later chapter. Do not confuse the deed with the deed of trust, which is described under Loan Documents.

b. Lien Waiver and/or Gap Indemnity

Buyers, lenders, and title insurance companies want assurance that no unexpected liens having seniority over the deed of trust will come to light after closing. A **lien waiver**, in general, is an affidavit that states there are no unrecorded liens on the property and that no third parties are legally entitled to file a lien within the statutory time period allowed. This document provides assurance and an inducement to the title company to issue a policy without exception to unrecorded liens or liens that may be filed by those who have recently provided services or materials in connection with alterations to the property. There are different forms of lien waivers, depending on the circumstances.

In the case of a purchase transaction involving a residence where no recent improvements have been made, the waiver will be signed only by the owner(s) of the property, and it will state that during the statutory time period allowed for filing liens prior to closing and recording, no services or materials have been provided in connection with the property, or in the case of minor alterations that all providers have been paid in full. The statutory time period allowed for filing liens may not expire until after the closing has occurred.

If improvements have recently been added to the property, such as a sunroom, and the construction is complete at the time of closing, the contractor(s) who performed the work or provided materials should sign an affidavit stating he (they) has been paid in full and that he (they) knows of no party eligible to file

Lien waiver
an affidavit that states that there are no unrecorded liens, particularly mechanics' liens, on the property to be conveyed.

a claim of lien against the property in connection with the services or materials provided. The contractor(s) waives any right to file a lien by the terms of this lien waiver. The owner will also sign this affidavit.

If the construction of improvements or alterations is in progress at the time of closing, it is unlikely the contractor(s) has been paid in full as his work is ongoing, so in this case the affidavit will contain language **subordinating** any potential lien he may be eligible to file in connection with his work to the lien of the mortgage or deed of trust. This ensures the lender's priority over the contractor's potential lien.

A lien waiver or subordination agreement should be prepared in connection with every closing in applicable states, even if only signed by the seller certifying that no alterations have been made, or by the borrower in the case of a refinance. If a lien waiver is not provided to the title insurance company, it will include an exception in the policy for general unrecorded mechanics' and/or materialmen's liens, which is undesirable as it excludes an important coverage for buyers and lenders.

A Gap Indemnity is an affidavit signed by the seller indemnifying the title insurance company against any encumbrances of record between the effective date of the title commitment and the closing. This provides an inducement to the title insurance company to provide gap insurance with the title policy, which covers this time period. Gap coverage is more common in commercial closings than in residential, and in fact, may only be applicable to commercial closings in some states. Further, gap coverage is not commonly used in all states, which is why title examination must be updated right before recording, to the very moment the deed and mortgage are recorded.

These affidavits will all contain language indemnifying the buyer, lender, and title insurance company against loss in the case of any untrue statement(s) therein. The appropriate forms are state-specific and are available from the title insurance company. The closing paralegal should prepare an appropriate affidavit for every closing, even in a refinance, in which case the borrower will sign the affidavit as opposed to the seller. In the cases where construction is involved, the paralegal should contact the service and material providers well in advance of closing for signature to ensure the document is executed by all parties before the closing occurs.

c. Substitute 1099-S

A substitute 1099-S for tax reporting purposes should be signed by the seller in each real estate transaction, with the exception of a closing where the seller is a corporation, which is an exempt entity. A copy of the signed substitute 1099-S must be provided to the seller by the closing agent either at closing or by January 31 of the year following the closing. If there are multiple sellers of the same property, a form must be signed by each, with his or her tax identification number and pro rata share of the gross proceeds shown. The exception to this is a married couple who files taxes jointly, who may both sign one form and provide one Social Security number. The closing paralegal may be responsible for handling the mailing and filing all his or her firm's 1099-S filings with the Internal Revenue Service at the beginning of each year.

Forms are available through the IRS website, www.irs.gov, but may also be generated by the seller's attorney or closing agent. Some states have additional withholding forms required in connection with the recording of documents, and the paralegal should familiarize himself/herself with these requirements. Software programs are available for electronic filing.

In the case of a refinance, there is no need for a substitute 1099-S, as it relates strictly to the exchange of money or services for property.

Subordinate
to place in a lower rank, class, or position; to assign a lower priority to.

d. Non-Foreign Status Affidavit

The Non-Foreign Status Affidavit is a certification pursuant to the Internal Revenue Code that the seller is not a non-resident alien, a foreign entity, or an entity whose owners, partners, or beneficiaries are foreign persons, as defined by the Internal Revenue Code and Income Tax Regulations. Tax must be withheld by the purchaser of an interest in real property located within the United States if the seller falls under any of these categories.

The Non-Foreign Status Affidavit may be combined with the substitute 1099-S, and should be prepared by the seller's attorney or closing agent as part of the seller's documents.

In the case of a refinance there is no need for a non-foreign status affidavit, as it relates strictly to the citizenship of the seller of real property.

e. Survey Affidavit

If a survey was done fairly recently and no improvements or alterations have been made to the property since the date of the survey, the title insurance company may accept a survey affidavit from the seller (or borrower in the case of a refinance), stating that no improvements have been made and indemnifying the lender against loss as a result of any untrue statement therein.

The survey affidavit form may be obtained from the title insurance company and should be prepared by the seller's attorney or closing agent as part of the seller's documents.

f. Bill of Sale

If **personal property** is to be sold in conjunction with the sale of the real property, a **bill of sale** should be included with the closing documents. Personal property might consist of a refrigerator, washer, dryer, blinds, or other items agreed upon between the buyer and seller. The bill of sale is generally prepared by the seller's representative along with the deed and other seller's documents. It is similar to a deed in that it conveys ownership, but only of the personal property. It may or may not contain warranties for the personal property.

Bill of sale
an instrument for conveying title to personal property.

Since the bill of sale does not convey an interest in the real property, it is not recorded in the public registry as are the deed and mortgage. Personal property should not be confused with "fixtures," like stoves, wall sconces, water heaters, sinks, and so forth, which are affixed to and conveyed as part of the real property, although there are exceptions that may be agreed upon, as in the case of a chandelier the seller wants to take because it is a family heirloom, or a window air-conditioner the seller wants to leave because he or she will not need it.

There will be no need for a bill of sale in connection with a refinance, as it relates strictly to the purchase of personal property.

g. Assignment of Warranties

The seller may have received warranties or guarantees from manufacturers related to some major components in the house being sold, such as the HVAC system, the roof, freezers or refrigerators, entertainment centers, and other expensive items. Frequently, these items will carry warranties guaranteeing maintenance-free performance for a certain period of time. The buyer will want to take advantage of these warranties, and so at the closing the seller will assign the warranties to the buyer. Manufacturer's warranties that are assigned to the home buyer on ovens, stoves, refrigerators and other appliances or systems, should not be confused with warranties found in the deed, such as the warranty of quiet enjoyment, further assurance, etc.

As with a bill of sale, there will be no **assignment** of warranties in a refinance, as it relates to the sale of personal property.

h. Affidavits Addressing Title Issues

The title search may reveal matters that appear to be in the property owner's name, but this cannot be confirmed by the public record. For example, if the seller's name is John Smith, the title research is likely to reflect many index entries in variations of that name. It is not the title paralegal's responsibility to decide whether these entries are against the actual seller, beyond the scope of the public records.

All questionable matters found should be reported to the title company, which may require that the seller sign an affidavit certifying that these encumbrances are not against him or the subject property, and indemnifying the title company against loss as a result of any untrue statements in the affidavit. A similar affidavit may be used in the case of a refinance, but will be signed by the borrower rather than the seller.

i. Settlement Statement/HUD-1

The settlement statement is an extensive itemization of the funds received and disbursed by the closing attorney or escrow agent in the sales or loan refinance transaction. Contrary to the seller's documents, the Settlement Statement is signed by both parties, and is prepared by the closing agent/attorney. The **RESPA** requires the use of the **HUD-1 settlement statement form** in residential closings when the loan is federally insured.

The settlement statement/HUD-1 provides a breakdown of the gross and net amounts due from the buyer (either in cash or loan proceeds) and the gross and net amounts to be paid to the seller. Essentially, it is a full accounting of the money changing hands in connection with the closing, showing the total incoming funds (including the new loan) and a breakdown of the disbursements from those funds to the entitled parties for services performed, such as payoff of the seller's loan, real-estate broker commissions, hazard insurance premium, appraisal fee, title search and title insurance premium, termite and other inspections, the property survey, mortgage insurance, recording fees, transfer taxes, as well as prorations between the parties of taxes and utility fees.

As stated above, certain charges such as taxes and utilities are **_prorated_**. For example, property taxes may be assessed and become a lien on the property on January 1. However, those taxes may not be due and payable until December 31. Therefore, if the property closes on June 30, the seller must pay the property taxes for the first half of the year, while the buyer is responsible for the property taxes for the second half of the year. These amounts are adjusted, or prorated, on the settlement statement.

The same principle applies to the proration of utilities. Water and sewer charges may be billed quarterly, and so the settlement statement will apportion or prorate the seller's and buyer's respective portions of those charges. Another item that may be prorated is fuel oil used for heating the house. If the seller filled the fuel tank in early March with 300 gallons of fuel oil (at a cost of, perhaps, $1,000), and the closing occurs two months later in May, the seller will be entitled to a rebate, or proration, of the fuel oil remaining in the tank at the time of closing.

The settlement statement accounts for all trust funds being received and disbursed in connection with the closing. In residential transactions, a HUD-1 form is used for purchase transactions and may be used for refinances as well. A HUD-1A form is an abbreviated version of the HUD-1 that may be used optionally for refinances. These forms and their instructions are available in the Forms section on the website of the Housing and Urban Development (www.hud.gov), but many firms use a software program that automatically populates and produces a HUD-1 or HUD-1A form based on the data the user (paralegal) inputs. These programs conveniently show the user when the settlement statement is out of balance. The amount received must be exactly the same as the amount disbursed. HUD-1 closing statement is Exhibit 11-2 and can be found on page 295.

The settlement statement is divided into two columns, one for the Buyer or Borrower's funds and one for Seller's funds. Each party's column contains two sections, one for credits and the other for debits. The difference between each party's total credits and total debits is the net amount due either to or from the corresponding party, and is shown at the bottom of each column. The form is set up so that Buyer's debits are at the top ("Gross Amount Due from Borrower") and credits are at the bottom ("Amount Paid by or in Behalf of Borrower"), and the sections in the Seller's column are reversed so that credits are at the top and debits are at the bottom. This is intentional: Some amounts will be reflected on both sides of the settlement statement, as a credit to one party and a debit to the other, and it is easier to see how these amounts are applied if they are adjacent to each other. The following are HUD-1 itemizations.

Purchase Price.   As stated above, certain figures will be shown on both sides of the settlement statement, as is the case with the purchase price, or "Contract sales price." Since the purchase price is paid by the Buyer to the Seller, that amount is shown both as a debit to the Buyer under "Gross Amount Due FROM Borrower" and as a credit to the Seller under "Gross Amount Due TO Seller" in the top section of each party's column. If the sale of personal property is included in the transaction, that amount is shown separately on the line titled "Personal property."

The Loan.   Other figures will only appear on one side since they only apply to one party, as is the case with the loan amount, which is a credit to the Buyer/Borrower and shown in the section entitled "Amount Paid by or in Behalf of Borrower" on the line entitled "Principal Amount of New Loan."

If the loan is an equity line or a construction loan, in which case the borrower may make "draws" from the principal over a period of time rather than receiving the full amount of the loan at closing, then only a portion of the loan proceeds will not be disbursed to the Buyer/Borrower at closing. In this case, only the draw amount will be shown in the figures column, because this is the amount being received and disbursed by the closing agent.

If the seller's existing loan is being assumed by the buyer, the current principal amount due will be inserted on both sides of the settlement statement, as a debit to the seller and a credit to the buyer. The current month's interest will be prorated separately, in the same way taxes are prorated between the parties, except the proration will be for the month rather than the year. If the seller has already made the monthly payment at the time of closing, the buyer's portion of the interest will be debited from the buyer and credited to the seller on the settlement statement, and vice-versa if not.

If the loan is a "purchase-money" loan, sometimes referred to as "seller financing," the principal amount of the loan is shown the same way as a loan assumption, as a debit to the seller and a credit to the buyer, but there is no proration of interest.

The lender will charge certain fees in connection with the processing and administration of the loan, the most significant of which is the origination fee, which is usually based on a percentage of the loan. It will also require reimbursement for various reports it may have ordered in connection with evaluating the risk and profitability of the loan, like an appraisal of the property, a flood certification and a credit report, and may charge additional fees for review of these reports.

These charges are shown on the second page of the HUD-1 (Settlement Charges) in the section entitled "Items Payable in Connection with Loan."

The lender may "net" its fees from the loan proceeds, meaning it deducts the fees from the loan proceeds before sending the wire or check, so the amount received by the closing agent is less than the amount actually disbursed by the lender. This seems efficient since the closing agent would only send the loan fees back to the lender shortly after receipt, but it can be tricky to make sure it is reflected properly on the settlement statement. The borrower must get credit for the entire amount of the loan because the entire amount was actually disbursed by the lender as if the closing agent had indeed received and returned the fees. But the settlement statement must also reflect the actual amount received so the trust accounting will be accurate.

Tax Proration.   Unless otherwise agreed, property taxes for the year during which the closing occurs are prorated between the Buyer and Seller, so that each party only pays for the time period he or she owns the property during that year.

If the current year's taxes have not yet been paid and the bill is available, the lender will likely require payment of the entire bill at closing to eliminate the chance of a delinquent payment, which could result in a tax foreclosure of the property. In this case, each party's pro-rata share is entered as a debit in his or her column, and the entire amount due is disbursed by the closing agent to the tax department after recording.

If the current year's taxes have already been paid by the Seller, the Buyer's pro-rata share is shown as a debit from the Buyer and a credit to the Seller, in both top sections under "Adjustments for items paid by seller in advance," resulting in a reimbursement to the seller for the buyer's pro-rata share.

If the current year's tax bill is not yet available at the time of closing, the proration may be calculated as an estimate based on the prior year's tax bill. In this case, the Buyer, as the new owner, is responsible for paying the taxes when the bill is available, so he or she should be reimbursed by the Seller for Seller's portion. The Seller's pro-rata share is shown on both sides as a debit from the Seller and a credit to the Buyer, in the bottom sections under "Adjustments for items unpaid by seller," resulting in an advance to the buyer for the amount he or she will pay on behalf of the seller.

If the property has been improved since the prior year's tax bill but the current year's bill is not yet available, the parties may sign a tax proration agreement stating that they will prorate the taxes when the bill becomes available, since the amount due may be significantly higher than the prior year due to the addition of improvements.

If personal property is included in the transaction, both real and personal property taxes are prorated. In a commercial transaction where the property is leased, the tenant may be responsible for paying taxes, and there is no need for the proration between the Buyer and Seller.

Assessments for infrastructure by a city, town, or county, for instance, curb and gutter, may be prorated in the same way as taxes, as indicated in the same sections on the settlement statement.

Rent/Homeowner's Association Dues Proration.   If the property is leased, one month's rent is prorated in the same manner as the taxes, except the proration is for the month during which the closing occurs rather than the entire year. Homeowners' association (HOA) dues are generally paid by quarter and should be prorated accordingly. The blank lines below the tax prorations and assessments may be used for additional prorations of costs to be split between buyer and seller, like oil or gas.

Earnest Money.   The earnest money is a deposit made by the Buyer prior to the closing, in accordance with the purchase contract. It is typically held in escrow by the broker or the title insurance agency/company, but is sometimes paid directly to the seller by the buyer at the time the purchase contract is executed. If the former, it is deposited into the closing agent's trust account prior to the closing and then disbursed to the Seller as part of his or her closing proceeds. It will be shown in the same way the loan funds are shown, as a credit to the buyer and therefore an incoming fund.

If the latter, it will be shown on both sides as a debit to the Seller and a credit to the Buyer toward the purchase price, but it will not be received and disbursed by the closing agent. The closing paralegal must make sure that, as with all closing funds, the earnest money deposit is in the trust account as "good funds" before the closing begins.

Settlement Charges (Page 2).   The second page of the HUD-1 form is a detail of additional charges to each party, which are totaled and brought forward to the corresponding columns on the first page, and therefore included in the amounts shown in the totals.

Broker/Realtor Commissions.   In the past, the seller paid the brokerage commission and the broker with the listing (listing agent) and the broker who secured the buyer (selling agent) were both considered agents of the seller. Now there are seller agents and separate buyer agents, and it is negotiable as to which party pays the commission to the buyer's agent, as is the amount paid to each broker. Frequently, the buyer's agent negotiates to be paid by the seller, but that is not always the case. The paralegal must confirm the negotiated commissions with both the listing agent and the selling agent to determine the proper allocation of payments and the paying party for the settlement statement.

Costs in Connection with Loan.   The following three sections are for fees and costs in connection with the buyer's loan:

1. "Items Payable in Connection with Loan" is for the fees the lender charges to the borrower, like the origination fee (which is typically 1% of the loan) and costs for third-party reports ordered in advance by the lender, such as the appraisal, environmental report, termite report, or flood certification. If the lender has "netted" or deducted its fees from the loan funds, these fees will be shown as having been *paid outside closing* ("POC"), because they are not being received and disbursed by the closing agent.

2. "Items Required by Lender to be Paid in Advance" includes the daily interest (or per-diem interest) for the partial month, prorated from the date of the loan to the end of the month. Interest for residential closings is paid in arrears (for the month prior). For example, a March 15 closing means the lender collects 17 days' per-diem interest (from March 15 to March 31), which will be the equivalent of the payment that would be due on April 1, except it is paid in advance. The first full monthly payment of principal and interest would therefore be due on May 1 under the note.

3. "Reserves Deposited with Lender" is for escrows for the mortgage insurance premium (if applicable), property insurance, and taxes for the current billing cycle. To determine the monthly escrow amount for taxes, the total amount due for the year should be divided by twelve. If the closing is in March and the first loan payment is due on April 1, and the taxes are due on December 31, then three months of taxes should be collected on the closing statement, to cover January through March, because the escrows for the months of April through December will be collected as part of the borrower's monthly loan payments. This method ensures the lender will have the full years' taxes in escrow to pay when due on December 31 (remember the buyer will receive a credit at closing for the seller's portion of the year, and will be responsible for paying the entire year's bill when due). Insurance escrows may be calculated in the same way, except the billing cycle may not be based on a calendar year.

Title Charges.　Title insurance is calculated based on a formula varying by state, and may be discounted in the case of a reissue rate, where the new policy is being tacked to a prior policy. An invoice for the title insurance premium is provided with the commitment, and the amount due should be inserted on the second page of the settlement statement. It is paid by the buyer in some states and the seller in others.

Government Recording and Transfer Charges.　Recording fees, excise/transfer taxes, and mortgage taxes vary by state. Transfer taxes are typically paid by the Seller, as are recording fees for releases and/or satisfactions of existing mortgages or deeds of trust in the Seller's name. Recording fees for the deed and mortgage or deed of trust are usually the Buyer's responsibility.

Additional Settlement Charges.　This section is for additional charges not falling into another specific category, for example, the surveyor's fee, the pest inspection (if ordered directly by buyer or closing agent rather than lender), overnight delivery charges or wire fees for delivery of the payoff to the existing mortgage holder, or payment by the Seller for outstanding taxes or utility bills not being prorated.

Loan Payoff.　A formal payoff statement should be obtained from the Seller's lender prior to closing (or borrower's in the case of a refinance). The payoff statement is the existing lender's promise to cancel the loan if the payoff is made accordingly. It should contain the amount of principal and accrued interest due, any late charges or other fees, and the per-diem, or daily interest on the loan. In years past, the closing paralegal could contact the seller's lender and easily obtain payoff information. But due to more recent privacy laws, the closing paralegal may not be able to obtain the payoff statement without written authorization or personal information from the seller, including, but not limited to, the loan account number and at least a portion of the seller's social security number. For this reason, the closing agent may require that the seller request the payoff statement. But as the seller may benefit from an error in the seller's favor, he or she should be asked to have the payoff statement forwarded directly to the closing attorney by the lender, and the paralegal should contact the lender to confirm its validity once it is received.

Exhibit 11-1 is a generic form of seller authorization for release of the payoff to the closing agent.

EXHIBIT 11-1 Request for Payoff Information

REQUEST FOR PAYOFF INFORMATION

1. Please provide me with a written payoff statement for _____
    (the projected payoff date) in connection with the following loan:

    Loan No.: _____   Original Loan Amount: $_____

    Loan Date: _____   Approximate Loan Balance: $_____

    Borrower(s): _____

2. Based on the information currently available to me, the mortgage, deed of trust, security deed and other collateral (if any)
    that secures repayment of the loan is identified as follows:

    Date: _____   Amount Secured: $_____

    Original Mortgagor(s): _____

    Original Secured Party: _____

    Recording Information: Recorded in Book _____ at Page _____ in the Register of Deeds of _____
    County, State of _____

    Property Address: _____

3. I confirm that I am authorized to request and receive a payoff statement. I am:

    ☐   Liable as a borrower for payment of the loan.

    ☐   Liable as a guarantor of the loan obligation.

    ☐   A record owner of the real property or other collateral that secures the repayment of the loan.

    ☐   The Closing Attorney for the following client: _____ who is:
           ☐ refinancing
           ☐ purchasing the property from _____

4. Please send the written payoff statement:

    ☐   By mail addressed as follows (insert name and address):

    _____

    ☐   By fax to: Fax No. _____ Attn: _____

    ☐   By PDF: Attn: _____

REQUESTING PARTY:

	Consent by: _____ (obligor)
By:	By: _____
Printed name:	Printed name: _____
Telephone number: _____	

If the amount shown on the payoff statement is as of a date earlier than the closing date, per-diem (daily) interest should be added to the total amount due to correspond with the date the funds will be actually received by the lender. If the payoff is being forwarded via overnight delivery of a check or via a late wire, or the closing is postponed for a few days, the amount disbursed must be adjusted accordingly.

The adjusted amount must be shown on the closing statement to accurately reflect the disbursement, so the potential date of receipt must be anticipated well in advance by the paralegal drafting the closing statement, and he or she should err on the side of caution when there is any question. An insufficient payoff will result in a refusal to cancel the mortgage by the existing lender, putting the new lender in a junior position, which is a breach of the terms of the loan and the lender's instructions to the closing agent. The payoff must be sufficient to pay the loan in full on the day it is received by the lender, not the day it is disbursed.

Some banks have, for example, a 2:00 p.m. cutoff and any funds received after that time are considered to be on the next day's accounting, so the payoff amount must be calculated in advance with this in mind. Say the closing occurs on a Thursday at 10:00 a.m. and the closing statement reflects the payoff as of the day of closing. But due to delays, the deed and mortgage are not recorded until 4:00 p.m. If the payoff is forwarded to the lender by hand-delivery of a check on the same day, it will still be insufficient in the case of a 2:00 cutoff. If the payoff is forwarded via wire, it may not be received by the lender until the next day, and certainly will be received on the next day if sent by overnight delivery of a check.

If the closing occurs on a Friday, at least three days' per-diem interest should be added since the payoff will not be received and credited until the following Monday. Many closing agents automatically add a certain number of days of daily interest, for instance, 30 days, to ensure a sufficient payoff. It is acceptable for the payoff to exceed the actual amount due; any overage should be refunded by the lender to its borrower (the seller). In some cases the lender will forward the refund to the closing agent as the paying party, in which case the closing agent will deposit the refund in trust and disburse it in turn to the seller.

Adding per-diem interest is generally reliable for a few days' difference between the payoff statement and the closing date, but if the postponement is more than a few days, or if it is postponed into the following month, a new payoff statement should be obtained to ensure accuracy.

In the case of payoff of an equity line of credit where draws may be made by the seller, the closing agent should obtain an additional form from the seller requesting that the lender *freeze* or *block* the line so that no further draws may be made after the payoff statement is issued. Consider this scenario: The payoff statement is received by the closing agent on December 1, 2014, and it shows the total payoff as $200,000.00 as of December 15, 2014. The paralegal drafts the settlement statement accordingly.

Then on December 10, 2014, the seller writes an equity-line check on the account in the amount of $5,000.00, increasing the amount he or she owes to the lender to $205,000.00, unbeknownst to the closing agent. Closing occurs on December 15, 2014, and the closing agent disburses the amount of $200,000.00 to the lender, which is now insufficient to pay the loan in full. If the seller does not agree to pay the additional amount due, the closing agent may be responsible for it. This situation goes from bad to worse if the closing paralegal does not follow up with the lender immediately after closing to verify the payoff was received and sufficient, as interest will continue to accrue on the $5,000 balance. And it goes from worse to catastrophic if the seller writes another check and draws new principal on the line of credit.

No matter how the payoff is forwarded to the lender, the paralegal should include a letter with a check, or send an e-mail immediately following a wire, specifically stating that the funds represent a *payoff* of the loan and requesting prompt cancellation of the mortgage of record. This language shows *intent* to pay the loan in full, and may be used in defense of the closing agent if there is a dispute. But there is no guarantee of any protection, and this must not be relied upon as a safety net. The closing paralegal should follow up with the lender until the mortgage has been canceled of record, for which there may be a statutorily allowed time period, but which may take much longer.

A payoff statement should be obtained for any existing UCC financing statement in addition to a mortgage, and it must be properly terminated of record in conjunction with the mortgage.

HUD-1 Page Three. The final page of the HUD-1 provides the borrower with a comparison of the estimated loan costs shown on the Good Faith Estimate and the actual costs as reflected on the HUD-1. It also provides a breakdown of the loan terms, to give the borrower a full disclosure and therefore a better understanding of all the costs and interest being paid in connection with the loan, including potential increases in the payment amount. The HUD-1 form is a federally regulated form, and it is essential that all figures be exact and transparent to the seller, the buyer, and the lender. Any pressure from the buyer, the seller, or any party's broker to deviate from the rules and regulations governing proper completion of the settlement statement should be resisted. Exhibit 11-2 is an example of a Settlement Statement (HUD-1).

EXHIBIT 11-2 Settlement Statement (HUD-1)

A. Settlement Statement (HUD-1)

B. Type of Loan

1. ☐ FHA 2. ☐ RHS 3. ☐ Conv. Unins. 4. ☐ VA 5. ☐ Conv. Ins. | 6. File Number: | 7. Loan Number: | 8. Mortgage Insurance Case Number:

C. Note: This form is furnished to give you a statement of actual settlement costs. Amounts paid to and by the settlement agent are shown. Items marked "(p.o.c.)" were paid outside the closing; they are shown here for informational purposes and are not included in the totals.

D. Name & Address of Borrower: | E. Name & Address of Seller: | F. Name & Address of Lender:

G. Property Location: | H. Settlement Agent: | I. Settlement Date:

Place of Settlement:

(continued)

EXHIBIT 11-2 *Continued*

J. Summary of Borrower's Transaction		K. Summary of Seller's Transaction	
100. Gross Amount Due from Borrower		**400. Gross Amount Due to Seller**	
101. Contract sales price		401. Contract sales price	
102. Personal property		402. Personal property	
103. Settlement charges to borrower (line 1400)		403.	
104.		404.	
105.		405.	
Adjustment for items paid by seller in advance		**Adjustment for items paid by seller in advance**	
106. City/town taxes to		406. City/town taxes to	
107. County faxes to		407. County taxes to	
108. Assessments to		408. Assessments to	
109.		409.	
110.		410.	
111.		411.	
112.		412.	
120. Gross Amount Due from Borrower		**420. Gross Amount Due to Seller**	
200. Amount Paid by or in Behalf of Borrower		**500. Reductions in Amount Due to seller**	
201. Deposit or earnest money		501. Excess deposit (see instructions)	
202. Principal amount of new loan(s)		502. Settlement charges to seller (line 1400)	
203. Existing loan(s) taken subject to		503. Existing loan(s) taken subject to	
204.		504. Payoff of first mortgage loan	
205.		505. Payoff of second mortgage loan	
206.		506.	
207.		507.	
208.		508.	
209.		509.	
Adjustments for items unpaid by seller		**Adjustments for items unpaid by seller**	
210. City/town taxes to		510. City/town taxes to	
211. County taxes to		511. County taxes to	
212. Assessments to		512. Assessments to	
213.		513.	
214.		514.	
215.		515.	
216.		516.	
217.		517.	
218.		518.	
219.		519.	
220. Total Paid by/for Borrower		**520. Total Reduction Amount Due Seller**	
300. Cash at Settlement from/to Borrower		**600. Cash at Settlement to/from Seller**	
301. Gross amount due from borrower (line 120)		601. Gross amount due to seller (line 420)	
302. Less amounts paid by/for borrower (line 220)	( )	602. Less reductions in amounts due seller (line 520)	( )
303. Cash ☐ From ☐ To Borrower		603. Cash ☐ To ☐ From Seller	

The Public Reporting Burden For this collection of information is estimated at 35 minutes per response for collecting, reviewing, and reporting the data. This agency may not collect this information, and you are not required to complete this form, unless it displays a currently valid OMB control number. No confidentiality is assured; this disclosure is mandatory. This is designed to provide the parties to a RESPA covered transaction with information during the settlement process.

L. Settlement Charges

700. Total Real Estate Broker Fees	Paid From Borrower's Funds at Settlement	Paid From Seller's Funds at Settlement
Division of commission (line 700) as follows :		
701. $ to		
702. $ to		
703. Commission paid at settlement		
704.		

800. Items Payable In Connection with Loan			
801. Our origination charge	$	(from GFE#1)	
802. Your credit or charge (points) for the specific interest rate chosen	$	(from GFE#2)	
803. Your adjusted origination charges		(from GFE#A)	
804. Appraisal fee to		(from GFE#3)	
805. Credit report to		(from GFE#3)	
806. Tax service to		(from GFE#3)	
807. Flood certification to		(from GFE#3)	
808.			
809.			
810.			
811.			

900. Items Required by Lander to be Paid in Advance			
901. Daily interest charges from to @ $ /day		(from GFE#10)	
902. Mortgage insurance premium for months to		(from GFE#3)	
903. Homeowner's insurance for years to		(from GFE#11)	
904.			

1000. Reserves Deposited with Lander			
1001. Initial deposit for your escrow account		(from GFE#9)	
1002. Homeowner's insurance months @ $	per month $		
1003. Mortgage insurance months @ $	per month $		
1004. Property Taxes months @ $	per month $		
1005. months @ $	per month $		
1006. months @ $	per month $		
1007. Aggregate adjustment	-$		

1100. Title Charges			
1101. Title services and lender's title insurance		(from GFE#4)	
1102. Settlement or closing fee	$		
1103. Owner's title insurance		(from GFE#5)	
1104. Lender's title insurance	$		
1105. Lender's title policy limits	$		
1106. Owner's title policy limit	$		
1107. Agent's portion of the total title insurance premium to	$		
1108. Underwriter's portion of the total title insurance premium to	$		
1109.			
1110.			
1111.			

1200. Government Recording and Transfer Charges			
1201. Government recording charges		(from GFE#7)	
1202. Deed $ Mortgage $ Release $			
1203. Transfer taxes		(from GFE#8)	
1204. City/County tax/stamps Deed $ Mortgage $			
1205. State tax/stamps Deed $ Mortgage $			
1206.			

1300. Additional Settlement Charges			
1301. Required services that you can shop for		(from GFE#6)	
1302.	$		
1303.	$		
1304.			
1305.			

1400. Total Settlement Charges (enter on lines 103, Section J and 502, Section K)		

(continued)

EXHIBIT 11-2 *Continued*

Comparison of Good Faith Estimate (GFE) and HUD-1 Charrges		Good Faith Estimate	HUD-1
Charges That Cannot Increase	**HUD-1 Line Number**		
Our origination charge	#801		
Your credit or charge (points) for the specific interest rate chosen	#802		
Your adjusted origination charges	#803		
Transfer taxes	#1203		

Charges That In Total Cannot Increase More Than 10%		Good Faith Estimate	HUD-1
Government recording charges	#1201		
	#		
	#		
	#		
	#		
	#		
	#		
	#		
	Total		
Increase between GFE and HUD-1 Charges		$ or	%

Charges That Can Change		Good Faith Estimate	HUD-1
Initial deposit for your escrow account	#1001		
Daily interest charges $ /day	#901		
Homeowner's insurance	#903		
	#		
	#		
	#		

Loan Terms

Your initial loan amount is	$
Your loan term is	years
Your initial interest rate is	%
Your initial monthly amount owed for principal, interest, and any mortgage insurance is	$ includes ☐ Principal ☐ Interest ☐ Mortgage Insurance
Can your interest rate rise?	☐ No ☐ Yes, it can rise to a maximum of %. The first change will be on and can change again every after . Every change date, your interest rate can increase or decrease by %. Over the life of the loan, your interest rate is guaranteed to never be lower than % or higher than %.
Even if you make payments on time, can your loan balance rise?	☐ No ☐ Yes, it can rise to a maximum of $
Even if you make payments on time, can your monthly amount owed for principal, interest, and mortgage insurance rise?	☐ No ☐ Yes, the first increase can be on and the monthly amount owed can rise to $. The maximum it can ever rise to is $
Does your loan have a prepayment penalty?	☐ No ☐ Yes, your maximum prepayment penalty is $
Does your loan have a balloon payment?	☐ No ☐ Yes, you have a balloon payment of $ due in years on
Total monthly amount owed including escrow account payments	☐ You do not have a monthly escrow payment for items, such as property taxes and homeowner's insurance. You must pay these items directly yourself. ☐ You have an additional monthly escrow payment of $ that results in a total initial monthly amount owed of $. This includes principal, interest, any mortgage insurance and any items checked below: ☐ Property taxes ☐ Homeowner's insurance ☐ Flood insurance ☐ ☐ ☐

Note: If you have any questions about the Settlement Charges and Loan Terms listed on tilts form, please contact your lender.

2. LOAN DOCUMENTS

The loan documents are provided by the lender and are, for the most part, complete and ready for signature when they are delivered as part of the loan package. Only the buyer/borrower will sign the loan documents.

a. Commitment Letter

The loan **commitment letter** is the lender's pledge to lend the borrower a specific amount of money to the buyer for a specific interest rate. This commitment, however, is only good for a specified period of time, for example 30-60 days, because of interest-rate fluctuations in the lending market. The paralegal may obtain information for the settlement statement or amortization schedule from the commitment letter, such as the amount of the loan, the interest rate, and certain fees to be reimbursed to the lender in connection with facilitation of the loan. The commitment letter should be included in the loan package.

> **Commitment letter**
> the lender's pledge to lend the borrower a specific amount of money for a specific interest rate. The commitment is usually good for only 30-60 days.

b. Promissory Note

While the deed conveys title, and the mortgage or deed of trust pledges the property as collateral for the loan, the promissory note sets out the actual terms for the repayment of the loan. The note should state the interest rate, the payment amount and the term of the loan (which may vary between 5 and 30 years), including the dates of the first and last payments, and on what day of the month the payments must be made. It may include a complete amortization table that shows each payment over the term of the loan, so the borrower may see how much of his or her monthly payment to the lender is applied to the principal and how much is applied to interest. There are software programs available for creating an amortization table if the borrower requests one and it is not included in the loan package. When using these programs, the loan date and the first payment date should be entered exactly in accordance with the loan terms to reflect the accurate amount of interest, since it is paid in arrears (for the month prior to the payment month).

A ***balloon payment*** is a single payment at the end of the loan term, and includes the entire remaining balance after all the scheduled amortized payments have been made. If a loan is amortized over 20 years it will include 240 payments. Sometimes borrowers want to pay the loan over a shorter term, knowing they will refinance the balance before the end of the shorter term. Say John Smith obtained a loan in a year when interest rates were high. He feels certain that in five years rates will be lower, or perhaps he plans to sell the property within the five-year term, so he amortizes the loan over 20 years, meaning the monthly payment will be the same as if the loan were paid over 20 years, but the loan will mature in five years.

Of course this means that at the end of five years, there will be a large outstanding balance, which he must either pay in full or refinance at the current rate. The balloon payment would be the 241st payment, hence the term "balloon," because it inflates or expands the debt. This may also be done using the ***last payment*** (the 240th in this case) rather than a balloon payment. This should not be confused with adjustment of the last payment to account for rounding, meaning the amount paid could not be divided into equal payments, and the last payment was slightly adjusted accordingly.

The promissory note will be prepared by the lender and included in the loan package, ready for signature at closing. Promissory notes do not always require notarization, but the lender will include it in the form if it is required.

c. Mortgage or Deed of Trust

If we have a deed, why do we need a mortgage or deed of trust? The mortgage or deed of trust serves a completely different purpose than the deed. The deed conveys actual title to the buyer; the mortgage or deed of trust conveys *an interest in* the title to the lender. Some states are mortgage states, and other states favor the deed of trust. But in either case, the purpose is the same: the document *pledges the property as security* to the lender in exchange for the lender's making the loan for the purchase of the property. Ultimately, the document says: "If I, buyer/borrower, default on my obligations under this mortgage/deed of trust or the promissory note, then lender may foreclose on my property."

The mortgage or deed of trust should include basic elements common to most states, including the names of the borrower and the lender, the name of the trustee in trust states, the amount of the loan, and the maturity date, as well as other language required by applicable statutes. It must also include a clear description of the note or other document being secured, as an incorrect identification may result in the mortgage being unsecured.

If the mortgage or deed of trust secures future advances, it should state the amount of the **first draw**, or **present obligations**. This may be applicable in the case of a construction loan, where the maximum amount of the loan is not advanced at closing, and draws may be made over time. If this amount is left blank, it must be completed before the document is recorded.

The paralegal should make sure the borrower name in the mortgage or deed of trust matches the loan commitment letter, note, and deed, and that the signature lines and notary acknowledgments conform exactly. He or she should make sure the borrower has initialed each page if required by the lender. The legal description in the mortgage should be identical to that in the deed, the title commitment, and the survey, if applicable. Some lenders require that the exact legal description from the survey be used in the mortgage, if applicable. The mortgage or deed of trust will be prepared by the lender and included in the loan package, but it may require that the closing attorney insert the legal description and other property identification, or other information unknown until closing, like the amount of present obligations in the case of future advances.

d. Good Faith Estimate

The Good Faith Estimate is a HUD form that is provided to the borrower by the Lender before the loan is approved, to give the borrower an idea of what settlement charges he or she will have to pay in connection with the loan. This helps the borrower to shop for the best rates, and keeps him or her from being surprised by charges in connection with the loan and closing that he or she was not prepared to pay. A copy of the Good Faith Estimate should be included in the loan package, and contains many of the figures needed for the closing statement.

e. Federal Truth In Lending Disclosure

The Truth In Lending ("TIL" or "FTIL") is an in-depth disclosure statement regarding the terms of credit, made in compliance with federal law. It contains some of the same information the note may contain, like the number of payments, the amount of each payment, and the day of the month the payments are due, but it addresses the loan costs in the aggregate as opposed to principal and interest only.

It provides the borrower with much more detailed information on the overall costs of the loan, most importantly:

i. *APR*, or the *Annual Percentage Rate*, not to be confused with the *interest rate*. The APR will be higher because it includes the interest rate and other previously paid finance charges;

ii. *Finance Charge*, or the entire amount the loan will cost the borrower if paid as scheduled, including interest and all premiums, fees, and finance charges; and

iii. *Total Amount Financed*, or the amount of the mortgage after deduction of points and certain closing costs.

The Truth In Lending Disclosure also provides other disclosures, like whether a prepayment penalty applies, whether the loan may be assumed by another party, and insurance requirements.

f. Loan Assignment

Frequently a loan is purchased by a separate lender before the loan has closed, and an assignment from the lender to the new lender is recorded immediately after the mortgage or deed of trust.

g. Right of Rescission

The Right of Rescission applies in cases of refinances and other non-purchase transactions. It gives the borrower three days to change his or her mind and cancel the contract with the lender before the loan closes. The rescission period begins after the borrower has signed the credit contract and has received the truth in lending disclosure and two copies of the rescission notice, and ends at midnight on the third day, including Saturdays, but not Sundays or legal holidays.

The rescission notice is prepared by the lender and will be included in the refinance loan package. The closing paralegal should calendar a reminder for the fourth day and proceed with updating the title research and recording the deed of trust, assuming the borrower has not exercised his or her right to cancel the loan contract.

h. Closing Instruction Letter

In addition to statutory requirements, the lender will have specific requirements that must be met in connection with the loan documents before the attorney or closing agent may be authorized to record documents and disburse the loan funds. The letter usually lists all the loan documents included in the package, specifies the required chain of events for closing the loan, and requires the attorney or closing agent's signature evidencing his or her acceptance and commitment to adhere to its terms. The paralegal should make sure these instructions are followed to the letter, as any breach will put the closing attorney at risk, especially if the lender incurs a loss as a result of the failure to fulfill the requirements.

i. Miscellaneous Loan Documents

There will usually be more forms included in the loan package, depending on the lender and the state. Examples of these include an Errors and Omission Agreement (the borrower's agreement to correct any typographical errors in the closing documents, a name affidavit (where the buyer's name appears more than one way on record, to certify the variations represent the same person), an Equal Credit Opportunity Act (ECOA) Disclosure, or an Occupancy Affidavit (the borrower's certification regarding whether he or she intends to occupy the collateral as his or her principal residence.

3. OTHER CLOSING DOCUMENTS

a. Property Survey

The survey is a physical inspection of the property performed by a licensed surveyor, to ascertain its correct boundaries, and to determine the location of any encroachments and/or easements, including those on record and those discovered by the surveyor in his or her field work. The surveyor's responsibility is to certify as to the physical status of the property based on his or her inspection, but it is the attorney's responsibility to review the survey and determine the legal implications of the matters shown. The survey should be reviewed carefully for any issues that should be disclosed to the buyer, lender, and/or title insurance company, and a copy should be provided to each. Typically the cost of the survey is the buyer's responsibility.

There are multiple types of surveys, but the ones most often used for closing purposes are "As-Built" surveys and those performed in accordance with the standards of the American Land Title Association ("ALTA"). ALTA surveys are generally used in commercial closings and contain much more detail than as-built surveys, including a list of the exceptions from the title commitment and the metes-and-bounds legal description.

The survey and the plat are similar, but the terms are not interchangeable. A *plat* is a recorded representation of the property, and it must be reviewed and approved by the appropriate governmental agency or municipality, usually the county, before recording. Some states may allow a *survey* to be recorded without the full review of a plat.

i. Guide for Drafting the Metes-and-Bounds Legal Description.

The paralegal may be asked to draft the legal description based on the survey. This can be a daunting task, but experience will sharpen his or her skills and make him or her a more valuable asset to the attorney.

Start by using a final sealed survey and not a preliminary drawing, so that if changes are made in the finalization of the survey, you will not miss updating them in your description. Legal descriptions should not be drawn from topographical maps, site plans, landscaping plans, or anything other than as-built, boundary, or ALTA surveys.

It is a good idea to position the survey so that the "North" arrow shown on the survey is up, even if that means the numbers and text are upside-down, so the parcel is properly oriented in your view.

First, identify the general location of the property in a brief paragraph or sentence that identifies the township, the county, and the state: "Lying in Friendship Township, Guilford County, North Carolina, and being more particularly described as follows:...."

Before beginning the actual description of the tract, note the distinction between *existing* and *new* markers/monuments. Surveyors attempt to locate *existing* corner or boundary markers/monuments (iron pins, concrete monuments, railroad ties) that were previously set, and base their drawings on those markers, as they prevail over newly placed ones. If an existing marker cannot be located, the surveyor may set a *new* marker in the ground (the terms "new" and "set" are interchangeable on surveys).

Start with a clearly defined BEGINNING point. The description should be written so that a person could take it to the site and physically find the beginning point from the references provided. The legal description should begin at an existing marker if possible, and if not, then from a point or new monument to which an existing monument can be *tied*. "BEGINNING at a point in the west margin of Main Street located 50 feet from an iron pipe" gives no more information about the location of the tie than it does about the beginning point. Use a monument or tie that is identified on a recorded plat if possible, or one that is identified as or tied to a geological survey monument. If you utilize a tie to a monument or point from an adjacent deed reference shown on a survey, be sure you have looked at that deed description to make sure it is still the corner you intend to describe. If a portion of the adjacent property has been sold, it may not be what was originally, say, the northwest corner, of the tract.

Sometimes the point of BEGINNING is established by basing it on a point of COMMENCEMENT, which is another word for a tie, but it is generally used where there are multiple calls between the tie and the point of beginning, to avoid confusion between the two.

After the beginning point is established, each line in succession should be described using the bearing or course (direction), and the distance (length) of the line, with semicolons separating the calls, generally formatted as follows: "…and running thence South 05° 27' 44" East 242.35 feet to an existing concrete monument marking the northwest corner of David Smith (see Deed Book 1234, Page 567);…" or "…thence South 05° 27' 44" East 242.35 feet to a new iron pipe to a point located on the east margin of the right of way of Main Street…." or even "…thence South 05° 27' 44" East 242.35 feet to a new iron pipe to a point located on the east margin of the right of way of Main Street, said pipe also marking the northwest corner of David Smith…."

The legal description should describe the parcel boundary entirely in either a clockwise or counterclockwise direction, but clockwise is generally preferred. In order to make all the calls "run" in the same direction, sometimes it is necessary to reverse the directions in a call in order to make it correct in your description. The surveyor may not necessarily describe the calls running in the same direction, especially in the case where two tracts share a common line. The same line may be described as running both North 45° East and South 45° West, and for the drawing itself, either is correct. But for the legal description only one will make the call run in the direction that makes it begin at one specific point and end at the other. It is a common mistake to reverse the first direction (North or South) and forget to reverse the second (West or East), which is why it is essential to plot your completed descriptions and check for closure errors.

It is rarely accurate to describe a line as the "northeast," "northwest," "southeast," or "southwest" line, particularly for street right-of-way margins. In most cases, the only line that should be described as such is one that runs exactly 45° in any direction. If a line is angled at more than 45°, it is more of a horizontal line than a vertical line, and the property line is therefore either a north line or a south line in the case of a basically square or rectangular tract. If it is angled at less than 45°, it is more of a vertical line than horizontal, and should be described as either an east or west line. If the tract is not a basic square or rectangle, and a north, south, east, or west line is staggered, consisting of multiple lines of varying directions, then the entire distance should be viewed as the north, south, west, or east line, rather than its parts being described independently as such. Using phrases like "…thence along the west line of John Smith the following eight (8) courses and distances…," or "…thence continuing along the west line of John Smith…," is very effective. Include as many references to adjacent property, roads, creeks, railroad rights of way, and so forth, as possible (including book and page numbers), particularly when recorded plat references are available. Be sure to identify monuments properly, as they control over calls in most states.

Remember to look at an entire north, south, east, or west line as a whole when determining which corner a monument marks. If the tract is, for example, a rectangle, but it is situated at an angle on the axis, then what appears to be the northwest corner may be better defined as the northernmost corner, or the westernmost corner. Use an identifier that cannot be interpreted more than one way and can only identify one corner of the tract. See Figure 11-1.

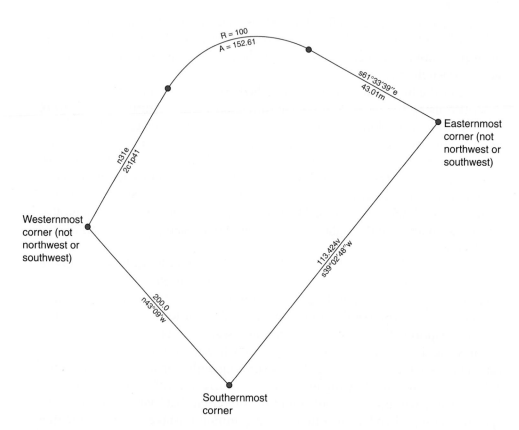

FIGURE 11-1

Many people are intimidated by the thought of describing curves. A curve is simply a portion of an entire circle. At least three elements of a curve are necessary in order to describe it effectively. The most common elements found on surveys are the radius, the arc length, the chord bearing, and the chord distance. Look at a curve on a survey, and then picture it continuing all the way around until it meets its beginning point, so that it is a full circle. The *radius* is the straight line from what would be the center point of that circle to any point on the circle itself (picture the hands of a clock). The *arc length* (sometimes simply called "length") is the distance of the actual curved line (lay a string along the curved line and mark it at the points where the curve begins and ends; then lay the string straight out on a measuring stick to determine the arc length). The *chord* is the imaginary straight line between the beginning and end points of a curve, and the *chord bearing and distance* make up the call that describes that straight line (draw a dotted line between the two points to see the chord). See Figure 11-2.

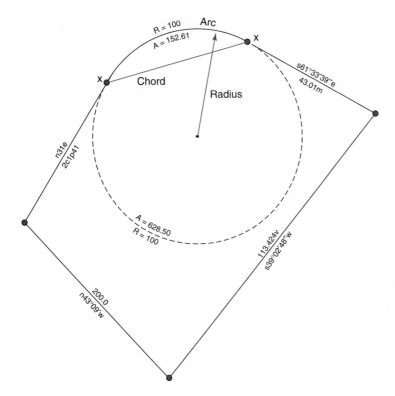

FIGURE 11-2 The elements of a Curve

This text assumes the curve is tangent (as depicted by the solid-line arc in the diagram above). Non-tangent curves (the dotted-line arc is an example of a non-tangent curve) are not addressed here.

The arc length will always be longer than the chord distance, even if by an amount small enough that it is not reflected in two digits. It is necessary to state whether the curve runs to the right or to the left. If you find this difficult to determine from an "aerial" view as you look at the drawing, imagine walking along the line, and decide whether you will be veering to the right or to the left when you get to the point of curvature. If the arc is very slight and looks like a straight line (which would mean the radius is a large number), and you cannot tell whether it runs right or left, draw it out both ways with a deed plotting software and compare the acreage to the survey.

The closure error will be the same whether the curve goes to the right or to the left because you are starting and ending at the same points, but the acreage will increase or decrease depending on whether the line is convex or concave to the tract. You will know whether the curve goes to the right or left when the acreage matches what is shown on the survey, but do not hesitate to call the surveyor and ask if you are unsure, or if you do not have plotting software. There are many ways to describe a curve effectively, but the following format is sufficient when provided with the radius, arc, and chord: "...thence along a curve to the right having a radius of 50.00 feet, an arc length of 127.25 feet, and a chord bearing and distance of North 66° 38' 58" East 95.98 feet to an existing iron pipe...."

If the tie line is shown as a curve on the survey, there is no need to provide anything other than the chord when describing the tie, as the tie is not part of the tract and is simply used to show the location of one point in relation to another.

The degree symbol may be found in the symbols library of most word-processing software programs and usually may be inserted with a keystroke shortcut. Straight quote and apostrophe marks should be used for the minutes and seconds symbols in all calls, as opposed to "curly" quotes.

Supplement the boundary-line description by adding additional information from the survey to identify the property. Be sure to state that the last line meets your beginning point, so that if the description contains an undiscovered closure error, the *intent* of creating closure is made clear. State that the property is the same as that shown in the prior deed in the chain of title, especially if that deed contains a superseded description, and include the recording reference for that deed. This makes your *intent* to describe the same property clear, even if your description does not describe it properly. These practices may give you, your attorney, and the client an extra layer of protection if an error is discovered in your description at some point. They may also provide a title insurance company with enough comfort to insure over the closure error.

At the end of the description, insert a reference to the survey, including the title, the date, the name of the surveyor, a lot number or lot name if applicable, and, if available, the job number. Include the acreage and add the words "more or less" to account for any minor closure error, which will be shown in the title block on the survey.

There is no need to use both a plat description and a metes-and-bounds description together, although it is not unusual to see it done. If the tract is platted, the plat description should be used since metes and bounds can vary between descriptions. In most states, a plat description prevails over a metes-and-bounds description, which makes the metes-and-bounds description superfluous in a case where both appear.

Never assume anything when looking at a survey. A point may look like it is situated in the centerline of a road right of way, but unless the surveyor has designated it as such, it is not necessarily in the exact centerline. A property line may appear to run along a right-of-way margin, but the drafter should look for the commonly used symbol for a right-of-way margin, which is a solid line broken at regular intervals by two short ones.

If you call a surveyor to obtain additional information that is not reflected on the survey, ask that the survey be revised to include it before adding it to your description. In some situations your attorney may feel it is sufficient to have the additional information faxed or e-mailed to you by the surveyor in lieu of having it added to the drawing (e.g., the additional information was minor or it was too late to add it to the final survey), so that you have backup in your file if there is ever a question as to why you added information to your description that was not shown on the survey.

Remember that you are limited to the information shown on the survey, even if that means your description is not as detailed as you would like it to be, but also remember that surveyors are usually flexible and willing to add information that you request be shown on the drawing, to the extent possible.

Surveyors are a great resource, and most are happy to help with questions. They understand that surveys are not always easy to read, especially if they contain so much information that it is difficult to match calls with lines, as happens often with ALTA surveys. There is only so much room on a drawing to insert the amount of information required, and sometimes the surveyor has no choice but to shift some data. Every description should be plotted, including those prepared by surveyors, as no person or software program can claim 100% accuracy.

b. Inspection Reports and Releases

Copies of the home inspection report, termite report, radon gas report, or well water and septic tank report are part of the closing documents. If any of those reports identifies a problem, the parties will decide on a course of action, which is negotiated prior to closing. Usually either the seller will agree to pay for the repairs or remediation, or will make adjustments to the purchase price to account for the cost of the repairs or remediation. But in any event, the seller will want the buyer to sign a **release** whereby the buyer *waives* any claims against the seller relating to the problem or problems identified in the reports.

Release
a promise by the promisor, usually written, to the promisee that relieves the promisee of an obligation owed to the promisor.

The release and waiver might be seen as the two sides of the same coin. Both consist of promises given by one who is assuming some risk of injury or damage in a transaction. In a release, the promisor is essentially saying to the promisee: "I am releasing you from any liability that you might otherwise owe to me."

With a **waiver**, the promisor is saying to the promisee: "I am waiving any legal claims that I may have against you if I suffer loss, damage, or injury as a result of your actions or omissions."

Waiver
a promise, usually written, in which the promisor gives up the right to pursue legal claims against another who otherwise may have been liable to the promisor.

The paralegal should recognize that in the case of dual representation, the closing attorney or agent may not ethically represent either party's interest in a dispute over repairs or remediation, and in *no* case should the paralegal make any statement or take any action on behalf of either party.

c. Hazard Insurance

The lender will require the buyer to insure the newly financed property against losses occasioned by fire, and depending on where the property is located, against losses resulting from high winds, hurricanes, tornadoes, hail, flooding, earthquakes, and other natural disasters. The premium for hazard insurance, which is sometimes referred to as property insurance, must be paid one year in advance, so the paralegal should check with the insurance company prior to preparing the settlement statement to ascertain whether the premium has been paid by the borrower before closing. If not, it should be added to the settlement statement as a debit to the buyer and disbursed to the insurance company after closing.

D. General Tips for Drafting of Documents

Most closing documents have statutory language that is required for them to be legally enforceable. In drafting documents, the proper approved form must be used, and any modification made to the form language in the draft must be called to the attention of the closing agent/attorney, to ensure no statutory language has been omitted. If there is no specific state bar–approved or generated form for the situation (e.g., a tax proration agreement), it is a good idea to use a form the closing agent or attorney has used previously as a starting point, and modify it accordingly. Such a sample form is sometimes referred to as a "go-by." Even the most experienced paralegals and attorneys rely on form books and sample documents, and most law offices will have a collection of such forms that they use on a regular basis.

Many legal documents contain "defined" terms, meaning shortened names serving as "nicknames" are substituted for those terms or party names within the documents. If the borrower's name is Timothy Andrew Baker, the first instance of his name may be followed by "(herein referred to as "Baker")" or simply, "("Baker")." Obviously, it is of utmost importance that names be properly spelled.

An Offer to Purchase and Contract may be referred to as the "Contract" or the "Agreement," or even the "OPC." There is no rule regarding what the defined term must be. The defined term is capitalized throughout the document to show it defines the name or agreement as if it were fully set out. It is important when drafting any legal document to be consistent. If the document is captioned as a "Contract," then that term should be used throughout the document, rather than using "Agreement" or some other term for the sake of variety; if terms are used interchangeably, this could cause confusion and ambiguity.

When inserting a reference to an exhibit attached to a document (e.g., the legal description), consider the difference between the phrases "See attached Exhibit A" and "See Exhibit A attached hereto and incorporated herein by reference." The latter is preferable as it specifies that the information on the exhibit is incorporated into the document as if it were fully set out in that space. References to exhibits should be underlined and/or in bold, so they are easily noted. Also, there should be consistency between the reference to the exhibit and the title of the actual exhibit, such as "Exhibit A" and "Schedule A."

E. Disbursement of Funds

Immediately prior to the closing, and sometimes not until the closing has begun and loan documents have been signed, the buyer's lender will send the loan funds to the attorney or escrow agent conducting the closing. These funds will be placed in the attorney's **trust account**, or in the title agency's **escrow account**, to be distributed to the various persons or entities to be paid, such as the:

1. Seller's Lender

In theory, the new loan funds are disbursed by lender to borrower/buyer, who then pays the purchase price to the seller, who then pays off his or her existing loan. But the loan funds do not actually change hands this way at the closing; they are disbursed by the lender directly to the closing attorney or agent, who disburses the payoff directly to the seller's lender after closing, so that neither buyer nor seller actually receives the gross funds in hand. But the result is that the majority of the new loan funds are most often used to pay off the seller's loan.

2. Holders of Existing Liens

Examples are a judgment creditor, or a governmental entity holding a tax lien against the property.

3. Real Estate Brokerage Commissions

A typical real estate commission is 6% of the sale price, so if the house sells for $250,000, the commission would be $15,000, which is often split evenly between the seller's (listing) broker and the buyer's broker.

4. Closing Attorney or Title Agency

Depending on where the property is located, the costs for the closing attorney or title agency may range from about $500 to around $2,000.

5. Property Surveyor

Cost for the average residential survey might cost between $300 and $800, depending on the region of the country where the property is located and the size of the property.

6. Title Insurance Company

The one-time premium for the title insurance policy could range from about $250 to more than $1,000.

7. Appraisal Company

The appraiser who issued an opinion of value and prepared a report for the new lender and/or buyer.

8. Hazard Insurance Company

A hazard insurance policy premium would run from $500 to several thousands of dollars per year, depending on where the property is located and its value; and finally

9. Seller

The seller is paid for his or her equity in the property.

Sale Price	less	Loan Payoff	less	Closing Costs	=	Seller' Equity
$250,000	less	$176,000	less	$1,000	=	$73,000

In most cases, the lender will not wire the loan funds or release the loan check to the closing agent until the day of closing, and sometimes it will require a copy of at least the executed note before releasing funds. As a result, timing, organization, and efficiency are essential on the day of closing.

Once the loan funds are received, applicable rules (including, but not limited to, settlement statutes, State Bar ethics rules, and the lender's instructions) govern what funds may be disbursed at what stage of the closing process. All closing funds must be paid into the closing agent's trust account via a method accepted by the state's ethics rules, most of which are limited to certified bank checks, attorneys' or brokers' trust/escrow account checks, and wires. Personal checks should not be accepted for closing funds as they may take up to ten days to post to the trust account, and will therefore not be "good funds" at the time of closing.

If the term "good funds" is interpreted in the most conservative and restrictive manner, all closing funds, that is, the loan proceeds, the earnest money, and any other incoming funds, must be deposited into the closing agent's trust account and considered "good funds" before documents may be recorded and the disbursements made to entitled parties. This means a check (even certified) has cleared and the funds have been posted to the closing agent's trust account, or that a wire has been confirmed as received by the bank and cannot be reversed.

In other words, the funds must have reached a "point of no return" where they cannot be retracted from the account due to a check bouncing or a wire being sent with an incorrect account number. It could also mean the bank providing the trust account has provided the closing agent with "provisional credit," meaning the bank is willing to assume a check that has been deposited but not yet posted to the account is good, and will allow the attorney to act and disburse as if the funds have indeed posted. Provisional credit is not given as freely as it was in past years for obvious reasons, and should never be assumed until obtained in writing.

There are exceptions to the restrictions on disbursements, and the closing agent or attorney will instruct the paralegal accordingly. In some cases, excise/transfer taxes and recording fees may be disbursed from trust funds prior to recording. This eliminates the "chicken-and-egg" issue of needing funds in order to record, but not being permitted to disburse them until after recording. But even these disbursements should not be made before the funds are considered "good funds" or the bank has given provisional credit.

In notice states, disbursements may be made prior to the recording of documents, as long as all documents are fully executed and have been forwarded to the closing agent for recording. But the closing agent should still have the documents recorded as soon as possible after receipt.

Trust account funds are held in trust by the closing attorney/agent for other parties, and their handling must be held to the highest level of ethics. If a closing disbursement is made from a trust account that also contains funds belonging to unrelated parties, and the funds are not yet considered "good funds," then the closing agent has, for all practical purposes, used someone else's money for the disbursement. His or her responsibility for the handling of these funds is the same no matter the amount. All disbursements should be authorized by the closing agent/attorney, for both his or her protection and the paralegal's.

Once the closing has been completed, the documents have been recorded, and proper written authorization to disburse has been obtained from the lender, disbursements may be made from the trust account. The first disbursement made should be the payoff, as it accrues interest daily and will be insufficient after a certain date. In addition, the paralegal should not assume he or she has until that date to deliver the payoff funds; the seller should not continue to pay daily interest on his or her loan after closing due to the paralegal's delay. The delivery instructions on the payoff statement should be followed, whether it means delivery of a check to a local branch or a wire to a specific account. If a check is delivered, a payoff letter should accompany it, and if a wire is sent, an e-mail should follow it to confirm receipt. In either case, written confirmation of receipt and sufficiency of the payoff should be obtained immediately from the lender.

Other disbursements should be made promptly via checks or wires, pursuant to the instructions given by the payees. A transmittal letter should accompany each check, and an e-mail or letter should follow each wire, so there is written evidence of the method and date of delivery.

F. Recording the Deed and Mortgage/ Deed of Trust

Recordation
the act or process of recording an instrument, such as a deed or mortgage, in a public registry. Recordation generally perfects a person's interest in the property against later purchaser's but the effect of recordation depends on the type of recording statute in effect.

Register
to enter in a public registry.

Register of deeds
a public official who records deeds, mortgages, and other instruments affecting real property.

One of the most important steps in the closing process is the **recording**, or **registering**, of the deed and the mortgage or deed of trust. This takes place at the office of the register of deeds in the county where the property is located, or in the Circuit Clerk/Clerk of Court in some states.

The purpose of recordation is to put the world on notice that the grantor has conveyed title to the property to the grantee. Recordation also diminishes the likelihood of subsequent fraudulent or erroneous conveyances of the same property by an unscrupulous seller. In that event, a title search conducted on behalf of the new buyer would quickly reveal that the seller was no longer the owner of the property, and may have been attempting to perpetrate a fraud on the new buyer.

As with most government services, a tax must be paid by the seller in conjunction with the recording of a deed conveying real property, generally referred to as *excise tax, revenue tax,* or *documentary stamps.* Excise tax is based on the purchase price of the property, and a typical fee might be $1 per $1,000 of the purchase price. In the example above, the formula is:

$$\$250,000 \text{ Purchase Price} \div \$1,000 = \$250 \text{ Excise Tax}$$

Thus, the seller would pay $250 in excise tax, which is indicated on the face of the deed. This may be referred to as tax *stamps,* a throwback to the early days of recording before technological advances, when stamps having an appearance similar to postage stamps were adhered to the front page of the deed to indicate the amount of excise tax. Some counties also charge an additional *transfer tax.* Some states also charge a tax on mortgages, or *mortgage tax,* calculated in the same way as transfer tax, but based on the amount of the loan.

The registry will also charge a fee for recording the documents, which is usually the buyer's responsibility. Recording fees are minimal compared to excise, transfer, and mortgage tax, and are most often based on the number of pages in each document.

The deed and mortgage or deed of trust should be recorded as quickly as possible after the closing, and, preferably, immediately following the closing. Some attorneys and escrow companies will have the documents that are to be recorded signed as soon as the closing begins and have the paralegal take them to the register of deeds or Clerk of Court, so that he or she may update the title examination while the closing proceeds, and record the documents immediately upon receipt of authorization from the attorney or escrow agent after the closing has been completed and requirements for recording are met.

The practice of recording immediately after closing may seem overly cautious, but it virtually assures that a fraudulent deed cannot be "slipped into" the chain of title before the real deed is recorded.

After the deed, mortgage, and any other applicable documents are recorded at the registry, copies or digital images are made of the documents and the originals are returned to the closing attorney or escrow agent, or directly to the buyer if the registry is so instructed. This process may be immediate, or it may take several days or even weeks, depending on the registry.

G. Priority of Title

If there is a claim by two or more persons to the same piece of real property, recording statutes can help the court decide who the rightful owner is. In such disputes, fraud is not necessarily involved. Sometimes a grantor who owns several tracts of land may confuse those tracts and convey the same property twice. Quite often disputes will arise between and among family members who may have been devised or gifted a deed of property by a now-deceased relative, and the grantee(s) never got around to recording the deed.

All states have adopted *recording statutes* by which the trier of fact—a judge or jury—will determine who holds title to the property. These statutes come in three varieties, described below.

> **Priority**
> the status of being earlier in time or higher in degree or rank; precedence."

1. PURE-RACE STATUTE

A pure-race statute declares that whoever wins the race to the register of deeds office and records a deed first is the owner of the property, regardless of whether she had notice of a prior conveyance by the seller to another.

Thus, a pure-race statute provides the *greater incentive toward prompt recording* of documents of conveyance, enhancing the completeness of title records and, hence, the security and marketability of title to real property.

EXAMPLE

Seller sells his property to Buyer 1 on January 15, and Buyer 1 records the deed on January 31.

Seller sells the *same* property to Buyer 2 on January 20, and Buyer 2 records the deed on the same day.

<u>Holding</u>: Even if Buyer 2 knows of the prior conveyance to Buyer 1, Buyer 2 will be deemed the owner of the property because Buyer 2 recorded his deed first.

There are only two pure-race states, Louisiana and North Carolina, but exceptions exist within each state to the pure-race model.

2. RACE-NOTICE STATUTE

Race-notice statutes hold that the person who records first will have priority of title and is deemed the owner of the property, if that person does *not* have actual or constructive notice of a prior unrecorded deed.

EXAMPLE

Seller sells his property to Buyer 1 on May 15, and Buyer 1 records the deed on May 31.

Seller sells the same property to Buyer 2 on May 20, and Buyer 2 records the deed on the same day.

<u>Holding</u>: Buyer 2 has priority of title and is deemed to be the owner of the property *if and only if* Buyer 2 did *not* have notice of the prior conveyance to Buyer 1 *and* records before Buyer 1.

Approximately half of the states have race-notice statutes.

3. PURE-NOTICE STATUTE

A recording act that gives priority of title to the party with the *most recent* claim, but only if he paid value for the property, and at the time was without notice of a prior *unrecorded* conveyance. The later purchaser need not record first to protect his interest.

Thus, pure notice statutes protect a subsequent (more recent) purchaser. Unlike a race-notice statute, time of recording is not important in determining ownership. Pure notice statutes do not require that the transferee of real property secure priority of recording as against a prior transferee.

EXAMPLE

Seller sells his property to Buyer 1 on July 1, but she does not record the deed.

Seller sells the same property to Buyer 2 on July 2 and he does not record the deed.

<u>Holding</u>: Buyer 2 will own the land if he paid value for the property, and did not have actual or constructive notice at the time of the conveyance, of the prior sale to Buyer 1. Further, the only way that Buyer 1 can prevail over the later buyer, that is, Buyer 2, is if Buyer 1 records her deed before title to the later conflicting deed is *acquired* by Buyer 2.

A large minority of states have pure-notice statutes.

SABO v. HORVATH

Supreme Court of Alaska
559 P.2d 1038
December 29, 1976

This appeal arises because Grover C. **Lowery conveyed the same five-acre piece of land twice**—first to William A. Horvath and Barbara J. Horvath and later to William Sabo and Barbara Sabo. Both conveyances were by separate documents entitled "Quitclaim Deeds." Lowery's interest in the land originates in a **patent** from the United States Government under *43 U.S.C. § 687a (1970)* ("Alaska Homesite Law").

Lowery's conveyance to the **Horvaths** was prior to the issuance of patent, and Lowery's subsequent conveyance to the **Sabos** was after the issuance of patent. The Horvaths recorded their deed in the Chitna Recording District on **January 5, 1970**; the Sabos recorded their deed on *December 13, 1973*. The transfer to the Horvaths, however, **predated patent and title**, and thus the Horvaths' interest in the land was recorded "outside the chain of title."

We affirm the trial court's ruling that **Lowery had an interest to convey** at the time of his conveyance to the Horvaths. We further hold that Sabo may be a "good faith purchaser" even though he takes by quitclaim deed. We reverse the trial court's ruling that Sabo had constructive notice and hold that a deed recorded outside the chain of title is a *"wild deed"* and does not give constructive notice under the recording laws of Alaska.

It should also be noted that prior to the conveyance to the Horvaths, Lowery had complied with a substantial portion of his obligation under the statute and regulations. He had filed his notice of location and his application to purchase and had lived on the land the required amount of time. Since *43 U.S.C. § 687a (1970)* does not prohibit alienation, we hold that at the time Lowery executed the deed to the Horvaths he had complied with the statute to a sufficient extent so as to have **an interest in the land which was capable of conveyance**.

Since the Horvaths received a valid interest from Lowery, we must now resolve the conflict between the **Horvaths' first recorded interest** and the **Sabos' later recorded interest**.

The Sabos, like the Horvaths, received their interest in the property by a quitclaim deed. They are asserting that their interest supersedes the Horvaths under Alaska's statutory recording system. AS 34.15.290 provides that:

> A conveyance of real property.... is void as against a subsequent innocent purchaser.... for a valuable consideration of the property.... whose conveyance is first duly recorded. An unrecorded instrument is valid.... as against one who has actual notice of it.

Since a "quitclaim" only transfers the interest of the grantor, the question is whether a "quitclaim" deed itself puts a purchaser on **constructive notice**. Although the authorities are in conflict over this issue, the clear weight of authority is that a quitclaim grantee can be protected by the recording system. We choose to follow the majority rule and hold that a quitclaim grantee is not precluded from attaining the status of an "**innocent purchaser**."

In this case, the Horvaths recorded their interest from Lowery *prior to* the time the Sabos recorded their interest. Thus, the issue is **whether the Sabos are charged with <u>constructive</u> knowledge** because of the Horvaths' prior recordation. Horvath is correct in his assertion that in the usual case a prior recorded deed serves as constructive notice pursuant to AS 34.15.290, and thus precludes a subsequent recordation from taking precedence. Here, however, the Sabos argue that because Horvath recorded his deed prior to Lowery having obtained patent, they were not given constructive notice by the recording system. They contend that since Horvaths' recordation was outside the chain of title, the recording should be regarded as a "wild deed".

It is an axiom of hornbook law that a *purchaser has notice only of recorded instruments that are within his "chain of title."* If a grantor (Lowery) transfers prior to obtaining title, and the grantee (Horvath) *records prior to title passing*, a second grantee who diligently examines all conveyances under the grantor's name from the date that the grantor had secured title would not discover the prior conveyance. The rule in most jurisdictions which have adopted a grantor-grantee index system of recording is that *a "wild deed"* does not serve as constructive notice to a subsequent purchaser who duly records.

Alaska's recording system utilizes a "grantor-grantee" index. Had Sabos searched title under both grantor's and grantee's names but limited his search to the chain of title subsequent to patent, he would not be chargeable with discovery of the pre-patent transfer to Horvath.

We could require Sabo to check beyond the chain of title to look for pre-title conveyances. While in this particular case the burden may not have been great, as a general rule, requiring title checks beyond the chain of title could add a significant burden as well as uncertainty to real estate purchases.

It is unfortunate that in this case due to Lowery's **double conveyances**, one or the other party to this suit must suffer an undeserved loss. We are cognizant that in this case, the equities are closely balanced between the parties to this appeal. Our decision, however, in addition to resolving the litigants' dispute, must delineate the requirements of Alaska's recording laws.

Because we want to promote simplicity and certainty in title transactions, we choose to follow the majority rule and hold that the Horvaths' deed, recorded outside the chain of title, does not give constructive notice to the Sabos and is not "duly recorded" under the Alaskan Recording Act, AS 34.15.290. Since the Sabos' interest is the first duly recorded interest and was recorded without actual or constructive knowledge of the prior deed, we hold that the Sabos' interest must prevail. The trial court's decision is accordingly.

Reversed.

CHAPTER SUMMARY

The *closing* is the final step in the real estate transaction in which title is conveyed from a grantor to a grantee. In most cases, the grantor will be the seller of the property, and the grantee will be the buyer. The seller conveys title in exchange for receiving funds from the buyer. Closings are conducted in most states either by an attorney or by an escrow agent acting on behalf of an escrow company. Paralegals are extremely important in the preparation and organization of the many legal documents that change hands at a closing.

Among the more important documents necessary to close a real estate transaction are the deed, mortgage or deed of trust, promissory note, title insurance commitment, property survey, settlement statement (often referred to as a *HUD-1 statement*, required under *RESPA*), termite and other inspection reports, and hazard insurance policy.

When the appropriate documents have been executed by the parties, the attorney or escrow agent will disburse the closing funds, most significantly the buyer's new loan on the property. These proceeds will be used to pay off the seller's loan, and to pay the seller for whatever equity the seller may have in the property. The proceeds will also be used to pay for the various reports, property survey, hazard insurance, prorated taxes and utility bills, brokers' commissions, attorneys' fees, and recording fees and taxes related to the recording of the deed and mortgage.

Immediately after closing the transaction, the deed and/or mortgage should be *recorded* at the register of deeds office in the county where the property is located. All states have adopted recording statutes that determine actual ownership in the event that there are conflicting claims of ownership of the property. The three types of statutes are: *pure-race statutes, pure-notice statutes,* and *race-notice statutes,* the last being the most common among the states.

CONCEPT REVIEW AND REINFORCEMENT

KEY **TERMS**

Assignment	Hazard Insurance	Recording
Closing	HUD-1	Register of Deeds
Closing Attorney	Lien	Release
Deed	Mortgage	RESPA
Deed of Trust	Mortgage Lien	Settlement Statement
Dual Representation	Notary Public	Truth in Lending Act
Escrow	Priority of Title	Tax Stamps
Escrow Agent	Pure-Notice Statute	Transfer Tax
Escrow Company	Pure-Race Statute	Waiver
Excise Tax	Race-Notice Statute	

CONCEPT **REVIEW** QUESTIONS

1. What is a closing, and what is its purpose?
2. What is TILA, and what is its importance as it relates to a closing?
3. What is RESPA, and how does it relate to a closing?
4. What is a settlement statement? What is a HUD-1 statement, and of what importance is it to the closing process?
5. What is the role of the closing attorney? What is dual representation, and what problems are associated with it?
6. What is the role of an escrow company? How, if at all, does it differ from the role of a closing attorney?
7. What is a "pure notice" statute?
8. What is a "pure race" statute?
9. What is a "race-notice" statute?
10. Why should deeds be recorded? Why should the recording of a deed take place as soon as possible after closing?

ETHICS

LET'S JUST **SHARE**!

Tony and Simon have known each other since they were children. They grew up in the same neighborhood, attended the same schools, and shared a dorm room throughout college. Simon moved away after college graduation but has recently decided to move back to his hometown and wants to purchase a house in the old neighborhood.

Tony owns several houses on the block and offers one of the houses to Simon at a terrific price, which Simon accepts. The men are still great friends so they decide to use the same lawyer to handle the paperwork for the transaction, which will save them money and time. They have agreed to all the terms and just need someone to memorialize the agreement.

Is it ethical for one attorney to handle the paperwork for both the buyer and the seller in a real estate contract? Why or why not?

Does a written client waiver cure any potential conflict of interest the attorney might encounter?

Is it wise for one attorney to handle the paperwork for both buyer and seller in a real estate contract? (As an example of the potential for problems in a dual representation scenario, see the exercise below.)

BUILDING YOUR PROFESSIONAL SKILLS

CRITICAL THINKING **EXERCISES**

1. Attorney has agreed to represent both Buyers and Sellers at closing of the residential property to be conveyed. Attorney and Paralegal, Buyer, and Seller are all seated around the large table in Attorney's conference room. Buyer and Seller are making small talk about the house, when Buyer casually mentions that she can't wait for her children to see and enjoy the large and expensive swing set in the backyard of the property.

The Sellers look at each other in surprise, and Mr. Seller emphatically states that the Buyers are mistaken, and that the Sellers will be taking the swing set to their new home. The Buyers protest, stating that the swing set is a "fixture" that is part of the real property, and therefore, should convey along with title to the property.

How should attorney handle this dispute in light of the fact that both the Buyers and Sellers are Attorney's clients?

Attorney's opinion, which she has yet to disclose to the parties, is that the Buyers are correct and the swing set is a fixture that should remain with the property due to its method of attachment to the land,
which is by spikes chained to the legs of the swing set being driven into the ground. Should Attorney inform Sellers of her legal opinion, or should she first try to negotiate a financial compromise between the parties?

Can Attorney offer part of her closing fee to compensate Sellers if they are willing to leave the swing set in exchange for a few hundred dollars cash?

2. The following events all took place in this year: Seller sells her property to Buyer 1 on June 1, telling Buyer 1 that he may take possession of the property on July 1. Buyer doesn't record the deed until June 30. In the meantime, Seller sells the same property a second time to Buyer 2 on June 15, informing Buyer 2 that she can take possession of the property on July 1. Buyer 2 records the deed that very same day, June 15.

On July 1, as you might have anticipated, Buyer 1 and Buyer 2 "meet" at the residence. Each claims to hold legal title to the same property that Seller sold to both of them.

Who is the lawful owner in a pure-notice state?

Who is the lawful owner in a pure-race state?

Who is the lawful owner in a race-notice state?

RESEARCH ON THE **WEB**

1. As to recording statutes, is your state a pure-notice, pure-race, or race-notice jurisdiction? Identify the specific statute that answers this question. Review the case annotations to the statute to get an overview of the importance of the statute and how it has been interpreted by the courts in your state.

2. Search the web for RESPA. When was this federal statute enacted? Locate the statute on the web, and identify the particular types of transactions to which it applies. For example, does it apply to commercial loans for the development of real property? Does it apply to long-term leases?

BUILDING YOUR **PROFESSIONAL** PORTFOLIO

1. As you now know, preparing for a closing can be a daunting experience for someone who is new to the process. After the deed, the most important document to be seen at a closing is the settlement statement. As we discussed earlier, a HUD-1 settlement statement is required in any closing involving federally insured loan funds.

   Using the HUD-1 exhibit in this chapter as a "go-by" or template, create your own hypothetical transaction. Fill in the necessary line items with numbers that you deem to be appropriate to determine how much money the buyer has to come up with at the closing, and how much the seller will receive at closing.

2. Contact your state bar association or department of real estate to determine what standardized forms they might have available. Are such forms mandatory; that is, must they be used at a closing, or may the escrow company or attorney use other forms?

chapter **12**

COMMON INTEREST COMMUNITIES

LEARNING OBJECTIVES

After reading this chapter, you should understand:

- The three most important legal documents for the creation of a common interest community

- The purpose of a declaration

- The purpose of the articles of incorporation

- Bylaws

- Three definitions of condominium

- How condominiums differ from homeowner associations

- How a cooperative differs from a condominium

- Conditions, Covenants & Restrictions (CC&Rs)

Common Interest Community
a form of ownership of real property where private ownership of one's individual unit is coupled with shared ownership of the common areas.

Association
the legal entity usually a nonprofit corporation that owns the common areas in a common interest community, whether the CIC is a condominium association or a homeowners association.

A. Overview of Common Interest Communities

A **common interest community** is one wherein *individual* ownership of real property is combined with the *shared*, or *common*, ownership of other real property in the same development. That is, one owns his or her dwelling unit and is automatically a member in a *homeowners association* that owns the *common areas* and common elements, such as recreational facilities, parking areas, sidewalks, and open spaces.

The concept of private ownership coupled with shared ownership probably dates back to the dawn of humanity. According to evidence found at ancient sites in Ethiopia and elsewhere, anatomically modern humans have lived on the planet for at least the last 195,000 years. At these ancient settlements, scientists have unearthed "common areas" such as communal fire pits and refuse dumps. Human nature being what it is—even 195,000 years ago—it would seem likely that the occupants of these ancient sites would have shared "ownership" of these common areas, while possessing, that is, "owning," their personal living spaces.

There is some disagreement as to when and where the first common interest community (CIC) was created in the United States, but there are a few examples of CICs to be found in New York City dating back more than 150 years ago to the mid-1800s. However, it wasn't until fairly recently—beginning in the 1960s—that common interest communities really began to grow in large numbers and popularity in the United States. This came about because of a 1964 amendment to the federal National Housing Act[1] that allowed the Federal Housing Administration (FHA) to insure home loans for condominiums. As a result, lenders felt more secure making loans for individual condominium units and were more willing to make loans for large condominium developments.

Common interest communities were not known under the common law, but rather they are creatures of *statute*, and every state in the Union has devised a statutory scheme governing the development, operation, and ultimate dissolution of the CIC. Common interest communities of one type or another have come to dominate the residential real estate market. This trend will accelerate as more and more of the post–World War II baby boom generation—those born between 1946 and 1964—retire and leave their single-family homes for life in a maintenance-free common interest community.

The various categories of CICs include *condominiums, cooperatives,* and *homeowners associations.*

B. Advantages and Disadvantages of CIC Living

Very few people who live in a common interest community are neutral concerning how they feel about this type of ownership of residential property; they either love it or hate it (and in the latter case, one wonders why they would buy into a CIC in the first place).

Advantages

There are several advantages to living in a common interest community, including:

1. Relative Affordability

Land prices have increased steadily, and sometimes dramatically, across the United States, but particularly in urban areas. To take an extreme example, during the height of the real estate boom in 2007, in San Francisco the median price of a home was approximately $650,000 (the median price meaning that half of the homes purchased in that year sold for less than $650,000, while the other half sold for more than $650,000).

A single-family residence on its own individual lot in any given area will almost always sell for a significantly higher average price then would a residence of the same square footage in common interest communities in the same area. Thus, the most affordable housing is to be found in common interest communities due to the *increasing scarcity of developable land*.

2. Amenities

Because the cost of building, operating and maintaining a CIC's common areas is shared by all of the homeowners in the development—who may number in the hundreds or thousands—amenities such as swimming pools and tennis courts

---

[1]P.L. 81-171.

are much more affordable than building a swimming pool or tennis court for one's own single-family residence. Thus, one may use and enjoy all sorts of recreational amenities, open spaces, and green belts for a relatively small price, which is reflected in an owner's regular dues payments.

Many of the more expensive homeowners associations cater to golfers, and the homes are built around common areas consisting of one or more golf courses. Some homeowners associations cater to boaters and docks and other boat-related facilities are part of their common areas. Perhaps the most unusual type of homeowners association is the fly-in, aviation, or airpark community, where the common areas are, among other things, runways and taxiways. The number of such associations is growing as traffic in major urban areas becomes heavier, and commuting times become longer. Many airpark common interest communities have covenants in their CC&Rs that require that the exterior of the hangar attached to one's home must match the exterior and architectural style of the home itself.

3. Maintenance

Many folks enjoy living in common interest communities because the unit owners, by virtue of their ownership of a dwelling unit, are members of the ***homeowners association*** that is the actual ***owner of the common areas***. One of the association's main purposes is to maintain the common areas and thereby relieve the owners of that burden. These maintenance duties are particularly important as they relate to landscaping. If you enjoy trees, plants, and flowers, but don't like mowing, trimming, or planting them, then living in a common interest community may be for you because those landscaping and maintenance chores are handled by the employees of the homeowners association.

4. Security

Having neighbors close by can be a source of comfort and security for many who live in common interest communities. Some CICs market themselves by touting their security features, which may include walls or fencing surrounding the community, gates and gate houses, on-site security guards, closed-circuit television monitors, a list of approved contractors, well-lit common areas, and other security measures.

Disadvantages

Some of the disadvantages listed below are simply the "flip side" of the advantages mentioned above.

1. Dues and Assessments

The payment of monthly, quarterly, or annual **dues** is what enables the association to build, operate, maintain, and improve the common elements and amenities like the swimming pool and tennis courts. Many owners in common interest communities will not, or cannot, use the amenities and do not appreciate having a portion of their dues go to subsidizing their neighbors' use and enjoyment of the hot tub. This fact sometimes creates friction between the users, and the non-users, of the recreational facilities.

Aside from the regular dues payments, an association's board of directors will sometimes find it necessary to impose a **special assessment** upon the owners. This may result from some type of natural catastrophe such as a tornado, hurricane, or earthquake. Or it could result from the need for an unbudgeted capital improvement, such as resurfacing a parking area or replacing a roof.

Dues
monies that are paid on a regular basis—monthly, quarterly, or annually—by unit owners for the routine maintenance of the common areas. Dues are typically assessed based upon an owner's pro rata square footage.

Special Assessment
a demand by the association for monies over and above an owner's regular dues payment, required for some emergency or special purpose.

In some cases, the need for a special assessment may be the result of poor management of the development by the board and/or management company, which may produce higher-than-expected maintenance expenses. Or, the association may have to prosecute, or defend against, a lawsuit that will necessitate the hiring of legal counsel, and perhaps the payment of a civil judgment.

2. Rules and Regulations

Common interest communities tend to have rules on top of rules. These rules are sometimes actually *covenants* written into the original documents that created the condominium or homeowners association, such as the Declaration or the Covenants, Conditions & Restrictions (CC&Rs). CC&Rs can be amended, but often require a "supermajority to do so, for example, a majority of 66%, 75%, or even up to 100% of the unit owners. The requirement of a supermajority of more than 66% can make it very difficult to amend the CC&Rs. Case law has generally held that rules that are written into the founding documents are *presumptively* valid and enforceable.

Other rules may have been enacted by a board of directors or successive boards of directors over many years. In order to be enforced by an association, courts have held that rules enacted by a board must be *reasonable* and applied in an evenhanded manner. Whether created by the founding documents or enacted by a board of directors, rules can, and do, control and limit many of the rights and privileges associated with traditional, single-family home ownership. Some of the areas that are typically governed by either covenants created by the developer or by rules passed by a board of directors are:

a. The amount and frequency of dues payments and assessments;
b. Fines and other penalties for infractions of the rules;
c. Residential color schemes;
d. Architectural styles;
e. Landscaping and types of plantings permitted;
f. Whether, and what type of fencing, is allowed;
g. The types of pets permitted (and even the size and weight of the pets);
h. Whether, and how frequently, a unit may be leased to non-residents;
i. Restrictions on the number and types of vehicles, and parking arrangements;
j. What you may, or may not, have on your patio or balcony (BBQs, laundry, or carpet, for example);
k. The size and type of signs, flags, or other symbols that may be posted in or on one's property; and
l. Just about anything else you can imagine.

The success or failure of common interest communities depends to a great degree on having, and enforcing, reasonable rules for the governance of the unit owners and their guests in the CIC. Some unit owners chafe under rules that they perceive to be not only unreasonable or unnecessary, but preferentially enforced— or not enforced—against certain owners who may be friends with some of the directors on the board.

3. Neighbors

Living in close proximity to inconsiderate or rude neighbors can make life in the common interest community a miserable proposition. Condominium units, especially the older developments, oftentimes do not have adequate sound insulation, which can be a source of continuous, even if unintentional, annoyance. Children can be loud and destructive. Behavior that would not merit a second notice in a single-family neighborhood can spark serious disputes in the close confines of a CIC.

C. Types of Common Interest Communities

1. CONDOMINIUMS

We typically think of a condominium project as being one or more, large, multistory buildings containing many individual condominium units. In these types of condominiums, unit owners do not individually own any land. As we shall see, this is not the only type of condominium arrangement, but as a preliminary, let us consider three definitions of the word "condominium."

a. Condominium is a *type of legal ownership*

The most familiar type of common interest community is the **condominium**. As with all common interest communities, ownership of one's individual condominium unit *necessarily* carries with it an undivided ownership interest in the common areas and common elements, as well. And so, the first definition of condominium is a *form of ownership*.

> Condominium
>
> a form of ownership of real property that combines ownership of one's individual unit with an undivided ownership interest in the common areas.

    The term "undivided" means that the owner of an individual unit has a right to use any and all portions of the common areas and common elements; in the common areas, there is no dividing line between what's yours and what's mine.

b. A condominium is an *individual unit*

A second definition of **condominium** refers to an owner's ***individually owned space*** in the condominium development. This space has been jokingly referred to as one's "box of air," because one only owns "from the paint to the paint" inside the condo unit.

> Condominium
>
> one's individual unit in a multifamily development.

c. A condominium is the *entire project*

The third definition of **condominium** refers to the entire condominium project or development, which would include all of the individual condominium units, as well as the common areas and elements. For example, one might say, "I live at the Del Boca Vista Condominiums."

> Condominium
>
> a multifamily project, including all of the individual units and common areas, developed in accordance with a state's condominium statutes.

2. HOMEOWNERS ASSOCIATION (HOAS)

The second type of condominium project is the homeowners **association**. These developments *appear* very much like a traditional single-family residential neighborhoods, that is, one where there are a freestanding houses with yards.

    In HOA developments, whether the units are freestanding or attached, the homeowner owns his or her individual unit, and also the land directly beneath his or her residence, sometimes referred to as the ***footprint*** of the building. In some associations, the owner does not own the yard space or green areas beyond the footprint. However, in other associations, homeowners may own some land extending beyond the footprint, in other words, a residential lot. Whether one owns just the footprint, or part of the land extending beyond the footprint, the common areas are owned and maintained by the homeowners association, of which the homeowner is necessarily a member.

    Thus, a homeowners association is technically a condominium because it combines individual unit ownership with common area ownership. The major differences between an association and a condominium are:

    a. In a homeowners association, owners own the land directly beneath their units (the footprint), and perhaps some land extending beyond the footprint; and

b. Because of (a) above, the overall development plan of an HOA is necessarily horizontal, rather than vertical as in a high-rise condominium project.[2]

Like condominiums, however, associations have boards of directors that are elected by the residents for the purpose of governing the association.

3. COOPERATIVES

Cooperative
a corporation that owns residential real property, including the individual units therein. The "co-op" leases the residential units to its shareholders.

Cooperatives, or simply co-ops, are *not condominiums* and, technically, are not even common interest communities because the members of the cooperative do not own the units where they live. Rather, the cooperative is a *corporation*, and the residents of the building do not own real property, but instead are shareholders in the corporation. The corporation owns the real property, and then leases each of the several units to the corporation's shareholders.

It is an interesting legal point that co-ops are sometimes controlled by the *corporate law* of the state wherein they are located rather than the law of real property.

Cooperatives are like condominiums and associations in that they are governed by an elected board of directors. Cooperatives ownership is found almost exclusively in the northeastern United States, and mostly in New York City.

4. PLANNED UNIT DEVELOPMENTS

Planned Unit Development
a special type of zoning, the purpose of which is to optimize the physical layout, uses, and density of large, multi-use developments. The term is also used to describe the real estate development itself.

A **planned unit development** (PUD) is sometimes confused with a condominium or common interest community. It is neither of those, and is not a form of ownership at all. Instead, it is a special type of *zoning*, and a mechanism whereby a parcel of land is zoned to allow the development of a single, usually very large community, which is, itself, sometimes referred to as a "planned unit development." Such a community often contains *mixed uses*, including residential (condominiums, associations, and/or apartments), retail shops, and small business. Thus, a planned unit development is a planning tool that facilitates the orderly, predictable development of what is primarily a residential subdivision.

In a planned unit development, the emphasis is on the word "planned." A plan of development will tend to optimize the *density* of the project, and the use and enjoyment of the amenities by the residents, particularly the greenbelts and open spaces. As land becomes more scarce and expensive, planning how a parcel is developed, used, and enjoyed becomes increasingly more important.

D. Documents Relating to Common Interest Communities

1. DECLARATION

Declaration
also known as the master deed, it is the legal document that creates the condominium when recorded at the office of the register of deeds in the county where the real property is located.

A **declaration** is the legal document that *creates the condominium* when it is recorded at the office of the register of deeds in the county or counties where the property is located. It is considered the most important of the CIC-related documents. The declaration is sometimes known as the *master deed*.

---

[2]In older condominiums, the shared ownership of the common areas was often accomplished by the residents owning the common areas as *tenants-in-common* (see Chapter 3 on Concurrent Ownership). For liability and other reasons, the tenants-in-common form of shared ownership of the common areas is no longer viable. In more recently developed condominiums, ownership of the common areas is through a non-profit condominium *association*—that is, a corporation—of which the unit owners are automatically members.

Whether we are discussing the traditional condominium or a homeowners association, both are common interest communities that have individual unit ownership coupled with (or more technically, "appurtenant to") shared ownership of the common elements, and, as such, both types of developments require a declaration.

Remember that we said earlier that condominiums are creatures of statute, and not the common law. So, when the declaration or master deed is recorded, the developer is simply *declaring* to the world that the property to be developed is, and will be, subject to the body of state statutes relating to the development, operation, and governance of condominiums.

Among other things, the Declaration should include:

a. The name of the condominium,
b. A legal description of the entire property,
c. The number of units in the condominium and their boundaries,
d. A description of the common elements and their boundaries, and
e. The conditions, covenants & restrictions (CC&Rs) that run with the land. Because they "run with the land," the CC&Rs will bind all future owners of the individual units to observe the specific conditions, covenants, and restrictions enumerated in the declaration.

a. Conditions, Covenants & Restrictions (CC&Rs)

The CC&Rs may restrict not only the number of units to be built in the project, but also their permitted uses and architectural styles, the type of landscaping, whether or not pets will be allowed, and a host of other restrictions on how future owners may use and enjoy their property. Because covenants do restrict the owners' use of their property, and because use restrictions on real property are generally disfavored in the law, if there is a legal dispute relating to the CC&Rs, the covenants must be strictly construed by the courts.

Strict construction means that the words of the covenant will be literally and narrowly interpreted by a court in the event of a lawsuit over a CC&R. If there is any **ambiguity** in the covenant, condition, or restriction, the court will find in favor of the homeowner, and the free use of his or her property. Strict construction looks at the letter of the law (or the covenant, in this case) rather than considering the spirit of the law (or covenant). Since CC&Rs will be strictly construed by a court of law in the event of a legal dispute, the developer should ensure that they are properly drafted by a law firm highly knowledgeable and experienced in the law of common interest communities.

> **Strict construction**
> an interpretation that construes words narrowly. This type of construction treats statutory and contractual words with highly restrictive readings.

> **Ambiguity**
> and uncertainty of meaning or intention as in a contractual term or statutory provision.

2. ARTICLES OF INCORPORATION

The hallmark of a common interest community is individual ownership of one's unit, appurtenant to membership in an association (corporation) that owns the common elements. The association, which owns the common areas and common elements, is a legal entity, and like all legal entities it must be created by natural persons. A condominium association or a homeowners association is formed by filing **articles of incorporation** with the jurisdiction's secretary of state. These entities are typically formed as *nonprofit* associations/corporations governed by state statutes enacted specifically for nonprofits.

The articles of incorporation—sometimes called the *corporate charter*—are similar to state constitutions and our federal Constitution (which replaced the

> **Articles of Incorporation**
> the legal document that creates the homeowners association that will own the common areas and common elements of the condominium. Articles are filed with the Secretary of State's office and are also known as the corporate charter.

Articles of Confederation) in that they paint in broad strokes the powers of the corporation/association, which may include articles relating to the following:

   a. The *purpose* of the corporation, for example, "to provide for the maintenance, operation, and governance of Del Boca Vista, and to promote the general welfare, health and safety of its residents."

   b. The *powers* of the corporation, such as "to levy and collect monthly dues from the unit owners, and any special assessments, as necessary. Dues and assessments shall be calculated based on a unit's square footage as a percentage of the square footage of all of the residential units."

   c. *Membership* in the association, for instance, "Each and every owner of a residential unit located in Del Boca Vista is also a member in Del Boca Vista Condominium Association. Membership in the Association may not be severed from the ownership of a unit."

   d. Powers and duties of the *Board of Directors* (sometimes called the board of managers): "The Board of Directors shall have the authority to determine the amount of monthly dues and special assessments to be collected from the unit owners for the purpose of operating and maintaining the common areas and common elements. In addition, the Board shall have the authority to levy fines against unit owners for violations of these CC&Rs, and any rules and regulations adopted by a board.... The Board shall have the authority to enact rules and regulations to effect the purposes and provisions of the Declaration and Bylaws."

   e. *Dissolution* of the condominium: "Del Boca Vista Condominiums may be dissolved only in accordance with the general statutes of this State."

EXHIBIT 12-1 Sample Covenants, Conditions & Restrictions

Sample Covenants, Conditions & Restrictions (CC&Rs)

Below is a copy of the CC&Rs that covers all the building development units in Alta Sierra. These CC&Rs are registered with the County Recorder's office, and are the original CC&Rs which all Alta Sierra units adopted and copied, with a couple of minor differences in a few of our 22 units.

(Sample CC&Rs)

ALTA SIERRA ESTATES

DECLARATION OF RESTRICTIONS

THIS DECLARATION, Made by ALTA SIERRA VISTA, INC., owners, this day of April 10, 1968.

WITNESSETH:

THAT, whereas, the above named corporation desired to restrict all that certain tract or parcel of land as shown upon the official map of "ALTA SIERRA ESTATES - ********* recorded in the office of the County Recorder of the County of Nevada, State of California, on April 10, 1968 in Book 3 of Subdivision Maps at page 4.

NOW, THEREFORE, ALTA SIERRA VISTA, INC., as owner of the above tract of land, hereby declares that said land is held and shall be held, conveyed, hypothecated, used, improved, and occupied subject to the following covenants, restrictions, easements, and agreements which are imposed pursuant to a general plan and shall create mutual equitable servitudes on each of the lots, plots, or parcels in said tract of subdivision and a privity of contract with reference thereto between the various owners thereof, their heirs, personal representatives, successors, and assigns, to-wit:

RESTRICTIVE PROVISIONS

Clause I - Use and Improvements

No buildings other than one detached single family private dwelling, private garage for the use of the occupants of such dwelling and other usual and appropriate outbuildings, strictly incident and appurtenant to a private dwelling shall be erected or maintained on all lots, except Lots 73, 74, 75, 76, and 83, which may be used for commercial purposes. No use whatsoever, except in connection with its use and improvement as a site and grounds of a private dwelling or commercial as above set forth shall be made of any lot or plot therein and furthermore, no driveway, road, right of way, or any easements for public or private use shall be granted for any reason whatsoever, across or through any lot in this subdivision to any other piece of property without approval in writing of the Architectural Committee.

Clause II - Temporary Dwellings

No trailers, garage, or other outbuildings shall be used as a temporary or permanent residence, nor shall any residential structure be moved on to the tract from some other location.

Clause III - Minimum Building Requirements

The construction of all dwellings on all lots, regardless of size of dwelling, must conform to F.H.A. or better specifications.

As to all lots, no dwelling shall be erected or permitted to remain thereon having a ground floor area, exclusive of open porches and garages, of less than 1,200 square feet for a one-story building.

Clause IV - Set Back of Buildings

No building or projection thereof shall be located nearer any street than twenty feet, except that an owner can obtain a variance from and upon the approval of the Architectural Committee.

No building shall be located nearer than five feet to any side lot line.

Clause V - Subdivision of Lots

Any re-subdivision of lots must conform with all county and state regulations applying thereto. Furthermore, no re-subdivision shall be allowed until the approval of the Architectural Committee is given for size and location as shown on a map to be supplied to the Architectural Committee.

Clause VI - Easements

Easements and rights of way, as indicated upon the recorded map of said subdivision, are reserved for the installation and maintenance of pole line, utilities, and other public and quasi-public uses. No buildings shall be placed upon such easements or interference be made with the free use of the same for the purpose intended.

Clause VII - Signs

No billboards or other advertising device shall be erected or placed upon any lot or plot in said tract, without the written permission of the Architectural Committee.

Clause VIII - Completion of Construction

Any residence or other building in said subdivision, the construction of which has been started, shall be completed without delay, except when such delay is caused by acts of God, strikes, actual inability of the owner to procure delivery of necessary materials, or by interference by other persons or forces beyond the control of the owner to prevent.

Financial inability of the owner or his contractor to secure labor or materials or discharge liens or attachments shall not be deemed a cause beyond his control.

In the event of cessation of construction of any building for a period of 120 days, where such interruption is not excused by the provision hereof, the Declarant hereof or any other owner of property subject to this Declaration shall have the right to enter upon said uncompleted property and remove the same or carry such construction work to completion, and the expense incurred in connection with the removal or completion of such building shall become a lien upon the land and improvements thereon upon which such a building is located which may be foreclosed either as a mechanics lien and/or as a mortgage made on real property.

Clause IX - Appearance of Yards

(continued)

EXHIBIT 12-1 *Continued*

Lots must be kept free of debris, junk cars, objectionable or unsightly materials, etc.

Clause X - Mail Boxes

Mail boxes are to be of that design and color set forth by the Architectural Committee.

Clause XI - Fences and Trees

No fence or hedge shall be erected or permitted to remain or allowed to grow to a height exceeding three feet nearer any street than the set back lines as indicated herein.

All pruning, cutting, and thinning of trees larger than four inches in diameter shall be controlled by the Architectural Committee.

Clause XII - Keeping of Pets, Animals, etc.

No lot or plot or building thereon in said tract shall be used for the keeping or breeding of any livestock or animals of any kind except for dogs, cats, or like pets, provided that they are not kept in numbers or under conditions objectionable to other residents in said tract. All yards, pens, and outbuildings used in connection with the keeping of said pets shall be located on the rear half of the respective lots and shall be adequately screened from view from any street. The keeping of horses is permissible on lots of one (1) acre or more in size, provided they are not kept in numbers or under conditions objectionable to other residents in said tract.

Clause XIII - Approval of Plans

No building, fence, wall, or other permanent structure shall be erected, altered, or placed on any plot in said subdivision until building plans, specifications, and plot plan showing the location of structures on the lot have been submitted to and approved in writing as to conformity and harmony of external design and as not interfering with the reasonable enjoyment of any other lot, by an Architectural Committee composed of Edward Pasteris, or the then manager, whoever he may be, and an additional two members to be appointed as follows: One representative from Alta Sierra Vista. Inc.. and one representative to be appointed by Edward Pasteris or the then manager.

Upon failure by the committee or its designated representatives to approve or disapprove such plans and specifications within fifteen days after the same have been properly presented, approval thereof will be deemed to have been made, provided the proposed construction complies with all the provisions otherwise of this declaration. If any member of the committee resigns or is unable to act, the remaining members shall appoint his successor. Pending such appointment, the remaining members shall discharge the functions of the committee. At any time, the committee may by recorded statement to that affect relinquish the right herein reserved to appoint and maintain the committee and at such time the then recorded owners of fifty per cent or more of the lots in said subdivision may elect and appoint a committee of three or more of such owners to assume and exercise all of the powers and functions of the committee specified herein.

No member of any Architectural Committee, however created, shall receive any compensation or make any charge for his services as such.

Clause XIV - Failure to Enforce

The various restrictive measures and provisions of this Declaration are declared to constitute mutual equitable covenants and servitudes for the protection and benefit of each lot in said subdivision and failure by Declarants or any other person or persons entitled so to do to enforce any measure or provision upon violation thereof shall not stop or prevent enforcement thereafter or be deemed a waiver of the right so to do.

Clause XV – Severability

The various measures and provisions of this Declaration are declared to be severable, and the invalidity of any one measure or provision shall not effect any other measure or provision.

Clause XVI - Subordination to Mortgages and Deeds of Trust

Nothing contained in this Declaration shall impair or defeat the lien of any mortgage or deed of trust made in good faith and for value, but title to any property subject to this Declaration obtained through the sale in satisfaction of any such mortgage or deed of trust shall thereafter be held subject to all of the restrictions and provisions hereof.

Clause XVII - Terms of Restrictions

These Covenants, Restrictions and Agreements shall run with the land and shall continue in full force and effect until February 1, 1981, at which time the same shall be automatically extended for successive periods of ten years unless by a duly executed and recorded statement of the then owners of fifty per cent or more of the lots in said subdivision, elect to terminate or amend these restrictions in whole or in part. Said Declaration of Restrictions can be amended or modified at any time when fifty per cent of the owners elect to do so.

Clause XVIII - Enforcement and Remedy

Each grantee of a conveyance or purchases under a contract or agreement of sale by accepting a deed or contract of sale or agreement of purchase accepts the same subject to all of the covenants. restrictions, easements, and agreements set forth in this Declaration and agrees to be bound by the same.

Damages for any breach of the terms, restrictions and provisions of this Declaration are hereby declared not to be adequate compensation, but such breach and/or the continuation thereof may be enjoined or abated by appropriate proceedings by the Declarant, or by an owner or owners of any other lot or lots in said subdivision.

3. HOA BYLAWS

Bylaws cover many of the same topics found in the articles of incorporation, but do so in a more precise and specific manner. That is, bylaws fill in the details of the broad strokes found in the articles of incorporation. For instance, the articles of incorporation or charter may require that annual meetings must be held to elect a board of directors. The details, or nuts and bolts, of how those meetings are to be conducted will be found in the bylaws. Regarding the annual meeting, the bylaws would specify:

Bylaws
the legal document that describes in detail how a homeowners association is to operate and conduct its business.

a. When and where the annual meeting is to be held,
b. The notice that must be given to each of the unit owners regarding the annual meeting,
c. What constitutes a quorum for the purpose of the election of the board members,
d. Who may vote in the elections of the board members,
e. Whether proxies are allowed in the voting process,
f. How the terms of the members of the board are to be staggered, and
g. That Robert's Rules of Order will govern the conduct of the meetings.

If the articles of incorporation are similar to a constitution, the bylaws are comparable to the statutes that put into effect the general goals and principles in the articles of incorporation and the declaration. Bylaws are not generally filed with the office of the secretary of state.

4. RULES AND REGULATIONS

Rules and regulations are enacted and enforced by the board of directors of the condominium or homeowners association. The authority of the board of directors to craft rules and regulations is derived from the declaration and/or bylaws. Rules and regulations govern the most mundane aspects of life in the association, such as:

a. The swimming pools, their hours of operation, what type of containers may be brought into the pool areas, and whether guests of the owners may use the pools and other recreational facilities, etc.;

b. The clubhouses, their hours of operation, whether alcoholic beverages may be sold or consumed in the clubhouses, whether shoes or swimming attire may be worn in the clubhouses, whether these facilities may be used for private parties, etc.;

c. Parking, and what types of vehicles may be parked where, and when. For example, many associations have rules prohibiting the parking of a unit owner's commercial vehicle or RV (recreational vehicle) anywhere but in a special lot reserved for them; and

d. Pets, and whether they are permitted in and on the property, and if so, what types of pets are allowed. In addition to limiting the types of pets that unit owners or their guests may have, pet rules may also govern the size and weight of such pets. Needless to say, pet rules and regulations are a frequent source of friction between pet owners and management.

To be enforceable and survive a court challenge, rules and regulations must be **reasonable** and promote the legitimate goals of the condominium or homeowners association, for example, the **health, safety, or general welfare** (does this remind you of a state's "police powers"?) of the unit owners and their guests. The following famous case illustrates the importance of our pets, but also the countervailing interests of our neighbors who may not be as enamored of Fluffy as we are.

NAHRSTEDT V. LAKESIDE VILLAGE CONDOMINIUM ASSOC.

Supreme Court of California
8 Cal. 4th 361; 878 P.2d 1275; 33 Cal. Rptr. 2d 63
September 2, 1994, Decided

Opinion

A homeowner in a 530-unit condominium complex sued to prevent the homeowners association from enforcing a **restriction against keeping cats**, dogs, and other animals in the condominium development. The owner asserted that the restriction, which was contained in the project's declaration, was "unreasonable" as applied to her because she kept her three cats indoors and because her cats were "noiseless" and "created no nuisance." Agreeing with the premise underlying the owner's complaint, the Court of Appeal concluded that the homeowners association could enforce the restriction only upon proof that plaintiff's cats would be likely to interfere with the right of other homeowners "to the peaceful and quiet enjoyment of their property."

Because a stable and predictable living environment is crucial to the success of condominiums and other common interest residential developments, and because recorded use restrictions are a primary means of **ensuring this stability and predictability**,

the Legislature in section 1354 has afforded such restrictions a presumption of validity and has required of challengers that they demonstrate the restriction's "unreasonableness" by the deferential standard applicable to equitable servitudes. Under this standard established by the Legislature, enforcement of a restriction does not depend upon the conduct of a particular condominium owner. Rather, the restriction must be **uniformly enforced** in the condominium development to which it was intended to apply unless the plaintiff owner can show that the burdens it imposes on affected properties so substantially outweigh the benefits of the restriction that it should not be enforced against any owner. Here, the Court of Appeal did not apply this standard in deciding that plaintiff had stated a claim for declaratory relief. Accordingly, we reverse the judgment of the Court of Appeal and remand for further proceedings consistent with the views expressed in this opinion.

Lakeside Village is a large condominium development in Culver City, Los Angeles County. It consists of 530 units spread throughout 12 separate 3-story buildings. The Lakeside Village project is subject to certain covenants, conditions and restrictions (hereafter **CC&R's**) that were included in the developer's **declaration** recorded with the Los Angeles County Recorder on April 17, 1978. Ownership of a unit includes membership in the project's homeowners association, the body that enforces the project's CC&R's, including the pet restriction, which provides in relevant part: "No animals, which shall mean dogs and cats, livestock, reptiles or poultry shall be kept in any unit." The CC&R's permit residents to keep "domestic fish and birds."

In January 1988, plaintiff Natore Nahrstedt purchased a Lakeside Village condominium and moved in with her **three cats**. When the Association learned of the cats' presence, it demanded their removal and **assessed fines** against Nahrstedt for each successive month that she remained in violation of the condominium project's pet restriction. Nahrstedt then brought this lawsuit against the Association. Nahrstedt also alleged she did not know of the pet restriction when she bought her condominium.

Subordination of individual property rights to the collective judgment of the owners association together with restrictions on the use of real property comprise the chief attributes of owning property in a common interest development. Inherent in the condominium concept is the principle that to promote the health, happiness, and peace of mind of the majority of the unit owners since they are living in such close proximity and using facilities in common, each unit owner must give up a certain degree of freedom of choice which he or she might otherwise enjoy in separate, privately owned property.

Restrictive covenants will **run with the land**, and thus bind successive owners, if the deed or other instrument containing the restrictive covenant particularly describes the lands to be benefited and burdened by the restriction and expressly provides that successors in interest of the covenantor's land will be bound for the benefit of the covenantee's land.

In California, as we explained at the outset, our Legislature has made common interest development use restrictions contained in a project's recorded declaration "enforceable…unless unreasonable."

Giving deference to use restrictions contained in a condominium project's originating documents protects the general expectations of condominium owners that restrictions in place at the time they purchase their units will be enforceable. This in turn encourages the development of shared ownership housing—generally a less costly alternative to single-dwelling ownership—by attracting buyers who prefer a **stable, planned environment**. It also protects buyers who have paid a premium for condominium units **in reliance** on a particular restrictive scheme.

Our social fabric is founded on the **stability of expectation and obligation** that arises from the consistent enforcement of the terms of deeds, contracts, wills, statutes, and other writings. To allow one person to escape obligations under a written instrument upsets the expectations of all the other parties governed by that instrument (here, the owners of the other 529 units) that the instrument will be uniformly and predictably enforced.

Under the holding we adopt today, the reasonableness or unreasonableness of a condominium use restriction that the Legislature has made subject to section 1354 is to be determined not by reference to facts that are specific to the objecting homeowner, but by reference to the common interest development *as a whole*. As we have explained, when, as here, a restriction is contained in the declaration of the common interest development and is recorded with the county recorder, the restriction is presumed to be reasonable and will be enforced uniformly against all residents of the common interest development **unless the restriction is arbitrary**, imposes burdens on the use of lands it affects that substantially outweigh the restriction's benefits to the development's residents, or violates a fundamental public policy.

We conclude, as a matter of law, that the recorded pet restriction of the Lakeside Village condominium development prohibiting cats or dogs but allowing some other pets **is not arbitrary**, but is rationally related to health, sanitation and noise concerns legitimately held by residents of a high-density condominium project such as Lakeside Village, which includes 530 units in 12 separate 3-story buildings.

E. Governance

1. BOARD OF DIRECTORS

To successfully govern and manage a homeowners association requires considerable patience and great interpersonal skills on the part of the directors on the board, and the on-site manager, if there is one. Not all associations are large enough to afford a full-time manager and operations staff, and so these responsibilities are often contracted out to local property management firms, landscaping contractors, maintenance contractors, and the like.

In smaller associations, dedicated members of the board and devoted individual homeowners sometimes voluntarily, and without pay, perform some of the landscaping and simpler maintenance tasks, which saves considerable sums of money for their fellow homeowners.

One of the main reasons for having a **board of directors** is to enforce the rules and regulations of the CIC. Rules and regulations are an absolute necessity in common interest communities. When created and used properly, rules provide stability and predictability to daily life in the community. One of the most important tasks for the governing board is the fair enforcement of the rules. Well-crafted and fairly enforced rules serve an economic function, because they can promote uniformity, which can increase the resale value of each of the individual units over what they would be otherwise.

Fair enforcement of the rules—as opposed to **arbitrary** and **capricious** enforcement—by the manager at the direction of the board of directors can resolve small problems before they grow into big problems. For example, if a unit owner or guest is creating a noise disturbance or violating some other rule or regulation of the community, a neighboring unit owner can make a complaint to the board of directors, which is obligated to enforce the community's rules.

The directors on the board of a common interest community—just like the directors of any corporation—have a **fiduciary** obligation to the corporation and its members/shareholders. A fiduciary is one who owes a duty of loyalty to another, meaning that a director must act in the best interests of the corporation, rather than for his or her own personal gain.

In a traditional neighborhood of single-family homes, if a neighbor is causing a disturbance or creating a nuisance, one would have to confront the neighbor and/or make a complaint to the police. The police might inform the complainant that, in order to obtain a remedy, she would have to either swear out a warrant against the violator and testify in court, or file a lawsuit. Neither of these options is particularly palatable or conducive to neighborhood harmony and solidarity.

In a common interest community, these problems can be handled quickly, usually informally, and without the need for further intervention by law enforcement or the court system. The board—sometimes through a property manager—will notify the offender that there has been a complaint (without identifying the complainant), and ask the resident to end the offensive conduct. If the resident persists, it is the association that will make the complaint to the police, impose a fine, and/or file suit against the offender for continuing violations of the association rules.

2. LIABILITY OF DIRECTORS

In the last 50 years or so, we have become a highly litigious society. Consequently, during the early days of condominium ownership—the 1960s and 70s—many owners of units in condominiums and associations, although concerned about their

Board of Directors
the governing body of a corporation or association, including condominiums and homeowners associations. At a minimum, a board usually consists of a president, vice president, secretary, and treasurer.

Arbitrary
founded on preference or prejudice, rather than fact.

Capricious
unpredictable or impulsive behavior.

Fiduciary
one who owes to another the duties of good faith, trust, confidence, and candor, and who must exercise a high standard of care in managing another's money or property.

communities, were very reluctant to run for a seat on the board of directors. You have heard the expression "No good deed goes unpunished." Nobody wants to be **sued for volunteering** as a director or officer of a homeowners association, especially when one is trying to help the community where he or she lives. As a result of lawsuits, many associations—especially smaller associations—found it difficult to fill seats on their boards of directors. This problem has been largely overcome in three ways:

a. Directors and Officers Insurance (D & O Insurance)

Directors and officers insurance policies protect boards and their individual officers and directors (and sometimes, managers and other staff employed by the association) when they have acted in **good faith** and **within the scope** of their duties as officers and directors of the association's board. These policies will cover the costs of defending against a lawsuit, and any judgment against an officer or director. However, the policies will not insure against grossly negligent decisions or actions. Nor will a D & O policy insure against intentionally tortious conduct by a director, such as assault, battery, false imprisonment, or intentional infliction of severe emotional distress.

> D & O Insurance
> an insurance policy that protects directors and officers, and sometimes the employees, of a homeowners association or condominium from liability when they have acted in good faith and within the scope of their duties.

    In some cases, the association itself will **indemnify** an officer or director who was sued as a result of some action taken, or not taken, on behalf of the association. By its indemnity, the association promises members of the board that it will reimburse any officer or director for legal fees or monetary judgments against the director(s) when acting within the scope of their board duties. Like D & O insurance policies, the association's indemnification of board members will not cover intentional torts committed by them.

b. The Business Judgment Rule

The **business judgment rule** is a common law (sometimes statutory) **rule of evidence** that protects officers and directors not only in condominium and homeowners associations, but in all types of corporations and other business entities. In some states the business judgment rule is created by statute, while in others it was created by case law, otherwise known as common law. Regardless of its origin, the rule protects the officers and directors against legal claims when a rational, good faith decision turns out to be ill-advised, unprofitable, or otherwise harmful to the association or its members.

> Business Judgment Rule
> a rule of evidence created by statute or common law that protects officers and directors of corporations and associations from liability for decisions made in good faith, but which are ultimately detrimental to the corporation's shareholders or association's members.

    As you can imagine, there are hundreds of decisions that are made by a board of directors in the average homeowners association. Some of these decisions are bound to result in negative and unintended consequences, and perhaps cost the unit owners thousands of dollars in special assessments, but that does not mean that the officers and directors will be liable for making a bad decision. The business judgment rule is a rule of evidence; the court will instruct jurors that there is a **rebuttable presumption** that the officers and directors have acted in the best interests of the association.

> Presumption
> a legal inference or assumption that a fact exists.

> Rebuttable Presumption
> an inference drawn from certain facts that establish a prima facie case, which may be overcome by the introduction of contrary evidence.

c. Statutes

Some states have enacted legislation that limits the liability of officers and directors in all instances except cases of gross negligence, or intentionally tortious conduct.

3. BUDGETING

Perhaps the most important function of the board of directors is to create a realistic **budget** for the maintenance of the common areas of the association. This is not as easy as it might seem because directors are elected. Like professional politicians,

> Budget
> an estimate of a property's anticipated income and expenses over a specified period of time, usually a year.

they are pressured by their constituents to keep dues as low as possible. Such pressure may cause the maintenance of the common areas to fall below that which is necessary to increase, or at least maintain, the value of the common areas, which may have negative consequences for the values of the individual units.

Aside from the routine maintenance of the common areas, the budget must allocate some portion of the regular dues to the **reserve fund**. This budget item is for major repairs and capital improvements. Such major repairs might include installing new roofs, resurfacing of parking areas, or renovating or replacing elements of the HVAC system. Capital improvements would include installing a new swimming pool, building a new clubhouse, or large-scale landscaping projects.

4. COMMON PROBLEMS IN THE CIC

Not surprisingly, many of the most common problems in a common interest community are related to the common areas, sometimes called the common elements. "Common" is defined as something that is shared or used by, or applies to, everyone. Thus, the common law of England applied to nobleman and pauper alike, that is, it was common to all (except, of course, the king).

In the same vein, the *common areas* are those parts of a condominium or homeowners association which may be used and enjoyed by all of the unit owners in the development. We have already identified some of these common areas, such as swimming pools, club houses, greenbelts and open spaces, parking areas, sidewalks, and roadways.

Disputes between the unit owners and the association that involve the common areas are often the result of poorly drafted declarations and bylaws filed by the developer. The *association* is obligated to pay for the maintenance of the common areas, while the homeowner has to pay for repairs to his or her individual unit. Which is to say that, in a dispute over the repair or replacement of what may be a common area, either the association or the homeowner is going to get hit in the pocketbook. The line of demarcation between what is common area property, and the property of an individual owner, is sometimes very blurred and indistinct. Consider the following example.

WHO OWNS THE SHUTTER...AND THE LIABILITY?

Suppose you own a townhouse in a homeowners association. Yours is one of four connected units in one of several buildings of the development. As such, you own your residence and the land beneath it. The Declaration that was filed by the developer back in 1970 simply states: "The Association is responsible for the maintenance of the common areas and the common elements."

One day, a shutter next to one of your second-story windows falls, hitting the mail carrier on the head as she is delivering your mail. Who is liable to the mail carrier will hinge (pardon the pun) on whether the shutter is a common element to be maintained by the association, or whether it is part of your real property to be maintained by you.

A well drafted declaration or set of bylaws would have addressed and answered this legal issue. Unfortunately, not all declarations and bylaws are as comprehensive and specific as they need to be.

To further complicate matters, there is a species of real property in an association known as a **limited common element**. A limited common element is part of the common area and therefore owned by all of the unit owners; however, it is reserved for the exclusive use of one or more unit owners, but fewer than all of the owners.

Reserve Fund
a portion of the regular dues that are set aside for major repairs to, and capital improvements on, the common areas.

Limited Common Element
common area owned by all the unit owners, but reserved for the exclusive use of one or more unit owners, and fewer than all of the owners.

The most typical example of a limited common element is a *parking space*. Parking spaces in high density condominium developments, especially in condominiums situated in large urban areas, are highly prized. Since the parking space is common area, the condominium association would normally be responsible for its maintenance, such as painting the lines, keeping it free of oil and other substances, and repairing cracks or potholes.

The declaration filed by the developer may provide either that:

a. The expense of maintaining the limited common elements is to be assessed against the unit owner(s) who benefits from the limited common element, or
b. That all unit owners are to pay the expenses related to all limited common elements.

In either case, a specific limited common element is *appurtenant to* ownership of a specific unit. That is, the limited common element known as parking space # 52 "belongs to" Unit # 52. When Unit # 52 is sold, the exclusive right to use parking space # 52 runs with the land, and will belong to the new owner of # 52.

Patios, *decks*, *walkways,* and *docks* are generally classified as *limited common elements* to be maintained by the association, but for the exclusive use of one or more individual owners. The declaration, however, is the final arbiter of whether a piece of real property is a common element, a limited common element, or individually owned.

STATE V. KOLCZ

Middlesex County Court of New Jersey, Law Division (Criminal)
114 N.J. Super. 408, 276 A.2d 595
April 7, 1971, Decided

This is an appeal of nine cases wherein the respective defendants were found guilty of *trespassing* by the Monroe Township Municipal Court. The incident occurred on January 26, 1971, at about 2 P.M., at the Rossmoor Community, "a planned retirement village."

Defendants are members of a group of citizens of the township who desire to change the present form of municipal government. They embarked upon this in the manner prescribed by circulating a petition to be signed by the required number of local citizens. On January 26, 1971 this group, one of whom is a member of the municipal governing body, went to Rossmoor with the intention of asking the residents to sign their petition. They intended to do this by going from *door to door* of the dwelling units, ringing doorbells and asking the residents if they care to sign the petition. Rossmoor is in part surrounded by a wall and there are gates with security guards. Upon arriving, the nine defendants were met by the president of one of the holding companies and by a lawyer, their visit apparently having been anticipated. They informed these two gentlemen of their intention and

were told that they could not enter upon the premises. Defendants nevertheless entered and went about their intended mission. Complaints for trespassing were then signed by the president in the municipal court.

Defendants, in their conversation with the representatives of the community on January 26, 1971 were informed that they could go to the community center and set themselves up in such a manner that residents could go to them if they desired to sign the petition.

During the course of the trial a representative of the Middlesex County Board of Elections testified. She said that the total number of registered voters in Monroe Township was 4,628 and of that number 990 resided within the confines of Rossmoor. [21%—Ed.]

The case of *Martin v. City of Struthers, 319 U.S. 141 (1943)*, involved an ordinance which made it unlawful for anyone distributing "handbills, circulars, or other advertisements" to ring a doorbell or otherwise summon homeowners to the door for the purpose of receiving such literature. A member of the Jehovah's Witnesses, who was convicted of violating the ordinance by distributing pamphlets to homeowners concerning a religious meeting, had her conviction reversed by the U.S. Supreme Court. The court ruled the ordinance to be an **unconstitutional invasion of the right of free speech and press**. In weighing the conflicting interests, Justice Black, in his opinion, said:

> Anyone familiar with political life realizes that campaigning door-to-door is one of the most accepted techniques of seeking popular support. Also, the circulation of nominating papers would be greatly handicapped if they could not be taken to the citizens in their homes. Furthermore, the dangers of distribution can so easily be controlled by traditional legal methods, leaving to each householder the full right to decide whether he will receive strangers as visitors.

Applying this principle to the case before the court, one cannot help but agree that there is no substitute for door-to-door communication.

In *Marsh v. Alabama*, a **company-owned town** [a quasi-government] sought to ban the distribution of literature of Jehovah's Witnesses. A direct conflict existed between an individual's First Amendment rights and the right of the owners of the town to prohibit the exercise of these rights. Justice Black explained:

> Ownership does not always mean absolute dominion. The more an owner, for his advantage, opens up his property for use by the public in general, the more do his rights become circumscribed by the statutory and constitutional rights of these who use it. When we balance the Constitutional rights of owners of property against those of the people to enjoy freedom of press and religion, as we must here, we remain mindful of the fact that the latter occupy a preferred position.

It appears that persons endeavoring to disseminate **political or religious** information are protected by the Constitution, but those wishing to canvass an area for **business purposes** must yield to other considerations.

This court believes that decisions relating to municipalities are equally applicable to Rossmoor, since it is in many essential regards a self-sufficient community. The corporate officers may speak for the citizens of Rossmoor on matters relating to health, welfare and safety. These officers may believe that it is their duty to protect the Rossmoor residents from annoying or obnoxious sales methods, but the court cannot allow the corporation to decide to bar what it knows to be a bona fide political endeavor.

Although the guaranties of free speech and free press will not be used to force a community to admit peddlers or solicitors of publications to the homes of its residents, such guaranties should be used to insure that each individual alone decides what **political** and **religious information** he wishes to receive.

This court is bound by legal principles reiterated by the United States Supreme Court. In applying these principles to the instant case the court feels that defendants were **exercising a legal right** in a legal manner and therefore *were not trespassers*. This court does not wish to open wide the gates of Rossmoor and thereby allow anyone to come in, at any time, for any purpose.

Nevertheless, this court feels compelled to hold ajar the gates of Rossmoor under the present circumstances. To hold otherwise would, in effect, create a political "isolation booth." The nine complaints of trespass are therefore dismissed.

F. The Common Interest Community as a Quasi-Government

Some common interest communities consist of thousands of residential units. These developments, in terms of both geographical size and population, dwarf the size and population of many small towns. For this reason, common interest communities and their governing associations have been referred to as **quasi-governments**, and their boards of directors compared with town councils.

Because common interest communities are quasi-governmental entities means that rights that must be honored by real governments, such as free speech,

Quasi
to some extent or degree; nearly; similar to.

must be allowed in privately-owned associations, even when such activities may be prohibited by the Conditions, Covenants & Restrictions, or the rules and regulations. The rights of private property ownership can conflict with First Amendment and other rights under the federal and state constitutions. Consider the following case:

QUASI-GOVERNMENTAL NATURE OF AN HOA

Suppose that Del Boca Vista, a large homeowners association located in southern Florida, has a covenant in its CC&Rs that prohibits all signs, other than FOR SALE signs, larger than 1' × 2'.

Ms. Hendricks in Unit B-113 hangs a large bed sheet in her bay window on which she has written: "Impeach the President of the U.S." The Board of Directors of Del Boca Vista receives a complaint about the sign, which is so large that it can be seen from the public road abutting the condominium development. The Board orders the manager to cite Ms. Hendricks for a violation of the CC&Rs.

Ms. Hendricks responds to the board with a letter in which she states that if the Board attempts to enforce the regulation by imposing a fine on her, Ms. Hendricks' sister—a well-known attorney in the area—"will sue the Association and each director on the Board for violating my First Amendment right to freedom of speech." Keep in mind that **political speech** has been described as the most important type of speech by the United States Supreme Court, and therefore, the most worthy of protection.

Who should prevail in this case, and why?[3]

See *State v. Kolcz* on page 331 regarding political speech in a condominium association.

This example underscores the fundamental tension that exists not only at Del Boca Vista and every other condominium and homeowners association, but in a free society in general. It is the tension and conflict between the rights of the *individual*, versus the rights of the *community*.

Ms. Hendricks, and each of us, have a right to freedom of speech. However, it is also true that Ms. Hendricks and all of the other unit owners in Del Boca Vista agreed to abide by the CC&Rs when they purchased their units.

G. Business Condominiums

In the past, doctors, lawyers, accountants, and other relatively small business firms were content to lease office space from a developer. Many of these professionals began to realize that owning their office spaces was much preferable to making ever-increasing monthly rental payments to a landlord. Thus were born business condominiums.

---

[3]There is a complicated and technical issue related to this question, regarding whether the homeowners association or condominium is a "**state actor**." Constitutional protections, such as due process and the right to free speech, *apply only against governmental entities* and not private persons. For example, some celebrities have their domestic employees sign contracts wherein the employees agree not to publish, or cause to be published, any article or book regarding the celebrity. Is this not a violation of the employee's right to free speech, which is protected by the First Amendment?

The answer is no, because the celebrity is not the state, nor acting on behalf of the state, and therefore, not a state actor. Thus, the celebrity-employer and the employee are free to negotiate the terms of their contract, including the employee's giving up the right to freedom of speech. If a government, or *quasi-government* like an HOA or condominium, attempted to negotiate such a contract with its employees, that action would be unconstitutional if the court found that the HOA or condominium was, in effect, a state actor.

Business condominiums are created and operated very much like residential condominiums. As the development of residential condominiums has grown, so has the development of business condominiums, and for the same reasons—the scarcity and increasing cost of real estate. Over the long term, real estate usually appreciates and so the owners of a business condominium will benefit from the appreciation in the value of the property. Another advantage of owning one's office space is greater input and control over decisions affecting the property, rather than relying on a landlord to make those decisions.

CHAPTER SUMMARY

A common interest community is one wherein *individual ownership* of real property is combined with the shared, or *common ownership* of other real property in the same development. That is, one who owns his or her dwelling unit is automatically a member in a homeowners *association* that owns the common areas.

Common interest communities are created *by statute*, and every state in the Union has devised a statutory scheme governing the development, operation, and ultimate dissolution of CICs.

There are several *advantages* to living in a common interest community, including relative affordability of housing, amenities such as swimming pools and tennis courts, maintenance of the common areas is provided by the association, security, and a board of directors to govern the association and enforce the rules and regulations.

Some of the *disadvantages* of association living are the payment of regular dues to maintain common areas and recreational facilities that you may not use; special assessments, rules, and regulations; and neighbors who may be less than considerate.

The types of CICs include condominiums, homeowners associations, and cooperatives. *Condominiums* and *associations* combine individual unit ownership with shared ownership of the common areas. *Co-ops* are not condominiums because the members of the cooperative do not own the units where they live. The cooperative is a *corporation*, and the residents of the building do not own real property, but instead are *shareholders* in the corporation. The corporation owns the real property, and then *leases* each of the several units to the corporation's shareholders.

A *planned unit development* (PUD) is a type of zoning, and a mechanism whereby a parcel of land is zoned to allow the development of a single, usually very large community, which often contains mixed uses such as residential, retail shops, and small business. Thus, a planned unit development is not a type of ownership, but a planning tool that facilitates the orderly, predictable development of what is primarily a residential subdivision.

The important documents relating to CICs are the *declaration*, which is the legal document that creates the condominium and is recorded at the office of the register of deeds in the county where the property is located; it is considered the most important of the CIC-related documents. The declaration is sometimes known as the *master deed*.

The *articles of incorporation* create the association—typically a non-profit corporation—that holds ownership of the common areas, and are filed with the secretary of state. The articles of incorporation are sometimes called the *corporate charter*.

Bylaws fill in the details of the broad strokes found in the articles of incorporation.

Rules and regulations are enacted and enforced by the board of directors and govern everyday life in the association, such as hours of operation of the recreational facilities, whether pets are allowed, and parking.

Governance of the association rests with the board of directors, which consists of homeowners elected by their fellow owners. Associations and their boards of directors are *quasi-governmental*. There is a fundamental tension that exists between the rights of the individuals who live in the association, and the rights of the community.

Directors and Officers (D & O) Insurance protects boards and their individual officers and directors when they have acted in *good faith* and *within the scope* of their duties as officers and directors of the association's board. Another protection for board members is the *business judgment rule* that protects officers and directors against legal claims when a good faith decision turns out to be harmful to the association.

Budgeting is one of the most important functions of any board of directors. When assessing and collecting regular dues from the members, a certain percentage must be allocated to the *reserve fund* for major repairs and capital improvements.

The *association* is obligated to pay for the maintenance of the *common areas*, while the homeowner has to pay for repairs to his or her individual unit.

A *limited common element* is part of the common area and therefore owned by all of the unit owners; however, it is reserved for the exclusive use of one or more unit owners, but fewer than all of the owners. The most typical example of a limited common element is a parking space, and patios, decks, walkways and docks are generally classified as limited common elements to be maintained by the association.

Business condominiums are growing in popularity with small business owners for the same reasons as residential condominiums have become so popular, that is, the rising cost of land. Condominium ownership allows owners to own more property for the dollar, and brings ownership within reach of more consumers.

CONCEPT REVIEW AND REINFORCEMENT

KEY TERMS

Amenities
Arbitrary
Articles of Incorporation
Association
Board of Directors
Budget
Business Judgment Rule
Bylaws
Capricious
CC&R
Common Area/Common
 Element

Common Interest Community
Condominium
Cooperative
Corporate Charter
Covenants
Declaration
D & O Insurance
Dues
Footprint
Homeowners Association
Indemnify
Individual Ownership

Limited Common Element
Master Deed
Planned Unit
 Development
Presumption
Quasi
Quasi-Government
Rebuttable Presumption
Reserve Fund
Rules and Regulations
Shared Ownership
Special Assessment

CONCEPT REVIEW QUESTIONS

1. What are the three most important legal documents for the creation of a common interest community?

2. What is a declaration, and what is its purpose? What types of information does a typical declaration contain? Where is the declaration filed? What is the synonymous term for the declaration?

3. What are articles of incorporation, and what is their purpose? Where are articles of incorporation filed? What is the synonymous term for articles of incorporation?

4. What are bylaws, and what is their purpose? Where are bylaws filed? How do bylaws differ from the declaration and articles of incorporation?

5. How would you define "condominium" as it relates to a form of legal ownership of real property? What are the other two definitions of the word "condominium"?

6. What is a homeowners association? Is a homeowners association a type of condominium as that term relates to a form of legal ownership? Why?

7. What is a cooperative, and in what part of the country are co-ops mostly found? Does ownership in a cooperative mean that one owns the real property? If not, what does a resident of a cooperative own? Does the resident of a co-op, technically speaking, live in a common interest community?

8. How is a cooperative different from a condominium?

9. What are CC&Rs? When are CC&Rs created? What are some of the rights of property ownership that CC&Rs limit in a common interest community?

10. Why are common interest communities sometimes referred to as "quasi-governmental"? What constitutional implications does this description have in relation to persons coming onto the association's property to go door-to-door and distribute political pamphlets? Does a board of directors have "police powers" that are similar to police powers belonging to a state or local government?

11. What is D & O insurance, and why is it necessary? What is indemnification, and in the context of common interest communities, who indemnifies whom?

12. What are "reserve funds," and when are they used? What are dues, and how often are they paid? What are special assessments, and when are they assessed against the unit owners in an association?

13. What is a "footprint," and how is it related to real property in an association? Does the term have any significance to a unit owner in a high-rise condominium?

14. What is the significance of the term "arbitrary and capricious" as it relates to the enforcement of rules and regulations in a common interest community?

15. What is a planned unit development? Is it a type of ownership of real property?

16. What is an example of a "limited common element"? How is a limited common element different from the common area? Who is responsible for maintaining limited common elements? Who is responsible for paying for the maintenance of limited common elements?

17. What is a fiduciary? Who in a common interest community owes a fiduciary duty to whom, and why?

ETHICS

A GO-BY IS GREAT, **BUT...**

Andy is a paralegal in a two-attorney law firm that specializes in common interest communities. One of the law firm's clients of long standing is the Vista del Sol Homeowners Association. Last week, Andy got a call from Petula, the president of Vista del Sol HOA, while both of the attorneys in the law firm were in court.

Petula told Andy that she needed to get a copy of a lease that the individual unit owners might use for renting out their units for short periods of time, not exceeding two weeks, if the Board of Directors decided to allow such rentals. Petula needed Andy to fax a copy of the lease immediately because the Board was just about to sit down for a meeting to consider whether to allow short-term rentals, and what type of language they would want to include in a standardized rental agreement.

Wanting to be a nice guy, and wanting to please a long-standing client, Andy told Petula that the law firm had drafted at least a half dozen such standardized rental agreements for other HOAs, and one as recently as a few weeks ago. Andy said that he would fax the most recent one to Petula right away, adding: "If it was good enough for some other HOA, I don't see why it wouldn't be good enough for Vista del Sol."

Has Andy engaged in the unauthorized practice of law? Why or why not?

If Andy had limited himself to just faxing the rental agreement prepared for the other HOA, without making the statement above, could he have avoided any and all questions about the unauthorized practice of law?

Should Andy have made a statement to Petula that the rental agreement that he was faxing wasn't necessarily suitable for Vista del Sol? Would that have negated any potential charges relating to the unauthorized practice of law?

How would you have handled this situation if you were Andy?

BUILDING YOUR PROFESSIONAL SKILLS

CRITICAL THINKING **EXERCISES**

1. Owners of apartment buildings have sometimes been held to be liable to a tenant if she is assaulted in her apartment by someone who is not a resident of the development. Liability may be imposed on the apartment owners if a jury decides that they have breached a duty of care to the tenant, for example, by failing to provide adequate locks, failing to keep the complex well-lit at night, or failing to prune large bushes in which a criminal could hide.

   If the context is changed from an apartment complex to a condominium development, would the same legal theories apply? That is, in a condominium, all of the unit owners are members of the association that owns the common areas. So, in the case where an owner is assaulted in his own unit, can he successfully sue the condominium association, of which he is a member? Does it make any difference whether the association is a non-profit corporation, or a for-profit corporation? What has common law traditionally held regarding these questions? Is the common law beginning to change in this area of premises liability?

2. Earlier in the chapter it was stated that a covenant in a CC&R is usually presumed valid by the courts if there is a dispute relating to it. However, use-restriction rules and regulations (e.g., "No residence may be painted any shade of red.") enacted by a board of directors do not enjoy that presumption of validity. Instead, courts will apply a "reasonableness test" to determine if a particular rule or regulation is enforceable against the residents of the association.

   In the case of *Hidden Harbor Estates v. Basso*, 393 So.2d 637 (1981) (emphasis added), the Florida Court of Appeals wrote:

*There are essentially **two categories of cases** in which a condominium association attempts to enforce rules of restrictive uses. The first category is that dealing with the validity of restrictions found in the declaration of the condominium itself. The second category of cases involves the validity of rules promulgated by the association's board of directors.*

*In the first category [restrictions in the declaration], the restrictions are clothed with a very strong **presumption of validity**.... Such restrictions are very much in the nature of covenants running with the land and they will not be invalidated absent a showing that they are **wholly arbitrary** in their application, **in violation of public policy**, or that they abrogate some fundamental **constitutional right**.... A use restriction in a declaration of condominium may have a certain degree of unreasonableness to it, and yet withstand attack in the courts.*

*The rule to be applied in the **second category** of cases [use-restriction rules passed by a board], however, is different. In those cases where a **use restriction** is not mandated by the declaration, but is instead created by the board of directors, the **rule of reasonableness** comes into vogue. The requirement of "reasonableness" in these instances is designed to somewhat fetter the discretion of the board of directors.*

The question is: Why is there different treatment for use restrictions created in the CC&Rs found in the declaration as opposed to use restrictions contained in rules promulgated by the board of directors? A hint...reliance.

3. In 2008, the residents of Del Boca Vista Homeowners Association (containing 700 residential units) elected a board of directors that turned out to be very lax in its enforcement of the rules and regulations in general, but particularly as to the rules regarding acceptable exterior paint colors.

Del Boca Vista, like many homeowners associations, has color charts for the colors that may be used on each block of the development. These approved colors are all pastels, but for the last four years, many residents disregarded the color schemes, and painted their homes in colors that were literally "off the charts." Some of the offenders painted their homes in the colors of their alma maters, such as forest green, crimson and gold, and burnt orange and Chicago maroon.

In 2012, a new board was elected after campaigning on a platform of uniformity and strict compliance with the color charts and the association's other architectural rules and regulations. Immediately upon taking office, the property manager, at the Board's direction, began imposing fines on 57 owners who had painted their homes with inappropriate colors in the preceding four years. In addition to the fines, the 57 owners were also required to repaint the exteriors of their homes in the appropriate association colors; in some cases, the cost of repainting could be as high as $10,000.

Several of the 57 owners who were cited by the manager showed up at the next meeting of the board of directors to complain that the citations were unfair and the Board's requirement that they repaint their homes was arbitrary, capricious, and an undue financial burden. Some of the owners have threatened to sue the Association and the Board.

If you were a member of the Del Boca Vista Board of Directors, what factors would you consider in trying to resolve these complaints? Did the Association waive its right to enforce the color schemes because there was little, if any, enforcement of the painting standards between 2008 and 2012? What are the values that the Association is attempting to uphold by its insistence on adhering to the color charts?

Does it matter if the color palettes were mandated in the original Declaration, or if they were merely rules adopted by a previous board, or boards? Must the Association provide due process to its members, that is, at a minimum, notice and an opportunity to be heard, or does due process only apply in civil and criminal judicial proceedings?

RESEARCH ON THE **WEB**

1. Find the statutory scheme for your jurisdiction that controls the creation and operation of a condominium. Is there a separate set of statutes that controls the creation and operation of homeowners associations? If so, note the similarities and differences between the two statutory schemes.

2. Search the web to learn how many "airport communities" are currently in existence in the United States. What famous actors (husband and wife) reside in such a community in Florida? Do you see the trend for the development of such common interest communities increasing or leveling off, and why?

3. Life in the association can be interesting, to say the least. Passions often run high at board meetings, sometimes over some of the simplest and most unimportant of matters. Run the following query, and variations thereof, to see how many hits you get:

   condominium or homeowners association & fist fight & meeting

4. Access the web and attempt to determine the earliest instance of common interest ownership that was created in your jurisdiction. Many of the earliest instances of common ownership relate to parks, for example, Grammercy Park in Manhattan. What type of property was owned in common…parks, meadowlands, grazing areas? When was the common interest created? What type of legal instrument created the common interest—deed, will, trust?

5. If you have access to LexisNexis or Westlaw, craft a query to determine the earliest case in the databases to use the word "condominium." What is the name of the case? From what jurisdiction does the case arise? In what year was the case decided? Is the word "condominium" used in the same sense that we understand it today?

BUILDING YOUR **PROFESSIONAL** PORTFOLIO

1. Draft a simple policy for Del Boca Vista condominium association regarding who may come onto the property for the purpose of soliciting from the residents. Will you allow every solicitor to enter the premises, or perhaps, no solicitor? Can you bar all solicitors from the property?

2. Draft a rule regarding what types of beverage containers are permitted in the swimming pool facility of your HOA.

chapter 13

REAL ESTATE DEVELOPMENT & INVESTMENT

LEARNING OBJECTIVES

After reading this chapter, you should understand:

• What a real estate developer does

• When and why a feasibility study may be required

• How a site analysis is different from a feasibility analysis

• How housing density is related to zoning

• How an option contract is different from an offer to purchase contract

• What the acronym "REIT" stands for

• What cash flow is, and its significance to the real estate investor or lender

Risk
the uncertainty of a result; the existence and the extent of a possibility of harm.

A. Overview of Real Estate Development

Real estate development is about **risk.** Developers, by nature, tend to be risk-takers who are willing to roll the dice on a given project. While developers seek to minimize their risk, there are many external factors that can turn a seemingly profitable venture into a money pit. While developers may make large financial profits, they can also sustain large financial losses as well.

As you will see in the following sections, there are several stages in the real estate development process. These *stages often overlap*, but sometimes, a new stage cannot be begun until a previous stage has been completed. Therefore, a developer may be compared with the conductor of an orchestra. Many different types of professions and professionals must be properly melded to bring about a successful conclusion to a real estate development project.

Below is a partial list of some of the professionals that a developer must be able to interact with, coordinate, or "orchestrate":

1. Land owners and sellers,
2. Real estate brokers,
3. Neighboring property owners,
4. Bankers and other lenders,
5. Attorneys,
6. Government officials,
7. Architects,
8. Interior designers,
9. Landscapers,
10. General contractors,
11. Subcontractors,
12. Marketing agents,
13. Leasing agents,
14. Tenants, and
15. Property managers.

After a high tolerance for risk, perhaps the most important characteristic of a successful developer is social, or people, skills. Because of the complexity of the development process, the "developer" may not be just a single person, but may be comprised of a team of individuals with specialized knowledge in one or more areas of the development process.

Real estate developers have occasionally been held in low esteem by members of the public. A relatively small percentage of developers are only interested in the quick buck, and consequently their projects are poorly designed and constructed. Some developers have built projects without any concern for the adequate protection of the environment, or without due consideration of the concerns and needs of neighboring property owners and tenants. Many developers have left partners, investors, and lenders holding the bag because of the developer's financial mismanagement (or worse).

Conversely, there are many developments and re-developments that might be deemed works of art, sometimes on a grand scale. Certain waterfront renovations and restorations come to mind, where lands that were once considered eyesores—and potential health hazards—have been reborn and transformed into beautiful parks, shops, restaurants, marinas, and residential spaces. Baltimore's Harborplace is a prime example of such a rebirth. Although most residents and tourists seem to approve of such renovations in general, these large developments are not without controversy.

Recall the case of *Kelo v. City of New London*. Putting aside the Supreme Court's questionable decision that allowed the City of New London to take private property, that project was an example of a waterfront development that went terribly awry, in spite of good intentions.

The waterfront projects are probably the most dramatic, expensive, and eye-catching of the real estate developments. But a real estate development may consist of just a few houses in a small subdivision, or a small office building. And so let us offer a couple of definitions:

> *Developer*—a person or organization that develops; a person who invests in and develops the urban or suburban potentialities of real estate

The definition above is not very helpful because it uses the word "develop" to define developer. So let's consider the root word:

> *Develop*—to bring out the capabilities or possibilities of something; bring to a more advanced or effective state; to cause to grow or expand.

Developers, at their best, will "bring out the capabilities or possibilities" of a parcel of real property, creating a benefit not only for the owners and tenants of the project, but for the community as a whole. Now we will examine the stages of the development process.

B. The Stages of Real Estate Development

There are many stages in the real estate development process, and some of the steps listed below happen simultaneously. As an example, although site acquisition is a stage that precedes the design stage, there is no reason that a developer cannot be consulting with architects about the developer's overall concept for the project. Stated differently, the developer must be adept at juggling several balls simultaneously.

1. AN IDEA

As you drive through the streets of your town, you will see houses, apartment buildings, shopping centers, office buildings, schools and hospitals, mini-storage facilities, and industrial buildings. Each of these developments came to be built only after someone came up with an idea to build it.

Ideas come to us in many ways. For the real estate developer, an idea for a project may come to mind because the developer knows that there is a *demand* in the community for a certain type of development; for example, there may be a demand for Class A office space in a particular city. The developer may glean this information from a variety of sources, including the developer's own knowledge of the local real estate market, market surveys, census and other demographic information, as well as input from real estate brokers, leasing agents, lenders, property managers, architects, contractors, and others in real estate–related occupations.

Armed with the knowledge that there is a demand for a particular type of real estate product, the developer will attempt to find a *developable, affordable site* that will meet the perceived demand for Class A office space. Large developers may employ full-time site-acquisition specialists to locate suitable parcels for development, or more typically, smaller developers will use local real estate brokers to find appropriate sites.

Sometimes, the idea process works in reverse. In that situation, the idea for a real estate development is not driven by demand, but rather the developer may be aware of a piece of property that is strategically located, and as yet undeveloped. With that particular parcel of land in mind, the developer attempts to ascertain the **highest and best use** of that parcel, that is, the use that will generate the most profit, which means that the developer must determine whether the parcel is best suited for the construction of residential units (for example, apartments and/or condominiums), office space, commercial/retail use, mini-storage, industrial, or institutional use, such as schools, hospitals, and so on, or perhaps some combination of these in what is called a **mixed-use development.**

> **Highest and Best Use**
> that use of a parcel of land that will generate the most profit.

To summarize, a developer may come up with an idea for a project by:

a. Knowing of a demand for a particular type of property (e.g., Class A office space), and then locating a site on which to build that type of property; or

b. Knowing that a particular site is available, and then determining what type of use—apartments, shopping center, etc.—to make of the property.

> **Mixed-Use Development**
> a single real estate development made up of two or more different property types, such as residential, retail, and office space.

The example above illustrates how an idea for a particular type of real estate development may be demand-driven. But an idea for a project may be sparked by a developer's creativity, like the famous line in the movie *Field of Dreams*, where a disembodied voice proclaims, *"If you build it, they will come."* At the end of the movie, the viewer sees a long line of cars coming in the night to visit a baseball field carved from an Iowa cornfield. This calls to mind an adage about (some) developers: "Developers don't build because there is a demand; they build because lenders will lend."

Understandably, prudent lenders are very reluctant to make loans based upon a developer's hunch or mere speculation, even when assured by the spirit-voice of the long-deceased baseball legend Shoeless Joe Jackson. This sounds logical, but the "build-it-and-they-will-come" philosophy caused the collapse of many lenders in the mid-to-late 1980s, during the so-called savings and loan crisis.

The flip side of the coin is that lenders may sometimes feel pressure to make loans when they have large amounts of cash on hand. When a lender makes a loan, it generates income from loan origination fees, service fees, and interest on the loan principal. Cash deposits sitting in a bank vault are not making any money for the lender, and for this reason, the lender might make loans that are less than prudent.

Like the expansion of the housing bubble in 2007, the savings and loan crisis in the 1980s was precipitated by extremely lax, and frequently criminal, lending practices. The savings and loan industry was deregulated by Congress in the early 1980s. A lot of money for construction loans became available, and lenders, enticed by large **loan origination fees** and commissions, were willing to make loans to anyone who claimed to be a developer. This easy money led to a tremendous amount of overbuilding, particularly in apartment construction. As a result, the vacancy rates soared, and the apartment developer-owners were unable to meet the debt service on the construction and permanent loans.

The solution in the 1980s was through the creation of the Resolution Trust Corporation (RTC), which bought up the real estate assets and bad loans of the hundreds of failed S&Ls. This **bailout** of the banking system ultimately cost the taxpayers approximately $125 billion (which was a lot of money in the 1980s). History would repeat itself in 2007, a mere 20 years after the S&L debacle, when the federal government once again had to step in and bail out the banking system in order to prevent a meltdown of the national and international economic systems.

2. FEASIBILITY ANALYSIS

Regardless of how an idea for a specific project comes to a developer, the developer will have made some quick, rough calculations to determine if a project will "pencil out." These calculations will inform the developer of the approximate price that should be paid to purchase a parcel, or parcels, of land for the development project. The developer will consider such factors as site preparation, construction and development costs to build the project, operating expenses of the completed project, cost of the construction and permanent loans, and the amount of rent that can be generated per square foot of leasable space.

However, lenders usually will not make multimillion dollar loans based upon a developer's rough calculations. Remember that lenders like to feel as safe and secure as possible when making loans. Because real estate development is inherently risky, lenders will seek to reduce that risk by requiring that a **feasibility study** be conducted before making a construction loan.

The cost of a feasibility study depends upon the size and complexity of the proposed development and may run from $25,000 into the millions of dollars.

Loan Origination Fee
a fee charged by a lender which is a percentage, usually 1%–2%, of the face amount of a loan, over and above the interest to be paid on the loan.

Bailout
the rescue of an entity or an industry, such as the banking industry, from financial trouble or possible collapse.

Feasibility Study
an analysis of several demographic and economic factors in a local market to determine if a proposed use of real property would be profitable.

A reputable developer realizes and will (reluctantly, perhaps) admit that feasibility studies, although expensive, are of value to the developer, as well as the lender. Besides reducing the lender's anxiety level, the study may warn the developer away from a particular use or project size, and thereby save the developer from possibly large financial losses.

Consider the case where a developer wants to build a 300-unit apartment complex. A proper feasibility study or analysis should take account of some or all of the following:

a. The *location* of the proposed development and its relationship to the project's prospective tenants: Is the development in a location where tenants would want to be? Are the surrounding areas and neighborhoods attractive? Remember that the three most important factors to consider in real estate are *location, location, and location.*

b. The *highest and best use* of the proposed development: single-family residential, apartments, retail, offices, mini-storage, industrial, institutional, or some type of mixed-use.

c. How much *demand* currently exists for the proposed type of development, and what percentage of that market can the developer capture?

d. What *competition* from other similar uses already exists in the vicinity of the proposed development, and are there other proposed projects that will be coming online in the next couple of years, and compete with the development under consideration?

e. What is the appropriate *unit-mix*—for example, if we are talking about an apartment project, what percentage of the units should be one, two, or three bedrooms; what is an appropriate rent structure for one-, two-, and three-bedroom apartments, considering the target market, for example, college students, young professionals, retirees, etc.?

f. What types of *amenities* would tenants expect under the proposed rent structure?

g. What is the anticipated *turnover rate* among tenants in this type of project? Using the example of the proposed development of an apartment project, the turnover rate would be much higher for college students than for retirees.

h. The *proximity* of public transportation, employment, shopping facilities, schools, restaurants, etc., to the proposed development.

i. What are the *per capita income*, and the *average household income*, in the neighborhood where the proposed project is to be built?

j. Are construction loans and permanent *loans currently available* at a reasonable interest rate for apartment projects.

The factors above relate to supply and demand, and financial considerations. However, since the 1970s, more and more cities and towns have become aware of the *environmental* consequences that may accompany large (or even relatively small) development projects. Therefore, from the inception of the project, the developer should have a good understanding of what is required by the environmental rules and regulations of the municipality where the project is to be built. Developers do not like surprises, and knowledge of environmental restrictions and requirements can save the developer time and money by avoiding development opportunities that would be prohibitively costly because of federal, state, or local environmental requirements. These requirements might include mitigation of traffic congestion, large open spaces in the project, and large-scale infrastructure improvements or upgrades, such as to water and sewer lines.

3. SITE ANALYSIS

Consider the case of the developer who has an idea to build about 300 apartment units on the south side of town. A feasibility study was conducted and indicated that there was a market for that many units in that part of town. The developer has made some preliminary inquiries of various lenders, some of which are amenable to making fairly large construction loans at this time.

The developer has had her eye on a 20-acre parcel, which has been on the market for more than four years, and looks promising as a development site. She has made an offer on the property contingent upon a favorable **site analysis,** which is a comprehensive study of the myriad factors that will determine whether the parcel is viable as the site for the development of the 300 units.

Among the many variables examined in a site analysis are:

a. The *topography* of the land, including any potential drainage problems, and whether parts of the property lie in a *floodplain* (which would make any lender very uneasy), or is in an active earthquake or hurricane region.

b. The availability of *utilities,* including water, sewer, electrical supply, and gas service. If these utilities are not readily available, the developer must calculate the additional cost to bring these utilities to the property.

c. *Environmental regulations* and requirements must be ascertained precisely. Heretofore, the developer has had a general knowledge of the requirements, but now it is time to determine exactly what the requirements are, and how much it will cost to comply with those requirements.

d. A *physical inspection* and study of the property is necessary to determine if there are any issues with toxins in the soil, underground fuel storage tanks, or other chemical hazards. Soil conditions must be analyzed to determine if the land is capable of supporting the proposed structures. Are there any existing structures that would need to be demolished and removed, or any encroachments by neighboring properties that would have to be remedied?

e. On the legal side, the developer should ascertain that the current *zoning* is appropriate for the proposed use. If not, the developer will have to request a zoning change or variance, which process can be time-consuming, expensive, and comes with no guarantee that the requested change in zoning will be granted by the city or county.

f. A preliminary *title examination* should be made to determine if there are any easements on or through the property, any unsatisfied liens on the property, or other encumbrances of record.

g. Are there any state or local *building codes* that might create impediments for the proposed use of the property, proposed construction materials, or layout of the improvements? Are there requirements relating to the density of housing, that is, the number of units allowed per acre of land, the minimum number of parking spaces, or the maximum amount of square footage for "impervious surfaces," such as sidewalks and parking lots, which will impact runoff into nearby streams and/or the local sewer system?

4. SITE ACQUISITION AND PERMITS

If you are the developer of the proposed 300-unit apartment complex, you want to make certain that you are ready to proceed with the development of your project immediately after the closing of the sale. You want everything to be nailed down

Site Analysis
the physical inspection and evaluation of a proposed building site to determine its suitability for development.

before committing to spend much of your own time and money, and becoming personally liable on a multimillion dollar construction loan. The construction lender feels the same way, and may not make the loan until most, if not all, of the purchase *contingencies* have been met.

You are already familiar with how real property is purchased. In development deals, the basic principles of contract law are the same—mutual assent (offer and acceptance) and consideration—but development transactions contain many more contingencies and conditions that must be satisfied prior to the closing. For example, the offer to purchase and closing may be contingent upon some or all of the following:

a. Appropriate zoning, or securing a zoning *variance* from the city or county government.

b. Several **permits** must be obtained from the state, county, or city governments relating to environmental compliance, building systems and materials, changes to streets and traffic signals, and installation and use of utilities.

c. *Loan commitments* for the construction and permanent loans must be gotten, at a certain interest rate and for a specific period of time.

> **Permit**
> a certificate issued by a federal, state, or local governmental agency allowing some action to be taken, for example, a building permit.

As with many businesses, time is money. If any of the above contingencies are not met, it may bring the development process to a grinding halt. If the developer has failed to incorporate the required environmental safeguards into the landscape design, the city will not issue a building permit. In the meantime, the cost of money (i.e., the interest rate on the construction loan) may increase, contractors and subcontractors may become unavailable, and there is always the risk that the city or town may demand further changes be made to the development.

Remember that offers to purchase include a *closing date*, which dictates the date by which the seller and developer-buyer must finalize the transaction and title is conveyed. Bear in mind that in making an offer to purchase the developer may have submitted a significant earnest money deposit with the offer. If the developer cannot meet some contingency written into the contract of purchase, a seller may not be willing to extend the closing date.

There has been a considerable amount of litigation relating to contingencies, which may require that the developer use "reasonable efforts," or even her "best efforts" to secure, for example, a change in zoning, or lender financing.

> **Best Efforts**
> diligent attempts to perform an obligation, as measured by what the reasonable person would do in the same or similar circumstances. It is a higher standard than reasonable efforts.

Best efforts is a higher standard than *reasonable efforts* but sometimes in the offer to purchase contract, the standard is not properly identified. Failing to properly identify the appropriate standard by which a developer must perform invites litigation.

The problem with contingencies in an offer-to-purchase contract has led many developers to employ an **option *contract*[1]** instead of an offer to purchase contract. An option is a contract in which the developer pays a sum of money to the seller of the property; in return, the seller gives the developer—who is also the prospective buyer—the exclusive right to purchase the property at a specific price, and within a specific period of time, typically, within 12 to 24 months.

> **Option**
> a contract in which the seller agrees, for a fee, to keep an offer to sell a property open for a specified period of time, and usually for a specific price. During the option period, the offer may not be revoked by the seller.

If the developer-buyer has not exercised the option to buy the property, the option contract simply *expires* at the end of the stated term, and the seller retains the option fee paid by the developer. This process avoids the legal issues related to

---

[1]Technically, the term "option contract" is redundant because an option, by definition, *is* a contract.

a developer's reasonable efforts versus best efforts, or delays caused by third parties such as a zoning board. There are only two possible outcomes:

a. Either the developer exercises the option to purchase within the specified option period, and buys the property, or

b. The option expires—unexercised—by the developer. In this case, of course, the seller and developer are always free to enter into a new option contract.

If the developer does exercise the option to purchase, the option fee paid by the developer to the seller may be applied against the purchase price—or not—depending upon how the option contract reads. Incidentally, and not surprisingly, the option contract must be in writing to satisfy the Statute of Frauds because it involves an interest in real property.

HYPOTHETICAL

Suppose that a developer has made an offer to purchase, including a $25,000 earnest money check, on a property where she hopes to construct an office building. At present, the property is zoned for residential use, not office. The developer has included in the offer a closing date of December 31 of this year.

The developer has included a contingency in the offer to purchase that requires the developer to use her "best efforts" to obtain a change in the zoning. The seller accepts the offer.

In the intervening months, the developer has used her best efforts to obtain a change in the zoning from residential to office use. Unfortunately, despite the developer's best efforts, the zoning board has dragged its feet in approving the requested zoning change. The December 31 closing date will almost certainly come and go before the zoning board issues the anticipated change for an office use.

This delay is certainly beyond the developer's control. If the developer cannot close as promised, but has used her best efforts to secure the change, can the seller rescind the contract and keep the developer's $25,000 earnest money deposit?

Is there additional information about the language in the offer to purchase that might help you to answer this question?

5. DESIGN

There are four principal types of design work in a real estate development:

a. Site Design

Site design is the process whereby the improvements—in our ongoing example, the 300 apartment units, parking spaces, and amenities—are best matched to the unique topography and characteristics of the site to create a project that is appealing in its own right, while it also complements and enhances the surrounding community.

Probably the most important constraint on the site designer is the *housing density* permitted by the local zoning code, that is, the number of apartment units allowed per acre. The site design must also take into consideration the optimal placement of apartment types, such as the best location for the three-bedroom units (usually occupied by families), two-bedroom units, and one-bedroom apartments. This layout may in turn be dictated by the siting of the amenities, parking spaces, and even the locations where the city has mandated that there be fire hydrants.

b. Landscape Design

The design of the project's landscaping is sometimes considered part of the site design. However, it is often contracted separately to a landscape design firm because of its importance to the marketing of the apartment units, and for the creation of a unique identity for the apartment community.

In almost every town and city in America, one may find apartment communities with names like The Oaks, The Pines, The Arbors, Cedar Woods, Stonegate, Rock Creek, Fairmont, Mountain View, and University Place. While not particularly original, these names do convey to the prospective tenant the developer's concept or vision of the property. And at least in theory, The Oaks Apartments will be populated by a significant number of oak trees.

Landscaping can add immeasurably to a development's attractiveness, marketability, and unique identity in the marketplace, each of which may positively contribute to profitability. But the developer must also take into account the expense of the ongoing maintenance and upkeep of the landscaping—the more flowers, bushes, trees, and water amenities on the site, the greater the expense.

c. Exterior/Architectural Design

Some developers consider their completed projects to be their legacies and, in a few cases, monuments to themselves. This may be a good thing if it encourages developments that are unique, well-constructed, and appeal to prospective tenants as well as the public.

But even beyond leaving a legacy, a developer is most concerned with making a profit. One of the best ways to ensure the marketability, and therefore profitability, of a development is for the developer to team up with an architect who will create ideas for **building exteriors** that are both unique, yet compatible with the building exteriors of the surrounding neighborhood structures.

An architect's choice of building **materials** and **design** will be influenced not only by the local neighborhood, but by the regional "neighborhood" as well. A stucco exterior is well-suited to Southern California, but would stick out like a sore thumb in New England. Adobe is perfect for Arizona and New Mexico, but you won't see many adobe homes in West Virginia. Custom, taste, and the availability of building materials vary by region and the architect's design will be informed accordingly.

Building design is dictated to a certain extent by local building materials, such as Georgia clay to make the bricks used in the construction of countless homes in the Southeast. But interestingly, the local and regional **climate** can influence building design as well. A-frame construction is very common in areas where there is heavy snowfall, such as the Great Lakes regions and New England. A flat roof on a house or other structure in such an environment would collapse and not survive the winter.

d. Interior Design

For the last 70 years, the average size of the American home, including apartments, has steadily increased, although there has been some reversal of this trend in the last few years. We like our space in this country, and a good interior design plan for our 1, 2, and 3-bedroom apartments will maximize the amount of space that can be used and enjoyed by the tenants.

Lighting, floor coverings, room colors, window size and placement, and ceiling height are all variables that can affect one's perception of the interior space. The talented interior designer can adjust these variables to make a room seem larger than it really is. Once again, like the landscaping and architectural teams, the interior designer's purpose is to enhance the marketability—and thereby, the profitability—of the real estate development.

6. FINANCING

There are actually *two types of loans* used to finance a real estate development, and often these loans are made by two separate lenders. The first type of loan is the **construction loan,** and the second type is the *"take out"* **or permanent loan,** which is funded by the lender sometime after the construction has ended and the project has come online.

A *construction loan* is riskier than a permanent loan, and is for a much shorter term, usually not more than 2–3 years, depending on the size of the development project. For these reasons, construction loans bear higher interest rates than permanent loans.

The permanent loan is for a much longer period of time, usually 20–40 years, just like a loan to purchase a house. It is also called a "take out" loan because it takes the construction lender out of the picture. The permanent loan carries a lower interest rate than the construction loan because there is less risk in that the project has already been built-out.

The construction loan and permanent loan are issued in the name of the development company, which is almost always a corporation. However, in making either type of loan, the lender will probably require that the developer *personally guarantee* the loan. If the development project is not completed, or if there is a loan default following completion, the lender can seize the development company's corporate assets. If those assets are not sufficient to satisfy the outstanding debt—and usually they would not be—then the lender can seize the personal assets of the developer.

In addition to the developer's personal guarantee of the loan, lenders often require that the developer purchase a **performance** or **completion bond.** This bond is a promise by an insurance company to the lender that, if the developer is unable to complete the project, the insurer will hire a qualified contractor, and pay for the materials, to finish the job. The premium paid by the developer to the insurance company to purchase the bond is a percentage of the amount being loaned by the lender on the project, typically in the range of 2% to 5%.

How does the developer pay personal and business expenses during the pendency of a 1–3 year project? Included in the construction loan is a *developer's fee*, which is either paid on a regular basis or is paid similarly to the draw received by a subcontractor. The developer's fee enables the developer to maintain an office, pay staff, and meet personal living expenses during a construction and lease-up timeline that extends for years.

7. CONSTRUCTION

The **general contractor** is responsible for the successful completion of the project's construction. Some developers—usually those with significant construction experience—act as their own general contractors, while other developers hire a general contractor to oversee the construction. Even if the developer hires a general contractor to direct the construction, the developer must still keep a close watch on construction costs, scheduling, and deadlines.

Managing the construction process is complicated even with the smallest real estate developments. There are often dozens of subcontractors who must perform correctly, safely, and efficiently, in the proper sequence, and at the proper time, for there to be a successful completion of the project.

Construction Loan
a loan for the construction of a real estate development. Construction loans are short-term, usually not more than 2–3 years, and carry a higher interest rate than the permanent loan because of the increased risk of default during the construction phase.

Permanent Loan
also known as the "take out" loan because it will replace the construction loan upon the completion and lease-up of the new development. Permanent loans usually have terms of 20–40 years, and a lower interest rate than the construction loan.

Completion Bond
also known as a performance bond, it is a promise by an insurer that it will pay to complete the project in the event of the developer's default. The completion bond is paid for by the developer, for the benefit of the lender.

General Contractor
the person or entity that has overall supervisory responsibility during the construction process for the completion of the project. The GC schedules the work of the subcontractors, and the delivery of the building supplies.

Delays are inherent in the construction process and are the major challenge to the general contractor. Delays may be the result of the weather, natural disasters, incompetent subcontractors, the non-availability of certain supplies or materials, lenders, government officials, strikes, wars, and almost any other natural or human cause.

Scheduling **subcontractors** is a major part of the general contractor's job. Keep in mind that some subcontractors cannot begin their work until other subcontractors have completed theirs. Additionally, subcontractors have to work at other job sites, and if there is a delay on our jobsite, some subs will have to tend to their other jobs, and may not be available again for months.

Many of the jobs listed below consist of a series of tasks, some of which must be approved by a city or county inspector before the subcontractor can move on to the next task. A partial list of the jobs to be performed by the various subcontractors, in quasi-chronological order, is given below.

a. ***Site preparation***. The land is graded with bulldozers and other large pieces of equipment, sewer lines are installed, and roads and sidewalks are constructed. Building foundations, if necessary, are excavated.

b. ***Footings*** are poured. These are concrete pads on which the building is constructed, and prevent the building from sinking into the ground. The foundation, if necessary, is built, usually using either masonry blocks, or poured in-place concrete.

c. On our 300-unit apartment jobsite, the ***subflooring*** and ***framing*** are installed. On high-rise building projects, ironworkers erect the steel skeleton, and concrete is poured in place for the flooring.

d. The ***exterior walls*** and ***roof*** are put in place, enclosing the building, and the windows are installed. This allows the subs working on the interior to begin work without worrying about weather.

e. ***Brick*** and ***stone*** subcontractors build the fireplaces in each of our apartment units, and install stone accents on the exteriors of the buildings.

f. The ***electrical, plumbing,*** and ***HVAC*** subcontractors will wire, plumb, and install their respective systems. City or county inspectors must inspect and approve these major systems before they are enclosed (in the next step).

g. The ***drywall*** subcontractor goes to work, and the ***floor covering*** is laid down. However, if the floor covering is carpet rather than stone or tile, for example, the carpet will be one of the very last items put in place.

h. ***Appliances*** are installed, usually by the suppliers.

i. ***Painting*** subcontractors paint the interior walls, molding, and trim.

j. ***Landscaping*** subcontractors plant trees, bushes, flowers and shrubs, sow grass seed or lay down sod, install and adjust the irrigation system, install and adjust exterior accent lighting, erect fencing, install signage, and complete construction of amenities such as waterfalls or fountains.

k. The property manager makes an ***inspection*** of each unit and creates a ***punch list*** in the process, which is a list of the several, hopefully minor, problems to be corrected before the units can be rented to tenants. These problems might include touchup painting, leaking faucets, inoperable light switches or electrical outlets, etc.

l. A ***certificate of occupancy*** must be obtained following a final inspection by the appropriate city or county agency, before any tenants can occupy the apartment units.

Subcontractors are paid out of the proceeds of the construction loan. "Subs" who work on the project for an extended period of time receive **draws**; that is, after completing 30% of the work, the subcontractor might be paid 25% of the

Subcontractor
one engaged in a building trade such as a plumber, electrician, or roofer, who works on a construction site under the supervision of the general contractor.

Draw
one of numerous periodic payments received by a subcontractor for work performed on a construction site. The amount of the draw is roughly equivalent to the pro rata amount of the work performed by the subcontractor.

contract price for the work to be performed. In other words, the developer retains a small percentage of the monies owed to the sub until the subcontractor has fully performed. The withholding is called a **retainage** and gives the developer some leverage over the subcontractors to ensure that the sub's work is completed properly and in a timely manner.

Once the sub has completed the work, the developer pays the final draw payment, plus any retainage that is owed. If the subcontractor is not paid some or all of the monies owed by the developer, the sub may file a **mechanic's lien** at the clerk of court's office. If the subcontractor and the developer cannot come to an agreement on paying off the lien, the sub can literally force the sale of the property being developed. This is rare, however, because if the developer is unable or unwilling to pay off the sub, the lender would probably step in, pay off the subcontractor, and then withhold that same amount from future disbursements of loan funds to the developer.

Before the permanent loan replaces the construction loan, the permanent lender will conduct a title search to determine if there are any mechanics liens that must be satisfied, since the permanent lender wants to be in the first position in terms of priority of lien.

8. MARKETING AND LEASING

During the construction phase, the developer should be marketing the project, making the community aware that a new apartment complex, office building, or shopping center will soon be available for lease, and opening for business. The *marketing strategy* will be different depending on the type of property that is being built. The target market for tenants in an apartment complex is very different from the target market for tenants for an office building, shopping center, or industrial development.

It is crucial that the new development, regardless of the type of property, be leased as quickly as possible. The permanent lender, which will pay off (or "take out") the construction lender, may not be obligated to make the permanent loan until a specific percentage of the apartment units, or square footage of the office building or shopping center, has been leased to tenants. Remember that the construction loan carries a higher interest rate than the permanent loan, and therefore, having the permanent loan in place will reduce the developer's monthly debt service by thousands of dollars.

In many situations, particularly with office and shopping center developments, the marketing of the property will be part and parcel of the leasing process. The developer will sign a contract with a real estate broker who specializes in the leasing of office or retail space. The broker receives a commission for each lease procured.

How quickly the property is leased depends to a great extent on *demand* in the rental market. Remember that the developer, early in the development process, commissioned a feasibility analysis that included a survey of the rental market. But that study may have been completed 18 to 24 months earlier, and markets can change almost overnight. If demand for apartment units or office space is still strong, as the survey indicated two years ago, then the project should lease up relatively quickly.

On the other hand, if demand has slackened, then in the case of the new apartment development coming online, we are likely to see banners proclaiming 3 MONTHS FREE RENT!

If the development is an office building or shopping center, you will not see banners advertising free rent, even though the developer may be offering significant **rental concessions.** Unlike residential developers, office developers do not want the business community to know that there are problems finding new tenants because it raises doubts about the property. Aside from lowering the rental rates,

Retainage
a small percentage of money withheld by the general contractor or developer from the draw paid to a subcontractor.

Mechanic's Lien
a claim filed with the clerk of court by a subcontractor or materials supplier in the event they are not paid for work performed on, or for building materials supplied to, a jobsite. If the claim or lien is not paid, the sub or supplier may force the sale of the real property to which the lien relates.

Rental Concession
something of value given by an owner of a commercial property to entice prospective tenants to sign a lease for space in the owner's building.

another method that a developer may employ to attract office and retail tenants is by offering **tenant improvements,** or TIs.

Whenever a tenant moves into a new office or retail space, the space has to be "improved" to suit the tenant's needs. These are *tenant improvements*, and could include items such as room dividers, carpeting, wall coverings, and kitchen upgrades; needless to say, TIs can be very expensive. When there is strong demand for new office or retail space, the market dictates that the tenant bear the cost of these improvements. Conversely, when the demand for space is soft, the developer must pick up some or all of the costs of the TIs. In either case, the developer's bottom line is affected, for better or for worse.

Tenant Improvement
an upgrade to office, retail, or other commercial space. If the demand for space is soft, the property owner may offer TIs at a discount, or even for free. Conversely, when demand for space is strong, the tenant usually pays for the TIs.

EXHIBIT 13-1 Commercial Lease Agreement

Commercial Lease Agreement

This Commercial Lease Agreement ("Lease") is made and effective _____, by and between _____ ("Landlord") and _____ ("Tenant").

Landlord is the owner of land and improvements commonly known and numbered as _____ _____ and legally described as follows (the "Building"):

[Legal Description of Building] _____

_____

THEREFORE, in consideration of the mutual promises herein, it is agreed:

1. Term:

Landlord hereby leases Premises to Tenant, for an "Initial Term" beginning _____ and ending _____. Landlord shall use best efforts to give Tenant possession as nearly as possible at the beginning of the Lease term. If Landlord is unable to timely provide the Premises, rent shall abate for the period of delay. Tenant shall make no other claim against Landlord for any such delay.

2. Rental:

Tenant shall pay to Landlord during the Initial Term rental of $_____ per year, payable in installments of $_____ per month. Each installment payment shall be due in advance on the first day of each calendar month during the lease term to Landlord. The rental payment amount for any partial calendar months included in the lease term shall be prorated on a daily basis.

3. Use:

Notwithstanding the forgoing, Tenant shall not use the Leased Premises for the purposes of storing, manufacturing or selling any explosives, flammables or other dangerous substance, chemical, or device.

4. Sublease and Assignment:

Tenant shall have the right with Landlord's consent, to assign this Lease to a corporation with which Tenant may merge or consolidate, to any subsidiary of Tenant, to any corporation under common control with Tenant, or to a purchaser of substantially all of Tenant's assets. Except as set forth above, Tenant shall not sublease all or any part of the Leased Premises, or assign this Lease in whole or in part without Landlord's consent.

5. Repairs:

During the Lease term, Tenant shall make, at Tenant's expense, all necessary repairs to the Leased Premises. Repairs shall include such items as routine repairs of floors, walls, ceilings, and other parts of the Leased Premises damaged or worn through normal occupancy, except for major building systems or the roof, subject to the obligations otherwise set forth in this Lease.

(continued)

EXHIBIT 13-1 *Continued*

6. Alterations and Improvements.

Tenant, at Tenant's expense, shall have the right following Landlord's consent to remodel, redecorate, and make additions, improvements and replacements of and to all or any part of the Leased Premises from time to time as Tenant may deem desirable, provided the same are made in a workmanlike manner and utilizing good quality materials. Tenant shall have the right to place and install trade fixtures, equipment and other temporary installations in and upon the Leased Premises, and fasten the same to the premises. All personal property, equipment, machinery, trade fixtures and temporary installations shall remain Tenant's property free and clear of any claim by Landlord. Tenant shall have the right to remove the same at any time during the term of this Lease provided that all damage to the Premises caused by such removal shall be repaired by Tenant at Tenant's expense.

7. Property Taxes:

Landlord shall pay all general real estate taxes and installments of special assessments coming due during the Lease term on the Premises. Tenant shall be responsible for paying all personal property taxes with respect to Tenant's personal property at the Leased Premises.

8. Insurance:

A. If the Leased Premises or any other part of the Building is damaged by fire or other casualty resulting from any act or negligence of Tenant, or Tenant's agents, employees or invitees, rent shall not be diminished or abated while such damages are under repair, and Tenant shall be responsible for the costs of repair not covered by insurance.

B. Landlord shall maintain fire and extended coverage insurance on the Building and the Leased Premises in such amounts as Landlord shall deem appropriate. Tenant shall be responsible for fire and extended coverage insurance on all personal property, including removable trade fixtures, located in the Leased Premises.

C. Tenant and Landlord shall, each at its own expense, maintain a policy or policies of comprehensive general liability insurance with respect to the activities of each in the premises with the premiums thereon fully paid on or before due date, issued by and binding upon some insurance company approved by Landlord, such insurance to afford minimum protection of not less than $1,000,000 combined single limit coverage of bodily injury, property damage or combination thereof. Landlord shall be listed as an additional insured on Tenant's policy or policies. Tenant shall provide Landlord with current Certificates of Insurance evidencing Tenant's compliance. Tenant shall obtain the agreement of Tenant's insurers to notify Landlord that a policy is due to expire at least ten (10) days prior to expiration. Landlord shall not be required to maintain insurance against thefts within the Leased Premises.

9. Utilities:

Tenant shall pay all charges for water, sewer, gas, electricity, telephone and other services and utilities used by Tenant on the Premises during the term of this Lease unless otherwise expressly agreed in writing by Landlord. In the event that any utility or service provided to the Leased Premises is not separately metered, Landlord shall pay the amount due and separately invoice Tenant for Tenant's pro rata share of the charges. Tenant shall pay such amounts within fifteen (15) days of invoice. Tenant shall not use any equipment or devices that utilizes excessive electrical energy or which may, overload the wiring or interfere with electrical services to other tenants.

10. Signs:

Following Landlord's consent, Tenant shall have the right to place on the Leased Premises, at locations selected by Tenant, any signs which are permitted by applicable zoning ordinances and private restrictions. Landlord shall assist Tenant in obtaining any necessary permission from governmental authorities or adjoining owners and occupants for Tenant to place or construct the foregoing signs. Tenant shall repair all damage to the Leased Premises resulting from the removal of signs installed by Tenant.

11. Entry:

Landlord shall have the right to enter upon the Leased Premises at reasonable hours to inspect the property provided Landlord shall not thereby unreasonably interfere with Tenant's business on the Leased Premises.

12. Parking:

During the term of this Lease, Tenant shall have the non-exclusive use in common with Landlord, other tenants of the Building, their guests and invitees, of the non-reserved common automobile parking areas, driveways, and footways, subject to rules and regulations for the use thereof as prescribed from time to time by Landlord. Landlord reserves the right to designate parking areas within the Building or in reasonable proximity thereto, for Tenant, Tenant's agents, and employees.

13. <u>Building Rules:</u>

Tenant will comply with the rules of the Building adopted and altered by Landlord from time to time and will cause all of its agents, employees, invitees and visitors to do so. All changes to such rules will be sent by Landlord to Tenant in writing.

14. <u>Damage and Destruction:</u>

Subject to Section 8-A. above, if the Leased Premises or any part thereof or any appurtenance thereto is so damaged by fire, casualty or structural defects that the same cannot be used for Tenant's purposes, then Tenant shall have the right within ninety (90) days following damage to elect by notice to Landlord to terminate this Lease as of the date of such damage. In the event of minor damage to any part of the Leased Premises, and if such damage does not render the Leased Premises unusable for Tenant's purposes, Landlord shall promptly repair such damage at the cost of the Landlord. In making the repairs called for in this paragraph, Landlord shall not be liable for any delays which are beyond the reasonable control of Landlord. Tenant shall be relieved from paying rent and other charges during any portion of the Lease term that the Premises are inoperable, and unfit for occupancy or use, in whole or in part, for Tenant's purposes. Rentals and other charges paid in advance for any such periods shall be credited on the next ensuing payments, if any. If no further payments are to be made, any advance payments shall be refunded to Tenant. The provisions of this paragraph extend also to any occurrence which is beyond Tenant's reasonable control and which renders the Leased Premises, or any appurtenance thereto, inoperable or unfit for occupancy or use, in whole or in part, for Tenant's purposes.

15. <u>Default:</u>

If default shall at any time be made by Tenant in the payment of rent when due as herein provided, and if such default shall continue for thirty (30) days after notice thereof in writing to Tenant by Landlord without correction having been commenced and thereafter diligently prosecuted, Landlord may declare the term of this Lease ended and terminated by giving Tenant written notice of such intention, and if possession of the Leased Premises is not surrendered, Landlord may reenter said premises. Landlord shall have, in addition to the remedy above provided, any other right or remedy available to Landlord on account of any Tenant default, either in law or equity. Landlord shall use reasonable efforts to mitigate its damages.

16. <u>Quiet Possession:</u>

Landlord covenants and warrants that upon performance by Tenant of its obligations hereunder, Landlord will keep and maintain Tenant in exclusive, quiet, peaceable and undisturbed and uninterrupted possession of the Leased Premises during the term of this Lease.

17. <u>Condemnation:</u>

If any legally constituted authority condemns the Building or such part thereof which shall make the Leased Premises unsuitable for leasing, this Lease shall cease when the public authority takes possession, and Landlord and Tenant shall account for rental as of that date.

18. <u>Subordination:</u>

Tenant accepts this Lease subject and subordinate to any mortgage, deed of trust or other lien presently existing or hereafter arising upon the Leased Premises and to any renewals, refinancing and extensions thereof, but Tenant agrees that any such mortgagee shall have the right at any time to subordinate such mortgage, deed of trust or other lien to this Lease on such terms and subject to such conditions as such mortgagee may deem appropriate in its discretion. Landlord is hereby irrevocably vested with full power and authority to subordinate this Lease to any mortgage, deed of trust or other lien now existing or hereafter placed upon the Leased Premises of the Building, and Tenant agrees upon demand to execute such further instruments subordinating this Lease or attorning to the holder of any such liens as Landlord may request. In the event that Tenant should fail to execute any instrument of subordination herein require d to be executed by Tenant promptly as requested, Tenant hereby irrevocably constitutes Landlord as its attorney-in-fact to execute such instrument in Tenant's name, place and stead, it being agreed that such power is one coupled with an interest. Tenant agrees that it will from time to time upon request by Landlord execute and deliver to such persons as Landlord shall request a statement in recordable form certifying that this Lease is unmodified and in full force and effect (or if there have been modifications, that the same is in full force and effect as so modified), stating the dates to which rent and other charges payable under this Lease have been paid, stating that Landlord is not in default hereunder (or if Tenant alleges a default stating the nature of such alleged default) and further stating such other matters as Landlord shall reasonably require.

19. <u>Security Deposit:</u>

The Security Deposit shall be held by Landlord without liability for interest and as security for the performance by Tenant of Tenant's covenants and obligations under this Lease. The Security Deposit shall not be considered an advance payment of rental or a measure of Landlord's damages in case of default by Tenant. Landlord may, from time to time, without prejudice to any other remedy, use the Security

(*continued*)

EXHIBIT 13-1 *Continued*

Deposit to make good any arrearages of rent or to satisfy any other covenant or obligation of Tenant. Following any such application of the Security Deposit, Tenant shall pay to Landlord on demand the amount applied in order to restore the Security Deposit to its original amount. If Tenant is not in default at the termination of this Lease, the balance of the Security Deposit remaining after any such application shall be returned by Landlord to Tenant. If Landlord transfers its interest in the Premises during the term of this Lease, Landlord may assign the Security Deposit to the transferee and thereafter shall have no further liability for the return of such Security Deposit.

No waiver of any default of Landlord or Tenant hereunder shall be implied from any omission to take any action on account of such default if such default persists or is repeated, and no express waiver shall affect any default other than the default specified in the express waiver and that only for the time and to the extent therein stated. One or more waivers by Landlord or Tenant shall not be construed as a waiver of a subsequent breach of the same covenant, term or condition.

25. Successors:

The provisions of this Lease shall extend to and be binding upon Landlord and Tenant and their respective legal representatives, successors and assigns.

26. Consent:

Landlord shall not unreasonably withhold or delay consent with respect to any matter for which consent is required or desirable under this Lease.

27. Performance:

If there is a default with respect to any of Landlord's covenants, warranties or representations under this Lease, and if the default continues more than fifteen (15) days after notice in writing from Tenant to Landlord specifying the default, Tenant may, at its option and without affecting any other remedy, cure such default and deduct the cost thereof from the next accruing installment or installments of rent payable until Tenant shall have been fully reimbursed for such expenditures, together with interest thereon. If this Lease terminates prior to Tenant's receiving full reimbursement, Landlord shall pay the unreimbursed balance plus accrued interest to Tenant on demand.

28. Compliance with Law:

Tenant shall comply with all laws, orders, ordinances and other public requirements now or hereafter pertaining to use of the Leased Premises. Landlord shall comply with all laws, orders, ordinances and other public requirements now or hereafter affecting the Leased Premises.

29. Final Agreement:

This Agreement terminates and supersedes all prior understandings or agreements on the subject matter hereof. This Agreement may be modified only by further writing that is duly executed by both parties.

30. Governing Law:

This Agreement shall be governed, construed and interpreted by, through and under the Laws of this State.

IN WITNESS WHEREOF, the parties have executed this Lease as of the day and year first above written.

[Date]
_____

_____

Landlord

_____

Tenant

9. PROPERTY MANAGEMENT

Professional property management is essential to the long-term success of the new development. Ideally, the developer will have consulted with a property management firm at the earliest stages of the development process. This is because experienced property managers can anticipate problems that the developer or architect can fix on the drawing board, even before they become problems.

An example of such a potential problem might be the location of HVAC components. The large compressors and other components can be noisy, and should be as far removed as possible from the leasable spaces, otherwise the developer will have one or more very unhappy tenants, who may decide to rent elsewhere.

Many, perhaps most, developers wish to sell their newly developed projects as soon as possible. A sale enables the developer to *cash out* of the project, make a profit, and move on to the next development. However, a sale at a price that will net a profit for the developer will be difficult unless two things happen. In considering the importance of the two items below, examine the factors from the prospective buyer's point of view:

First, the project—be it apartments, an office building, or a shopping center—must be substantially leased. That is, a significant percentage of the apartment units or an office building's leasable square footage must be occupied by paying tenants. This is the job of the leasing broker. Developments that are fully leased, or almost so, reduce the risk for the new buyer because the buyer knows that tenants are "locked in" under the terms of their leases.

Second, a prospective buyer wants to see a **stabilized cash flow** that will cover the costs of ownership, such as mortgage payments, common area maintenance, insurance, taxes, and utilities. Stabilizing the cash flow is the job of the **property manager.** A just-completed development can have all sorts of problems similar to growing pains. Curing these problems may cost a significant amount of money that will probably be paid for out of the property's cash flow. These extraordinary costs can make the property appear to be unprofitable.

Additionally, all of the new tenants may not have yet moved in, and those who have taken possession may have received some upfront rental discounts and/or significant TI concessions. It may take a year a more after completion of the project for the kinks to be worked out and for the income stream to stabilize. Only then can a prospective buyer get a true picture of how the property will perform over time. This knowledge will inform a buyer about how much to offer the developer for the purchase of the property.

Finally, one may wonder who, or what, can afford to purchase developments that cost millions, hundreds of millions, or even billions of dollars. For the purchase of really expensive properties, there are three important players: insurance companies, pension funds, and **REITs** (real estate investment trusts). Each of these entities manages huge amounts of cash, which must be invested to provide a return for shareholders or pensioners. Real estate, when well-located and properly managed, can provide a relatively safe return on investment, with the possibility of appreciation of the property, and thereby, in the value of one's shares of ownership.

In *Lucas v. South Carolina Coastal Council,* the developer's legal problems arose when the State of South Carolina made changes to its environmental regulations that deprived him of any use of the two lots he wanted to develop. Significantly, the State made the changes to its environmental laws *after* Lucas had purchased the lots for development.

Stabilized Cash Flow
occurs when the income and expenses on a new income-producing property have become relatively steady and predictable.

Property Manager
the individual or firm charged with the day-to-day operations of an office building, shopping center, or apartment complex. The property manager will attempt to maximize income, and minimize expenses, while maintaining an appealing environment for the tenants.

REIT
a real estate investment trust is an entity through which individuals may invest in large real estate projects in the hopes of obtaining a return on their investment.

LUCAS V. SOUTH CAROLINA COASTAL COUNCIL

Supreme Court of The United States
505 U.S. 1003; 112 S. Ct. 2886; 120 L. Ed. 2d 798
June 29, 1992, Decided

Opinion

In *1986*, petitioner [developer] David H. Lucas paid *$975,000 for two residential lots* on the Isle of Palms in Charleston County, South Carolina, on which he intended to build single-family homes. In *1988*, however, the South Carolina Legislature enacted the Beachfront Management Act, which had the direct effect of barring petitioner from erecting any permanent habitable structures on his two parcels. A state trial court found that this prohibition rendered Lucas's parcels "valueless." This case requires us to decide *whether the Act's dramatic effect on the economic value of Lucas's lots accomplished a taking* of private property under the Fifth and Fourteenth Amendments requiring the payment of *"just compensation."*

In the late 1970's, Lucas and others began extensive residential development of the Isle of Palms, a barrier island situated eastward of the city of Charleston. Lucas in 1986 purchased the two lots at issue in this litigation for his own account. No portion of the lots, which were located approximately 300 feet from the beach, qualified as a "critical area" under the 1977 Act; accordingly, *at the time Lucas acquired these parcels, he was not legally obliged to obtain a permit* from the Council in advance of any development activity. His intention with respect to the lots was to do what the owners of the immediately adjacent parcels had already done: erect single-family residences. He commissioned architectural drawings for this purpose.

The Beachfront Management Act [of *1988*] brought Lucas's plans to an abrupt end. Under the Act construction of occupiable improvements was flatly prohibited. The Act provided no exceptions.

Lucas promptly filed suit, contending that the Beachfront Management Act's construction bar effected a taking of his property without just compensation. Lucas did not take issue with the validity of the Act as a lawful exercise of South Carolina's police power, but contended that the Act's *complete extinguishment of his property's value* entitled him to compensation regardless of whether the legislature had acted in furtherance of legitimate *police power* objectives. Following a bench trial, the court agreed. Among its factual determinations was the finding that "at the time Lucas purchased the two lots, both were zoned for single-family residential construction and ... there were no restrictions imposed upon such use of the property by either the State of South Carolina, the County of Charleston, or the Town of the Isle of Palms." The trial court further found that the Beachfront Management Act *decreed a permanent ban on construction* insofar as Lucas's lots were concerned, and that this prohibition "deprived Lucas of any reasonable economic use of the lots, ... and rendered them valueless." The court thus concluded that Lucas's properties had been "taken" by operation of the Act, and it ordered respondent to pay "just compensation" in the amount of $ 1,232,387.50.

The Supreme Court of South Carolina reversed. It found dispositive what it described as Lucas's concession "that the Beachfront Management Act was properly and validly designed to preserve ... South Carolina's beaches." Failing an attack on the validity of the statute as such, the court believed itself bound to accept the "uncontested ... findings" of the South Carolina Legislature that new construction in the coastal zone—such as petitioner intended—*threatened this public resource*. The court ruled that *when a regulation respecting the use of property is designed "to prevent serious public harm," no compensation is owing* under the Takings Clause regardless of the regulation's effect on the property's value.

Two justices dissented. They would not have characterized the Beachfront Management Act's "primary purpose as the prevention of a nuisance." To the dissenters, the chief purposes of the legislation, among them the promotion of tourism and the creation of a "habitat for indigenous flora and fauna," could not fairly be compared to nuisance abatement. As a consequence, they would have affirmed the trial court's conclusion that the Act's obliteration of the value of petitioner's lots accomplished a taking. We granted certiorari....

On the other side of the balance, affirmatively supporting a compensation requirement, is the fact that regulations that leave the owner of land without economically beneficial or productive options for its use—typically, as here, by requiring land to be left substantially in its natural state—carry with them a heightened risk that *private property is being pressed into some form of public service* under the guise of mitigating serious public harm. The many statutes on the books, both state and federal, that provide for the use of eminent domain to impose servitudes on private scenic lands preventing developmental uses, or to acquire such lands altogether, suggest the practical equivalence in this setting of *negative regulation* and *appropriation*.

We think, in short, that there are good reasons for our frequently expressed belief that when the owner of real property has been called upon to *sacrifice all economically beneficial uses* in the name of the common good, that is, to leave his property economically idle, he has suffered a *taking*.

It is correct that many of our prior opinions have suggested that "harmful or noxious uses" of property may be proscribed by government regulation without the requirement of compensation. For a number of reasons, however, we think the South Carolina Supreme Court was too quick to conclude that that principle decides the present case. The "harmful or noxious uses" principle was the Court's early attempt to describe in theoretical terms why government may, consistent with the Takings Clause, affect property values by regulation without incurring an obligation to compensate—a reality we nowadays acknowledge explicitly with respect to the full scope of the State's *police power*.

The transition from our early focus on control of "noxious" uses to our contemporary understanding of the broad realm within which government may regulate without compensation was an easy one, since the distinction between *"harm-preventing" and "benefit-conferring" regulation is often in the eye of the beholder*. It is quite possible, for example, to describe in *either* fashion the ecological, economic, and esthetic concerns that inspired the South Carolina Legislature in the present case. One could say that imposing a servitude on Lucas's land is necessary in order to prevent his use of it from "harming" South Carolina's ecological resources; or, instead, in order to achieve the "benefits" of an ecological preserve. A given restraint will be seen as mitigating "harm" to the adjacent parcels or securing a "benefit" for them, depending upon the observer's evaluation of the relative importance of the use that the restraint favors.

Whether Lucas's construction of single-family residences on his parcels should be described as bringing "harm" to South Carolina's adjacent ecological resources thus depends principally upon whether the describer believes that the State's use interest in nurturing those resources is so important that *any* competing adjacent use must yield.

When it is understood that "prevention of harmful use" was merely our early formulation of the police power justification necessary to sustain (without compensation) *any* regulatory diminution in value; and that the distinction between regulation that "prevents harmful use" and that which "confers benefits" is difficult, if not impossible, to discern on an objective, value-free basis; it becomes self-evident that noxious-use logic cannot serve as a touchstone to distinguish regulatory "takings"— which require compensation—from regulatory deprivations that do not require compensation. *A fortiori* the legislature's recitation of a noxious-use justification cannot be the basis for departing from our categorical rule that total regulatory takings must be compensated. If it were, departure would virtually always be allowed. The South Carolina Supreme Court's approach would essentially nullify *Mahon's* affirmation of limits to the *noncompensable exercise of the police power*.

Where the State seeks to sustain regulation that deprives land of all economically beneficial use, we think it may resist compensation only if the logically antecedent inquiry into the nature of the owner's estate shows that the proscribed use interests were not part of his title to begin with. This accords, we think, with our "takings" jurisprudence, which has traditionally been guided by the understandings of our citizens regarding the content of, and the State's power over, the *"bundle of rights"* that they acquire when they obtain title to property. It seems to us that the property owner necessarily expects the uses of his property to be restricted, from time to time, by various measures newly enacted by the State in legitimate exercise of its police powers; "as long recognized, some values are enjoyed under an implied limitation and must yield to the police power."

The "total taking" inquiry we require today will ordinarily entail analysis of, among other things, the degree of harm to public lands and resources, or adjacent private property, posed by the claimant's proposed activities, the social value

(continued)

of the claimant's activities and their suitability to the locality in question, and the relative ease with which the alleged harm can be avoided through measures taken by the claimant and the government (or adjacent private landowners) alike. The fact that a particular use has long been engaged in by similarly situated owners ordinarily imports a lack of any common-law prohibition (though changed circumstances or new knowledge may make what was previously permissible no longer so). So also does the fact that other landowners, similarly situated, are permitted to continue the use denied to the claimant.

The question, however, is one of state law to be dealt with on remand. We emphasize that to win its case South Carolina must do *more than proffer the* *legislature's declaration* that the uses Lucas desires are inconsistent with the public interest, or the conclusory assertion that they violate a common-law maxim such as *sic utere tuo ut alienum non laedas* [use what is yours in a way that does not harm what is another's].

South Carolina must identify background principles of nuisance and property law that prohibit the uses Lucas now intends in the circumstances in which the property is presently found. Only on this showing can the State fairly claim that, in proscribing all such beneficial uses, the Beachfront Management Act is taking nothing.

The judgment is reversed, and the case is remanded for proceedings not inconsistent with this opinion.

C. Real Estate Investment

Real estate investment and financing can be complicated. What is offered below is a broad and simplified review of some of the most important concepts involved in real estate investment. An investor will apply the concepts below to decide whether to purchase an existing apartment complex, office building, or shopping center, and for what price. The same concepts are also employed by developers and construction lenders to analyze the viability of projects yet to be built.

1. RATE OF RETURN

Rate of Return
the amount of profit generated as a percentage of the amount one has invested.

Return
the amount of profit generated by one's investment in real estate, the stock market, precious metals, or some other type of investment.

Whether one invests in real estate, the stock market, gold bullion, or pork belly futures, the first question that comes to the investor's mind is: "What can I make on my investment?" Phrased differently, the investor is asking: "What will be the **rate of return** on the money I invest?" But the concept of **return**—what can be made on one's investment—must always be considered in the context of the risk that the investor is willing to assume.

If you had $1,000 to invest, would you prefer to invest in a real estate deal where you *could* make 20% on your investment (or perhaps lose your entire $1,000 investment)?

Or, would you prefer to make a guaranteed 5% by investing in a Treasury bill? The 5% return is virtually guaranteed because T-bills are backed by the full faith and credit of the United States.

Among other factors, your answer will depend upon your tolerance for risk. The general rule to be remembered is that *safer investments*—those having less risk, such as U.S. Treasury bills—*offer lower returns* than more risky investments such as real estate developments.

On a grander scale, suppose that you have $100,000 in cash and decide to purchase a home. After you have lived in the house for a year, you sell it for $110,000. What is your rate of return? The answer is 10% because:

Example # 1: $10,000 profit ÷ $100,000 invested = .10, or 10%

2. LEVERAGE

Using the same example, let's see how you can increase the rate of return on your investment by using the concept of **leverage.** This time, you purchase the same house for the same price of $100,000.

However, in this scenario, you only have $10,000 in cash to put down on the purchase price, and consequently, you have to borrow $90,000 from the bank. Once again, a year later you sell the house for $110,000. What is your rate of return? The answer is 100% (!) because:

Example # 2: $10,000 profit ÷ $10,000 invested = 1.0, or 100%

In Example # 2, you increased your rate of return tenfold over your rate of return in Example # 1. You accomplished this by using **leverage**, which is sometimes called **OPM** ("other people's money").

In Example # 2, you doubled your money in just one year and that sounds great. But you accomplished this at considerably *greater risk* than you had in Example # 1. In the first example, you purchased the property outright, and therefore, did not have to make any monthly mortgage payments to a lender. In the second example, however, you borrowed $90,000 and there was some risk that you would not have been able to make the monthly mortgage payments (if you had lost your job, or became ill for an extended period of time) and the bank might have foreclosed on the property. Of course, the monthly payments would reduce your rate of return somewhat, but for the sake of simplicity, we have ignored that factor.

And so while leverage can increase an investor's rate of return, there is also significant risk associated with the use of leverage. Real estate developers, who are by nature risk-takers, usually want to leverage their investments in their projects as much as possible by using more of the lender's money (OPM). The lender, on the other hand, feels much more comfortable if the developer has more of his or her cash invested in the project. The percentage that the lender is willing to loan on the development, or purchase, of a property is called the **loan-to-value ratio (LTV).** Using the same numbers as in Example # 2 above, we can see that the loan-to-value ratio was 90%:

LTV = $90,000 bank loan* ÷ $100,000 purchase price = .90, or 90%

(* you put $10,000 of your own money towards the purchase price)

3. CASH FLOW AND NOI

Cash flow is a term used to describe the *flow of money into, and out of, an investment*, in this case, a real estate investment property. Let us look again at the 300-unit apartment complex that you recently developed. The market analysis that you commissioned almost 3 years ago suggested that the local market could absorb 300 apartment units and the following mix of apartment sizes, which recommendations you adopted. The breakdown of the total of 300 units, is given below, along with the rental rate for each type of apartment:

90 1-bedroom apartments (30% of the units) @ $600/unit = $54,000/month
150 2-bedroom apartments (50% of the units) @ $800/unit = $120,000/month
60 3-bedroom apartments (20% of the units) @ $1,000/unit = $60,000/month

Gross Scheduled Income = $ 234,000/month
× 12 months
Annual GSI = $ 2,808,000

Thus, the *gross scheduled income* is the maximum possible rental income under the current rental-rate structure. The GSI is rarely achieved. If it is, that condition will not last for long because the owners of the project would correctly intuit that market demand for the units is high, and therefore, rents should be raised.

The following is an example of an annual Cash Flow statement. If the investment property is not new, its *actual* cash flow statements for the last few years will be available for review by a prospective lender or buyer. On the other hand, if the investment property was just recently completed, projected (estimated) numbers are all that will be available for review. However, these projections can be compared with data compiled by the Institute of Real Estate Management (IREM) or other professional associations for similar existing properties in the same or similar locations. Based on the actual or estimated numbers, a bank will determine how much to loan, and a buyer will use to determine how much to pay for the property:

$2,808,000	Gross Scheduled Income (GSI)
− 421,200	− Vacancy and Credit Loss (15% of GSI)
$2,386,800	= Effective Gross Income (EGI)
− 1,074,060	− Expenses (45% of EGI)[2]
$1,312,740	**= Net Operating Income (NOI)**
− 960,000	− Debt Service ($12M @ 7% for 30 years)
$ 352,740	= Cash Flow (annual)

Net Operating Income
the line item on a cash flow statement indicating the profitability of an income-producing real property. The NOI is important because it is used by real estate buyers, sellers, and lenders to derive an estimate of a property's fair market value.

The **net operating income** (NOI) figure is in bold because it is the most important number for a prospective lender or buyer. The NOI is a measure of how profitable a property is, or can be, with effective management. Note that the debt service is itemized *after* the NOI, and is therefore not a component of the NOI. Consequently, the financing of the property—whether it is highly leveraged (a high LTV) or is owned free and clear—does not affect the NOI. Thus, by looking at the NOI, the prospective buyer can see how well a property performs *regardless of the financing* in place.

A lender will use the NOI to determine how much it will lend to a buyer to purchase the project. Lenders and experienced acquisitions analysts can look at a cash flow statement and determine if any of the numbers appear to be "fudged," or are questionable. They are assisted in their analyses by statistics gathered and published by the Institute of Real Estate Management (IREM) in Chicago, Illinois.

There are two methods to value large investment properties, each of which makes use of the NOI:

a. Capitalization Rate

The capitalization rate, or "cap rate," enables a prospective buyer or prospective lender to determine the approximate value of a property based on its net operating

---

[2]Expenses include everything from advertising to maintenance to supplies. In the typical apartment complex, the largest line item under the Expense category is usually for the employees' compensation (management, maintenance, and landscaping). Dishonest sellers have been known to understate expenses, which increases the NOI, making the property appear more profitable. The higher NOI would (falsely) indicate a higher profitability, and therefore, a higher selling price.

income (NOI). The formula for determining value by using the capitalization rate is very simple:

Value of Property = Property's NOI ÷ Market Cap Rate

Using the net operating income from our cash flow analysis above:

Value of Property = $1,312,740 ÷ .10 (10%), therefore ...

Value of Property = $13,127,400

Based upon the value derived by using a cap rate of 10%, a prospective buyer might offer the seller of the property somewhat less, for example, $12,500,000. Let's assume that the seller counters at $13 million, and the buyer accepts.

Informed by the value derived by using a cap rate of 10%, a lender might be willing to loan the prospective buyer 80% (i.e., a loan-to-value ratio of 80%) of the final purchase price of $13 million:

$13,000,000 Purchase Price × .80 LTV = $10,400,000 Loan Amount

This means that the buyer will have to come up with 20% of the purchase price, or $2,600,000.

The question may have entered the reader's mind: How do the buyer and lender know what an *appropriate cap rate* is? The answer comes from the local and regional real estate markets. The lender and buyer (and seller) will review the numbers for transactions within the last couple of years involving sales of similar types of property. For each sale of each property, information can be obtained regarding the purchase price and the NOI, which will yield a cap rate for each transaction. An average of all the cap rates might produce the .10 that we used in the example above.

Another way of looking at the capitalization rate is that it measures the amount of cash generated by the property (reflected in the NOI) when compared with the purchase price of the property.

Some investor-buyers may use their own preferred capitalization rate. For example, a prospective buyer might feel that he or she requires a higher rate of return, say a 12% cap rate, than the average market cap rate of 10%. Assuming the same net operating income as above, this means that the investor-buyer, needing a higher return, would offer *less* for the property:

Value of Property = $1,312,740 NOI ÷ .12 (12%) Buyer's Preferred Cap Rate

Value of Property = $10,939,500

On the other hand, a large institutional investor might be willing to settle for a lower capitalization rate for a Class A property in a hot real estate market. That buyer would be willing to trade short-term cash flow for long-term appreciation. Assuming the same net operating income as above, this means that the investor-buyer would offer *more* for the property:

Value of Property = $1,312,740 NOI ÷ .08 (8% Buyer's Cap Rate)

Value of Property = $16,409,250

As you can see from the examples above, regardless of what cap rate is used by a prospective buyer or lender, an accurate NOI is critical to the analysis. Since the NOI comes from the cash flow statements generated by the *seller*, buyers and lenders must carefully review the property's reported income and expenses. Some sellers have been known to overstate the income, or understate the expenses, or both. That practice results in a higher NOI, and consequently, a higher sales price, than would otherwise be the case.

b. Discounted Cash Flow/Present Value

The second method to determine a property's fair market value is called *discounted cash flow* (DCF), or *present value* (PV) analysis. Like the cap rate analysis that we examined in the previous section, DCF relies heavily on a property's net operating income (NOI).

However, unlike cap rate analysis, which uses a property's most recent cash flow statement and NOI, discounted cash flow analysis (DCF) uses the most recent cash flow statement and NOI and projects those several years into the future. Using some complicated mathematical formulas, the future income stream (the future NOIs added together) are then *discounted* to a *present value*. Thus, we get the two names for this method: discounted cash flow, and present value analysis.

The future cash flows have to be discounted—or reduced—to a present value because all of us would rather have $1,000 cash in hand *today* than a promise or hope of receiving $1,000 in cash over the next few years. And so that future $1,000 is actually less valuable than the $1,000 cash in hand today. To determine how much the hoped-for, future $1,000 is really worth, an investor-buyer would determine an appropriate percentage rate by which to discount the future income stream. The discount rate is similar to the capitalization rate studied in the previous section. The following three important factors will be considered by the investor to generate an appropriate discount rate:

i. *Inflation*. Inflation occurs when the prices of products such as gasoline, building construction materials, food, etc. increase over time. This means that $1 spent next year on a product will buy less of that product than if you bought it today. The inflation of a product's price reduces the value of a dollar that you will spend (or receive) next year.

ii. *Risk*. Every investment has a certain amount of risk associated with it. Let's say that you purchased a very nice, 10-unit bed and breakfast on the Carolina coast. This looks like a great investment: before buying, you verified the seller's cash flow statements, which accurately reflect a profitable operation. The B&B is in good physical shape and is located on a prime beachfront lot, and tourists flock to the area. In spite of all that upside, there is significant risk to your investment because of the hurricanes that visit the Carolinas almost every year.

iii. *Opportunity Cost*. This term simply means that $1 received a year from now is worth less than $1 in hand today because the investor will have to forgo any better investment opportunities that come along in the intervening year, and cannot use that future $1 to purchase anything today.

The two methods of valuing a property described above—capitalization rates, and discounted cash flow/present value analysis—each has its limitations. An investor seeking to purchase a large income-producing property would likely use both methods and then make an offer based on the method that produced the lower fair market value for the property to be purchased.

The valuation analysis gets even more complicated when depreciation of the improvements, tax regulations, and a few other factors are thrown into the mix.

CHAPTER SUMMARY

A *developer* is someone who will bring out the capabilities or possibilities of a parcel of real property, creating a benefit not only for the owners and tenants of the property, but for the community as a whole. There are several stages to the development process, which may overlap during the development process, including:

An Idea—the developer may (i) have an idea about demand for a particular property type (apartments, offices, shopping center), and then find the property on which to build, or (ii) have the property, then brainstorm as to how it can best be utilized, considering its *highest and best use.*

Feasibility Analysis—this study analyzes several factors to determine if the local market will support a proposed use. It considers variables such as (i) the *location* of the proposed development; (ii) the *highest and best use* of the proposed development; (iii) how much *demand* currently exists for the proposed type of development and what percentage of that market can the developer capture; (iv) does *competition* from similar developments already exist in the vicinity; (v) the appropriate *unit-mix*; (vi) the *amenities* that tenants would expect under the proposed rent structure; (vii) the anticipated *turnover rate* among tenants in this type of project; (viii) would allowing *pets* be a benefit or a detriment to the marketing of the units; (ix) availability of bus lines, shopping, schools, restaurants, etc., to the proposed development; (x) the per capita income and average household income in the neighborhood of the proposed project; (xi) *availability of loans*, both construction loans and permanent loans; and (xii) *environmental issues.*

Site Analysis—this is an analysis of the particular land parcel, rather than a rental market. Among the many variables examined in a site analysis are (i) the *topography* of the land, including drainage, floodplain, earthquake or hurricane regions; (ii) the availability of *utilities*; (iii) *environmental* regulations; (iv) a physical *inspection* and study of the property to determine if *toxins* are in the soil, and *soil* conditions to determine if the land is capable of supporting the proposed structures; (v) the current *zoning*; (vi) a preliminary *title examination*; and (vii) *building codes*, permitted density of housing, that is, the number of units allowed per acre of land.

Site Acquisition & Permits—Offers to purchase developable property will contain many contingencies, which can present problems for the developer. The problem with contingencies has led some developers to employ an *option contract* instead of an offer to purchase contract. An option contract is one in which the developer pays a sum of money to the seller of the property; in return, the seller gives the developer the exclusive right to purchase the property at a specific price, and within a specific period of time. The option contract must be in writing to satisfy the Statute of Frauds, because the option contract involves an interest in real property.

Design—There are four types of design work in a real estate development:

1. *Site Design*—the process whereby the improvements are best matched to the unique topography of the site to create an appealing project.
2. *Landscape Design*—the design of the project's landscaping is sometimes considered part of the site design. It is very important to the marketing of the development.
3. *Exterior/Architectural Design*—the architect's job is to create building exteriors that are unique, yet compatible with those of the surrounding neighborhood structures. An architect's choice of building materials and design is influenced by the local and regional neighborhood. Custom, taste, and the availability of building materials vary by region and the architect's design will be informed accordingly. Local and regional climate can influence building design.
4. *Interior Design*—Lighting, floor coverings, room colors, window size and placement, and ceiling height are all variables that can affect one's perception of the interior space. The talented interior designer can adjust these variables to make a room seem larger than it really is.

Financing—there are two types of loans used to finance a real estate development, and usually two separate lenders. The first is the construction loan, and the second type is the "take out" or permanent loan. A *construction loan is riskier than a permanent loan*, and is for a much shorter term, and bears a higher interest rate than a permanent loan. The permanent loan is for a much longer period of time, usually 20–40 years, just like a loan to purchase a house. The lender will probably require that the developer *personally guarantee* the loan. Lenders often require that the developer purchase a *performance* or *completion bond*.

Construction—the *general contractor* is responsible for the project's construction. Even if the developer hires a general contractor to direct the construction, the developer must still keep a close watch on construction costs, scheduling, and deadlines. Scheduling subcontractors is a major part of the general contractor's job. A *certificate of occupancy* must be obtained before tenants can occupy the apartment units. The withholding of funds to a sub is called a *retainage*.

If the subcontractor is not paid some or all of the monies owed by the developer, the sub may file a *mechanic's lien* at the clerk of court's office.

Marketing and Leasing—the marketing strategy will be different depending on the type of property that is being built. The target market for tenants in an apartment complex is very different from the target market for tenants in an office building or shopping center. A method that developers employ to attract office and retail tenants is by offering *tenant improvements, or TIs*.

Property Management—professional property management is essential to the long-term success of the new development.

Insurance companies, pension funds, and REITs can afford to purchase developments that cost millions, hundreds of millions, or even billions of dollars. Each of these entities manages huge amounts of cash, which must be invested to provide a return for shareholders or pensioners. Real estate, when well-located and properly managed, can provide a relatively safe return on investment.

Real estate investment is an attempt to generate a return (profit) on monies invested in a project. The general rule is that safer investments—those having less risk—offer lower returns than more risky investments.

Leverage can increase the rate of return on one's investment by using OPM ("other people's money"), but also increases the investor's risk. The percentage that the lender is willing to loan on the development, or purchase, of a property is called the *loan-to-value ratio* (LTV).

Cash flow is a term used to describe the flow of money into, and out of, an investment. The *Gross Scheduled Income* (GSI) is the maximum possible rental income under the current rental-rate structure. The *Net Operating Income* (NOI) is the most important number for a prospective buyer, and is a measure of how profitable a property is. The Institute of Real Estate Management (IREM) publishes statistics on the performance of income-producing properties.

There are two methods to value large investment properties, each of which makes use of the NOI: (i) the *capitalization rate*, or *cap rate,* enables a prospective buyer or prospective lender to determine the approximate value of a property based on its net operating income (NOI). Another way of looking at the capitalization rate is that it measures the amount of cash generated by the property (reflected in the NOI) when compared with its purchase price. The formula is: Value of Property = Property's NOI ÷ Market Cap Rate

The second method to determine a property's fair market value is called *discounted cash flow* (DCF), or *present value* (PV) analysis. (DCF) uses the most recent cash flow statement and NOI and projects those several years into the future. Using some complicated mathematical formulas, the future income stream (the future NOIs added together) are then "discounted" to a present value. Thus, we get the two names for this method: discounted cash flow, and present value analysis.

The following three important factors will be considered by the investor to generate an appropriate discount rate: (i) *Inflation* occurs when the prices of products increase over time, (ii) *Risk*, and (iii) *Opportunity Cost*, which means that $1 received a year from now is worth less than $1 in hand today because the investor will have to forgo any better investment opportunities, and cannot use that future $1 to purchase anything today.

CONCEPT REVIEW AND REINFORCEMENT

KEY **TERMS**

Amenities	Draw	Marketing
Bailout	Environmental Regulations	Mechanic's Lien
Best Efforts	Feasibility Study	Mixed-Use Development
Building Codes	Floodplain	Net Operating Income
Cap Rate	General Contractor	Offer to Purchase
Cash Flow	Gross Scheduled Income	OPM
Completion Bond	Highest and Best Use	Option
Construction Loan	Housing Density	Performance/Completion Bond
Developer	Leverage	Permanent/Take-Out Loan
Development	Loan Origination Fee	Permit
Discounted Cash Flow/Present Value	LTV	Personal Guarantee

Property Manager	Risk	Tenant Improvement
Rate of Return	Site Analysis	Topography
REIT	Soil Conditions	Turnover Rate
Rental Concession	Stabilized Cash Flow	Unit-Mix
Retainage	Subcontractor	Utilities
Return	Target Market	Zoning

CONCEPT **REVIEW** QUESTIONS

1. What does a real estate developer do? Why are some developers sometimes held in low esteem by the public?

2. What is a feasibility analysis? What factors or variables should a good feasibility study examine? Who is it that requires a feasibility study, and why?

3. What is a site analysis? What factors or variables should a good site analysis examine? How is a site analysis different from a feasibility analysis?

4. What is meant by a property's "highest and best use"? How is that relevant to the development process? If a property is developed, is there any law or regulation that requires that it be developed to its highest and best use?

5. What is a property's unit-mix? Why is it significant? How might a proper unit-mix improve the profitability of a development? Conversely, how might an improper unit-mix decrease the profitability of the development?

6. What is housing density, and what is its significance to a developer? How is housing density related to zoning?

7. How would you define turnover rate? Is a high turnover rate good or bad for the owner of income-producing real property? Do you think that there would be a higher turnover rate in an apartment project, or in an office building? Why?

8. Why is a permanent loan sometimes referred to as a "take-out" loan? Does a permanent loan usually carry a higher or lower rate of interest than the construction loan? Why? How is the term "personal guarantee" related to either a construction loan or permanent loan?

9. What is a performance or completion bond? When would it become important in the development process? Who does the performance bond benefit? Who has to pay for it?

10. What is an option contract? How is it different from an offer to purchase contract? Why do some developers prefer using an option contract to "tie up" land, rather than making an offer to purchase on the property?

11. What does the acronym "REIT" stand for? What does an REIT do, and why?

12. What is cash flow, and what is its significance to the real estate investor or lender? On the real estate cash flow statement, what would an investor or lender probably consider the most important number? Why?

13. What is the capitalization rate? For what purpose is a cap rate used? How does a lender or investor determine what is an appropriate capitalization rate? What is the relationship between the capitalization rate and the net operating income?

14. What is discounted cash flow analysis? How is it related to present value analysis? Who uses discounted cash flow or present value analysis, and why?

15. What is leverage? What is OPM? How is leverage related to OPM? What effect does leverage have on one's rate of return? For the investor (or lender), is there any particular problem associated with leverage?

16. What is a rate of return, and why is it significant to an investor? What is an example of an investment (not necessarily a real estate investment) that would yield a very safe return? What is an example of an investment (not necessarily a real estate investment) that would carry a high risk for the investor? As an investor, would you be willing to take on a greater risk for the possibility of a greater return? Or conversely, would you prefer a safer investment but with a lower rate of return? Why?

17. What is gross scheduled income? How do you determine gross scheduled income? How is gross scheduled income related to the net operating income?

ETHICS

JUST SIT AND **LISTEN**

John is an associate in a very busy real estate law practice that represents several real estate developers. He is under consideration for partnership this year and has been working non-stop to ensure he exceeds the billable hour requirement set by the firm.

One of John's many clients is a developer who is one of four defendants in a relatively minor lawsuit involving just a few thousand dollars. One of the other defendants is being deposed today at the office of the plaintiff's counsel.

As a result of John's very busy schedule, he inadvertently calendared a meeting with an important new client at the same time that the deposition is scheduled. Instead of trying to reschedule the meeting with the new client, John asks his paralegal, Roberto, to attend the depositions in his place. John instructs Roberto to "just sit in and listen and report back anything of interest."

If Roberto merely attends the deposition and "just sits and listens" pursuant to John's instructions, has Roberto engaged in the unauthorized practice of law?

If Roberto takes notes and examines exhibits at the deposition, has he engaged in the unauthorized practice of law?

If John's developer-client, who is one of the four defendants, attends the deposition, should Roberto tell the developer-client why John is not present? What, if anything, should Roberto say to the developer-client?

Is John, or another attorney from his firm, obligated to be present at the deposition?

BUILDING YOUR PROFESSIONAL SKILLS

CRITICAL THINKING **EXERCISES**

1. In the case of *Lucas v. South Carolina Coastal Council*, which is found in this chapter, the State of South Carolina had very legitimate environmental concerns relating to its coastline. A state's authority to legislate in the areas of the public's health, safety, morals, and general welfare goes back hundreds of years, and is known as the state's "police power."

   Mr. Lucas was a real estate developer who had purchased two coastal lots. Lucas planned on building an expensive home on each lot, which would generate significant profits for him. Property rights—both real and personal—and the right to the profits that flow from property ownership, are deeply rooted in the Fifth and Fourteenth Amendments to the United States Constitution.

   The Fifth Amendment states in part: "*... nor shall private property be taken for public use, without just compensation.*"

   The Fourteenth Amendment states in part: "*... nor shall any State deprive any person of life, liberty, or property, without due process of law ...*"

   Of the two amendments quoted above, which do you think has more relevance to the *Lucas* case? Why?

   Do you agree with Justice Scalia's majority opinion that found in favor of Mr. Lucas? As a result of that opinion, did the State of South Carolina have to allow Mr. Lucas to build on his two lots?

   How is the *Lucas* case similar to, or different from, the case of *Kelo v. City of New London*? What were the consequences for the developer in each case?

2. The town of Smallville in your state is currently the site of a small satellite campus of Big State University. There had been a few reports in the local press that the Smallville campus may experience tremendous growth over the next 5 to 10 years. As a developer of residential apartment units, you are quite intrigued by this news. However, you are aware that state tax revenues are down, and the state legislature is having a difficult time balancing the budget, and so an expansion of the satellite campus may not occur at all. But you are also aware that there are several other developers in the region who would be more than eager to compete against you to develop apartments in Smallville, should the expansion eventuate.

   What can you do now to improve your chances of having developable property in Smallville available to you if the state finds money for the expansion in the next few years?

3. You are the vice-president of acquisitions for a major REIT. The president of the REIT has just informed you that the company has raised approximately $200 million, which it must invest over the course of the next two years. You offer to accept a raise of $100 million, but the president, who is humorless, ignores your kind offer.

   Continuing, the president asks you which regions and sub-regions of the country you believe will experience long-term (i.e., in the next 10 to 20 years) growth, and whether those locations would provide suitable opportunities for real estate development and investment.

   What regions and sub-regions do you identify, and why?

RESEARCH ON THE **WEB**

1. We have made the point in this chapter that real estate development is a very risky proposition. To validate that conclusion, run the following query on the Internet:

   "developer & bankruptcy"

   To reduce the number of hits, add the name of your state to the query.

   To further reduce the number of hits, add the name of your city, or the nearest large metropolitan area.

How many hits have you generated with each filter?

2. Using the Internet, attempt to locate statistical information regarding the number of new residential units (apartments and owner-occupied) that have been built in your jurisdiction in each year for the last 10 years for which data is available. Is the trend up, down, or stable?

3. Go online to determine if there are lenders—banks, S&Ls, or otherwise—who are advertising or offering to make loans for the development of income-producing properties.

BUILDING YOUR **PROFESSIONAL** PORTFOLIO

1. There are numerous accounting programs that can generate cash flow statements and other financial statements for the owner of income-producing real estate. Use the cash flow statement for the 300-unit apartment complex as a go-by or template to generate your own cash flow statement for an apartment complex that you are familiar with in your community. From the local Apartment Guide you can get a good idea of the number of units, unit mix, and rent structure at a given apartment complex. From that data, you can determine the Gross Scheduled Income for the property.

Depending on the local economic and rental market conditions, you can guesstimate a figure for the second line item, that is, Vacancy and Credit Loss. The more difficult the local economic conditions, the higher the Vacancy and Credit Loss figure will be. Subtracting Vacancy and Credit Loss from the Gross Scheduled Income will give you the Effective Gross Income.

From the EGI you will have to subtract the property's expenses. Generally, the expenses for residential apartment units will be in the neighborhood of 40% to 50% of the EGI. The remainder after subtracting the expenses from the EGI is the net operating income.

Next, estimate the current monthly debt service on the property. You may be able to determine when the property was purchased, and for how much, by searching your county's online property and tax records. If that information is not available, make an informed guess as to the property's current value.

After you have derived the current estimated fair market value, determine the approximate loan amount by using an 80% loan-to-value ratio. You will then have to find an amortization calculator (several available online) to determine the monthly or annual debt service. If you subtract the debt service from the NOI, the remainder is the property's Cash Flow.

GLOSSARY

Abstract of Title—a summary of the history of a piece of real property, showing not only the grantors and grantees, but also liens and other encumbrances that may affect the quality of title of the property.

Accretion—the slow accumulation of sand or soil through the action of water, thereby increasing the size of the affected property.

Acknowledgment—a formal declaration made in the presence of an authorized officer, such as a notary public, by someone who signs a document and confirms that the signature is authentic.

Adverse Possession—the process by which one who is essentially a trespasser may obtain lawful title to real property by openly, exclusively, and actually possessing and using it for a specified number of years.

Affirmative Covenant—a formal promise by the covenantor to take some specific action, or do some specific thing.

Agency—a fiduciary relationship wherein the agent acts on behalf of a principal and, in the process, may bind the principal to a contract. In real estate transactions, the agent will be the real estate broker.

Agent's Duty to Perform—the obligation of the agent to act in accordance with the terms of the agency agreement. The duty to perform includes the agent's subsidiary duty to obey, and the duty of diligence.

Agent's Duty to Render an Accounting—the agent's obligation to report to the principal on the monies received, and disbursed, by the agent on the principal's behalf.

Airspace—the space above a parcel of real property that may be used by commercial aircraft. Airspace must be above a minimum safe altitude, or else air traffic may constitute a nuisance.

Ambiguity—that which is reasonably susceptible to two different interpretations.

Amortization Schedule—a listing of the periodic payments indicating how much of any given payment is applied against principal, and how much is applied to the interest component of the loan.

Amortize—to pay off a debt over a period of time, usually in equal payments, for example, monthly payments, with a portion of each payment paying off interest and a portion paying off principal.

Annexor—one who attaches or affixes personal property to real property.

Appraisal—the process of determining an opinion of value by a licensed appraiser, which is used by a lender to determine the amount to be loaned for the purchase price.

Arbitrary—founded on preference or prejudice, rather than fact.

AREA—this acronym may help you remember the four natural ways by which the land and boundaries may be changed: accretion, reliction, erosion, and avulsion.

Articles of Incorporation—the legal document that creates the homeowners association that will own the common areas and common elements of the condominium. Articles are filed with the Secretary of State's office and are also known as the corporate charter.

Assignee—one to whom rights are transferred by the assignor.

Assignment—the transfer of one's rights to another.

Assignor—one who transfer rights to another.

Association—the legal entity that owns the common areas in a common interest community, whether the CIC is a condominium association or a homeowners association.

Avulsion—the sudden removal of land caused by a change in a river's course or by flood.

Bailout—the rescue of an entity or an industry, such as the banking industry, from financial trouble or possible collapse.

Beneficiary—one who receives real or personal property under a will.

Bequest—a gift of personal property (other than money) made in a will.

Best Efforts—diligent attempts to perform an obligation, as measured by what the reasonable person would do in the same or similar circumstances. It is a higher standard than reasonable efforts.

Bilateral Contract—a promise made in exchange for a return promise.

Bill of sale—an instrument for conveying title to personal property.

Black Letter Law—bedrock principles of common law that have developed over the centuries. It is black letter law, for instance, that we each owe a duty of care to those around us to act in a manner so as not to create an unreasonable risk of harm to them.

Blockbusting—the illegal practice by real estate brokers or agents who are attempting to generate sales of real estate by frightening homeowners in a segregated neighborhood by telling them that a racial, ethnic, or religious minority is beginning to move into their neighborhood.

Board of Directors—the governing body of a corporation or association, including condominiums and homeowners associations. At a minimum, a board usually consists of a president, vice president, secretary, and treasurer.

Boilerplate—language in a contract that has become standardized, and therefore, is rarely negotiated.

Broker—one who facilitates the purchase of real property by assisting buyers and sellers in coming to an agreement on the terms and conditions of the transaction. Brokers are licensed by the state wherein they conduct business.

Budget—an estimate of a property's anticipated income and expenses over a specified period of time, usually a year.

Bundle of Rights—describes the nature and extent of an owner's or tenant's interests in the land.

Business Judgment Rule—a rule of evidence created by statute or common law that protects officers and directors of corporations and associations from liability for decisions made in good faith, but which are ultimately detrimental to the corporation's shareholders or association's members.

Bylaws—the legal document that describes in detail how a homeowners association is to operate and conduct its business.

CAM Charges—common area maintenance charges that are billed monthly, quarterly, or annually to the tenants for things such as parking lot repair, snow removal, signage, utilities, and mechanical maintenance.

Capricious—unpredictable or impulsive behavior.

Cash Flow—the money flowing into (income) and the money flowing out of (expenses) a property or other investment over time.

Caveat Emptor—Latin for "Let the buyer beware." It meant that the seller of property had no affirmative duty to disclose defects in the property, even hidden defects.

Chain of Title—the ownership history of a piece of real property, showing the grantors and grantees who owned the property over a period of time.

Closing—the final step in a real estate transaction during which the grantor (usually a seller) conveys title to the grantee (usually a buyer), most often in exchange for financial consideration.

Closing Date—the deadline by which the closing of the transaction must occur. At closing, the seller transfers title to the property to the buyer in exchange for the buyer's payment of the sale price to the seller.

Cloud on Title—a defect or potential defect in the owner's title to a piece of land arising from some claim or encumbrance such as a lien, easement, or court order.

Collateral—property that is pledged as security for a loan. The real property being purchased is pledged as collateral in the mortgage or deed of trust as security for the loan.

Color of Title—a writing or other evidence purporting to show that a claimant to property, such as an adverse possessor, is the actual owner of the property.

Commitment letter—the lender's pledge to lend the borrower a specific amount of money for a specific interest rate. The commitment is usually good for only 30-60 days.

Common Interest Community—a form of ownership of real property where private ownership of one's individual unit is coupled with shared ownership of the common areas.

Common Law—law that has been developed by courts, rather than legislative bodies.

Community Property—real or personal property acquired by either or both spouses during their marriage; the marital property is split equally between the divorcing parties.

Competent—of a suitable age, usually 18, and mental capacity to engage in a legal transaction, for example, the conveyance of real property.

Completion Bond—also known as a performance bond, it is a promise by an insurer that it will pay to complete the project in the event of the developer's default. The completion bond is paid for by the developer, for the benefit of the lender.

Condemnation—the legal process by which government exercises its rights of eminent domain.

Condition Precedent—in a contract, an event that must occur before a party is obligated to perform under the contract.

Condominium 1. —a form of ownership of real property that combines ownership of one's individual unit with an undivided ownership interest in the common areas; 2. one's individual unit in a multifamily development; 3. a multifamily project, including all of the individual units and common areas, developed in accordance with a state's condominium statutes.

Consideration—that which motivates or induces another to enter into a bargain or agreement. Consideration may consist of either a promise, or a performance.

Construction Loan—a loan for the construction of a real estate development. Construction loans are short-term, usually not more than 2–3 years, and carry a higher interest rate than the permanent loan because of the increased risk of default during the construction phase.

Contract—an enforceable agreement between two or more persons to do, or not to do, some act.

Cooperative—a corporation that owns residential real property, including the individual units therein. The "co-op" leases the residential units to its shareholders.

Counteroffer—an offeree's new offer that varies one or more terms of the original offer. A counteroffer both rejects and terminates the original offer.

Covenant—a formal promise in a contract or deed, and often relating to real property.

Covenantee—the person or entity to whom a covenant or formal promise is made in a contract or deed.

Covenantor—the person or entity making a formal promise in a contract or deed, and often relating to real property.

Curtesy—under common law, the rights of a widower, following the death of his wife, to property owned by her. Curtesy has been replaced in most states by statutes that specifically allocate the type and amount of property to be received by the surviving spouse.

D & O Insurance—an insurance policy that protects directors and officers, and sometimes the employees, of a homeowners association or condominium from liability when they have acted in good faith and within the scope of their duties.

de facto—Latin "in fact"—having effect even though not formally recognized in the law.

de jure—Latin "as a matter of law"—existing as a matter of law, or as a result or consequence of a legal act.

Declaration—also known as the master deed, it is the legal document that creates the condominium when recorded at the office of the register of deeds in the county where the real property is located.

Dedication—a gift of real property to a local, state or federal government.

Deed—a written legal document that proves title to, and ownership of, real property.

Deficiency Judgment—a judgment for the difference between what the borrower owed to the lender and the proceeds from the foreclosure sale.

Devise—a gift of real or personal property made in a will, although it is most commonly understood to mean a gift of real property.

Disclosure Statement—a checklist that includes the major components of a house, and that the seller may be required to fill out. The seller will indicate on the checklist any defects in the condition of the components. Disclosure statements were introduced in response to the doctrine of caveat emptor.

Dominant Estate—the estate or parcel of land that benefits from an easement.

Dominion and Control—the terms are somewhat synonymous, and therefore, redundant. The exercise of dominion and control over one's property implies the ability to exclude all others from possessing or enjoying it.

Dower—under common law, the rights of a widow, following the death of her husband, to property owned by him. Dower has been replaced in most states by statutes that specifically allocate the type and amount of property to be received by the surviving spouse.

Draw—one of numerous periodic payments received by a subcontractor for work performed on a construction site. The amount of the draw is roughly equivalent to the pro rata amount of the work performed by the subcontractor.

Dual Agency—when a broker represents both buyer and seller in the same transaction. Dual agency is fraught with the danger of ethical conflicts, and is therefore illegal in some states.

Dues—monies that are paid on a regular basis—monthly, quarterly, or annually—by unit owners for the routine maintenance of the common areas. Dues are typically assessed based upon an owner's pro rata square footage.

Easement—a type of servitude in which one acquires the right to use another's land for a specific purpose.

Easement Appurtenant—an easement conveyed by one landowner—the servient estate—to benefit another (usually adjoining) parcel of land, the dominant estate.

Easement by Necessity—an easement created by operation of law because the easement is indispensable to the reasonable use of nearby property, such as an easement connecting a parcel of land to a road; without such an easement, the landowner would suffer some substantial detriment.

Easement by Prescription—an easement created as a result of one's long and continuous use of another's property.

Easement in Gross—an easement to benefit a specific person or entity, such as the electric company, rather than another parcel of land.

Eminent Domain—the power of federal, state, or local government to take private property for a public use, and for which it must pay just compensation.

Encumbrance—an encumbrance is a broader term than "lien," and encompasses liens, as well as claims against, or interests in, a property that may reduce its value, such as an easement or possible legal claim against the property, which would cloud the title.

Equitable Distribution—in states other than community property states, marital property is split equitably based on several factors, rather than evenly.

Equitable Right of Redemption—the right of a borrower in foreclosure to pay off the entire loan balance at any time up until the foreclosure sale.

Escheat—occurs when ownership of real or personal property passes to the state because the decedent has died without a will, and there are no persons qualified to receive the property under the statutes of intestate succession.

Escrow—a legal document such as a deed, or property such as money, held by a person not a party to the real estate transaction, that is, the escrow agent. Upon the satisfaction of the conditions in the contract for sale of the property, at the closing the escrow agent will deliver the deed to the buyer, and will disburse proceeds to the seller.

Estate—the nature and extent of one's legal rights and interests in a given parcel of real property.

Eviction / Summary Ejectment / Unlawful Detainer—these are the different names used in various states for the legal process by which a tenant is removed from a rental property, whether residential or commercial. These actions, especially in residential cases, are usually litigated in small claims court.

Exclusive Agency Listing Agreement—this offers less protection to a broker because if the property owner finds a buyer, she will not have to pay a commission to the broker. If the listing broker or another broker procures a buyer, seller must pay a brokerage commission to the listing broker.

Exclusive Right to Sell Listing Agreement—the listing contract preferred by brokers because it offers the most protection to the broker. The broker will be paid a commission regardless of who sells the property.

Express Easement—an easement that is created by the written agreement of the parties.

Fair Housing Laws—federal and state laws enacted to prevent discrimination in the sale or rental of housing.

Feasibility Study—an analysis of several demographic and economic factors in a local market to determine if a proposed use of real property would be profitable.

Fiduciary—one who owes to another the duties of good faith, trust, confidence, and candor, and who must exercise a high standard of care in managing another's money or property.

Financing Statement—a document filed in the public records to notify third parties, usually buyers and lenders, of a secured party's security interest in goods or real property.

Fixed + Percentage Lease—a lease payment that has a flat monthly rate, plus a percentage of the tenant's gross or net retail receipts.

Fixed Lease—a flat monthly rental paid by the commercial tenant just like the flat rate paid by an apartment renter.

Fixture—an item of personal property, which by virtue of its attachment to real property, and the intent of the annexor, becomes real property itself.

Fixture—personal property affixed or attached to real property that becomes part of the real property.

Four Unities—a joint tenancy, in addition to the right of survivorship, must also carry with it the four unities of possession, interest, time, and title (PITT).

Fraud—intentionally deceiving another as to a material fact. Fraud also includes concealment of a material fact by one who has an affirmative duty to disclose such material information.

General Contractor—the person or entity that has overall supervisory responsibility during the construction process for the completion of the project. The GC schedules the work of the subcontractors, and the delivery of the building supplies.

General Warranty Deed—the best kind of deed because it contains the most warranties or guarantees from the grantor, and thereby, the greatest protection for the grantee.

Grantee—one to whom real property is conveyed.

Granting Clause—language in a deed that transfers some or all of a grantor's interest in real property to a grantee.

Grantor—one who conveys real property to another.

Habendum Clause—language in a deed that describes the extent of the estate being conveyed by the grantor to the grantee.

Heir—a spouse or relative of a decedent who has died intestate (without a will) and is entitled by a state's intestacy statutes to some or all of the decedent's real and personal property.

Highest and Best Use—that use of a parcel of land that will generate the most profit.

Historic/Heritage District—sections or neighborhoods in a city or town where, for historic or architectural reasons, zoning regulations require the preservation of the exteriors of the local buildings, and may prohibit their demolition.

Holographic Will—a will that was handwritten by the testator.

HUD—The Department of Housing and Urban Development.

HUD-1—a settlement statement required by federal law that is a full accounting of the money changing hands in connection with a closing.

Implied Easement—an easement implied from the facts and circumstances relating to a parcel of real property. The conduct of the parties may also shed light on whether an easement has been created by implication.

Incident (to)—dependent upon, subordinate to, arising out of, or otherwise connected with something else, which is usually of greater importance.

Inter Vivos ("between the living") Gift—a transfer of property by gift from a living person to another living person.

Interest—the amount of money paid by a borrower for the use of the borrowed funds.

Interest Rate—the percentage of the loan amount that a borrower must pay to a lender in return for the use of the borrowed money.

Intestacy Statutes—a state's body of laws that determines who qualifies as an heir of an intestate, and is thus entitled to receive the intestate's real and personal property.

Intestate—one who dies without a will.

Intestate Succession—the state statutes that determine how a decedent's real and personal property is to be distributed when that person has died intestate, that is, without a will. The persons taking the decedent's property by intestate succession are called heirs.

Judicial Foreclosure—a method of foreclosure that is very similar to a regular lawsuit, and requires the filing of a complaint, service on the borrower, a formal hearing, and the opportunity to appeal.

Jurat—(from the Latin, "to swear") a certification added to an affidavit or deposition stating when and before what authority the affidavit or deposition was made.

Just Compensation—usually, the fair market value of a property paid to a land owner by the government for taking part or all of the owner's real property under its power of eminent domain.

Landlocked—when there is no access to a parcel of land by way of a public road.

Latent Ambiguity—a defect in the legal description of a property in a deed that is hidden, or not obvious. A latent ambiguity does not necessarily void the deed, and may be cured by extrinsic evidence.

Lease—a contract—either written or oral—that conveys an interest in real property that is known as a leasehold estate. The holder of a leasehold estate has fewer rights in the "bundle of rights" than would the owner of a fee simple.

Legacy—a gift of personal property, which is often a gift of money, made in a will.

Leverage—the ability to increase the rate of return from an investment by using other people's money (OPM).

License—a right to use real property for a short period of time, and which right is revocable without notice or legal process, at the will of the licensor.

Lien—a legal claim, right, or interest that a creditor has in another's property, lasting until the debt or duty that it secures is satisfied.

Lien waiver—an affidavit that states that there are no unrecorded liens, particularly mechanics' liens, on the property to be conveyed.

Life Estate—an estate held only for the duration of a specified person's life, usually the possessor's life.

Limited Common Element—common area owned by all the unit owners, but reserved for the exclusive use of one or more unit owners, and fewer than all of the owners.

Limited Warranty Deed—also known as a Special Warranty Deed. Because this type of deed offers fewer warranties or guarantees to the grantee than a general warranty deed, it is not preferred by grantees.

Lis pendens—a pending lawsuit; a notice, recorded in the chain of title to real property, required or permitted in some jurisdictions to warn all persons that certain property is the subject matter of litigation, and that any interest acquired during the pendency of the suit are subject to its outcome.

Litigation Law Firm—the process of seeking a remedy at law; a lawsuit.

Littoral Rights—the rights of landowners whose properties abut a lake, ocean, or sea.

Loan Origination Fee—a fee charged by a lender which is a percentage, usually 1%–2%, of the face amount of a loan, over and above the interest to be paid on the loan.

Loan-to-Value Ratio—the ratio (percentage) of the loan amount to the fair market value of the property to be purchased.

Magistrate—a judicial official, usually appointed rather than elected, who presides over small claims court and who renders a judgment.

Marital Estate—the property acquired during a marriage that will be distributed upon divorce.

Market Comparable—a property that has recently sold and is compared with the subject property to derive an appropriate list price for the subject property. It is important that the sale of the "comp" property be in the same neighborhood as the subject property, and have been sold recently.

Marketable Title—a title that is free of any defects that could diminish the value of the property, and impair the owner's ability to guarantee quiet enjoyment of the property to a grantee.

Material Breach—a breach by one party to a contract that is so significant that the non-breaching party is relieved from performing under the terms of the contract.

Material Information—that which would be important to a reasonable person in making a financial decision, for example, of whether to buy or sell real property.

Mechanic's Lien—a claim filed with the clerk of court by a subcontractor or materials supplier in the event they are not paid for work performed on, or for building materials supplied to, a jobsite. If the claim or lien is not paid, the sub or supplier may force the sale of the real property to which the lien relates.

Minor/Partial Breach—a breach by one party to a contract that is relatively insignificant, and therefore, does not relieve the non-breaching party of the duty to perform under the terms of the contract. When the breach is minor, the breaching party is said to have substantially performed.

Mirror-Image Rule—for there to be an acceptance of an offer, the offeree may not change, add, or qualify any of the offeror's terms.

Misrepresentation—negligently conveying erroneous, material information to one to whom a duty of care is owed regarding the information being conveyed.

Mixed-Use Development—a single real estate development made up of two or more different property types, such as residential, retail, and office space.

Mortgage—a pledge of real property as collateral/security for a loan.

Mortgagee—the lender receiving the pledge of real property from the borrower as collateral for a loan.

Mortgagor—the party giving the pledge to the lender as collateral for a loan. Thus, the mortgagor is the borrower.

Multifamily Residential Property—two or more attached apartment rental units.

Navigable Waterways—bodies of water that are capable of accommodating vessels used to transport commercial goods. Navigable waterways are regulated by federal maritime law.

Negative Covenant—prohibits or restricts an owner's use of his property; it is also called a restrictive covenant.

Net Operating Income—the line item on a cash flow statement indicating the profitability of an income-producing real property. The NOI is important because it is used by real estate buyers, sellers, and lenders to derive an estimate of a property's fair market value.

Non-Navigable Waterways—bodies of water that are not capable of accommodating vessels used to transport commercial goods, and are regulated by state law.

Notary Public—a person authorized by a state to administer oaths, certify documents, and attest to the authenticity of signatures.

Nuisance Per Se—a nuisance in and of itself, at all times, under all circumstances, and regardless of the surrounding land uses. A nuisance per se always involves a violation of a statute or ordinance.

Nuncupative Will—an oral will.

Offeree—the person to whom an offer is made.

Offeror—the person who makes an offer to another.

Open Listing Agreement—an ad hoc contract whereby seller agrees to pay a commission to any broker who procures a buyer. Seller also reserves the right to sell the property herself without having to pay a commission at all.

Opinion of Title—a certification offered by an attorney, after reviewing the title search and abstract of title, concerning whether a parcel of real property is marketable.

Option—a contract in which the seller agrees, for a fee, to keep an offer to sell a property open for a specified period of time, and usually for a specific price. During the option period, the offer may not be revoked by the seller.

Patent Ambiguity—an obvious mistake in the legal description of real property, and is found on the face of the deed. A patent ambiguity renders the deed void.

Percolating Groundwaters—waters that are dispersed throughout an underground soil layer or layers, but do not flow through an existing water channel.

Permanent Loan—also known as the "take out" loan because it will replace the construction loan upon the completion and lease-up of the new development. Permanent loans usually have terms of 20–40 years, and a lower interest rate than the construction loan.

Permit—a certificate issued by a federal, state, or local governmental agency allowing some action to be taken, for example, a building permit.

Personal Property—sometimes called chattel, is all property that is not real property.

Planned Unit Development—a special type of zoning, the purpose of which is to optimize the physical layout, uses, and density of large, multi-use developments.

Police Power—is the authority that state and local governments have had for centuries to legislate in the areas of the public health, safety, morals, and the general welfare.

Possession—is the exercise of dominion and control over property, whether real property or personal property.

Power of Sale—a clause found in a mortgage or deed of trust that allows the lender to foreclose without giving the borrower the right to a formal judicial hearing.

Presumption—a legal inference or assumption that a fact exists.

Primary Mortgage Market—banks, employee credit unions, and savings and loan associations that make residential mortgage loans directly to borrowers.

Principal (1)—the person for whom an agent acts. In most real estate transactions, the principal will be the seller of the property.

Principal (2)—the amount of money borrowed from the lender.

Priority—the status of being earlier in time or higher in degree or rank; precedence.

Probate—the judicial process by which a testamentary document is established to be a valid will; to administer a decedent's estate.

Profession—an occupation requiring advanced training and education, and often adhering to a professional code of ethics.

Profit—an easement to enter the land of another, coupled with the right to take something of value from the land.

Promissory Note—a written promise to pay a debt of a specific sum of money, for a specific term, and at a stated interest rate.

Property Manager—the individual or firm charged with the day-to-day operations of an office building, shopping center, or apartment complex. The property manager will attempt to maximize income, and minimize expenses, while maintaining an appealing environment for the tenants.

Public Trust Doctrine—the doctrine that holds that lands beneath navigable waterways—for example, river beds, lake beds, or sea beds—are owned by the state in trust for its citizens, even though the waterway and vessels using it are governed by federal regulations.

Puffing—the expression of an exaggerated opinion about real or personal property that is being sold to another. Puffing is "just sales talk," and is generally not considered to be tortious conduct.

Quasi—to some extent or degree; nearly; similar to.

Quitclaim Deed—a deed wherein the grantor makes no warranties or guarantees to the grantee, but simply conveys any interest that the grantor *may* have in the property. Quitclaim deeds are commonly used to quiet title in will contests and divorce actions.

Rate of Return—the amount of profit generated as a percentage of the amount one has invested.

Real Property—is land, anything affixed to the land, and rights appurtenant to the land.

Rebuttable Presumption—an inference drawn from facts that establish a prima facie case, but which may be overcome by the introduction of contrary evidence.

Recordation—a deed is recorded or registered at the office of the Register of Deeds to put the world on notice of one's ownership of real property, and to make a record of when such notice was filed, in the event of a competing claim of ownership.

Redlining—the illegal practice by lending institutions when they refuse to make loans on properties in areas that are considered undesirable and poor financial risks, or to the people living in those areas.

Register—to enter in a public registry.

Register of deeds—a public official who records deeds, mortgages, and other instruments affecting real property.

REIT—a real estate investment trust is an entity through which individuals may invest in large real estate projects in the hopes of obtaining a return on their investment.

Release—a promise by the promisor, usually written, to the promisee that relieves the promisee of an obligation owed to the promisor.

Reliction—the increase in land area due to the gradual subsidence or receding of a river or lake.

Remainderman—the third person to whom the property is conveyed at the end of a life estate.

Rental Concession—something of value given by an owner of a commercial property to entice prospective tenants to sign a lease for space in the owner's building.

Reserve Fund—a portion of the regular dues that are set aside for major repairs to, and capital improvements on, the common areas.

RESPA—the Real Estate Settlement Procedures Act is a federal law that requires lenders to provide home-buyers with information about known or estimated settlement costs.

Restitution—a tort claim designed to prevent unjust enrichment of another in the absence of a contract between the two parties.

Retainage—a small percentage of money withheld by the general contractor or developer from the draw paid to a subcontractor.

Retaliatory Eviction—when a landlord evicts a tenant solely because the tenant has exercised rights under the law, such as the right to organize a tenant's union.

Return—the amount of profit generated by one's investment in real estate, the stock market, precious metals, or some other type of investment.

Reverter or Reversion—the return of the property to the original grantor; this frequently occurs at the end of a life estate.

Riparian Rights—the rights of landowners whose properties abut rivers or streams to the use of the water.

Risk—the uncertainty of a result; the existence and the extent of a possibility of harm.

Runs with the Land—when a right or obligation relating to land is binding on successive owners.

Sanctions—penalties imposed on a broker or agent by the state's department or division of real estate. Sanctions include monetary penalties, and/or the suspension or revocation of an agent's or broker's license.

Scope of the Agency—the extent of an agent's authority to act on behalf of a principal.

Secondary Mortgage Market—large financial institutions, including Fannie Mae and Freddie Mac, which buy bundles of mortgages from primary mortgage lenders, and thereby enable the primary lenders to continue making loans for the purchase of real property.

Seisin—a term that goes back to feudal England, and is synonymous with the concept of title or ownership. If you are "seized" of the property, you have the right to convey the property.

Self-dealing—occurs when an agent participates in a business deal that benefits the agent to the principal's detriment, or possible detriment.

Self-help Eviction—the removal of a tenant by a landlord without the use of the legally required process. Self-help evictions have the potential for violence and therefore are banned in most states.

Servient Estate—the estate or parcel of land that is burdened by an easement.

Servitude—a right or obligation in land that runs with the land.

Setback Requirement—a zoning restriction that requires that a structure be built at some minimum distance from a street or a neighbor's property line.

Single-Family Residence—a free-standing house having its own surrounding yards.

Site Analysis—the physical inspection and evaluation of a proposed building site to determine its suitability for development.

Small Claims Court—a court designed to enable litigants to proceed *pro se* (without a lawyer) in order to quickly and inexpensively resolve suits involving relatively small amounts of money.

Sovereign—a governmental entity possessing independent and supreme authority. Every state in the United States is a sovereign, as is the federal government.

Special Assessment—a demand by the association for monies over and above an owner's regular dues payment, required for some emergency or special purpose.

Spite Fence—a fence erected solely to injure an adjoining landowner by shutting out or diminishing the landowner's light, air, or view.

Stabilized Cash Flow—occurs when the income and expenses on a new income-producing property have become relatively steady and predictable.

Statute of Limitations—the time in which a lawsuit must be filed by a plaintiff.

Statutes of Frauds—laws in every state that hold that certain types of contracts must be in writing. The prime example is a contract for an interest in real property. Oral leases for less than a year, for example, are a common exception to the statutes of fraud.

Steering—the illegal practice by a broker of manipulating, directing, or "steering" a buyer or renter of one race into a neighborhood comprised mainly of residents of the buyer's (or renter's) own race.

Strict construction—an interpretation that construes words narrowly. This type of construction treats statutory and contractual words with highly restrictive readings.

Subcontractor—one engaged in a building trade such as a plumber, electrician, or roofer, who works on a construction site under the supervision of the general contractor.

Subject Property—the property that is being listed for sale by the broker.

Subordinate—to place in a lower rank, class, or position; to assign a lower priority to.

Subterranean Waters—also known as groundwaters, are water sources that exist under the surface of the earth. There are two basic types: underground streams and percolating groundwaters.

Suit to Quiet Title—an action brought by a plaintiff who seeks to have a court determine that plaintiff is the owner of a piece of real property. Also called a "quiet title action."

Surface Waters—bodies of water found on the surface of the earth, such as rivers, streams, lakes, and oceans.

Tacking—the joining of consecutive periods of ownership or possession by different persons and treating them as one continuous period.

Takings Clause—a clause found in the Fifth Amendment to the U.S. Constitution, and practically every state constitution, that allows the taking of private property for a public use, but only on the condition that the government pay just compensation to the property owner.

Tenancy—in the context of a leasehold estate, a tenancy defines the quality and duration of the tenant's interest in the property.

Tenancy at Sufferance—a tenant who has held over—remained in the property—after the expiration or termination of the lease agreement.

Tenancy at Will—a leasehold that lasts for as long as the landlord and tenant agree. This is a very informal arrangement, which may be terminated at the will of either party, with reasonable notice.

Tenancy for Years—the most common type of leasehold, which lasts for a fixed period of time.

Tenancy from Period to Period—a leasehold for successive, continuous, and discrete periods of time. There is no specific termination date, and a rental period may "roll over."

Tenant Improvement—an upgrade to office, retail, or other commercial space. If the demand for space is soft, the property owner may offer TIs at a discount, or even for free. Conversely, when demand for space is strong, the tenant usually pays for the TIs.

Termination of Easement—easements may be terminated in several ways, including by agreement of the parties, expiration, merger, or abandonment.

Testator—1. one who dies with a valid will, 2. the person who makes a will with the intent of leaving real or personal property to one or more beneficiaries.

Time Is of the Essence—a clause in a contract that requires that a particular act, such as a closing on real property, must occur by a specific date.

Title—in the abstract is the right of ownership. Title also means the evidence of ownership rights; with real estate, evidence of ownership or title is by deed.

Title Insurance—a policy issued by a title insurance company that protects the buyer of a property against losses related to a defect in the title of the real property.

Title Search—a thorough search of all types of public records to discover any liens or other encumbrances that may affect the quality of the title of the property to be conveyed.

Transactional Law Firm—the law office activities that pertain to the negotiation and the making of deals relating to real estate.

Trespass to Land—the intentional tort by which one enters, or causes an object to enter, the land of another. Trespass also includes refusing to leave another's real property after being ordered to do so.

Triple Net Lease—a lease in which the tenant pays its pro rata share—based on square footage—of the property taxes, property insurance, and CAM charges.

Truth in Lending Act—also known as the Consumer Credit Protection Act, the TILA is a federal statute that requires full disclosure of the terms of consumer loans, including mortgage loans, including the interest rate, the annual percentage rate, and the term of the loan.

Underground Streams—waters that flow through subterranean water channels.

Unilateral Contract—a promise made in exchange for a return performance.

Unity of Interest—each joint tenant has the same percentage interest in the property, and the same type of estate, or bundle of rights.

Unity of Possession—the right to use and enjoy the whole property, not just a part of it.

Unity of Time—each joint tenant must have acquired his or her ownership interest at the same time.

Unity of Title—each joint tenant acquired title to the property by way of the same conveyance, that is, by the same deed or will.

Upset Bid—a bid that overturns the winning bid at a foreclosure sale. State law will dictate the amount or percentage by which the upset bid must exceed the winning bid, and the length of time after the foreclosure sale in which the upset bid must be submitted to the clerk of court.

Void—without legal force or effect, a nullity; the word is generally used in regard to a contract.

Voidable—a contract or conveyance that is valid until it is voided at the option of the grantor.

Waiver—a promise, usually written, in which the promisor gives up the right to pursue legal claims against another who otherwise may have been liable to the promisor.

Warranty—a promise or guarantee made by the grantor and found in a deed.

Warranty of Habitability—a clause in a lease agreement—either express or implied by law—requiring a landlord to provide safe and clean premises, and working electrical, plumbing, and heating systems.

Waste—any use of the property by the life tenant that unreasonably reduces the value of the life estate.

Will—the legal document that describes how one's real and personal property is to be distributed upon death.

Will Contest—the litigation of a will's validity, usually based on allegations that the testator lacked capacity or was under undue influence.

INDEX